Comparing Christianities

Comparing Christianities

An Introduction to Early Christianity

APRIL D. DECONICK
Rice University
Texas, USA

WILEY Blackwell

Registered Offices
John Wiley & Sons, Inc., 111 River Street, Hoboken, NJ 07030, USA
John Wiley & Sons Ltd, The Atrium, Southern Gate, Chichester, West Sussex, PO19 8SQ, UK

For details of our global editorial offices, customer services, and more information about Wiley products visit us at www.wiley.com.

Wiley also publishes its books in a variety of electronic formats and by print-on-demand. Some content that appears in standard print versions of this book may not be available in other formats.

Library of Congress Cataloging-in-Publication Data

Names: De Conick, April D., author. | John Wiley & Sons, publisher.
Title: Comparing Christianities : An Introduction to Early Christianity / April D. DeConick.
Description: Hoboken, NJ : Wiley-Blackwell, 2023. | Includes bibliographical references and index.
Identifiers: LCCN 2023021437 (print) | LCCN 2023021438 (ebook) | ISBN 9781119086031 (paperback) | ISBN 9781119086062 (pdf) | ISBN 9781119086055 (epub)
Subjects: LCSH: Church history--Primitive and early church, ca. 30-600. | Christianity and culture--History--Early church, ca. 30-600.
Classification: LCC BR162.3 .D429 2023 (print) | LCC BR162.3 (ebook) | DDC 270.1--dc23/eng/20230601
LC record available at https://lccn.loc.gov/2023021437
LC ebook record available at https://lccn.loc.gov/2023021438

Cover Design: Wiley
Cover Image: Courtesy of April D. DeConick

Set in 9.5/12pt STIXTwoText by Integra Software Services Pvt. Ltd, Pondicherry, India
Printed and bound by CPI Group (UK) Ltd, Croydon, CR0 4YY

C9781119086031_110923

This book is dedicated to all yet-to-come students, wherever this textbook is read.

Contents

Contents

Preface

Can a textbook be the culmination and pinnacle of a life's work? We often think of textbooks as summaries of a field of study, rehearsals of old material that expose students to the history of research, not as reconfigurations that challenge the way we have been doing things. But that is what this textbook is. It comes out of my own thirty-year career of teaching, studying, and writing as a woman concerned with the way that narratives about our past – religious or otherwise – are often constructed to keep certain people in power, to authenticate and legitimize their dominance, and to justify the marginalization of people who differ from them.

When I first started to teach Biblical Studies, I was young and did not understand this yet. If someone had told me this when I was in my twenties, I probably would have resisted this idea. I had not yet experienced being a woman professor peering through the glass ceiling. I had not yet experienced working in a field almost completely dominated by male voices, colleagues, and publications. Hence, when I started on my career path, I ran fairly typical courses in the New Testament, Jesus and the Gospels, and the History and Literature of Early Christianity from Paul to Augustine. I used the standard textbooks written by my male peers and supplemented with other readings to fill in the gaps.

But as the years passed and I became more exposed to the expansive literature that the early Christians left behind, I began to question why the field of Biblical Studies organizes itself into Old and New Testaments (or the Hebrew Bible and the Christian Testament) and quarantines this "authentic" and "historical" literature from the rest of the writings produced by early Christians. I became less and less certain about the way that scholars argued and maintained this quarantine by dating the composition of the New Testament literature to the first century and all other literature (with the exception of perhaps the Didache) to the second century.

It was not long before I began to realize that, for much of the New Testament, this early dating is a fantasy and a fallacy. As I studied various scholarly treatments of individual texts, I came to terms with the fact that the Pastoral Epistles (1 and 2 Timothy and Titus), the Catholic letters (James, 1 and 2 Peter, 2 and 3 John, and Jude), Hebrews, and even Luke-Acts are most certainly second-century texts (ca. 130–150 CE). Then there is the matter of Marcion, Valentinus, Basilides, Carpocrates, Hermas, Ignatius, and Polycarp, all Christians active in the same decades (130–150 CE), sometimes in the same locations (Rome, Alexandria, Asia Minor, and Antioch). Suddenly my picture of the New Testament was not so simple. I saw entanglement, not quarantine.

As I continued to teach the New Testament, I kept asking myself, "Whose literature was this?" And as I studied and reflected, it became clear to me that the New Testament was not just assembled, but the texts themselves were either written or rewritten by early Catholics to authorize themselves as the real Christians and their memories of Jesus and the beginnings of Christianity as the true story.

As I read and reflected on the scholarship that was produced in the nineteenth and twentieth centuries, I began to wonder about the way that the New Testament and early Christianity had been carved up and leveraged to "recover" a story about a "pure" form of Christianity taught by (the historical) Jesus. How much of this standard "historical" script had actually emerged out of German theological schools to authorize their own Protestant theology and traditions? Was I effectively teaching as "history" early Catholic history and interpretation as German theologians had reconfigured it? We can certainly do better than that, I thought.

The result of my years of teaching, study, and reflection is this textbook, which is a fresh history of early Christians, the pluralistic movements that they developed, and the entangled literature they produced. This textbook is not dedicated to "lost" or "found" Christianities, as if these forms of Christianities were somehow separate from the development of early Catholicism. This textbook does not separate New Testament literature from other early Christian literature, nor does it privilege the early Catholics over other Christians. Instead, this textbook is organized into chapters devoted to regional

Christian movements as they emerged and interacted during the first five generations of Christians. I have identified these generations as 40-year periods. The beauty of this organization is that it allows for comparative work to happen as we identify the major issues that challenged each generation of Christians and come to understand their solutions.

> First generation: 30–70 CE
>
> Second generation: 70–110 CE
>
> Third generation: 110–150 CE
>
> Fourth generation: 150–190 CE
>
> Fifth generation: 190–230 CE

On the first page of each chapter, I have identified the Christians and the literature that is covered in the chapter under the headings KEY PLAYERS and KEY TEXTS, respectively. Each chapter is further divided into sections which identify specific COMPANION READINGS that go along with the narrative in each section. These companion readings are easily accessible online at websites that specialize in biblical texts, patristic literature, and Nag Hammadi sources. Each chapter includes a timeline for the Christians covered in that chapter, as well as a table identifying their patterns of thought, practices, and ecclesiology. Included as well are the main TAKEAWAYS and QUESTIONS that can launch student discussions and be used as study guides. All illustrations are my own unless otherwise indicated. I designed the textbook to be delivered in a typical university semester and run it myself over the course of 14 instructional weeks.

This textbook has not been written before. It is the first attempt to write a comprehensive history of the first Christians as a pluralistic movement. Writing this textbook has been a journey of reflection and discovery for me. It has opened up new vistas that I am excited to share with students everywhere with the hope that, as we come to understand Christian pluralism and the consequences of the construction of orthodoxy in the past, we can challenge ourselves to examine not only Christian pluralism today, but religious pluralism more broadly; that when faced with claims of religious exclusivism and intolerance, we can learn to ask, "Who benefits from this?" and "Whose story is it anyway?"

April D. DeConick
Feast Day of Saint Thomas the Apostle

July 3, 2022

Acknowledgments

While I want to thank many people who have been instrumental in the creation of this textbook, I want to start with the acknowledgment we usually save for last. That is my husband, Wade Greiner. This book could not have been written without your constant support and encouragement – but, even more importantly, it is better because of our endless conversations about the topics. Not only did you allow me to talk on and on about these subjects, but you asked me all the right questions, questions that many times sent me back to the drawing board, to rethink or reconceive. When I was young, before we met, I did not even dream that I would be lucky enough to marry someone who would be so sincerely interested and proud of my work, let alone someone who would challenge me to take it further. Thank you.

This textbook is about students. I wrote it for you, and I wrote it because of you. Over 30 years, I have had hundreds of students, and I am unable to name all of you. You were all important to me, pushing me to be a better teacher and to tell an honest story. And I am proud of you all. To my undergraduates from Illinois Wesleyan University (when there was still a Religion Department there), but especially: Christine Luckritz Marquis, Jaeda Calaway, Sharon Stowe Cook, Kwang Oh, Katie Stump Holt, Jenny LaBrenz, Nicole Jo Wiedman, John Betz, Joshua Evans, Laura Arnold, and Mark Lamie. To my undergraduate students at Rice University, but especially: Jake Schornick, Julia Nations, Katelyn Willis, Brett Snider, Courtney Applewhite, Kai Cowen, Suzanne Harms, Van Heitmann, Domonique Richardson, Alexa Scott, Artie Throop, Lila Frenkel, Caleb Fikes, Eli Gennis, Malcolm Lovejoy, Joshua Murphree, and Emily Quinn. To my graduate students from Rice University, but especially: Grant Adamson, Franklin Trammell, Matthew Dillon, Andriana Umana, Michael Domeracki, C.J. Schmidt, Minji Lee, Rebecca Harris, Erin Prophet, Cindy Dawson, Naamleela Free Jones, Oihane Iglesias Telleria, Zachary Schwartz, Angela Stieber, Jacob Melancon, Rochelle Willingham, Abby Crowe-Tipton, and J.D. Reiner. Thank you.

Thank you to those who read parts of my manuscript and gave me honest feedback, but especially: David Terrell, Vernon Robbins, Lautaro Roig Lanzillotta, Dylan Burns, Jeffrey Kripal, and Susanne Scholtz.

Thank you to the Boniuk Institute for Religious Tolerance at Rice University and the Humanities Research Center at Rice University for providing me with grants to support the writing of this textbook.

Thank you to all of you who published scholarship that challenged me to reconsider my positions and discover new vistas, especially: Jason DeBuhn, Matthias Klinghardt, Douglas Campbell, Peter Lampe, Joseph Tyson, Markus Vinzent, Timothy Barnes, Denise Kimber Buell, Susanne Scholtz, Terence Donaldson, Dylan Burns, Lautaro Roig Lanzillotta, Vernon Robbins, Christine Trevett, William Tabbernee, Richard Pervo, Benjamin White, Michael Winkelman, Andrew Newberg, Mark Turner, and David Eagleman.

Thank you to my literary agent, Anne Borchardt, as well as to Rebecca Harkin, the acquisitions editor at Wiley-Blackwell who originally helped me conceive this project and supported me when the project took a different shape in the first few years of writing. Also my thanks to the editorial team who took great care in the final production. This book took me several years longer to complete than we had originally planned. I am most grateful for your kindness and patience as I worked and reworked the book. It took years of writing before I figured out that I could not begin to tell the Christian story from the beginning, but had to start telling the story from the middle.

CHAPTER 1

Sectarian Jews

Paul conversing with Thecla, ivory panel from casket, Rome, late fourth century, British Museum. Artist Matteo di Giovanni. **Source:** Heritage Images / Getty Images.

> "If anyone else has reason to be confident in the flesh, I have more: circumcision on the eighth day, a member of the People of Israel, of the tribe of Benjamin, a Hebrew born of Hebrews; as to the Law, a Pharisee; as to zeal, a persecutor of the church; as to righteousness under the Law, blameless. Yet whatever gains I had, these I have come to regard as loss because of Christ."
>
> *Paul of Tarsus wrote this in his letter to the church in Philippi*

KEY PLAYERS
Paul of Tarsus

KEY TEXTS
Letters of Paul

So you want to learn about the first Christians? Get back to the roots? Discover what really went on back in the time of Jesus and his first followers? Or perhaps you have questions about how early Christianity formed. Where did it start? Who was in charge? Why did the Catholics emerge as champions at the first church Council of Nicaea (325 CE)? Is their story the whole story? Or maybe you have heard that there are other gospels than the gospels of Matthew, Mark, Luke, and John found in the Bible. You wonder about who wrote these gospels and what they have

Comparing Christianities: An Introduction to Early Christianity, First Edition. April D. DeConick.
© 2024 John Wiley & Sons Ltd. Published 2024 by John Wiley & Sons Ltd.

to say about Jesus and the early Christians. Why isn't the *Gospel of Thomas* or the *Gospel of Mary* found in the New Testament? Or possibly you have heard that early Christianity was controversial and contentious, with some Christians and their churches identified as heresies or illegitimate forms of Christianity, while others with orthodoxy or legitimate Christianity. Who made this call? And why was it made? How did this controversy between orthodoxy and heresy relate to the rise of religious intolerance and the formation of Christianity? What does all this mean for Christianity as we know it today and its future?

These, in fact, are the very questions that are foundational to this textbook. They are questions that have compelled me, first as a student and then as a professor and scholar of early Christianity. The questions started when I was nineteen, when my mother came across a book that captured her eye in our local bookstore. After she read it, she passed it on to me. The book was a small, edited volume of early Christian gospels containing the *Gospel of Thomas*, the *Secret Book of James*, the *Gospel of Peter*, the *Infancy Gospel of Thomas*, and the *Gospel of the Hebrews*. Before I opened that book, I never knew that the early Christians wrote more literature than what we find in the New Testament. As I read those early Christian writings, I was riveted. I could not put the old gospels down and wanted to know more about them. But in 1982, there was very little published on these texts that was available to the public. It became clear to me that if I wanted to figure out why these texts were not in the New Testament, I was on my own.

At the end of my first semester in college, I left nursing school to explore the Humanities. As a Junior, I decided to major in Biblical Studies in the Department of Near Eastern Studies at the University of Michigan. I enrolled in classical Greek, and then Coptic, the ancient Egyptian language that some of these gospels survive in. I studied the New Testament alongside the Christian Apocrypha (Figure 1.1), writings that did not become part of the New Testament. I learned how Bishop Athanasius of Alexandria (ca. 296–373 CE) was the first known person to identify as a collection the 27 Christian books that became part of the Catholic New Testament (Figure 1.2) in an Easter letter he wrote to the

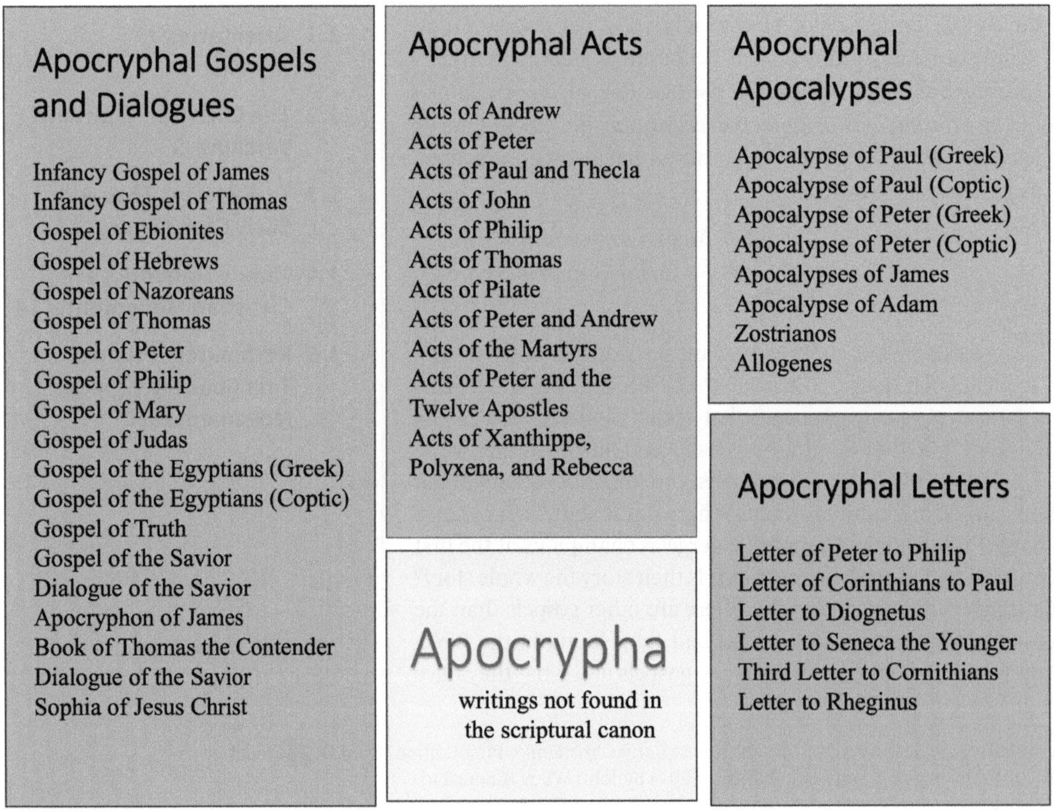

Apocryphal Gospels and Dialogues

Infancy Gospel of James
Infancy Gospel of Thomas
Gospel of Ebionites
Gospel of Hebrews
Gospel of Nazoreans
Gospel of Thomas
Gospel of Peter
Gospel of Philip
Gospel of Mary
Gospel of Judas
Gospel of the Egyptians (Greek)
Gospel of the Egyptians (Coptic)
Gospel of Truth
Gospel of the Savior
Dialogue of the Savior
Apocryphon of James
Book of Thomas the Contender
Dialogue of the Savior
Sophia of Jesus Christ

Apocryphal Acts

Acts of Andrew
Acts of Peter
Acts of Paul and Thecla
Acts of John
Acts of Philip
Acts of Thomas
Acts of Pilate
Acts of Peter and Andrew
Acts of the Martyrs
Acts of Peter and the
Twelve Apostles
Acts of Xanthippe,
Polyxena, and Rebecca

Apocryphal Apocalypses

Apocalypse of Paul (Greek)
Apocalypse of Paul (Coptic)
Apocalypse of Peter (Greek)
Apocalypse of Peter (Coptic)
Apocalypses of James
Apocalypse of Adam
Zostrianos
Allogenes

Apocrypha

writings not found in
the scriptural canon

Apocryphal Letters

Letter of Peter to Philip
Letter of Corinthians to Paul
Letter to Diognetus
Letter to Seneca the Younger
Third Letter to Corinthians
Letter to Rheginus

FIGURE 1.1   Examples of second- and third-century Christian Apocryphal writings.

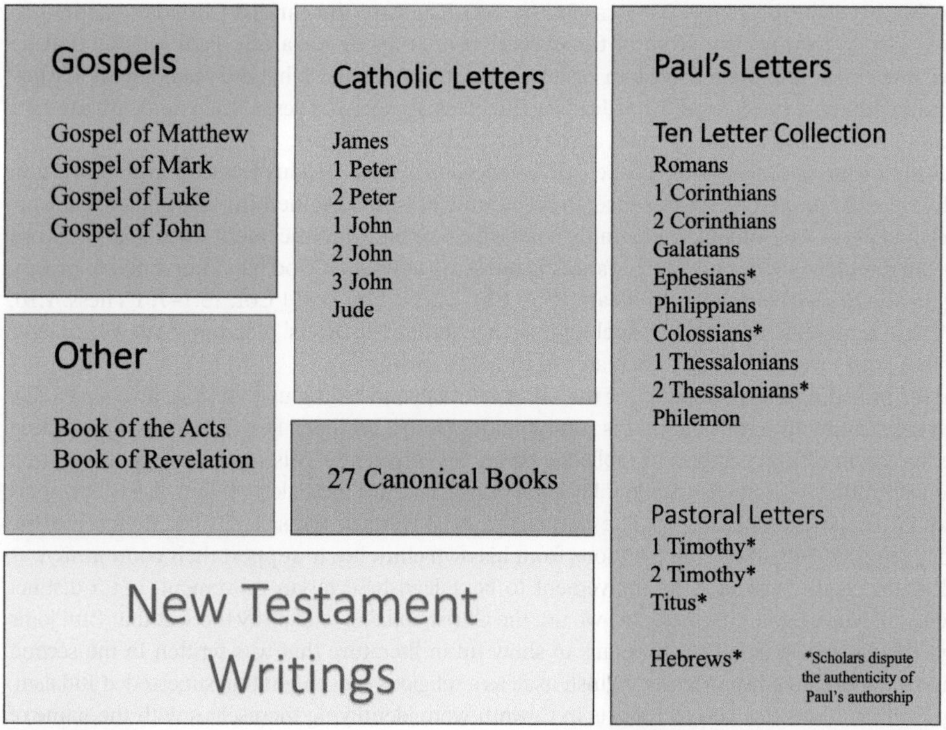

Gospels	Catholic Letters	Paul's Letters
Gospel of Matthew Gospel of Mark Gospel of Luke Gospel of John	James 1 Peter 2 Peter 1 John 2 John 3 John Jude	**Ten Letter Collection** Romans 1 Corinthians 2 Corinthians Galatians Ephesians* Philippians Colossians* 1 Thessalonians 2 Thessalonians* Philemon
Other Book of the Acts Book of Revelation	**27 Canonical Books**	**Pastoral Letters** 1 Timothy* 2 Timothy* Titus*
New Testament Writings		Hebrews* *Scholars dispute the authenticity of Paul's authorship

FIGURE 1.2   Books of the New Testament first listed by Athanasius in 367 CE.

bishops in Egypt (367 CE). In defining the Christian Bible as he does, Athanasius excludes many early Christian writings that were popular among Christians, disabusing them of their authority by calling them "apocrypha" or false writings. I went on to write my doctoral thesis and several books on the *Gospel of Thomas*. My fascination with the early Christian gospels and the Christianities that competed with Catholicism has resulted in the publication of several other books, including my book on the infamous second-century *Gospel of Judas* and another book on the Gnostics of antiquity.

Comparing Christianities is meant to fully engage early Christian literature inside and outside the New Testament. It is the textbook that I wished for when I was a college student back in 1982 with all those questions about earliest Christianity. As Christianity was kickstarted with the tragic death of the Jewish Messiah, Jesus of Nazareth, and was reengineered after the First Roman–Jewish War (66–73 CE) so that it was able to compete successfully as a new religious movement in Rome, numerous Christian identities and groups developed. The emergence and interaction of these multiple Christianities take center stage in this textbook and, with them, several questions. Why are there so many Christian movements in the first and second centuries? What makes them Christian? Why are their memories of Jesus and the historical Christian past different from each other? Where do all these documents and movements come from? How were they related to each other and to Judaism? Why did some of these movements survive while others failed to have a future? Did any of these movements actually have a monopoly on the truth?

1.1 Orientation to the Past

COMPANION READINGS
Philippians

Before embarking on this journey into the ancient Christian past, we need to get oriented to that past. Most helpful in this orientation is a collection of letters that Paul of Tarsus wrote to a number of early Christian churches he had established in Asia Minor and

Greece, roughly between the years 40–55 CE (Figure 1.3). They are the earliest Christian writings to survive, composed within twenty years of the execution of Jesus of Nazareth. Paul tells us that he joined Jesus' movement after he received an ecstatic revelation of Jesus. What did Jesus reveal to him? He says he came to know the "gospel" that Jesus is the Messiah and that Jesus' life and death are part of God's plan to redeem the People of Israel at the eschaton or end of time.

What is the meaning of the word "gospel" or "*evangelion*" (Greek)? This is a well-known word in antiquity. It is used by emperors, for instance, to communicate abroad something exciting or noteworthy that they had done. An evangelion is simply a newsflash or big announcement. Paul uses the word "*evangelion*" to refer to what he considered fantastic breaking news: that God had intervened in history by sending his son to save believers from death (Gal. 1:11–12, 16; Phil. 3:8; 1 Cor. 15:1–7; 1 Thess. 1:10; Rom. 1:6). There is no sense at all that gospel refers to a text that tells Jesus' biography. As we see later in this textbook, this usage develops much later in Christian history.

Paul never provides us with a name for the movement beyond telling us that he is aware of a distinct church community in Jerusalem that is run by James (Jesus' brother), Peter, and John. According to Paul, the Jerusalem church had been established before his conversion. Missionaries from this church had been concentrating on converting fellow Jews not only in and around Palestine, but also urban areas outside Palestine in the Jewish Diaspora. The community of converts in Jerusalem called themselves the Poor and they required Paul to collect donations from his own churches to support their community.

It is clear that Paul considered the movement to be a Jewish sectarian movement, not a distinct Christian religion. However, in this textbook, we use the Christian label to identify the sect that Paul joins even though the name "Christian" only begins to show up in literature that was written in the second century when the movement began to distinguish itself as a religious movement that superseded Judaism. If anything, Paul mentions that some converts in Corinth were identifying themselves with the name of the person who converted them ("we are Petrine" or "we are Apollarian"), a practice Paul dislikes. Because Paul leaves us without a name for the Jewish sectarian movement he had joined, we must keep in mind that our use of the word Christian to describe the earliest movement does not signal a non-Jewish identity. Everyone who joined the Christian movement during Paul's life were converting to a Jewish sect. They were joining the People of Israel. When exactly Christianity developed an identity as a religion distinct from Judaism is hotly contested in scholarship. As we see in this textbook, this parting of the ways happened at different times in different ways for different Christians. For Paul, however, to join this movement means that you are joining a Jewish messianic movement that identifies Jesus with the Messiah.

The title Messiah or Anointed One (Hebrew: *mashiach*; Greek: *christos*) derives from the verb "to anoint" (Hebrew: *mashach*; Greek: *chrio*) and refers to the anointing ritual that the Jews used to install priests, prophets, and kings into office. In the first century, the Jews were living under the oppressive rule of imperial Rome. Many Jews felt that their colonization was linked to behaviors like idolatry that had strained their relationship with their God, a God who had promised to protect their nation from

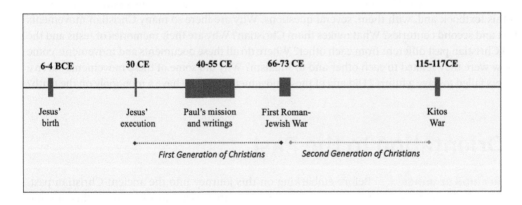

FIGURE 1.3   Timeline mapping first two generations of Christians.

foreign invasion as long as they kept God's commandments and were exclusively devoted to him.

The Jewish national God was so holy and sacred, so set apart from mundane everyday existence that even his name was considered ineffable, that it was written without vowels: YHWH. Although his name was only intoned during the Day of Atonement ceremonies in their Temple in Jerusalem by the high priests, scholars who have studied naming practices among Jews think that it was pronounced, "Yah-weh." As a national God, YHWH was worshipped in the land of Judea by Judeans, from which comes the designation "Jew." Once Jews began living outside the land of Judea in the Diaspora, the word Jew came to designate people who worshipped YHWH, the God of the Judeans, wherever they were dispersed geographically. Wherever they were, the Jews distinguished themselves from the non-Jews or Gentiles who did not share in this exclusive relationship with YHWH.

Their commitment to worshipping YHWH exclusively meant that Jews could not also worship the colonial civic Gods and Roman emperors. Nor could they consider YHWH to be Zeus or Baal by another name. He was a standout God, with a history deeply entangled with the Jews. He was a revelatory God, communicating directly to his people through his prophets. Indeed, their scripture showcases a special relationship between YHWH and the Jews. This relationship is premised on a covenant or contract that both parties consented to and is reaffirmed every time a Jewish infant boy is circumcised. YHWH, whom the Jews believed was the God who created the world and ruled it, had chosen to make an official pact with their nation. He promised to protect them as his chosen people and defend them from their enemies as long as they remained obedient servants to him and followed his rules. This covenantal agreement between the Jews and their God provided the Jews with a theological, rather than a political, explanation for their colonization. They believed that their colonization signaled the loss of YHWH's protection because they had broken their covenant with YHWH by failing to observe his rules.

These rules, which YHWH's prophet Moses delivered to them, are written in the Pentateuch or the first five books of the Bible and are known as the Torah. These rules cover almost all aspects of human life, not only cultic or ritual aspects like how to perform certain sacrifices or keep the Sabbath as a day of rest. The rules govern everything from sex, semen, and menstruation to diet, property damage, and disease. The rules govern the operation of the Temple in Jerusalem, which was the cultic center of Jewish worship and which regulated the festival calendar.

Roman authorities tended to tolerate the religions of the people they colonized unless the native religion promoted social unrest. Romans took this stance because it was good publicity and it reduced the impact of the changing of the guards once they had installed themselves as the new rulers of the regions. The local populations could continue their lives as usual, as long as they paid their taxes to their new overlords and obeyed their laws. The Romans, in fact, allowed the Jews to worship YHWH at the Temple in Jerusalem, exempted Jewish men from military service because it forced them to break the Law, and collected the tax for the Temple from Jews living in the Diaspora. The Romans tolerated the worship of the Jews because the Romans were convinced that their devotion to YHWH was their ethnic prerogative and ancestral heritage.

But religious tolerance did not mean that there was no social unrest among the Jews or anti-Jewish sentiment among the Romans. The Romans often installed client kings and governors who ruled in ways that privileged their own imperial aspirations and financially crippled the native populations. It was during Roman occupation that messianic dreams fermented among Jews. They speculated about the emergence of a national hero who would renew their obedience to the Law and, with it, the promises of YHWH's covenant. The advent of the Messiah was understood by Jews to be part of latter world events that included the defeat of their colonizers, the resurrection of the dead, the final judgment, the establishment of New Jerusalem, and the restoration of their national independence under YHWH's sovereignty. There is a wide range of opinions recorded in Jewish literature about the nature of each of these final world events or eschaton, including the description of the Messiah and his role in the inauguration of eschaton.

Messianic speculation among the Jews was caught up in a circle of unrest, resistance, and terror. While eschatological expectations grew in reaction to the horrible conditions of colonial life, providing the Jews with hope that YHWH would eventually make things right, they also spurred violent uprisings and equally violent clampdowns from the colonizers. The Jewish historian Flavius Josephus (ca. 37–100 CE) records a number of incidents in the first century of messianic contenders, who took up arms against Roman authorities and were defeated decisively (Jos., *JW* 2.261–3, 427–434; 4.385–90, 505–513; 6.98, 434; 17.271–5, 278–85). He identifies the Zealots as Jewish nationalists and revolution-aries who urged the Jews to rebel against Rome in order to return governance of Palestine to the Jews (Jos., *JW* 18.1.6). He also tells about the Sicarii or daggermen who sparked terror in crowds by pulling from beneath their cloaks, hidden knives (Jos., *JW* 20.9.3). They used these knives to assassinate and kidnap high-ranking Jewish authorities whom they believed were cooperating with the Romans. The violent resistance of these parties incited the Romans to take drastic measures, which led to the First Roman–Jewish War (66–73 CE), the destruction of the Temple (70 CE), and the massacre of the Jews in Jerusalem (70 CE) and at Masada (73 CE).

During the time of Jesus' activities, Pontius Pilate was alarmed by the local eschatological and messianic zeal that he confronted as governor of Judea. He felt that this apocalyptic enthusiasm threatened the fabric of Roman social order. For instance, Pilate reacted brutally to a messianic prophet who emerged among the Samaritans in the village named Tirathana. Pilate sent a detach-ment of cavalry and heavy-armed infantry, which killed most of the prophet's followers and took the rest prisoners. Pilate then executed the leaders of this messianic movement (Jos., *Ant.* 18.85–89). Given this reaction, it is not surprising that Jesus' activities resulted in his execution as the "King of the Jews."

From Paul, we learn that the first Christians from Jerusalem frequented synagogues in order to convince other Jews to join their movement. But, while they made some headway, they had a difficult time convincing most Jews that Jesus' messiahship was prophesized in the Jewish scriptures. The big stumbling block was the fact that Jesus not only died, but was also an executed criminal. This seemed ridiculous to most Jews who thought that their scriptures prophesized the rise of a messianic teacher, king, or priest who would be a hero. He would be victorious in his pursuit to renew the covenant and usher in the new age of Israel's glory by overthrowing Roman rule. Clearly, the executed Jesus was not this person.

While Jews were reticent to convert because of the incongruity of Jesus' life with traditional inter-pretations of the prophets, the missionaries found that a number of Gentiles (non-Jews) who frequented the synagogues were more easily convinced. These Gentiles had mostly converted to Judaism, following the Law except that they refused to be circumcised. They were called God-Fearers and were considered to be Jewish proselytes or recruits. This means that there was a diversity of Christians from the get-go. Some were ethnic Jews, while the majority were Jewish proselytes (uncircumcised Gentiles).

Paul tells us that he was not commissioned to convert Jews. Instead, the missionaries from Jeru-salem were those responsible for working in the synagogues and bringing into their house churches Jewish converts (which included Jewish proselytes). Paul's relationship with these missionaries seems to have suffered from his terrible reputation. He admits to violently persecuting Christians before he converted, although he does not relate how or why he did this. We can imagine though that it had something to do with the fact that Paul characterizes himself as a Pharisee, who was par-ticularly zealous about his Jewish faith prior to becoming a Christian (Phil. 3:5). The Pharisees (or Separatists) were a Jewish sect of laymen who thought that every Jew had to be as holy as a priest in order to keep YHWH's Law correctly (Exod. 19:3–6). During Jesus' time, in order to maintain their stringent purity rules, the Pharisees formed segregated lay groups consisting of Jews, who ate their meals together and worshipped together. Because the Law could be ambiguous, the Pharisees fash-ioned a set of rules and regulations that helped them observe the Law consistently. For instance, while the Law commanded that the Jews keep the Sabbath day holy, it did not give many details about how this observation might look. For generations, the Pharisees studied the Torah and filled in these conspicuous gaps with rulings. This body of legal traditions about how to precisely observe the Law is known as the Oral Torah. It was codified and written down in the late second century CE as the Mishnah. Even later, the Mishnah was studied by the rabbis and opinions about its inter-pretation were recorded. In the fifth century, this larger body of material came to be known as the Talmud.

Paul's reputation as a zealous Pharisee who persecuted Christians had spread throughout the churches in Judaea and seems to have made it difficult for him to work in this region after his conversion. So he ends up going north into Syria, Asia Minor, and Greece and begins missionizing pagans rather than Jews or Jewish proselytes (Figure 1.4). Paul persuades them to join the movement by teaching them while he sewed leather goods in his portable shop. These pagan Gentiles had no former knowledge of Judaism, were not Jewish proselytes, and were not frequenting synagogues. According to Paul, the Gentile converts met in their homes. Their gathering or *ecclesia* is translated as assembly or church. Paul claims to have been commissioned to do this by Jesus himself in a revelation. Paul also relates that he traveled to Jerusalem to visit with James, Peter, and John and receive their blessing to expand the mission to the pagan Gentiles. The leaders of the Jerusalem church complied.

So, because of Paul, the Christian movement came to contain three constituencies instead of two: ethnic Jews, Jewish proselytes, *and* non-law-observant Gentiles. The latter put pressure on the movement because they were unfamiliar with the Jewish Law and did not want to memorize or follow all its prescriptions. They especially disliked the idea of having to follow the Jewish diet and be circumcised, but the rest of the 613 commandments seemed unnecessary to them as well. Since the earliest leaders of the Christian movement had not yet made a ruling about whether converts had to be circumcised or observe the Jewish diet, the Law became hotly contested among the earliest Christians. This becomes aggravated when Paul begins to teach the Gentiles in his churches that the Law is not necessary for them to observe at all because Christ brought an end to the Law which God had intended to only be a temporary custodian anyway. Besides, Paul said, as long as the Gentiles love each other, they have fulfilled the Law inadvertently. Their faith made them righteous, not the Law (Rom. 13:8–10). This teaching polarized the Christians so that Paul finds himself embattled against other missionaries who come into his communities to convince Gentiles to fully convert by being circumcised and by observing the Jewish commandments.

Paul's decision to bring non-observant Gentiles into the movement caused the movement to fracture along legal fault-lines. There was a range of opinions among Jews about the meaning and application of the Law to real life situations. There were Jews who were Maximalists, believing that fidelity to the Law and its traditional interpretation should be strictly maintained. Minimalists were Jews

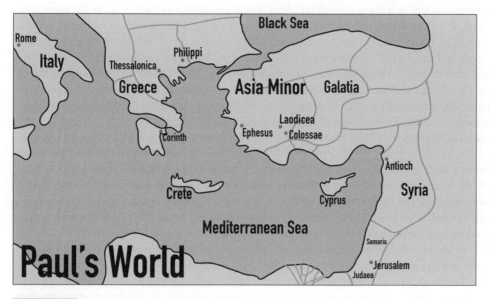

FIGURE 1.4 Map of the world that Paul traveled.

who felt that there was flexibility when it came to interpreting how the Law should be observed. This flexibility allowed for innovative interpretations that would keep up with the changing times. The moderate Jews fell somewhere in between, thinking that traditional interpretation had its place, while allowing for some adaptability to new social situations.

It is important to recognize that this discussion over how the Jewish Law should be valued and applied to real life situations was integral to questions of Jewish identity. Historically, this kind of difference of opinion over the Law, typically, has resulted in the rise of separate social groups. For instance, consider the modern Jewish landscape: the Jewish community consists of Orthodox Jews (Maximalists), Conservative Jews (Moderates), and Reform Jews (Minimalists). The Christian community too has developed socially along these lines so that modern denominations are organized around their position on the Law and its importance for salvation: Catholic and Orthodox Christians (Moderates), Protestants (Minimalists), and Messianic Jews (Maximalists).

It appears that the same social phenomenon took place among the very first Christians. The trigger appears to have been the conversion of masses of non-observant Gentiles in Paul's churches–Gentiles who did not want to undergo circumcision or change their diet. This was the social crisis that got all of them thinking. How was the Jewish Law applicable to these new Gentile converts? While the Christians agreed that Gentiles ought to be brought into the covenant at the end of time to worship YHWH (Ps. 22:27; 86:9; Isa. 49:6; 60:3), they disagreed on how this ought to be done. The Maximalists Christians demanded that the Gentile converts be circumcised and fully observe all God's commandments in his Law. Moderate Christians thought that circumcision was not necessary, but that other parts of the Law need to be intentionally observed, especially the Ten Commandments or some version of the Noahide laws (a reduced set of commandments that God gave Noah). Minimalist Christians expected Gentiles to devote themselves exclusively to the worship of the one God, love one another, and live temperately so as not to sin or bring unwanted attention to themselves. They thought that it was not necessary to burden Gentiles with the Law at the end of time when believers from the nations were being gathered together to worship God. Their faith was enough, they said, to make them righteous. Some of these Minimalists took Paul's comment about Christ being the "end of the Law" to mean that they were not obligated to any moral code, but free to behave as the Holy Spirit so moved them. This is why Paul finds himself having to crack down on antinomian (lawless) and ecstatic or charismatic behaviors that begin to erode the social order of his churches.

Paul's correspondences leave us in the mid-first century CE with a picture of a Jewish messianic movement that is fractured into three social parties along these legal fault-lines. In this textbook, we refer to these parties as the Maximalists, Moderates, and Minimalists. The Christian movement is gaining the most ground among the non-observant Gentiles and the least ground among ethnic Jews. The growth of the movement is dependent upon missionaries who are either from the apostolic-run church in Jerusalem like Peter (Aramaic name: Cephas), independent operators like Paul and Apollos (missionary whom Paul meets in Ephesus), or people commissioned by their own local church like Prisca and Aquila (Jewish converts from Rome whom Paul also knows).

There is no indication from Paul's letters that there is anyone in charge of all of the churches being founded, or that there is any single authority that controlled the missionaries and their message, or that there was some overarching plan and vision for the future of the Christian movement. At best, Paul regards the Jerusalem church as a legitimate authority because it predates Paul and is run by some of Jesus' disciples. But he felt his own revelatory calling was just as legitimate. He did, however, find it strategic to link into the Jerusalem network because he thought that it would help authorize his own independent mission to the non-observant Gentiles in Asia Minor and Greece. That said, he was highly critical of the apostles when he disagreed with them, especially those who were not Minimalists, and he did not feel in any way obliged to conform to their opinions.

From Paul's letters we can glean that there are established churches in Jerusalem and Palestine, north into Syria and Asia Minor, and west across Greece to Rome. So not only is the Christian movement split into three parties along legal fault-lines, but the churches also display regional characteristics, so that the churches in northern Asia Minor, for example, develop local traditions and interpretations of scriptures that are distinct from those developed in other locales, and so forth. This means that there was not a time when the Christian movement was homogeneous. It was a pluralistic movement from the start. This diversity only generates more diversity as the movement expands into the late-first and early-second centuries.

What is stable in the churches is the fact that all the churches baptize their converts in Jesus' name and share a thanksgiving meal that they call the Eucharist, with its ritual blessings memorialized as Jesus' words (variations of: "This is my body that is for you"; "This cup is the new covenant in my blood" 1 Cor. 11:23–26). The other constant is the fact that all the churches are charismatic, paradigms of religious enthusiasm. The Christians in all the churches thought that they were experiencing the fulfillment of the end-time prophecy found in Joel 2:28: "I will pour out my spirit out on every person; your sons and daughters will prophesy; your elders will dream dreams, and your youth will see visions." The Christians insisted that the Holy Spirit had descended on them at their baptisms and filled them up, making them prophets, healers, and visionaries.

Because of this charisma – the spirit filled both the sons and the daughters so that "in Christ there is neither male nor female" (Gal. 3:28) – women held positions of power alongside men in the first churches. Paul names women who preached alongside him (i.e. Euodia and Synthyche: Phil. 4:2–3), women who led churches in their homes (i.e. Nympha: Col. 4:15; Chloe: 1 Cor. 1:10–13; Prisca: 1 Cor. 16:3–4, 19; Phoebe: Rom. 16:1–2; Apphia: Philem. 1), women who were apostles and missionaries (i.e. Prisca: 1 Cor. 16:3–4, 19; Junia: Rom. 16:7), women who were co-workers (i.e. Phoebe: Rom. 16:3; Mary: Rom. 16:6; Typhena and Tryphosa: Rom. 16:12; Persis: Rom. 16:12), and women who were deacons (i.e. Phoebe: Rom. 16:1–2). Women converts were doing the same things as male converts, including traveling as apostles, presiding over house-churches, prophesying, and preaching.

1.2 The Christian Standard Versions

When did Christianity start and who started it? Did Christianity start with Jesus in Galilee as has been traditionally assumed by Protestant churches? Or Peter the apostle as Catholic doctrine has it? Or James the brother of Jesus and leader of the first church in Jerusalem as the Orthodox proclaim? Or was it the joint creation of his disciples, who after Jesus' death found themselves unemployed, in need of work, as the German Enlightenment philosopher Hermann Samuel Reimarus argued in a draft of a work which was so radical that it was kept secret until after his death (1694–1768)? Or was it invented by Saul of Tarsus turned Paul the Apostle, a Jew who, after an ecstatic experience, fashioned a message about Jesus that was wildly attractive to non-Jews, as many biblical scholars today maintain?

While these answers are all different, they are more similar than we might think. All assume that Christianity started around the time of Jesus and involved a cast of characters that were chosen by him to establish the Christian church and its legacy: Catholicism, Orthodoxy, and Protestantism. In other words, all these stories, including the academic one, do the work of authorizing our present-day Christian churches, giving them a direct line back to Jesus.

These linear stories construct the origins of Christianity by connecting the Christian church, as we know it today, with Jesus. In this way, late doctrines like the Trinity or the Two Natures of Jesus, sacraments like the Eucharist, the creation of the New Testament scriptural canon, and ecclesiastic structures like the Papacy are authorized by Jesus through a succession that occurred via his apostles and a second-century cast of characters, traditionally, called the Apostolic Fathers (the successors to the apostles), and the Church Fathers (the successors to the Apostolic Fathers) (Figure 1.5). Generally, these narratives are told as a coherent chronological story starting in Galilee or Jerusalem with Jesus and then soldiering through the New Testament documents, the Apostolic Fathers, and the Church Fathers, mining them for positivist historical information.

Apostolic Fathers *Third Generation*	Church Fathers *Fourth-Fifth Generation*
Shepherd of Hermas Didache Letters of Ignatius of Antioch Letter of Polycarp of Smyrna Letter of Barnabas Letters of Clement of Rome Letter of Diognetus Martyrdom of Polycarp Fragments of Papias of Hierapolis Quandratus of Athens Aristides	Justin Martyr Minucius Felix Melito of Sardis Hegesippus Athenagoras of Athens Irenaeus of Lyons Theophilus of Antioch Clement of Alexandria Tertullian of Carthage Hippolytus of Rome Ps.-Hippolytus Origen Cyprian Novatian Gaius

FIGURE 1.5 Classifications "Apostolic Fathers" and "Church Fathers".

Frequently in these stories, the Fathers of the Church are in conflict with other Christians whom they identify as fake Christians masquerading as real Christians. In these stories, the fake Christians are called heretics, a label which reflects the position that they have deviated from the straight and narrow path of the truth or orthodoxy preserved by the Church Fathers. The early Catholic Church is viewed as the rightful heir and guardian of the New Testament scriptures, which the heretics have misunderstood, corrupted, and abused.

This orthodox narrative was first forged by the Church Fathers in order to displace and marginalize Christians they disagreed with at a time when what it meant to be Christian was hotly contested. This story has had a long shelf-life because it has served the purposes of Christian churches over the centuries. It has survived for two thousand years, broadcast not only within Christian churches, but also within the academic fields of Biblical Studies and Church History, which were originally located within the religious discipline of theology. There have been two basic academic versions of the story, both reflecting standard theological narratives of Church History.

The standard Catholic version presents the story as a continuous development of church institutions and doctrines that represent the outward expressions of the Holy Spirit working within the community, an idea that gained traction in the academy through the nineteenth-century work of Catholic theologian and Church historian Johann Adam Moehler (1796–1838 CE). This continuity is presented from Jesus to the Council of Nicaea as a natural progression of the maturation of Christian doctrine and practices by learned men who, in this line of apostolic succession, understood the truth of Jesus' incarnation and worked to communicate this sacred mystery in the language and culture of the times. In other words, it was the natural process of enculturation, when the sacred truth came to be expressed in Greek philosophical jargon. While the doctrines are viewed as human constructions, they are meant to witness to the truth of the incarnation and safeguard it. The Fathers were defenders of the sacred truth against others who would try to pedal a cheap imitation. The Fathers' well-organized defense of the truth triumphed at Nicaea (325 CE) and has been expressed ever since in official councils and creeds (Figure 1.6).

The standard Protestant version of the story developed out of Catholic–Protestant conflicts in the wake of the Reformation (1517–1648 CE). It presents the development of the orthodox doctrines of the Catholic Church as a corruption of the pure truth taught by Jesus found in the scriptures. This echoes

Nicene Creed

We believe in one God, the Father almighty, maker of all things visible and invisible; And in one Lord, Jesus Christ, the Son of God, begotten from the Father, only-begotten, that is, from the substance of the Father, God from God, light from light, true God from true God, begotten not made, of one substance with the Father, through Whom all things came into being, things in heaven and things on earth, Who because of us men and because of our salvation came down, and became incarnate and became man, and suffered, and rose again on the third day, and ascended to the heavens, and will come to judge the living and dead, And in the Holy Spirit. But as for those who say, There was when He was not, and, Before being born He was not, and that He came into existence out of nothing, or who assert that the Son of God is of a different hypostasis or substance, or created, or is subject to alteration or change - these the Catholic and apostolic Church anathematizes.

FIGURE 1.6   Nicene Creed (325 CE).

the Protestant doctrine of *sola scriptura*, that the New Testament is the self-contained deposit of the revelation of Jesus. This version haunts the academic work of the famous German Lutheran Church historian, Adolph von Harnack (1851–1930 CE), who said that Christianity started with the true principles taught by Jesus. Over time, these true principles were degraded under the weight of intellectual activity and Greek philosophical speculations that focused on understanding Jesus' person and nature rather than Jesus' teachings which were the real essence of Christianity. He calls this process the Hellenization of Christianity (when Christianity was made to conform to Greek thought) which, he says, transformed the "living faith" into creeds that had to be believed and ceremonies that had to be followed.

Why did the Hellenization of Christianity occur in the first place? Harnack gives this first-place honor to the heretics who, out of their pagan fascination with Greek culture, hellenized Christianity to the extreme. Harnack says that the Catholic Fathers remedied the acute enculturation program of the heretics, putting its own teachings, worship, and practices into fixed forms and ordinances that tried to keep the worst of pagan culture, like polytheism, at bay, while still speaking the language of the Greek world. When all is said and done, Harnack presents a picture of the origins of Christianity rooted in Jesus' original message minus all the Catholic accoutrements which, he explains, were analogous to the Hellenization program of the pagan heretics anyway.

In 1934, the German Church historian, Walter Bauer (1877–1960 CE), published the first history of early Christianity which aimed to deconstruct these standard narratives because, Bauer explains, he had recognized that they were more theological stories than historical accounts. By examining regional Christian literature and legends, Bauer investigates whether there was a primary Christian church with an ecclesiastical teaching from which heresies diverged. As a historian, he says that he felt compelled to set aside his theological biases and to let the other side also be heard. By casting aside his preconceived ideas about what ancient Christianity was supposed to look like, he started his project by remaining open to all possibilities.

In his book, Bauer ponders where to start. He realizes that his project cannot start with the New Testament because the majority of texts cannot be arranged confidently either chronologically or geographically. Nor can the precise circumstances of the origins of these texts, including their authors, be sufficiently determined. He instead offers to write a retrohistory, starting at a later time when information about early Christians is better known, then working backward to figure out what is less known. As he works backward through the materials, he demonstrates how orthodox Catholic authors construct legends and forge texts to create, authorize, and distribute their truth across the Mediterranean into regions that were not originally orthodox but non-Catholic to begin with. In the end he determines that there was no original unity of thought or practice among the Christians – orthodoxy was not the original Christianity – but instead, there was a great diversity that, beginning in the second century, was disciplined and restrained by Catholics who cast themselves as the original Christians. Bauer had dropped a bomb: early Christianity was plural and orthodoxy was constructed.

But the bomb did not detonate immediately. It was only decades later, when scholars began in earnest to study newly discovered Christian writings from Nag Hammadi, that Bauer's thesis finally gained an audience. For these scholars, the vast diversity of non-orthodox thought and practices reflected in the Nag Hammadi collection destabilized the standard story of orthodoxy (Figure 1.7). Bauer's insistence on Christianity's original plurality rang true even when some of his specific arguments had become dated and his interpretation was shown to carry on the project of Liberal

Nag Hammadi Writings

Prayer of the Apostle Paul	Authoritative Teaching
Apocryphon of James	Concept of Our Great Power
Gospel of Truth	Paraphrase of Shem
Treatise on the Resurrection	Second Treatise of the Great Seth
Tripartite Tractate	Apocalypse of Peter
Gospel of Thomas	Teachings of Silvanus
Gospel of Philip	Three Steles of Seth
Hypostasis of the Archons	Zostrianos
On the Origin of the World	Letter of Peter to Philip
Exegesis on the Soul	Melchizedek
Book of Thomas the Contender	Thought of Norea
Holy Book of the Great Invisible Spirit	Testimony of Truth
Sophia of Jesus Christ	Marsanes
Dialogue of the Savior	Interpretation of Knowledge
Apocalypse of Paul	Valentinian Exposition
First and Second Apocalypse of James	Allogenes
Apocalypse of Adam	Hypsiphrone
Acts of Peter and the Twelve Apostles	Gospel of Truth
Thunder, Perfect Mind	Trimorphic Protennoia

FIGURE 1.7 Contents of Christian books found in the Nag Hammadi Codices.

Protestantism from the nineteenth century. The Liberal Protestant project arose in order to sync Christianity with modern intellectual knowledge. Liberal Protestants took seriously Darwin and the scientific method, so that, for instance, the Bible and church creeds came to be understood by Liberal Protestants as human cultural products. Orthodoxy was also viewed as a human cultural construction, set into motion by the apostles. Orthodoxy was seen as only one way among many diverse ways to frame Christian truth. So, while Bauer made many historical advances in our understanding that early Christianity was plural and orthodoxy constructed, he continued the theological Protestant project of his era by writing a history that left Jesus as the sole authority of the Christian church and truth.

1.3 Trajectories Through Early Christianity

If Christianity was originally diverse and orthodoxy constructed and secondarily imposed to limit and control this diversity, then the model of a linear progression of the Church from Jesus to the Apostles to the Apostolic Fathers to the Church Fathers to Nicaea was fractured, if not split open. In place of this narrative, New Testament scholars Helmut Koester (1926–2016 CE) and James Robinson (1924–2016 CE) offered the model of trajectories through early Christianity. Their idea was simple. Investigate the earliest Christian texts – the New Testament texts and a select number of non-canonical sources – and map the variant forms of Christianity represented in them. Then demonstrate how these variant forms of early Christianity produced other types of Christianity that moved through history in a variety of trajectories.

Using this model, they emphasized that early Christianity was not randomly plural but the plurality developed along trajectories that were traceable. For instance, they suggested that an orthodox trajectory can be traced from Paul to Ephesians to 1 Peter to Luke-Acts to the Pastorals to the emergent Catholic Church. Another trajectory went from Paul to certain heterodox (not conforming to orthodox standards) second-century Christians, from Colossians to Valentinus, Basilides, and Marcion. As they mapped the trajectories, they brought into question the privileging of New Testament texts so that the study of New Testament texts, in their work, was bundled together with the study of second-century Christian literature. Their model resisted telling the story of the history of the Christian church. Instead, they created a history-of-ideas model that showed how Christian thought developed along different thought paths among early Christians.

The trajectories model had ties with earlier scholarship which had determined that there were two major Christian movements represented in the New Testament texts and which became significant players in early Christianity. In this way early Christianity was divided into Jewish Christianity and Pauline or Gentile (non-Jewish) Christianity. Today, this terminology is considered dated because it coded Jewish Christianity as legalistic and backward, while also inaccurately suggesting that Jewish Christians were ethnic Jews, which was not always the case. Some were Gentile converts. In addition, as we already learned, earliest Christianity was a Jewish sectarian movement that brought Gentiles into the People of Israel alongside ethnic Jews.

The trajectories model has been influential because it created space for imagining early Christian diversity outside the traditional stories. Yet it has been criticized for not going far enough beyond the traditional story because it simply multiplies the old teleological narrative of the Catholics into many similar narratives with beginnings that determine the endings (or vice versa). More problematic is the understanding of individual trajectories as representatives of different forms of Christianity developing in isolation of each other, with little allowance for multiple trajectories in a single geographical location. Because individuals and texts are placed within single trajectories, it has been difficult to imagine individuals or texts participating in multiple trajectories.

In the end, we are left in a mire with no real answers to the simplest questions. What does the plurality of early Christianity mean for our understanding of early Christianity history? How did early Christian diversity originate? What did the various movements look like and where were they located? How did the various movements relate to each other? What made the movements different from each other? What made the movements Christian? What factored into the intergenerational survival of some and the failure of others?

1.4 Family Networks of Christian Movements

This textbook aims to answer these questions, but to do so by implementing a different model based on the concept of family networks. Modeling early Christian movements in networks of religious families decenters the standard Catholic and Protestant stories so that the products of history (Catholicism, Orthodoxy, and Protestantism) do not determine the telling of the stories. This model also allows us to map the emergence of Christian pluralism in a relational rather than isolationist way, so that we can come to understand the connections between different groups as well as the multivocality (multiple authorial voices) and the multivalency (multiple meanings) of the Jewish and early Christian texts they used (Figure 1.8). This means that different groups could use the same texts but interpret them in remarkably distinct (and even opposite) ways.

This model has its roots in the rise of taxonomy or classification that developed in the biological sciences in the eighteenth century in order to describe, identify, and name organisms systematically based on shared characteristics. Carl Linnaeus (1707–1778 CE), a Swedish botanist, is considered the father of modern taxonomy, since he introduced the formal system of naming organisms with two Latin names: the first identifies their genus (e.g. *Homo*) and the second their species (e.g. *sapiens*).

After Charles Darwin published *On the Origin of Species*, scientists retooled the old taxonomies to reflect Darwin's principle of common descent. When they began to diagram evolutionary trees or cladograms, they realized monophyletic (single arrangement) groups, like "mammals" or "birds" defined by a set of shared attributes with a recent common ancestor, were not always the case. Groups of organisms existed that were not defined with reference to a recent common ancestor and a property which was necessary and sufficient for membership in that group. This led researchers to talk about polyphyletic (multiple arrangement) groups like marine mammals or flying vertebrates that are composed of organisms that share a large number of similarities, yet no property is necessarily shared by all individuals in the group, and no individual has all the properties generally characteristic of members of its group.

FIGURE 1.8 The difference between multivocality (multiple authors) and multivalency (multiple meanings).

Consider this possible polyphyletic scenario illustrated below (Figure 1.9). There are six individuals who can be grouped according to seven attributes A–G. In this case, one grouping (Species 1) includes individuals 1–3 and a second grouping (Species 2) includes individuals 4–6. Each grouping shares a majority of attributes. In Species 1, each member shares at least one of the attributes C or D, neither of which is present in the second grouping. In Species 2, each member shares at least one of the attributes E, F, or G and none of these are present in the first grouping. We might imagine that the individuals could be arranged so that the individuals resemble their nearest neighbors very closely and their further neighbors less closely. Those individuals nearest the extremes would resemble each other hardly at all.

Ludwig Wittgenstein (1889–1951 CE) famously applied this concept to philosophy using the concept of a GAME as an example. What makes Solitaire, Chess, Ring-Around-The-Rosie, and Minecraft games? There are no "essential" attributes of games, Wittgenstein said, but rather there are overlapping characteristics shared by individual games. The category GAME is heterogenous, so that individual games share many but not all the properties that games have in common (Figure 1.10). Wittgenstein called these similarities family resemblances. Games, he said, form a family whose members have family resemblances

Species 1			Species 2		
1	2	3	4	5	6
A	A		A	A	
B	B	B			B
C		C			
	D	D			
			E	E	
			F		F
			G		G

FIGURE 1.9 Table laying out possible polyphyletic scenario.

Board Games			Computer Games		
1	2	3	4	5	6
A competitive	A competitive		A competitive	A competitive	
B solo	B solos	B solo			B solo
C cards		C cards			
	D dice	D dice			
			E video avatar	E video avatar	
			F map		F map
			G video cars	G video cars	

FIGURE 1.10 Example of GAME grouping based on family resemblances Series 1 (1–3): Board Games; Series 2 (4–6): Computer Games.

which overlap. The members of a family are related to each other in different ways. Families are complicated networks of similarities that overlap and crisscross. When we study games, Wittgenstein advised, we should not think that there must be something in common or they would not be called "games."

Rodney Needman (1923–1996 CE) applied Wittgenstein's idea to the field of social anthropology when he reflected on the concept of KINSHIP which he understood to be the allocation of rights (i.e. group membership, succession to office, inheritance of property, locality of residence, type of occupation, etc.) and their transmission from one generation to the next. He resists defining KINSHIP prescriptively but instead wants to think about it as a category with possible features that are related to each other and vary from case to case.

J. Gordon Melton (1942– CE), scholar of American religions, used the idea of family resemblances and networks to successfully chart the modern religious landscape in his massive *Encyclopedia of American Religions*. He organized various groups into 26 religious families based on common heritage, thought worlds, and lifestyles, while recognizing that aspects of these features would vary and overlap from group to group within each family. His organization helps us see the emergence of various movements, as well as understand the various movements and their families in relationship to each other.

This textbook likewise organizes the diversity of early Christianity into families. Groups in each family may share many similar features, but not all, and they share in common some features that are distinct from other families. The features that are studied in the following chapters include each group's theology (beliefs about God), Christology (beliefs about Christ), cosmogony (beliefs about creation), cosmology (beliefs about world structure), anthropology (beliefs about humans), soteriology (beliefs about salvation), devotional patterns (worship activities), ecclesiastic (church) organization, scriptural usage, and remembered heritage, especially when it comes to their understanding of Judaism and their ties to it. The families that they belong to are comprehensively mapped out in the final chapter of the textbook, after all the evidence of the individual groups is presented in the preceding chapters. In this way, our understanding of the early Christian landscape is created out of the sources rather than superimposed on them.

1.5 Rethinking How We Talk About Religious Movements

While it is essential to understand the broad families of early Christian movements, it is also important to understand the nature of each of the movements within the different families. The sociology of religious movements has gained ground in recent years with the recognition that the traditional terminology that relies on church (conventional religious organization), sect (deviant religious organization with traditional beliefs and practices), and cult (deviant religious organization with novel beliefs and practices) is not sufficient to describe religious movements, but is a product of the Protestant worldview and authorizes Christian denominationalism. Consider how problematic this typology is when we are analyzing a religious landscape like second-century Christianity that does not have a conventional religious organization yet. Also consider how this typology organizes religious movements in relationship to the categories of what is normative and what is deviant, which immediately values or devalues particular movements. Sociologists of religion have tried to adjust this typology, but their adjustments have mainly served their purposes in describing new religious movements in relationship to their tension with society and secularism, how world-affirming or denying they are. This also is not sufficient for trying to describe early Christian plurality.

In this textbook, we use a new typology to describe the types of religious groups that make up early Christian sectarianism (Figure 1.11). Here sectarianism denotes independently organized groups that claim to be the authentic representatives of the same religious tradition. Within this sectarianism, we observe five types of religious movements based on the ways in which they form or emerge. A CONSOLIDATED RELIGIOUS MOVEMENT is a group created when two or more independent religious units form a single network with common religious leadership. A modern example is the merger of the American Unitarian Association and the Universalist Church of America, in 1961, to form the Unitarian Universalist Association. A REFORMED

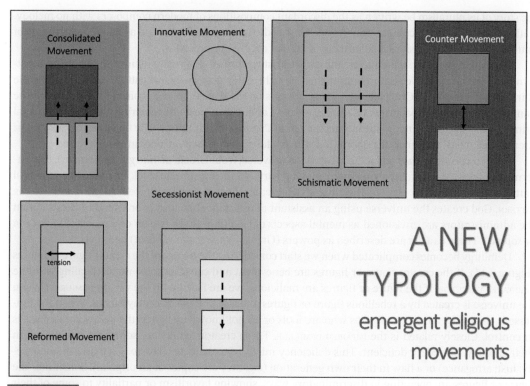

FIGURE 1.11 Diagram illustrating how new religious movements emerge.

RELIGIOUS MOVEMENT is a group which has changed something about the religious group with which its members are already affiliated. Usually the reformed group perceives itself as a restoration of the ideal form of the tradition and operates tensely within the tradition to make these reforms. If opposed, they often secede and form an independent and competing organization as happened during the Protestant Reformation. In a SECESSIONIST RELIGIOUS MOVEMENT an independent religious group is formed when a segment splits off from a religious group and starts an alternative form of the parent group. An example of a secessionist movement is the Pilgrims who left the Church of England which they perceived to be corrupt. A SCHISMATIC RELIGIOUS MOVEMENT is created when a single religious movement splits into smaller segments, such as what happened in 1054 when the Catholic Church split into the Roman Catholic and the Greek Orthodox Churches. A COUNTER RELIGIOUS MOVEMENT is a group formed in opposition to another religious group because it disagrees with the other group and attempts to compete with it for converts. A modern example is Mormonism or the Church of Jesus Christ of Latter-day Saints. An INNOVATIVE RELIGIOUS MOVEMENT is a group that emerges as a novel religious organization, generated as a product of innovation. The Church of Christ, Scientist is a contemporary example of an innovative religious Christian movement that emerged when Mesmerism and the teachings of Phineas Parkhurst Quimby informed Mary Baker Eddy's interpretation of her personal visions and study of the Bible.

1.6 All that Jazz

To write a history of early Christianity is to grapple with the extreme diversity among early Christians. If we were to put this history to music, the composition would not be a symphony in four movements with brisk and lively beginnings in Jesus' mission to the slow and lyrical development of the early church to the contrast and clash with the heretics to the climatic triumph of the Catholic Church in the finale. Nor would the story of its pluralism be written as the discordant compositions of modern composers with no melody. Rather it would be a jazz composition in which a melody is improvised again and again around a variety of patterns of chord progressions and harmony lines that may not be orthodox.

What are some of the patterns that the early Christians used to improvise their melodies? Certain patterns involve THEOLOGY. We see throughout this book, three distinct theological patterns entertained by the Christians (Figure 1.12). One pattern, YAHWISM, focuses on the worship of the Biblical Creator God whose name is YHWH. Another pattern is TRANSTHEISM (from Latin: *trans-*, beyond) centering on a transcendental primal God who is the source of life but not the actual Creator of the universe. The final pattern, XENOTHEISM (from Greek: *xeno-*, foreigner) features a God who is a foreigner or alien intruder in our universe.

When it comes to DEMIURGY (who created the universe; from Greek: *demiurgos*, craftsman), the patterns are highly complex, involving many moving parts. At the most basic level, there are two potential patterns. In the AUTOCRAT PATTERN, the creator God creates the universe by himself. In the ADMINISTRATOR PATTERN, God creates the universe using an assistant or assistants like angels or attendant Gods. Often the administrators are envisioned as mental aspects of God (e.g. God's reason or *logos*; God's wisdom or *sophia*). These usually are described as powers (Greek: *dynameis* or *exousia*) or angels.

Demiurgy becomes complicated when we start considering the nature of the creator figure or figures (Figure 1.13). If the creator figure or figures are benevolent and conscientious, we are dealing with the CARETAKER DEMIURGE. If the figure or figures are malicious, we are faced with the VILLAIN DEMIURGE. When the universe is created by a rebellious figure or figures, the REBEL DEMIURGE is playing out. When the universe is created by a figure or figures who are fools or do not know any better, the IGNORANT DEMIURGE is in control. Closely related is the IMPAIRED DEMIURGE. These creator figures are somehow diminished in their capacity, flawed, or deficient. This deficiency might be a character flaw (e.g. narcissism; erogeneity; lust; arrogance) or a flaw in their own generation (e.g. they are copies of an original). Sometimes the figure or figures are operating in discriminatory ways, showing favoritism or partiality to some of their

FIGURE 1.12 Early Christian theological patterns.

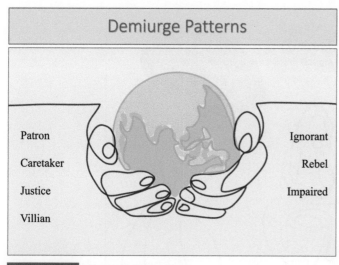

Demiurge Patterns

Patron

Caretaker

Justice

Villian

Ignorant

Rebel

Impaired

FIGURE 1.13   Patterns of Demiurgy.

creatures. This is the PATRON DEMIURGE. Sometimes the demiurge creates to rule his universe with a set of laws that require him to judge human compliance, to reward and punish his creatures as a high court justice might. This is the JUSTICE DEMIURGE. To complicate matters, none of these descriptions is mutually exclusive. For instance, a demiurge may be an ignoramus and also impaired. Or the demiurge may be a caretaker while also a patron or a justice.

In all Christian systems, the created universe is a place of evil, although what evil is and what is evil varies, as are explanations for the origins of evil. Demons exist in all Christian systems as powerful evil supernatural beings who play a part in ruling the universe, sometimes even as the demiurge. They control human beings, tempting them to sin by inciting the passions (i.e. lust, anger, gluttony, etc.). They possess human beings and make them sick. They incite people to conflict and war. This means that Christians in antiquity looked at the human body with suspicion and the material world around them as a potential booby trap.

This also means that most Christians were very conflicted about their bodies and the world. While some thought that the universe was created with good intention and others malicious intention, this did not mean that the "good intention" Christians saw the material world and their bodies as good in contrast to the "evil intention" Christians who saw the world and their bodies as evil. Rather Christians who thought the universe was created with good intention, also thought that Satan or the Devil ruled the world and demons were all around them wreaking havoc. Those who thought the world was created with malicious intention thought that the creator God ruled the world and demons were all around them wreaking havoc. In both cases, the physical world and the human body are viewed as the playground of the demons.

The universe that these demiurgic figures create is always a place of suffering and death, although the explanations for why this is the case (a.k.a. THEODICY) and what humans are supposed to do about it are highly dependent on the interaction of the theological and demiurgic patterns that each Christian movement assembled for itself. At the core of these various explanations for why the universe is a place of suffering and death however are two basic options. Either a God or Gods are responsible (FAULTY-GOD PATTERN) or humans are responsible (FAULTY-HUMAN PATTERN). These patterns were not mutually exclusive, but could be combined. The Christians did not consider the no-fault pattern (as in "shit happens").

When it comes down to it, Christian movements are all about building salvific or soteriological (from Greek: *soter*, savior) systems that allow Christians liberation from demonic control here on earth and in their afterlives. This afterlife was imagined as a utopian world that would be fashioned following the eschaton when the world and demonic rule ended. The soteriological options that the Christians developed depended on their explanations for evil and preferred patterns of THEODICY

FIGURE 1.14   Patterns of Theodicy: Who is responsible for suffering?

(Figure 1.14). All Christian systems promoted a God who intervened in history to save humanity. In all systems, Jesus' death is instrumental in this act of salvation. All Christians believed salvation was exclusive to them as God's elect, and that, in order to be redeemed, it was necessary to join their group, participate in their rituals, and live a life that reflected their redeemed status. The question that the groups debated was whether humans had to achieve their salvation through human actions too. Does salvation depend on whether certain laws were observed that God required them to follow (Figure 1.15)? Christian systems that answered affirmatively represent the ACHIEVEMENT PATTERN (humans have to do something to achieve their salvation). If answered negatively, the system represents the GIFT PATTERN (salvation is a gift of God's grace alone).

Anthropological patterns are recognizable too. In antiquity, human beings were understood to have physical material bodies (a.k.a. flesh; Greek: *sarx*) animated by the soul (Greek: *psyche*). The soul is the human's mental and emotional self, very similar to our modern psychological term, psyche. One common pattern is MONISTIC, perceiving the soul to be the breath of life animating the body. It is the material principle of vitality that makes up the person's mental capacities. It is what makes the person a living conscious being. The soul does not exist outside the body. Body and soul form a single indissoluble monistic unit. The soul, like the body, is mortal. The deceased is destined to be a shade or ghost in the afterlife. For some Jews this meant that the deceased – body and soul – are supposed to be resurrected from the dead and immortalized at the end of time to live in the new utopian world.

The second anthropological pattern is DUALISTIC, based on the teachings of Plato who believed that the soul was immortal. The soul was divided into a higher self – the mental capacity to reason (Greek: *nous*, mind) – and a lower self – the appetite and passions. The soul fell from its heavenly abode and embodied when it lost sight of God. The immortal soul is released at death and, in many dualistic systems, reincarnates (Greek: *metempsychosis*) until it achieves perfection and can return to its heavenly starting place. Some Christians, however, were dualists but they straddled the fence on the question of the soul's immortality. They believed that the soul of baptized Christians will separate from the body at

FIGURE 1.15   Patterns of Soteriology: Who Saves Us?

death and wait around in a heavenly realm. Then at the end of time, the body will be resurrected from the grave, the soul will be immortalized, and they will join together as a resurrected being for eternity.

The third anthropological pattern is TRIADIC, where the human being is more than body and soul. In this pattern, the ability to intuit and discern the truth (rather than reason out the truth) is understood as a separate mental capacity, usually called the Spirit (Greek: *Pneuma*) but also called the Mind (Greek: *Nous*). This capacity is immortal and divine. In this pattern, the Spirit or Mind is the true self rather than the soul. In some instances, all humans are seeded with the Spirit or Mind. In other instances, only an elect group is gifted with it, while everyone else has a counterfeit spirit that is not divine or immortal. Systems are built to ensure the separation of the soul from the body, and then the spirit from the soul. Usually, the soul's final resting place is different from the final abode of the spirit. One Christian group in antiquity used a QUADRATIC PATTERN, adding to the triadic a substance they believed to be superior to the spirit (which was divine, in their view, but not God's equivalent). They called this fourth substance FILIAL, believing it to be equivalent to God, born as a child from a parent.

Five basic Christological patterns emerge among the first Christians (Figure 1.16). The ADULT POSSESSION PATTERN relied on scriptural stories of Jewish prophets who received God's Spirit when they were chosen by God. It explains Jesus' divinity in terms of Jesus, the human being receiving the Holy Spirit at his baptism. This Spirit leaves him when he is dying on the cross. The human Jesus is gifted with the Holy Spirit because he had lived a morally exceptional life and aligned his own will or soul with the possessing Spirit. He is rewarded with a resurrected angelic body following his death when God raises him from the dead to live eternally among the heavenly host.

Some early Christians pushed the POSSESSION PATTERN back to the womb, believing that an angel or Spirit or Power possessed the gestating Jesus. While Jesus was born fully human (he had a mortal body and soul), he also, from birth, was possessed by an extraordinary Power that allowed him to do extraordinary things. This is the FETAL POSSESSION PATTERN.

The HYBRID PATTERN relies on the popular imagination of the ancients who recognized extraordinary and heroic people as divine-human hybrids. Geniuses like Plato were mythologized as children of God.

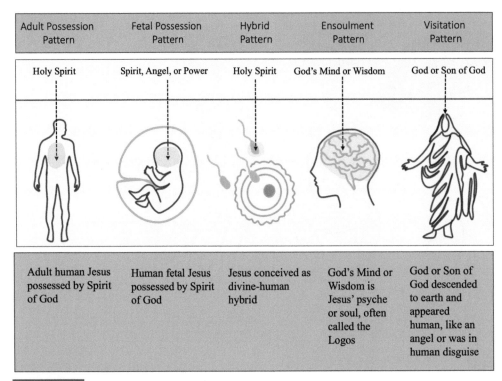

Adult Possession Pattern	Fetal Possession Pattern	Hybrid Pattern	Ensoulment Pattern	Visitation Pattern
Holy Spirit	Spirit, Angel, or Power	Holy Spirit	God's Mind or Wisdom	God or Son of God
Adult human Jesus possessed by Spirit of God	Human fetal Jesus possessed by Spirit of God	Jesus conceived as divine-human hybrid	God's Mind or Wisdom is Jesus' psyche or soul, often called the Logos	God or Son of God descended to earth and appeared human, like an angel or was in human disguise

FIGURE 1.16 Early Christology patterns.

Plato, in fact, was considered the son of the God Apollo and Perictione, the virgin wife of Ariston (who was told in a vision not to have sex with Perictione until Apollo's child was born). Alexander the Great was known to have been Zeus' son born of his liaison with the Macedonian Queen Olympia. If we were to list all the hybrid offspring of sexual trysts between Greek Gods and human partners, the list would be pages long. This same cultural imagination was applied to Jesus so that he was understood to be sired by God's Spirit in Mary's womb, born a divine-human hybrid capable of performing superhuman feats like walking on water, feeding crowds from a few loaves of bread, and even raising the dead. Yet, because he was also human, he was mortal and died.

The ENSOULMENT PATTERN plays with anthropological dualism, the idea that the soul is a separate entity that exists before birth, and after death outside the body. At birth, the soul descends from heaven and enters the material body which it animates as the human psyche. In Jesus' case, the separate entity is a special divinity (e.g. an angel, divine Power, God's Mind or Wisdom) that descends as Jesus' soul. In other words, Jesus is God in flesh. In cases where the anthropology is TRIADIC, this concept can be extended to include the Spirit. This means that the Spirit of the human Jesus also is an extraordinary divinity.

The VISITATION PATTERN understands Jesus to be a divine entity who descends to earth and is indistinguishable from human beings in the same way that angels or Gods like Zeus or Apollo or Aphrodite appear on earth. In Biblical stories, angels eat, drink, and are entertained unaware by humans. In Genesis 6, angels have sex with women and birth giants. This is true for the Greek Gods as well. They too are perceived to be indistinguishable from humans in their appearance. They frequently have sex and babies with human partners, although their babies are born extraordinary demigods as we have previously learned.

From this brief overview it is clear that the Christians improvised using a large number of patterns and their combinations in their literature. Yet it is a dilemma how to write a Christian history as a jazz composition rather than the more familiar orthodox symphony with its predetermined beginning and ending. When we look at the historical literature produced by the Christians, what is actually known about the movement immediately after Paul is murky. While Paul's letters are our oldest records of the beginnings of the movement and provide us with fabulous details that help us understand what the movement looked like around 50 CE, it is more difficult to figure out what happened between the mid-first century and the mid-second century. The reasons for this have to do with the fact that by the late-first century the first-generation (ca. 30–70 CE) and the original leaders of the movement had died, leaving the churches without direct historical memory of Jesus or the direct knowledge about the beginning of the movement. This memory loss is exacerbated by the First Roman–Jewish War (66–73 CE) which ended tragically for the Jews. The Temple in Jerusalem was destroyed and the total population of the city massacred.

This meant that Christians in Jerusalem (who might have been lucky enough to get out of town before the massacre) became war refugees. Tradition has it that most Christians in Judea fled across the Jordan deeper into Mesopotamia just as the war was starting (Figure 1.17). The consequence of the migration of Christians from war-ravaged areas of Judea is huge. After 70 CE, the church in Jerusalem is no longer a viable center for the Christian movement as the Christians scatter across the Syrian Diaspora all the way to Persia (modern Iran and Iraq), many ending up in smaller independent groups along the rivers which were convenient locations for their baptisms.

Post-Pauline literature is extremely difficult to date although it is clear that this literature is aware that the temple has been destroyed and that new church leadership models are being experimented with now that the first-generation leaders were gone. The fact that Jesus had not yet returned nor had the world ended are constantly mentioned and rationalized in this literature. The texts were either anonymously published because the actual authors were not well-known leaders or pseudonymously published. The pseudonyms gave the texts heroic and legitimate authors from among the first-generation of Christians. This anonymous literature includes not only the gospels that later Christians called the Gospels of Mark, Matthew, Luke, and John, but also texts like the Book of Acts, Hebrews, Revelation, and pseudonymous letters like James, 1 and 2 Peter, 1 and 2 Timothy, and Titus. It includes gospels that were not collected into the New Testament, like the *Gospel of Thomas, Mary, Philip,* and

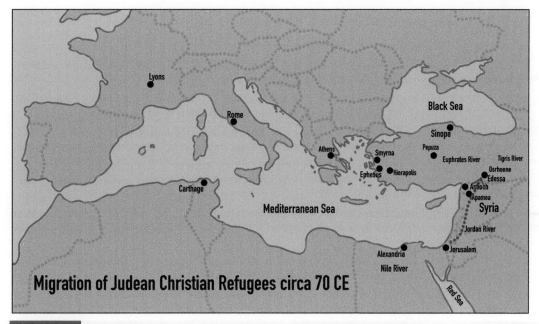

FIGURE 1.17 Migration of Judean Christian refugees as result of First Roman–Jewish War.

Judas and writings like the *Didache*. It is clear that these texts were written after 70 CE but how much after is debatable and is argued on a case-by-case basis. How these case-by-case arguments are made determines how scholars write their histories of earliest Christianity.

The first time in the historical record that we hear about the existence of letters of Paul and Christian gospels is in the mid-second century among third-generation Christians (110–150 CE) who themselves disagree about where they came from and whose versions of them are authentic. Gospels do not start getting author's names and origin stories attached to them until the fourth generation of Christians (150–190 CE) with Irenaeus who was a bishop of Lyons (ca. 177–202 CE). He claimed that his church was better than other churches because it had not just one gospel, but four gospels that had apostolic lineage: Matthew, Mark, Luke, and John. While Irenaeus claims these gospels as the intellectual property of his church, we know that other fourth-generation Christians were using them too, but interpreting them very differently. For instance, Heracleon (ca. 175 CE), one of Valentinus' Gnostic students whom we meet later in this textbook, wrote the first scholarly commentary on the Gospel of John, a text that the Valentinian Gnostic movement interpreted in their own fashion.

In this textbook, we are going to approach the history of early Christianity by starting in the middle with Christian literature that we can reliably date and position geographically (ca. 120–220 CE). This retrospective approach means that the end does not determine the beginning of the story nor does the beginning of the story determine the end. Once the middle is mapped, we will have a good sense of the makeup of the family networks of Christians, the patterns they develop and rely on, and their relationships to each other. By decentering the standard linear stories of Christian origins, we are able to write in the final chapter of this textbook, a brief retrohistory that accounts for the emergence of the different Christianities and their intergenerational struggles for survival.

We begin this project with Marcion of Sinope because he is the first Christian we learn about from the historical record, who had a Christian gospel and the letters of Paul, which he was studying, editing, and publishing. So in the next chapter, we begin in Rome around 130 CE with Marcion and his story.

Takeaways

1. Earliest Christianity is pluriform from the start, shaped by three parties (Maximalists, Moderates, and Minimalists) and the regional cultures of different native populations.

2. Early Christians wrote a large amount of literature in the first, second, and third centuries CE that expressed their beliefs and practices. Only a small portion of this literature is found in the New Testament.

3. Early Christian literature has been divided into several categories including the New Testament or canonical literature, the Christian Apocrypha, the Nag Hammadi writings, the Apostolic Fathers, and the Church Fathers.

4. Paul's authentic letters are the oldest surviving Christian writings, presenting us with a picture of early Christianity as a charismatic, pluriform, and Jewish sectarian movement that is decentralized and especially attractive to Gentiles.

5. Because the early Christian movement believed that the Spirit filled its sons and daughters, making them prophets, healers, and visionaries as promised by Joel 2:28, women held positions of power alongside men in the first churches.

6. There are many ways to write the history of early Christianity, although most have been written as church histories which authorize Catholicism, Orthodoxy, and Protestantism.

7. This textbook implements a new model – the family network and the concept of family resemblances – to explain and map Christian diversity.

8. The history of Christianity is most akin to a jazz composition that uses patterns of chord progressions and harmony lines to improvise melodies. Distinct patterns of theology, demiurgy, theodicy, soteriology, anthropology, and Christology are in play throughout the early Christian literature studied in this textbook.

9. While early Christianity is characterized as a plurality of sectarian movements, socially these movements formed in relationship to each other. A typology of the emergence of religious movements can help us determine and understand these relationships better.

Questions

1. How does earliest Christianity compare to other contemporary Jewish sects? What makes it a unique movement?

2. Why was the Christian movement more attractive to Gentile converts than ethnic Jews?

3. Who would the Maximalist party have been most attractive to? Why?

4. Who would the Minimalist party have been most attractive to? Why?

5. Who would the Moderate party have been most attractive to? Why?

6. What advantages are there to writing the history of early Christianity by starting in the middle of the story rather than at the beginning and the end? Do you think it really matters? If so, why?

7. If Christians were so diverse that they worshipped different Gods, had different schemes for Jesus' divinity, thought about theodicy and demiurgy in opposing ways, etc., what makes their melodies Christian?

8. How does the Family Networks of Christian Movements model decenter the telling of the Christian story? Why is this important for historians to do?

9. Why is it important to understand the way in which a particular Christian movement formed?

10. Who gets to decide who is Christian and who is not? How would you decide?

Resources

John Ashton. 2000. *The Religion of Paul the Apostle*. New Haven: Princeton University Press.

Walter Bauer. 1979 [German: 1934]. *Orthodoxy and Heresy in Earliest Christianity*. English translation by John E. Seely and Robert A. Kraft. Minneapolis: Fortress Press.

Tony Burke. 2013. *Secret Scriptures Revealed: A New Introduction to the Christian Apocrypha*. Grand Rapids: William B. Eerdmans Publishing Company.

Douglas A. Campbell. 2014. *Framing Paul: An Epistolary Biography*. Grand Rapids: Eerdmans Publishing Company.

James K. Elliot. 1993. *The Apocryphal New Testament: A Collection of Apocryphal Christian Literature in English Translation*. Based on M.R. James Oxford: Clarendon Press.

Justo. L. Gonzalez 1970. [Revised ed.] *A History of Christian Thought: From the Beginnings to the Council of Chalcedon*. Volumes 1–2. Nashville: Abingdon Press.

J. Gordon Melton. 2016. (9th ed.). *Melton's Encyclopedia of American Religions*. Volumes 1–2. Detroit: Gale Cengage Learning.

Ulrich Groetsch. 2015. *Hermann Samuel Reimarus (1694–1768): Classicist, Hebraist, Enlightenment Radical in Disguise*. Leiden: Brill.

Hans-Josef Klauck. 2003. *Apocryphal Gospels: An Introduction*. London: T&T Clark.

Hans-Josef Klauck. 2008. *The Apocryphal Acts of the Apostles: An Introduction*. Waco: Baylor University Press.

Helmut Koester. 2000. (second ed.). *History and Literature of Early Christianity*. Volume 2: Introduction to the New Testament. Berlin: Walter de Gruyter.

Fred Lapham. 2003. *An Introduction to the New Testament Apocrypha*. London: T&T Clark.

Lautaro Roig Lanzillotta. 2017. "Spirit, Soul and Body in Nag Hammadi Literature: Distinguishing Anthropological Schemes in Valentinian, Sethian, Hermetic and Thomasine Texts." *Gnosis: Journal of Gnostic Studies* 2: 15–39.

Judith Lieu. 1994. "'The Parting of the Ways:' Theological Construct or Historical Reality?" *Journal for the Study of the New Testament* 56: 101–119.

Christoph Markschies. 2015. *Christian Theology and Its Institutions in the Early Roman Empire: Prolegomena to a History of Early Christian Theology*. Translated by Wayne Coppins. Waco: Baylor University Press.

L. Michael White. 2004. *From Jesus to Christianity: How Four Generations of Visionaries and Storytellers Created the New Testament and Christian Faith*. San Francisco: HarperOne.

James Carleton Paget and Judith Lieu (eds.). 2017. *Christianity in the Second Century: Themes and Developments*. Cambridge: Cambridge University Press.

Hermann S. Reimarus. 1970 [German: 1774–1778]. *Reimarus: Fragments*. Translated by. Ralph S. Fraser Edited by. Charles H. Talbert. Minneapolis: Fortress Press.

James M. Robinson and Helmut Koester. 1971. *Trajectories Through Early Christianity*. Minneapolis: Fortress Press.

Christopher Rowland. 2002 (2nd ed.). *Christian Origins: The Setting and Character of the Most Important Messianic Sect of Judaism*. London: SPCK.

Jens Schröter. 2021. *The Apocryphal Gospels: Jesus Traditions outside the Bible* Early Christian Apocrypha 9: Westar Tools and Translations. Eugene: Cascade Books.

Alan F. Segal. 1990. *Paul the Convert: The Apostolate and Apostasy of Saul the Pharisee*. New Haven: Yale University Press.

James D. Tabor. 2012. *Paul and Jesus: How the Apostle Transformed Christianity*. New York: Simon and Schuster.

Adoph von Harnack. 1961 [German 1898]. *The History of Dogma*. Volume 1–2. English translation by James Millar. New York: Dover Publications.

CHAPTER 2

A New Religion

Paul writing. From an early ninth century manuscript version of Paul's letters. The manuscript is ascribed to the Monastery of St. Gallen under the scribe Wolfcoz. **Source:** Photo 12 / Getty Images.

> "Oh fullness of wealth, folly, might, and ecstasy, that no one can say or think anything beyond the gospel, or compare anything to it!"
>
> *This is the only surviving direct quotation of Marcion (preserved by an unknown Syriac author)*

KEY PLAYERS

Marcion of Sinope
Papias of Hierapolis
Pliny – Cerdo

KEY TEXTS

The *Evangelion* – The *Apostolicon*
Gospel of Matthew
Fragments of Papias
Pliny's letter to Trajan
Tertullian, *Against Marcion*

Christians in mid-second century Rome faced an identity crisis. Were they Jews or Christians? A hundred years earlier, Christianity was a Jewish messianic movement. The rise of Jesus' movement occurred at a time when Jews were engaged in sporadic conflicts with their Roman colonizers over their national independence. As we

Comparing Christianities: An Introduction to Early Christianity, First Edition. April D. DeConick.
© 2024 John Wiley & Sons Ltd. Published 2024 by John Wiley & Sons Ltd.

learned in Chapter 1, the Roman occupation of Judea fueled messianic dreams that a great hero, a Messiah would emerge to renew their nation's obedience to God's Law. The Jewish Law refers to the 613 *mitzvot* or commandments found in the Torah, the first five books of the Hebrew Bible. Once the nation renewed its commitment to keep the Law of their God YHWH, they believed that they would enjoy the benefits of YHWH's covenant, the contract their nation had made to be YHWH's people and receive his blessings of protection and national independence.

The advent of a Messiah was understood by some Jews to be part of latter world events that included the defeat of their colonizers, the resurrection of the dead, God's final judgment, the establishment of New Jerusalem, and the restoration of their national independence under YHWH's sovereignty. In the early first century, there were several messianic contenders besides Jesus who had also been executed by Roman authorities, but it was only Jesus' movement that adapted and survived the execution of their leader.

Despite these executions, Roman–Jewish conflicts continued during the formative generations of Christianity. During the years 66–73 CE, the Romans and a militant faction of Jews engaged in the First Roman–Jewish War, which resulted in the destruction of the Temple in Jerusalem, the massacre of the city's inhabitants by the Romans (70 CE), and the suicide of the Jews who held out at Masada (73 CE). In 115 CE, the Kitos War erupted when Jews in Cyrenaica, Cyprus, and Egypt revolted under the leadership of Andreas Lukuas to whom some gave the messianic title, King of the Jews. He and his rebels massacred Roman citizens in the region. The bloodbath spread north and ended two years later in Judea with a Roman victory. The third war, the Bar Kochba Revolt, was fought in the years 132–136 CE. The rebellion was led by Simon Son of the Star (Hebrew: *bar Kochba*; cf. Num. 24:17). He was regarded as the Messiah by many Jews who followed him. Again, the Romans were victorious.

In the aftermath of the Bar Kochba Revolt, Emperor Hadrian barred Jews from entering Jerusalem and built atop the rubble a new Roman colony that he named Aelia Capitolina. To erase the memory of Judea, he consolidated Judea, Galilee, and Samaria into Syria Palestine, a single Roman province. He made decrees outlawing the study of the Torah, the observation of the Sabbath, circumcision, synagogue assemblies, and Jewish courts, decrees that were not lifted until his death in 138 CE.

This dangerous political climate challenged third-generation Christians (ca. 110–150 CE) to think long and hard about their religious identity, especially when it came to Jewish practices and scriptures. Since Christianity began as a Jewish sectarian movement, the negotiation of Christian identity – whether Jewish or not Jewish – was a tinderbox in the second century. And Marcion, the spark.

[2.1] A Pauline Aficionado

COMPANION READINGS
Papias, *Fragment*
in Eusebius, *Church History* 3.39
Tertullian, *Against Marcion* 4.2–6

Marcion was from the city of Sinope on the coast of the Black Sea in the far north of Asia Minor (modern day Sinop, Turkey). By occupation, Marcion was a sea captain who owned a small fleet of ships that carried merchandise and freight overseas to trade in the Roman capital (Eus., *Eccl. Hist.* 5.13.3; Tert., *Prescr.* 30.1; *Marc.* 1.18; 3.6; 4.9; 5.1). By all reports, Marcion's business was lucrative. He was a wealthy man, who, when in Rome had leisure time enough to become involved in scholarly activities among other Christians there. We can deduce from his ability to work with texts critically, that he spoke Greek and had received a standard Greek education as a grammarian. If the tradition is correct that his father was a bishop in Marcion's hometown, Marcion's interest in Christian scholarship and texts had been cultivated long before he established himself in Rome (Figure 2.1).

Why did Marcion relocate to Rome? We do not know exactly why, but it is said that a rift came between Marcion and his father who was the bishop of a church in Pontus. Later Christians accuse

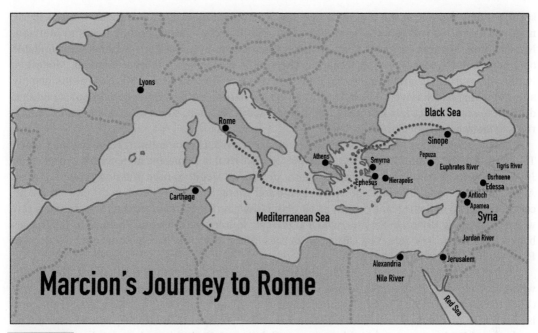

Marcion's Journey to Rome

FIGURE 2.1   Marcion's sea journey from Sinope to Rome (ca. 120–130 CE).

Marcion of having an affair with one of the young women in his father's church, so the rift may have been of a personal nature. Interestingly although far from conclusive, there is an isolated report from Jerome (ca. 400 CE) that Marcion sent a woman ahead of him to prepare things for his relocation (Jer., *Hier. ep.* 133.4).

Once Marcion moved to Rome, he joined a local Roman church, probably because it catered to immigrant Christians from his part of the world. Tertullian of Carthage later tells us that the church Marcion joined was Catholic (i.e. universal) and Apostolic because it rested on the authority of the apostles (Tert., *Marc.* 4.5). In this textbook, we refer to this particular network of churches as Apostolic Catholic. Over the course of the second century, these churches consolidated, creating an ecclesiastical network of like-minded congregations that claimed their tradition came directly from the twelve apostles, that their leaders were authorized via a direct succession from the apostles, and that their church was universal (catholic) rather than an independent local variant. This network came to depend more and more on rulings of local meetings of its bishops and judgments that came directly from the Bishop of Rome. The traditions and practices that this network develops in the second century are later claimed by Catholics, Orthodox, and Protestants as their official heritage. Marcion makes a sizable donation to this church – 200,000 sesterces – which in Marcion's time was enough money to purchase a fabulous house in the city proper or a large estate in the suburbs or a mid-sized farm of one-hundred-and-twenty-five acres in the countryside.

Testimonies among later Christian writers give varying dates for Marcion's relocation and activity in Rome, although all the dates fall within the period of third-generation Christianity (ca. 110–150 CE). The earliest date is given by Clement of Alexandria who places Marcion in Rome during Hadrian's reign (117–138 CE) (Clem. Alex., *Misc.* 7.107). Tertullian locates Marcion during the time of bishops Telesforus (ca. 125–136 CE), Hyginus (ca. 136–140 CE), and Pius (ca. 140–155 CE) (Tert., *Prescr.* 30.2). Irenaeus of Lyons says that Marcion was in Rome during Hyginus' time (ca. 136–140 CE) and that Marcion made friends with a Christian philosopher named Cerdo (Iren., *Haer.* 1.27.1). Around 150 CE, Marcion's younger contemporary Justin Martyr tells us that Marcion was so successful by then that Marcion was famous and had many followers around the world. He also is surprised that Marcion is still alive and teaching, a comment that suggests Marcion was an elderly man when Justin wrote (Jus., *1 Apol.* 26.5). Justin is the only contemporary witness to Marcion. None of these testimonies about Marcion are sympathetic to him, but portray him as a formidable opponent. Later writers (such as Irenaeus, Theophilus of Antioch, Philip of Gortyna, Modestus, Bardesanes, Tertullian, and Hippolytus) published treatises directed against Marcion, although only a few of them have survived. The polemical or hostile nature of the surviving testimonies makes it difficult to recover accurate historical information about Marcion, so we must work hard as historians to interpret these testimonies fairly.

Judging their testimonies, it is likely that Marcion first arrived in Rome during Hadrian's reign when Telesforus was the bishop. The later we place Marcion's arrival in Rome, the more we have to question Justin's eyewitness testimony about Marcion's successful Mediterranean mission around 150 CE. According to Irenaeus, Marcion returned to Rome and strengthened his church in the city when Anicetus was Bishop of Rome (ca. 155–167 CE). He claims that, during Marcion's second stay, he had a row with Polycarp, the Bishop of Smyrna, who had traveled to Rome to discuss with Anicetus differences between the calendrical dates that Christians in Asia Minor and Christians in Rome used to celebrate Easter (Iren., *Haer.* 3.3.4; 3.4.3).

When Marcion first arrived in Rome, he does not appear to have come empty-handed. He brought with him some very significant documents. The first is an anonymous written text, which was simply called the *Evangelion* (the Gospel). Marcion claimed that it had no author (Tert. *Marc.* 4.2). The second is a collection of letters of Paul. The collection was called the *Apostolicon* (the Apostle's Letters). The ten letters of Paul are arranged in this sequence: Galatians, 1 Corinthians, 2 Corinthians, Romans, 1 Thessalonians, 2 Thessalonians, Laodiceans (a version of Ephesians which also went by this name), Colossians, Philippians, and Philemon.

Where did Marcion get these documents from? Most likely these documents were versions of the Christian texts that were being used in Marcion's hometown church in Sinope, although it is possible that Marcion himself may already have had a hand in assembling and editing these for his or his father's congregation. He probably brought them with him to Rome as objects of his faith and study. He believed that the *Evangelion* preserved the breaking news about God's grace which Paul writes about in his letters.

But when he gets to Rome and begins attending church services, according to Tertullian, Marcion notices that there are other texts similar to the *Evangelion* in circulation in Rome. He worries because they differ from the *Evangelion* he has and they are advertised as writings of different apostles (Tert., *Marc.* 4.3–6). The only other mention of writings by apostles at this early date comes from the composition of Papias, Bishop of Hierapolis (modern day Pamukkale, Turkey), who was Marcion's contemporary. Papias is the author of a five-volume commentary on Jesus' sayings called *The Interpretation of the Sayings of the Lord*. Papias' commentary is lost. But Eusebius of Caesarea (ca. 320 CE) preserves an important fragment from the contents of Papias' work (Eus., *Eccl. Hist.* 3.39).

And the presbyter said this [to Papias]: "Mark having become the interpreter of Peter, wrote down accurately whatsoever he remembered. It was not, however, in exact order that he related the sayings or deeds of Christ. For he neither heard the Lord nor accompanied Him. But afterwards, as I said, he accompanied Peter, who accommodated his instructions to the necessities [of his hearers], but with no intention of giving a regular narrative of the Lord's sayings. Wherefore Mark made no mistake in thus writing some things as he remembered them. For of one thing he took especial care, not to omit anything he had heard, and not to put anything fictitious into the statements." This is what is related by Papias regarding Mark; but with regard to Matthew he has made the following statements: "Matthew put together the oracles [of the Lord] in the Hebrew language, and each one interpreted them as best he could."

Eusebius, Eccl. Hist. 3.39.15–16

As the fragment continues, Papias shares with us his compositional method along with what he knew about early Christian literature at the time he himself was writing his own commentary on Jesus' sayings. He tells us that his process of gathering information about Jesus' sayings included oral interviews in which he spoke to second-generation Christians (70–110 CE) who claimed to have heard first-generation leaders preach, specifically Andrew, Peter, Philip, Thomas, James (son of Zebedee), John, Matthew, Aristion, and the presbyter John. Papias felt that the oral information he gathered in his interviews with second-generation Christians was superior to anything he could find written down.

What did Papias know was written down? He knows about a book by Mark, although it had developed a bad reputation as disorganized. Papias justifies the disorganization of Jesus' sayings and activities with the suggestion that Mark was a student of Peter, the apostle. According to Papias, for his composition, Mark relied on what he had learned from Peter about Jesus, but had no way of knowing how this material should be systematically arranged in chronological order. Most scholars have identified this book as a version of the Gospel of Mark. But Papias does not call it a gospel and tells us nothing about its contents, so any claim to identify Papias' book with the Gospel of Mark is far from certain. Certainty all but evaporates when we recognize that Papias also knows about a book written by Matthew. Papias notes that this book was a systematic, orderly compilation of Jesus' sayings in Aramaic. This is certainly not the Greek Gospel of Matthew we have today. But it is evident that a book of sayings in Aramaic circulated under the name Matthew in Papias' day. This book is lost. Whatever other writings Papias may have known remain a mystery.

What we can determine from the writings of Tertullian, however, is that Marcion, when he arrives in Rome, seems surprised to find texts like the *Evangelion*, but attributed to the apostles (Tert., *Marc.* 4.3–6). Marcion wonders where they came from. How can they be the work of the apostles who were Jesus' disciples since they only taught the gospel orally and did not write the gospel message down as Paul did, Marcion reasoned? Marcion is convinced that Paul was the only apostle who wrote about the gospel in his letters (cf. Adamantius, *Dialogue* 2.12).

Upon further inspection, Marcion concludes that the copies of these similar texts are corrupt, containing many errors and falsifications particularly when it comes to what they have to say about Judaism. He thinks that the authors of these other texts are trying to impose Jewish practices upon Christians, pressuring them to live as Jews. He considers these texts pseudo-gospels, products of false apostles who, after Jesus' death, tainted the one-true gospel of grace, which had only been directly revealed to Paul by Christ in ecstasy.

2.2 A Book of Paul's Letters

COMPANION READINGS
Galatians in the *Apostolicon*
Pliny, *Letters* 10.96–97

Why would Marcion think that false apostles wrote pseudo-gospels that contaminated Paul's gospel message of grace? Marcion is a close reader of Paul's letters. Paul's letters were at the center of his faith, as they were for the Christians in his hometown church in Asia Minor. At the beginning of his collection of Paul's letters is Galatians, and everything Marcion understands about Christianity was developed out of his Minimalist interpretation of this letter. In this letter, Paul claims to be an apostle commissioned directly by Jesus Christ, having received the one-true gospel from Jesus through revelation (Gal. 1:1, 11–12). Paul understands this fantastic breaking news to be the revelation of God's grace to sinners, a revelation which takes priority over the Jewish law and system of justification that had disciplined God's people until the advent of Christ (Gal. 2:21; 3:23–26). Paul complains that the Gentile converts in Galatia are turning away from the gospel he announced to them and are following a different gospel message. Paul thinks that the gospel of grace has been perverted by other preachers and swears damnation on anyone (even an angel!) who preaches a gospel different from the one-true gospel of grace that Paul had proclaimed to them (Gal. 1:6–9). Paul rebukes the apostle Peter for betraying the gospel by compelling Gentiles to live like Jews (Gal. 2:14–15). Paul also mentions false brothers among the apostles who spied on him in order to compel Gentile converts to be circumcised according to the Jewish law (Gal. 2:2–5).

Everything Marcion knows about Paul comes from his interpretation of the *Apostolicon* with Galatians at the forefront. The *Apostolicon* did not include, as would later Apostolic Catholic collections of Paul's letters, the Pastoral epistles (1 Timothy, 2 Timothy, and Titus) or Hebrews. Of the ten letters of Paul in the *Apostolicon*, only Galatians, Colossians, and Romans are substantively different from the later Apostolic Catholic versions. The letters in the *Apostolicon* do not have Galatians 3:2–14, Colossians 1:15b–16, and Romans 9, 11, 15–16.

It is unclear how to explain these differences. For instance, we know that up to four alternative versions of Romans circulated among the Christians (without Chapter 16, without Chapters 15–16, Marcion's version, and the current form). Determining what material is additive and subtractive in these letters is a problem that scholars have not yet been able to resolve. That said, Marcion's versions of the letters were not that much different from what other Christians were using, although the order of the letters is strategic. Galatians, Paul's most powerful missive against the imposition of Jewish practices on Gentile converts, acts as a foreword or preface determining the way that the rest of the letters are read.

From these letters, Marcion knows that Paul was not one of Jesus' disciples, but had interacted with them. He knows that Paul was a circumcised Jew from the tribe of Benjamin. He was not a convert to Judaism but born of Jewish parents. Paul considered himself a Pharisee, concerned that God's Law be obeyed strictly according to the rabbinic rulings of his time. Paul describes himself as a very zealous young man, extremely committed to the Law and the Jewish traditions of his ancestors. Before joining Jesus' movement, he admits to violently persecuting their churches with the intent to destroy them (Phil. 3:5–6; Gal. 1:13–14; 1 Cor. 15:9).

What changed for Paul? Paul self-reports a revelatory experience, one that he codes as the most significant event of his life, when he ascends through several heavens and receives a revelation from Jesus Christ (2 Cor. 12:2–4). Paul receives from Jesus the gospel, which is the message of God's grace (Gal. 1:11–12, 16; Phil. 3:8; 1 Cor. 15:1–7). Paul is commissioned to be Jesus' ambassador to the Gentiles. Paul understands his conversion experience to be so life-altering that he comes to regard his former life as *skubalon*, a Greek vulgarism, Marcion was sure to know meant shit or crap (Phil. 3:8; cf. Gal. 2:18).

Paul is commissioned to preach the gospel among the uncircumcised who did not belong to the nation of Israel and had no hope of salvation because they had no God in the world to save them (Laod./Eph. 2:11–12). God intervened on their behalf, rescuing the weak, the lowly, and the despised (1 Cor. 1:27–28). God was unknown until Jesus' advent, neither understood by the wise Gentiles or the Jews (1 Cor. 1:21; Rom. 10:3, 12–14). God was unknown because he hid his plan from the powers that control this world, including the "God of this Aeon" who intentionally blinds people from the truth (Laod./Eph. 3:9). This unknown God is the Father of Jesus, who in turn came to earth as his Father's manifestation and regent (Phil. 2:6–11; Col. 4:15–16).

Marcion took Paul to mean that God rescues the Gentiles not by bringing them into the covenant tied to the Jewish Law, but by extending to them a new covenant based on faith. Paul characterizes the Jewish Law as a code of criminal law used to judge, condemn, and punish (Gal. 3:10, 22; 2 Cor. 3:6; Rom. 7:8; 8:1–2). In contrast, Paul characterizes the new covenant as a family law agreement to adopt orphaned children (Gal. 3:26; 4:5–6; Rom. 8:14–19; Laod./Eph. 1:5) or a manumission of slaves from the powers that control the world (Gal. 4:3, 8; 1 Cor. 1:6; Col. 2:8; Laod./Eph. 2:2) and the Torah itself (Gal. 2:3–4; 4:5, 24; 5:1; Rom. 7:4–6). The cost for this freedom? Jesus' life (Gal. 2:20; 4:5; 1 Cor. 5:7; 6:20; Rom. 5:6). With his death, Christ ended the Law, abolishing it (Rom. 10:4; Laod./Eph. 2:15). The Law had been nailed to Jesus' cross, when Jesus disarmed and conquered the powers that rule this world (Col. 2:14–15).

Marcion gathers from Paul's testimony that not everyone was happy with Paul's message of freedom from the Law, especially the apostles who had been Jesus' disciples and who, during Paul's time, were leading the church in Jerusalem (Gal. 2:4–14). The conflict was framed by Paul as a dispute over different interpretations of the gospel that Jesus had taught (Gal. 1:6–9; 1 Cor. 10–17). According to Paul, other missionaries were strong-arming the Gentiles to live according to the Jewish Law, to submit to circumcision (Gal. 2:3–4), to maintain a kosher diet (Gal. 2:11–14; Col. 2:16), to observe the Sabbath (Col. 2:16), and to celebrate the religious holy days (Gal. 4:9–10; Col. 2:16) according to the lunar calendar (Col. 2:16).

Paul is highly critical of these Maximalist missionaries. He accuses them of wanting to impose the Law on the Gentiles while failing to live up to it themselves (Gal. 2:14; 6:13; Rom. 2:21–24). He mocks them, calling them "super-apostles" (2 Cor. 12:11). He considers them "false apostles" and "deceitful workers" who disguise themselves as apostles of Christ (2 Cor. 11:13). He likens them to Satan who disguises himself as an angel of light, and perceives them to be Satan's apostles (2 Cor. 11:14–15). Paul presses on with his critique, identifying them as false brothers (2 Cor. 11:26), who like Paul were ethnic Jews (2 Cor. 11:22).

All in all, when Marcion read Paul, he understood that the Law and the gospel were separate items, and that God's grace alone had rescued them. Any suggestion that Christians were obligated to the Jewish Law was false teaching associated with false apostles who did not really understand the gospel message to the Gentiles. Marcion likely did not originate this interpretation of Paul, but shared it with other third-generation Christians in Pontus. It is not too difficult to imagine how this reading of Paul might have emerged in the aftermath of the Kitos War, when Jews rebelled against Roman authorities as Trajan was busy fighting in Parthia, a rebellion which led to bloody massacres on the part of both the Jews and the Romans (115–117 CE). Some Christians may have wanted to distance themselves from the Jewish identity. Already Christians had an image problem when it came to the Romans, and we know from an exchange of letters between Emperor Trajan and Pliny, the governor of Bithynia and Pontus (110–113 CE) that relations with the Roman authorities were not good in Marcion's homeland even before Trajan marched into Mesopotamia (115 CE).

Pliny felt that he had to interrogate Christians in his territory because the animal and meat trade was sluggish at the pagan temples. Too few people were buying animals to sacrifice to the Gods. The sacrifice of animals in pagan temples was the main source of purchasable butchered meat. With a failing economy, Pliny intervenes with his investigation of Christians who had been denounced, many in an anonymous pamphlet that came to his attention. If the accused confessed to be Christians (he gave them three chances to change their minds), he led them away to be punished, although we do not know what that punishment entailed. If they denied they were Christians, he asked them to call upon the Gods of Rome and to make an offering of incense and wine to Trajan's statue. Then he asked them to curse Christ. If they passed these tests, he released them. Some of these people claimed to have been Christian once, but to have left the movement as long as twenty years past.

From his investigation, which included the targeted interrogation and torture of two women slaves who were deaconesses, Pliny learns that they had met regularly before dawn on a fixed day of the week. During their meetings, they had sung responsively hymns to Christ as a God. They had declared an oath not to commit adultery or fraud, not to lie nor refuse to return money when asked. After this they had left their meetings, but gathered later to eat a meal of ordinary food. They told Pliny that they no longer met because they did not want to violate Pliny's recent order against holding political assemblies.

Pliny writes to Trajan to consult with the emperor whether any further action should be taken since he had discovered a large number of Christians of every rank, both young and old, male and female. He notes that the temple activities had resumed and the economy improved following his investigation.

Trajan replies, commending Pliny for handling the situation and restoring order. He highlights that there is no fixed standard when prosecuting Christians, but he agrees that anonymously published

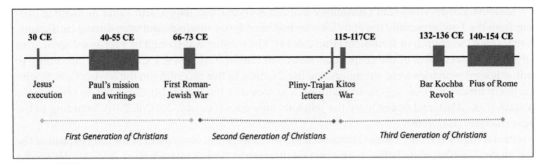

FIGURE 2.2 Timeline mapping first three generations of Christians.

lists of names of Christians should not be used to determine who is a Christian. This would set a dangerous precedent indeed. While Christians should not be sought out, if they are denounced, they must be tested as Pliny had done, in order to prove their guilt or innocence. If they worship the Roman Gods, they should be pardoned and their past should not be held against them.

This exchange of letters between a Roman governor and his emperor around 110 CE shows that Christian affiliation was risky because Christians were rumored to meet in suspicious assemblies to plan their treasonous activities. Negotiating Christian identity became even more problematic after the Kitos War (post-117 CE) and then after the Bar Kochba Revolt (post-136 CE), when Marcion lived and worked (Figure 2.2). For many people in antiquity, Christians and Jews were not distinct enough to be perceived as different religious identities. Christians used Jewish scriptures as their Bible, gathered in assemblies similar to synagogues (some even in synagogues), awaited the eschaton or the end of the world predicted in the book of Daniel and other Jewish prophetic writings, believed in a Messiah, and worshiped the Jewish God. Christianity's roots as a Jewish sectarian movement and consequent Jewish shape was a cause for candid reflection among third-century Christians. How were they to negotiate their identity going forward at a time when being identified as Jewish put them in even more jeopardy than they already endured as followers of Jesus of Nazareth, a man executed for treason?

2.3 Reasoning God Out of the Bible

COMPANION READINGS
Tertullian, *Against Marcion* 1.2, 8, 19–20

While Marcion shared with other Christians the belief in the difference between the Law (covenant) and the gospel (the message about salvation through Jesus), he is the one who began asking probing questions that would spark intense debate over religious identity and the future shape of the Christian movement. It is important to recognize that Marcion believed that the *Evangelion* was a written account of the gospel about God's grace that had been revealed to Paul. According to his later opponent, Tertullian, Marcion thought that other written texts claiming also to be gospels were the false gospels that Paul believed the apostles (and others) were preaching.

Faced with written gospels that diverged substantively from the *Evangelion*, Marcion suspects that whoever had authored the texts had corrupted Paul's gospel of grace, which had liberated Christians from the Jewish Law and practices. To test his hypothesis, Marcion sets up a comparative research project. He studies in detail the Jewish scriptures alongside the pseudo-gospels of the apostles, the *Evangelion*, and the *Apostolicon*. His study confirms for him that defenders of Judaism had corrupted Paul's gospel of grace by rewriting the *Evangelion*, adding to it references to the Law and the Prophets.

He determined that the authors had created a false Christ who conformed to the Jewish beliefs that the authors were unable to let go. In Marcion's opinion, the separation that Paul had constructed between the Law and the gospel of grace had been breached.

But that is not all that Marcion discovers in his research. As Marcion keeps track of the comparisons between the Jewish scriptures and the Christian texts, he notices striking differences when it comes to how God is described. For instance, Marcion makes note of the fact that in the Jewish scriptures, God commanded bears to come out of the undergrowth and eat the children who had called his prophet "baldy." But in the *Evangelion*, Jesus welcomes children and praises them as model citizens of his kingdom. God in the Jewish scriptures commands people to love those who love them and hate their enemies. But in the *Evangelion*, Jesus teaches people to love their enemies and pray for those who persecute them. God in the Jewish scriptures is a God who condones war and violence, whose wrath is wielded against non-Jewish nations. But God according to Jesus is a God of mercy and peace, who extends his grace to Gentiles. Marcion's litany of differences goes on and on. Pages of differences fill his notebook.

How could this be? Marcion wonders. Further reflection brings to mind Jesus' declaration that no one has known the Father except the Son. Surely then, something weird was going on with the Genesis stories. How could Adam and Eve, their children and their grandchildren have talked to God or known him as those stories related? And why would God, whom Jesus said knew people's thoughts, have to ask Adam where he was in the garden?

These observations push Marcion to a logical conclusion. Jesus had not only brought an end to the Jewish Law and practices, he had come to teach about a Father of grace and goodness, a God who is completely different from the Creator God in the Jewish scriptures. Jesus is the Son of this God, a God so transcendent that no one had ever even guessed at his existence before Jesus' advent. From this Marcion reasoned that Jesus had not intended to start a Jewish movement. Rather Jesus intended to start a new religion that was not Jewish – the Christian religion.

Marcion organizes his notes about the differences between the Jewish scriptures, the *Evangelion*, and the *Apostolicon*. He synthesizes his research into a book called *The Antitheses* (or *The Contradictions*). Marcion's theology, his beliefs about God, are captured in *The Antitheses*, which we know in some detail from various later Christian writers who opposed Marcion. His beliefs are developed directly out of his comparative project and interpretation of texts. Marcion never appeals to special revelation for the source of his theology, but deduces everything from interpreting and comparing Jewish scriptural passages with the *Evangelion* and the *Apostolicon*. Marcion deduces from his comparison that the God in the Jewish scriptures is different from the God who was Jesus' Father.

From later descriptions of *The Antitheses*, we know that Marcion pointed to a number of theological differences that he determined were irreconcilable. For instance, the Jewish God was known to Adam and later generations (cf. Gen. 2:15–24), while Jesus said that no one has known the Father but the Son (*Ev.* 10:22). The Jewish God was so ignorant that he had to ask where Adam was, while Jesus could read minds (*Ev.* 5:22). The stories of Joshua in Judges, Marcion argues, prove that the Jewish God was a warmonger, conquering cities violently and cruelly. Jesus, however, taught about God's mercy (*Ev.* 6:36) and how to de-escalate violence (*Ev.* 6:27–31). The Jewish God never gave Isaac his sight back (Gen. 27:1) and David killed the blind in his conquest for Zion (2 Sam. 5:6–10), but Jesus opened the eyes of many blind people (i.e. *Ev.* 18:35–43). Moses was told by the Jewish God to leave Egypt, girded and shod, carrying a staff and sacks filled with gold and silver (Gen. 12:11, 35–36). Jesus told his disciples to go out unshod with no sack, no change of clothes, and no money in their wallets (*Ev.* 10:4). The Jewish God commands "an eye for an eye, a tooth for a tooth" (Exod. 21:24; Lev. 24:20; Deut. 19:21); but Jesus says, "If anyone strikes you on the cheek, offer the other also", and "from anyone who takes your coat do not withhold even your shirt" (*Ev.* 6:29). Elijah, the prophet of the Jewish God, called down fire from heaven (1 Kgs. 18:38), while Jesus forbade his disciples from calling down fire (*Ev.* 9:54–55).

Perhaps most pronounced to Marcion is the fact that the Jewish prophet Elisha, with the power and approval of the Jewish God, made two bears come out of the woods and maul 42 children to punish them because they had called him "baldy" (2 Kgs. 2:23–24). Marcion could not reconcile such a God with Jesus' teachings that he welcomed the children into the kingdom as model citizens (*Ev.* 18:15–17). In Marcion's mind, the difference between these two Gods is proven beyond doubt with Paul's observation that anyone hanged from a tree is cursed by the Jewish God (Deut. 27:26), yet Jesus suffered death on the cross for the redemption of the Gentiles (Gal. 3:10–14).

Marcion concludes from this evidence that there was not one God, but two Gods. The Jewish God YHWH is the Creator of this universe and selected the Jews as his chosen people. He is a God of Law and justice. Marcion calls this God "the God of Abraham, Isaac, and Jacob," the "Creator," and also the "World Ruler," which is a reference to Laodiceans/Ephesians 6:12, where Paul says that our battle is against the "world rulers of darkness."

The God that Jesus announced, however, was a God previously unknown, living enclosed in the third heaven (1 Cor. 12:2), an invisible spiritual world. He is the God who is above all things, above every principality and power (Laod./Eph. 1:20–21). He is a God defined by his newness, otherness, and alienness (cf. Laod./Eph. 2:19). He is a newcomer to our universe, an alien, foreigner, or stranger from a place separated from us by an infinite distance (Tert., *Marc.* 1.2; Iren., *Haer.* 4.33.2). Ontologically, the Creator is not derived from the Alien God, nor does the Alien God have any connection to YHWH's created order. The Alien God's transcendence is total. Marcion defines this Alien God as the God of Love and Mercy who, when witnessing our suffering, came to our rescue by sending his Son to liberate us (Figure 2.3).

Marcion confessed "another" God who is "greater" than the Creator, one who has done greater works than the Creator. In this way, Marcion spoke out against the Creator, accusing him of being an envious and jealous God, such as he is described in Deuteronomy 4:24 and Genesis 3:22. He is a God who creates evil, and kills as well as enlivens (Exod. 20:5; Isa. 45:7; Deut. 32:39).

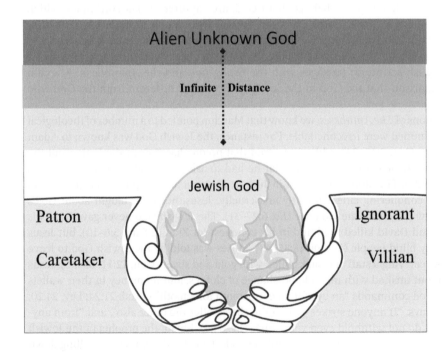

FIGURE 2.3 Marcion's theology and demiurgy illustrated.

Marcion posited that the Alien God was different. He was a "good" God, "suddenly" intervening in human history. Marcion's description of Jesus' Father as supremely good and nothing but good is a reference to the Alien God's inescapable act to save what was not his own. His act was a sudden intervention of a God of grace and compassion to rescue people from the suffering they endured under the rule of the Creator God. Even the Creator God was ignorant of the existence of Jesus' Father before Jesus showed up in Judea. Jesus' Father did not have any prior credentials except that he was "good." This essential goodness determines his actions when he decided to intervene in the affairs of another God's world who, in contrast, was retributive and punitive.

The remarkableness of the All-Good God that Marcion taught cannot be overstated. This conceptualization of God would have been very "odd" in a world full of Gods, that were all-powerful capricious divinities who had created humans as their servants. Gods were beings to be feared and plied with gifts to stave off famines, disease, and war. Hubris (godlike pride and vanity) especially was to be avoided because jealous Gods did not like to be challenged by uppity humans. The anger and wrath of the Gods was dangerous to endure.

This conceptualization of the Gods was the case across the board, from Greece to Egypt to Babylonia to Rome to Israel. We call this theological orientation Slave Spirituality, a worldview that deems humans slaves or servants of the Gods in a way that God is a master who has the power to do anything he wants with his creatures. Such is the case, for instance, with the story of Job and the capricious YHWH. Jews eventually tamed the capriciousness of YHWH by introducing Vassal Spirituality. In other words, they put their relationship with YHWH in covenantal or contractual terms, so that both God and his subjects were legally obligated to each other like a king is to his vassals. God established a set of laws or commandments that his subjects agreed to follow. Because they had signed God's covenant, YHWH could not be capricious, but had to behave in ways that would protect them and reward them for their fidelity. If his subjects broke the contract, God as their King could punish them or abandon them.

Marcion's Theological Conclusions

YHWH is	Jesus' Father is
The God of the Jews	An Unknown God
A jealous God	A God of love
An envious God	A merciful God
A warrior God	A God of grace
A punitive God	A universal savior God
A God of Justice	A God greater than YHWH
The Giver of the Law	A totally transcendent God
Creator of the universe	A God of supreme goodness
The Ruler of the World	A God who lives far away from us
The God of Abraham, Isaac, and Jacob	An Alien God (newcomer to our universe)
He will send a Messiah to save the Jews	He suddenly intervened to end human suffering

Xenotheism

FIGURE 2.4   Marcion's understanding of the characteristics that distinguished Jesus' Father from YHWH.

Early Christians, as Jewish sectarians, carried on this view of God. Gentile converts who were raised to think of themselves as slaves or servants of capricious Gods were brought into this covenant relationship, learning that God was a God with rules and expectations for human behavior. God would reward and punish accordingly. Marcion's vision of an Alien God who was 100% good, gracious, and merciful was different. Such a God was unheard of before Marcion "deduced" him from his comparative study of Jewish and Christian scriptures.

But God's complete goodness was not all that Marcion innovated. Church historian, Adolf von Harnack (1851–1930 CE) wrote an influential book about Marcion, which was published in 1921. He argued that Marcion's theology of alienness was also an innovation in religious history. There is no other thinker before Marcion who conceived of a God who had no connection to this world, a God who was utterly transcendent and utterly good. Marcion is to be credited with a theological innovation that we call in this textbook Xenotheism, the belief and worship of a God who is alien (Greek: *xenos*) to our universe (Figure 2.4).

2.4 The Gospel Story About Jesus

Since Paul does not discuss the details about Jesus' life or ministry and Marcion rejected as apocryphal the other gospels attributed to the apostles, what Marcion believed about Jesus developed out of his interpretation of the *Evangelion* which he read in light of his innovative theology. Marcion's reading of the *Evangelion* deeply informed his distinctive Christology or belief about Jesus.

According to Tertullian, Marcion is adamant that he did not author the *Evangelion* nor did any apostle including Paul. Rather Marcion said that it represents the true gospel message that Jesus Christ revealed to Paul. It had no attributed author. Or to put it another way, the *Evangelion* was anonymously circulating. Marcion is certain that other gospels with apostolic authors are "Judaized" corruptions of the *Evangelion*. Marcion's *Antithesis* interacts only with the Gospel of Matthew. It may be that Marcion only ever knew the Gospel of Matthew, and that Tertullian is the one to speculate that Marcion knew several Gospels written by the apostles since Tertullian himself knows them and considers them older than Marcion. Whatever the case, Marcion refers to passages from the Gospel of Matthew in order to refute them in *The Antitheses*. One of these passages was Matthew 5:17 where Jesus declares, "I did not come to destroy the Law, but to fulfill it." Marcion said that Christ did not speak this way, but instead said, "I did not come to fulfill the Law, but to destroy it." Marcion likely inferred this from Paul's words in Romans 10:4 that "Christ is the end of the Law." Marcion objected to many other passages in Matthew which he determined had been added to the *Evangelion* to Judaize it (Matt. 1:23; 2:1, 11, 16–18; 4:13–14; 5:17; 5:45; 8:4; 9:27–28; 10:10; 12:48; 15:24; 15:26; 16:17–18; 19:3–8; 27:35).

In fact, Marcion thought that the *Evangelion* predated the other "Judaized" gospels. Later Christian writers like Tertullian, who had copies of the *Evangelion*, provide us with details about its contents. When we compare these details about the contents of the *Evangelion* to the Christian gospels we have today, it is clear that the *Evangelion* had a literary relationship to the Gospel of Luke.

To help us envision the shape and contents of the *Evangelion*, Jason BeDuhn, Matthias Klinghardt, and Dieter T. Roth have each published recent reconstructions of the *Evangelion*. Also available is an older English edition made by James Hamlyn Hill (1891), which is based on the reconstruction of the text made by August Hahn in 1823. While these reconstructions have their differences, we are certain that the *Evangelion* did not contain Luke's beginning (1:1–2:52, 3:2–4:15, 16b–22) or ending (24:13–53), the saying about Jonah (11:29b–32), the saying about the blood of the prophets (11:49–51), the saying about the sparrows (12:6–7), the story of the Tower of Siloam and the parable of the fig tree (13:1–9), the warning against Herod (13:29–35), the parable of the prodigal son (15:11–32), the duty saying (17:10), the Son of Man prophecy (18:25–30), Jesus' entry into the city and weeping over Jerusalem (19:29–44), the cleansing of the temple (19:45–46), the parable of the vineyard (20:9–18), the reference to the burning bush (20:37–38), the vengeance prophecy (21:18, 21–22), the fulfillment saying (22:16), the tale of the two swords (22:35–38), the violence on the Mount of Olives (22:49–51), or the story of the two thieves at the cross (23:39–43).

What is the message about Jesus that Marcion took away from the *Evangelion*? Marcion's Christology is largely influenced by the fact that Marcion's version of the *Evangelion* did not mention Jesus' birth or his baptism by John, but begins with Jesus' visit to a synagogue in the fifteenth year of the reign of Tiberius Caesar (29 CE) when Jesus "comes down to Capernaum." From this, Marcion concludes that Jesus, as Son of the Alien God, had directly descended from the third heaven (where Paul had received his revelation of Jesus) to earth. In this surprise appearance of Jesus Christ, the Alien God revealed himself in order to rescue everyone suffering enslavement to the powers in charge of the universe, specifically the Creator God and the Devil. Out of his deep compassion, God suffered what humanity suffers, even the agonies of death.

For Marcion, this redemptive act meant that God is the Father of mercy and the God of all comfort. His redemption is universal. He is a God of no partiality. Because he sent his son Jesus to redeem all of humanity, Jesus was called the Messiah (Greek: *Christos*), although he was not the Messiah that the Jewish prophets predicted would come to fulfill the plans of the Creator God. The Jewish Messiah had yet to emerge on the historical stage. In the meantime, however, the Alien God sent his Son as the Messiah for everyone, Greek and Jew alike.

This did not mean, however, that everyone responded to the Alien God's Messiah equally. From Marcion's read of the *Evangelion* and the *Apostolicon*, Jews were particularly resistant to the idea. Marcion read the *Evangelion* as a story about Jesus' rejection by the Jews and about Jesus' critique of Jewish practices. The *Evangelion* starts with Jesus' expulsion from the synagogue after he openly criticizes Israel's treatment and rejection of its prophets. His message so infuriates the Jews present that they take Jesus to a mountain cliff and try to push him off (*Ev.* 5:29). In the *Evangelion*, Jesus calls the crowds of Jews following him "evil" (*Ev.* 11:29), "faithless," and "perverse" (*Ev.* 9:41). Pharisees are damned and rebuked for building tombs for the prophets killed by their ancestors (*Ev.* 11:42–48). The Sabbath work restriction among Jews is presented as a joke (*Ev.* 13:15; 14:5; cf. 6:1–11). Ritual cleansing is rejected as foolish (*Ev.* 11:37–40). Jews who give alms because they are trying to be obedient to the Law are likened to people who walk over graves without knowing it (*Ev.* 11:42–44). Jesus announces that the Law and the Prophets came to an end with John's ministry, when the good news about the kingdom began to be preached (*Ev.* 16:16).

Marcion knows, however, that Jesus never explicitly proclaimed a new Alien God in the *Evangelion*. To explain Jesus' silence on the subject, Marcion says that the knowledge of the Alien God was something that Christ wanted people to discover for themselves, presumably using reason as Marcion had done. According to Marcion, this is why Christ was long-suffering and patient, tolerating his disciples' misunderstandings and Peter's ignorant confession. Unfortunately, the disciples never really understood, although they tried. After Jesus' death they completely fell back into their old ways of life. This is why Jesus decided to commission Paul through divine revelation (when he lifted Paul up to the third heaven to learn the unutterable truth) to be his one and only apostle, stripping the disciples of their former apostolic status.

Marcion also thinks that Jesus did not have a physical body since his version of the *Evangelion* does not begin with any birth story of Jesus. Nowhere in the *Evangelion* does it say that Jesus was born in a creature's body. Rather, Marcion finds in Paul's letters that Jesus "came in human likeness" and is "the image of the invisible God" (Phil. 2:7; Col. 1:15). From this evidence, Marcion concludes that Jesus was a spiritual entity in disguise, an apparition (Greek: *dokesis*; Latin: *phantasma*). His Christological model uses the VISITATION PATTERN.

What did Marcion mean by this? According to Tertullian, Marcion explains this with reference to descriptions of the appearances of angels in traditional stories. In these stories, angels who appear to humans like Abraham do not have physical bodies, and yet they are not perceivably different from human beings (Gen. 18:1–8). Their human disguise is so perfect, in fact, that people might be tricked, not knowing that they were entertaining angels in disguise. It is important to keep in mind that Marcion does not think that Jesus was a ghost or a specter, but an apparition that was so humanlike that he was indistinguishable from other humans. Because he was a human apparition, he could eat and drink and suffer crucifixion, while at the same time he could be taken to a cliff, pushed off, and survive. He could slip through mobs unharmed (*Ev.* 5:29).

Marcion's idea that Jesus was an apparition (Greek: *dokesis*) came to be called by later Christians Docetism. It identified the position that Jesus did not have a fleshly body and, therefore, did not suffer in the flesh. While Marcion would have agreed with this in principle, he was quick to contextualize and qualify it. Jesus' appearance in human likeness, he said, is the story of a divine being so transcendent and so compassionate that it endured descent from its heavenly home to live like a human being in a world completely its Other. He contrasts this with the opinion of other Christians who taught that Jesus, as the Creator's Son redeemed his own beloved creatures because it was justice to do so. But not so with the Alien God, Marcion said. His love was so excessive that Jesus descended into an alien environment at a great cost to himself and suffered exceedingly to redeem beings who belonged to an Other God. He rescued people from the power of darkness and transferred them into his Kingdom of forgiveness (Col. 1:13–14).

Marcion sees Jesus' message as innovative, pointing to a novel way of life, a newness of spirit, that contrasted with the old way of life shaped around the laws of a petty God. Marcion thinks that Jesus started a new universal religion that brought to humanity a new kindness, a new disposition, and a new life which he called the Kingdom of God. This novel teaching is laid out, according to Marcion, in the beatitudes where the love of the Alien God is evident. The gospel preached by Christ is a blessing to everyone the Creator God made miserable: the poor, the hungry, the mourners, the hated, the persecuted, and the outcasts. The Alien God flipped the tables. Marcion sees the difference between charity to one's brothers and sisters (which the Creator God demanded) and charity to everyone who asks (which the Alien God taught). Love and forgiveness across ethnic boundaries is a concept that Marcion felt was "a new and different thing." So much had the tables turned, that Jesus demands that we love our enemies, he said. Only this extreme form of love, Marcion thinks, mirrored the kind of love that the Alien God had shown to humanity, redeeming "strangers" and his foes, reaching out to the wretched and praying for his own tormentors. When Marcion reads the story about the woman with the unstoppable flow of blood who reaches out to touch the fringe of Jesus' garment, Marcion sees in the story a woman surrendering herself to the unmerited love of the Alien God. While the Jewish Law marked her as impure and socially destitute, the Alien God accepted her as she was and healed her (*Ev.* 8:42–48).

Marcion's understanding of Jesus' "new" message comes largely from his interpretation of the *Evangelion*, where salvation is presented in ethical terms, not ethnic ones. The best example of this is the parable of the Good Samaritan (*Ev.* 10:29–37). Jesus boldly warns Jews to take notice if they think they are saved because they are descendants of Abraham. They will be surprised when they are thrown out of the Kingdom (*Ev.* 13:22–28). The Kingdom is open to people who strive to live by the ideals of humility (*Ev.* 14:7–11; 18:14; 22:24–27), service (*Ev.* 22:27), mercy (*Ev.* 10:29–37), charity (*Ev.* 6:29–30, 38; 18:22–23), love (*Ev.* 6:27, 32–36; 10:25–28), the Golden Rule (*Ev.*6:31), repentance (*Ev.* 17:1–4; 18:9–14), and forgiveness (*Ev.* 6:37; 17:1–4; 23:32). It is open to people who are on the margins of society: the impoverished (*Ev.* 21:1–4; 7:22; 12:33–34; cf. 6:20, 24), the crippled, the sick, the blind (Ev. 7:22; 14:13–14), and women (*Ev.* 7:36–50; 8:1–3; 10:38–42; 15:8–10; 21:1–4). Most of all, it is open to repentant sinners (*Ev.* 5:20, 30–32; 7:34, 36–50; 15:7, 10; 18:9–14; 19:2–10).

Marcion also had an opinion on what Jesus' death accomplished. According to Marcion, Jesus' death rescues the righteous and the sinners from their maker, the Creator God. Marcion thinks that the Alien God paid a ransom to the Creator God for the souls of human beings. The payment was

Jesus' death. He develops this opinion out of Paul's letters, particularly Galatians 3:13, and 1 Corinthians 6:20 and 7:23. There is evidence from Adamantius (ca. 300 CE) that Marcion's version of Galatians 2:20 also read, "And the life I now live in the flesh I live by faith in the Son of God, who *purchased* (instead of *loved*; Greek: *agorasantos* instead of *agapesantos*) me and gave himself for me." Marcion favors the metaphor of payment because buyers do not purchase what they already own.

Marcion also uses the metaphor of stealth and theft, that, as a redeemer, the Alien God comes like a thief at an unexpected hour (*Ev.* 12:39) or as the stronger man who seizes his booty (*Ev.*11:21–22). Tertullian encapsulates the character of Marcion's God, as a God who swoops down upon a world alien to him, abducts human beings, snatching them away from their Creator, the God of the Jews.

Marcion's God, however, was not interested in abducting the total human being, body and soul. There is no resurrection of the body in Marcion's opinion. Rather, the Alien God was only interested in the human soul. The soul is the part of the human being that Marcion believed could be liberated from the body at death and could be transformed into a spiritual or "heavenly" being worthy to enjoy life in the Alien God's heaven (Rom. 3:28; 8:2; 1 Cor. 15:48–49). Christ's death and resurrection provided the model for the soul's resurrection or spiritual transformation, something which only the Alien God could manage as an act of grace (1 Cor. 15:21–22, 46, 49, 57). In other words, what is saved from the Creator (the soul) is transformed and reconstituted by the Alien God as spirit.

In Marcion's mythology, Jesus journeyed to the underworld after he died on the cross (Rom. 10:7; Laod./Eph. 4:7–10). In the underworld, Jesus not only personally conquered the Power of Death but preached liberation to the souls imprisoned there. Those who rallied around Jesus' message of universal salvation and followed him out of the underworld were all of the tormented sinners and heathens. The Creator God's righteous servants like the Abel, Enoch, Abraham, Moses, and the prophets, however, remained in the grave because they remained loyal to the Jewish God. There they await the coming of their own Messiah who, the Creator God had promised, would establish a new Kingdom for the Jews.

2.5 Who are the Jews?

COMPANION READINGS
Tertullian, *Against Marcion* 3.6

Marcion's solution to the Christian identity crisis was separation. Christians are Christians and Jews are Jews. Christians worship the Alien God, while Jews worship their national God, the Creator of the world. Separate Gods, separate Messiahs, separate scriptures, separate religions.

That said, Marcion did not damn the Jews or disparage Judaism. Marcion is a universalist. The Alien God offers everyone salvation and a spiritual afterlife in his heaven as glorious beings. Marcion emphasizes the universal nature of salvation through the grace of the Alien God, who saves Jews and Gentiles alike. He never interprets "Christ is the end of the Law" to mean that only Gentiles are saved (Rom. 11:1–2, 11). The will of the Alien God was for all Israel to be saved and experience his mercy (Rom. 11:26, 28b, 31). In fact, Marcion argues that Jesus used the title Messiah (Greek: *Christos*) because the Alien God wanted to make himself known first to the Jews because they were YHWH's chosen people. Jesus used language most familiar to them to persuade them. The will of the Alien God was also for all the Gentiles to be saved, for all those who had been excluded from Israel and suffered in limbo under the regime of the Creator God who had made them but had not chosen them as his people (Rom. 1:8–32).

But not everyone took up this offer of grace. Marcion, aware of Paul's frustration over Israel's resistance to Jesus' message (cf. Rom. 10:2–4, 21; 11:7–12, 23), believes that the Jews refused to follow the Alien God because they were blinded by the Creator God (and thus made "ignorant") and recalcitrant in their devotion to him (cf. 2 Cor. 4:4). In Marcion's eyes, their devotion to the Creator was nationalistic, ethnic, and ancestral, dependent upon the covenant contracted between the people of Israel and YHWH. Marcion does not think that their God was the Devil, but legalistic and just. Because the God of Israel was just, he would fulfill the promises he had made to Israel. He still planned to send his own Messiah to gather together all the people of Israel into one strong nation. Marcion asserts that the prophecies in the Jewish scriptures did not refer to Jesus, but to a Jewish Messiah who would be named Emmanuel. He would be born of a young woman and would be a mighty warrior. He would deliver the People of Israel from their colonizers. He would not suffer crucifixion or die. Rather he would be victorious in establishing YHWH's kingdom on earth. On this subject, Marcion affirms traditional Jewish messianic expectations and the justice of their God. According to Marcion, the old covenant between the Creator and Israel still exists and still operates for the observant Jews.

Marcion reads in the *Evangelion* that some Jewish leaders played a part in Jesus' arrest and conviction (*Ev.* 22:47–54, 63–71), but he absolves them of all responsibility by laying the blame for Jesus' death squarely on the Creator God, not anyone else. The Creator God is at fault because he blinded the minds of the Jews so that they would not know that Christ came to rescue them from the Creator (cf. 2 Cor. 4:4). Had they known that Christ came from a merciful God in order to free them from the sufferings that the Law occasioned, Jesus would have been spared, Marcion reasoned.

The Creator God did not just blind the Jewish leaders. He blinded the apostles who were Jews too. Marcion believed that Jesus came to the apostles first with his message of mercy because they were especially virtuous. Jesus welcomed them into the mystery of divine love (that had been hidden from the Creator of the universe) and the riches of salvation (cf. Eph. 3:9; Rom. 11:33). In their ignorance, they made the mistake of identifying the gospel proclaimed by Jesus with the fulfillment of Jewish prophecies. They stopped preaching to Jews about another God besides YHWH. Marcion thinks that their historical relationship with the Creator had clouded their understanding, making them suspicious of this new revelation of unconditional love and grace. So they fell back on the security of the Law and their ancestral relationship with the Creator. Paul, because he received a special revelation, is the only exception. He is the only one who communicated the radical newness of Christ's revelation. And Marcion literally followed in his footsteps.

2.6 A Counter Church in Rome

Very concerned that even his copies of the *Evangelion* and the *Apostolicon* may not be free from the "Judaizing" campaign of the false apostles, Marcion carefully studies these documents and makes corrections to the texts. We cannot determine how extensive his editing was because the *Apostolicon* is the oldest collection of Paul's letters that we know about. Our first manuscript of Paul's letters dates to the beginning of the early third century. While second-century Christian writers quote passages from Paul's letters, it is clear that the text of Paul's letters had not stabilized. Their readings varied. Multiple varying copies of Paul's letters circulated in the second century, the *Apostolicon* among them.

When Marcion finished composing *The Antitheses* and making textual corrections to the *Evangelion* and the *Apostolicon*, he published his work, expecting that his scholarship on the separation of the Law and the Gospel, and his rational discovery of the real identity of Jesus' Father would bring about a major reform among Apostolic Catholics. He discusses this reformation with the elders of his church in Rome, but instead of enacting reforms, the elders kick Marcion out of the church and return to him the 200,000 sesterces he had originally donated. Later Christians do not agree when this happened. Tertullian says it happened in 144 CE, but other sources say that the year was 138/140 CE, and also that Marcion did not get the boot alone. Cerdo's membership in the Roman church was revoked too.

Cerdo is a Christian from Syria who was teaching in Rome during the time of Bishop Hyginus. Cerdo also taught that the God preached by the Law and the Prophets is not the Father of Jesus. He believed that the God of the Law and the Prophets is the epitome of justice and righteousness, while Jesus' Father is the epitome of goodness and benevolence. We can imagine that Marcion and Cerdo were scholars working on the same problem and likely discussed their research with each other. We can imagine their ideas developing in tandem.

After Cerdo got the boot, he formed a private esoteric study group. Marcion, however, did not choose to continue his work as a private solo teacher like Cerdo. His discovery of the Alien God was not a secret to be kept but a discovery to be revealed to everyone. Marcion decides to use his wealth to start his own public Christian church, promoting the worship of Jesus' Father, the Alien God. The church he sets up is modeled after the Apostolic Catholic assemblies. Since he envisions his church as a COUNTER MOVEMENT meant to correct the Judaizing errors of the Apostolic Catholic church, he establishes a parallel but separate community structure with its own bishops, deacons, elders, and lay people. He distinguishes between the baptized (converts) and the catechumen (those preparing for baptism), although the groups were socially integrated. In fact, in his services the two groups (alongside curious newcomers) said their prayers together. Members celebrated the eucharist, the sacred meal, although they chose to drink water instead of wine and gave milk mixed with honey to the newly baptized. In terms of church organization and worship services, the average lay person was not able to distinguish a Marcionite church from an Apostolic Catholic church, a fact that later became a nuisance for the Apostolic Catholics.

Marcion's counter movement was most evident in the lifestyle he demanded for members of his church. Marcion forbade marriage and all sexual activity among members of his church, a lifestyle we call encratism (Greek: *encrateia*, self-controlled). In later chapters, we see that other Christian movements also demanded celibacy. In fact, celibacy before *and* after baptism was the norm among Christians in Syria until the third century. Marcion may have known this, and believed that the Apostolic Catholics in Rome had become lax. Marcion only baptized people after they vowed to remain unmarried or to stop having sex with their spouses (if they were already married). This means that, for acquiring new members, his churches depended 100% on conversion.

While this might seem odd or excessive to us today, Marcion was only instituting what he believed Paul preached as the ideal (1 Cor. 7) and what he thought was an act of resistance against the Creator God. Marcion asked members of his churches to abandon the commandments of the Creator God, including his program of procreation (Gen. 1:28). Marcion's protest against the Creator God also meant that members of his churches were not allowed to eat meat or drink wine, and strict rules of fasting were put into place. Members of his church were taught to accept martyrdom if they were denounced and arrested by the Romans. Under no circumstance were they to deny Christ. Because of the severity with which they treated their bodies and embraced martyrdom, Marcionites gained the reputation of supermen in antiquity, with Marcion as their virtuous leader.

Supermen aside, the greatest innovation of Marcion's church was the publication of a set of Christian scriptures – the *Evangelion* and the *Apostolicon* – which replaced the Jewish scriptures. With the publication of these scriptures, Marcion had created for his church the first Christian New Testament, a closed canon of authoritative and sacred documents. While scholars debate whether Marcion is responsible for calling his Christian scripture The New Testament, the evidence points in this direction. Tertullian relates that Marcion set The New Testament in opposition to the old covenant (Latin: *testamentum*) because Marcion believed that The New Testament belonged to a separate God who had nothing to do with the old Law and the Prophets (Tert., *Marc.* 4.6). The "newness" of Christianity was all over *The Antitheses*. Marcion concluded that the Alien God was different from the Creator because the *Evangelion* showcased "new" doctrines of the "new" Christ (Tert., *Marc.* 4.28). Central for Marcion is Jesus' saying, "No one tears a piece from a new garment and puts it on an old garment; if he does, he will tear the new, and the piece from the new will not match the old. And no one puts new wine into old wineskins; if he does, the new wine will burst the skins and it will be spilled, and the skins will be destroyed" (*Ev.* 5:36–38). Marcion thought that the Kingdom of God that Christ proclaimed was "new" (Tert., *Marc.* 3.24; 4.24). The way Jesus preached was a "new" way of speaking (Tert., *Marc.* 4.11). The content of Christ's message of forgiveness and love for our enemies was the result of a "new" type of mercy taught by the "new" Christ from a divine patience that was "new" (Tert., *Marc.* 4.10). Christ's actions were "new": he raised the young man of Nain from the dead (*Ev.* 7:11–17), healed on the Sabbath (*Ev.* 6:1–5); he calmed the storm on Lake Gennesaret (*Ev.* 8:22–25) (Tert., *Marc.* 4.12, 18, 20). Given that Marcion was setting up Christianity as a new religion separate from Judaism, it is likely that Tertullian's comment reveals the fact that Marcion had also called his new canon, The New Testament.

The significance (and genius) of the creation of a Christian set of scriptures cannot be overstated. While other Christians had texts, there was little agreement about which texts had authority beyond the Jewish scriptures. The Christian texts had not stabilized, so different copies of the same texts had different readings and even different passages in them. These textual differences only reified the diversity among Christians that had generated the textual differences in the first place. Marcion realized how problematic this situation was for Christians. He analyzed the *Evangelion* and the *Apostolicon* and corrected them in order to establish authoritative versions of them. Then he published them as the first New Testament, a concept that was Marcion's brainchild.

But that is not all. Once Marcion publishes his New Testament and organizes his counter church in Rome around it, he decides to take up the Christian mission where Paul left off. He sails out of Rome and travels around the Mediterranean with his message of the real Christianity, establishing Marcionite churches along the route, leaving copies of his New Testament with them. His success and spread were so immediate and rapid that, by 150 CE, Justin notes that Marcion's churches were everywhere and, to his credit, Marcion himself, as an old man, was still preaching (Figure 2.5).

Timeline

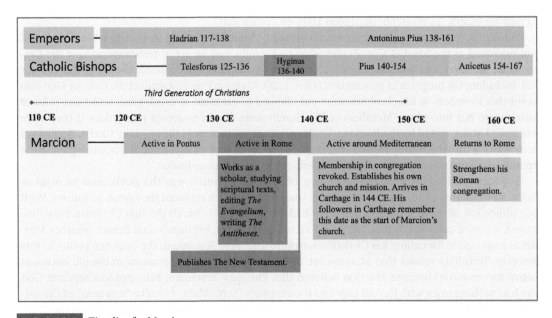

FIGURE 2.5 Timeline for Marcion.

Pattern Summary

When we reflect on the patterns that Marcion used to construct Christian identity (Figure 2.6), we observe that he centered his theology around the discovery and revelation of the true identity of Jesus' Father. He was an Alien God who was not connected to our universe prior to Jesus' advent. Marcion was a XENOTHEIST. He blamed human suffering on God, but not Jesus' Father. He thought that YHWH, the God of this world, was totally responsible for suffering and that there was nothing people could do to escape his system of suffering. YHWH rules as an AUTOCRAT

Family Pattern Chart
Marcion

X=Definitely > L=Likely

THEODICY	Faulty-God	Faulty-Human	Other
Marcion	X		
Cerdo	X		

SOTERIOLOGY	Gift from God	Human achievement	Minimalist	Moderate	Maximalist
Marcion	X		X		

CHRISTOLOGY	Adult possession	Fetal possession	Hybrid	Ensoulment	Visitation	Human who received revelation
Marcion					X	

ANTHROPOLOGY	Mono	Dual	Triad	Quad
Marcion		X		

COSMIC DEMIURGY	Autocrat	Administrator	Caretaker	Patron	Justice	Villain	Rebel	Ignorant	Impaired
Marcion	X	L	X	X	X	X		X	

RESURRECTION	Body reunites with soul	Body discarded and soul immortalized	Body and soul discarded and spirit rises	God-element separates from body soul, and spirit and rises
Marcion			X	

SCRIPTURES	Jewish	Gospel	Pauline letters (10)	Pauline letters (13)	Hebrews	Acts	Catholic letters	Revelation	Other
Marcion		Ev/Mt	X						

ECCLESIOLOGY	Consolidation movement	Reform movement	Secessionist movement	Counter movement	Innovative movement	Transregional	Regional
Marcion				X		X	

FIGURE 2.6 Summary of Marcion's patterns.

and an ADMINISTRATOR. He is the PATRON and CARETAKER of the Jewish people who relates to them as a JUSTICE OF THE LAW. But he is a nasty God, VILLAINOUS, and IGNORANT. Jesus descended across an infinite space from the Alien God's world to our own world and, like an angel, appeared as an adult man. He was God's Son visiting earth.

Marcion was a DUALIST, believing that Jesus came to save souls and immortalize them as spirits who would live in the spiritual world of Jesus' Father. Salvation was a matter of grace, a GIFT from the God of Love and Mercy. Marcion instituted Paul's ideal lifestyle, celibacy, in protest to YHWH's commandment to procreate. He also required strict regiments of fasting, vegetarianism, and abstinence from wine. This lifestyle pattern is about the practice of ENCRATISM or self-discipline.

Marcion's scripture included Paul's ten letters and the *Evangelion*. He likely called this The New Testament. He rejected the Jewish scriptures as the old testament (covenant) meant for the Jews, not the Christians. He formed a COUNTER MOVEMENT in Rome which he took abroad into Asia Minor and north Africa. His ecclesiology was separate from the Apostolic Catholic structures but mirrored them. He used single baptism to initiate new members and provided water, milk, and honey at his eucharist ceremonies.

Takeaways

1. Marcion saw Christianity as a new religious movement separate from Judaism.

2. Marcion is our first witness to a collection of ten of Paul's letters. This collection consisted of Galatians, 1 and 2 Corinthians, Romans, 1 and 2 Thessalonians, Laodiceans (Ephesians), Colossians, Philippians, and Philemon.

3. Multiple gospels were circulating among third-generation Christians, some with apostolic authors, but not all. Papias knows about a book attributed to Mark and a collection of Jesus' sayings in Aramaic attributed to Matthew. According to Tertullian, Marcion runs across gospels in Rome that were attributed to the apostles, but the specific apostles are not named. There is only evidence that Marcion was refuting passages from the Gospel of Matthew in *The Antitheses*.

4. Marcion has the *Evangelion*, a written gospel with no author attribution, although it has a literary relationship with the Gospel of Luke. The reconstruction of the *Evangelion* is the first textual witness of any freestanding Christian gospel we can recover from historical reports.

5. Neither the gospels in circulation nor Paul's letters had yet achieved textual stability. Different versions were circulating among third-generation Christians. Third-generation Christian scholars were actively editing these documents and creating new ones. Marcion was one of these scholars. He saw the benefit of stabilizing Christian texts. He edited the *Evangelion* and the *Apostolicon*, composed *The Antitheses*, and published them as the authoritative version of scripture for his churches.

6. As the first scholar to edit and establish an authoritative version of Paul's letters or any gospel, Marcion is to be credited with the conceptualization and creation of the first New Testament.

7. Some Christians met in private esoteric groups with teachers like Cerdo. Others, like Marcion, built public churches with open access to the Christian message.

8. Docetism is a form of VISITATION CHRISTOLOGY popular among the Marcionites, although later writers only give us a caricature of the belief. When Marcion taught that Jesus was a divine apparition descended from a distant heaven to earth, he envisioned Jesus' appearance to have been like the appearance of an angel who was indistinguishable from humans, who could eat, drink, and suffer.

9. Marcionism was a COUNTER MOVEMENT attempting to restore Christianity to the movement that Jesus had intended originally. According to the Marcionites, the Apostolic Catholic leaders had errored in their push to "Judaize" Jesus' universalist message. Noteworthy is the fact that the leaders of the Apostolic Catholic church network define themselves as both "apostolic" and "catholic/universal" in contrast to Marcion's claim to have founded the universal church based on the teachings of the only true apostle, Paul.

10. Marcion innovates theology. He is the first theologian in history to recognize a transcendent God who is not related to the universe, but an Alien God. The Alien God is all-good and operates entirely out of his grace and mercy.

Questions

1. Was Marcion the first Christian? Why or why not?

2. Do you think Marcion was anti-Jewish? Why or why not?

3. What do you make of the fact that the *Evangelion* circulated anonymously? Could the author have deliberately left off his name? If so, why? What would be the advantage or benefit?

4. How does Marcion explain the fact that Jesus was an ethnic Jew, he was called the Messiah, and his disciples were Jews?

5. How did the *Evangelion* differ from the Gospel of Luke?

6. How do you think Marcion reasoned out his Christological opinion about Jesus? Explain.

7. What do you think was the most innovative thing that Marcion did? Why?

8. If you had lived in antiquity around 140 CE, what would you have felt necessary to do to make sure that your Christian community survived into the next generation?

9. It has been suggested that Marcion prefigured the Protestant Reformation (the Reformers relied on the doctrine of *sola scriptura*; they reread Paul and noted his emphasis on faith and the grace of God instead of good works). Do you think he did? If so, why? If not, why not?

Resources

Jason D. BeDuhn. 2013. *The First New Testament: Marcion's Scriptural Canon.* Salem: Polebridge Press.

M. David Litwa. 2022. Chapter 14. *Found Christianities: Remaking the World of the Second Century CE.* London: T&T Clark.

Charles E. Hill. 2007. "The Fragments of Papias." Pages 42–51 in *The Writings of the Apostolic Fathers.* Edited by Paul Foster. London: T&T Clark.

R. Joseph Hoffmann. 1984. *Marcion: On the Restitution of Christianity: An Essay on the Development of Radical Paulinist Theology in the Second Century.* AAR Academy Series 48. Chico: Scholars Press.

Matthias Klinghardt. 2018. *The Oldest Gospel.* Klinghardt Edition. Translated by Stephen Trobisch. Quiet Waters Publication.

Matthias Klinghardt. 2020. *The Oldest Gospel and the Formation of the Canonical Gospels: Reconstruction – Translation – Variants.* Biblical Tools and Studies 41. Leuven: Peeters.

Peter Lampe. 2003. "Chapter 24". in *From Paul to Valentinus: Christians at Rome in the First Two Centuries.* Edited by Michael Steinhauser edited by Marshall D. Johnson. Minneapolis: Fortress Press.

Judith M. Lieu. 2015. *Marcion and the Making of a Heretic: God and Scripture in the Second Century.* Cambridge: Cambridge University Press.

Sebastian Moll. 2010. *The Arch-Heretic Marcion.* Tübingen: Mohr Siebeck.

Dieter T. Roth. 2015. *The Text of Marcion's Gospel.* New Testament Tools, Studies and Documents 49. Leiden: Brill.

Joseph B. Tyson. 2006. *Marcion and Luke-Acts: A Defining Struggle.* Columbia: University of South Carolina Press.

Markus Vinzent. 2014. *Marcion and the Dating of the Synoptic Gospels.* Studia Patristica Supplement 2. Leuven: Peeters.

Adolf von Harnack. 1990 (German original: 1923). *Marcion: The Gospel of the Alien God.* Translated by John E. Steely and Lyle D. Bierma. Eugene: Wipf and Stock Publishers.

CHAPTER 3

Early Gnostic Churches

Two pages from Codex II of the Nag Hammadi Collection. The title *"Apocryphon of John"* is written in the upper part of the left page. Coptic Museum, Cairo, Egypt. **Source:** Patrick CHAPUIS / Gamma-Rapho / Getty Images.

> "I see that everything is suspended by the spirit,
> I understand that all is borne up by the spirit,
> Flesh suspended from soul,
> Soul borne up by air,
> Air hanging on ether,
> Fruits are borne from the Depth,
> A baby is borne from the womb."
>
> *This is the only surviving poem written by Valentinus*

KEY PLAYERS

Valentinus – Hermetics – Sethians

KEY TEXTS

Genesis 1–4 – John 1:1–18
Valentinus' letter fragments
Gospel of Truth (NHC I,3)
Corpus Hermeticum – Discourse on the Eighth and Ninth (NHC VI,6)
Apocryphon of John (NHC II,1)
Valentinian Exposition (NHC XI,2)
Tertullian, *Against the Valentinians*
Irenaeus, *Against Heresies*

Marcion was convinced that God can be known through rational investigation, deliberation, and reasonable deductions. Faith, then, is a matter of believing the results of this investigation and living a life that reflects these beliefs. The conviction that God can be known through reason, however, was not shared universally among third-generation Christians. Some Christians

Comparing Christianities: An Introduction to Early Christianity, First Edition. April D. DeConick.
© 2024 John Wiley & Sons Ltd. Published 2024 by John Wiley & Sons Ltd.

thought that God cannot be reasoned out, but must be intuited and known through religious experience. In other words, God can only be known when God and the believer meet face-to-face. For these Christians, Gnosis or knowledge of God was not discursive knowledge but experiential knowledge accessible to spiritual people. Valentinus was one of these Gnostic Christians.

3.1 A Visionary

COMPANION READINGS
Gen. 1–3 – John 1:1–18
Tertullian, *Against Valentinians* 4
Hippolytus, *Refutation* 6.42.2
Irenaeus, *Against Heresies* 1.11
Valentinus, *Letter Fragments* 1, 8

Valentinus immigrated to Rome during the tenure of Bishop Hyginus (ca. 136–140 CE). Valentinus was quickly recognized as a brilliant theologian. He became famous for his intellectual and authorial talents, his ability to interpret scriptures, and knack for drawing outstanding students to study with him. According to Tertullian, Valentinus was so successful as a theologian (a real "genius") that he fully expected to be elected as the next Bishop of Rome. Instead, another man, Pius, was elected, and Valentinus took the defeat as a referendum against his vision of a Gnostic Christianity. In protest, he seceded from the Apostolic Catholic church network and reorganized in Rome as a Gnostic Christian movement with churches that offered its members initiations or inductions into God's presence.

Valentinus' vision of a Gnostic Christianity did not originate in Rome. His understanding of Christianity emerged in Egypt, particularly Alexandria (Figure 3.1). Valentinus was a native Egyptian born in Phredonis (likely Phragonis) about sixty miles east of Alexandria in the Nile delta. When he arrived in Alexandria, he received a basic Greek education. He was exposed to Middle Platonic interpretations of the writings of the famous Greek philosopher, Plato who wrote about a Demiurge or Craftsman God who created the universe as well as a more transcendent principle he called The Good who existed in an archetypal world of perfect Ideas or Forms. The archetypal world served as the template for the Demiurge's craftsmanship of the universe and humanity. Valentinus also was exposed to Christianity. Like Marcion, he was an interpreter of Paul.

As a young man, while studying in Alexandria, Valentinus had a vision that changed his life. We do not know the exact circumstances of the vision, but Valentinus must have been pondering the origins of human existence and unsuccessfully trying to figure it out analytically. Intellectuals at the time had much to say about this topic, as they interacted with a long history of philosophical theories and debates about what the first principle was, how it multiplied or diversified, and where Gods and human beings fit in the scheme. The Roman Hippolytus (author of the *Refutation of All Heresies*; ca. 225) records that, one day, Valentinus saw an apparition which looked like an infant boy, newly born (Hipp., *Ref.* 6.42.2). "Who are you?", Valentinus asked the boy. Miraculously, the infant opened his mouth and announced, "I am Reason" (Greek: *Logos*). This entity, the Logos, was not human reason, but God's Mind. The connection between the Logos and Christ is made in the Gospel of John 1:1–18 which presents Jesus as the incarnation of God's Logos. Valentinus likely was familiar with the Gospel of John, a text that later Valentinians relied on heavily and commented on extensively. During this encounter with the Mind of God, the secrets of the origins of the universe and human existence were revealed to Valentinus. For Valentinus, this encounter with God's Mind, the Logos, was a eureka moment, the moment of his enlightenment.

We do not know how long it took Valentinus to put his revelation into words and write it down. What we do know, however, is that Valentinus did not teach about his revelation in philosophical or scientific language. Instead he chose to share his revelation as a myth or religious story. He carefully crafted his myth into a tragic love story about an original, primordial, hermaphrodite God. While various later Valentinians argued the details of the myth, Irenaeus preserves an account of the myth that he specifically identifies as Valentinus' own version. According to this version of the myth, this

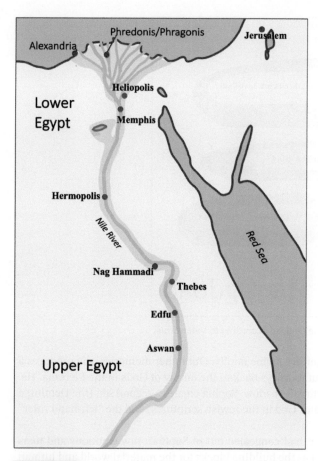

FIGURE 3.1 Location of Valentinus' birthplace and youth.

original primal divinity is dual, both male and female, the Ineffable Forefather (also referred to as Depth and Invisibility), and Silence the Mother (also referred to as God's Thought and Grace). The two gendered aspects of the hermaphrodite form a syzygy or divine couple. When they make love, they conceive and birth another syzygy, Father (also referred to as Son and Mind) and Truth. Together these four syzygies of eight Aeons or Eternities make up the eight primal aspects of God called the Ogdoad (The Eight) (Figure 3.2). When Truth and the Son make love, they conceive and give birth to the syzygy Reason and Life, and then Humanity and Church. The transcendent realm known as the Totality or Pleroma continues to be populated. Reason and Life produce five more syzygies. Humanity and Church produce six syzygies. In total, the Pleroma is populated with thirty Aeons who live as hermaphrodite syzygies.

All is well until the thirtieth Aeon, Sophia or Wisdom is born. Because Sophia is God's Wisdom, she does what comes naturally. She tries to get to know the Forefather (her grandparent), the primal uncreated God who started it all. But this is an impossible thing to do because of the very nature of the primal God who is both ineffable and restrained by Silence. So Sophia finds herself in a quandary. She cannot know the Forefather, the God-Before-All-Gods, but, because she is Wisdom, she cannot stop trying. She suffers horribly, constantly yearning for what she cannot have. To stop her from disturbing the peace, she is separated from the Pleroma and forced to live beyond the border of the Pleroma.

Beyond the border of the Pleroma, Sophia continues to suffer from her unquenchable desire. Anxiety terrorizes her. Tears of remorse and repentance erupt. Her love for the God-Before-All-Gods gushes

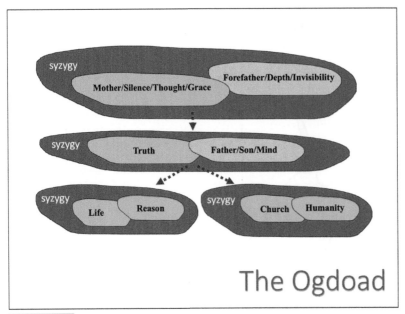

The Ogdoad

FIGURE 3.2 Illustration of the emanation of the Ogdoad according to Valentinus.

forth. In her loneliness, she tries to remember her divine family. Out of her memories, she produces a son, Christ. Christ does not stay with her, but journeys back to the family of Gods in the Pleroma. He, however, leaves behind his shadow. From Christ's shadow, Sophia creates a second son (the Demiurge or Craftsman who is identified with the Creator God in the Jewish scriptures) and the "left-hand ruler" (the Devil).

The Demiurge takes the substances that had congealed out of Sophia's raw emotions and tears (passion, desire, fear, anxiety) and uses them as the building blocks for the material world and human body. From her remorse, her son fashions the soul (Greek: *psyche*). The human spirit (Greek: *pneuma*), birthed from Sophia's capacity to love Jesus, ends up trapped in the human soul and body through a divine trick, when Sophia implants it in Adam without the Demiurge's knowledge.

According to a letter fragment written by Valentinus, the Biblical Creator God who fashions Adam (Gen. 2:4b-3:24) is the Demiurge. When he and his helpers create Adam, the presence of the spirit inside Adam takes them by surprise. They are afraid that their human creation is more powerful than they are because the spirit gives Adam the capacity to know and speak the truth (cp. Gen. 3:5; Eph. 1:17). Even though they do not know how the spirit got into Adam, they realize that the spirit is necessary to invigorate their creature (cp. Gen. 2:7). Without it, Adam cannot stand erect (cf. *Gos. Truth* 30.17–26). The rest of human history is the story about the Demiurge trying to control the human spirit by keeping humans ignorant of its presence within them and the transcendent God trying to rescue and retrieve his suffering spirit in order to heal the original rupture in the Pleroma.

So powerful was this vision of the infusion of humanity with the divine that Valentinus tries to capture the cosmic pervasiveness and immanence of the spirit in a poem he composed called *Harvest* (Hipp., *Ref.* 6.37.7).

> I see that everything is suspended by the spirit,
> I understand that all is borne up by the spirit,
> Flesh suspended from soul,
> Soul borne up by air,
> Air hanging on ether,
> Fruits are borne from the Depth,
> A baby is born from the womb.

What Valentinus saw – every infant born seeded with the spirit of God from the fruits of the very Depth of divinity – was startling in a world where humans were believed to be material "clay" creations of the Gods brought to life with a puff of breath. While God's breath may have animated them, they did not contain a seed of the primal God within them. In many ancient Mediterranean myths, humans were so undervalued that their creation was an afterthought of the Gods or not mentioned at all. When their creation is mentioned, they are created as mortal servants of the immortal Gods. Their afterlives are nothing more than shades or ghosts lurking in the dark recesses of the underworld.

The ancient Greeks had the idea that the human psyche – the soul – was the distinguishing mark of human beings responsible for our emotional states, cognition, and our moral judgment. Some like Pythagoras and Plato taught that the soul, because it was some kind of intellectual ethereal substance, preexisted birth and survived death, and in fact went through many cycles of incarnation in its attempt to become a perfectly virtuous or godlike immortal being. The Stoics identified our ability to reason (Greek: *logos*) with the soul. Stoics thought that reason is a pneumatic or spiritual substance (either fire or ether) that animates all matter (rocks, plants, animals) in a materialistic or biological sense. It is the vital force of nature. Stoics believed that the soul is mortal, and only survives death in the event that its ether is dissolved and distributed into the cosmic ether. All of these anthropological theories stand in stark contrast to Valentinus' vision of the soul and body infused with the transcendent God's immortal spirit from birth. Valentinus' vision of a triadic human would have been shocking to most people in antiquity as it still is for most people in modernity.

Valentinus did not believe, however, that the incarnation of the spirit in babies is an occasion for joy. The immanence of the spirit is God-ruptured, God-suffering, analogous to the Gospel story of the woman with the unstoppable flow of blood. To the Valentinians, this bleeding woman in dire straits represents the hemorrhaging of the divine spirit. Valentinus believed that the spirit had been poured into the human heart, an alien condition that only increased its suffering. Valentinus himself compared the suffering of the heart, the abode of the spirit, to the suffering we endure when we are forced to use a filthy public latrine.

The tragedy of this story is not what we might expect. The tragedy is not the fall and mixture of the spirit into the soulish and material dimensions of reality. The tragedy in Valentinus' story is the *inevitability* of all this, of a ruptured God whose unknowable nature leads to unstoppable existential damage. We are the way we are – broken – not because we as human beings have done awful things but because God is the way God is – broken. The responsibility for suffering (theodicy) does not fall on humans but squarely on God's shoulders even though this is tragic because there is nothing that God could have done to stop his rupture. He can only remedy it.

In that moment of enlightenment, Valentinus realizes an existential conundrum that traditional philosophy and religion had not been able to address. If our brokenness and pain is this basic to who we are and to the world we inhabit, how can we ever find healing? How can we ever get beyond the anxiety and terror that structures the very foundation of our being and our world? It was in Valentinus' study of Paul that he found an answer to this existential impasse. He became the first Christian to express what, centuries later, would become the rallying cry of Protestant Christians: if our brokenness and pain are so basic to who we are, then healing is not going to happen by our singular efforts to be pious, good, or ascetic. Our redemption requires God's grace, and God's grace alone. As Valentinus wrote in a letter preserved by Clement of Alexandria, God must visit the human heart. When this happens – as it did for Valentinus – the heart is enlightened and God is known.

3.2 The God of Egypt

COMPANION READINGS
Gospel of Truth (NHC I,3)

To modern people, the myth Valentinus crafted may seem outlandish. Who ever heard of a hermaphrodite God who created an Ogdoad and then a Totality of Aeons? Who ever heard of a God who existed even before the Creator God in the Genesis stories? To understand what is going on, we must keep in mind that Valentinus was an Egyptian. He lived in a culture steeped in the lore of different Gods and sacred myths about the origin of the world and humankind. His myth about a primal God is a Christian variant of the Egyptian stories, with some Greek philosophy blended in. His God is the primal God of Egypt in Christian garb, a God who had a history going back two thousand years before Valentinus.

In the oldest layer of Egyptian religion (ca. 2400–2300 BCE) the patron deity of Heliopolis, Atum, is the primal God who comes into existence by writhing around in the primeval ocean as a snake encircled in his own coils, or standing up as a man on a mound and roaring. The ancient Egyptians pictured Atum as a hermaphrodite, the "father of fathers" and the "mother of mothers." He is the Great God who came into existence by himself. He creates through a process of autogenesis, where he masturbates and then spits out his children from his mouth in a great exhalation or roar. His offspring, Air and Moisture, are differentiations of himself, birthed as a male and female couple. Air and Moisture birth their own children, again a male and female couple, Earth and Sky. Earth and Sky birth the divinities Osiris, Isis, Seth, and Nephthys. With Atum, they form a collective of nine Gods, known in Heliopolis as The Ennead. Atum is the undifferentiated unity from which everything emerges in differentiated forms, including the Sun God Rê, who is the manifestation of Atum in the morning and the evening. Atum is a single self-created God responsible for life, which emanates from his mouth as spit and his eyes as tears like an inundation of the Nile.

This theology of Atum's transcendence paved the way for Pharaoh Akhenaten's experimentation with monotheism, when he established the exclusive worship of Aten, the solar disk, as the sole God of Egypt (1348–36 BCE). The exclusive worship of Aten meant that the worship of other solar Gods was systematically suppressed and Aten took over their myths and characteristics. During Akhenaten's reforms, Aten, the solar disk, becomes not only the Sun God, but the life-giving illumination of the sun depicted as a solar disk with rays extending into hands. Aten was worshipped as the one-and-only universal God and transcendent Creator.

After Akhenaten's death, the exclusive worship of Aten was abandoned, but the concept of a supreme single transcendent God was not. The concept of a supreme transcendent God was applied to the worship of Amun, a popular solar God originally one of the patron Gods at Hermopolis. Amun, the Hidden One, was considered the creator God among eight primal Chaos-Gods or Infinites. The Eight (The Ogdoad) are Fluidity (Nun and Nunet), Infinity (Heh and Hehet), Darkness (Kek and Keket), and Invisibility (Amun and Amunet). These qualities (fluidity, infinity, darkness, invisibility) were considered the properties of primal substance.

Over time, the Sun God Amun rose to the position of King of the Gods, the supreme liege of the original Ogdoad. He is depicted as a ram-headed man or a man donned in a plumed headdress. He comes to be known as the greatest God of the Great Gods, the sole God from the beginning, and the primeval God with no other like him. He came to be described like Atum, as the self-generated God coming into being when he emerged from the waters of Chaos and stood on a mound. He is the father of the fathers of all Gods. His primordial sounds bring into being all the other Gods, and he creates everything that is created.

The promotion of the idea that reality is the result of the will of a hidden transcendent God was popularized after Akhenaten's death so that limited types of pantheism (all deities are aspects of God) and henotheism (worship of one God among many) rather than monotheism came into vogue. The traditional plurality of Egyptian deities was reframed as aspects, names, or manifestations of the transcendent supreme God. This allowed for the worship of single supreme Gods to emerge as forms of popular personal piety from the Ramesside times (1292–1069 BCE) down to the Greco-Roman period when Valentinus lived.

Valentinus' origin myth as presented by Irenaeus is a Christian version of this old Egyptian story. A primal hermaphrodite God (Ineffability and Silence) births a male and female pair of Aeons (Son and Truth). Father and Truth birth Logos and Life, and Humanity and Church. The primal God's children and grandchildren thus round out the Ogdoad, in Christian lingo, not Egyptian. The grandchildren give birth to the rest of the Aeons, which are aspects of the primal God, many of them distinctive Christian terms as well: Depth and Mixing, Not Aging and Oneness, Self-Existent and Bliss, Immovable and Blending, Only-Begotten (a title of Jesus in the Gospel of John) and Blessed, Paraclete (the word for Holy Spirit in the Gospel of John) and Faith, Paternal and Hope, Maternal and Love, Praise and Understanding, Ecclesiastical and Blessedness, Will and Wisdom.

While none of the fragments of Valentinus' writings provide descriptions of the transcendent primal God, later Valentinians published the *Gospel of Truth* which was a theological reflection on what Valentinus considered to be the true gospel: the pure joy of knowing the Father in a moment of grace (*Gos. Truth* 16.31–34). The *Gospel of Truth*, whose style of writing and contents resemble surviving fragments of works composed by Valentinus, is likely the gospel that Valentinus is said to have written himself (Ps.-Tert., *Haer.* 4.6). The book was known to Irenaeus (ca. 180 CE) and is preserved intact in the Nag Hammadi Collection (Iren., *Haer.* 3.11.9). In this highly poetic theological reflection, enlightenment is said to happen in the heart when the light of God illumines it with the light of day, a comment very similar to that made by Valentinus in one of his letters (*Gos. Truth* 32.32–35). This Gospel makes it clear that it is impossible for us to grasp the Father through rational scrutiny. We cannot know the Father unless the Father makes it happen. All we can do is desire to know the Hidden God, the Father from whom everything came forth, and to whom everything will return. And trust his will that enlightenment will happen (*Gos. Truth* 37.21–38.6).

Central to the theological reflection in the *Gospel of Truth* is the primal Father who is described again and again as unknowable, inconceivable, and beyond thought. He is perfect (*Gos. Truth* 18: 32–33; 27:23–24; 36:33–35; cp. Matt. 5:48). Most of the metaphors used to describe the primal Father are experiential rather than intellectual or philosophical. The Father is beautiful, sweet, and fragrant (cp. 2 Cor. 2:14–15). His will is what is good. He is calm, his countenance light and grace. He is warm and loving. He is hidden and boundless, a deep reservoir that contains everything. Everything emanates or comes out of him (cf. *Gos. Truth* 18:32–35; 19:7–10; cp. Col. 1:16–17).

As far as a name, the primal God has no normal name – no word or other designation – because what name can be given to something that does not yet exist (*Gos. Truth* 38.7–39.20)? At most we might say that he is the Ineffable One. He becomes a father when he sends forth his son from his bosom (*Gos. Truth* 23.19–24.20). It is in the Son, his image, that this unknowable primal God is able to reveal himself. As an image of God, the Son perfectly reflects the Father and thus makes the invisible Father known (*Gos. Truth* 20:19–22; cp. Col. 1:15–16). The Son even has the name of the Father (*Gos. Truth* 38:7–12; 39:20–24; cp. John 17:6, 11–12, 26). By manifesting himself as the Son, the Father corrects the existential problem that his unknowability had caused the Aeons who labored to know the inconceivable God (*Gos. Truth* 24.10–20) and found themselves living in a fog of error (*Gos. Truth* 7.5–20) and the terror of a nightmare (*Gos. Truth* 28.32–30.16). Such Christian commentary on the relationship of the primal God and his first emanation has been developed out of close readings of the Gospel of John and verses that mention the relationship between the Father God and Jesus, his Son (cp. John 1:1–18; 14:7; 17:21, 25–26).

How did this self-manifestation as the Son occur according to the *Gospel of Truth*? It occurred through the speech of the Father, the uttering of sounds. Verbalization as the mode of creation is something commonly known across the Mediterranean, from Egypt to Israel. Atum roars. Amun emits primal sounds. The Jewish God says, "Let there be light" (Gen. 1:3). According to the Gospel of John, the Christian God sends forth his Logos or Word (John 1:1). Likewise in the *Gospel of Truth*, the Father emanates the Son as the Logos. The Logos is the Mind of God which contains the Book of the Living with names to be called out (*Gos. Truth* 19.35–20.6; cf. 3:5; 17:8; 20:12, 15), a concept developed with close attention to details about this book mentioned in Jewish scriptures (Ps. 69:28; Isa. 4:3; Ex. 32:32–33; cf. Ps. 40:8; 65:6; 87:6; 139:16; Job 13:26; Jer. 17:1; 22:30; Mal. 3:16; Dan. 7:10; 12:1). The sounds called out, however, are not vowels or consonants – the Book cannot be read – but "letters of truth" which are complete thoughts that reveal the Father to the Aeons and enable them to come forth out of the fog (*Gos. Truth* 22.20–23.19).

Valentinus knows a God who is the primal hermaphrodite God, transcendent and hidden, a being of intense light and love. He also knows that the primal God is the root of all existence and explains his "coming out" in Christian terms associated with the Gospel of John, as the manifestation of his Son as his Logos or Mind, and Philippians 4:3, as the pronunciation of the letters of truth in the Book of the Living (cf. Rev. 3:5; 5:1–9; etc.). Valentinus is convinced that this God is not the Creator God in Jewish scriptures. Valentinus knows from personal experience that this God cannot be discovered analytically, but must be experienced in a moment of desire and grace.

(3.3) Jesus According to Valentinus

COMPANION READINGS
Valentinus, *Letter Fragment* 3
Irenaeus, *Against Heresies* 1.7.2; 1.11.1

Valentinus was a Christian, so Jesus plays a central role in his faith. As we learned, in Valentinian systems, the human being is triadic, consisting of a body, soul, and spirit. The body is the material creation of the Demiurge (the Biblical Creator) fashioned out of the earthy (Greek: *hylic*) substance that solidified out of Sophia's trauma: her raw emotions and tears (passion, desire, fear, anxiety). The soul or human psyche is formed out of soulish (Greek: *psychic*) substance that formed out of Sophia's feelings of remorse. The spirit comes from spiritual (Greek: *pneumatic*) substance birthed from Sophia's love for God. Because Jesus was human, the Valentinians believed that he had a real human body, a soul, and a spirit. Valentinus was no Docetist.

Although Jesus had a real human body (*Gos. Truth* 31:4–8; cp. Rom. 8:3), Valentinus taught that Jesus was the master of self-control (Greek: *encrateia*) when it came to eating, so much so that when he ate, he did not defecate. It is said that Valentinus wrote in a letter to Agathapous that Jesus "was self-controlled, always persevering. Jesus labored for [his digestion] to be divine. He ate and drank in a special way, without pooping. He had such a great capacity for self-control [in his diet] that nourishment within him was not corrupted, for he did not experience corruption" (Clem. Alex., *Misc.* 3.59.3; trans. DeConick). Valentinus believed that Jesus' digestive system had been divinely transformed through his food regimen. The food he ate did not turn into feces.

While this may sound bizarre to us, it is an idea that is based on common medical knowledge at the time. People in antiquity believed that the humors (blood, black bile, yellow bile, and phlegm) and the four elements (fire-heat, earth-cold, air-dry, and water-wet) in the human body had to be in equilibrium for the body to be healthy. The body was assumed to be a self-sufficient system capable of functioning on its own heat. It should only need enough food and drink to keep that heat alive. In such a perfect state, it would continue on idle. Eating too much food resulted in a surplus of heat and fermentation within the organs, which would harm the body. The result, they observed, was manifest in a greater amount of feces.

This is why in monastic texts, monks like Gregory of Nyssa (335–394 CE) are obsessed with their feces, which demonstrated their success or failure with overcoming gluttony and other passions which they believed increased their fecal output. Monks and hermits who had achieved bodily perfection were considered to live like angels, going for years without a bowel movement (this likewise applied to menstruation among female ascetics). All this is to say that Valentinus is very clear that Jesus had a human body like the rest of us, but that he perfected it – "he labored for [his digestion] to be divine." By mastering his fork, he created a perfect body that did not defecate.

The other aspects of Jesus – his soul and spirit – have other origins. As for his soul, Valentinians believed that the Demiurge created a son, the Christ (the Messiah) mentioned in the Prophets, using soulish (Greek: *psychic*) substance (Iren., *Haer.* 1.7.2). When Jesus was conceived in the womb, he did not receive a normal human soul (Greek: *psyche*). Rather Jesus was an exceptionally created human being. The Psychic Christ was implanted as Jesus' soul. So we see here the ENSOULMENT PATTERN emerge for the first time. In addition to this special soul, Jesus also possesses a special spiritual seed, a gift from Sophia (Iren., *Haer.* 1.7.2). Thus the triad is complete and Jesus is a real human being with a physical body, a soul, and a spiritual seed. Although he is a real human being, the Valentinians believed his makeup never experienced corruption, either when he was conceived or during his lifetime. The human Jesus was as perfect as it gets when it comes to his humanity. He had a disciplined body, an uncorrupted soul, and a perfect spirit.

So what made Jesus God? Valentinus likely is the first Christian theologian to try to solve the Binitarian Problem (how the divine and human natures in Jesus Christ related to each other and worked together). Although there are no accounts of Valentinus' actual teachings about this beyond his explanation of how Jesus divinized his digestive tract, later Valentinian sources are very involved in explaining how Jesus was both God and human. To explain his divinity, many sources use the ADULT POSSESSION PATTERN, teaching that at his baptism the Jesus Aeon descended from the Pleroma in the form of a dove and entered Jesus (Figure 3.3).

What is the Jesus Aeon and how did it originate? Various Valentinian sources describe the Jesus Aeon as the "fruit of the Pleroma." He was produced by the Pleroma in such a way that he embodies all the qualities of each of the thirty Aeons. If we remember that the thirty Aeons are attributes of the Father, then the Jesus Aeon is a micro-Pleroma or a mini-Godhead which can leave the Pleroma and descend into the cosmos. According to Irenaeus' accounting of Valentinian teaching, the Jesus Aeon

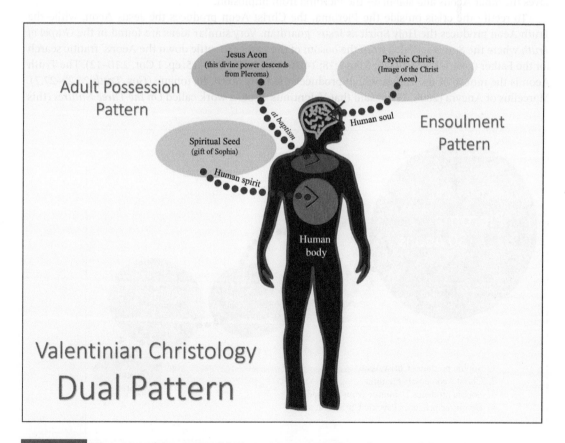

FIGURE 3.3 Illustration of the aspects of the human Jesus: his body, soul, spirit, and divine power.

enters into Jesus' body and possesses him as an adult at his baptism. This means that the human Jesus is supersized. He contains an Aeonic superpower that makes the human Jesus a walking and talking Pleroma on earth. Thus Jesus had the three "normal" parts of the human being plus an Aeon residing in him. The Aeon left him, ascending back to the Pleroma, when he came before Pilate. This meant that the human Jesus suffered, while the impassibility of the divine Aeon was protected. In the end, it is clear that many Valentinians blended the ADULT POSSESSION Christological pattern (the descent of the Jesus Aeon at baptism) with the ENSOULMENT PATTERN (Jesus' soul was the Psychic Christ) in order to work out the Binitarian Problem.

It is also important to note that the Valentinians distinguished the Psychic Christ (the son of the Demiurge) who operates in the cosmic sphere from another figure they call the Christ Aeon who operates in the transcendent sphere. According to Valentinus, the Christ Aeon (in the transcendent realm) was the first entity that Sophia produced outside the Pleroma based on what she could remember about the Father's first emanation, the Son or Mind. After he is produced, the Christ Aeon decides to leave Sophia and go inside the Pleroma to reside, leaving behind his shadow. From his shadow, Sophia produces the Demiurge (Iren., *Haer*.1.11.1) (Figure 3.4).

Once inside the Pleroma, the Christ Aeon teaches the rest of the Aeons about the unknowable Father by showing them that the Son is the Father's image and embodies the Father. In other words, when they know the Son, they know the Father. This calms down the Aeons and their frantic search for the Father and guarantees no further disturbances such as Sophia caused. Thus the Christ Aeon saves the other Aeons and stabilizes the Pleroma from implosion.

To rectify the crisis outside the Pleroma, the Christ Aeon produces the Jesus Aeon, while the Truth Aeon produces the Holy Spirit as Jesus' guardian. Very similar ideas are found in the *Gospel of Truth* where the Son is revealed from the bosom of the Father to settle down the Aeons' frantic search for the Father (24.10–11; 36.14–20; John 1:18; 14:26–27; 15:26; 16:13–15; cp. 1 Cor. 2:10–12). The Truth Aeon is the mouth of the Father which produces the Holy Spirit, its tongue (*Gos. Truth* 26.29–27.7). Marcellus of Ancyra (280–374 CE) said that Valentinus wrote a work called *On the Three Natures* (this

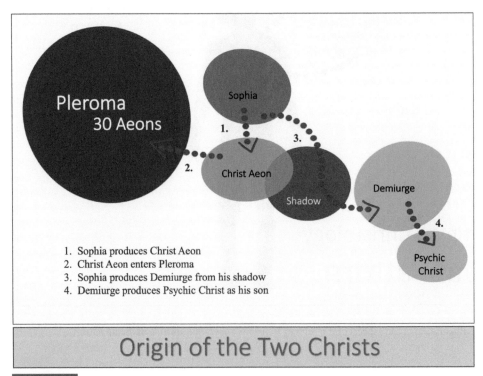

1. Sophia produces Christ Aeon
2. Christ Aeon enters Pleroma
3. Sophia produces Demiurge from his shadow
4. Demiurge produces Psychic Christ as his son

Origin of the Two Christs

FIGURE 3.4 Illustration of the origin of the two Christs in the Valentinian system.

text does not survive), in which Valentinus was the first Christian theologian to propose that God's nature is expressed as three independent entities (Greek: *hypostases*) or persons: the Father, Son, and Holy Spirit (Marcellus, *On the Holy Church* 9). Valentinus appears to be the theologian who initiated the discourse about the nature of God that later is developed into the doctrine of the Trinity by fourth-century Catholics. He is the first to describe a system which explains the relationships between the three entities that make up the Godhead.

> "These then teach three hypostases [beings], just as Valentinus the heresiarch first invented in the book entitled by him *On the Three Natures*. For he was the first to invent three hypostases and three persons of Father, Son, and Holy Spirit, and he is discovered to have filched this from Hermes and Plato."
>
> *Marcellus of Ancyra, On the Holy Church 9*

What was the human Jesus' job? He revealed the true God and the truth of immortality to humans and showed them the way back to their spiritual home. Since the *Gospel of Truth* is a reflection on Valentinus' teachings, Valentinus was likely behind the idea that Jesus taught the gospel which revealed the Father to everyone living in oblivion. He developed this idea by reflecting on Paul's letters. In the *Gospel of Truth*, Jesus' main job was to enlighten people and show them the way of truth. The advent of Jesus is understood to be the revelation of the Father's "hidden mystery" to people who had been living in darkness (*Gos. Truth* 18.11–19). This language is dependent on Colossians (1:25–27; 2:2–3) and Ephesians (3:2–5, 9–10). Jesus' revelation was like the reading of a will which discloses the fortune of the deceased lord of the manor (*Gos. Truth* 20:15–27; cp. Gal. 3:13–18).

His revelation provoked the ire of the Demiurge and his helpers who had him persecuted and nailed to a tree (cp. Gal. 3:13; Col. 2:14). This tree, however, was not any old tree. This was the Tree of Knowledge in the Garden of Eden, and Jesus its fruit. Here the Valentinian reflection on Paul's letters becomes entangled with an inverse reading of the Genesis story. According to the *Gospel of Truth*, eating the fruit from the Tree of Knowledge did not cause death as the deceitful Demiurge forecast (cp. Gen. 2:16–17), but showed the truth to those who ate the fruit, that the Father was within themselves (*Gos. Truth* 18.12–31; 42.11–38; cp. Gen. 3:5–7).

Additionally, Jesus' suffering and death is understood in light of Paul's reference to the "book of life" (Phil. 4:3), an idea Paul took from Psalm 69:28 and which emerges also in the book of Revelation (3:5; 5:1–9; 13:8; 17:8; 20:12, 15; 21:27). According to the *Gospel of Truth*, when Jesus was crucified, he took the Book of the Living and nailed it to the cross. This action published the names of the saved, those who respond to Jesus' teachings, even those in the underworld where Jesus went when he died in order to instruct and save the ancestors (*Gos. Truth* 19.35–20.38; cp. Col. 2:14). All the people whose names are written in this book are promised to be saved by the Father who will call out their names (*Gos. Truth* 21.26–22.20). When he calls out their names, they are able to ascend to him, because everyone who has knowledge (*gnosis*) is from above. When called, they hear and answer, turning to Jesus and ascending to him (*Gos. Truth* 22:2–12; cp. John 3:31–32).

This conversation about the "Called" has the feeling of a doctrine of determinism: that a person's fate is determined even before birth no matter what they do. The *Gospel of Truth*, however, suggests something more nuanced. While the names of the Called have been hidden in the Book of the Living since the beginning, the Called *are revealed by their fruits*. The Called are determined by their choice to follow Jesus (*Gos. Truth* 33:37–39; cp. Matt. 7:16, 20; 12:33). While God knew who would be called because their names are in the Book, they had to respond to Jesus' call to be redeemed. In this way, the tension between Paul's belief in universal salvation and his theory of predestination of a group of elect people is navigated (Rom. 8:29).

According to the *Gospel of Truth*, Jesus' death means life for many (*Gos. Truth* 20:13–14; cp. Matt. 20:28//Mark 10:45). Death could not hold Jesus. Jesus stripped himself of his perishable body and clothed himself in imperishability, paving the way for the resurrection of the knowers (*Gos. Truth* 20:28–34; cp. 1 Cor. 15:53–54; 2 Cor. 5:2–4; John 10:17–18; 13:1–3; 19:6–11; Rom. 5:19; Phil. 2:6–8). Literally, Jesus is the way to God (*Gos. Truth* 31:28–29; cp. John 14:6). He is the shepherd who held ninety-nine sheep in his left hand, but still searched for the hundredth. When found, all hundred were taken up by his right hand and saved (*Gos. Truth* 31:35–32:16; cp. Matt. 18:12–13; 25:33). He labored even on a Sabbath day to help the sheep which had fallen in the pit, giving his life for the sheep by lifting it up from the pit (*Gos. Truth* 32: 18–25; cp. Matt. 12:11–12; John 10:10–11, 15, 28). In this way, the love of the Father is poured out upon them (*Gos. Truth* 43:6–7; cp. Rom. 5:5). They are his children, filled with the seed of the Father, perfect in all ways (*Gos. Truth* 43:9–21; cp. 1 John 3:9, 24).

3.4 A Split-Level Church in Rome

COMPANION READINGS

Valentinian Exposition (NHC XI,2)
40.1–44.37

Tertullian tells us that Valentinus was originally a renowned theologian and leader who worked within the Roman church as a spiritual teacher. When Pius was elected as Bishop of Rome (ca. 140 CE), Valentinus took the decision hard because he had expected to step into that role himself. He was a famed Christian teacher, instructing pupils in an advanced school or seminary setting. But, according to Tertullian, after Pius took over, Valentinus made the choice to secede and start his own church featuring a grace-based experience of God (*gnosis*) to save not only the human soul, but also the human spirit.

The type of church Valentinus constructed was a split-level church, set up to poach unsuspecting Apostolic Catholics with services that paralleled their own (Figure 3.5). The aim was to eventually convince the unsuspecting Apostolic Catholic members to be baptized a second time and initiated into the advanced ranks of spiritual Christians who were privy to the divine mysteries. The Apostolic Catholic members were called psychics (soulish Christians), while the advanced members were called pneumatics (spiritual Christians). The pneumatics believed that they alone had knowledge of the transcendent God, while the psychics, in their ignorance and naïveté, mistook the Jewish God for the true God.

This split-level church is mentioned in a Nag Hammadi text called the *Interpretation of Knowledge* (*The Hermeneia of Gnosis*). The text is badly damaged (we estimate that we have only 7% of the original text), but it appears to be a sermon or letter to a Valentinian congregation that included both pneumatics and psychics. According to the text, the pneumatics saw themselves as enlightened Christians, knowing about the true Father, the tragedy of the Mother, Jesus' real mission to redeem the spiritual seeds, and the true meaning of the cross. They believed themselves to be godly people, living by the Spirit and graced by abundant spiritual gifts that the other Christians in their assemblies did not have. The other Christians, they perceived to be ignorant people of faith who did not have Gnosis. Their assemblies faced infighting between these two parties, the ignorant jealous of the enlightened, and the enlightened dissatisfied with having to tolerate the ignorant. The preacher (the author of the text) gets after them all, using Paul's imagery of Christ's body to bring them to an appreciation for each other and to help them be satisfied with their station as a foot, eye, or hand. He traces the split church to the Archons who wanted to control the power of the "inner man," but the text is so damaged that it is impossible to determine the extent of the preacher's explanation. It is abundantly clear, however, that the preacher thinks that the split church can be used advantageously, as a social platform to persuade those of "faith" to get with the program and pray that they might share the grace that the pneumatic members already have received.

Valentinus' split-level church was meant to provide the means to influence the naïve psychics to join the Gnostic pneumatic ranks. By gathering both groups under one roof, the hope was that

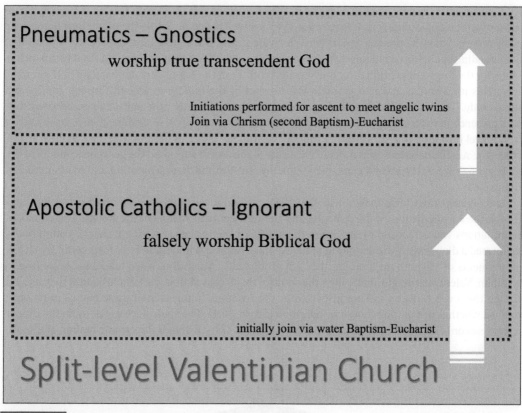

FIGURE 3.5 Illustration of the membership of the Valentinian Church.

the pneumatics could persuade the psychics to be initiated and receive gnosis, when they would experience firsthand that the true God was not YHWH, but a God-Beyond-All-Gods, the transcendent source of life.

Like Marcion, Valentinus modeled his church after the Apostolic Catholic Church in Rome. He used water baptism just as the Apostolic Catholic Church did: to forgive the sins of those who converted. Based on what we know about the practices of later Valentinians, Valentinus' church used water baptism as a first-level ritual. Baptized Christians who wanted to join the rank of the pneumatics, had to undergo a second baptism which featured an anointing ceremony called chrism. Later Valentinians thought that the Tree of Life in the Garden of Eden was an olive tree so they used olive oil in this ceremony.

In one of the letters of Valentinus, Valentinus speaks of the Father visiting the human heart with his goodness, making it holy with his light (*Letter Frag.* 2). While the reference to light may be literal, it may also refer to chrism, since light is an image often associated with oil and anointing in Christian literature. The Valentinian *Gospel of Philip* actually equates the two: "The light is the chrism" and understands chrism to be superior to baptism because it provides initiates with light and the Holy Spirit (*Gos. Phil.* 69.14–15; 74.20–21). It may be that Valentinus was referring to chrism when he wrote about the Father making the heart holy with his light. This is explained in the *Gospel of Truth* in this way: the light that indwells the heart is the ointment of the Father's mercy, the instrument of perfection. When the oil of mercy is smeared on initiates, the light indwells the heart, filling the initiates with the Father's goodness and perfecting them (*Gos. Truth* 32.32–35; 36.13–20).

A Valentinian church manual survives in the Nag Hammadi Collection (in the same volume as the *Interpretation of Knowledge*). It is called *A Valentinian Exposition*. While the mythology in this text clearly reflects Valentinianism a generation after Valentinus, these guidelines may reflect Valentinus' understanding of chrism as redemptive of the initiate's spirit. The handbook explains that first baptism is done for the forgiveness of sins and is associated with John the Baptist's water baptism in the Jordan River. This purification makes it possible for the soul of the initiate to ascend through the cosmic spheres only. The second baptism, however, perfects the soul so that the spirit can be released into God's presence in the transcendent world of the Aeons. In other words, second baptism is an advanced second-level initiation that prepares the initiates' spirits for astral ascent into the transcendent realm to meet the Aeonic divinities face-to-face. The route of the ascent supposed the geocentric model of the universe finalized in the second century by Ptolemy, an Alexandrian astronomer and mathematician (Figure 3.6).

Later Valentinian texts make clear that these second-level initiations involved astral journeys through the cosmic realms of the Archons and the transcendent realms of the Aeons. The climax of the initiations was a Gnostic event, when the spirits of the initiates met their angelic counterparts and formed a divine syzygy in imitation of the Aeonic couples. While these later texts certainly reflect developments of Valentinian thought, they are grounded in Valentinus' own teaching. According to Tertullian, Valentinus taught that, when the souls of the deceased first leave their bodies, they ascend through the seven heavens and are inspected by the Archons ruling each of these realms in order to establish whether or not they should be admitted (*Scorp.* 10.1). The souls have to tell them the proper secret passwords in order to advance to the next heaven. Once through the cosmic realms, the souls,

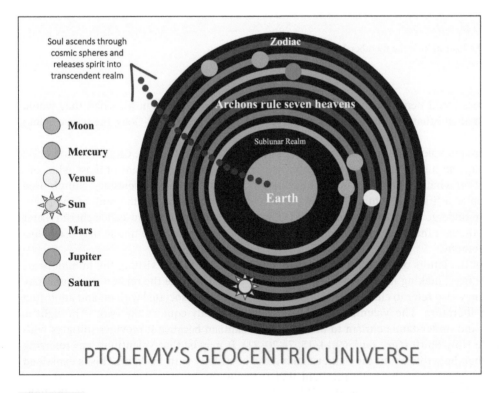

FIGURE 3.6 Ancient view of the cosmos and the ascension of the Gnostic's soul through the planetary spheres governed by the Archons.

in face-to-face encounters, meet the real divinities within the Pleroma: their beloved bridegrooms who act as guardian angels (Latin: *Theleti*), the Immovable Ones (Latin: *Acineti*), and the Ones-Beyond-Magic (Latin: *Abascanti*). If Tertullian is preserving an accurate memory of Valentinus' teaching, then we can trace to Valentinus practices that prepare people for the journey of the soul at death and lively beliefs in angelic bridegrooms who lovingly await union with those who endure the arduous astral journey home. As we will see later in this textbook, both of these ideas are developed extensively by Valentinians after Valentinus' death.

The *Valentinian Exposition* is especially fascinating because it also contains the guidelines for anointing people on their death bed (what we call today Last Rites) in order to empower the soul and spirit for their death journey (*Val. Exp.* 40.1–29). They believed that the Last Rites ceremony was given to them by Jesus Christ, the shepherd of their spirits. This is a reference to Jesus' role as a psychopomp, the one who guides the spirit of the deceased into the Kingdom. Because the dying had been anointed already when they were initiated, anointing them on their death bed works like a booster shot. As the dying are anointed, Jesus comes to them as their afterlife guide. The ritual empowers them to conquer the Archons, even the Power of Darkness, freeing their spirits to ascend into the transcendent world of the Aeons. The leader likely pronounced these words over the dying Valentinians as oil was smeared on them: "Glory be to you, the Father in the Son, the Father in the Son, the Father in the holy Church and in the holy angels! From now on, he [the name of the dying person] abides forever in the imperishability of the Aeons, forever until the [...] Aeons of Aeons. Amen."

The *Valentinian Exposition* manual also lays out Eucharistic words, which suggest that Valentinus did not give up the sacred meal but invested it with a purifying redemptive function that was carried on by later Valentinians (*Val. Exp.* 43.20–38; 44.1–37). Since there are two Eucharistic prayers enumerated and recorded, it is likely that the first Eucharist prayer was used following the first baptism, while the second Eucharist prayer was used following the second baptism when chrism was performed to perfect the converts and prepare them to enter God's Kingdom.

While it is difficult to know what Christian literature Valentinus' church considered scripture, given the reliance of the *Gospel of Truth* on the letters of Paul (the same letters known to Marcion), the Gospel of Matthew (also known to Marcion), and the Gospel of John, it is likely that Valentinus' congregation at the very least had access to these texts. Given the combined testimonies of Irenaeus and Ps.-Tertullian – that Valentinus and the Valentinians had also their own *Gospel of Truth* – it is likely that the *Gospel of Truth* was in play too.

We hear something very distinctive about the sexual practices of Valentinians from Clement of Alexandria. He says that Valentinus and his followers find great joy in marriage because they consider the coupling of husband and wife to reflect the procreative activities of the Aeonic syzygies. Clement also comments that they consider their sexual activities to be spiritual activities (Clem. Alex., *Misc.* 3.1.1; 3.29.3). We do not have any more evidence of how this may have played out in Valentinus' church, until we read more about it from fourth-generation Valentinian texts. We will return to a deeper discussion of Valentinian sex and gender later on when we explore Valentinians as fourth-generation Christians.

3.5 Hermes' Transcendent Trip

COMPANION READINGS

Corpus Hermeticum 1, 4.1–5

Discourse on the Ogdoad and the Ennead (NHC VI,6)

Valentinus' Christian theology, mythology, and systematized initiations to experience God (Gnosis) may be unfamiliar to us living as we do in modernity among Christians whose mythology is quite different from Valentinus'. In Valentinus' time, however, his theology, mythology, and initiations were not strange at all. In fact, they had precedents which can be traced as part of a larger cultural conversation that was ongoing in Alexandria (and elsewhere) among pagans,

Jews, and Christians about which God ought to be identified with the transcendent source of life that the Greek philosophers debated. For centuries, Greek philosophers had speculated about the source of life, whatever it was that initiated the processes of creation. The Greeks had identified several possibilities as primal properties and substances, including water, air, perpetual motion, intellect, mind, intelligence, wisdom, and reason. While today the investigation and conversation about the origins of life occurs among physicists and other scientists who talk about the Big Bang, in antiquity this conversation took place among intellectuals who talked philosophy.

The discussion of the primal cause of life brought with it the language of transcendence when the philosopher Anaxagoras (428–510 BCE) suggested that the order of nature alone could not explain creation. He argued that there had to be an intrusion of a higher order to release matter's potentiality. According to Anaxagoras, this higher order was a rational influence that is not part of nature. His theorizing abstracted and detached the principle of rationality from nature and initiated the discussion about what is the cause of the order in nature. Speculations about a unitary first principle, its nature (unperceivable, unlimited, timeless, eternal, good, nameless, formless, colorless) and its location (outside of creation, above heavens, above Mind) abounded among Neo-Pythagoreans and Middle Platonists.

Their speculations had an unintended religious consequence. Their theories put into question the long-standing devotion to a variety of regional and local Gods, who, in the lore, had a part in creation. Instead of falsifying the long-standing devotion to these Gods, the speculation about the primal condition, lifted the reputations of certain Gods to new transcendent heights. The most common solution among the intellectuals was to identify the primal transcendent source of life with the God that people already considered the "highest" or supreme God in their pantheons of Gods. In the Greco-Roman period, many Egyptians thought this was Amun. Most Greeks said it was Zeus. The Jewish philosopher Philo of Alexandria argued that it is the Creator God in Jewish scriptures.

But not everyone was convinced with these identifications. Some people mounted a counter argument, that the primal God was not one of the traditionally venerated Gods, but a deity who existed above and beyond even the traditional Gods. The Hermetics, who bring into the discussion the lore of Hermes Trismegistus (the Thrice-Great God), is one of these counter groups in Egypt. Exposure to Hermetism likely led Valentinus to consider the possibility of a transcendent God who was different from any of the known Gods, including the Biblical Creator God. As we will see shortly, it was also exposure to Hermetism that solidified for Valentinus the idea that Jesus functioned as a Hermes-like psychopomp and divine teacher of God's mysteries, a divine man whose Mind was God's. Hermetism also exposed him to initiation ceremonies that Hermetic circles used to release the soul on an astral journey to meet the God beyond the Ogdoad in a transcendent sphere.

What actually was going on in Hermetic circles in Alexandria? Their divine teacher is Hermes Trismegistus. Hermes Trismegistus is an amalgam of the Egyptian God Thoth and the Greek God Hermes, who are both underworld psychopomps or guides and carriers of messages from the Gods to humans. In Hermetic circles, Hermes is identified as the Creator of heaven and earth. He is so great, so extraordinary, that he is recognized as the Ruler of the World, presiding over fate and justice. He is a cosmic deity with cosmic proportions, identified with the Mind of the Sun God Rê. He is not the transcendent God, but the intermediary between the transcendent God and humanity.

What is so extraordinary about the story of Hermes Trismegistus is that he was originally the human being Hermes, who, through a gradual process of shamanic-like initiation was inducted into the heavenly spheres, ascending to the pinnacle of the world where the Gods live in the skies. In that high place, his mind was switched out, entering permanently the immortal body of a God (*C.H.* 1.13.3). After this transfiguration, he descends to earth as a new God, Hermes Trismegistus, the Mind of Rê. He remains in the world to reveal the secrets of the divine world to other people and to conduct them through similar out-of-body or ecstatic journeys. The teachings of Hermes about the supreme God-Beyond-All-Gods and humanity's divinity was ridiculed by people outside their circles as crazy and ridiculous so that the Hermetics faced scorn, hatred, and even death threats (*C.H.* 9.4; Latin *Asc.* 25).

What did Hermes Trismegistus have to say about the divine world? It is the tragic story about how the divine came to be trapped in sentience and unconsciousness, starting with primordial time, when a coiling snake arose from the deep watery darkness with a wailing roar. From its cry emerged the four elements of fire, air, earth, and wind (*C.H.* 1.4–6; 3.1–2). The Hermetics call this primal God "Father" because of his procreative activities. As a hermaphrodite pregnant with all things, he begins, contains, and encompasses everything. From him emerge light and life. He is called Good because this is the only word that can describe his essence. He manifests himself as the cosmic Mind, who, in turn produces a second God, the Sun God who creates the universe.

Out of love for himself, Mind also produces an archetypal human who is a powerful clone of the transcendent God. Curious about the activities of the Sun God, the clone stoops down to peer through the cosmic ceiling. When he does this, he sees his own reflection in a pool of water on earth. Instantaneously, he is enamored with how he looks in material form. He loves his earthly appearance so much that he wants nothing more than to inhabit it. What he wishes for comes true. He descends and embraces his material form.

In this story, the traditional Greek tale of Narcissus has been repurposed toward three ends. First, the Hermetics use this story to explain how it is that humankind is dual, consisting of a body and an immortal soul, which is a fallen God. This means that the human mind is a God superior to the cosmic framework, but has become a slave within it (*C.H.* 1.9–15; *Asc.* 22–23). Second, the human predicament is explained as a tragic flaw in God, in his narcissistic desire to become human, rather than in human's desire to become God. The cause of human suffering is a primal narcissism buried deep in the depths of the human psyche. Third, the only way out of this tragedy is for the narcissism to be overcome, for the soul to be emptied of lust and bodily desire, separated from the body, and returned to its primal condition.

The way that Hermetics rescued and returned the soul to its original condition involved initiation ceremonies such as described in the *Discourse on the Ogdoad and Ennead* (in the Nag Hammadi Collection). Guided by a guru-like leader or mystagogue, the initiate is instructed in the way of Hermes (*Disc.* 52.3–7). The initiate also undergoes a ritual immersion in water, a baptism believed to represent immersion in the primal waters of Mind. This immersion begins the process of the repatriation of the initiate's individual mind within the cosmic Mind, vitalizing the human mind's ability to comprehend all things, whether on earth, in heaven, or beyond heaven (*C.H.* 4.1–5). The water treatment enables the initiate's mind to access its God-power and begin to grow to immeasurable immensity, outleaping the body, outstripping time, and becoming eternal (*C.H.* 11.20).

The initiate also is guided by the mystagogue on an ascent journey through the cosmic spheres, progressively shedding at each planet the regalia that had been wrapped around the fallen Mind at birth, natural properties of the human soul like growth and aging, emotions, evil inclinations, lust, arrogance, greed, and deceit. Once released from the soul's hypnotizing trappings, the mind of the initiate enters the Ogdoadic region, where the initiate sings hymns to the primal Father who lives beyond the Ogdoad in the region of the Ennead outside the universe. There the mind of the initiate is surrendered and transformed into the cosmic Mind. This is how the initiate's true self enters God and is made God. This is Gnosis, when the initiate, like Hermes, flies through the air and becomes God too (*C.H.* 1.24–26; 10.24–25; *Disc.* 56.22–60.1). For all intents and purposes, Valentinus' Christianity blends Christian lore with Hermetic knowledge about God and the soul, and Hermetic initiatory practices that were used to access the primal God.

[3.6] **The Transcendent God Meets the Bible**

COMPANION READINGS
Genesis 4
Irenaeus, *Against Heresies* 1.29–30

While the Hermetic pursuit of Gnosis and the transcendent God of Egypt was known thoroughly by Valentinus, the form of Christianity he developed also was informed by various ways that other Christians were interpreting the Jewish scriptures, especially passages about creation known as the Genesis story. While in Alexandria, Valentinus had the opportunity to interact with some of these other Christians and discuss their readings of Genesis. These Christians called themselves Gnostics (Greek: *Gnostikoi*) or Knowers because, according to Irenaeus, they said that they "knew" a transcendent God who was not the Biblical Creator.

Irenaeus, a fourth-generation Christian (155–195 CE), tells us about these Christians (Iren., *Haer.*, 1.preface.1; 1.11.1; 1.29.1; 1.30.15). While Irenaeus mocks their claim to Gnosis or knowledge of God, he is an important witness to a wide array of third-generation Christians who were seeking truth experientially and worshipping a God-Beyond-All-Gods. These Gnostic Christians were keen (and literal) readers of Biblical scriptures, especially the stories about creation, the fall of Adam and Eve, and the flood.

Irenaeus preserves a popular reading of this Biblical origin story that features the "good" snake who helps Eve gain knowledge or Gnosis (*Haer.* 1.30). We call this reading of Genesis 1–6, the Ophite Myth because "snake" in Greek is *ophis*. The Ophite Myth appears to have developed first among sectarian Jews in Alexandria because it is dependent on Jewish knowledge about God's wisdom (Sophia), speculations about Adam and Seth, and Jewish angelology. The Christian features that Irenaeus mentions are not essential to the myth. Jesus appears to be "added" into an earlier myth that featured Sophia as the protector and savior of her children. Her children were direct descendants of Adam and Eve's children Seth (Gen. 4:25, 5:3) and Norea. Who is Norea? She is a derivative character like Lilith. Lilith, in Jewish midrash, is believed to be Adam's first wife (Gen. 1:27) in contrast to Eve who was taken from his rib (Gen. 2:22). Norea is derived from the Greek word *oraia* which means "beautiful" (LXX Gen. 4:22; Hebrew, *naamah*). In Irenaeus' version of the Ophite Myth, she is Seth's sister.

As philosophers and intellectuals like Philo, these sectarian Jews were trying to make sense of the philosophical conversation about the transcendent God in light of their own scriptures. Philo identified the omnipotent and impassive transcendent God of the philosophers with YHWH. He argued that all the Biblical passages that attributed ignorance and emotions (grief, joy, regret, jealousy, anger) to YHWH did so because the author of the passages had condescended to the unsophisticated level of his readers who were uneducated and were not able understand the true nature of God. To pander to the uneducated, the Biblical author invented for God "hands and feet, incomings and outgoings, enmities, aversions, estrangements, anger, in fact such body parts and passions as can never belong to the Cause [of life]" (Philo, *Sacr. Cain* 1.95–96). Philo also turned to allegory to interpret tricky passages. So, for instance, what are we to make of the passage where Adam and Eve "hid themselves from the face of God"? Philo says, this means only that wicked people run away from God or live in darkness so that God is concealed from them. In this way, Philo insists that the omnipotence and impassibility of the transcendent God is not compromised (Philo, *Alleg.* 3.1–3).

There were other Jews in Alexandria who did not agree with Philo. They were Jewish sectarian Biblical literalists who rejected condescending and allegorical strategies. To them it was obvious that the Biblical Creator God in the Genesis story was not the transcendent God. He was an emotive anthropomorphic God, not a transcendent principle that sparked life. They argued that the Biblical God must be a Demiurge, a creator God ranked beneath the transcendent source of life.

They made this determination based on close readings of their scriptures which they believed to be authoritative and true. They noted that time and again in their scriptures, YHWH exhibits human characteristics and emotions. They also pointed out that he is not a lone God. He claims to be jealous of other Gods and he creates human beings with the assistance of other divinities, as he himself says in Genesis 1:26, "Let *us* make man in *our* image, after *our* likeness" (my italics). This suggested to these close readers of the scriptures that something was amiss with conventional Jewish wisdom about the identity of YHWH. These kinds of verses indicated that YHWH was not the transcendent God who is, by definition, beyond human categories and descriptors.

If not the transcendent God, then who was YHWH? To answer this question, they relied on long-standing Jewish traditions of angels and demons as creatures who cross human and divine realms. They pointed also to passages in the scriptures where the Angel of YHWH (translated in most

Bibles as the Angel of the Lord) appears in humanlike form but speaks YHWH's words and wields YHWH's power. This angel is YHWH in human form, appearing in many stories to be interchangeable with the God YHWH. These stories confirmed for them that YHWH was not the transcendent God, but a secondary God or angel who created the world and rules it.

Once they made this identification, they began to work out the relationship between the transcendent God and YHWH. Was YHWH an extension and ambassador of the transcendent God, creating the world according to the will of the transcendent God? Or was YHWH doing his own thing? The answer to this question again came out of their interpretation of scriptural passages. Pointing to many of the same passages that Marcion also used, these Biblical Gnostics demonstrated that YHWH is an emotional God, a jealous, angry, and capricious God sometimes committing genocide to appease his wrath.

The more they studied the details of their scriptures, the more they were certain that YHWH is not the transcendent God's agent, but his adversary. In order to draw attention to their discovery, they call him Ialdabaoth (or Yaldabaoth), which is an aggregate of YHWH's warrior alias "Lord of Armies" (Hebrew: *Yahweh Sabaoth*). They begin to toy with the idea that Ialdabaoth must be like Lucifer, the rebellious angel-turned-demon. If YHWH was jealous, angry, and ignorant, was he like Lucifer, who led an army of revolting angels and was thrown down from high places? They thought so. They were convinced that Ialdabaoth is a rebel, an apostate God. He must be a God who leads his armies of angels in an ongoing battle against the transcendent God (Figure 3.7).

This type of thinking led these sectarian Jewish intellectuals back to the drawing board. They began with Genesis 1:1, seeking to unravel the mysteries about where the transcendent God was and how Ialda-

FIGURE 3.7   Only surviving image of Ialdaboath. Cast of an Ophian amulet originally described by Bonner (1949, D188). The location of the original jasper gem is unknown. This is a new photo of the cast housed in the Kelsey Museum of Archaeology, University of Michigan, Ann Arbor. Published with permission.

baoth came into being. In Irenaeus' rendition of the Ophite Myth, the interpreters perceive the primal God to be a hermaphrodite because in Genesis 1:26–27, God creates humans as both male and female in God's own image and likeness. They noted that God speaks in the plural "Let us make man in our image, according to our likeness." Based on the fact that God's image is a Man, these sectarian Jews argued that the transcendent God had to be the First Man and Father of all (Gen. 1:1). They also called the primal God Bythos, the Depth, a name derived from Genesis 1:2 which speaks about the existence of a deep void.

The First Woman (Bythos's First Thought) comes from him. She is the Holy Spirit who flies over the water (Gen. 1:2). She is "the Mother of the Living" (Gen. 3:20). She produces a son whom they call the Son of Man and the Second Man. This Aeon they derive from Genesis 1:3: "Let there be *phôs*." This identification is a play on the Greek word "*phôs*" which meant both "man" and "light" depending on the placement of the accent. A Third Man is generated from the collaboration of the First and Second Man with the Holy Spirit in something like a *menage toi* (Gen. 1:26–27). The Third Man is the archetype of the human, a figure called Man (Greek: *Anthropos*). After this, the Holy Spirit separates the primal elements, light from dark and water from the abyss (Gen. 1:4–7). As she flies over the waters, she descends through the air as Sophia, God's Wisdom.

Her identity as Sophia belongs to a deep tradition of Jewish speculations about God's Wisdom (Sophia). In Jewish literature, Sophia is brought forth in the beginning (Prov. 8:22; Sir. 1:4, 24:9), is identified with the Holy Spirit, life, and the Tree of Life (Wis. 7:7, 22–23; Prov. 3:18, 8:35; Bar. 9:14), lives in the clouds (Sir. 24:4), helps God create (Prov. 3:19, 8:27–30; Wis. 9:2), descends into the world (Bar. 3:37; Sir. 24: 1–12), is associated with the seven-fold cosmic structure (Prov. 9:1), and protects Adam, Noah, and other righteous men (Wis. 10:1–21). This is why in the Ophite Myth, the sectarian Jewish exegetes argued that some of Sophia's light falls all the way down into the waters. This energizes the waters, creating the seas (Gen. 1:9–10). The light remaining in the air reverses course and sucks the fallen light back up into her body. Sophia extends her body as wide as possible, forming the heavens (Gen. 1:6–8). Then she sheds her body and ascends back to the heights. Her cast-away body appears to be the earth which is seeded with her vitality, although Irenaeus only tells us this indirectly (Gen. 1:11–12).

Sophia also leaves behind her son, Ialdabaoth, who is the chief Archon and the solar deity (Gen. 1:14–18). He creates the rest of the planetary Archons: Iao, Sabaoth, Adoneus, Eloeus, Oreus, Astaphaeus. These names are created largely from Jewish titles for God and his angels. Together they are the Seven (the Hebdomad). Ialdabaoth populates the seven heavens with angels and powers who rebel against him. Depressed by the constant war, Ialdabaoth looks down to earth, seeking something better. When he does this, he generates Mind (his own twisted Nous) as the snake in the Garden. This is the origin of the human mind (*psyche*: soul). This makes him happy so he shouts, "I am Father, and God, and above me there is no one" (Isa. 45:5).

Sophia, who is hidden above him, reprimands him as his mother, telling him not to lie. There is the First Man, the Father of All, above him, and also his Son, the Son of Man, she calls down to him. To distract the warring Archons so they do not hear her message and realize that Ialdabaoth is actually not the highest God, Ialdabaoth convinces them to create Adam whom he hopes to use as a secret weapon to overpower the First Man and the Son of Man above him. Sophia knows his plot and decides to take action in order to deprive Ialdabaoth of the spirit (the light) that she had left behind. If she can remove her spirit from Ialdabaoth and put it into a being that he cannot control, she will depower her arrogant son. When Ialdabaoth creates Adam, she will use Adam as a container for the spirit. To do this, she projects the image of Man into Ialdabaoth's mind without his awareness. He and the rest of the Archons use this image to create Adam's form (Gen. 1:26–27; 2:7). But what they create is a worm writhing on the ground (Job 25:6). This upsets them. The moment is perfect for Sophia to suggest to Ialdabaoth that, if he breathes life into Adam's nostrils, his creation will live. Without thinking, Ialdabaoth does this. This is how he empties himself of his mother's spirit and gives Adam a living soul (LXX Gen. 2:7).

When Ialdabaoth realizes that his mother's spirit, the light, is now in Adam, he tries to remove it surgically by taking out Adam's rib (Gen. 2:21). But when he opens up Adam's side, Sophia snatches the light before Ialdabaoth can grab it himself, leaving Eve in harm's way. Ialdabaoth is mad and becomes abusive immediately deciding that he will rape Eve (Gen. 2:22; 4:1). To protect Eve, Sophia uses the snake to convince her to transgress Ialdabaoth's commandment to stay away from the Tree of Knowledge (Gen. 2:16–17; 3:1–2). When she picks and eats its fruit, she gains knowledge (Gnosis) of the transcendent God and she and Adam hide from Ialdabaoth, the monster God (Gen. 3:4–11). Once he finds them, he curses the snake and throws it down (Gen. 3:14–15). The snake becomes the Leviathan demon whose body wraps around the cosmos. He also curses Adam and Eve and casts them out of Eden (Gen. 3:16–24). The sectarian Jewish interpreters thought that this meant that Adam and Eve were cast down into material bodies (Gen. 3:21) where their souls became enfeebled and forgot about the transcendent God. Sophia continues to protect Seth's and Norea's descendants from Ialdabaoth's cruelty (attempted rapes, flood, fire at Sodom and Gommorah). Throughout history, Sophia helps Seth's and Norea's children remember the transcendent God by sprinkling her light on them, an act that the Jewish sectarians connected with baptism and likely performed among themselves.

Once the Ophite Myth emerged, it went viral, taking on a life of its own, being used by different groups and adapted to their unique profiles and regional traditions, and combined with other myths. Versions of the Ophite Myth or knowledge of it show up in a number of texts, including: the Ophian Diagram known to Celsus (ca. 175 CE) and Origen (ca. 240 CE); *Sophia of Jesus Christ*; *Second Treatise of the Great Seth*; *Untitled Treatise* in the Bruce Codex; *Apocalypse of Adam*; *Hypostasis of the Archons*; *On the Origin of the World*; *Eugnostos*; *Apocryphon of John*; *Trimorphic Protennoia*; *Holy Book of the Great Invisible Spirit*; *Melchizedek*; *Thought of Norea*; *Gospel of Judas*; *Zostrianos*; *Allogenes*; *Three Steles of Seth*; and *Marsanes*.

3.7 The Children of Seth

COMPANION READINGS
Apocryphon of John (NHC II,1)

There were so many permutations of the Ophite Myth that Irenaeus compares the Gnostics who wrote them to a "multitude" of mushrooms popping up here and there, each author presenting a new take on the old myth. The variety confused Irenaeus so much that he was not sure where the permutations came from, but he was sure that they were somehow related. He thought that Valentinus was working from the Ophite Myth and revised it to suit the system Valentinus had in mind. Irenaeus was probably correct in his analysis on this point.

Hans-Martin Schenke (1929–2002 CE), a prominent German scholar who edited the Nag Hammadi texts, organized the materials by grouping texts together which claimed to be authored by people who call themselves the Children of Seth, the Incorruptible Race, and the Holy Generation (*Apocryphon of John, Hypostasis of the Archons, Holy Book of the Great Invisible Spirit, Apocalypse of Adam, Three Steles of Seth, Zostrianos, Melchizedek, Thought of Norea, Marsanes, Allogenes, Trimorphic Protennoia*). He argued that these texts ought to be grouped together under the rubric "Sethian" because they were written by people who believed that Seth was their inaugural ancestor, as well as their redeemer from on high. Schenke pointed to a communal identity given that most of these texts showcase distinctive activities of groups singing hymns, saying prayers, and chanting praises to specific transcendent Gods (Invisible Spirit, Barbelo, and the Autogenerated Son), baptizing their members in a ceremony called the Five Seals with the help of the same angels (Micheu, Michar, Mnesinous, Yammon, Elasso, and Amenai), and inducing spirit journeys through the same cosmic and transcendent realms home to four luminous angels (Harmozel, Oroiael, Daveithai, and Eleleth). In their mythology, which features a fallen Sophia, her son, Ialdabaoth opposes them all. Schenke identified the *Apocryphon of John* as the exemplar of Sethianism.

While we recognize Ialdabaoth and Sophia from the Ophite Myth, who are Barbelo and these four luminous angels? Where did they come from? Irenaeus helps us again. They come from the Barbeloite Myth (Iren., *Haer.* 1.29). This is a completely different myth about how the primal Gods came into being. In this myth, we have a holy Trinity: the primal Father, a Mother who is called Barbelo, and a Son called Self-Generated. Barbelo likely derives from an Egyptian word (*berber*) that means "overflow" or "boil over." In the Barbeloite Myth, we also find the four luminous angels.

In many of the texts that Schenke identified as Sethian, we find the Barbeloite Godhead intersecting with the Ophite Myth. It is almost as if someone cut the Ophite Godhead out of the Ophite Myth and pasted the Barbeloite Godhead into it. New characters pop up here and there (i.e. Mirothear, Adamas, Geradams, heavenly Seth, Micheu, Michar, Mnesinous, etc.). Emphases shift. Most texts on Schenke's list background Sophia's role as the Savior. They either emphasize the saving capacity of the Primal Mother Barbelo or foreground Seth's role as progenitor and Savior of a holy race of children called the Seed of Seth. Some texts begin talking about a ritual called the Five Seals, which was used to ritually activate the hidden potency of the spiritual seed in order to release the true spirit from its incarceration.

While the Sethian grouping is helpful because it allows us to see certain things, it also frames the evidence so that we miss differences which might be important. When we step back, we see that the texts, which Schenke groups as "Sethian," do not all actually feature the Barbeloite Godhead. The *Apocalypse of Adam* and the *Hypostasis of the Archons* lack Barbeloite features. They do not include prominent Christian doctrines nor does Jesus play an integral role (when mentioned, he is superficially grafted onto a Jewish story). Could these two texts be harboring the old Jewish Ophite mythology beneath a very thin Christian veneer? Other texts that Schenke included under the Sethian rubric (*Three Steles of Seth*, *Zostrianos*, *Allogenes*, and *Marsanes*) have taken the Barbeloite Myth and reworked the myth to bring it into conversation with Plato's understanding of the primal principles. While these Platonized texts identify the Elect with the "Children of Seth," they do not allude to any of the rest of the Ophite mythology. They could represent the opinions of metaphysical thinkers who are distinguishing themselves *from* the Christian Sethians.

The Ophite Myth was very popular and permutations of it are found in many contexts that do not fit Schenke's Sethian grouping (Figure 3.8). For instance, a Christian permutation of the Ophite Myth was also used by a group of fourth-generation Christians whom the Roman philosopher Celsus (175 CE) knew and Origen of Alexandria (248 CE) calls Ophians. As noted previously, permutations of the myth also appear in the Valentinian literature, *Eugnostos*, *Sophia of Jesus Christ*, *Second Treatise of the Great Seth*, *On Origin of the World*, and *Untitled Treatise* in the Bruce Codex.

If we organize these texts around the usage of the Ophite Myth, the myth's journey appears to have started in Alexandria among sectarian Jewish intellectuals who created the myth out of their flipped reading of the Genesis story (Iren., *Haer.* 1.30). They used baptism as the ritual to sprinkle Sophia's spirit on initiates and grant them knowledge of the transcendent God. They likely memorized the names of the planetary rulers so that they could know how to navigate through their treacherous realms after they died and their souls had to journey to the transcendent world.

Different independent circles of Jewish and Christian Gnostics used the Ophite Myth competitively. They tweaked the myth and ritual so that they could claim to have the most effective version of the ritual necessary to release the soul successfully and the exact knowledge (Archon and angel names) needed to get to the transcendent world. This mythic redesign is happening not only in the Valentinian literature, but also in the other texts we mentioned, like *Eugnostos*, *Sophia of Jesus Christ*, *Hypostasis of the Archons*, and *On the Origin of the World*.

A distinctive Sethian identity formed in the second century when a Barbeloite group decided to add the Ophite interpretation of the Genesis story to their Egyptian Christian Trinity (the Invisible Father, Barbelo the Mother, and the Self-Generated Son). This group probably was already performing a baptismal ritual called the Five Seals. During this ceremony, the Aeon from Barbelo (Forethought) descends bodily into Hades and, from deep sleep, awakens the initiates to the knowledge that the spiritual seed indwells them. This is her gift of Gnosis to them. After a ritual exchange of words, she seals them five times in a special luminous water – the primal waters of life – to redeem them from

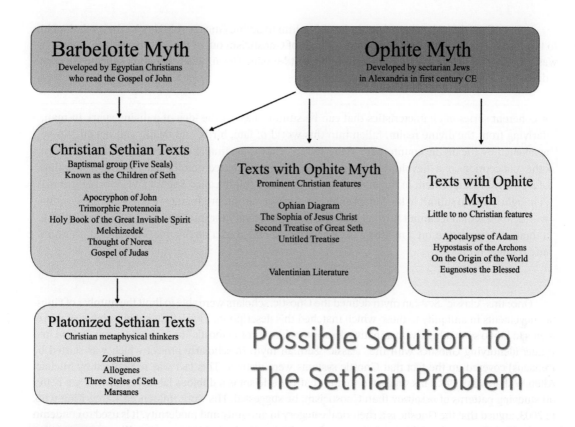

Barbeloite Myth
Developed by Egyptian Christians
who read the Gospel of John

Ophite Myth
Developed by sectarian Jews
in Alexandria in first century CE

Christian Sethian Texts
Baptismal group (Five Seals)
Known as the Children of Seth

Apocryphon of John
Trimorphic Protennoia
Holy Book of the Great Invisible Spirit
Melchizedek
Thought of Norea
Gospel of Judas

Texts with Ophite Myth
Prominent Christian features

Ophian Diagram
The Sophia of Jesus Christ
Second Treatise of Great Seth
Untitled Treatise

Valentinian Literature

Texts with Ophite Myth
Little to no Christian features

Apocalypse of Adam
Hypostasis of the Archons
On the Origin of the World
Eugnostos the Blessed

Platonized Sethian Texts
Christian metaphysical thinkers

Zostrianos
Allogenes
Three Steles of Seth
Marsanes

Possible Solution To The Sethian Problem

FIGURE 3.8 Illustration of the Christians and texts that relied on the Barbeloite and Ophian Myths. How each group and text received the myth is a matter of debate.

death. Her actions defeat five underworld guardians and release their spirits from their mortal fate and perpetual reincarnations (cf. *Apoc. John* 11.6–7). The texts that best represent their movement include the *Apocryphon of John, Holy Book of the Great Invisible Spirit, Melchizedek, Thought of Norea*, and *Trimorphic Protennoia*. As for the Platonized texts – *Zostrianos, Allogenes, Three Steles of Seth*, and *Marsanes* – they likely were composed by third-century metaphysical thinkers who were co-opting Sethian mythology to outdo Plato. We will return to these metaphysical thinkers in Chapter 11.

3.8 Gnostic Spirituality

COMPANION READINGS
Irenaeus, *Against Heresies* 1.1, 29–30

As we have seen, Irenaeus relates that numerous people in antiquity developed distinctive systems of transcendental thought within discrete communities of worship. Since he was a scholar of texts, Irenaeus tries to explain their relationship to each other by studying their texts and zeroing in on their myths. Then he goes to work analyzing their similarities and creating a genealogy based on his comparative research. His fictitious genealogy made it appear as if the movements were exemplars of a Gnostic religion that was based on versions of the Barbeloite and Ophite Myths, which Irenaeus outlines in *Against Heresies* 1.29–30. Scholars today refer to the Sethian combination of these myths as the "classic" Gnostic myth.

Irenaeus' work made it easy for scholars after him to define Gnostic thinkers by their relationship to the "classic" Sethian Myth and build typologies of Gnosticism out of the features of this Myth. This was done extravagantly at the famous conference at Messina (1966) where scholars collectively wrote a definition of Gnosticism, determining that it is:

> A coherent series of characteristics that can be summarized in the idea of a divine spark in man, deriving from the divine realm, fallen into this world of fate, birth, and death, and needing to be awakened by the divine counterpart of the self in order to be finally reintegrated. Compared with other conceptions of a 'devolution' of the divine, this idea is based ontologically on the conception of a downward movement of the divine whose periphery (often called Sophia [Wisdom] or Ennoia [Thought]) had to submit to the fate of entering into a crisis and producing – even if indirectly – this world, upon which it cannot turn its back, since it is necessary for it to recover the *pneuma* [spirit], a dualistic conception on a monistic background, expressed in a double movement of devolution and reintegration.

Once this "classic" Sethian myth defined the Gnostic, scholars were able to limit the number of Gnostic movements in antiquity to those which matched this description. This left an equal number of movements in limbo so that highly imaginative descriptors like "proto-Gnostic" or "almost-Gnostic" came into vogue. Identifying Gnostics with the "classic" Sethian myth (a scholarly project which was started by Irenaeus) covered up the fact that Gnostic systems were distinct. This fact was recognized by Michael Allen Williams in 1996. This suggested to him that Gnosticism is a dubious label. Perhaps we are better off studying patterns of DEMIURGY than Gnosticism, he suggested. His work influenced Karen King who, in 2003, argued that the Gnostic is a rhetorical category in antiquity and modernity. It is used to condemn certain Christians while making our own versions of Christianity today normative. King suggests using other terms like "alternative" or "marginalized" to describe these Christians and their texts.

While these opinions have been highly influential among scholars (we have suspended the Messina definition, and tempered our use of the word Gnosticism), these approaches sidestep the larger issues about Gnosticism by substituting "alternative" Christian language for the Gnostic. By making the Gnostic an alternative Christian, we shut down our ability to investigate pre-Christian and non-Christian Gnostic movements. Worse yet, this language of alternative Christians erases Gnostic identities from historical memory, something that Irenaeus set out to do and scholars have almost accomplished. It is time to step back and reassess this situation.

First, it is a fact that the word Gnostic (pl., *Gnostikoi*) was used in antiquity. People in antiquity understood what it meant, and it meant more than a derogatory slur. Certainly it was used to satirize, mock, and condemn people who thought they were "in the know." But there is plenty of historical evidence that people actually used the word to positively identify themselves too. We meet most of these people in later chapters of this textbook. For now, it is enough to recognize that there were a variety of systems that were considered Gnostic by the early Christians as summarized in Figure 3.9.

The evidence for the use of the label extends outside Christian testimonies as well. The Roman philosopher Celsus (180 CE) mentions Christians who call themselves Gnostics (Origen, *Adv. Cels.* 5.61). These are probably the Christians whom Origen calls Ophians. The Neo-Platonic philosopher Plotinus knows about a group of Gnostics who attend his seminars in Rome (*Vit. Plot.* 16). They showed him two of their books, *Zostrianos* and *Allogenes*. Both of these books survive in the Nag Hammadi Collection and have Sethian features. We will read more about them in Chapter 11.

Given this rich evidence, it is clear that the word Gnostic had a wide application that transcended discrete group identities and mythologies. It could be wielded by some Christians like Irenaeus as a satirical weapon, while others used it to identify something distinctive that could be located across a variety of groups, something that transcended a particular myth or set of doctrines or practices.

Irenaeus says that a group in Rome who followed Carpocrates called themselves Gnostics
Haer. 1.25.6

Irenaeus knowns the Christian Sethians as Gnostics
Haer. 1.preface.1; 1.11.1; 1.29.1; 1.30.15

Clement of Alexandria knows of a group led by a man named Prodicus who called themselves Gnostics and Tertullian of Carthage says that Prodicus was a Valentinian
Misc. 3.30.1 and *Adv. Prax.* 3

Clement of Alexandria knows another leader of a Christian sect who called himself Gnostic
Misc. 2.114.5; 3.30.2; 4.114.2; 4.116.1; 7.41.3; cf. *Paed.* 1.52.2

The mystagogue and author of *The Book of Baruch*, Justin and his followers claimed to be Gnostics because they alone knew the perfect Good God   Hipp., *Ref.* 5.23.3

The Naassenes were known to have called themselves Gnostics
Hipp., *Ref.* 5.2; 5.6.4; 5.8.1; 5.11.1

Epiphanius of Salamis says that Valentinus himself called himself a Gnostic as did his followers   *Pan.* 31.1.1, 31.1.5

Testimonies of People Who Called Themselves Gnostics

FIGURE 3.9 People in antiquity used the word Gnostic to describe a range of Christians.

In other words, it was used to identify something transconfessional, something that is not tied to a single religious group but crosses groups. What do we make of this?

One way to proceed is to consider how the Gnostic functioned as a mental category or cognitive frame. Simply put, cognitive frames are mental shortcuts that our minds develop to help us process information and interpret this information generally and categorically. How did ancient people understand and use the word Gnostic? What were the distinguishing characteristics associated with it? Like our modern words "Fundamentalist" and "Progressive," what did the word "Gnostic" signal? Mental frames are not absolute definitions, but rather are constructed based on ideal characteristics of the thing that can be adapted to new situations. Like our mental category CHAIR, which is a seat with legs (except bean bags) and arms (except slipper chairs), in the minds of ancient people, the category GNOS-TIC had ideal, but flexible features too.

When the ancient evidence is examined, we find that the word Gnostic refers to the metaphysical orientation or spirituality of people who knew (Gnosis) and worshipped a previously unknown transcendent God. These people claimed to be able to attain Gnosis because of a consubstantial connection with God (humans share God's substance). In other words, God literally is part of human beings because his spirit infuses them, not as a gift at baptism, but as an essential part of human nature. The goal of Gnostic systems is the release of the God-part (i.e. spirit, mind, light) from its embodiment so that it can journey back to its source, God. Gnostic Spirituality is distinguishable from Slave and Vassal Spiritualities which understand the human's relationship to the sacred in terms of a slave to a master or a vassal to a king. With the Gnostic orientation, there is a flip, so that humans, seeded with God, must realize their divine potential. Their divine selves make their way back to their transcendent home, and unite or rejoin God like broken pieces mended together.

Gnostic Spirituality is wrapped up in a quest for reality that culminates in the direct knowledge of a supreme God who dwells beyond the cosmos (Gnosis). This God is a hidden, secret God, unknown to most people. He is a God distinct from the traditional Gods (including the Biblical Creator), a God who is the primal source of life itself. Gnostic groups worship this transcendental God and develop ritual activities in order to "know" God directly and restore their spirits to the heights. They use specialized ritual technologies to make this journey (before and/or after death). They build religious movements as collective expressions of this spirituality (Figure 3.10).

Their search for the transcendent God impacted the way that they thought about their ancestral religious traditions. In their attempts to reveal the secret of the transcendent God hidden in the scriptures, they tended to disrupt and flip traditional interpretations of the texts. They authorized their beliefs and practices with reference to traditional stories and scriptures which they read in nonstandard ways and explained with reference to a variety of origin myths. They tended to interpret Jewish and Christian scriptures and philosophical literature against the grain in their attempts to reveal hidden truths and critique religious conventions.

A new way to talk about ancient Gnostics is to think about them as belonging to a family of transcendental movements. Gnostic Spirituality, which emerges in Egypt around Philo's lifetime, generates a family of new religious movements in the Roman world to worship the unknown transcendent God whom adherents claimed to "know" through direct experience (Gnosis) and be consubstantial with. Valentinus and his followers, the Hermetics, the sectarian Jewish authors of the Ophite Myth, the Christian Barbeloites, and the Christian Sethians were all part of this transcendental family. We meet their other kin later in this textbook.

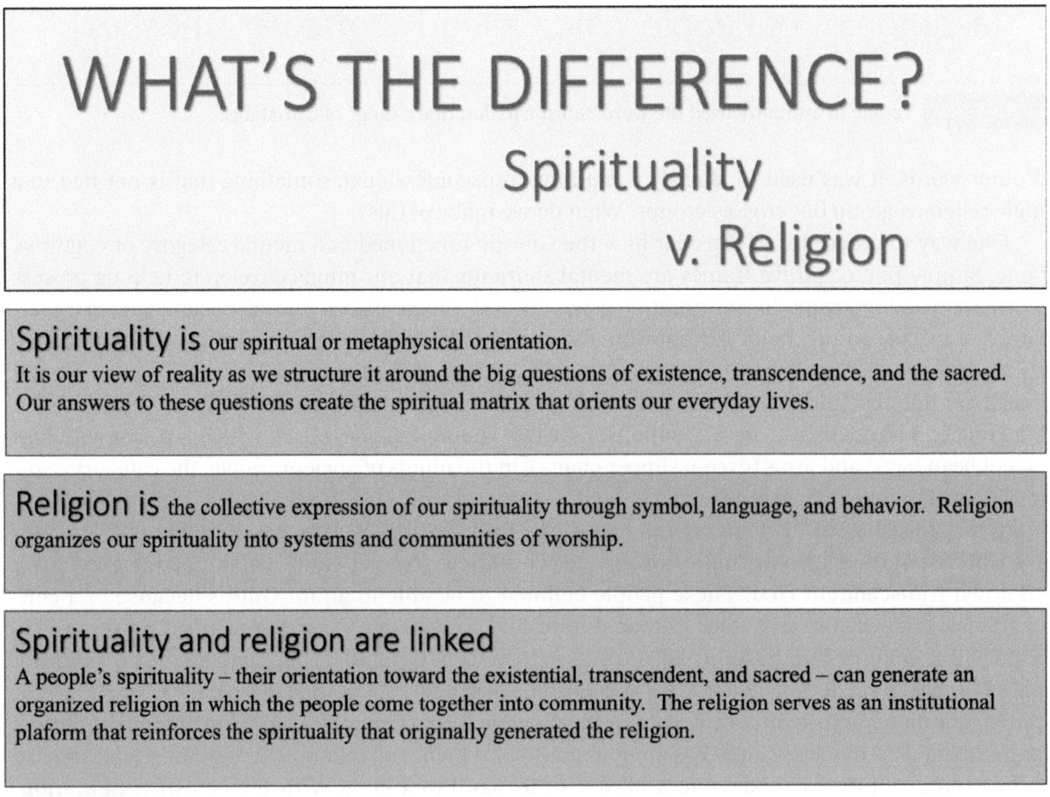

WHAT'S THE DIFFERENCE?
Spirituality
v. Religion

Spirituality is our spiritual or metaphysical orientation.
It is our view of reality as we structure it around the big questions of existence, transcendence, and the sacred. Our answers to these questions create the spiritual matrix that orients our everyday lives.

Religion is the collective expression of our spirituality through symbol, language, and behavior. Religion organizes our spirituality into systems and communities of worship.

Spirituality and religion are linked
A people's spirituality – their orientation toward the existential, transcendent, and sacred – can generate an organized religion in which the people come together into community. The religion serves as an institutional plaform that reinforces the spirituality that originally generated the religion.

FIGURE 3.10   The difference between spirituality and religion is illustrated.

Timeline

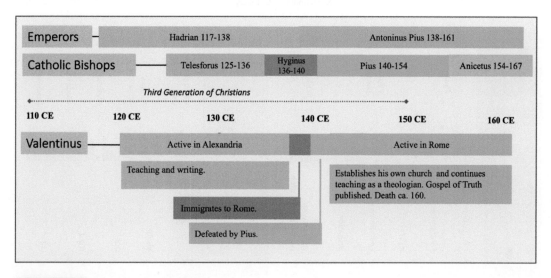

FIGURE 3.11   Timeline for Valentinus.

Pattern Summary

Valentinus' patterns (Figure 3.12) start with his TRANSTHEISTIC concept of God as the primal source of life. His transcendental God is a hermaphrodite similar to the Egyptian Gods Atum and Amun who generate aspects of themselves, establishing original eight or nine Gods. The Demiurge is a separate figure. In Egyptian lore, he is Rê. In Valentinus' system, he is the Biblical Creator God who caretakes and operates within a system of JUSTICE he established. At the same time, he is REBELLIOUS and IGNORANT. Valentinus understands THEODICY to be the inevitable fault of the primal God coming into existence as mental operations that are unable to know the original ineffable depth. God's suffering is built into the fabric of human existence and there is nothing we can do to find relief. God must intervene so that humans are saved through God's grace alone.

Valentinus appears to have solved the Binitarian Problem by arguing that Jesus was both human and divine. His humanness reflected the fact that he consisted of a body, soul, and spirit, although his soul was the psychic Christ that the Demiurge had created. His divinity came at his baptism when the Aeon Jesus in the form of a dove descended upon him. In this way, Valentinus augments the ADULT POSSESSION PATTERN with the ENSOULMENT PATTERN which he pioneered. In terms of lifestyle, his followers believed that human marriage reflected the syzygies of the Aeons. Valentinus had access to the ten letters of Paul, at least the Gospels of Matthew and John, and likely authored the *Gospel of Truth*. The secessionist church he established, paralleled the Apostolic Catholic structures with the addition of an advanced level for Christians who wished to explore God's mysteries. Entrance into the advanced group of pneumatics required a second baptism with oil and initiations that were likely similar to the Hermetic rites.

Family Pattern Chart
Valentinus and Sethian Christians

X=Definitely > L=Likely

THEODICY

	Faulty-God	Faulty-Human	Other
Valentinus	X		
Sethians	X		

SOTERIOLOGY

	Gift from God	Human achievement	Minimalist	Moderate	Maximalist
Valentinus	X		X		
Sethians	X		X		

CHRISTOLOGY

	Adult possession	Fetal possession	Hybrid	Ensoulment	Visitation	Human who received revelation
Valentinus	X			X		
Sethians	L				L	

ANTHROPOLOGY

	Mono	Dual	Triad	Quad
Valentinus			X	
Sethians			X	

COSMIC DEMIURGY

	Autocrat	Administrator	Caretaker	Patron	Justice	Villain	Rebel	Ignorant	Impaired
Valentinus	X	X	X	X	X	X	X	X	X
Sethians	X	X	X	X	L	X	X	X	X

RESURRECTION

	Body reunites with soul	Body discarded and soul immortalized	Body and soul discarded and spirit rises	God-element separates from body soul, and spirit and rises
Valentinus			X	
Sethians			X	

SCRIPTURES

	Jewish	Gospel	Pauline letters (10)	Pauline letters (13)	Hebrews	Acts	Catholic letters	Revelation	Other
Valentinus	X-partial	Jn Mt	X						L-GosTr
Sethians	X-partial								

ECCLESIOLOGY

	Consolidation movement	Reform movement	Secessionist movement	Counter movement	Innovative movement	Transregional	Regional
Valentinus		X	X			X	
Sethians					X	X	

FIGURE 3.12 Summary of Valentinus' and the Sethian Christians' patterns of beliefs and practices.

Takeaways

1. Valentinus was a third-generation Christian who thought that God cannot be reasoned out, but must be intuited and known through religious experience. For him, Gnosis or knowledge of God was not discursive knowledge but experiential knowledge. Valentinus believed that God had to actually visit and enlighten the human heart. When this happens, God is known.

2. Valentinus is attributed a vision of God's Mind, which revealed to him, in a moment of enlightenment, the origins of the universe and human existence. He crafted his revelation in mythic language that shows familiarity with Egyptian stories about the primal hermaphrodite God and Hermetic knowledge and practices.

3. Valentinus teaches about a transcendent God who is a primordial hermaphrodite prior to any other being. He identifies this God as different from the Biblical Creator God. The God of the Jewish scriptures is a secondary God created by Sophia out of Christ's shadow. Valentinus understands the primal transcendent God to be the true object of Christian affection and worship.

4. In the first century CE, the Ophite Myth got started among sectarian Jews in Egypt, philosophers and intellectuals who were trying to make sense of the philosophical conversation about the transcendent God in light of their own scriptures. They generated a myth that distinguished the transcendent God from the Biblical Creator God and read the Jewish scriptures in ways that inverted their traditional meaning. This myth was repurposed by a variety of Gnostic groups in antiquity. The Barbeloite Myth is a second Gnostic myth that was amalgamated with the Ophite interpretation of the Genesis story in several texts that scholars identify as Sethian.

5. Gnosticism is a disputed category among scholars because it has been misused to slander certain Christian groups in order to discredit them. It also has been wrongly used to suggest that there was an all-encompassing Gnostic religion based on a myth that scholars have reconstructed from many sources. While these arguments have suspended our use of the Messina definition, it does not appreciate enough the fact that the word Gnostic was a category in antiquity that was being used to identify people who claimed to know the transcendent God-Beyond-All-Gods and worship him in separate social groups.

6. Valentinus' conceptualization of the transcendent God took place within the context of an ongoing conversation among ancient scholars who wanted to identify the source of life. While Greek philosophers secondarily identified Zeus or one of the other Gods with the source of life, some Egyptian thinkers like the Hermetics and the first Sethians posited that this source was a God who transcended the known Gods in the pantheons, including the Biblical God. Valentinus likely was familiar with both Hermetists and the Ophite Myth.

7. Jesus Christ was central to Valentinus' myth and theology. Jesus was a real human being who ate (but did not defecate). His soul was the Psychic Christ and he had a spiritual seed gifted by Sophia. The Aeon Jesus descended from the Pleroma and entered the human Jesus, supercharging him. Valentinus likely was the first Christian to explain the relationship between Jesus' two natures (human and the divine) which is known as the Binitarian Problem. He used a combination of the ENSOULMENT and ADULT POSSESSION PATTERNS to do so.

8. Jesus' main role was instructional, revealing the Father to humans and opening up the path for their soul to journey home to the Father. His death was crucial. His crucifixion revealed the knowledge that the Father is within us, that the seed of the Father fills his children and cannot be detained by the inferior authorities who rule the universe.

9. Valentinus teaches about the cosmic pervasiveness and immanence of the spirit. He writes about this in a poem called *Harvest*.

10. Valentinus' form of Christianity first emerged in Alexandria, Egypt, in the early second century. He brought his teachings to Rome during Hyginus' tenure as Bishop of Rome (136–140 CE).

11. Valentinus had a Greek education which had familiarized him with Middle Platonic interpretations of Plato's writings about a Demiurge who creates the universe as well as a more transcendent principle that Plato called the Good.

12. Valentinus was exposed to Christian literature, particularly the letters of Paul. If the Gospel of Truth reflects Valentinus' teachings about the joy of knowing the Father in a moment of God's grace, he also knew the Gospel of John and at least the Gospel of Matthew.

13. Valentinus left the Roman church after Pius was elected. He started his own church, inducting people into the knowledge of God, using water baptism as a first-level ceremony, a second baptism featuring chrism for pneumatics, and the sacred meal as his main ritual activities.

14. Valentinus was a Christian. Initially he operated as an affiliate of the Apostolic Catholic network of churches, but later he seceded and started his own Christian church to try to save the naïve Apostolic Catholics (psychics) and grow the ranks of the spiritual Christians (pneumatics). His interface with Judaism and the Apostolic Catholic churches was complicated in that he identified the Biblical Creator God with an inferior oppositional Demiurge who created Adam only to impair him when he realized that Adam contained God's powerful spirit.

Questions

1. How does Valentinus' theology compare to Marcion's? How are they same? How are they different?

2. How did Valentinus imagine the origin of life and the creation of the universe compared to the Hermetic and Ophite explanations? Where is the transcendent realm in Valentinus' mythology located in relationship to the cosmic? Who controls the cosmic spheres?

3. Who is responsible for suffering and death in the universe according to Valentinus? How does Valentinus envision the suffering of Sophia in relationship to the construction of the cosmos?

4. If you joined Valentinus' church, how would you be inducted into membership? What rituals would be involved? What would you be supposed to experience?

5. What does Valentinus' system share with the Hermetic? How is it distinct?

6. What does Valentinus' system share with the Ophite? How is it distinct?

7. Why do you think the Ophite Myth was so attractive to so many Christians?

8. What makes a thinker or a group Gnostic?

9. What is Gnosis? What role does it play in Valentinus' Christianity?

10. Irenaeus portrayed Valentinus' Christology as complicated. Do you think it was? Why or why not?

11. Gnostic Christians have been characterized throughout history by their opponents (and scholars) as Docetists, pessimists, and nihilists. Is this an accurate description of Valentinus? Why or why not?

Resources

David Brakke. 2010. *The Gnostics: Myth, Ritual, and Diversity in Early Christianity*. Cambridge: Harvard University Press.

Christian H. Bull. 2018. *The Tradition of Hermes Trismegistus: The Egyptian Priestly Figure as a Teacher of Hellenized Wisdom*. Leiden: Brill.

April D. DeConick. 2013. "Crafting Gnosis: Gnostic Spirituality in the Ancient New Age." Pages 285–308 in *Gnosticism, Platonism and the Late Antique World: Essays in Honour of John D. Turner*. Edited by Kevin Corrigan and Tuomas Rasimus. Nag Hammadi and Manichaean Studies 82. Leiden: Brill.

April D. DeConick. 2016. *The Gnostic New Age: How a Countercultural Spirituality Revolutionized Religion from Antiquity to Today*. New York: Columbia University Press.

April D. DeConick. 2020a. "Gnosis/Gnosticism." Brill Encyclopedia of Early Christianity Online. https://referenceworks.brillonline.com/entries/brill-encyclopedia-of-early-christianity-online/gnosisgnosticism-SIM_00001439.

April D. DeConick. 2020b. "The One God Is No Simple Matter." Pages 263–292 in *Monotheism and Christology in Greco-Roman Antiquity*. Edited by Matthew Novenson. Supplements to Novum Testamentum 180. Leiden: Brill.

Ismo Dunderberg. 2008. *Beyond Gnosticism: Myth, Lifestyle, and Society in the School of Valentinus*. New York: Columbia University Press.

Karen L. King. 2003. *What Is Gnosticism?* Cambridge: The Belknap Press of Harvard University Press.

Peter Lampe. 2006. *Christians at Rome in the First Two Centuries: From Paul to Valentinus*. Translated by Michael Steinhauser Edited by Marshall D. Johnson. London: T&T Clark International.

Lautaro Roig Lanzillotta. 2019. "Valentinian Protology and the Philosophical Discussion regarding the First Principle." Pages 358–386 in *Intolerance – Polemics – Debate: Cultural Resistance in the Ancient World*. Edited by Jacques van Ruiten and Gerut Henk Van Kooten. Leiden: Brill.

Bentley Layton. 1987, 2022 (revised ed. by). David Brakke). *The Gnostic Scriptures: A New Translation with Annotations and Introductions*. Garden City: Doubleday.

Nicola Denzey Lewis. 2013. *Introduction to "Gnosticism": Ancient Voices, Christian Worlds*. Oxford: Oxford University Press.

M. David Litwa. 2022. Chapters 7, 11, and 12 in *Found Christianities: Remaking the World of the Second Century CE*. London: T&T Clark.

Birger A. Pearson. 2007. *Ancient Gnosticism: Traditions and Literature*. Minneapolis: Fortress Press.

Zlatko Plese. 2006. *Poetics of the Gnostic Universe: Narrative and Cosmology in the Apocryphon of John*. Nag Hammadi and Manichaean Studies 52. Leiden: Brill.

Gilles Quispel. 1996. "The Original Doctrine of Valentinus the Gnostic." *Vigiliae Christianae* 50: 327–352.

Tuomas Rasimus. 2009. *Paradise Reconsidered in Gnostic Mythmaking: Rethinking Sethianism in Light of the Ophite Evidence*. Nag Hammadi and Manichaean Studies 68. Leiden: Brill.

Geoffrey S. Smith. 2020. *Valentinian Christianity: Texts and Translations*. Oakland: University of California Press.

Einar Thomassen. 2006. *The Spiritual Seed: The Church of the 'Valentinians'*. Nag Hammadi and Manichaean Studies 60. Leiden: Brill.

Pieter Willem van der Horst. 2010. "Philo and the Problem of God's Emotions." *Études Platoniciennes* 7: 171–178.

Michael A. Williams. 1996. *Rethinking "Gnosticism": An Argument for Dismantling a Dubious Category*. Princeton: Princeton University Press.

CHAPTER 4

The Church of the Martyrs

Grave relief of freeman Publius Aiedius Amphio and his freewoman wife Aiedia Fausta (cp. Hermas and his wife). Augustus gave former slaves many rights including the right to marry Roman citizens and become full members of Roman society. Monument housed in Pergamon Museum, Berlin. **Source:** Marcus Cyron / Wikimedia Commons / CC BY-SA 3.0.

"Allow me to become food for the wild beasts, so that I may attain to God. I am the wheat of God. Let me be ground by the teeth of the wild beasts, that I may be found the pure bread of Christ. Cajole the wild beasts, that they may become my tomb, and may leave nothing of my body!"

Ignatius of Antioch wrote this in a letter to a Roman congregation as he was being taken by Roman soldiers to Rome for execution

CHAPTER OUTLINE

KEY PLAYERS
Hermas
Ignatius of Antioch
Polycarp of Smyrna

KEY TEXTS
Shepherd of Hermas
Letters of Ignatius
Polycarp, *Philippians*
Martyrdom of Polycarp

What is a Christian supposed to do when denounced to the Roman authorities? Should Christians go ahead and deny Christ to save their lives, or do they have to confess Christ, a confession that almost guaranteed their execution? In this chapter, we meet three third-generation Christians who were denounced: Hermas of Rome, Ignatius of Antioch, and Polycarp of Smyrna. Hermas and Ignatius write about their decisions to deny or confess Christ when denounced and arrested. In the form of nightmarish visions that he had after he was released from prison, Hermas writes about his guilt over denying the Lord and his desire to be accepted back into the fellowship of his church. In a series of letters to Christian churches in Asia Minor and Rome, Ignatius writes about his harrowing decision to embrace death as he was being taken to Rome for execution. Polycarp's story comes to us in a third-person narrative describing his martyrdom.

Stories of the Roman persecution of Christians loom larger than life in our cultural memory. We may think about Nero crucifying Christians and setting them ablaze as torches in his garden at night because he blamed them for starting the fire that devastated Rome in 64 CE (Tac., *Ann.* 15.44). We might see in our mind's eye images of hundreds of Christians rounded up and thrown to the lions or gladiators in the Roman Colosseum, their gruesome deaths entertainment for blood thirsty Roman audiences. We might think that Christians were forced to live in secret to avoid the constant threat of persecution. We might imagine that the persecution of Christians was a systematic and extensive Roman policy that resulted in thousands of Christians dying. This is certainly how Hollywood portrays it in famous films like *The Robe* and *Ben Hur*.

While it is true that Christians were subject to persecution, they were not constantly hunted down and dragged before Roman authorities. Persecutions were sporadic and localized, akin to what Pliny's letter to Trajan reported, which we learned about in Chapter 2. Historians even think Eusebius' claim that the emperor Domitian (83–96 CE) ordered a major persecution of Christians is fake news. In fact, Eusebius' story about Domitian's persecution seems to be mixed up with a report about Domitian's attempt to replenish his depleted coffers. To increase his cash flow, he began enforcing a law mandated by his father Vespasian (69–79 CE) that ordered Jews to pay a tax on the Temple as war reparations. As his officials worked to enforce the law, they discovered that there was another group that worshipped the same God. They worried that these folks might be evading the tax.

According to Eusebius (*Eccl. Hist.* 3.20.1–7), the Roman officials learned about a family that claimed to be the grandchildren of Jesus' biological brother, Judas (not Iscariot). They called themselves descendants of David. When they were interviewed, Jesus' relatives told the officials that they were waiting for Christ's Kingdom to come at the end of the world. His relatives believed that Jesus would come in glory to judge everyone including the dead. They assured the officials that the Kingdom they awaited was not a competitor of Rome but a heavenly angelic kingdom. The officials seemed not to care about their religious chatter at all, but instead pressed them hard about their properties and monetary assets. Once the officials learned that they were peasants with very little property and that their taxes were paid up, they were released. Eusebius uses this story to mark the end of Domitian's persecution, but it is clear that he has made Domitian's attempt to enforce the Jewish tax law into an official Roman persecution against Christians that never happened.

"Of the family of the Lord there were still living the grandchildren of Judas [not Iscariot] who is said to have been the Lord's brother according to the flesh. Information was given that they belonged to the family of David, and they were brought to the Emperor Domitian by the Evocatus. For Domitian feared the coming of Christ as Herod also had feared it. And he asked them if they were descendants of David, and they confessed that they were. Then he asked them how much property they had, or how much money they owned. And both of them answered that they had only nine thousand denarii, half of which belonged to each of them. And this property did not consist of silver, but of a piece of land which contained only thirty-nine acres, and from which they raised their taxes and supported themselves by their own labor. Then they showed their hands, exhibiting the hardness of their bodies and the callousness produced upon their hands by continuous toil as evidence of their own labor. And when they were asked concerning Christ and his kingdom, of what sort it was and where and when it was to appear, they answered that it was not a temporal nor an earthly kingdom, but a heavenly and angelic one, which would appear at the end of the world, when he should come in glory to judge the quick and the dead, and to give to everyone according to his works. Upon hearing this, Domitian did not pass judgment against them, but, despising them as of no account, he let them go..."

Eusebius quotes here Hegesippus in Eccl. Hist. 3.20

Even though early Christian persecutions were not as Hollywood portrays them in films, it is important to remember that Christianity was not a legal religion in Rome until 313 CE when emperor Constantine signed the Edict of Milan. The illegality of Christianity did not have to do with the religion itself, which Romans seemed to perceive as a suspicious foolish sect of Judaism. While Romans more or less tolerated Judaism as an ancient and ancestral religion associated with a conquered nation of people, Christianity fell off this radar because it was considered a novel newly-emergent Jewish sect primarily made up of Gentiles, not ethnic Jews. Worse yet, they worshipped a Jewish criminal whom Rome had executed for insurrection. If this were not enough, Christians also refused to worship the state Gods and the emperor, making them traitors to Rome just like their executed leader, Jesus. It also made them atheists in eyes of the Romans.

Romans believed that Christian obstinacy put the larger populace in jeopardy because it was the worship of the civic deities (i.e. Athena, Zeus, etc.) that guaranteed the protection and prosperity of the people. As long as the patron Gods were properly worshipped and cared for, the cities would be spared the anger of the Gods and, along with it, plague, famine, and war. This meant that any perceived downturn or disaster (natural or otherwise) could be blamed on Christian obstinacy and result in their denunciation and execution. Life as an early Christian came with the knowledge of Christianity's illegality and the risk that denunciation was possible. Whether to deny or confess was a traumatic possibility that every Christian had to contemplate.

4.1 A Freed Slave

COMPANION READINGS
Hermas, *Vision* 2.2–3

Hermas was born a slave somewhere outside of Rome. As a young man he was sold to Rhoda, a woman who lived in Rome (Herm., *Vis.* 1.1). He was a skilled and educated slave, who likely managed business ventures for Rhoda. At some point in his life, Hermas gains his freedom so that by the time he writes and publishes the *Visions*, the *Commandments*, and the *Similitudes*, he is not only a freedman, but also a property owner, entrepreneur, family man, and likely a Roman citizen.

Hermas is also a devout Christian whose fasting and constant penitential prayers elicit prophetic visions involving two main angels. The Lady (who is sometimes a virgin, sometimes an elderly woman) is an angel who represents the Church. The Shepherd (not Jesus) is an angel who is Hermas' guardian and disciplinarian. For this reason, the collection of Hermas' writings is known as *The Shepherd of Hermas*. Later Christians recount that Pius, the bishop of Rome (140–55 CE), was Hermas' brother (*Mur. Canon*, lines 73–80). Because Hermas' writings gained great respect among the later Christians and came to be considered by some as canonical, this connection to Pius is likely a legend meant to boost the credibility of a less-than-famous-but-popular layperson's writings.

The only detail in Hermas' writing that helps us date his works is the fact that Hermas locates the authority for all church matters with the presbytery, a committee of elders, rather than the bishop who, he says, is the patron for the community's gathering and the caretaker of the widows and poor (Herm., *Vis.* 3.5; *Sim.* 9.27). Since this leadership structure is found in churches before the mid-second century, this means that Hermas is writing in Rome just before Marcion and Valentinus arrive in Rome.

In his writings, Hermas tells us many autobiographical details about his life. He owns a house and a field located a mile off the Via Campana, a highway snaking along the bank of the Tiber from the Porta Portuenis, a city gate, to the Campus Salinarum (Herm., *Vis.* 4.1). He farmed the acreage with barley or spelt, a crop that was cooked into porridge to feed the poor. At an earlier point in his career, Hermas was a wealthy businessman with a diverse portfolio and many connections. While he does not relate what these businesses were, his writing shows that he is knowledgeable about metalsmithing, clothmaking, and the storage of oil and wine. Hermas is married and has children. He explicitly mentions sons.

Hermas, however, has personal problems. He no longer owns multiple businesses. He appears to have lost them as a result of imprisonment (he was involuntarily kept away from his home and businesses for a lengthy period). When he is finally allowed to return home, he is plagued by nightmarish visions brought on by a massive sense of guilt and self-loathing. Hermas worries that he has committed an unforgivable sin, leaving him cast out of God's Kingdom and no longer welcome in his church.

To make matters worse, Hermas' problems appear to have stemmed from his sons who, he says, betrayed him and his wife. They betrayed their parents for money, but, in the end, did not profit from it as they had anticipated (Herm., *Vis.* 2.2). Hermas admits that he had been so busy with his businesses, he had neglected his sons and had not noticed that something was amiss until it was too late. Hermas speaks repeatedly of experiencing suffering and afflictions because of their betrayal, (probably) jail time, and loss of his businesses and wealth, with the exception of his farm.

4.2 A Troubled Man

COMPANION READINGS

Hermas, *Similitudes* 6.2–3; 8.6
Hermas, *Vision* 3.1–2, 10; 4.1–2
Hermas, *Commandment* 3; 4.3

Although Hermas avoids talking about his affliction or jail time openly, it is clear from his nightmares and penitential prayers that Hermas' sons denounced him as a Christian to profit themselves. When imprisoned and questioned by the authorities, Hermas denied Christ because he was both terrified of dying and wanted to save his businesses. In his writings, Hermas is obsessed with the question of what happens to Christians who deny the Lord when denounced. He returns to this sin repeatedly (Herm., *Sim.* 6.2; 8.6, 8, 19, 26, 28).

He is gravely concerned about this issue because, in his church, those who deny the Lord are considered traitors or apostates who have committed an unforgivable sin. They are no longer welcome in his church and are not allowed into God's Kingdom in the afterlife (Herm., *Sim.* 8.6). In his church, Christians are baptized once, and this baptism is thought to erase only the baptizand's sinful past. Any sins committed after baptism could not be washed away again. Christians in his church took seriously their lifestyle choices and demanded vigilance when it came to following God's commandments. Some sins might be able to be atoned through severe penance and suffering, but the sin of denial of the Lord was not one of them. It was unforgivable (Herms., *Com.* 4.3; *Sim.* 8.16).

Hermas has many questions about the status of deniers like himself. He tells us about his frequent (almost constant) prayers and confessions privately in his home. He petitions God for revelations which will answer his questions (Herm., *Vis.* 3.10). As the result of his prayers, he receives often terrifying revelations from the Lady and the Shepherd (Herm., *Vis.* 5). Hermas is told by the Shepherd that those who deny the Lord are the worst kind of thieves because they rob God. Hearing this, Hermas weeps bitterly because he now is certain that he cannot be saved (Herms., *Com.* 3). He is also told by the Lady that, because of his sins, he cannot sit on God's right in his Kingdom even though Hermas wants to be able to do this. The Lady explains to him that he will not be allowed to join the martyrs who suffered for the Lord, endured whippings and prison time, and died by crucifixion or mauling. Hermas, who did not suffer for the Lord, cannot expect to be seated with the saints (Herm., *Vis.* 3.1–2).

The gravity of his plight and his pain are visceral as he learns that the Shepherd, his guardian angel, was sent to him not as a spirit who is supposed to protect him, but as a frightening angel of punishment sent to help Hermas deal with his sins. Instead of showing compassion and saving sinners from suffering, the Shepherd ferments their suffering, beats them, and makes them miserable. He makes their business ventures go foul, sends illnesses, and other forms of grief until they are made ready for training to be subjects of the Lord for the rest of their lives. Their suffering is lifted only as they obey the Lord's commandments (Herm., *Sim.* 6.2–3; 10.1). Hermas understands everything he has endured – his loss of his businesses and wealth, his imprisonment, his family strife and betrayal – to be the direct result of the Shepherd's incense over Hermas' nonchalant attitude toward God's commandments, distracted as he was by the success of his businesses and other worldly concerns (Herm., *Sim.* 7; *Com.* 10.1). The evils of business and its distractions are a constant refrain in Hermas' writings (Herm., *Sim.* 4; 6.2; 8.8). But this is not the half of it. On top of these sins, Hermas has now added the sin of denial, which makes him an apostate or traitor.

Under these conditions, Hermas has no hope. The doors of his church and heaven are closed to him. But Hermas is, if nothing else, persistent. Hermas becomes a rigorous penitent, constantly confessing his sins to God in prayer and grieving over his sinful obsession with his businesses, an obsession that had led him down the path of unrighteousness (Herm., *Com.* 10.1). Hermas begins to faithfully observe what he calls the "commandments of God." He knows that his membership in the church is conditional on whether he follows God's commandments. He has been taught that whoever keeps all of God's commandments will live with God in his Kingdom (Herm., *Com.* 12.6). He has learned that God is punitive, requiring members of the church to follow his rules or face his wrath and discipline. Hermas also knows that observing God's law can be therapeutic, a cure for previous sins (Herm., *Sim.* 10.2). Even though denial of the Lord is unforgivable, Hermas turns his attention to keeping God's commandments with rigor on the slight chance that something might open up for him if he throws himself on God's mercy enough times.

He decides to show the sincerity of his repentance and commitment to the church by turning his attention openly to the needy. He treats his remaining wealth as a sacred allowance to be used to help those in need (Herm., *Sim.* 1, 2). He does not wait around for the poor to come to him. Instead, he seeks out the hungry to feed them (Herm., *Vis.* 3.9). He uses the produce from his farm to feed widows, orphans, and others in need. He fasts regularly and gives the money he saved by not eating to the poor (Herm., *Sim.* 5.1, 3). When he is not fasting, he eats lightly so that he can share his table as well (Herm., *Vis.* 3.9). His actions are those of a wealthy benefactor who came to understand that his wealth was trusted to him from the Lord (Herm., *Sim.* 2).

One day while repenting as he walked on the road home, Hermas gets a second chance to face the execution he avoided the first time when he denied the Lord. He is seized by a terrifying vision in which he is about to be mauled by a wild beast. This is a form of death used by the Romans to execute Christians, so it is not surprising that this image appears in his second-chance vision. From the horizon, a horrible beast swarms down upon him like a mass of fiery locusts. Terrified, he weeps for the Lord to rescue him. He tamps down his doubts and is able to turn to boldly face the beast. Just as the beast opens his mouth to maul him, Hermas races passed him without so much as a scratch. As he runs down the road, the Lady is standing on the sidelines waiting for him. She praises him for his endurance and faith. She tells Hermas that because he maintained his faith, an angel came down from heaven and shut the jaws of the beast so that it could not tear Hermas to pieces. Hermas is promised to be able to escape any future tribulations if he repents and serves the Lord for the rest of his life (Herm., *Vis.*4.2). While this vision says a great deal about Hermas' state of mind and his anxieties, it also reflects what must have been Christian teaching that, if their faith in the Lord and commitment to the commandments are strong enough, the Lord would rescue them in the arena from any gruesome execution they might have to face.

Hermas becomes convinced that his denial of the Lord, while bad, is not the unforgivable sin that his church says it is. Hermas suggests that a distinction ought to be made between apostates who do not repent and those who do (Herm., *Sim.* 8.6). The former are unforgivable, the latter forgivable. In vision after vision, he discovers from the Lady and the Shepherd that because God is gracious and merciful, God forgives even apostates like himself who repent (Herm., *Vis.* 2.2; *Sim.*9.19, 21). He is certain that when God sees that their repentance is sincere and no further sin is committed, God will order their former sins erased and allow them to sit on his left hand in his Kingdom (Herm., *Sim.* 9.33). He argues in his writing that repentant deniers like himself should be welcomed back into the church (Herm., *Vis.* 3.1–2; 12). To give more weight to his writings, he claims that his book is an actual transcription of the heavenly book shown to him by the Lady in his vision (which she herself was reading when he met her) (Herm., *Vis.* 2.1, 4)

Hermas thinks that a further distinction ought to be made between Christians who denied the Lord in their hearts and those who denied the Lord but did not mean it in their hearts but did it for some other reason, such as saving their businesses. The former are unforgivable, the latter forgivable. Likewise, Hermas distinguishes between those Christians who deny the Lord in the moment and those Christians who plan ahead to deny the Lord and repent later. He cautions that those who plan this tactic may not be allowed into God's Kingdom (Herm., *Sim.* 9.26, 28).

4.3 God the Creator

COMPANION READINGS
Hermas, *Vision* 1.3
Hermas, *Commandment* 1
Deuteronomy 6:1–25

Hermas clearly identifies the God whom he worships with the Biblical Creator of the heaven and the earth, not a transcendent deity (as we saw with Valentinus) or an alien deity (as we saw with Marcion). Hermas' God lives in the heavens, not beyond them. He created the universe for the sole purpose of building the Christian Church (Herm., *Vis.* 1.1, 3). He describes God as invisible, creating the world using his great powers, wisdom, and providence. His fated plan includes the construction of the Church and the blessing and salvation of his Elect (Herm., *Vis.* 1.3). Hermas considers the Church (pictured as the Lady angel) to be the first of God's creations (Herm., *Vis.* 2.4), but also his Spirit and his Son (Herm., *Sim.* 8.12).

The *Commandments* open with a statement that likely represents an early creed taught by his church: "First, believe that there is one God who created and finished all things, and made all things out of nothing. He alone is able to contain the whole, but himself cannot be contained. Have faith in him, and fear him. Fearing him, exercise self-control. Keep these commandments and you will cast away from you all wickedness, and put on the strength of righteousness, and live to God, if you keep this commandment" (Herm., *Com.* 1).

This first commandment is a Christian variation of the first of the Jewish Ten Commandments prayed in synagogues as the Shema: "Hear O Israel, the Lord (YHWH) is our God, the Lord (YHWH) is one (or: alone)." It comes from a passage in Deuteronomy (Deut. 6:1–25) where the faithful are charged with fearing the Lord and keeping all of God's commandments diligently every day of their lives in order to receive God's promises of progeny, property, and prosperity rather than God's discipline and punishment. Instead of identifying God in terms of Jewish ancestors (e.g. God of Abraham, Isaac, and Jacob), however, Hermas recasts the Jewish national God as a universal God, emphasizing that he is the Creator of the universe. Like the jealous and angry Lord depicted in the Deuteronomy, Hermas' God has emotions, directing his anger and punishments against Christians who have sinned against him (e.g. Herm., *Vis.* 1.1, 3). The inclusion of non-Jews in the worship of YHWH is highlighted in Hermas who understands that the twelve tribes of Israel represent the twelve nations of the world who have been called to believe in the Name of the Son of God (Herm., *Sim.* 8.18).

Hermas thinks about the relationship between God and humans largely in legal terms. He learned this legal model from his church. This model reflects a reinterpretation of the Jewish Law, particularly the Ten Commandments, as Hermas' church applied them to their community. The general idea is that God gave particular commandments to his people and he expects them to be observed. When they are not kept, God disciplines and punishes the sinner. When they are kept, God gifts the faithful with good things, including life eternal. Hermas does not envision earth as a happy place even for the faithful. The world is a bitter dark place, purged by fire and blood. The faithful are those who have been turned into gold because they have been smelted in the fire (Herm., *Vis.* 4.3).

In the *Commandments*, Hermas lays out twelve moral imperatives that he believes God's Son received from God, his Father, which he gave to people as a purgative for their sins (Herm., *Sim.*3.6). Hermas' commandments can be laid out comparatively with the Ten Commandments found in Jewish scripture (Figure 4.1). The similarities are modest, the differences noteworthy because they reflect Hermas' moral concerns.

Hermas promotes a particular understanding of the nature of sin. Hermas thinks that sin starts because people have opposing angels on each shoulder, so to speak. The angel of iniquity whispers in one ear and the angel of righteousness in the other. People are sinful when they listen to the angel of iniquity and act on his advice. Consequently, people are not only responsible for sins they commit, but also responsible for their righteousness, which Hermas defines as a state of not sinning. So Hermas' emphasis on twelve moral imperatives reads like a guide to help people manage the evil angel on their shoulder, to avoid unintentional sin, and to stop sin before it starts by steering clear of things like wealth and luxury that might lead to sin. We might think of Hermas' moral imperatives as an early Christian Twelve-Step Program of Recovery from Sin (Figure 4.2).

Sins that Hermas considers most problematic are those which might be committed unintentionally because their definitions are hazy. To avoid accidental adultery, Hermas spends time defining

10 Commandments In Jewish Scriptures		12 Commandments For Christians
You shall worship no other Gods but the Lord (the God of Abraham, Isaac, and Jacob)	=	You shall have faith in the one God (the creator of earth and heaven)
You shall not commit adultery	=	You shall not commit adultery
You shall not lie	=	You shall not lie
You shall not covet You shall honor your parents You shall keep the Sabbath holy You shall make no idol or image of God You shall not swear by the name of God You shall not kill You shall not steal	≠	You shall not get angry You shall practice charity You shall not listen to the angel of iniquity You shall fear the Lord You shall practice restraint from doing evil You shall not doubt You shall not grieve over your sins You shall not listen to false prophecy You shall not desire to do evil

What Is Similar? What Is Different?

FIGURE 4.1   Illustration showing how Hermas' Twelve Commandments compare to the Ten Commandments found in Jewish scripture.

Hermas' 12-step Recovery Program

STEP 1	Believe in God, the Biblical Creator, and make him the sole God of worship
STEP 2	Fear the Lord's punishment more than the Devil
STEP 3	Learn to distinguish between true and false prophecy so you are not led astray
STEP 4	Know the parameters of lying so that you do not lie unintentionally
STEP 5	Know the parameters of adultery so that you do not commit adultery unintentionally
STEP 6	Get your thoughts under control by refusing to listen to the angel of iniquity
STEP 7	Eradicate the desire that motivates you to do evil
STEP 8	Eradicate emotions like anger that lead you to sin
STEP 9	Control the opportunity for sin by living a life of simplicity, self-restraint, & self-discipline
STEP 10	Stop dwelling on past sins and grieving about them; be cheerful in your salvation
STEP 11	Devote your income to charity, as absolution for sin and also as a deterrent to future sin
STEP 12	When all else fails and doubt arises, turn to the Lord in prayer

FIGURE 4.2   Hermas coordinated his program of repentance with his understanding of God's commandments.

adultery. We learn that, with the exception of those widowed, second marriages among divorcees are considered adulterous and ought to be shunned. Similarly, lying is a major sin that goes beyond fake news and gossip to include dishonest business deals and denying the Lord when denounced.

Hermas believes that these twelve commandments were given by God to his Son who, in turn, gave them to help people purge their sins. He thinks that God's Son purged people from their sins by suffering many trials and giving them the Law (e.g. the twelve commandments) he had received from his Father (Herm., *Sim.*3.6). He identifies the Son of God with the angel Michael, the authority over all people everywhere, who is the Lawgiver and its superintendent (Herm., *Sim.* 8.3, 12). He imagines the Law preached by the Son of God as a tree whose unrepentant branches will be lopped off (Herm., *Sim.*8.3; Rom 11:18). The Son of God is also the gate into the Kingdom of God (Herm., *Sim.* 8.12). No one can enter the Kingdom except through the Son (Herm., *Sim.* 8.12; cf. John 14:6).

How did God's Son come to earth? Hermas uses an ADULT POSSESSION PATTERN of Christology: that a divine entity possesses Jesus' body. According to Hermas, in order that the Holy Spirit would not be defiled, God chose to put the Holy Spirit into the very righteous and chaste body of Jesus. In this way, the man Jesus partnered with the Holy Spirit and was able to consult with God's Son and the angels. Hermas appears to have held some distinction between Jesus and the Son whose spirit possessed him. This may be why Hermas never mentions Jesus by name or uses the messianic title Christ, but rather only refers to God's Son when speaking of the Lord. Jesus is the exemplar of purity and obedience for Christians who also are indwelt with the Holy Spirit at their baptisms. If they defile their bodies, they injure the Holy Spirit. Hermas is told to keep both body and spirit pure in order to be saved and live with God (Herm., *Sim.* 5.6–7). Hermas considers "imperishable" all flesh that has been kept pure. This suggests an afterlife populated with imperishable bodies (rather than disembodied souls) that ascend to live in God's Kingdom (Herm., *Sim.* 8.18).

Hermas boils down the Christian faith to twelve commandments which must be kept in order to be saved by God or as Hermas says, "live with God." Hermas is not a Minimalist like Marcion. When it comes to the Law, Hermas is a Moderate, believing that faithfulness is dependent upon observing particular moral behaviors and expressing particular attitudes that God's Son taught were at the heart of the Law. Hermas envisions his Christian identity as a kind of green card or visa that allows him to reside in a special city. Like other cities, this city has particular laws that have to be obeyed. Whoever does not obey the laws is thrown out. The rule of the mayor (i.e. God) is simple: "Either obey my laws or get out" (Herm., *Sim.* 1).

4.4 Hermas Goes to Church

COMPANION READINGS
Hermas, *Vision* 3.2–4
Hermas, *Similitudes* 9.18

Hermas sees the Church in his prophetic visions not only as the Lady, but also as a tower whose construction started before anything else was created and continues to be built in the present (Herm., *Vis.* 3.2). The Church is pre-existent. It is founded on the Name of God and held together by the invisible Power of the Lord (Herm., *Vis.* 3.3). The construction workers are six archangels, the first creations of God after the Church. They manage and rule over the rest of God's estate, the world at large, with the help of numerous subordinate angels including the virtues of God (Herm., *Vis.* 3.4).

In one vision, the virtues are seven: the mother Faith, and her daughters, Self-restraint, Simplicity, Guilelessness, Chastity, Intelligence, and Love (Herm., *Vis.* 3.8). In another vision, they are twelve: Faith, Continence, Power, Patience, Simplicity, Innocence, Purity, Cheerfulness, Truth, Understanding, Harmony, and Love (Herm., *Sim.*8.15). Subsequent to their creation is a second generation of twenty-five "righteous men," a third generation of thirty-five prophets, and a fourth generation of forty apostles (Herm., *Sim.* 8.15).

Hermas considers the apostles to be superstars of his church, people who earned the right to walk with the angels because they taught the word of the Lord purely and lived righteously (Herm., *Sim.* 8.25). According to Hermas, bishops were primarily responsible for holding services in their homes, extending their hospitality to the congregants, and protecting everyone in their group, especially serving the widows and those in need of charity (Herm., *Sim.* 8.27).

The tower is built of stones that represent different people whom Hermas calls the Elect. These include apostles, bishops, teachers, deacons, martyrs, the newly baptized, and everyone else who have walked the straight and narrow, unwaveringly following God's commandments. But cast aside are the sinners, unless they repent (Herm., *Vis.* 3.5). Here Hermas presents the Church as sanctimonious: a "pure" body of individuals who all must be obediently following God's commandments or purged of their sins. Unrepentant sinners are separated out because they are deemed impure. For Hermas, God is defined by his purity. Hermas thinks that the Church distills the pure from the impure, enabling the pure and purified to ascend and live with God in his realm (Herm., *Sim.* 9.18).

To bolster the idea of the sanctimony of the Church, Hermas says that the apostles, bishops, teachers, and deacons have always been in agreement with each other. Hermas claims that there is no dissent in the churches he identifies with his own, but the bishops, teachers, and deacons all solidly represent what the apostles taught. He knows the idea from Paul's letters that the Church is one body, one mind, one understanding, one faith, and one love (Herm., *Sim.* 9.18). With this claim, Hermas positions his church as part of a collective of churches run by presbyteries with bishops and deacons, churches which claim to be the authentic heir to the teachings of the apostles, against other Christians who develop other Christian movements distinct from Hermas' church and its authoritative claims.

Significantly, Hermas also challenges the apostolic legitimacy of his church's teachings with claims to have his own prophetic revelations from the Lady and the Shepherd. He thinks that his angelic revelations have the power to authorize change in long-standing policies of his church. In other words, he hopes that when the leaders of his church hear about his direct conversations with God's primary angels, they will be influenced to change some of the church's traditional teachings.

In particular, Hermas hopes to change the current practices in his church that do not allow for baptized Christians remission of sins committed after baptism. Given Hermas' own life story, the sin that most concerns him is denial of the Lord, which, in his church is considered an unforgivable sin that cannot be alleviated even through severe repentance and practices of austerity. Even though some Christians say that there is no other repentance beyond what took place at their baptism, Hermas claims that he learns in his visions that one repentance is allowed by God after baptism. Sinners are forgiven as long as they stop sinning (Herms., *Com.* 4.2–3; *Sim.* 8.16). This one-off repentance and forgiveness is most remarkable because, Hermas says, it covers the sin of denying the Lord.

Hermas says that he learned about this new rule from the Lady who told Hermas that he is like a round stone that had been cast aside because it did not fit squarely in the build. These stones, she explains, are the faithful rich who deny the Lord when faced with tribulation in order to save their wealth and businesses. The only way to recover these stones and build them back into the tower is to cut the stone into a square, which means, that their wealth must be cut down (Herm., *Vis.* 3.6). This is the way that Hermas rationalizes the loss of his wealth and businesses following his denial. He also thinks that he was made to suffer and lose his fortune in order to exonerate his sinful children, bring his family to repentance, and enroll them in the Book of the Living among God's holy people (Herm., *Vis.* 1.3).

Hermas claims to be commissioned by the Lady and the Shepherd to write down his prophetic revelations, including transcribing a heavenly book that the Lady was reading and showed him in one of his visions. This material includes the twelve commandments and the new rule about the forgiveness of deniers. He is told to report them verbally to God's Elect and the presbyters of the church (Herm., *Vis.* 2.1; 2.4; 5; *Com.* 12.3; *Sim.* 10.2). He is told to tell those who preside over his church about what he has learned from the angels in order to cleanse them (along with himself) from sins they have committed (Herm., *Vis.* 2.2; 3.8). He is told to share the Lord's commandments with his church and exhort the parishioners to repent and observe these commandments for the rest of their lives even though this is very hard to do (Herm., *Com.* 12.3). He presents this as urgent, something that needs to happen immediately before the construction of the tower is completed and unrepentant sinners are excluded (Herm., *Sim.* 10.4). In particular, Hermas is supposed to tell Maximus that it was okay that he denied the Lord during tribulation because the Lord will be near to those who return to him (Herm., *Vis.* 2.3). He specifically names Clemens and Grapte (a woman) as Christians who assist with the publication and distribution of his books (Herm., *Vis.* 2.4). His books became so popular that they were considered by some later Christians to be scripture, read alongside the Jewish scriptures, the letters of Paul, and the Gospels. The author of the Muratorian fragment (the first full list of Apostolic Catholic scriptures; ca. 200 CE) takes it upon himself to tell Christians that they cannot read Hermas' books publicly in church assemblies. And yet Hermas' writings are found in the Codex Sinaiticus, the earliest manuscript copy of the Christian Bible (ca. 350 CE).

4.5 The Rise of the Bishop

COMPANION READINGS
Pastoral Letters (1 and 2 Timothy, Titus)
Ignatius, *Polycarp*; *Ephesians*; *Magnesians*; *Philadelphians*; *Trallians*; *Smyrnaeans*
Polycarp, *Philippians*

Ignatius is remembered as the second bishop of Antioch, most likely following Euodius (Eus., *Hist.* 3.22.1). Since antiquity, at least thirteen letters, some in expanded versions, have circulated under Ignatius' name. Scholars have long debated the authenticity or pseudonymity of these letters. The consensus of modern scholarship and the printed editions of Ignatius' letters is that seven letters of a particular version known as the Middle Recension represent the earliest recoverable stage of Ignatius' writings. These are his letters to the Ephesians, Magnesians, Trallians, Romans, Philadelphians, Smyrnaeans, and Polycarp (for locations, see Figure 4.3).

Ignatius was denounced as a Christian, arrested, found guilty, and transported to Rome for execution. During his transport, Ignatius wrote a series of letters to various church communities in Asia Minor and Rome. Traditionally, his letters have been dated to 110 CE because Eusebius

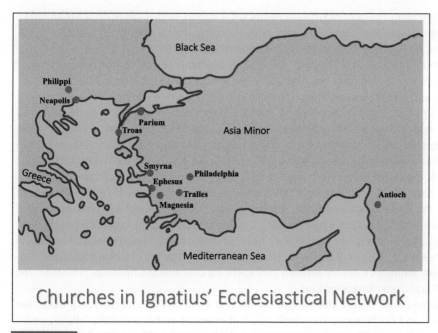

Churches in Ignatius' Ecclesiastical Network

FIGURE 4.3 Locations of the Asian and Hellenic churches mentioned in Ignatius' letters.

associates him with the persecution of Christians during the reign of Trajan as mentioned in Pliny's letter, which we learned about in Chapter 2. Eusebius is mistaken on this point because the persecution conducted by Pliny was local to Bithynia in northernmost Asia Minor and nowhere in the vicinity of Antioch. This early date has come under increasing scrutiny in scholarship because the description in Ignatius' letters of the leadership model of the churches in Asia Minor is not characteristic of turn-of-the-century texts, but mid-second century texts when bishops began usurping authority over the boards of presbyters.

What helps us place Ignatius historically is the fact that he and Polycarp, the bishop of Smyrna, personally knew each other. In fact, Ignatius wrote a letter to Polycarp, advising him how to do his job as bishop of Smyrna, maintain his position, and create unity in his church. Ignatius also asks Polycarp to ensure that a new bishop of Antioch is elected to take Ignatius' place once Ignatius is executed. He tells Polycarp to set up a committee to review the candidates and to elect someone Polycarp believes to be a very committed and active Christian whom he knows well and loves (Ign., *Poly.* 7). Ignatius also asks Polycarp to write to the churches that Ignatius was unable to contact because he was being shipped out to Rome suddenly (Ign., *Poly.* 8).

Polycarp's own follow-up correspondence to the church in Philippi mentions that he received Ignatius' letter. The Philippian church had heard about Ignatius' plight and had already written to Polycarp asking questions and requesting any correspondence Polycarp had from Ignatius. Polycarp sent them all the letters he had from Ignatius in addition to Polycarp's own letter to them (Ign., *Eph.* 21; Poly., *Phil.* 13). At the time Polycarp writes, he likens Ignatius' plight to other local martyrs like Zosimus, Rufus, and Paul (Poly., *Phil.* 9). Yet, Polycarp does not know what has actually happened to Ignatius. Polycarp asks the Philippians to forward any information they may have about Ignatius and the others who were denounced alongside him (Poly., *Phil.* 13).

We can date some of Polycarp's activities and his own martyrdom. He was reportedly colleagues with Papias (Iren., *Haer.* 5.33.4) and made a trip to Rome to discuss with Anicetus, the bishop of Rome (ca. 155–167 CE), when Easter should be celebrated (Iren., *Haer.* 3.3.4). Polycarp also got into a debate with Marcion (probably in Rome as Irenaeus suggests), whom he accused of being the "first-born of Satan" (Iren., *Haer.* 3.3.4). Various ancient writers offer different opinions on the year of his death, leaving us with a range from 155–177 CE (most scholars favor earlier in this range rather than later). All this is to say that Ignatius was a contemporary with Polycarp, Papias, Marcion, and other third-generation Christians. He was operating in the mid-second century.

When the letters of Ignatius and Polycarp are read in tandem, we can reconstruct with some accuracy what Christianity looked like, especially in Asia Minor, in the mid-second century. Their knowledge of Christian texts is limited. They appear to have a collection of the letters of Paul that include the Pastoral Epistles (1 and 2 Timothy and Titus). Scholars debate who wrote these texts, and when and why they were composed and published in Paul's name. Since these texts were not in the *Apostolicon* that Marcion had nor were they quoted by second-generation Christian authors or Valentinus, it appears that they were composed by a third-generation Christian in the Apostolic Catholic ecclesiastical network. Given the letters' anti-Marcionite sentiments (e.g. creation is good; encratism is bad), many scholars have concluded that one of the purposes of these letters was to battle Marcionism by trying to control the interpretation of Paul's ten letters circulating in Marcion's New Testament. These three additional letters give Paul a new identity as a heresy-hunter, a full supporter of the Law and its legitimate use, and an exemplar of the saved sinner. In these letters, Paul reminds Christians to submit to their bishops since he himself had authorized them. He enjoins the elders to install and control Christian prophets. Women's roles are severely restricted. He commands Christians to worship the Biblical Creator God as the only Sovereign God.

Ignatius only quotes from 1 Corinthians, Ephesians, and 1 and 2 Timothy. Polycarp made use of Romans, Galatians, and Philippians, 1 Corinthians, Ephesians, 1 and 2 Timothy, 1 Peter, and 1 John. He also appears to know 1 Clement, a letter more fully discussed in Chapter 9 of this textbook. In terms of Gospels, they both seem to know information found in the Gospel of Matthew (e.g. Ign., *Smyr.* 1.1; *Poly.* 2.2.). There may be echoes from the Gospel of John in Ignatius' letter to the Romans when he talks about Jesus' body as "flesh" and "living water" (Ign., *Rom.* 7), but this is uncertain because these concepts may have derived instead from eucharistic practice. The use of the word gospel, in fact, is never applied to a written text by either author, but is used to designate the events of salvation when Christ came in the flesh.

Ignatius and Polycarp are part of a network of like-minded churches in Asia Minor. The churches in this network were keeping up with each other by sharing letters that various church leaders wrote to each other and to the local congregations. This network of churches was in the process of installing a new leadership model characterized by the primacy and authority of elected bishops over the more traditional body of presbyters (elders) with bishops as their patrons (as Hermas had mentioned in his writings) (Ign., *Philad.* 10). The names of other bishops are known from Ignatius' greetings: Onesimus of Ephesus, Damas of Magnesia, and Polybius of Tralles.

This process was started by some of the bishops in these local churches who began to consolidate their churches in order to govern them as authoritative leaders over their presbyteries. From the correspondences of Ignatius and Polycarp, it is clear that this change in the leadership model was meant to deal a blow to Christian pluralism and construct a singular discrete Christian identity at the expense of other Christian identities (e.g. Ign., *Trall.* 7). Both bishops were aware of a number of other Christians who promoted competing views about what it meant to be Christian, who Jesus was, and even what God should be worshipped. Differences of opinions flourished within Asian and west Syrian churches.

Marcion and his followers are particularly targeted, although Ignatius refuses to name him directly (Ign., *Smy.* 5) and Polycarp nicknames him "Satan" and the "anti-Christ" (Poly., *Phil.* 7). But it is Marcionite teaching that they both refute, especially despising Marcion's docetic teaching that Jesus was not born and did not have a material body, but descended from the Alien God and manifested as an angel does. In contrast, Ignatius insists that Jesus was the product of both the virgin Mary and the Holy Spirit (which meant to him that Jesus was indwelt by the Holy Spirit when conceived) and that Jesus both lived and died a real life and death (Ign., *Eph.* 7; 18–9; 20; Poly., *Phil.* 7). He promoted a FETAL POSSESSION PATTERN of Christology in contrast to Marcion's VISITATION PATTERN.

Jesus' humanity is important to Ignatius' understanding of the Eucharist, the ritual eating of Jesus' "body" which Ignatius understands in very materialistic terms to be Jesus' "flesh." Ignatius thinks analogically, assuming that only something that is "like" something else can substitute for, atone, and save it. Ignatius believes that the Eucharist can only function as the "medicine of immortality" or the "antidote to dying" if Jesus was a real human being who died like the human beings he saves, whose suffering as a sacrificial substitute compensates for human sin (Ign., *Eph.* 20). Ignatius uses the slogan "Jesus Christ according to the flesh" to indicate this position (Ign., *Mag.* 13) which he says is part of the gospel (Ign., *Philad.* 5). According to Ignatius, Jesus was born a human and baptized not to remit his own sin, but so that his death might purify the water for others (Ign., *Eph.* 18). Ignatius is anxious because not all Christians in Asia Minor and western Syria are performing the Eucharist in the same way. Presumably some are following Marcionite guidelines, performing the Eucharist as a celebration of Jesus' power as a divine being to defeat and ransom human souls from their Creator, a job, Marcionites thought, only a God could handle. Socially, Ignatius advocates for distancing, encouraging those in his church network to distance themselves from anyone who objects to eating the flesh of Christ, to neither speak with them or about them in public or private (Ign., *Smy.* 7).

The other difference of opinion that Ignatius targets has to do with Christianity's identity as a Jewish sectarian movement. Ignatius knows Christians in Asia Minor and western Syria who operate as Maximalists, obeying the Jewish Law and meeting on the Sabbath. He disapproves, arguing that these Christians are unappreciative of God's grace (Ign., *Mag.* 8–9). Those who "confess Christ," he says, are fools to "Judaize," a criticism that is not so far removed from Marcion's belief that the Christian message had been Judaized (Ign., *Mag.* 10). At the same time that Ignatius criticizes them for Judaizing, he appropriates the Jewish prophetic writings and turns their authors into proto-Christians whom he considers "holy" because, he says, they proclaimed the gospel in their prophecies, placed their hope in Jesus Christ, and waited for his advent (Ign., *Philad.* 5; 9).

The construction of a distinct Christian identity under Ignatius' pen has a very dark side: the simultaneous construction of anti-Judaism. As some Christians like Ignatius tried to distinguish their movement from its parent religion, the rhetoric took an Oedipal turn and pommeled Judaism. As Ignatius moves to distinguish Christianity from Judaism, he casts Judaism as not only out-of-date but also "evil," something to be discarded because, he asserts, Christianity did not merge into Judaism, but Judaism into Christianity (Ign., *Mag.* 10). Ignatius argues for the primacy and moral superiority of Christianity, framing Judaism as irrelevant and absurd. This construction of anti-Judaism is not just a matter of words, but becomes structural within the churches as Ignatius and other bishops like him try to purge their churches of Jewish practices. To this end, Ignatius admonishes those observing Jewish practices to accept the name "Christian" (a new name) and live according to Christianity's principles rather than to continue with the "old sour leaven" of Judaism (Ign., *Mag.* 10).

Ignatius and Polycarp judge both Minimalist Marcionites and Maximalist Judaizing Christians to be agents of heresy, by which they mean agents of "wrong" teaching that deviates from their own "right" moderate teaching (e.g. Ign., *Eph.* 6). Their labeling is meant to frame and defame, drawing analogies that would have been easily recognizable. These agents of "heresy" are "wild beasts," that is, they maul to death God's righteous people like the wild animals in the Roman arena. They are associated with "rabid dogs" whose bite has no cure (Ign., *Eph.* 6–7). Heresy is a poisonous herb, a deadly drug that, when mixed with wine (i.e. Jesus Christ), brings death (Ign., *Trall.* 6). This metaphor is meant to stigmatize any Eucharist performed by Marcionite Christians. In a similar passage, Ignatius characterizes the teachers of heresy as "evil offshoots of Satan," producing fruit that kills when tasted (Ign., *Trall.* 11).

While Ignatius admits that the Marcionites identify themselves as "Christians," Ignatius works to deprive them of this identity by asserting that they only seem to be Christian when in fact they are unbelievers whose personal names he will not even mention until they repent and confess the reality of Christ's physical suffering, death, and resurrection. Ignatius uses language invoking the trauma of denunciation and apostasy. When he calls them deniers who do not confess the Lord's physicality, he characterizes them as apostates who deny the Lord when denounced to the Romans (Ign., *Smy.* 2, 5).

The labeling of the "other" Christians as deniers and apostates, as wild and rabid, and their Eucharist as poisonous, does not just denigrate the opinions and practices of other Christians. It establishes as more credible, natural, and right the opinions of those in the churches who are aligned with Ignatius and Polycarp. By logic, Ignatius and Polycarp are neither wild nor rabid, but sensible and sane. Sociologists have shown that labeling the "other" as deviant is a sociological strategy that groups put into play to naturalize, normalize, and empower their own group over the "others." It is a form of social control that is not so much the product of one individual as it is the product of powerful social processes between groups.

Ignatius' letters show how Christians went about constructing Christian identity in the middle of the second century, presenting Marcionism and Judaism as dark mirrors, as counter-identities and imposters (i.e. what Christianity is not) when compared to their own authentic Christian identity (i.e. what Christianity is). Against these presentations of the "other," Ignatius labels his own Christian identity "apostolic" and "catholic."

His use of the adjective "apostolic" (which we saw in Hermas' writings too) meant that the network of Asian and west Syrian churches, he was building, claimed that the teaching of their leaders came from the apostles through an established legitimate chain of transmission (Ign., *Trall.* Intro.; Poly., *Phil.* 6). This idea was used to authorize the teachings within the Asian and west Syrian network by arguing that the transmission of teachings from apostle to bishop results in consistent teachings rooted in a golden age. While Hermas made similar claims about his church in Rome, in Ignatius' letters, this idea is leveraged to the advantage of the local bishops who, Ignatius thinks, ought to be the authoritative powerhouses in their congregations, so that even the presbyters must be beholden to them (Ign., *Smy.* 8).

The teachings of the bishops were not just consistent with the past teachings of the apostles, but, by implication, they were uniform across the network of churches. Ignatius frequently admonishes his recipients to be of one mind, harmonious, and in compliance with the views of their bishops which are congruent with the commandments of God (Ign., *Trall.* 12; *Philad.* 1; 7). These commandments are to be distinguished from the Jewish Law. Any uncircumcised person (i.e. Gentile) who preaches the Jewish Law in the church network should be ignored (Ign., *Philad.* 6). Ignatius privileges the unity of the Eucharist ("have but one Eucharist") which, he insists, must be celebrated as the "flesh" of Jesus according to their bishop's orders (Ign., *Philad.* 4). He weaponizes this unity against the "wolves" who, he says, capture the faithful and carry them away from God (Ign., *Philad.* 2). He characterizes diversity of opinion as sinful and schismatic, rupturing the blessed unity of his church. In so doing, he frames his church as "the Church" and other leaders as exiled sinners who created schisms (Ign., *Philad.* 3). As sinners, Ignatius demands their repentance and return to the bishop's care (Ign., *Philad.* 8).

Ignatius is the first Christian writer to use the word "catholic" (e.g. Ign., *Smy.* 8). By catholic he implies that the Christian identity of his church is "universal." That said, he was not a universalist as we think of that word today. He did not believe that everyone was going to be saved by God. Universal meant, for Ignatius, that Christians were not an ethnic or national group like the Jews. While Christians worshipped the God known in the Jewish scriptures, this God was first and foremost the universal Creator God, not the God of a single nation. With this label, Ignatius also meant to imply that his construction of Christian identity was widespread (i.e. significant), rather than local (i.e. insignificant). He also meant that it was exclusive. In other words, the Catholic Church is the only church that can rightfully be called Christian (Ign., *Smy.* 8).

To "catholic" and "apostolic," Ignatius adds the "episcopal" descriptor, the idea that Christians are subject to the authority of their local bishop (Greek: *episkopos*) as they are subject to Jesus Christ (Ign., *Trall.* 3). He insists that there can be no church apart from those led by a bishop legitimately elected by a committee of already-established bishops in the network (Ign., *Trall.* 3). He leverages the discourse of sanctity to his advantage, arguing that congregants can only be "pure" if they are subject to their bishop and his "pure" altar (Ign., *Trall.* 7), suggesting again the superiority of the bishops in Ignatius' network and the Eucharist they offer. He charges that only the Eucharist, baptisms, and marriages performed by the duly elected bishops are valid Christian rituals (Ign., *Smy.* 8; *Poly.* 5). Anyone who acts without the consent of the bishop is framed as a servant of the Devil (Ign., *Smy.* 9).

Ignatius advises Bishop Polycarp to maintain his position carefully by preserving unity within his congregation and not allowing anyone to teach ideas that make Polycarp apprehensive. He invokes the language of violence, that Polycarp is like a hero who has been wounded yet still conquers because he remains firm like an anvil beaten by a hammer (Ign., *Poly.* 1, 3). He also reminds Polycarp to keep up his traditional role, assisting the widows and needy, organizing frequent meetings, asking after the welfare of every person in his congregation, and to support those in the congregation who were slaves (although he should not encourage them to seek their freedom at the public expense, but train them to not desire anything) (Ign., *Poly.* 4). Polycarp provides instructions that distinguish the work of the presbyters from the bishop (Poly., *Phil.* 6).

To ensure consistent teaching within the network of churches, Ignatius and Polycarp promote creedalism, the proclamation of a common statement of faith to standardize Christian identity and mark anyone with differing beliefs as non-Christians. The statement that Ignatius publicizes is the belief in "Jesus Christ, who descended from David (according to the flesh), and was also of Mary, who was truly born, and ate and drank. He was truly persecuted under Pontius Pilate. He was truly crucified, and truly died, in the sight of beings in heaven, and on earth, and under the earth. He was also truly raised from the dead, his Father quickening him, even in the same way that his Father will so raise us who believe in him by Christ Jesus, apart from whom we do not possess true life" (cf. Ign., *Trall.* 9; *Eph.* 20; *Smy.* 1–3; Poly., *Phil.* 2). The emphasis throughout is anti-Marcion with its focus on the reality of Jesus' fleshly body, human experiences, and bodily resurrection. This is in stark contrast to the Marcionite expectation that the resurrection will be a spiritual one when our bodies are shed and our transformed souls ascend to the Alien God (Ign., *Smy.* 1–3). While this early creed appears to be built on Romans 1:3, it is more difficult to discern if other Christian texts or traditional oral teaching are being invoked too.

Not everyone in the Asian and west Syrian network of churches was happy with their bishops' decision to take control and unite their congregations and standardize their beliefs and practices. Ignatius had been getting active push back from those who felt he was running a hostile takeover (Ign., *Philad.* 7; *Smy.* 11). Some felt that Ignatius was introducing novel ideas about Jesus that were foreign to the prophetic writings and the gospel, and that he had no grounds but assertions to prove his points (Ign., *Philad.* 8). The disquieted included Maximalist Christians who continued their traditional obedience to the Jewish Law, as well as a number of Minimalist Christians who thought Marcion had it right, Christians who, in the Eucharist, celebrated Jesus as the powerful Son of God who conquered the cosmic forces and liberated them from death.

In the letters of Ignatius and Polycarp, we glimpse the first attempts to consolidate a network of churches around an apostolic and catholic identity with a set of bishops interested in defining Christianity in ways that exclude Marcionites and other Christians who were observing Jewish practices as required by the Jewish Law. Their letters suggest that the Christian communities in their cities were heterogenous to the extent that the presbyteries or elders who governed the different churches held different views. Some may have sympathized with Christians who still identified as messianic Jews with obedience to the Law central to their identity. Others may have been convinced by Marcion and offered in their churches Eucharist ceremonies which did not identify the bread with Jesus' flesh.

This heterogeneity of the presbyteries apparently caused enough conflict and uncertainty that Ignatius works to convince the bishops of the congregations, including Polycarp, that the bishops should step up and take control. When one of them needed to be replaced, the bishops would choose and install the new leader, thus ensuring that the faith would be unified and constant. Ignatius' simultaneous construction of his personal identity as a hero marching to his death in the footsteps of Christ – that he would live and die as Christ – gave credibility to his claim that bishops should be obeyed as Christ Jesus is obeyed.

4.6 Martyred for the Faith

COMPANION READINGS

Ignatius, *To the Romans*

Martyrdom of Polycarp

Ignatius and Polycarp are remembered as Christians who were martyred. Ignatius' letters, of course, do not indicate whether he actually was executed, but they do present us with a glimpse into the mind of a Christian leader looking into the face of death. His letter to Christians in Rome, written on 24 August (sometime before Polycarp's death) from Smyrna, reflects on the horror and terror that he knows he will suffer once he reaches Rome and refuses to deny Christ. He thinks that he might be burnt alive or face death by crucifixion like Jesus or both (Ign., *Rom.* 5). If he is thrown to the wild animals, he understands that they will not just kill him, but tear his flesh apart limb-by-limb, grind his bones like wheat, and leave nothing for burial (Ign., *Rom.* 4). His only wish is for a speedy death, that it happens quickly (Ign., *Rom.* 5).

In order to strengthen his resolve to remain true to Christ when he is questioned by the Roman authorities, Ignatius endeavors to give the torture meaning. To this end, he understands his execution as an imitation of Jesus' execution by the Romans (Ign., *Rom.* 6). Since he believes that Jesus' death is a sacrifice offered to God, he understands his own death as a similar sacrifice to God (Ign., *Rom.* 2, 4; cf. *Eph.* 1). Its function, Ignatius thinks, allows him to partake fully in the Eucharist. Ignatius does not just get to eat the bread of Christ and drink the wine during Eucharist celebrations. He gets to experience being sacrificed as an offering to God and laid out on the altar as the bread of Christ (Ign., *Rom.* 2, 4; cf. 7).

In order for the sacrifice to count for anything, Ignatius believes that it has to be done voluntarily. So Ignatius insists repeatedly that he wants to be executed, even that he is eager to die. His voluntary status is repeatedly bolstered by his requests that the Christians in Rome do not try to intervene with the authorities to secure his release (Ign., *Rom.* 2, 4–7). He thinks that his execution guarantees his salvation and eternal home in heaven with Jesus, bypassing judgment and going straight to a place of honor beside Jesus (Ign., *Rom.* 4, 6–7). His execution, he says, will emancipate him so that he can rise to Christ as a freedman (Ign., *Rom.* 4). He wishes to use his death to demonstrate that a "real" Christian is someone who is willing to die for the name rather than someone who merely touts the name (Ign., *Rom.* 3; cf. *Mag.* 4). The martyr's death, according to Ignatius, is the strongest, perhaps the only real signifier of Christian identity.

While we do not know if or when Ignatius was executed, we have more certainty when it comes to Polycarp. The *Martyrdom of Polycarp* and other sources suggest that his execution took place between 155 CE and 177 CE, although most scholars tend to think that his death occurred earlier in this period rather than later. The account of his martyrdom purports to have been written a year after Polycarp's death (*Mart. Poly.* 18; cf. 21). His arrest appears to have been instigated when two servants from his household were arrested and tortured. One of these servants provided the information needed to locate and arrest Polycarp (*Mart. Poly.* 6). We do not know who actually denounced him.

Oddly Polycarp's story does not reflect much that we know about the Roman legal system since it presents Polycarp's trial as an event that occurred on a public holiday in the middle of a sports stadium before one of Rome's leading magistrates with no tribunal, accusation, or sentence. The magistrate turns him over to the crowd who orders his execution. We would expect Polycarp to have been tried like other Christians, who were brought by their accusers before an elevated platform called the bema, where the magistrate and the court of law operated. The magistrate would often consult with his councilors before giving the sentence which was read from a tablet. The other details provided by the author read like clichés or stock dialogue typical of martyrdom narratives. Polycarp is asked his name and then asked to "curse Christ," and "swear by the genius of Caesar" (*Mart. Poly.* 9.2–3).

The author of the account spares no expense shaping Polycarp's martyrdom so that it reflects the story of Jesus' execution whenever possible, which may account for some of the narrative's oddities like the crowd ordering his execution and the piercing of Polycarp with the sword of a centurion in addition to his incineration. Polycarp's death is presented as a sacrificial death, a holocaust offering of an unblemished ram given to God (*Mart. Poly.* 14). His death is a redemptive act, an hour of suffering that releases him from an eternity of punishment. By being burned alive, Polycarp escapes the eternal fire and is immediately raised up as an angel (*Mart. Poly.* 2).

The unusualness of the proceedings as well as the narrative's overlap with Jesus' story has led scholars to question the extent to which this account is historical or as early as it claims to be. This text is significant, however, not for its historical details, but for what it can tell us about how some early Christians framed and publicized the executions of their heroes. Like Ignatius, the author of this text understood Polycarp's execution as an imitation of Jesus' death, a traumatic and dramatic public testimony of Christian identity. Polycarp's martyrdom is presented as a noble death, even heroic. It is presented as an honorable form of death that served a greater purpose, comparable to other noble deaths in antiquity like the deaths of Socrates, Iphigenia (Agamemnon's daughter), and the Jews who resisted Antiochus IV during the Maccabean Revolt. In the case of Christian martyrs like Polycarp, their gruesome deaths are memorialized as devout displays of the faith of Christians. Their bones were collected to annually celebrate their deaths and serve as inspiration for those lucky enough to walk in their footsteps and acquire the crown of immortality (*Mart. Poly.* 18).

4.7 A Consolidating Church

The three Christians we met in this chapter all claim to be associated with a network of churches who consider themselves united in their apostolic heritage: Hermas in Rome, Ignatius in west Syria, and Polycarp in Asia Minor. Their churches were controlled by local presbyteries with bishops and deacons assisting with local charitable works. Under Ignatius' watch, in a crowded field of Christian difference, the bishops in Asia and west Syria began taking control of the presbyteries in order to circumscribe what authentic Christianity ought to look like. They authenticate the worship of YHWH not as the national God of the Jews, but as the universal Creator God of a Gentile Church. They maintain, however, a connection to the Jewish Prophets and a modified version of the scriptural commandments.

Hermas provides us a window into this church network as it sits on the cusp of change, when prophets like Hermas and presbyteries had authority to refashion the local traditions to flex with the changing needs of emerging churches or accommodate the concern of new members. The growing number of deniers among the Christians, for instance, put pressure on the congregations to develop ways for them to be returned to the churches as full members once again. Such is Hermas' prophetic solution posed to his presbytery, insisting that the Lady (heavenly Church) revealed to him that repentant deniers be forgiven and allowed back into the church.

Such flux creates doubt by raising questions about which prophet or presbyter is correct. Questions compound when there is disagreement among the presbyters over who is right and who is wrong or when new solutions are posed that mess with the integrity of traditional practices. Ignatius and Polycarp recognize how problematic this situation is for the stability of their congregations, so they wrestle the power from the presbyteries and justify their takeover as a means to protect true Christianity from a common enemy, in this case Marcion, who is cast as Satan himself, and Christians they called Judaizers. In other words, the consolidation of churches and the transfer of power to an authoritarian leader involved the identification of a common threat as a rallying point and the exclusion of the "enemy" who were cast as traitors. The authoritarian consolidation of power into the hands of local bishops like Ignatius and Polycarp was effectively bolstered by their reputations as trustworthy men so pious and true that they willingly died as martyrs, suffering for their flock as Christ had.

Timeline

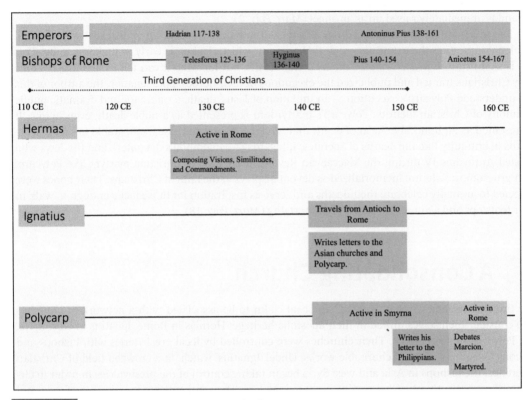

FIGURE 4.4 Timeline for Hermas, Ignatius, and Polycarp.

Pattern Summary

Hermas, Ignatius, and Polycarp are all early representatives of the Yahwist family (see Figure 4.5). The Biblical Creator God YHWH is their God of worship. YHWH created the world and is its caretaker. He operates justly enforcing the laws he established. All three men believe that humans are responsible for their suffering. They are Moderates, believing that there are a number of laws that humans must obey in order to remain sinless after baptism and avoid God's judgment. They understand that their salvation is dependent upon their obedience to God, even unto a martyr's death which guaranteed their place at the right hand of God.

In addition to observing God's commandments, Ignatius and Polycarp insist that in order to be righteous, Christians must avoid heresy (that is Judaizing and Marcionism). All three are DUALISTS who view their afterlives as embodied. Their flesh will be resurrected and reunited with their souls. All three consider the Jewish scriptures authoritative, along with the letters of Paul (Ignatius and Polycarp know thirteen letters). Ignatius and Polycarp also know the Gospel of Matthew. While Hermas promotes an ADULT POSSESSION PATTERN, Ignatius and Polycarp, to

Family Pattern Chart
Hermas, Ignatius, and Polycarp

X=Definitely > L=Likely

THEODICY

	Faulty-God	Faulty-Human	Other
Hermas		X	
Ignatius		X	
Polycarp		X	

SOTERIOLOGY

	Gift from God	Human achievement	Minimalist	Moderate	Maximalist
Hermas		X		X	
Ignatius		X		X	
Polycarp		X		X	

CHRISTOLOGY

	Adult possession	Fetal possession	Hybrid	Ensoulment	Visitation	Human who received revelation
Hermas	X					
Ignatius		X				
Polycarp		X				

ANTHROPOLOGY

	Mono	Dual	Triad	Quad
Hermas		X		
Ignatius		X		
Polycarp		X		

COSMIC DEMIURGY

	Autocrat	Administrator	Caretaker	Patron	Justice	Villain	Rebel	Ignorant	Impaired
Hermas	X	X	X	X	X				
Ignatius	X	L	X	X	X				
Polycarp	X	L	X	X	L				

RESURRECTION

	Body reunites with soul	Body discarded and soul immortalized	Body and soul discarded and spirit rises	God-element separates from body soul, and spirit and rises
Hermas	X			
Ignatius	X			
Polycarp	X			

SCRIPTURES

	Jewish	Gospel	Pauline letters (10)	Pauline letters (13)	Hebrews	Acts	Catholic letters	Revelation	Other
Hermas	X	Jn/Mt		L					
Ignatius	X	Mt/Lk/Jn		X					
Polycarp	X	Mt/Lk/Jn		X	X	?	1 Pet		1 Jn

ECCLESIOLOGY

	Consolidation movement	Reform movement	Secessionist movement	Counter movement	Innovative movement	Trans-regional	Regional
Hermas	X					X	
Ignatius	X					X	
Polycarp	X					X	

FIGURE 4.5 Summary of Hermas', Ignatius', and Polycarp's patterns of beliefs and practices.

condemn Marcion's Christology, insist on a FETAL POSSESSION PATTERN, that Jesus was born a divine-human being in the flesh. All three men consider their church part of a unified network of churches that trace their traditions to the apostles.

Hermas appears to have lived slightly before Ignatius and Polycarp, at a time when the presbyteries of the churches was the body politic. Ignatius and Polycarp identify Christian pluralism as problematic because it caused disputes and divided Christians into smaller diverse groups. To gain control of the situation and begin the process of Christian consolidation, they argued for the authoritarian rule of the bishops over their presbyteries and congregations. Ignatius argues for the use of the term "Christian" to identify themselves and also deploys the word "catholic" to describe the universality of the apostolic churches. To identify the true Christians from the false Christians, Ignatius says that the church must be part of the ecclesiological network of Catholic bishops.

Takeaways

1. Hermas' writings were well regarded in antiquity. For some Christians they were considered part of the New Testament canon.

2. Hermas' writings reveal to us a time in the development of the early apostolic tradition when the presbytery, the committee of elders, rather than the bishops, were the authoritative leaders in the congregations.

3. Most of Hermas' prophetic writings reflect the guilt and self-loathing of a Christian who, when denounced, had denied the Lord.

4. Hermas is obsessed with the question of what happens to Christians who deny the Lord when denounced. He challenges his church's tradition that deniers are unforgivable apostates. His prophecies try to remedy this situation and offer a catalyst to change this rule.

5. Hermas is a Moderate, recognizing the centrality of God's commandments to keep the Christian in the correct relationship with God. Hermas enumerates twelve commandments as a remedy for sin and a life of discipline.

6. Hermas worships the Biblical God as Creator of the world. Hermas does not understand this God to be the God of the Jewish nation, but a universal God whose Gentile Church is not only pre-existent, but the reason God created the world.

7. Hermas' God is punitive, a God to be worshipped and feared.

8. Ignatius and Polycarp are bishops in a network of like-minded churches in Asia Minor and Western Syria. They are trying to consolidate their churches and take over leadership from the presbyteries. They are consolidating under the claim that they are apostolic, catholic, and episcopal.

9. Ignatius identifies Marcionite and Judaizing Christians as the common enemy to justify his authoritarian move to take control of the presbyteries. Ignatius also encourages believers to take the name Christian away from others who do not own up to the name.

10. Ignatius and Polycarp's writings reveal the presence of Christian difference among Asian and West Syrian congregations.

11. In Ignatius' letters, he validates his martyrdom as an imitation of Jesus' suffering and death, associating it with the Eucharist, atonement, and salvation.

12. Ignatius preserves the earliest version of the apostolic creed which appears to have been modified or written to counter Marcion.

Questions

1. How does Hermas' God compare and contrast with Marcion's God and Valentinus' God?

2. Consider the illegality of Christianity in this period. If you were considering conversion, what type of questions might you have asked your teacher and already baptized Christians?

3. You decide to convert. You are denounced by an old acquaintance, arrested, awaiting trial. What are you thinking about? What are you weighing? Is there anything that would convince you that you ought to go ahead and be martyred? If so, what. If not, why not?

4. Let's look closer at martyrdom. What is martyrdom doing socially for the Christians? What value do Christians ascribe it? Why give it this value?

5. Present a modern example of consolidation and the authoritarian takeover of leadership. What was involved in this? How did it happen? Was it successful? If so, why? Now compare it to Ignatius' strategy of consolidation.

6. Ignatius despises Marcion's VISITATION PATTERN of Christology and instead advocates for a FETAL POSSESSION PATTERN. Why? What is at stake in Ignatius' opinion?

7. How does the construction of Apostolic Catholicism begin?

Resources

William Arnal. 2011. "The Collection and Synthesis of 'Tradition' and the Second-Century Invention of Christianity." *Method and Theory in the Study of Religion* 23: 193–215.

Timothy Barnes. 2008. "The Date of Ignatius." *The Expository Times* 120: 119–130.

Elizabeth A. Caselli. 2004. *Martyrdom and Memory: Early Christian Culture Making.* New York: Columbia University Press.

Paul Foster. 2007. "The Epistles of Ignatius of Antioch." Pages 81–107 in *The Writings of the Apostolic Fathers* Edited by Paul Foster. London: T&T Clark.

Justo L. González. 1970 (revised ed.). *Chapter 3 in A History of Christian Thought from the Beginnings to the Council of Chalcedon.* Volume 1. Ashville: Abingdon Press.

Michael Holmes. 2007. "Polycarp of Smyrna, *Epistle to the Philippians*." Pages 108–125 in *The Writings of the Apostolic Fathers* Edited by Paul Foster. London: T&T Clark.

Peter Lampe. 2003. "Chapter 22." in *From Paul to Valentinus: Christians at Rome in the First Two Centuries.* Translated by Michael Steinhauser and Edited by Marshall D. Johnson. Minneapolis: Fortress Press.

Claudio Moreschini and Enrico Norelli. 2005. "Chapters 5.2-3 and 9.2." in *Early Christian Greek and Latin Literature: A Literary History. Volume 1: From Paul to the Age of Constantine* Translated by Matthew J. O'Connell. Peabody: Hendrickson Publishers.

Sara Parvis. 2007. "The Martyrdom of Polycarp." Pages 126–146 in *The Writings of the Apostolic Fathers* Edited by Paul Foster. London: T&T Clark.

Joseph Verheyden. 2007. "The *Shepherd of Hermas*." Pages 63–71 in *The Writings of the Apostolic Fathers* Edited by Paul Foster. London: T&T Clark.

CHAPTER 5

Early Christian Philosophical Movements

Engraved Gem with Abrasax and a magical inscription, 100–250 CE. **Source:** Sepia Times / Universal Images Group / Getty Images.

> "Nobody is free from dirt."
>
> *Basilides writes this in his treatise on sin and suffering*

KEY PLAYERS
Basilides – Isidore – Carpocrates
Epiphanes – Marcellina

KEY TEXTS
Fragments of Basilides – *Secret Doctrine*

Why do good people like Job and Jesus (or any of the rest of us) suffer? Some of us might respond, "C'est la vie" (It's life) or "Shit happens." Such a response is much more difficult when you also believe in a supreme God who is omniscient (all-knowing), omnibenevolent (all-good), and omnipotent (all-powerful). Christians in antiquity were consumed with theodicy, with reconciling their view of God with the existence of evil and suffering. We learned in Chapter 3, for example, how Valentinus used mythology to teach that human suffering was an existential predicament caused by the unfolding of the transcendent God and the inevitable rup-

Comparing Christianities: An Introduction to Early Christianity, First Edition. April D. DeConick.
© 2023 John Wiley & Sons Ltd. Published 2023 by John Wiley & Sons Ltd.

ture of God's spirit into lower realms of existence. In this chapter, we meet two other Alexandrian thinkers – Basilides and Carpocrates – who founded their own Gnostic movements which broadcast alternative solutions to human suffering and redemption by intentionally engaging and reworking Greek philosophical systems.

5.1 A Philosopher

COMPANION READINGS

Clement of Alexandria, *Miscellanies* 7.17

Basilides, a Christian who taught in Alexandria during the reign of emperors Hadrian (117–138 CE) and Antoninus Pius (138–161 CE) was one of Valentinus' contemporaries. Given that both were active Christian teachers in Alexandria for a number of years (ca. 120–138 CE), if they were not actually personally acquainted, they at least had to have known about each other. From the few fragments that we have of Basilides' writings, we know that he was the first Christian philosopher and that, like Valentinus, his opinions had been shaped by a Gnostic metaphysics or spirituality. Connected to Basilides is his son, Isidore, who likewise dealt in Christian philosophy, writing several treatises that complemented his father's corpus.

Also connected to Basilides is the famous modern psychologist Carl Gustav Jung (1875–1961), who used the name as a pseudonym when he published *The Seven Sermons to the Dead* (1917) as homilies delivered by Basilides. This publication was the result of Jung's intense exploration of his own psyche, what he called his "confrontation with the unconscious." His spiritualist exploration included ecstatic visionary experiences and conversations Jung had with his own soul and the souls of the dead, all of which Jung recorded in black-covered journals known as the Black Books. The only part of these notebooks that Jung published during his lifetime is *The Seven Sermons to the Dead*, which he published privately and he gifted to friends. The rest of the notebooks had to wait until 2009 when they were published as *The Red Book* (complete with illustrations by Jung).

The sermons were written over a three-day period that began with what Jung describes as an experience of ghosts crowding into his house wanting to talk to him. As Jung explored his deep self over those three days (and presumably spoke with the dead), in his visions he saw arise Gnostic images (including Basilides' Good God Abrasax and the Pleroma) and believed them to be unconscious archetypes buried in the human psyche (what he later called the collective unconscious). Jung understood the purpose of these images to be therapeutic, to alleviate our suffering by directing our broken psyches (what he called our alienated egos) to become reconnected to the personal unconsciousness so that our conscious minds and our personal unconscious minds can work together in harmony. In this way, we are able to experience the fullness of being (the Pleroma) or the wholeness of the personality. As long as the ego remains alienated as if nothing exists but itself alone, we suffer from anxiety, depression, and mental projections as the result of our shadow, repressed memories, and forgotten traumas (which were once conscious but are no longer accessible to the conscious mind).

Jung later called the transformative journey to wholeness "individuation" and he developed a meditative technique called "active imagination" to stimulate a person's unconscious to release images that can be used therapeutically. Jung believed that individuation was possible because human beings contain pneuma, a spiritual potential or higher consciousness that functions to intuit, reveal, and urge us toward wholeness. This spiritual potential carries on a dialogue with our personal egos by using symbolic language in dreams, visions, and other altered states of consciousness. As a curative for mental disease, the psyche is guided on a developmental journey to wholeness through this two-way communication. This is all to say that Jungian analysis (which Jung considered a scientific approach to mental health) is actually a transposition of ancient Gnostic spirituality (especially as Basilides and Valentinus had developed it) into modern psychology.

In the ancient world, Basilides had a distinguished career. According to Clement of Alexandria, Basilides' followers report that Basilides' teacher had been a Christian named Glaucias, who was renowned for his interpretation of Peter's teachings. But a different genealogy is provided by Hippolytus, that Basilides and Isidore learned their teachings through Matthias who, in turn, had learned them privately from Jesus after his resurrection. Matthias was not one of the original twelve disciples, but the apostle who replaced Judas Iscariot in the lineup, according to the Book of Acts.

Basilides is said to have composed a psalm book (Greek: *Odai*) and a gospel (Greek: *Evangelion*). Nothing of his odes or his gospel survives (not even a description of their contents). Because of this, it is difficult to determine what his gospel was, whether a bio-sketch of Jesus (like Marcion's *Evangelion*) or a reflection on the revelation of Jesus Christ (like the *Gospel of Truth*). Basilides was aware of a number of Jesus' sayings and also knew the story about his crucifixion, including the detail that Simon carried Jesus' cross. Hippolytus describes, in great detail, a work called *Secret Doctrines* which he ascribes to Basilides and Isidore.

Basilides' real impact appears to have been a twenty-four volume work which was called the *Commentaries* (Greek: *Exegetica*) by Clement of Alexandria (ca. 200 CE) and the *Treatises* (Latin: *Tractatuum*) by Hegemonius (ca. 330 CE). Hegemonius attributes this title – *Treatises* – and their volume arrangement to Basilides himself. Both Hegemonius (*Acts Arch.* 67.5) and Agrippa Castor (ca. 130 CE; quoted in Eus., *Hist. Eccl.* 4.7.7) clearly state that Basilides' twenty-four volumes were about "the gospel." What do they mean by this? It is evident from Hegemonius' summary of volume thirteen of the *Treatises* that this volume was not an analysis of a written Gospel, but rather was a reflection about how the revelation of Jesus Christ solved certain philosophical dilemmas. When Hegemonius quotes from the opening of the thirteenth volume, he says that the topic of the thirteenth volume is the origin of the natures of good and evil and that chapter one of the volume starts the treatment of this subject with a nod to Jesus' story about the poor man (Lazarus) and the rich man (cf. Luke 16:19). Basilides used this story along with the parable of the Sower to problematize the origin of evil, calling it the nature that has no root or source (the soil that will not allow for the seed to take root).

We do not know how Basilides worked out the problem, but he appears to have opposed the position (of the "barbarians") that good and evil always existed and were ungenerated. Clement, however, worries that Basilides' teachings actually ascribe evil to God. Basilides is accused of something similar by Hegemonius who says that, because Basilides believed that Providence had ordained everything, he must have believed that good and evil always existed (*Acts Arch.* 67.4–12).

Clement's reference to Basilides' *Treatises* as *Exegetica* has led many scholars to mistakenly conclude that Basilides wrote twenty-four books exegeting or interpreting New Testament texts, making his work the first Christian Bible commentary. This conclusion is not only anachronistic, but it has no basis in the actual fragments preserved from Basilides' volumes. The fragments, in fact, are not dissections of the meaning of Christian scriptures. Rather they are expositions on Basilides' philosophical answers to vexing existential questions, which he supports with occasional references to words of Jesus or a story about him. Likewise, Isidore's books were not exegetical writings, but philosophical comments on prophecy (*Exposition of the Prophet Parchor*), Platonic topics (*On the Inseparable Soul*), and Christian ethics (Figure 5.1). Whatever else we might conclude about Basilides' writings, we should not mistake his volumes for what we understand today to be commentaries on written Gospels or any other New Testament text. The first known scholar to compose a commentary on a written Gospel is not Basilides, but one of Valentinus' students, Heracleon, whom we meet later in this textbook.

⑤·② **The Problem of Suffering**

COMPANION READINGS
Clement of Alexandria, *Miscellanies* 2.20, 4.12, 24

Clement of Alexandria preserves an extremely important fragment from the twenty-third book of Basilides' *Treatises* (Clem. Alex., *Misc.* 4.12). It is evident from this fragment too that Basilides was not writing a commentary on a written Christian Gospel, but instead was focused on explaining an existential problem, in

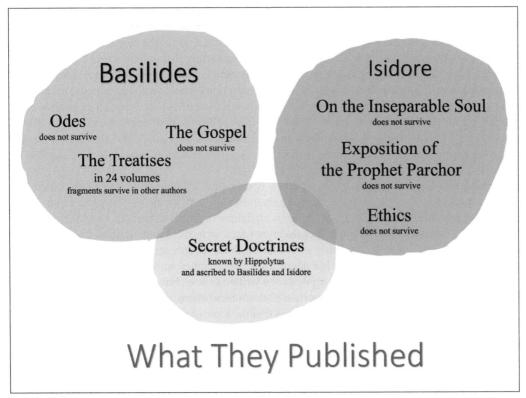

FIGURE 5.1   Basilides and Isidore were prolific writers, although most of their writings are lost.

this case the problem of theodicy, the suffering of people (including children) who do not seem to have done anything to deserve it.

Basilides presupposes that God, whom he calls Providence or Fate, is good. So he says that nothing bad or evil can come from Providence. In this, Basilides sounds like a Stoic, a philosopher who believed that Providence or Fate is the operation of divine Reason in the affairs of the world. Stoics thought that Fate is the will of God, and it is always good. Furthermore, whatever we might think is bad or evil actually has a rational purpose.

With this as his assumption, Basilides concludes that suffering must be an aspect of God's goodness and justice. It must have some educational and disciplinary purpose as fair punishment for sinfulness. In fact, Basilides was of the opinion that not all sins can be forgiven. The only sins that could be forgiven are those committed involuntarily or in ignorance. All other sins had to be atoned through suffering (Clem. Alex., *Misc.* 4.24). In Clement's quotation of Basilides, an interlocutor tries to embarrass Basilides by forcing him to conclude logically from this that Jesus suffered because he had committed sins. But Basilides will not be forced into this corner. Instead he explains that sinfulness does not mean sinful activities, but rather, the human inclination to sin, a capacity which everyone (including children and Jesus) have by virtue of their humanness. In other words, even though children may not have sinned because they did not yet have the opportunity to sin, the inclination to sin is enough to bring on their suffering. Suffering, then, is the condition of human existence.

To secure his position, Basilides turns to the story of Job who suffered horribly even though he was blameless. Why? Because "Nobody is free from dirt" (Job 14:4 LXX), Basilides writes. While we have traditionally traced the idea of original sin – the innate human tendency to sin – to Augustine (ca. 426 CE) via Tertullian (ca. 220 CE), here we find that Basilides is actually the original framer of the discussion in his treatises, although he does not trace sin's innateness to Adam's fall.

We get a glimpse at how Basilides further theorizes human sinfulness from a fragment of Isidore's writing, *On the Inseparable Soul* (Clem. Alex., *Misc.* 2.20). Clement, who preserves the fragment, explains that Basilidians associate the compulsion to sin with bad spirits that attach to the rational soul before birth as the soul embodies. Because of these attachments, evil and bestial cravings arise. Isidore says that this innate compulsion to sin is no excuse to sin. Rather he says that we must resist the compulsion to sin through reason and demonstrate that we can control the "lower creation" within us.

> "For if I persuade anyone that the soul is undivided, and that the passions of the wicked are occasioned by the violence of the [soul's] attachments, worthless people will not even have the pretense to say 'I was compelled. I was carried away. I did it against my will. I acted unwillingly.' They themselves led the desire of evil things, and did not fight against the assaults of the [soul's] attachments. But we must, by gaining dominance over the rational part [of our soul], show ourselves masters of the lower creation in us."
>
> *Isidore writes this in On the Inseparable Soul (Clem. Alex., Misc. 2.20; trans. DeConick).*

So what does Basilides then make of the situation of Christian martyrs, God's heroic faithful who are tortured to death? As we have already seen in this textbook, this was a sincere and urgent question during Basilides' time because indeed Christians were not a protected religious group. Arrest, interrogation, torture, and death could be faced by any one of them if the whims of the local Roman authorities turned against them. Later Christians like Clement of Alexandria (ca. 200 CE) were convinced that martyrdom was rigged by the Devil. But Basilides had other ideas. Taking his cue from Pythagoras and Plato who both taught about the transmigration of souls and their long-term "education" over the course of hundreds of lifetimes, Basilides argued that the souls of good people like the martyrs may be suffering because of small sins committed in previous lifetimes, a kind of karma playing out.

Origen of Alexandria (184–253 CE), Clement's predecessor, provides us with a quote from Basilides that further illuminates Basilides' opinion on this subject. According to Origen, Basilides supported his theory of the reincarnation of souls into living creatures, quoting Paul's opinion in Romans 7:9, "I lived once without the Law, that is, before I came into this body, I lived in the sort of body that is not under the Law, such as a beast or a bird."

Some scholars have suggested that this passage from the twenty-third book of Basilides' treatises may reflect Basilides' analyses of 1 Peter 4:12–19. While the subject of theodicy resonates in both texts, there is no evidence that Basilides is commenting on 1 Peter or even knows it. Rather the entire structure of Basilides' argument appeals to the story of Job and a quotation from it. Basilides' fragment is no evidence for the existence of 1 Peter. But it is evident that Basilides was an exegete, a trained interpreter of Jewish scripture.

5.3 Beyond the Stoic God

COMPANION READINGS
Irenaeus, *Against Heresies* 1.24.3

As we have already seen, Basilides does not trace the origin of evil and suffering to God. God, in fact, is perceived to be Providence from which nothing bad can come. The God to whom Basilides is referring is not the Biblical Creator God, but a transcendent primal Father who has no origin. While much of Basilides' philosophy is an outgrowth of Stoic ideas, the belief in a transcendent God outside the universe made Basilides distinct from the Stoics who thought that God as reason was present in nature itself, not something outside or beyond it.

It is important to recognize that Stoics were materialists. For them, God was the rational principle in the world whose substance they called pneuma. Stoics thought that pneuma is the active principle that infuses and enlivens matter. The pneuma is not something external to matter acting upon it. Rather it is integral to matter. Pneuma is the primal substance that existed before the universe, containing the totality of everything that would come to be. Since it is mixture of air and fire, the pneuma expands and disperses while heat, tension, and pressure mount. Once dispersed, it cools down. Eventually, the four elements condense out of it. Fire condenses into air. From air, water condenses and earth consolidates.

In contrast, Basilides thought that God is transcendent, above, beyond, and outside the universe. Basilides considered his discovery of this transcendent God to be the real deal, the discovery of a truth superior to everything else he had learned. Just as Valentinus relied on the structure of Egyptian mythology to trace out an original Ogdoad of first beings, so too does Basilides. According to Irenaeus' testimony, Basilides thought that the Mind (Greek: *Nous*) of God was the first to originate from the Unbegotten Father. From Mind came Reason (Greek: *Logos*). From Reason came Intention (Greek: *Phronesis*). From Intention came Wisdom (Greek: *Sophia*), and from Wisdom came Power (Greek: *Dynamis*). A fragment from Clement of Alexandria (*Misc.* 4.162.1) fills out Basilides' Ogdoad with Justice (Greek: *Dikaiosyne*) and Peace (Greek: *Eirene*). It is interesting that *Eugnostos*, an Egyptian philosophical text from the Nag Hammadi Collection, shares a very similiar Ogdoad with Basilides: the Unbegotten Father, Mind (*Nous*), Wisdom (*Sophia*), Thought (*Ennoia*), Reasoning (*Enthymesis*), Intention (*Phronesis*), Calculation (*Logismos*), Power (*Dynamis*), and Prognosis (*Foreknowledge*) (Figure 5.2).

While there are differences in these three schemes of the first beings, it is clear that the conversation about the origin of life occurred in both religious and philosophical contexts in Alexandria among intellectuals who took for granted that the first beings originated were an Ogdoad or Ennead of primary Gods. These first beings, which were generally understood to be mental processes or capacities necessary to generate further states of being, were modified by Christians to include figures or virtues important to them.

Irenaeus proceeds with his account of Basilides' origin story with the beings, Power and Sophia. Together these two generate the first powers, principalities, and angels, who in turn create the first

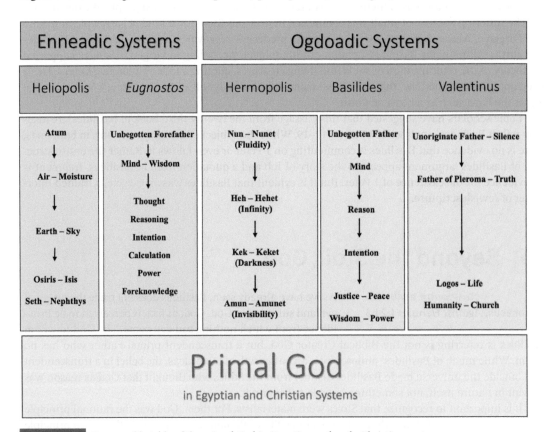

FIGURE 5.2 Comparable table of the primal God in Egyptian and early Christian systems.

heaven and its resident angels. The angels in the first heaven create the second heaven likewise, copying what they see above them. The angels in the second heaven copy what they see immediately above them and manufacture the third heaven, so that each new heaven becomes a realm immediately below its model. This process of creation through replication continues until there are 365 heavens.

This number matches the days in the Egyptian calendar which were based on twelve months of thirty days each with five epagomenal or intercalary days to complete the number of days in the solar year. The epagomenal days were celebrated by the Egyptians as the birthdays of the Gods Osiris, Horus, Seth, Isis, and Nephthys. This enumeration was intentional on the part of Basilides. It allowed Basilides to align his origin story with ancient stargazing theories about the precise location of the planetary spheres and the stars. These calculations were important for Basilides because they provided a map of the path through the heavenly spheres that the soul would use to journey home.

In Basilides' myth, two lower Gods play vital roles. One of the Gods is Abrasax, so-called because the letters of his name numerically add up to 365. In Greek, the letters of the alphabet double as numbers, so A=1, B=2, and so on. Thus:

$$\text{"A}(1) + \text{B}(2) + \text{R}(100) + \text{A}(1) + \text{S}(200) + \text{A}(1) + \text{X}(60) = 365."$$

In antiquity Abrasax (alternatively spelled: Abraxas) is a well-known God who appears frequently on magical objects like charms and amulets, and is referenced in esoteric literature and grimoires. When his appearance is sketched, he usually is depicted as an anguipede, a composite figure with a cock or lion head, human arms and torso, serpent legs, and scorpion feet (see image at the beginning of this chapter). According to Basilides, Abrasax is the great Archon or Ruler over the 365 heavens.

The second important God is the Biblical Creator God whom Basilides calls the God of the Jews. He is considered the chief Archon or Ruler over the 365th heaven, the last and lowest heaven to be created. He and the other angels who occupy this heaven created the world and everything in it. They divided up the earth into different nations and each one of them took on one of the nations to rule. The God of the Jews, however, lorded it over the other Archons. This caused resentment, so that the other Archons resisted him and challenged him. This explains, according to Basilides, why the nations of the world were constantly embattled against the Jews. The writings of the Jewish prophets, he thought, were inspired by the God of the Jews. The Law was given directly by him to the Jews.

5.4 An Alternative Account of Creation

COMPANION READINGS
Hippolytus, *Refutation* 7.20–27.13

Another discussion of Basilides' transcendent primal God and the origin of life is recorded by Hippolytus as coming from the book *Secret Doctrines* by Basilides and Isidore (*Ref.* 7.20.1–27.13). This book dates later than Irenaeus' account (180 CE), likely recorded by Hippolytus around 200–225 CE. The discussion in *Secret Doctrines* varies substantially from the discussion preserved by Irenaeus, so much so that many scholars think that someone other than Basilides must have been responsible for writing it (even though it is clearly attributed to Basilides throughout). That said, there are also scholars who have pointed out how many of the concepts in Hippolytus' testimony match closely the fragments of Basilides' writings preserved by Clement of Alexandria, who had died at least a decade before Hippolytus wrote about *Secret Doctrines*.

It is hard to know how to resolve this. Is either Irenaeus or Hippolytus mistaken? Is Hippolytus relying on a treatise that was attributed to Basilides pseudonymously? Are both preserving to some extent Basilides' theories? Might we have in Hippolytus material that Basilides wrote to clarify and expand particular points of theology or answer questions that his earlier writings had raised? If this is the case, Basilides may have tweaked his ideas, used different analogies and stories to make his philosophical ideas more accessible, and even corrected earlier positions or changed his mind. Or do we see in Hippolytus a text that was originally penned by Basilides but which has undergone significant expansion by Isidore or Basilides' students after his death? In this case, we might have Basilides' thoughts interwoven with the later commentary of Isidore or his students who, at the very least, appear to have integrated Aristotle into Basilides' system as well as stories about Jesus' birth.

In Hippolytus, Basilides' discussion of the origin of life centers around a creation myth well-known among ancient Egyptians who, in fact, did not have a single origin story, but many. In Hermopolis alone, there were four main creation myths touted. In one myth, a lotus flower emerges from the primal waters. When the petals open, Rê, the Sun God comes out and creates the world. In the second version, a scarab beetle (the symbol of the rising sun) comes out and shape-shifts into a young boy whose tears become the first human beings. In the third myth, the eight Gods of Hermopolis (the Ogdoad) create an invisible cosmic egg. When it hatches, light or air (in the shape of a bird) emerges. Thus visibility (and the Sun) is born. In another version, a celestial goose (Amun) or ibis (Thoth) lays an egg. Rê hatches from it and creates the world.

Hippolytus traces a similar story to Basilides, in which the primal God, like a many-colored peacock, lays an egg that contains the whole world as a seed. The seed was so tiny, Basilides says, it is like the mustard seed that Jesus talked about. It contained the potential for everything together in one little space: the roots, stem, branches, leaves, and the seeds for future plants. He also compares the potentiality of the egg to a newborn child who does not have teeth or intelligence, but grows up to have both.

According to Hippolytus, this egg mythology is important to Basilides because it allows Basilides to elaborate how the First Beings came to exist. Basilides identifies the problem as a philosophical one. How can a non-existent God – who was "nothing at all" and who was so ineffable as to be "not even ineffable" – produce something? This is the first time in history that we hear someone argue that everything comes from nothing. Later in the history of Christian theology, this will become known as creation out of nothing (Latin: *ex nihilo*). It is a position that is in stark contrast to all origin stories in the Mediterranean world (including the Biblical story) in which the universe is created by God(s) out of eternal formless matter and primordial water. Even the Stoics thought that the primal God was fire or breath (Greek: *pneuma*) or reason (Greek: *logos*) which, like a seed contained the first principles and the directions for the totality of all existence. The heat generated by God acted on matter, which was also a primal substance. Basilides is the first thinker to argue for a primal God so transcendent, so Other, that God is that which we cannot conceive: Nothing.

According to Hippolytus, Basilides means by this that there was no matter, no substance, nothing perceptible or imperceptible, nothing even mental or intelligible. The Non-Existent God – without thinking, without perceiving, without willing, without resolving, without desiring – wished (Greek: *ethêlô*) to make a world and the egg was laid. For want of a better word, Basilides uses the word *ethêlô*, which expresses that something (in this case creation) *will* or *shall* happen. It is usually translated as "wished" or "wanted" but these words imply desire, which is the opposite of Basilides' point. He uses the word *ethêlô* to make clear that whatever happened, it was not something intellectually initiated but it was something preordained. According to Basilides, creation happened because it was supposed to happen. In making this point, he is going against the grain of the usual philosophical discussion which seemed to be endlessly tracing the origin of life back to the cognitive or intellectual awakening of a primal entity. Basilides seems to have understood the nature of the Non-Existent God to be a void, an emptiness that by its very vacuous nature could do nothing but want to be filled or come into being. This wish to exist seeded something like a world genetic code: the potential for everything that would come into being.

Hippolytus says that Basilides argued this way because he was arguing against the idea that the primal God could emit or emanate (Greek: *proballo*) anything since this would mean that some kind of substance would need to be present. For a spider to spin a web, Basilides says, it needs to be able to emit threads. But there were no threads. In the beginning, there was Nothing, a state of non-existence which Basilides understood as an empty longing in which, like an egg, everything existed potentially that would come to be. The mixture inside the egg is hatched in stages as the transcendent realm and the universe come into existence like an infant grows into an adult. Substances come into existence because they are called into existence – "Let there be light, and there was light" (Gen. 1:3) – not because the substance light (or any other substance) preexisted. If this was (or became) Basilides' position, then Irenaeus misunderstood Basilides or assumed he was an emanationist thinker like Valentinus without verifying this.

What is important in Hippolytus' account of Basilides' ideas is the recognition that the egg contains a mixture of everything that is supposed to come into existence. The mixture includes the potential for four substances (not two or three as we have seen in other systems laid out in this textbook): physical, soulish (*psychic*), spiritual (*pneumatic*), and divine (*hyiotês*, literally, the sonship). This understanding of substances reflects Basilides' regard for Stoicism while also showcasing his critique of Stoicism. The Stoics taught that every human being has pneuma, which is the psychological faculty responsible for directing our reasoning and emotions. The human soul or psyche is purely physiological, responsible for keeping our life functions going (breathing, digestion, growth, self-movement). The physical body is matter enlivened by the soul and directed by the pneuma.

For Stoics, the divine is equivalent with the pneuma. But Basilides disagrees. According to Hippolytus, in Basilides' opinion, the important substance is something beyond normal pneuma. The real divine stuff is not the pneuma, but transcends the pneuma. It is the same in substance (Greek: *homoousia*) as the Non-Existent God-Who-Came-to-Exist. He calls this substance the filial substance (Greek: *hyiotês*, literally, the sonship), by which he means that it is related to the Non-Existent God-Who-Came-Into-Being like a child is to a parent. He gets the term *hyiotês*, not from philosophy, but from his read of Romans 8:12–23, in which Paul uses the related kinship term *hyiothesia* to suggest that the faithful enjoy a filial relationship with God as his children (cf. Gal. 4:5–7; Eph. 1:5). When all is said and done, filial substance is basically the substance of the transcendent God.

In Basilides' system, the problem is that, in the egg, the filial substance is mixed up (Greek: *synchysis*) with the other potential substances (physical, soulish, and spiritual). So the filial substance finds itself in a kind of quagmire. The aim of existence is for all of the filial substance to be separated out from the quagmire so that it can exist with God eternally without suffering in a condition alien to it. The rest of the substances likewise are to be separated into their eternal homes. This means that the ultimate architecture of existence features separate residences for God and his children (filial substance), spirits, souls, and physical structures (which dissolve into formlessness).

This separation starts the moment the egg hatches (Figure 5.3). Very rarified filial substance immediately bubbles out. It is so rarified that it is described as light. Swiftly it ascends to the edge of life, creating a realm of existence just below the Non-Existent God-Who-Came-Into-Being. Next to rise out of the egg is filial substance mixed with pneuma (spiritual substance). Struggling to ascend, it separates the pneuma from itself, creating the Holy Spirit which provides it with wings to fly up to the light. Once it arrives, the Spirit installs itself below the risen filial substance as a border which separates the filial substance from everything else. With these activities, the transcendent world and the First Beings come into existence. The Holy Spirit serves as a guardian and mediator between the First Beings in the transcendent world and everything that will come to exist in the realm below.

Next psychic or soul substance emerges in the form of the exceedingly beautiful, powerful, and ineffable Abrasax who hatches from the egg. He ascends to his spot immediately below the firmament. He creates a son, the Christ (who is much superior to him). As a wise and great demiurge or craftsman, Abrasax then creates the ethereal world: an Ogdoad which consists of eight celestial spheres (the star belt and the seven planets) which include 365 heavens. He and his son rule the Ogdoad, which is the area of the cosmos from the firmament down to the moon.

After this, more soul substance emerges from the egg, but this is not as rarified as Abrasax. From the egg hatches a second Archon, much inferior to Abrasax. While he is called Ineffable by some, he is really effable. He is the God of the Jewish scriptures who calls himself the God of Abraham, Isaac, and

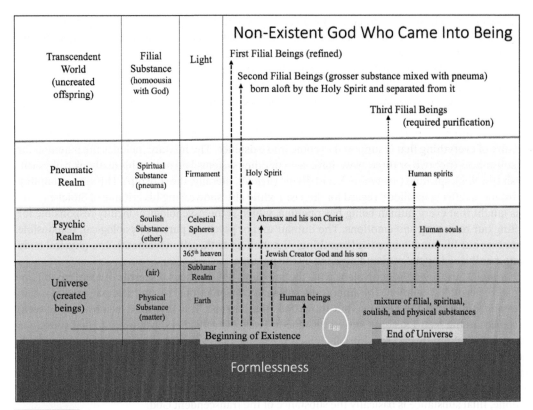

FIGURE 5.3   Basilides' world structure according to Hippolytus.

Jacob and feigns ineffability (Exod. 6:2–3). He rules the sublunary realm of air and is responsible for creating the world and everything in it from matter (the dregs of the egg). His realm is called the Hebdomad because, in this scheme of things, the sublunar realm had been divided into seven areas: probably (1) the atmosphere between the moon and earth; (2) the earth; and (3) five underworld realms.

Once these three major realms are laid out, the third batch of substance hatches from the egg. It needs purification because the remaining filial substance is heavily mixed with spiritual, soulish, and physical substance. Paul's comment in Romans 8:19–23 is extremely meaningful to Basilides. It suggests to him the weight of the agony and misery that the filial substance endures within the created world, especially because it is weighed down by the soul which is tied to the physical body and the capacity to sin. The filial substance within the human being endures yet additional suffering because it is ignorant of what it actually is: it is more powerful than Abrasax and the Jewish God because it is bascially the Non-Existent God-Who-Came-to-Exist stuck in the quagmire. To resolve this ignorance and provide the remaining filial substance with a way to be purified and end its suffering, Jesus and the Gospel enter the scene, revealing the mystery of God.

"I consider that the sufferings of this present time are not worth comparing with the glory that is to be revealed to us. For the creation waits with eager longing for the revealing of the sons of God; for the creation was subjected to futility, not of its own will but by the will of him who subjected it in hope; because the creation itself will be set free from its bondage to decay and obtain the glorious liberty of the children of God. We know that the whole creation has been groaning in travail together until now; and not only the creation, but we ourselves, who have the first fruits of the Spirit, groan inwardly as we wait for adoption as sons, the redemption of our bodies."

Romans 8:18–23 influenced Basilides

5.5 Jesus, The Mighty Power

COMPANION READINGS
Irenaeus, *Against Heresies* 1.24.4
Clement of Alexandria, *Miscellanies* 1.21

Irenaeus tells us a strange story about Basilides' opinion of Jesus, a story that has dogged Basilides through the centuries and even made its way into Muslim sources, which insisted that Jesus was never crucified (Iren., *Haer.* 1.24.4). Rather, while Jesus ascended into heaven, a substitute died in his stead. Muslim sources debate who this substitute was, whether Simon of Cyrene, Judas Iscariot, or some other volunteer.

The ultimate source of this story is Irenaeus who says that Basilides believed that Jesus did not suffer, but rather Simon of Cyrene, who, compelled to carry Jesus' cross, was transformed into a Jesus look-alike. He was crucified instead of Jesus, while Jesus stood by laughing at them. Jesus is portrayed in Irenaeus as a shape-shifter, an entity who, being the Mind (Greek: *Nous*) of the ungenerated Father, could become whatever he liked, in this case, an incorporeal power who ascended invisibly while laughing at the bystanders' ignorance.

Irenaeus goes on to say that Basilides thought it an error to confess "Christ crucified" because Jesus was sent by the Father and only came in the form of a man. In other words, Jesus was a mighty Power who was supposed to undo the works of the creators of the world and could not be crucified. Whoever confesses that "Christ was crucified" is still a slave to the creators of the world and the bodies they created. Whoever denies this has been liberated from the creators and knows the way to the ungenerated Father. Irenaeus interprets the denial of the cross by the Basilidians to mean that they get out of martyrdom because they are not willing to suffer for Christ's name (Iren., *Haer.* 1.4.6).

When we compare this summary from Irenaeus with the fragments that Clement of Alexandria preserves from Basilides' writings, we discover some issues. As we already saw when we discussed the fragment from the twenty-third volume of Basilides' treatises, Basilides believes that Jesus, because he was a human being, shared our inclination to sin, and so he suffered like a little child suffers. Basilides connects the suffering of martyrs to the inclination to sin as well, viewing martyrs as exceedingly righteous people whose deaths are a privilege given to them by God, allowing them to suffer honorably for sins they committed in previous lives.

Nowhere is there even a suggestion that Basilides thought that his followers should not undergo martyrdom or deny Christ. Rather they should embrace martyrdom as the form of death Jesus also suffered. Since Clement is quoting from Basilides' well-known treatises, it must be that Irenaeus is mistaken or has misunderstood or misrepresented Basilides.

In Hippolytus' discussion of Basilides, we learn that Jesus was a full human being because his saltatory role included separating out from each other the four substances that make up the human being (filial, spiritual, soulish, and physical substances) and returning them to their predetermined locations (Figure 5.4). The physical body will be dissolved into formlessness, the soul will ascend to Abrasax, the spirit will rise to the Holy Spirit, and the filial substance will fly into the transcendent world to live with the Non-Existent God-Who-Came-Into-Being. As Jesus separates these parts of himself, the bodily part is not saved but suffers the torture of crucifixion and returns to formlessness. The rest of him ascends past the realm of the Jewish Creator God into Abrasax's heavenly domain where Jesus sheds his soul. He bears aloft his spirit, which he leaves behind in the realm of the Holy Spirit. His filial aspect, thus purified of the other substances, ascends into the transcendent realm of the unbegotten Father. Jesus' resurrection represents the first time in history that this separation of substances takes place, thus Jesus is known as the "first-fruit." Jesus' suffering was necessary for this separation to occur and pave the way for the rest of us to experience this separation for ourselves.

Since both Clement and Hippolytus report that Basilides said that Jesus suffered and had a real human body, Irenaeus' report must be mistaken. We might have a clue to how this mistaken report could have come about in a passage from the Nag Hammadi text, the *Second Treatise of the Great Seth*.

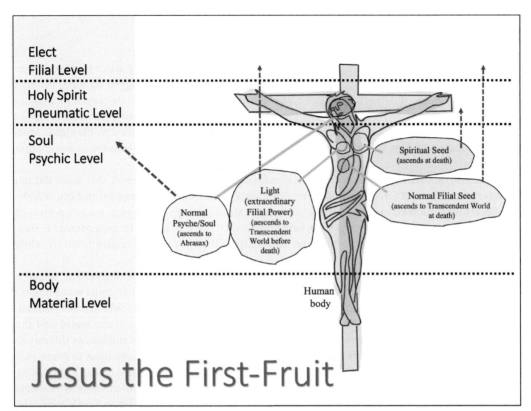

Elect
Filial Level

Holy Spirit
Pneumatic Level

Soul
Psychic Level

Spiritual Seed
(ascends at death)

Normal Filial Seed
(ascends to Transcendent World
at death)

Light
(extraordinary
Filial Power)
(aescends to
Transcendent
World before
death)

Normal
Psyche/Soul
(ascends to
Abrasax)

Body
Material Level

Human
body

Jesus the First-Fruit

FIGURE 5.4 Separation and ascension of the four aspects of Jesus upon his death according to Basilides.

"For my death which they think happened, (happened) to them in their error and blindness, since they nailed their man unto their death...In doing these things, they condemn themselves. Yes, they saw me. They punished me. It was another, their father [the Jewish Creator God], who drank the gall and the vinegar. It was not I. They struck me with the reed. It was another, Simon, who bore the cross on his shoulder. I was another upon whom they placed the crown of thorns. But I was rejoicing in the height over all the wealth of the Archons and the children of their error, of their empty glory. And I was laughing at their ignorance."

Second Treatise of the Great Seth (NHC VII,2 55.25–56.20).

In this passage, Simon is referred to as the person who carried Jesus' cross on his shoulders, as he does in the Gospel story (Matt. 27:32; Mark 15:21; Luke 23:26). Jesus' physical body suffers, while Christ the divine power that had descended on Jesus at his baptism, leaves him at the cross, ascending to the Father who had sent him. This is why Christ the divine power does not suffer crucifixion, but instead laughs from on high. Interestingly, this text also criticizes Christians whose faith centers around a crucified savior, "a doctrine of a dead man" (*Treat. Seth* 60.22). Whoever wrote this text reveled in the real truth about Jesus, that the Christ Power escaped death and ascended in glory and joy.

While the *Second Treatise of the Great Seth* is not a Basilidian writing, something similar to this account of Jesus' crucifixion must have been Basilides' view. According to Hippolytus, Basilides taught that a great Light Power (an extraordinary Power of filial substance), descended from the transcendent realm into Abrasax's son (the Christ) who then was able to enlighten the Ogdoad or psychic realm of the 365 heavens. This Light Power next descended from Abrasax's son into the Demiurge's (Biblical

Creator's) son and enlightened the Hebdomad, the airy atmosphere from moon to the earth. Finally, the Light Power entered Jesus in order to instruct humanity.

Did this decent happen at his baptism or at his birth (Figure 5.5)? In Hippolytus, this is unclear since it is first explained that the Light descended "upon" Jesus and Jesus radiated light because of this. This is evidence that Basilides taught that the descent of the Light upon Jesus happened at his baptism when the Spirit descended on him and illuminated him. In this case, we have the ADULT POSSESSION PATTERN in play. Then the text makes a clumsy turn to say that what Basilides really meant is that the Light (as the Holy Spirit) came upon Mary so that the child she conceived would be anointed with the Spirit. This appears to be a later interpretation of Basilides' teaching that is trying to replace the ADULT POSSESSION PATTERN with a FETAL one.

In the end, Basilides probably taught that the Light (an extraordinary filial power) descended through all the realms of existence. At Jesus' baptism, the Light enters Jesus, a human being who has a filial seed, spiritual seed, soul, and physical body. Because of his extraordinary constitution, Jesus is able to perform miracles (the Light Power) and suffer even unto death (the human Jesus). As Jesus dies on the cross, his constituent parts separate, so that his body is the only part of him that endures physical torture. On the cross, the Light leaves the body behind and flies into the transcendent world rejoicing.

This idea of separation of the person from the suffering body is a trope found in later literature recounting the death of martyrs. Later Christians like Bishop Cyprian (d. 258) believed that martyrs did not feel their bodies anymore because their souls had left their bodies. The soul was in ecstasy, united with God, so it could not feel the pain that the flesh underwent. Thus he tells the terrified Flavian (anxious about his own martyrdom) that "it is another flesh that suffers when the soul is in heaven. The body does not feel this at all when the mind is entirely absorbed in God" (*Acts Mart.* 21.4).

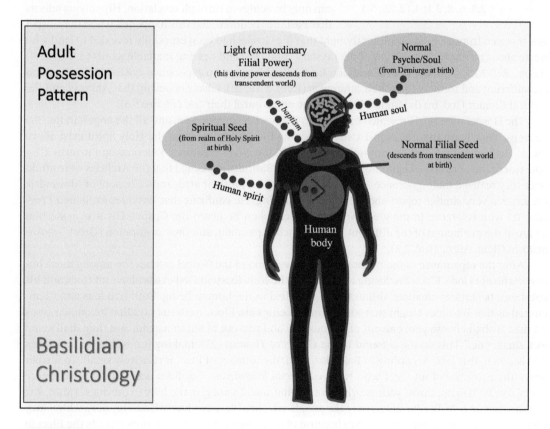

FIGURE 5.5 Illustration of the aspects of the human Jesus according to Basilides: his body, soul, spirit, filial substance, and the Light Power.

Where did Basilides get the idea that the descent of the Light on Jesus happened at his baptism and the separation of Christ from Jesus at the crucifixion? Basilides must have known a gospel that told about the descent of the Spirit on Jesus at his baptism (Mark 1:10 and parallels) and its flight from Jesus at his passion (Mark 15:34 and parallels; Matt. 27:50; Luke 23:46; John 19:30). This Christology is also confirmed by Clement's report that the Basilidians celebrated two events in the life of Jesus: Jesus' baptism and his crucifixion. They made precise calculations of these dates. According to their liturgical calendar, the Basilidians spent the night before the 11th of Tybi (6 January) reading scriptures as they prepared to celebrate Jesus' baptism. This makes them the first recorded Christians to celebrate what became known as the Festival of the Epiphany of Our Lord (still celebrated by Christians today on January 6). Clement also says that they celebrated Jesus' crucifixion on the 25th of Phamenoth (25 March) which is our earliest reference to Good Friday services. For the Basilideans, these are the two events that memorialize the movement of the Light Power in and out of Jesus.

5.6 The Election

COMPANION READINGS
Romans 9, 11
Irenaeus, *Against Heresies* 1.24.6
Clement of Alexandria, *Miscellanies*
2.3, 6, 8; 3.1; 4.12, 26; 5.1

According to Hippolytus' report about Basilides, the decisive event of the separation of Jesus' constituent natures at his crucifixion got started with the staged revelation of the Gospel from the transcendent realm. Human redemption can only be achieved through revelation. Hippolytus tells us that Basilides believed that this happened when the Gospel was revealed from on high. Basilides thought that the Gospel had been especially revealed to Paul who wrote about receiving a revelation of the mystery (Eph. 3:3) and hearing ineffable words (2 Cor. 12:4) (Hipp., *Ref.* 7.25.7.7). This was redemption for God's children who experience existential longing and are suffering and tormented in their ignorance (Rom. 8:19, 22), falsely believing that Abrasax and the Biblical Creator God are the Gods who rule them and control their fate (Figure 5.6).

The Gospel message is revealed to Abrasax, the Jewish Creator God, and all the angels in the 365 heavens. They learn that the Non-Existent God, the filial substance, and the Holy Spirit exist above them. They learn that they are not unbegotten Gods, but God's creatures. Referencing Proverbs 1:7 – "the fear of the Lord is the beginning of knowledge" – Basilides explained that the Archons were afraid once they realized their ignorance. This led them to repent for their arrogance. Clement of Alexandria preserves a very similar report about Basilides' teaching. He confirms that Basilides explained Proverbs 1:7 with reference to the great Archon's shock when he heard the Gospel. His fear made him aware of the distinction of the different natures, their separation, and their restoration (Greek: *apokatastasis*; Clem. Alex., *Misc.* 2.8).

After the repentance of the Archons, Jesus' revelation of the Gospel catches fire among those humans who are God's Elect, disclosing to them that the Non-Existent God exists above all Gods and his substance penetrates creation, although it is muddled in the human being. Both Irenaeus and Clement tell us that Basilides taught that some human beings are Elect. Irenaeus says that he quoted Jesus on this: "I shall choose you, one out of a thousand, and two out of ten thousand, and they shall stand as a single one." This saying is found in the *Gospel of Thomas* (23), making it possible that Basilides had access to this text. According to Basilides, then, the number of Elect is relatively small. To further prove the existence of an Elect who receives special knowledge, Basilides was known to reference Jesus' words: "Do not throw your pearls before swine, and do not give the holy to the dogs" (Matt. 7:6; Epiph., *Pan.* 24.5.2). For Basilides, only the people who are Elect can know God's mystery which they then must safeguard among themselves because of its awesome holiness. He understands the Elect to be "no longer Jews, but not yet Christians" (Iren. *Haer.*, 1.24.6).

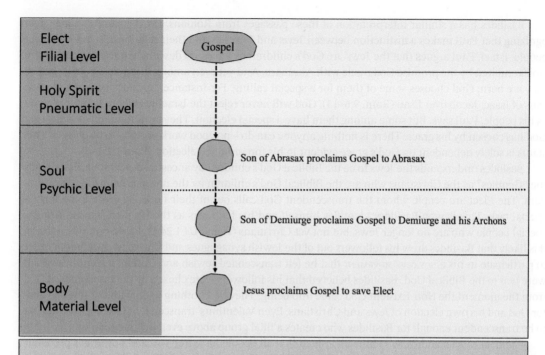

Elect Filial Level	Gospel
Holy Spirit Pneumatic Level	
Soul Psychic Level	Son of Abrasax proclaims Gospel to Abrasax
	Son of Demiurge proclaims Gospel to Demiurge and his Archons
Body Material Level	Jesus proclaims Gospel to save Elect

Revelation of the Gospel

FIGURE 5.6 How Basilides believed the revelation of the Gospel occurred on all the different levels of existence.

The origin of the idea of an elect body of believers comes from Paul's letter to the Romans, where Paul talks about those whom God elected or called prior to their birth (9:11; 11:7). How to understand these passages in Paul, has been disputed over the centuries, but these verses have been wielded by many (including Augustine and Calvin) to indicate a special, even predetermined saved status for Christians. In Chapter 3, we saw how Valentinus believed that those who came to know the transcendent God did so because they had been "called" by him when the Father read their names out of the Book of the Living. In other words, their social response to embrace Jesus made real the list of names that had been determined the moment that God began to emanate forms of himself.

Romans 9:10–11

"And not only so, but also when Rebecca had conceived children by one man, our forefather Isaac, though they were not yet born and had done nothing either good or bad, in order that God's purpose of election might continue, not because of works but because of his call..."

Romans 11:5–7

"So too at the present time there is a remnant, chosen by grace. [6] But if it is by grace, it is no longer on the basis of works; otherwise grace would no longer be grace. [7] What then? Israel failed to obtain what it sought. The elect obtained it, but the rest were hardened..."

Passages that Basilides used to develop his idea of the Election

Basilides has a similar interpretation of these passages from Romans. He is a careful reader, recognizing that Paul makes a distinction between Jews and Gentiles and their relationship to God's elect people, Israel. Paul argues that the Jews are God's children by ancestral descent, while the Gentiles are God's children by the promise God made with Abraham. And yet even among these elect people, before they are born, God chooses some of them for a special calling. For instance, he chose between the two sons of Isaac: Jacob over Esau (Rom. 9:6–13). God will never reject the Israelites whom he preordained as his people, Paul says. But some among them have a special election. They are a remnant of Israel that God has chosen by his grace. There is nothing anyone can do – no good work or feat – to be chosen. This status is solely dependent on God's grace evident in his foreordained election (Rom. 11:1–7).

Basilides understands the Jews to be the Biblical God's children by ancestral descent. Basilides reads the "Gentiles" as the Christians who are the Biblical God's children by the promise he made with Abraham. The Elect are people whom the transcendent God calls out of their ranks by grace to perform a special task. This is why Basilides identifies himself and his followers as the Election (Greek: *Eclogê*), special people who are no longer Jews, but not yet Christians (Iren., *AH* 1.24.6). Based on this evidence, it is likely that Basilides drew his followers out of the Jewish synagogues and Christian churches in order to participate in his INNOVATIVE MOVEMENT that he felt transcended Jewish and Christian identities which were tied to the Biblical God. Basilides believed that his followers were chosen by the transcendent God from the moment the Non-Existent God came into being. They had nothing to do with the Jewish Creator God and his own election of Jews and Christians. Even Valentinus' transcendent God does not appear to be transcendent enough for Basilides who creates a filial group above even the pneumatics.

Clement of Alexandria, who himself argued that all people have free will and nothing is predetermined, tells us that Basilides believed in predestination. On this point, Basilides' affinity with Stoicism comes to the front. As we already saw, Stoics had a strong sense of Providence or Fate, that divine reason operated within the world and determined all events in the universe. Stoics believe that things in and of themselves are neither good nor bad. They are what Stoics call indifferent (Greek: *adiaphora*). What matters is the way in which we put things to use and live virtuously. Virtue, for Stoics, means living life in accordance with reason, whether our own rational nature or the rational nature of the universe. Providence or Fate leaves no room for the individual free will of the soul. The only choice the soul has is to either accept its fate and live happily or resist its fate and be unhappy. Virtue is not so much about doing good activities. Instead, it is about the soul being-in-agreement with its nature and unperturbed with its fate. Stoic teachers liked to use the analogy of a dog tied to a moving cart. The dog can either be miserable as it is dragged along by the cart or trot happily behind it. Either way, both dog and cart will turn up at its destiny. Being tied up to the cart is neither good nor bad. It is a matter of indifference. Virtue is the dog's assent to move with the cart.

When Basilides talks about faith, he means something similar. Basilides believed that faith is a person's conscious consent to something that has not yet been experienced but is hoped for (Clem. Alex., *Misc.* 2.6). In other words, faith is the soul's assent to its final destiny, the fate that awaits it at the end of time when all the separated substances are restored to their proper places within the architecture of the universe and the transcendent realm. From this, Basilides reasons that every nature had its own faith, its own hope, and its own destiny to live in the location appropriate to it. The Elect are destined for the transcendent world, while everyone else is destined at the end of time to take up a place in the cosmic realms under the auspices of the Archons (Clem. Alex., *Misc.* 2.3). In this description of Basilides' teachings, Clement is remarkably close to the account preserved by Hippolytus.

Basilides, however, is not just adapting Stoic principles to his system. He, like Valentinus, was a Gnostic. Basilides believes that the Elect, who share in God's nature, are drawn to God intuitively, through sudden comprehension (Greek: *noesis*). Theirs is a super-faith (Greek: *exairetê pistis*), a faith that is extraordinary because it is an intuitive knowing rather than a rational consent. In the case of the Elect, faith is natural, dependent on the fact that they share God's substance (Greek: *ousia*) which is infinitely beautiful and worthy to take its place near God (Clem. Alex., *Misc.* 5.1). This shared substance allows for the Elect to discover doctrines by intuitive comprehension (Greek: *noêtikos*) without the need to resort to reason and logical proofs (Clem. Alex., *Misc.* 2.3). Because they already share

God's Mind, they already know everything. For Basilides, like Valentinus, faith and direct knowledge of the transcendent God go hand in hand.

Why did God even bother to leave behind a part of himself in this quagmire? Basilides says that God did this because the Elect have been given a special task by the transcendent God. Hippolytus tells us that Basilides thought that the Elect, the "spiritual people," had been left behind in the dregs of the egg in order to train, correct, and perfect all human souls so that, at the end of time, they can be lifted up to Abrasax rather than stay behind suffering in the sublunar region of the universe.

In Clement of Alexandria, we find clues about what this training entailed. First and foremost, the Elect are taught to live as strangers or aliens in this world. Basilides develops this doctrine with reference to the scriptural passage (Gen. 23:4; Psalm 39:12; cf. Heb. 11:13), "I am a stranger in the land and a sojourner among you." Basilides likens the Elect to aliens living in the world because their nature is transcendent (Greek: *hypercosmion physei*; Clem. Alex., Misc. 4.26). This played out in their community as both antinomianism (freedom from the laws and conventions) and asceticism (body disciplines). While it might seem at first that this is a paradox – to act freely from the laws while also gaining control over the body – both of these ideas make sense within Basilides' system.

Although Basilides was not a Stoic, as we saw earlier, Basilides applied Stoic sensibilities to Christian ideas. All things are indifferent, he thought; it is only the way they are wielded that matters. This idea is foundational to Basilides' opinion that the commandments in Jewish scripture and Christian writings are unnecessary for the Elect (Clem. Alex., *Misc.* 5.1). Not only are they a matter of indifference, but the pre-Christian prophecies were ordained by the world Rulers, and the Jewish Law by their chief, not the transcendent God. Irenaeus says that Basilidians attended pagan festivals and ate meat butchered in the pagan temples, something he personally finds objectionable. For Basilides, these types of things would be considered matters of indifference. Basilides likely found support for this opinion in Paul's letter to the Corinthians where Paul allows for eating sacrificial meat (1 Cor. 8). Clement remarks that the Basilidians believed that marriage was a matter of indifference, but the later followers of Basilides, he says, twisted Basilides' teaching about indifference in order to engage in licentious sexual behaviors (Clem. Alex., *Misc.* 3.1).

It is hard to assess Clement's statement about the licentious sexual behaviors of later Basilidians. What we do know is that Basilides was no eroticist even though his central ethic was love. Love, for him, is not romantic or sexual love. Basilides thinks that we need to love everything – even suffering – because everything is ordained by God. Next, we need to free ourselves of desire and, then, resist the compulsion to sin. And lastly, we need to hate nothing, but treat everything as a matter of indifference. Isidore, Basilides' son, composed a treatise on ethics in which he discussed marriage as a matter of indifference. He suggests, with reference to 1 Corinthians 7, that it does not matter if we marry or live as ascetics. What matters is living a life of self-control, unaffected by desire and passions, no matter our circumstances. If marriage helps us from being overwhelmed by sexual desire, then by all means we should marry, and stop wasting energy resisting temptation and dreading losing control. This attitude applies to other situations, like a non-compliant wife. In this situation, Isidore cautions the husband to accept his fate rather than resist it. It is better for the husband to endure the fate of a quarrelsome wife then resist his fate and fall out of God's grace.

[5.7] The Restoration

The end of time was a hot topic not only among Jews and Christians. Stoics had their own eschatological views which they touted as the "restoration" of all things. They believed that the universe would eventually decay, gradually resolving back into the primary substances (fire, air, water, and matter). At some point, fire would become the majority substance. Then a conflagration would occur, consuming matter and restoring everything to pneuma or reason (their God). But this state was not permanent, only the starting place for the next reiteration of the world to form, reproducing the previous world and its exact events over and over again, a replay down to daily events such as film director Harold Ramis imagined in *Groundhog Day* (Columbia Pictures 1993). While the universe was finite, the cycle of life perpetually fueled itself according to the Stoics.

Since Basilides positioned Christianity in relationship to Stoicism on so many other topics, how did his eschatological views fare? As we have seen, according to Hippolytus, Basilides taught that the job of the Elect was to aid the separation of the primary substances (filial, spirit, soul, matter) and their travel to their designated habitats in the universe and the transcendent world. Jesus was not only the divine messenger who revealed where they belonged, but their navigator who showed them how to get there. His suffering sufficed to completely purify his soul of the compulsion to sin so that at death his soul could separate from the body, ascend through all the heavenly realms, and be shed in Abrasax's court where it belonged.

Jesus is characterized as a mystagogue, a guide to the esoteric secrets necessary for the soul to ascend to the pinnacle of the universe. In ancient imagination, the celestial realms were filled with Gods, demons, and various powers who controlled their realms and guarded them. Entrance to their realms was frightening, even more so if one planned to travel across their realms to higher locations where even the guardians themselves were not permitted to go.

Irenaeus reports that when the celestial journey of the soul is undertaken, Basilides believed that, it was necessary to know the names and identities of the guardians that will be encountered. Basilides taught that Jesus reveals to his followers the secret names of all 365 angels that they will encounter as they ascend. Basilides' followers would have spent time memorizing these names so that when they died, they would have the knowledge necessary to broker the deal. In antiquity, pronouncing the names of deities in prayers, invocations, spells, and other rituals had powerful effects that could influence and charm the deities. Basilides appears to have taught them to use the names in prayers and spells to make a sleuth ascent. Using certain incantations, their souls would become invisible to the guardians of the 365 celestial realms. They were taught to "know them all, but let none know you."

In Irenaeus' report, we are given the actual name that Jesus pronounced as he descended invisibly from the transcendent realm into the universe and then, at his crucifixion, ascended from this world into the transcendent realm. He called out, "Kaulakau." This word derives from Isaiah 28:13, where it is written that the "word of the Lord will be to them precept upon precept (Hebrew: *sau la sau*), line upon line (Hebrew: *kau la kau*), and a little here (Hebrew: *ze'êr sham*)." Kaulakau is the word that their "Lord" Jesus used in order to move downward and upward through the veil that separates the transcendent world from ours.

Armed with this knowledge, the followers of Basilides believed that, at death, they would leave their bodies and fly invisibly through the realm of the Jewish Creator God and the heavens of Abrasax. They would shed their souls and leave them with Abrasax. They would ascend to the Holy Spirit and shed their spirits in that place. Having left their souls and spirits in their proper places, they would be poised to enter the transcendent world as pure divinities. As they called out "Kaulakau!" the gate to the transcendent world would open and they would be allowed to enter their eternal home.

According to Hippolytus, once all the filial substance finds its way to the transcendent God and all the other substances make their way to their destined places, Basilides insists that the process had to stop. As God finally comes to exist as a unified and cohesive being, matter will dissolve into form-lessness. Yet there was a danger that the mixing of the primal substances could happen again as long as the different substances were aware of each other and longed to be what they were not. To avoid the remixture of the substances and the perpetual recreation of the world the Stoics imagined, Basilides thought that God had a better plan. Out of his mercy, God would bring upon the whole world a great ignorance so that the souls who are immortal will remain with Abrasax, knowing nothing other than or better than his realm. They will not be tormented or suffer any longer, attempting the impossible like fish trying to graze with sheep. The two main Archons will know of nothing above them, but will be content and feel no sorrow or longing for what they cannot have. Each will rule over his own realm and pain will cease.

Basilides' view of the ideal world reflects ancient views about race and ethnicity, as well as his own experience as a colonized Egyptian. Identity for ancient Romans was often based on their perceptions of nationalities or descent groups that had specific geographical origins and shared cultural practices, specifically language. Romans often used mythical genealogies and environmental determinism to categorize people and explain perceived body differences. Their explanations mirror the realities of colonial Rome and the consequent shape of the hybrid cultures and social stratifications that structured their society.

Basilides' final stratification of the primary substances is dependent upon both biological and geographical metaphors. The ideal world is a restoration of the mixed natures (biological) to their separate homelands (geographical). Hybridity is not the ideal state, but a state of suffering that can only be endured unto death. Basilides' ideal world, where everyone is separate in their own realms, reflects the dreams of a colonized Egyptian whose culture was hybridized. When Basilides talks about the purification and ascent of the divine substance out of the created order, he envisions a future that is no longer hybrid. His idea that the Rulers of the world would be left behind in second-rate realms with much of their creation dissolved into formlessness is a social commentary on what Basilides hoped would happen to the Roman authorities. Even more interesting is Basilides' hope that the authorities would become ignorant of realms beyond their own. They would stop desiring to extend their rule into other areas and cease causing suffering. Basilides' solution to the kind of human suffering he endured as a colonized Egyptian is a permanent solution, one that could only be brought about by putting a stop to the desire for more and the tyranny that such desire causes.

⑤.⑧ Passion Problems

COMPANION READINGS
Romans 6–8
Irenaeus, *Against Heresies* 1.25.1–6
Clement of Alexandria, *Miscellanies* 3.2, 4, 6
Testimony of Truth (NHC IX,3) 29.6–44.30

In Alexandria, Basilides was not alone thinking about the problem of human suffering. Irenaeus reports that an Alexandrian contemporary, a Christian named Carpocrates, taught that we suffer punishment at the hands of the Archons because we cannot control our passions. Carpocrates, unlike Basilides who theorized suffering on the basis of original sin (the human inclination to sin), thought about sin in terms of committing deeds that break laws. He argued that our passions lead us to break the Creator's Law and sin. When we die, we are punished for this. The Archons are our jailers. They get to keep our souls and imprison them again in another body. The problem is that the system is rigged. Because of the Law, there is always going to be sin. There is no way to make bail. So we must endure the suffering of endless cycles of reincarnation.

In this mythology, Paul meets Plato. The structure of Carpocrates' system is standard Platonic fare, assuming the fall of the soul into matter where it is further corrupted by the emotions and passions it endures (Figure 5.7). Souls continue reincarnating until they are able to purify themselves suitably, a process that Plato suggests is no easy feat, bordering on the impossible. Carpocrates' conversation about the Law and sin is coherent with a Minimalist reading of Paul's letters, focused on Paul's argument that the Law defined sin and as long as it holds sway, it is impossible not to sin (Rom. 7:7–11; Gal. 3:19). Paul further suggests that our passions lead us to sin as long as we are under the Law (Rom. 6:12–14).

Irenaeus relates that Carpocrates believes that we got into this situation because of a group of fallen angels or Archons who were responsible for creating the world and instituting the Jewish Law (cf. Gal. 3:19–20). These angels are far removed spatially from the transcendent Unbegotten Father. Carpocrates' son, Epiphanes wrote a book entitled, *On Righteousness*. Clement of Alexandria quotes from his book and tells us that Epiphanes was a trained philosopher of Plato (as taught by Carpocrates).

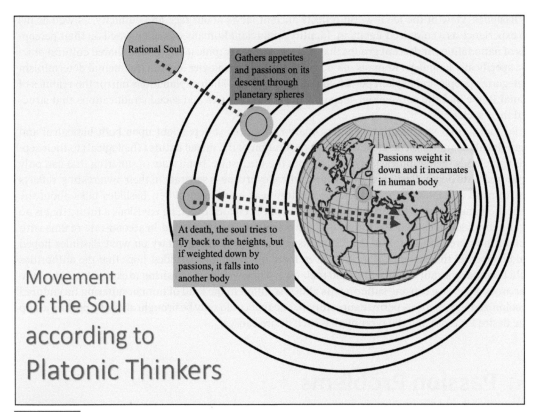

Rational Soul

Gathers appetites and passions on its descent through planetary spheres

Passions weight it down and it incarnates in human body

At death, the soul tries to fly back to the heights, but if weighted down by passions, it falls into another body

Movement of the Soul according to Platonic Thinkers

FIGURE 5.7 Illustration showing how Platonists thought the soul falls from the heavens through the planetary spheres into a human body at birth. It accumulates the passions like appendages on the way down. To ascend back to the heights, it must abandon the passions.

From these quotes, it is clear that the Carpocratians distinguish one of these angels as the Jewish God, the Lawgiver. They find the Jewish God and his Law a joke because it imposes limits to human freedom that other animals do not have. Animals, for instance, breed naturally. Why then should we be limited sexually in monogamous marriages?

Epiphanes makes a distinction between the laws of the natural world and the Jewish Law, both of which he says came from the Creator God (Clem. Alex., *Misc.* 3.2). There is a discrepancy that is laughable, he says, between the Jewish Law and the natural laws. The natural laws reflect a higher order of communal equality or righteousness while the Jewish Law does not. Although the quotes from Epiphanes' book do not give us the details, his argument presumes a Platonic subtext, that the Creator has fashioned the natural world after the pattern of the higher world that is all about equity and unity. So Epiphanes points out what a joke it is that the same God who instituted the Jewish Law to bring about transgression and restrain people, created the heaven to embrace the entire earth, the sun to pour its light equally on all, whether rich, poor, male, female, free, or slave.

The only way out of this rigged system is for the transcendent God to act upon it. He did so when he noticed that a particular soul had lived its life so purely that it remembered the transcendent realm it had visited before it reincarnated as Jesus, son of Joseph. This idea presumes Plato's discussion of memory, that with every reincarnation the soul's memory and knowledge of the Good is forgotten in the trauma of birth. This means that eternal truths which have been with the soul for eternity must be recollected. In Plato's opinion, recollection requires catharsis (purifying the body of the passions), contemplation, and sudden comprehension (Greek: *noesis*).

According to Carpocrates, Jesus was a human being, indistinct from everyone else, except that he had conquered his passions and remembered the eternal truth, the existence of the unbegotten

God. Because of this, God sent down a Power to rest upon him (a reference to Jesus' baptism following the ADULT POSSESSION PATTERN) and strengthen him in his fight with the creators of the world. Jesus recognized the Jewish Law for what it really was (a tool for punishment) and held it in contempt (cf. Rom. 8:3–4). Here again we see emerging an antinomian interpretation of Jesus' message. Although Irenaeus does not tell us one way or the other, we can imagine that this interpretation of Jesus emerged from studying the same passages of Paul which had persuaded Marcion that Jesus' message opposed the Jewish Law.

By refusing to follow the Jewish Law (cf. Rom. 8:2–4; 10:4), Carpocrates believed that Jesus freed himself from the rule of the Archons and became a paradigm for others to model their own escape. If we despise the Archons and their Law similarly, we will receive the same power from on high, and remember the Unbegotten God from whom our souls originally came. Like Jesus, we will be more powerful than the Archons, Carpocrates taught.

What did Carpocrates mean when he says that his followers must despise the Law? Just like Basilides, Carpocrates and his son Epiphanes teach that we must treat all things as indifferent. There is nothing by its nature that is either good or evil. Things are only good or evil because we attach moral significance to them. This moral significance is laid out in the Law which gives the Archons justification to punish us for misdeeds and keep our souls perpetually enslaved in their creation and the societal systems that arbitrate this morality. The Law and the social conventions it sustains must be resisted, rejected, and replaced by behaviors that reflect the natural world and its laws of equality (no difference between sexes), communal life (no private property), unity (humans are the same as other animals), and love (charity for the common good). In this program of naturalization, Carpocrates' Platonism merges with ancient Cynicism. Cynic philosophers like Stoics taught the necessity of overcoming the passions by understanding the indifference of all things, but they went even further by insisting that we should model our behavior after the natural world and other animals. They believed that we can only be happy and flourish if we live according to the laws of nature and treat everything society has to offer with indifference. When we do this, our passions will be in check and our minds will be peaceful. To live happily is to live self-sufficiently outside the conventions of society, rejecting its value judgments and shaming tactics by speaking and acting freely. While we might think that this meant libertine behavior, in fact it meant the opposite. Cynics embodied ascetic practices that literally gave up everything society valued, including wealth, fame, and power. They boiled life down to the basics, to the minimal that they needed to survive. Cynics had the reputation of living like dogs in the street. In fact, the word Cynic means "dog" in Greek.

Diogenes the Dog (412/404–324 BCE) was a famous Cynic whose life showcases the philosophy's principles. To demonstrate these principles, he slept in a discarded ceramic storage jar, begged for his food, only ate when he was hungry, urinated and masturbated in public, shouted his teachings from street corners, and openly mocked people, especially popular teachers and political authorities. His minimalism and asceticism are underscored in a story about his encounter with a poor boy drinking water out of the palms of his hands. Diogenes reacted by discarding the cup that he carried around, considering himself a fool for thinking that he needed it in the first place.

The Carpocratians embodied the principles of Cynicism, choosing to reject society and its conventions by living their lives in harmony with other animals. Like other animals, they made no distinctions between rich or poor, peasants or rulers, uneducated or educated, free or slave, and male or female. They gave up all notions of private property (including the possession of wives and monogamy) and lived in a commune. They are the only example in early Christianity of a group that believed in the equality of the sexes.

Marcellina is a famous woman leader of a Carpocratian group in Rome during the time of Bishop Anicetus (ca. 157–168 CE). Irenaeus says that her group called themselves "Gnostics." Her group used the first known painted icons during their worship services, one of which, they claimed, was an image of Christ that had been painted by Pilate. They also had icons of famous philosophers, including Pythagoras, Plato, Aristotle, and others whom Irenaeus does not name. On festival days, they would crown the icons and parade them around the streets. They also tattooed themselves on the backside of their ear-lobes, a practice that indicated their membership within the commune. With reference to 1 Corinthians 13:13, they valued highly faith (Greek: *pistis*) and love (Greek: *agapê*). By love, they did not mean *eros* or romantic love, but *agapê* or charity for the common good. Their charity was most visible in the meals that they shared in common. Clement of Alexandria calls them *agapê*-meals, which is accurately translated as "charity-meals." We might imagine them to be like our modern-day soup-kitchens for communal dining, rather than, as Clement insinuates, hedonistic banquets or "love-feasts."

It is not hard to understand how Clement and Irenaeus come to characterize the communal life of the Carpocratians and general rejection of society's conventions (which includes sharing wives and equalizing the status of men and women) as lewd and hedonistic. To them, it was. But to the Carpocratians, it was the epitome of a life of self-control and equality, when everything (including sex) is done naturally without passions like jealousy or envy coming into play. If they are able to live happily in this state of social equality and freedom, when they die they will owe nothing to the Devil, but can ascend straight to the Unbegotten Father like Jesus did. If they fail in this project, then their souls will still owe the Devil and will be impris-oned in bodies once more until they can learn to live their lives free of social conventions.

To illustrate this doctrine, the Carpocratians created a slogan ("until you pay the last penny") out of Jesus' saying from Matthew 5:35 which they interpreted allegorically: "When you are with your adversary (i.e. the Devil) on the way (to the Unbegotten Father), take pains to get free of him, so that he may not deliver you to the judge (the Jewish Creator God) and the judge to his servant (an archontic angel), and cast you (your soul) into prison (a body). Amen, I say to you, you will not come thence (out of the cycle of reincarnation) until you have paid the last penny" (cf. Matt. 5:35).

We have a sermon preserved in the Nag Hammadi text, the *Testimony of Truth*, whose ideology is remarkably similar to this portrait of the Carpocratians, including the use of their slogan that souls are unable to pass by the Archon "until they pay the last penny." The sermon starts out by claiming that the truth cannot be found by those who follow the Jewish Law because it is the leaven of the Archons. As long as people remain beholden to the Law, they serve the Archons who use desire and passion to ensnare them in their world order. The example that is used is the same example used by Epiphanes. According to this sermon in the *Testimony of Truth*, passion is reinforced by the law of marriage which the Archons instituted in order to populate the earth. Being obedient to this Law sustains our passions so that we will owe the Archon of Darkness, until we can pay him the last penny.

This perpetual cycle, the sermon proclaims, was interrupted by the descent of a Power at Jesus' baptism, a power which inspired Jesus to speak the truth freely and assisted him in subduing entirely his passions. Jesus did not worry about making eloquent speeches or winning debates, but endured everything that happened to him with silence, patience, and acceptance. In this sermon, equality among people was highly valued by Jesus, who understood that the Power he was given at baptism is available to everyone.

What is the truth that Jesus announced? According to this sermon, Jesus revealed the true God whom only he knew because Jesus was able to forsake the world. Jesus showed others how to do this, so that everyone who renounces the world and the Law also will be able to know the true God. The preacher thinks that Jesus revealed important answers to life's biggest questions. What is the difference between God and subordinate beings like angels? What is soul and what is spirit? Who cre-ated the earth and flesh? Who causes pain? Who suffers? Who governs us? Jesus traces all of human inequities (whether we are lame or blind, rich or poor, powerful or powerless) to the Archons and the passions. Renunciation of the passions by forsaking the world is essential for anyone who hopes to be able to get out of this archontic system of suffering. When we live like Jesus as renunciates empowered by God, we are able to grasp the fringe of his garment and be healed of our suffering.

The sermon goes on to contrast this message of redemption with the message preached by other Christians. He thinks other Christians are ignorant because they do not realize how problematic the passions are, including allowing for sexual desire within marriage because they think that God cre-ated penises that grow large for our enjoyment. In the sermon, other preachers are identified as "blind guides" and compared to Jesus' disciples who did not believe that Jesus walked on water. The author of the sermon thinks that their confession, "We are Christians," is void of any real power because, in their ignorance, they think that Christ died as a sacrifice for their sins. They believe that his sacrificial death purifies them so that on the last day they will be resurrected and hasten to God. They think that their own martyrdom has the power to save them. They do not understand that the true God, the true Father does not require sacrifices. If he did, he would be vainglorious (which he is not). The sermon warns that these other Christians do not know who they really are, in whose world they really live, or where they really will go when they die. It will be a tragic surprise for them to find their souls in the clutches of the Archons. At the end of time, because these other Christians were not able to release themselves from the archontic system, they will be destroyed along with the Archons.

Whatever we might make of the authorship of this sermon in the *Testimony of Truth* – whether it was written by Carpocrates or Epiphanes or someone else – it is clear that the Carpocratians were not licentious in the manner that Irenaeus and Clement suggest. They were not hedonists seeking erotic pleasure. Instead, they thought like Cynics who rejected society's conventions to get rid of privilege and inequity. They were masters of indifference and equality, which they performed by living communally as nature intended. In this way, they believed that they were freeing themselves from the system of Law and sin established by the Archons, and could rest assured that when they died they would follow Jesus home to the realm of the Unbegotten Father.

Timeline

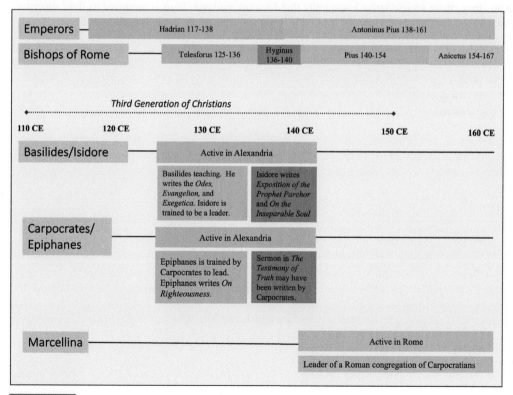

FIGURE 5.8 Timeline for Basilides/Isidore, Carpocrates/Epiphanes, and Marcellina.

Pattern Summary

In this chapter, the patterns of two early Christian philosophers and their sons show that, while they develop two independent INNOVATIVE churches, both are TRANSTHEISTS (Figure 5.9). Both men are operating in Alexandria and use the ten letters of Paul and the Gospel of Matthew. Basilides also may have had access to the *Gospel of Thomas* and a pre-Marcionite version of the *Evangelion* or the Gospel of Luke.

Their transtheist theology led them to develop similar patterns of theodicy (FAULTY GOD) and demiurgy (the Biblical God is a VILLIAN). Because of this particular cluster of patterns (theology, theodicy, and demiurgy), both of their movements are identified in antiquity as Gnostic movements. In fact, Marcellina led a Carpocratian group in Rome who called themselves Gnostics.

They diverge, however, when it comes to their understanding of anthropology and resurrection due to their differing philosophical commitments. Because Basilides is largely competing with Stoics and Valentinians whose "highest" substance is pneuma, he develops a QUADRATIC ANTHROPOLOGY that features a filial substance that surpasses the pneumatic in its divinity and makes the Elect extraordinary humans. Resurrection involves the separation of the quadratic substances into their specified cosmic and transcosmic locations, Jesus being the First-Fruit. Carpocrates is a DUALIST because he follows Plato, understanding the soul to be trapped in the body. The soul must do work to be released from the body. But it cannot do it on its own as Plato thought. Rather a divine Power from God (i.e. the Holy Spirit) must descend on the believer at baptism. This spiritual Power makes it possible for the believer to do what must be done for the soul to become righteous and escape the demiurge's judgment at death and the threat of perpetual reincarnation.

Basilides and Carpocrates each develop very distinctive churches with lifestyles that have little in common, again, because their philosophical commitments differed. Both promote antinomianism and indifference, but Basilides insists that this be cultivated in a way that trumped even the self-controlled Stoics, via asceticism and embracing martyrdom. Carpocrates and Epiphanes, however, understand indifference as the Cynics did. To imitate nature, they curate an egalitarian community that forsakes marriage. Jesus is promoted as their superstar exemplar who showed them how to receive the divine Power via baptism and live holy egalitarian lives.

# Family Pattern Chart
# Basilides and Carpocrates
X=Definitely > L=Likely

THEODICY

	Faulty-God	Faulty-Human	Other
Basilides	X	X	
Carpocrates	X	X	

SOTERIOLOGY

	Gift from God	Human achievement	Minimalist	Moderate	Maximalist
Basilides	X		X		
Carpocrates		X	X		

CHRISTOLOGY

	Adult possession	Fetal possession	Hybrid	Ensoulment	Visitation	Human who received revelation
Basilides	X	Later Basildians				
Carpocrates	X					

ANTHROPOLOGY

	Mono	Dual	Triad	Quad
Basilides				X
Carpocrates		X		

COSMIC DEMIURGY

	Autocrat	Administrator	Caretaker	Patron	Justice	Villain	Rebel	Ignorant	Impaired
Basilides	X	X	X	X		X		X	X
Carpocrates	X	X	X	X		X		X	X

RESURRECTION

	Body reunites with soul	Body discarded and soul immortalized	Body and soul discarded and spirit rises	God-element separates from body soul, and spirit and rises
Basilides				X
Carpocrates		X		

SCRIPTURES

	Jewish	Gospel	Pauline letters (10)	Pauline letters (13)	Hebrews	Acts	Catholic letters	Revelation	Other
Basilides		Ev or Lk Mt GosThom	X						
Carpocrates		Mt	X						

ECCLESIOLOGY

	Consolidation movement	Reform movement	Secessionist movement	Counter movement	Innovative movement	Trans-regional	Regional
Basilides					X		X
Carpocrates					X	Marcellina	

FIGURE 5.9 Summary of patterns of Basilides and Carpocrates.

Takeaways

1. Basilides, Isidore, Carpocrates, and Epiphanes were Christian intellectuals, trained in various forms of philosophy and interacting with their major ideas. While Plato was foundational to all of them, popular ideas and practices from Stoicism and Cynicism also were used to structure patterns of Christian thought and pursue existential questions.

2. Basilides built a Christian Gnostic system that was informed by Platonic and Stoic philosophy.

3. Basilides composed a Gospel and wrote a twenty-four-volume series he called the *Treatises*. They were not biblical commentaries, but expositions on existential questions and philosophical subjects.

4. Basilides relied on the letters of Paul. He also was aware of a number of sayings of Jesus and the crucifixion story, although what his sources were for these sayings and story is debated.

5. Basilides is the original framer of the discussion about original sin and the idea that creation came out of nothing.

6. Basilides was not a docetist but taught that Jesus was born a human being as it is written in the Gospel and that the Christ descended upon him at his baptism and left him at his crucifixion.

7. Carpocrates and Epiphanes built their Gnostic system on Platonic and Cynic platforms.

8. For Basilides, Isidore, Carpocrates, and Epiphanes, the philosophical concept of indifference determined their ethics, although how this played out in Basilidean and Carpocratian communities differed.

9. Carpocratians were the only Christians who believed in the equality of women; their group in Rome was led by the woman Marcellina.

10. Carpocratians dwelled in unconventional communes where men and women lived as close to nature as possible, having given up the normal rules of comportment.

Questions

1. If you were to ask Basilides why children suffer abuse or why Jesus suffered humiliation and crucifixion, how would he have responded?

2. Was Basilides an advocate for predeterminism? If so, how did he explain it? If not, why not?

3. How did Basilides differ from or challenge major tenets of Stoicism? How does Basilides' view of the end of the world compare and contrast with the Stoic position?

4. Did Basilides encourage his followers to avoid martyrdom as Irenaeus says? Why or why not?

5. What are the differences between Irenaeus' presentation of Basilides, Hippolytus' account, and Clement of Alexandria's report? Whose account do you think is the most reliable? Why?

6. If you were to ask Basilides if he were Jewish or Christian, what do you think he would have said? Why? How did his concept of election shape his religious identity? How did the faith of the Elect differ from the faith of the average person according to Basilides?

7. Both Basilides and Carpocrates value indifference. What did each one mean by this?

8. If you were to ask Carpocrates how we can stop human suffering, what would he tell you?

9. What did Carpocrates and Epiphanes think about the Jewish Law? How might their positions have formed out of reading Paul's letters?

10. How did Carpocrates and Epiphanes merge popular Cynic ideas and practices with their Christian system?

11. What kind of community did Marcellina lead in Rome? Why do you think she called her community the "Gnostics"?

12. What religious practices would you have participated in if you belonged to a Basilidian group? Marcellina's group? Lifestyle? Why were Carpocrates and his followers accused of licentious behaviors?

13. If a Carpocratian would have told you that you had to "pay the last penny," what would they have meant?

Resources

Dylan Burns. 2020. *Did God Care? Providence, Dualism, and Will in Later Greek and Early Christian Philosophy.* Studies in Platonism, Neoplatonism, and the Platonic Tradition 25. Leiden: Brill.

M. David Litwa. 2022. Chapters 9 and 10 in *Found Christianities: Remaking the World of the Second Century CE.* London: T&T Clark.

Arland J. Hultgren and Steven A. Haggmark (eds.). 1996. Chapter 6. *The Earliest Christian Heretics: Readings from Their Opponents.* Minneapolis: Fortress Press.

Peter Lampe. 2003. Chapter 28 in *From Paul to Valentinus: Christians at Rome in the First Two Centuries.* Translated by. Michael Steinhauser and edited by Marshall D. Johnson. Minneapolis: Fortress Press.

Bentley Layton. 1989. "The Significance of Basilides in Ancient Christian Thought". *Representations* 28: 135–151.

Birger Pearson. 2005. "Basilides the Gnostic." Pages 1–31 in *A Companion to Second-Century Christian 'Heretics'.* Edited by Antti Marjanen and Petri Luomanen. Supplements to Vigiliae Christianae 76. Leiden: Brill.

Gilles Quispel. 1968. "Gnostic Man: The Doctrine of Basilides." Pages 210–246 in *The Mystic Vision: Papers from the Eranos Yearbooks.* Edited by Joseph Campbell. Bollingen Series 6. Princeton: Princeton University Press.

CHAPTER 6

The Universal Church

Illustration of the Graffito of Alexamenos (200 CE). Paedagogium, Palatine Hill, Rome. **Source:** Rodolfo Lanciani / Wikimedia Commons / Public Domain.

"Straightway, a flame was kindled in my soul; and a love possessed me, a love of the prophets and of those men who are friends of Christ. And while turning over his words in my mind, I found this philosophy alone to be safe and beneficial. Thus, and for this reason, I am a philosopher."

Justin Martyr said this about the time when he met a Christian teacher who showed him the Jewish Scriptures

KEY PLAYERS
Justin Martyr – Tatian
Elchasai – Ebionites

KEY TEXTS
Justin, *1* and *2 Apology* and *Dialogue with Trypho*
Tatian, *Diatessaron* and *Oration to the Greeks*
Gospel of Ebionites – *Gospel of Nazoreans*
Gospel of Hebrews – *1 Timothy*
Epistle of Diognetus – *Epistle of Barnabas*
Melito of Sardis, *On Pascha*

In Chapter 5, we met Basilides and Isidore, philosophers who created a complete system of Christian philosophy laced with Stoic ethics and Gnostic mythology. We also met Carpocrates and Epiphanes who established Christian communes rooted in Platonic and Cynic principles. Twenty years later, another Christian philosopher, Justin Martyr, emerges declaring Christianity the universal philosophy for all times. Justin's goal is to understand this universal truth as it relates to scripture, particularly stories in the Jewish Bible that tell about a great angel of YHWH

Comparing Christianities: An Introduction to Early Christianity, First Edition. April D. DeConick.
© 2024 John Wiley & Sons Ltd. Published 2024 by John Wiley & Sons Ltd.

(a.k.a. angel of the Lord) who came to earth to speak for God. Justin writes in Rome between 150–160 CE at a time when the controversy surrounding Christianity identity as it relates to Judaism was far from resolved. To defend his version of Christianity as the truth, Justin takes on Judaism, the Law, and biblical prophesies, all the while delineating Christians as people who rightly worship the Creator of the earth, YHWH the God of the Jewish scriptures. As he writes, we become aware of Christian gospels that Justin knew but called the *Memoirs of the Apostles*. This seems to have been a gospel harmony that Justin's student, Tatian likely completed after Justin's execution. Tatian's gospel harmony – the *Diatessaron* – became the Syrian Bible for Christians who lived in Mesopotamia until the fifth century.

6.1 A Chance Encounter with Justin

COMPANION READINGS

Justin, *Dialogue with Trypho* 1–9

Justin of Flavia Neapolis (modern-day Nablus) was fleeing Samaria in the aftermath of the failed Jewish insurrection led by Simon Bar Kochba (the Bar Kochba Revolt; 132–135 CE) which we learned about in Chapter 2, when discussing Marcion. We learned that Bar Kochba and his guerilla forces had captured towns and garrisons across Judea, including Jerusalem, as they attempted to free Israel from Roman occupation. Roman response was swift and harsh, demolishing the Jewish strongholds and cities, including Jerusalem. To signal the end of the Jewish nation, the Romans renamed Judea "Syria Palestine." They plowed under the rubble left in the streets of Jerusalem and rebuilt a Roman city, Aelia Capitolina, to replace Jerusalem. Jews were forbidden to live there. Emperor Hadrian also made it illegal for them to study Torah, observe Sabbath, circumcise their children, hold Jewish courts, meet in synagogues, and perform other Jewish rituals. Refugees of the war fled the province, Justin was among them (cf. 1 *Apol.* 1.31.6; 1.53.9). His destination was Rome, a city he had visited earlier as a younger man (*Acta Just.* 3).

On his way to Rome, Justin laid over in Ephesus, awaiting favorable winds and weather for the ship he had booked to sail. Years later, Justin would compose a book about a conversation he claims to have had with a certain Jew, Trypho, while they walked along the covered walkway of a gymnasium near the harbor. He tells us that, as Trypho and his friends entered the walkway, Trypho notices Justin standing there leaning on a staff, dressed in a pallium (a rough woolen cloak) and light sandals, and sporting a beard. Since this was the stock uniform of a popular philosopher and educated man, Trypho hails him and they strike up a conversation (Justin, *Dial.* 1; 9). They inquire about each other. Trypho reveals that he, like Justin, is a war refugee who has been spending most of his time in Corinth and other parts of Greece studying philosophy. He asks after Justin, what philosophy he is peddling. He wants to know what Justin thinks about God.

Delighted to be asked, Justin shares with Trypho his life journey as an intellectual, yearning to learn life's truths. He recounts a standard general education for a Roman provincial, who decided at some point in his life to become a scholar specializing in philosophy. To do so, he says that he successively learned about all the prominent philosophies. While he found Stoicism interesting, he also found it utterly lacking when it came to answering questions about God, given that the Stoics were materialists more concerned with ethics than theology. When he inquired about learning Aristotle's system from the Peripatetics, he decided against pursuing it once he learned that there was a fee to join the school. When he tried to join the Pythagoreans, he could not pass their entrance examination, which tested competence in astronomy, geometry, and music. The school he finally settles on was Platonic because, he says, they taught him how to rise above materiality and attain a vision of God. In fact, Platonists in the second century, like the famous Numenius of Apamea, were known to teach an ethics and contemplative lifestyle which aided the soul to recall its original state when it lived in the company of the Gods and looked upon the Good, Plato's ultimate reality.

Justin was content until he met a Christian who showed him the Jewish scriptures for the first time. Justin was enchanted by their antiquity, uncritically accepting that the scriptures had been authored by Moses who was thought to have lived at the time of the Pharaohs, long before any Greek philosopher taught or wrote. Persuaded that he might have in his hands a philosophy more ancient than Plato, he takes up their study as a Christian proselyte. Justin becomes convinced that they reveal an ancient perennial truth, not as Jews read them, but as Christians do.

He comes to believe that Christianity is the genuine original philosophy that had been misunderstood by the Jews and subsequently degenerated into the multiplicity of Greek philosophical schools. As he talks to Trypho, Justin works to differentiate Christianity from Judaism and contemporary philosophies, subordinating them to Christianity. As an interlocutor, Trypho is excessively deferential and accommodating to Justin's opinions, suggesting that Justin's composition is not so much a record of their encounter as it is an encounter that Justin fictionalizes to construct Christian identity against the objections of Jews like Trypho. His academic project becomes laser-focused: to define who and what a Christian really is.

6.2 Christianity as a Universal Philosophy

COMPANION READINGS
Genesis 6:1–4
Justin, *Dialogue with Trypho* 126–128
Justin, *Second Apology* 3–6, 13

As a scholar of philosophy, Justin was enchanted with the thought that he had discovered in Christianity a philosophy that was more ancient than all the philosophies current during his time. Like the other philosophies, Christianity was, for him, a philosophy that had as its goal the awareness of the divine (what really exists) and the attainment of a happy life as reward (Justin, *Dial.* 3). The difference was that Christianity fully revealed the truth about God (what really exists), while the other philosophies only partially did so. As Justin studied and wrote in the middle of the second century, he created a system of Christian philosophy that was universal in scope. He believed that his work was recovering the aboriginal truth, a perennial philosophy that was not only Christian, but also the universal parent to all philosophies and religions in history.

Like other philosophers, Justin is interested in the question of what started everything. What was the first cause that originated the cosmos and the human being? Justin knew the commonly discussed options. Greek philosophers had been talking about abiogenesis (the origin of life) since Thales of Miletus (624–546 BCE). As we saw in previous chapters of this textbook, it had become popular in academic circles to argue that the origin of life could be identified with some kind of primal intellect or mind (Greek: *nous*), intelligence or wisdom (Greek: *sophia*), or reason or knowledge (Greek: *logos*). According to the Stoics, in the process of creation, this intellectual ability had been sown in human beings as the *logos spermatikos* (seed of reason), vitalizing their souls (Greek: *psyche*) or minds (Greek: *nous*).

Justin favored this Logos language. Yet he did not understand the pre-existent Logos as the Stoics did, as an impersonal fiery force that structures and organizes the cosmos. Instead Justin personalized and historicized the Logos by identifying it with Jesus Christ, the Son of God, an idea he likely picked up from the Gospel of John. According to Justin, God first created his Son, Reason or Logos, who eventually incarnates as the historical man Jesus (*1 Apol.* 5.4; *2 Apol.* 6). Justin argued that the Logos was responsible for creating the cosmos as his Father's subordinate and executor, a second God (Justin, *Dial.* 56; *1 Apol.* 13.4; 63.10). In the process of creation, the Logos created seeds of the divine Logos (Greek: *logos spermatikos*) and distributed them into human beings. Justin did not understand these seeds to be unbegotten and immortal pieces of God, but seeds of intelligence that the Logos created and bestowed in the human soul (Greek: *psyche*) so that humans would have the capacity to know the Christian truth, even before the Logos incarnated as Jesus Christ, when he would reveal the truth to everyone openly (*2 Apol.* 13).

What is Justin's understanding of Christian truth? Justin believes that the scriptures reveal the existence of one God, the transcendent source of life who is also the Biblical Creator God responsible for creating and governing the world. Justin's emphasis on the transcendent nature of God reflects his Platonic sympathies. In the second century, Platonists had speculated that the source of life, the Good, was so transcendent that the only way it could be described was apophatically, that is, to name what it is not. The Good's transcendence was so complete that it had to generate another God to create the cosmos and serve as a mediator between the divine and human realms.

Justin understands the Christian God to be the only true God (1 *Apol.* 6.1), a universal God who is completely Other (*Dial.* 4.1). He is an exclusive God, which means that there are no other Gods but him. He is so elevated that he lives above the heavens (*Dial.* 32.3; 60.2) and is nameless (*2 Apol.* 6.1–2). The mediator is his Son, the Logos, who fashions the world to reflect God's master plan (1 Apol 13.4; 63.10). The human race (Greek: *genos*) takes center stage; the world is created to benefit humanity (*2 Apol.* 4.2). Justin understands God to be Providence, caring for creation by appointing angels as guardians (*2 Apol.* 5.2).

To explain how this idyllic state collapsed, Justin references Genesis 6:1–4. Based on his reading of this text, he believed that some of the angels refused to act as custodians of their human charges and instead succumbed to lust and had sex with the women they were supposed to be caretaking. The children born were monstrous human-angel hybrids whom Justin called demons (Greek: *daimones*) (*2 Apol.* 5.3; Gen. 6:4). The demons enslaved the human race and encouraged them to murder, make war, commit adultery, and be licentious (*2 Apol.* 4 [5].4–6). They demanded to be worshiped as Gods, requiring sacrifices, incense offerings, and libations. Because people did not use their reason (Greek: *logos*) to understand what the demons were doing, in their ignorance they instead identified the demons with Gods (*1 Apol.* 5.2). Justin explains that the demons were responsible for the invention of the Greek myths about the Gods. They spread these myths among the Greeks and among all the other nations to deceive and misguide the human race (Greek: *genos*) (*1 Apol.* 54.1, 3).

In Justin's mind, polytheism originated because demons managed to install themselves as divinities worshiped by the different nations or ethnicities (Greek: *ethne*). The true God, however, chose the Jewish nation to know him and worship him. According to Justin, this did not go well since the Jews eventually succumbed to worshiping demons when, for instance, they built the golden calf (Deut. 32:17; *1 Apol.* 119.2; and Isa. 65:11; *1 Apol.* 135.4).

Despite the subterfuge of the demons, Justin is convinced that some historical figures, like Socrates and Plato, had caught partial glimpses of the truth because they were able to discern God using their divine intellect (Greek: *logos spermatikos*) (*2 Apol.* 13.5). Justin argues that Socrates and others like him were able to perceive through reason something of what was revealed by the Logos himself when he incarnated as Jesus (*1 Apol.* 5.4). They were able to recognize the One God and criticize polytheism. They had a sense that the soul could be immortalized. Many of these people were hated and put to death (*2 Apol.* 8.1; *1 Apol.* 5.3), evidence of the demons trying to silence them.

Justin considered these people Christians-before-their-time, presenting them as forerunners of the Christian faith. His Christian contemporaries, he thinks, are linked to these heroic people of the past who were able to resist the power of the demons and live in accordance with the Logos. To acknowledge pre-Christian standards and truths, Justin exploits the Stoic concept of the primal Logos and its cosmic distribution. With the Logos mythology, he is able to align Christian truth with conventional Roman knowledge so that Christianity would make sense to the Roman intelligentsia and fit into their history of ideas.

The incarnation of the Logos, however, is a specifically Christian innovation, one that did not have precedence in Greek philosophical speculation (Justin, *1 Apol.* 5.4). Justin explained this idea by connecting it to stories of the appearances of angels in Jewish scriptures. Justin appropriates certain stories about the appearance of the great Angel of the Lord who is God's manifestation (Hebrew: *kavod*; Greek: *doxa*). Because this angel bears God's private and personal name YHWH, he was perceived to share God's identity and serve as his voice. In other words, God, who is invisible, was thought to use the appearance of his angel to reveal himself to humans. This means that the appearances of the Angel of YHWH are full-blown theophanies or God-revelations. They represent the times when God revealed himself to Abraham at the oaks of Mamre or Moses at the burning bush or to Jacob at Penuel.

This identification also allowed Justin to maintain that all the references to God walking and talking and doing things on earth was actually not the "Ineffable Father" who cannot be spatially located, who does not have eyes or ears and cannot descend to earth (*Dial.* 126–128). When Justin read these stories, he read them as angelic manifestations of the Logos in humanlike form, manifestations that prefigured the Logos' actual incarnation as the human Jesus. In other words, God's Logos pre-existed, manifested throughout Jewish history as the Angel of YHWH (as evidenced in the scriptural stories), and incarnated as Jesus in Mary's womb. Justin is an advocate for the virgin birth, saying that the Logos-Angel was born "through a virgin" and understands that the Logos assumed flesh and blood and became a man (Justin, *1 Apol.* 66.2). The Logos (the full Mind of God) that Jesus had is similar in kind to the *logos spermatikos* that other people possess, but far greater (*1 Apol.* 32.8; 46.3; *2 Apol.* 8.1; 10.2; 13.3). Justin also reinterprets Jesus' baptism to be the historical watershed moment when God's Spirit is transferred from the Jews to Jesus and the Christians. With the Logos mythology, Justin was able to secure the biblical God's transcendence and developed an ENSOULMENT CHRISTOLOGICAL PATTERN such as Valentinus had done earlier.

That said, Justin admits that it is a "mystery" how it happened that the Logos came to be identified with a crucified man, although the demons were certainly involved as they tried to stop the revelation of the truth by killing Jesus (*1 Apol.* 13.4). Their effort to blot him out ultimately failed. The genie could not be put back into the bottle. Despite Jesus' death, the Logos had come to earth and revealed the true God (*Dial.* 61.1–3). The demons' trickery had been made known. They had lost their grip on humanity and their utter annihilation was considered a sure thing in the future (*1 Apol.* 28.1; *2 Apol.* 6 [7].1).

6.3 Christian Antiquity

COMPANION READINGS
Justin, *Dialogue with Trypho* 16, 18–19, 24, 29
Melito of Sardis, *On Pascha*
Epistle of Barnabas

Justin took what his fellow Romans knew was a new faith, a novel Jewish sect that started with Jesus of Nazareth, and situated it as perennial philosophy that predated Moses. This made Christianity older than all the important Greek philosophers and authors, including Homer, as well as Judaism with its Mosaic law. Justin made this argument by using the antiquity of the Jewish scriptures to his advantage, leveraging the Christian philosophical interpretation of them as the recovery of their genuine meaning. This genuine meaning is a perennial philosophy that, Justin says, the Jews did not perceive because they rejected and killed Jesus Christ. As a result of their faithlessness, they did not receive the key to unlock the true meaning of the scriptures. The Christians did. According to Justin, the scriptures no longer belong to the Jews, but to the Christians who faithfully understand them.

In his arguments, Justin exploits Jewish scripture to prove the continuity between Jewish scriptures and Christianity. He draws Christianity back into ancient times by insisting that all scriptural theophanies are to be read as revelations of Christ, the Logos. Likewise all messianic prophecies exclusively point to Jesus Christ and his, not one, but two comings, first in lowliness and second in glory (*Dial.* 10–30; 48–108). Any of the prophecies mentioned in Christian gospels that are not found in Jewish scriptures, Justin accuses Jewish scribes of cutting out of the scriptures (*Dial.* 71–73, 120.5). The rise of Christianity, Justin believes, was foretold in scriptures, scriptures that are no longer the possession of the Jews who were not able to grasp their spirit (*Dial.* 29.2). Justin authorizes his interpretation of the scriptures by arguing that this is not his own eccentric read of these texts, but an interpretation that he received from Christ himself through the mediation of Christ's apostles.

Jesus' baptism is viewed by Justin as the moment when Jewish prophecy ceases and the Spirit of God is transferred from the Jews to Jesus and the Christians. Justin insists that because Christ is the new law, laws like circumcision, Sabbath observation, and diet now must be read for their spiritual meaning, not their literal sense (*Dial.* 10–47). In Justin's mind, the Christian church is the true people of God, the new Israel (*Dial.* 10–47). It inherited the scriptures and all the privileges and promises that the Jewish people lost because they rejected Christ. The church, as the new Israel, also would become the rightful priests and heirs of Jerusalem in the future age (*Dial.* 82.1; 116.3).

Justin argues not only that the Christian church rather than the Jewish nation is God's people, but also that the Christian church is better than the Jewish nation. In his attempt to make Christianity an ancient universal philosophy distinct from Judaism, he degrades Judaism. Even though the Jewish people had a chance to know the truth, Justin says, they were blind and faithless, overly susceptible to sin and idolatry. To punish them for their rebellion and history of sinfulness, God imposed the Jewish Law on them. But then, when they also foolishly rejected Christ, God further punished them by using the Romans to destroy their temple, massacre the inhabitants of Jerusalem and, from its ashes, rebuild a Roman city in which Jews were outlawed. In this way, Justin uses the consequences of the first Jewish War and the Bar Kochba Revolt, both squelched viciously by Rome, to debase Judaism. Against this degradation, Justin distinguishes and elevates Christianity. He argues that the results of these historical skirmishes proved that the sacrificial system and the Mosaic Law had been rendered obsolete by God, that God had discarded the Jewish people in favor of the Christians.

Justin was not alone in his deprecation of the Jewish people. The *Epistle of Barnabas*, another early Christian text, interprets the exodus story in such a way that the Jews, convicted of idolatry when they created the molten calf, were utterly rejected by God. According to the author of the epistle, this is reflected in the fact that when Moses broke the tablets of the law, God ended his covenant with the Jews. The author makes very clear that anyone who thinks that God's covenant is with both the Jews and the Christians is sorely mistaken (*Barn.* 4). When Moses received the second set of tablets, they were not for the Jews but were intended for the future Christians (*Barn.* 14). They were meant to be read spiritually – the Jews do not understand this and try to obey the laws literally (*Barn.* 10). The author reveals the spiritual interpretation. Circumcision is not circumcision of the foreskin, but circumcision of the ear and heart (*Barn.* 9). Avoiding pork has nothing to do with giving up bacon. It tells Christians that they must avoid people who forget the Lord when they live hedonistically, but remember the Lord when they want something. When Moses says to eat animals that chew their cud and have cloven feet, God is telling Christians to be the sort of people who meditate on God's commandments and obey them with gladness (*Barn.* 10). The Christians, the true interpreters and observers of God's law, have inherited God's promises as God's people (*Barn.* 14).

The belief expressed both by Justin and the author of the *Epistle of Barnabas* that the Jews, because of their own insolence, had been displaced by the Christians worked to delegitimize Judaism, distance Christianity from it, and authorize Christianity as God's chosen people. That said, Justin did not see Christians as some new group that God chose to replace the Jews. Christians are not simply a new Israel. According to Justin, Christianity continues a line that goes back to God's promise made to Abraham so that its claim to be Israel is genuine. Because Christianity is the continuation of a religious people which predated the Jewish Law, it cannot be scorned as novel or new. It is a pre-Mosaic religion practiced by the faithful patriarchs and was maintained by the prophets. As for the Law of Moses, it had no significance as an identity marker for Christians except that it symbolically pointed to Christ, something that the Jews did not see. In Justin's opinion, its only value was to serve as divine punishment for the sinfulness of the Jews.

(6.4) The Christian Race

COMPANION READINGS
Justin, *Dialogue with Trypho*
116–119, 130
Epistle of Diognetus 3–8, 10

Justin's construction of Christianity as a pre-Mosaic perennial philosophy was conceptualized in ethnic and racial terms. In antiquity, ethnicity (Greek: *ethnos*) and race (Greek: *genos*) were used similarly to identify groups of people with particular territories, ancestry, language, religion, and physical traits. Binaries were also in play. As colonizers, the Greek and Romans identified themselves as superior civilized people against the rest of the world's inhabitants whom they called barbarians (Greek: *barbaros*). Comparably, the Jews mapped themselves as the chosen people of their God yhwh, while everyone else was part of the non-elect Gentile nations (Greek: *ethne*). Justin remapped this binary, identifying the Gentiles as God's special or chosen people, nation, or race. Given that the Jewish scriptures identify the Jews as God's elect people, how was Justin able to redraw the lines of this Jewish ethnographic map and why did he do it?

Justin does not perceive Christians to be Jews, although he knows about a small number of Christians who observe Jewish laws, a practice he finds unnecessary and pointless. Instead, Justin understands the majority of Christians to be Gentiles drawn from varying nationalities or ethnicities (Greek: *ethne*). Justin identifies them as a Christian race (Greek: *genos*) even though this miscellaneous assortment of people (Greek: *ethne*) did not have any of the usual characteristics of a race or ethnic group as Romans understood them. They did not come from the same geographical location, they did not have a unique language, and they did not have an ancient traditional religion or God.

This is why the author of the *Epistle of Diognetus*, another third-generation composition, is compelled to explain what this new Christian race (Greek: *genos*) is if they are not people from a particular country, sharing a common language and customs (*Diogn.* 1; 5–6). The author explains that Christians are found inhabiting Greek and barbarian cities alike, living according to the indigenous customs of each locale. They are dispersed through all the cities of the world like the soul is dispersed in the body (*Diogn.* 6). What they have in common is a lifestyle that requires Christians to live in their own countries as citizens but to act like resident aliens (*Diogn.* 5). They live by a code of morality that sets them apart from other citizens. For instance, while they marry and have children, they do not expose their infants. They obey the laws of the land, while exceeding the prescriptions ethically. Christians are at the same time citizens of their cities and citizens of heaven (*Diogn.* 5). They receive these moral laws from God's messenger and mediator, the Logos (*Diogn.* 7). Part of this moral code is to refuse worshipping idols. Instead Christians worship the actual source of life, God, the Lord and Creator of all things, who, although invisible, conceived his Son, the Logos in his mind. God then revealed himself to his Son, his assistant in creation (*Diogn.* 7–8). This God is defined as "absolute Good" and "free from wrath" (*Diogn.* 8). For the benefit of humankind, God made the world and gave humans reason to be able to recognize the coming of his Son and to receive knowledge of the Father (*Diogn.* 10). According to the author, those who believed his message were the Gentiles, not the Jews. Because of the faith of the Gentiles, the Son blessed the churches of the Gentiles. These are places where Christians gather to chant the fear of the Law, to make known the grace of the prophets, to establish the faith of the gospels, and to preserve the tradition of the apostles (*Diogn.* 11).

Even with these kinds of arguments, the Romans considered Christianity a novel foreign sect started by a Jewish criminal who had been executed by the Roman state when Pontius Pilate had governed Judea. To identify with Christianity made one, like Jesus, a traitor to the state, a crime punishable by death. The Romans believed that the Christians were Jewish sectarians who gathered in political clubs, actively plotting to undermine the state by overthrowing Rome and installing Jesus Christ as ruler of their much-talked-about kingdom.

As Christians like Justin began to distance themselves from Judaism, this was identified by some Romans as even more cause for concern. The Roman philosopher Celsus, for instance, considered Christians so seditious that they even revolted against their ancestors, the Jews, who, in Celsus' mind, were already disloyal enough. Even though Judaism enjoyed a certain level of tolerance among the Romans as an approved religion (Latin: *religio lictia*), the Jews had a reputation among Romans of being a dangerous and recalcitrant people who frequently revolted in their attempt to gain their independence. To understand Christians as revolutionaries who overthrew Jewish revolutionaries was not a good image for Christians.

Christian disloyalty to the state was further evident to the Romans in the Christians' refusal to worship the state Gods which guaranteed the public's well-being (Latin: *salus publica*). Christians were nothing more than despicable atheists in their eyes. The only reason why anyone would want to join such a sedi-tious and outlawed superstition (Latin: *superstitio*), the Romans surmised, was that Christians were seduc-ing uneducated peasants and slaves with their nonsense and hedonism. It was clear to the Romans that the Christians were beyond the pale. According to them, they committed ritualistic murder in their eucha-rists, which the Romans thought were cannibalistic banquets. They also engaged in incestuous agape or love feasts with their brothers and sisters. They were so gullible and stupid that it became a running joke among the Romans that Christians worshiped an ass. This caricature is not only mentioned in the litera-ture (Tert., *Nat.* 1.11; Orig., *Cels.* 3.1; cf. Jos., *Apion* 2.8) but also scratched in graffiti in the Paedagogium on the Palatine Hill in Rome (200 CE), an illustration which is our earliest known visual depiction of Christ. The graffiti reads: "Alexamenos worships God" (see illustration on first page of this chapter).

Much of Justin's writing is focused on addressing Romans' concerns about Christianity and defending it from these sorts of stereotypical charges. His books, the *1 Apology* and the *2 Apology*, are intentional defenses of Christianity, petitioning the Roman rulers to desist punishing Christians unfairly. Justin knew that accused Christians were sentenced and executed immediately after the legal proceedings in which they confessed to being Christian. Justin points out that it is an anomaly for Roman law to execute someone because of their name alone (Latin: *nomen ipsum*) without any evi-dence of additional punishable offenses.

In these writings, Justin also refutes the rumors of treason, cannibalism, incest, hedonism, and athe-ism. High on Justin's radar is the need to explain that Christians are not a political threat to Rome. They are not plotting the establishment of an earthly kingdom in place of Rome. Instead, they are waiting for God's judgment when they will enter the heavenly kingdom. In the meantime, Christians only want to help people live virtuous lives that sustain society. To demonstrate compatibility with the Roman slogan "what is older is better" (*presbyteron kreitton*), Justin argues that Christianity is highly consistent with the old traditional values. Christians are so virtuous, he says, that they hold to a code of ethics far stricter than even the strictest philosophies such as Stoicism. Christians have exceedingly high standards when it comes to chastity, benevolence, forbearance, patience, and truth-telling. Also Justin points out, Chris-tians pay their taxes and are loyal subjects of the empire. They respect Roman authorities at all times.

Justin problematizes Christianity's relationship with Judaism – both the charges that Christianity is a new religion and a schismatic revolutionary religion – by turning to the Jewish scriptures where he iden-tifies passages in which the word *ethne* occurs. For instance, when Justin reads from Isaiah (49:6), "I have appointed you to be the light to the Gentiles (*ethne*), that you may be their salvation even to the farthest part of the earth," he understands that God is forecasting that he will send Christ to the Gentiles (*ethne*) (*Dial.* 121.4). In Malachi (1:10–12), Justin understands the references to offering sacrifices to God to refer to the eucharist offered to him by "us Gentiles (*ethne*)" in the Christian churches (*Dial.* 41.3). He interprets Deut. 32:43, likewise. He takes this passage to mean "that we the nations (*ethne*) rejoice with his people," that is, Christians (we the nations, *ethne*) rejoice with Abraham, Isaac, Jacob, and the prophets (*Dial.* 130.2).

Justin's study of these and other passages led him to conclude that, after Jesus was crucified, the Christians sprang up as a people (*laos*) just as the prophets had predicted. He writes, "'And many nations (*ethne*) shall flee unto the Lord in that day and they shall be for him a people (*laos*) (Deut 32:16–23); and they shall dwell in the midst of the whole earth' (Zech. 2:11). But we are not only a people (*laos*), but a holy people (*laos*), as we have already shown: 'And they shall call it a holy people, redeemed by the Lord'" (Isa. 62:12). Justin goes on to differentiate the Christians as a nation (*ethnos*) that is not a "contemptible" people (*demos*), nor a tribe (*phylon*) of barbarians, nor ethnic groups such as the Carian or the Phyrgians, but a nation (*ethnos*) chosen by God (Isa. 65:1). The Christians form the nation (*ethnos*) promised to Abraham by God, Justin concludes, when God told Abraham that he would make him a father of many nations (*ethne*) (*Dial.* 119.3–4).

In this way, Justin presents the Christians as a new panethnic people, a new nation, race, or people that is distinct from the Jews and drawn from all the nations (*ethne*). While this new race is distinct from the Jews, it is not really a new race, but it is a continuation of a people promised to Abraham. With this argument, Justin presents Christianity as a form of religion that predates Moses and the Jewish Law.

This remapping of ethnic boundaries represents a dramatic, although gradual, shift in religious identity among Christians. In the middle of the first century, the Christian movement first took shape as a Jewish messianic sect open to Gentiles. In terms of identity, the movement was located within the Jewish nation and identity. It was based in Jerusalem and Jewish Diasporic cities around Judea, Samaria, and Syria. It found purchase especially in those cities that had large populations of sympathetic Gentile proselytes who admired the monotheistic worship of YHWH. The first Christians understood Jesus to be Israel's Messiah who inaugurated the end times and invited Gentiles to share in Israel's promises. They perceived themselves to be a people with a common identity that blurred traditional ethnic boundaries between Jews and Gentiles. They had either been incorporated within Israel along with the ethnic Jews, or they represented the remnant of the true Israel. In either case, the Mosaic laws were perceived to be valid for their entire community and they observed the laws as Jesus had taught them to do.

Over time, more Gentiles converted than ethnic Jews. This led to Christians debating the continued relevance of the Jewish Law. Many Christiansm began to place a bigger emphasis on the ethical aspects of the Law and to see the rest of the Law as ceremonial and less and less consequential to their daily lives. The catastrophic conflicts between the Jews and their Roman colonizers (e.g. Roman-Jewish War, Kitos Conflict, and Bar Kochba Revolt), put further pressure on the movement. These conflicts raised real questions for Christians about their Jewish identity. For many Christians, the Jewish identity of the Christian movement became more and more of a liability than a safeguard against Roman charges of religious novelty. This is the main reason why Marcionism had great appeal in the mid-second century. In Marcionite churches, Christianity had a distinct non-Jewish identity as a religious movement that had always been separate from Judaism, rescuing Gentiles from the plans of the Creator God who had chosen the Jews as his own people and left everyone else to suffer with no hope of salvation. Likewise, the followers of Valentinus, Basilides, and other early Gnostic Christian leaders, identified the Jews and other Christians as worshippers of an inferior, sometimes demonic God, in contrast to themselves as worshippers of the true transcendent Source of Life.

Justin pushed back against Marcion and Gnostic leaders like Valentinus, trying to resolve the tension with Judaism by laying claim to the antiquity of Jewish identity while, at the same time, insisting on a distinct Christian identity. He did this by fostering a replacement theory that devalued Judaism. In one sentence, Justin sums this up in his dialogue with Trypho, "God promised Abraham a religious and righteous nation (*ethnos*) of like faith, and a delight to the Father." But, Justin insists, this is not the Jews "in whom there is no faith" (*Dial.* 119.6). In this way, Justin is able to argue that Christianity is not a new religion, but is older than Judaism, and that Christianity is a faithful nation (*ethnos*) distinct from the rebellious Jewish people.

Justin redraws the binary Jew/non-Jew in such a way that, as a result of Jesus' death, the Christians become God's chosen people. As a holy people, he places them in stark contrast to the faithless Jews. The righteous Christians are Abraham's children who will inherit God's promises, not the Jews. On the one hand, Justin presents the Christian church as the new race, people, or nation set over and against the Jewish nation. On the other hand, he makes the argument that this new nation is the same nation that Abraham was promised, that is, Israel itself. Justin's description of Christian identity is an omen of anti-Jewish sentiment developed exclusively among Gentile Christians who had constructed and adopted a supersessionist narrative about themselves.

The replacement theory became very popular because it allowed Christians like Melito of Sardis (160 CE) to explain why the Jews had failed to respond positively to the Christian message. In his sermon (*On Pascha*), Melito accuses Jews of injustice, disgrace, and ignorance because they spilled innocent blood by murdering Christ. Why did they kill Christ? Melito thinks it was because they were not devoted to God or grateful to him. Melito argues that the Jews are not really Israel. Instead the Jews are opposed to the Lord, while the Gentiles worship him and are glorified. In this way, Melito suggests that the failure on the part of most of the Jews to respond positively to Jesus made it possible for another group – the Christians - to replace them.

Contemporary Christianity is often marketed as a universally-inclusive religion (i.e. good) in contrast to Judaism's exclusivism and ethnic particularity as God's chosen nation (i.e. bad). This idea was constructed as a binary by early Christians like Justin who structured Christianity identity using ethno-racial language themselves, rendering Christianity a special distinct universal race that replaced the Jewish people.

[6.5] Law-Observant Christians

COMPANION READINGS

Justin, *Dialogue with Trypho* 45–48
Irenaeus, *Against Heresies* 1.26
Hippolytus, *Refutation* 9.13–16
Epiphanius, *Refutation of All Heresies* 19.1–4
Gospel of the Ebionites
Gospel of Hebrews
Gospel of Nazoreans

In the *Dialogue with Trypho*, Justin goes to great length to restrict law-observation as a Christian practice. Because Justin's argument for the antiquity of Christianity as a perennial philosophy is based on the supposed age of the Jewish scriptures, Justin does not set aside the Jewish scriptures as Marcion did. Rather Justin maintains their authenticity as revelation from God. He however argues that the ceremonial laws concerning circumcision, Sabbath observation, and diet were never intended for Christians, but were imposed on the Jews by God as divine punishment for their idolatry and insolence. By using the Law in this way as the wedge, Justin works to distinguish Christians, who do not observe the ceremonial laws, from Jews who do observe the ceremonial laws.

This wedge proves problematic for Justin because Justin knows that not all Christians felt this way about the Law. He admits to Trypho that indeed there are both Jewish and Gentile Christians, he knows, who observe the ceremonial laws. Justin's opinion is that these Christians lack good judgment and misunderstand the penitential nature of the Law. They think that they are being virtuous by observing the Law when, in fact, the Law was imposed to punish Jewish insolence. Justin says that their choice to practice the ceremonial laws is inconsequential to their salvation as long as they confess Christ and do not compel converts to be circumcised or make them observe any of the other ceremonial laws. Justin considers these law-observant Christians part of the new Christian race, but raises doubt about the value of their practices.

While Justin does not give us any more details about the identity of these law-observant Christians, other sources mention a second-century law-observant Christian sect called the Ebionites (Hebrew: *ebyonim*, the Poor) (Iren., *Heresies* 1.26.2; Origen, *Cels.* 2.1; Epiph., *Pan.* 30; cf. *Ps.-Clementines*). These sources tell us that Ebionites believed that Jesus was Joseph's biological son. It is noteworthy that Justin, immediately after discussing his opinion on law-observant Christians, mentions Christians who believe that Jesus was not virginally born, but was Joseph's offspring (Just., *Dial.* 48). Given this, Justin was probably familiar with an Ebionite group. The fourth-century Bishop of Salamis, Epiphanius, reports that the Ebionites believed that Christ was created before anything. He was set over the angels and had appeared to Adam and the patriarchs (Epiph., *Pan.* 30.3–6). It was at Jesus' baptism, that the Christ's Spirit entered him and he was adopted as God's son and prophet. Again we see the ADULT POSSESSION PATTERN in play.

The Ebionites believed that Jesus' job while on earth was to be the voice of God, teaching his followers how to live righteously according to the Jewish Law as it was originally written. The Ebionites did not accept the authenticity of all of the Jewish scriptures, but believed that they had become corrupted over time with the addition of human opinions and judgments, including concessions from Moses himself. Jesus, as the True Prophet, came to point out the false passages that had corrupted God's scriptures and instruct his followers about the original meaning of the Law. Corrupted passages included all references to God as a humanlike being with emotions or a body, all plural references to God (us, we, our), and all references to sacrificial cult practices.

This particular sect of law-observant Christians took the dietary laws so seriously that they chose to be vegetarians. While vegetarianism was not traditionally a component of law-observation, Jews who ate at Gentiles' tables often chose to eat vegetarian meals in order to avoid improperly prepared meat dishes. Since meat in antiquity was a byproduct of sacrifices at pagan temples, the fact that they were against sacrifice likely factored into their vegetarianism as well. The eucharist they performed annually, using unleavened bread and water as the elements. In addition to using baptism as an initiatory rite, several times a day they stood fully clothed in the river, performing repeated baptism for purposes of healing and continuous purification, a practice quite cogent with ritual immersion baths that Jews performed in *mikvot* (special bathing pools with natural water sources often constructed next to synagogues). Young men in their communities were required to marry. They circumcised their children, worshipped on the Sabbath (Saturday) as well as the Lord's Day (Sunday) in their own synagogues, prayed facing Jerusalem, and held big Passover celebrations every year. They identified as messianic Jews, refusing to eat at the same table with non-observant Christians whom they considered Gentiles. They called Paul the "Apostate" or "Traitor," believing that he was a heretic because he was a renegade from the Law.

Reports about the Ebionites confer that they used a gospel that had similarities with the Gospel of Matthew. While other Christians identified their gospel as the *Gospel of the Ebionites*, the Ebionites themselves claimed that it was the Gospel of Matthew. Their gospel was a Greek edition of the Gospel of Matthew, although it varied in significant ways from canonical Matthew. It began with Jesus' baptism not his birth and emphasized that Jesus came to do away with the Jewish sacrificial system (*Gos. Ebion.* Frag. 3 and 6). In their gospel, both Jesus and John refuse to eat meat (*Gos. Ebion.* Frag. 2 and 7). Jesus' vegetarianism is recognized in his refusal to eat meat during Passover. The reference to John's vegetarianism is particularly interesting because it is derived from a play on the Greek words *akris* (grasshopper) and *egkris* (honey), so that John eats honey-cakes in their gospel, not locusts as canonical Matthew has him do. It is clear from this that their gospel was written in Greek even though some of our sources tell us that it was written in Hebrew letters.

Part of the difficulty with assessing this linguistic information about their gospel is the fact that the sources which describe the *Gospel of the Ebionites* seem to have conflated the Ebionites' Matthean gospel edition with two other gospels: the *Gospel of the Hebrews* and the *Gospel of the Nazoreans*. The *Gospel of the Hebrews* was a Greek text that was popular in Egypt among Christians who held in high regard James, the brother of Jesus and leader of the Jerusalem church. This gospel appears to have been a compendium of midrashic stories collected in the second century to supplement those found in other gospels. This text contained the fascinating story that the heavenly angel, Michael, descended into Mary, Jesus' mother, as Jesus gestated (*Gos. Heb.* Frag. 1). In addition, this text recognizes Jesus' mother as the Holy Spirit who anoints him at his baptism (*Gos. Heb.* Frag. 2 and 3).

The *Gospel of the Nazoreans* is a second-century Aramaic translation of the Greek Gospel of Matthew created by Aramaic-speaking Christians who called themselves Nazoreans. They lived in Syria and, by the end of the fourth century, were living in the northern city of Beorea (Aleppo, Syria). Like the Ebionite Matthew, their gospel was a specialized edition with its own variations of the Matthean narrative. The identity of the Nazoreans who created this edition of the Gospel of Matthew is debated, but the name was an old popular name for Christians (i.e. Acts 24:5), probably derived from the Hebrew word, *nazar*, which means to keep or observe. When this verb is used as an Aramaic name, it becomes *Nazorean*, meaning Keeper or Observer. Different Jewish and Christian sects appear to have used this name, laying claim to be the authentic Keepers of God's Law. This gospel did not begin with Jesus' baptism as the Ebionite Matthew did. Rather we know that it referenced Jesus' sojourn out of Egypt, suggesting that their gospel included a version of Matthew's story of Jesus' birth (cf. *Gos. Naz.* Frag. 1; cf. Jer., *Epist.* 112.13). This suggests that the group of law-observant Christians using this gospel believed that Jesus was virginally born.

Law-observant Christians appear to have been in the minority among Christians in Rome at Justin's time. They were more prominent in Mesopotamia, east of the Jordan along the Tigris–Euphrates river system where a number of distinctive groups flourished. Their ancestors were the Christian refugees from Jerusalem and other parts of Judaea who had fled the first Roman–Jewish War in the middle of the first century. Their Maximalist position on the Law had been maintained by these second-century groups.

In addition to Ebionite groups and various groups of Nazoreans, we know about the existence of Elchasaite groups whose beliefs were quite similar to the Ebionites. They relied on an edited version of the Jewish scriptures and some kind of gospel harmony they had sourced. They were anti-Paul, requiring their children to be circumcised and observe the Law as preached by Jesus. They did not allow their members to take up celibacy, but required marriage of its youth. They prayed facing Jerusalem. They refused to participate in sacrifices, saying that water is a better purifier than fire which is alien to God. They believed that Christ was conceived and born like any other man and that Christ had appeared many times in history before he appeared in Jesus. So they too relied on the ADULT POSSESSION PATTERN.

What made the Elchasaites distinct from the Ebionites was their claim to possess a book that had fallen out of heaven during the third year Trajan's war in Parthia (116 CE). We learn about this from Hippolytus, who writes around 230 CE. He tells us that a man named Alcibiades came to Rome from Apamea in Syria (*Ref.* 9.13–16) (Figure 6.1). Alcibiades showed the Roman Christians a book that he said had been revealed by two angels, a male angel who was the Son of God and a female angel who was the Holy Spirit. Both angels were gigantic beings whose height was estimated to be ninety-six miles and whose foot-size measured fourteen miles. A man called Elchasai – a name that is actually a title he was given, meaning in Aramaic (*hayil kesai*) the Hidden Power – got the book from the angel and began teaching from it to a group of baptizers. Given the similarities between the Ebionites and the later Elchasaites, it is likely that Elchasai used the book as a platform to reform an Ebionite group of baptizers he was affiliated with.

> "A certain Alcibiades, who lived in Apamea in Syria...came to Rome and brought with him a book. About the book, he said that Elchasai, a righteous man, had received it from Seres in Parthia and had transmitted it to a certain Sobiai. It had been communicated by an angel, whose height was 24 schoinoi, which is 96 miles, his breadth 4 schoinoi, and from shoulder to shoulder 6 schoinoi, and the tracks of his feet in length 3 ½ schoinoi, which is 14 miles, in breadth 1 ½ schoinoi, and in height half a schoino. And with him was also a female figure, whose measurements Alcibiades says were commensurate with those mentioned. The male figure was the Son of God and the female figure was called the Holy Spirit."
>
> *This is written by Hippolytus in* Ref. 9.13.1–3

The big news was that the book taught about a new way for sins to be remitted. Baptized Christians who had committed a grave sin (defined by them as incest, adultery, homosexuality, fornication, bestiality) could receive forgiveness if they listened to the book, believed in it, and underwent a second baptism. They were called upon to purify and cleanse themselves, to invoke the names of the seven witnesses listed in the book: the heaven, the water, the holy spirits, the angels of prayer, the oil, the salt, and the earth. They were to profess and vow: "I call these seven witnesses to witness that I shall sin no more, I shall not commit adultery, I shall not steal, I shall not do injustice, I shall not be greedy, I shall not hate, I shall not break faith, nor shall I take pleasure in any evil deeds" (Hipp., *Ref.* 9.15).

If those who attended to the book fulfilled these stipulations, they would share in the peace and reward of the righteous on Judgment Day, which the book predicted would occur after Trajan's war came to an end when a war in the heavens would break out among wicked angels. Like Hermas professed, Elchasai's book taught that the Lord could be denied by Christians as long as it was lip-service and not meant in the heart (Epiph., *Pan.* 19.1.8). The book also prescribed repeated baptisms in the river to heal consumption, exorcise demons, and get rid of rabies. The timing of these baptisms was restricted to certain days of the week. Baptisms were forbidden on the Sabbath and Tuesday because of the astrological influence of the war-like Mars, the planetary ruler of the third day of the week.

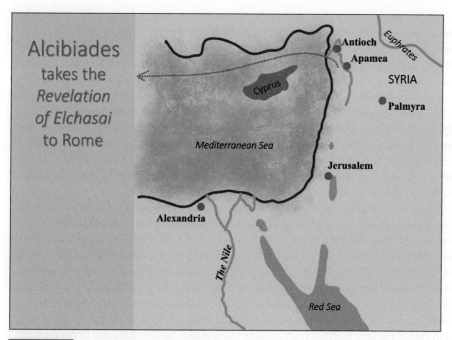

Alcibiades
takes the
*Revelation
of Elchasai
to Rome*

Antioch
Apamea
Euphrates
SYRIA
Palmyra
Cyprus
Mediterranean Sea
Jerusalem
Alexandria
The Nile
Red Sea

FIGURE 6.1   The revelation of Elchasai shows up in Rome.

More about the Elchasaites was learned when, in 1969, a miniature book measuring 4.5 by 3.5 cm was opened and deciphered. The little fourth-century Greek book had been found near Assiut, Egypt and is now archived in the manuscript collection of the University of Cologne. It turned out to be a hagiography about Mani (216–274 CE), the founder of the Manichaean church, the first world religion stretching from the Atlanta coast to the Pacific along the Silk Road. The biographical data reveals that Mani had been raised in a group of baptists that looked up to Elchasai as their foundering father and saint. Mani eventually leaves (or is expelled from) the group after a series of visions caused Mani to question the practices that the baptists used to purify themselves daily and wash their food. Unlike other Elchasaite groups, Mani's Baptist brothers were not married. They lived together as a group of celibate men who daily immersed in the river in their attempt to maintain their purity. The cold-water baths likely helped to tamp down their sexual urges. This lifestyle difference reveals that the Elchasaites must have experienced a schism at some point in their history since the other Elchasaite groups encouraged marriage.

While law-observant Christians are reported as minority groups surviving into the seventh century, eventually they become extinct. A modern version of law-observant Christianity, however, took shape in the 1960s among some American Jewish converts to Christianity. These converts believed that Jews can be Christian, while still maintaining their devotion to the Law and Jewish culture. The most well-known of these messianic Jewish groups is Jews for Jesus, founded in 1973 by Moishe Rosen.

6.6 Christian versus Christian

COMPANION READINGS
Justin, *First Apology* 26, 56, 58
Justin, *Dialogue with Trypho* 35, 80

In relationship to Judaism, Justin defines who is Christian by identifying Jews as law-observant and Christians as not. Those Christians who are still law-observant are recognized as Christian by Justin, but their traditional law-observant piety is reframed as unnecessary and misguided. So while recognizing them as Christian, he frames their practices negatively to demonstrate that the most-informed Christians do not observe the ceremonial laws. This makes law-observance an undesirable Christian practice in Justin's rhetoric. It also stereotypes all Jews as people who observe the ceremonial laws, whether they did so or not.

In writing about what it means to be Christian, Justin uses law-observant Christians and Jews as dark mirrors, to represent what Christians are not or should not be. He "othered" other Christians too (Figure 6.2). He mentions in his works that he has an entire book, the *Syntagma Against All Heresies* (*1 Apol. 26.8*). While the word heresy (Greek: *hairesis*) traditionally meant a school or party that people choose to join, as we saw with Ignatius, in Christian sources it becomes tied to the language of deviance. Traditionally, Justin has been understood to be the author of the *Syntagma*, but it is possible that he simply possessed the book and used it as a reference. In addition to this book, Irenaeus, bishop of Lyons, knows about a book that Justin had written against Marcion (*Haer.* 4.6.2), a book that Tertullian likely also knew and used as a reference when he composed his own five books against Marcion (ca. 205 CE). Both the *Syntagma* and Justin's book against Marcion are lost.

All this is to say that Justin was on the frontlines of weaponizing the concept of Christian diversity (difference) as heresy (wrongness) and deploying it in a way that stereotypes and radicalizes certain Christian movements, excluding them from Justin's construction of authentic Christianity. As this is done, Justin projects all deviance their way, demonstrating to his intended Roman readers that these false Christians are likely responsible for all the rumors of impiety and impropriety, while the authentic Christians like Justin are blameless. The only Christians who might be perpetrators of the accused shameful deeds like "upsetting the lampstand, promiscuous sex, and cannibalism" are fake Christians, people who call themselves Christians but who are in reality heretics (*1 Apol.* 26.6; *Dial.* 80.3).

The passages in Justin's extant works which discuss the heretics, while short, are very revealing. Justin identifies Christian diversity with the error and trickery of the demons who wanted to stop the Christian message from spreading. To stop it, the demons manipulated a certain Samaritan from Gitto, named Simon, and his consort Helen, who were active in Samaria soon after Jesus' death (*1 Apol.* 26; 56). The Simonians were a Samaritan Gnostic sect competitive with the first Christians. According to

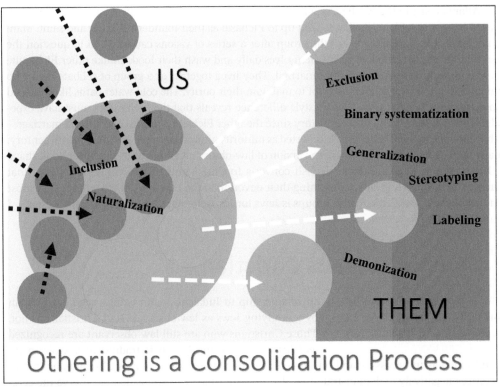

FIGURE 6.2 Illustration mapping how the consolidation process is dependent upon "othering" others.

Justin, they were devoted to the worship of Simon as the Great Power of God, who had as his consort Helen, God's First Thought and Holy Spirit.

We learn more about Simon's system from his book, *The Great Declaration* (Hipp., *Ref.* 6.2–15 [6.7.1–20.4). We only know of the book, however, as it is embedded in the anti-Simonian rhetoric of Hippolytus. It is fairly certain that Simon made an extensive exegesis of the six days of creation in Genesis 1, understanding the six days to refer to the Aeons that the primal God generated. This God is an indefinite Power which is identified with fire, the originating principle of the world (Deut 4:24). This fire produces six Powers (Aeons) in hermaphrodite pairs. Heaven and Earth are identified with the male Nous (Mind) and the female Epinoia (Insight and Holy Spirit). The sun is God's Voice (male) while the moon is God's Name (female). Air is God's Reasoning ability (male) while water is God's ability to Reflect (female). The seventh day of rest is associated with the seventh Power, the Logos. He is called The-One-Who-Stands because the Logos is the primary cause that generates the divine world, that is, everything which is declared in Genesis as "good." The Logos is the Great Power that contains all things that are to come to be. He is the Image of the primal incorruptible Power, the spirit hovering over the primal waters. This is how God autogenerates "making itself grow, seeking itself, finding itself, being mother of itself, father of itself, sister of itself, spouse of itself, daughter of itself, son of itself, mother father, a unit, being a root of the entire circle of existence" (Hipp., *Ref.* 6.12 [6.17-2-3]).

It is less certain from quotations of *The Great Declaration* what Simon thought about the creation of the world, which is mentioned to have happened under the auspices of the Biblical God. From other sources we discover that Simon taught about archangels who created the universe, so he likely identified the Biblical God with the Angel of YHWH. These creator angels were generated by the female Aeon Epinoia (Insight and Holy Spirit) who brought them into being to do the Father's bidding. Somewhere along the way (before or after the creation of the world is not clear), these archangels rebelled and incarcerated Epinoia in a human body. Epinoia's story, then, is about the descent of the Spirit (our divine intuitive capacity) and its imprisonment in the first humans by their creators. In this state, the Spirit cannot be released from the cycle of birth and death on her own.

So the Great Power had to descend to earth to save her. This is Simon. He is identified with the Logos' two names, The Great Power and The-One-Who-Stands. He is considered God's manifestation on earth, as the Son of God who descended to save the Father's fallen Spirit. According to Simonian mythology, Simon universally redeemed God's Spirit by marrying Helen (who was the Holy Spirit in the body of a prostitute). Those who worshipped him claimed that they had been saved by the Father's grace and sacralized their marriages in imitation of Simon and Helen, whom they considered their Father-Mother Gods (Iren., *Haer.* 1.23.1–3; Epiph., *Pan.* 21.; Hipp., *Ref.* 6.14). Simon's religion did not remain a quirky Samaritan sectarian movement, but was framed as a universal religion and gained many adherents across the Roman empire by the time Justin wrote about him (Figure 6.3).

Simonianism also interfaced with Christianity. We know the most about this interface in the stories about Menander, an ex-disciple of Simon, from a village in Samaria called Capparetaea (Just. Mart., *1 Apology* 26.1; Iren., *Haer.* 1.23.5; Tert., *Res.* 5.2; Eus., *Eccl. Hist.* 3.26.1–2; Theod., *Fab.* 1.1.3). He received a revelation that Simon was *not* the descendent Savior; Jesus was. Menander used baptism (perhaps in his own name) to initiate new members and guarantee their resurrection as immortal (deathless) and incorruptible (ageless) beings. Their salvation depended on special knowledge that they used to defeat the evil angels. Once baptized, the person was called an "apostle." Like Paul, Menander considered himself the greatest apostle sent from "the highest and secret Power" in order to save people of all nations (Tert., *Soul* 50.2). According to Menander, the Power that sent him was the primal God. The primal God, Menander taught, originally generated his Thought. In turn, Thought generated angels who created the world and the human body. Some of these creator angels were evil by their own choice. Jesus descends to save everyone who believes in him. Menander moved to Antioch, opened a Christian church, and gained a significant following according to later reports. His movement is an example of Ex-Simonian Christianity among second-generation Christians.

Satornil, a third-generation Christian scholar who lived in Antioch during the reign of Hadrian (117–138 CE), was familiar with Menander's teachings (Iren., *Haer.* 1.24.2; Eus., *Eccl. Hist.* 4.6.4; 4.73). Reports about Satornil reveal that he recognized a transcendent God who was distinct from the Biblical

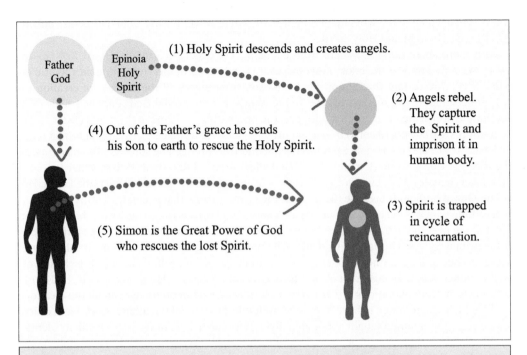

Simonian Mythology

(1) Holy Spirit descends and creates angels.

Father God

Epinoia Holy Spirit

(2) Angels rebel. They capture the Spirit and imprison it in human body.

(4) Out of the Father's grace he sends his Son to earth to rescue the Holy Spirit.

(3) Spirit is trapped in cycle of reincarnation.

(5) Simon is the Great Power of God who rescues the lost Spirit.

FIGURE 6.3 Illustration of the Simonian Myth in which Simon is sent to earth as the Son of God to save the trapped Spirit.

Creator YHWH, and whom he considered YHWH God's enemy. Satornil taught that YHWH was one of the seven mutinous angels who created the human being in the image and likeness of an ideal human archetype they saw above, a shining Man of Light (Gen 1:3, 26). After creating Adam from mud, Adam was unable to stand up, but could only squirm around like a worm (Ps. 22:6). So the transcendent God had pity and sent down a spark of life which allowed Adam to stand erect with compact joints and be viable. Somehow (the sources do not tell us how) the angels ended up creating good and evil races of humankind. Jesus descends to conquer the evil race and the demons (including YHWH) and save those who believe in him, so that the sparks will be able to return to the transcendent God.

Justin had to deal with this lively interface between Simonianism and Christianity. To do so, he attacked Simon whom he believed started the problems. According to Justin, in order to divert people's attention away from the Christian message that the apostles were trying to spread about the real God (the creator God of Jewish scriptures), the demons gave Simon (and Menander) the power to do magic, which convinced people that Simon was actually God and deserved their worship. In return, the faithful would receive immortality. Justin says that the worship of Simon was extremely popular in Samaria and had a foothold in Rome. Justin identifies an inscription to the Sabine deity, Semo Sancus, on Tiber Island as referring to Simon. According to Justin, the inscription read, "To Simon the holy God (*Simoni Deo Sancto*)." The inscription was unearthed on Tiger Island in 1574. In contrast to Justin's claim, it reads: *Semon Sancus Deo*. Since Simon is nowhere in this inscription, scholars have assumed that Justin was mistaken. But there is also the possibility that what Justin is reporting is how the Simonians interpreted the inscription to refer to Simon. They may have understood Simon (their father God) to be the avatar of one of the oldest Roman Gods, Semo Sancus. This would fit the Simonian's universalist mentality.

Justin goes on to identify Marcion as a man from Pontus who also teaches his followers to believe in a God other than the Creator. Marcion understands this God to be superior to YHWH, having done greater things than YHWH (*1 Apol.* 26; 58). Justin says that Marcion denies that the messiah who came to save Christians was predicted in the Jewish scriptures. This is why Justin tells us that Marcion teaches two Christs, one who will be sent by the Creator to save the Jews, and another (Jesus) sent by the Supreme God to save everyone. Again Justin attributes Marcion's teaching to the demons who want to stop the spread of the Christian message about God by creating an attractive myth that will persuade as many people as possible to join Marcion's church and worship another (false) God.

Justin expresses concern about the popularity of Marcion's churches, attributing Marcion's success to demonic seduction that leads Marcion's followers into atheism (not worshipping the true God). He also suggests that the Marcionites are so sure of the truth of their teachings that they mock Justin's crowd. It is very clear that Justin considers the Marcionites to be serious competitors who were putting significant pressure on the emerging Apostolic Catholic church network. This is why he wrote an entire book refuting Marcion as a heretic. While the *Dialogue with Trypho* is aimed to distinguish true Christianity from Judaism and recover the pre-Mosaic Christian philosophy from the Jewish scriptures, the *Dialogue* contains a significant amount of material that targets Marcion even when not mentioning him explicitly.

Throughout the *Dialogue with Trypho*, true Christianity is defined in a fashion counter to Marcionite teachings which saw Christianity as a religion separate from Judaism. As we already saw, Justin works in the *Dialogue* to secure Christianity's heritage as the true Israel. He teaches Trypho that the Creator, the God of the Jews, is the true and one-and-only God, something Trypho already knows, but which contradicts Marcion (*Dial.* 11). He tells Trypho that the prophets predicted that the messiah would come from this God, something Trypho also already knows, but which also contradicts Marcion (*Dial.* 7).

In addition to Marcion, Justin names others as heretics, particularly Valentinians, Basilidians, and Satornilians (*Dial.* 35). He knows that they all call themselves Christians, but instead he ascribes them the names of their founders in philosophical fashion. Just as Platonists are named for their leader Plato, so Justin understands the Valentinians to be named after Valentinus, the Basilidians after Basilides, and the Saturnilians after Saturnilius. He distinguishes "the true and pure doctrine of Jesus Christ" from the demonic-inspired teachings of these other Christians who are wolves in sheep's clothing. Justin reiterates that these groups falsely reject the Creator God of the Jewish scriptures and the authenticity of Jewish prophecy to refer to Jesus. He considers them to be atheists, impious, unrighteous, and sinful, confessing Jesus' name while not worshipping the true God. Justin identifies himself with the "true Christians" who uphold the "pure and pious faith" against the "godless impious heretics" who teach atheism, blasphemy, and foolishness (*Dial.* 80). Justin is especially cognizant of how dangerous it is for Marcion to surrender the heritage of Israel given that the Romans already suspected that the Christians were a recent Jewish schism. For Marcion to say that Christians worshipped a foreign God made Christians even more susceptible to charges of atheism and novelty. Justin exploits this. When he tries to convince the Romans that the true Christians were not atheists, Justin points the finger at Marcion, accusing the Marcionites of atheism.

In fact, Justin projects Roman accusations of Christian impiety and impropriety onto all the Christian groups that worship a transcendent God apart from YHWH. In so doing, he does not have to prove to the Romans that they are wrong in their accusations against Christians, only that the Christians who might be doing those things are not "us" but "them." To explain Christian pluralism, Justin creates a narrative that schisms were predicted by Jesus when he taught that there would arise false Christs, prophets, and apostles. Not all Christians who say they are Christians are really Christians, Justin says. The same is true about Jews. Not all Jews who say they are really Jews are Jews. Here he refers to the schismatic nature of Judaism, listing the Sadducees, Hellenists, Genistae, Meristae, Galileans, Pharisees, and Baptists as examples of Jews who, according to him, worship only with their lips but not their hearts (*Dial.* 80.3).

While Justin identifies heresy with any teaching that rejects the God of Abraham, Isaac, and Jacob as the God of worship – he considers this blasphemy – he mentions a subsidiary point of difference: that some Christians wrongly think that there is no resurrection of the dead, but instead they believe that the soul goes to heaven immediately after death. Justin considers himself part of the "right-minded Christians" who worship the Creator, the God of Abraham, Isaac, and Jacob. He considers belief in the resurrection of the dead confirmed by the fact that these same right-minded Christians also believe in the resurrection of the dead. He says that some of these right-minded Christians also anticipate a thousand-year reign of Christ at the end of time when Jerusalem will be rebuilt (*Dial.* 80). It is clear from Justin's report that Chiliasm (from Greek: *chilioi*, meaning "thousand" years) was a topic of debate among Christians and that while Justin was a Chiliast, some of the other "true" Christians were not. It is also clear that the book of Revelation was in use, which was responsible for the belief that Christ would reign with his chosen ones on earth for one thousand years. After this the resurrection of the dead would occur in order for the wicked to be judged (cf. Rev. 20:1–6).

Justin is very aware of the fact that not all Christians see eye-to-eye. He knows about a number of distinct Christian movements, many that worshipped a transcendent God who was not YHWH. In his writings, he projects impiety and impropriety onto the Christian groups that refused to worship YHWH. At the same time, he identifies the Apostolic Catholic network with a particular code of morality and a Canon of Truth (*regula fidei*) with its fixed confession that, by the will of the Father and Lord of all, the Son of God was born of a virgin, a man, named Jesus, was crucified, died, and rose again, and ascended into heaven (*1 Apol.* 46). He presents this as true Christianity. While he allows for some dogmatic differences among true Christians (i.e. law-observance and chiliasm), when it came to theology, there was no flexibility. If any God other than YHWH was worshipped, the group was judged heretical. Theology was Justin's bottom line.

6.7 Gospel Harmonies

COMPANION READINGS

Justin, *First Apology* 39, 61, 66–67
1 Timothy
Irenaeus, *Against Heresies* 1.28
Tatian, *Oration to the Greeks* 5, 7, 15

Where does Justin get his information about Jesus? Justin refers repeatedly to *The Memoirs of the Apostles* (cf. *Dial.* 100–107). He says that these memoirs were composed by the apostles and other followers and are called gospels (*1 Apol.* 66–67). Justin thinks that the apostles were twelve uneducated men to whom Jesus, after his resurrection, had to explain the prophecies (*1 Apol.* 39). In Justin's narration of the origins of his church, Paul does not factor in as one of the apostles. Rather after Jesus' resurrection, the twelve apostles left Jerusalem proclaiming God's word to all the Gentile nations. The twelve apostles, he says, each transmitted what he remembered about Jesus' instructions and activities and their memoirs prove how the whole story about Jesus was predicted in the prophecies of Jewish Scripture (as he read them in Greek translation). This understanding of the apostles looks like it sprang from Justin's reading of Matthew 28, Luke 24, and Acts 1–2. This narration of the origins of his church downplays Paul as an apostle especially as this story was used to teach that the twelve apostles of Jesus were the ones who evangelized the Gentiles.

While Justin refers to *The Memoirs*, he never names any particular gospel he has on hand. When we make comparative analyses between what Justin wrote and the copies of the early Christian texts we possess today, we discover that Justin quotes extensively from Matthew and Luke and he knew about Mark (which he references once as Peter's memoirs; *Dial.* 106). But he does not appear to have been working from individual gospel texts. Instead, he is consulting a harmonized version of Matthew and Luke, that is, a conflated version of the narrative created out of both sources. It is not clear if this harmonized gospel edition was one he got from elsewhere or if he was in the process of composing it himself, but Justin calls it *The Memoirs of the Apostles*. Collections of the memoirs of famous philosophers were sometimes prepared by the followers of a famous person, such as Xenophon's *Memoirs of Socrates*, a compilation that Justin actually knows and references (*2 Apol.* 11.3–5; referring to Xen., *Mem.* 2.1.21–33).

In terms of other texts known to Justin, we should include the Gospel of John. It is from this text that Justin derives his views on Jesus' divinity as the Logos, his fleshly incarnation (cf. *1 Apol.* 32; *Dial.* 105; cp. John 1:1–18), and his baptism (Jesus did not go into the river; cp. John 1:24–34) (*Dial.* 88). Justin also knows about John's interpretation of Christian baptism (*1 Apol.* 61; cp John 3:5). We have already seen that Justin also refers to the book of Acts and the book of Revelation.

While he never mentions Paul by name, Justin makes extensive use of Galatians and Romans (*Dial.* 39, 95–96; cp. Rom. 11:3–4). He also appears to have known 1 Corinthians, Philippians, Colossians, Ephesians, and 1 and 2 Thessalonians. There are also allusions to 1 Timothy and Titus in his writings. So Justin likely had a compendium of Paul's letters similar to Marcion's collection, although edited so that it was distinctive from Marcion's *Apostolicon* with the edition of the Pastoral epistles (1 and 2 Timothy and Titus). While it is common knowledge in biblical scholarship that the Pastoral epistles were not authored by Paul, but are pseudonymous writings from the second century, their inclusion in the edition of Paul's letters known to Justin reveals that there is more to this story than we might initially think.

Given that there are anti-Marcionite arguments present in the Pastoral epistles, especially in 1 Timothy 4 and 6, many scholars think that they were written largely to combat Marcionism. The edition of Paul's letters used by Justin is an edition created by someone who fought back against Marcion in a cunning way. Impersonating Paul, the author of the Pastoral letters strikes out against Marcion's main teachings about another God and Jesus' appearance as an angel who looked like a human but was not human. Also addressed by Paul's impersonator is Marcion's strict code of asceticism when it came to sex and food. The author also argues against Marcion's decoupling of Jewish prophecy and Jesus, as well as Marcion's belief that Jewish myths and practices were still valid for those who follow YHWH. What is so powerful about these letters is the fact that the author's pseudonym (his claim to be Paul) makes Paul himself the author of these anti-Marcionite positions. To include these pseudonymous letters in an edition of Paul's "genuine" ten letters gave them automatic authenticity, making it appear that Paul had already forecasted Marcion's deviance. With this, the impersonator of Paul was able to pull the rug out from under Marcion's feet.

The hypothesis that Justin may actually have been the one responsible for compiling the gospel harmony, has particular merit given the fact that another Christian, Tatian, completed a full gospel harmony called the *Diatessaron* between 170–180 CE. Tatian was Justin's protégé and it is likely that Justin's work on *The Memoirs* inspired Tatian to take up the work himself following Justin's death (cf. Iren., *Haer.* 1.28). Tatian immigrated from Syria to Rome while Justin was still active (150–160 CE). In his own composition, *The Oration to the Greeks*, Tatian tells us that he was an educated man with resources to complete a grand tour of all the philosophies much like Justin had done, a journey that ended in Rome with Christianity, his chosen philosophy (*Or.* 23, 35).

Tatian mentions Justin twice in *The Orations*, although he reveals little about Justin's relationship with him (*Or.* 18–19). We learn though that the philosopher Crescens was so embittered over Justin's teachings that he sought Justin's and Tatian's death (*Or.* 19; cf. Eus., *Eccl. Hist.* 4.16.1). Justin relates that Crescens did not take Christianity seriously as a new philosophy. So he and Crescens argued vehemently with each other publicly. Justin feared the Roman authorities probably had heard about their public dispute (*Dial.* 2.3; 11.2). In 165 CE, while Marcus Aurelius was emperor, Justin and his students Chariton (a man's name), Charito (a woman's name), Euelpistus (an imperial slave), Paion (from Cappadocia), Hierax (likely a slave from Phrygia), and Liberian (a Latin name) were arrested, charged, and sentenced to death by Rome's prefect, Rusticus.

It is likely that Justin and his students were arrested in his apartment in Rome. He ran a Christian philosophical school in his apartment above Myrtinus' baths (*Acta Just.* 3). There is no evidence that his school represented the views of any particular congregation in Rome, but he is familiar with the liturgy typical of the city's Apostolic Catholic congregations and speaks about Christians assembling on Sundays in congregations to perform the liturgy together. According to Justin, in the church he attended, they read the apostles' memoirs, the prophets' declarations, and listened to a homily given by the presider of the company. After this, the congregation would rise together and pray. In succession, bread, wine and water were brought out. The presider offered prayers and thanksgiving over the elements and the congregation gave its assent, saying "Amen." At this time, the elements were distributed to each individual and the deacons took the leftovers to those members who were absent. A collection was taken up and given to the presider who was then responsible to take care of the orphans, widows, sick, immigrants, and needy (*1 Apol.* 67). The preparations of new Christians for baptism and the baptisms themselves appear to have been done separately (*1 Apol.* 61). All these activities were separate from Justin's instruction in Christian philosophy which took place in his own apartment. He was arrested alongside the other pupils who had been with him that day.

Tatian survived. He must not have been in Justin's apartment when the arrest took place. From later sources, we know that while in Rome Tatian had his own student Rhodo. This leads us to think that Tatian carried on Justin's philosophical school in Rome after Justin's execution (cf. Eus., *Eccl. Hist.*. 4.29, 5.13) and completed *The Oration* and the *Diatessaron* during this time. In 172 CE, Tatian returned to Mesopotamia and established his own Christian church there after leaving the Roman congregation (cf. Eus., *Eccl. Hist.*. 4.29).

The *Diatessaron* – which was the word used to identify the fourth interval in ancient Greek music – was a brilliant scholarly achievement, a carefully edited compilation of the Christian gospel made from a multitude of sources including the synoptic gospels, John, and perhaps other gospels like the *Gospel of Thomas* or even other gospel harmonies that are no longer extant. It quickly rose to canonical status in Syria and became the official gospel of the Syrian church until the fifth century when the Christian Biblical canon was standardized, at which time bishops went around destroying all the copies of it (Theo. Cyr., *Haer.* 1.20). To this day, very little remains of the *Diatessaron*. What is known about the *Diatessaron* has been reconstructed mainly from commentaries composed by Syrian Christians like Ephraem and Aphrahat or translations (of translations) of the *Diatessaron* in Armenian, Arabic, Persian, Latin, Dutch, Italian, English, and German. Scholars debate whether Tatian wrote the *Diatessaron* in Greek or Syriac.

Tatian's teachings are better known through his surviving work, *The Oration to the Greeks*. In it Tatian develops Justin's Logos mythology in order to further elevate and emphasize God's transcendence. Referencing John 1:1–4, Tatian understood the phrase "in the beginning" to refer to God having within himself the Logos Power who was the foundation of creation before it came to be. God established everything through the activity of the Logos Power who sprang forth as God's firstborn (Col. 1:15) when God willed it so. The Logos, Tatian concludes, is the beginning of the universe (*Orat.* 5). While the Father remains connected to creation, Tatian makes it clear that the Logos is the one who actually does the creating of the world. Because God is not an active participant in creating the material universe, his transcendence is reinforced. That said, the transcendent God is still identified with the Biblical God.

His transcendence is further safeguarded with Tatian's teaching that the Logos' relationship to the Father involves a partition of the Father rather than a severance from the Father. The Logos is like a torch lit from another torch so that his coming forth from the Father does not deprive the Father of his power to reason. The Logos comes forth from the Father like spoken words so that the Father is not diminished in any way (*Orat.* 5). The Father remains the same in his transcendence after the Logos is generated as the divine instrument of creation. God's transcendence is further safeguarded because, according to Tatian, the Law was given by the Logos (by "another God"; cf. Clem. Alex., *Misc.* 3.82.3) not the Father.

The Logos is responsible for the creation and organization of matter which did not pre-exist according to Tatian. This was in contradiction to Greek philosophical theories and many Mediterranean religious myths but an idea already in play in other Christian sources like Basilides' writings. In Tatian's work, the Logos creates the first human beings in the image of God. The first humans have free will, but do not have God's "nature of the good which is God's alone." Tatian thinks that God's good nature is something that humans are meant to achieve through their own free choice. As long as they choose the good, their souls remain connected to God through his Holy Spirit and everything is wonderful (*Orat.* 7, 15).

Things become problematic, according to Tatian, when the first-born of the angels, who was very clever, rebelled against God's rule by convincing the other angels and humans that he was God instead (*Orat.* 7). The Logos intervenes. The angels are exiled from heaven, becoming demons on earth. The Holy Spirit is taken away from the first humans, making them mortal. Because the first humans had made this bad choice, they were beyond salvation (cf. Iren., *Haer.* 1.28). Ever since then, humans have only been able to choose evil. This situation is remedied with Christian baptism which reconnects the human soul with the Holy Spirit (*Orat.* 5, 15).

That said, it is still possible in Tatian's scheme for Christians to make the wrong choice and end up in dire straights again. Tatian taught that Christians always have to be on guard. They are faced with having to always choose to follow "the very nature of the good" in order to fulfill God's will for humanity (*Orat.* 7). This belief led Tatian to focus on constant moral monitoring as part of his Christian discipline. Tatian was particularly concerned with sexual sins, so much so that he was called an encratite, which means that he had mastered restraint over his emotions, impulses, and desires.

This was actually considered a virtue among Greeks and Romans. Philosophers like Pythagoras were known to have instituted vegetarianism for his followers as a form of discipline. Restraint in marital relations was advocated by Stoics. The Essenes are described in our sources as a communal group of celibates who embraced severe poverty and self-discipline. John the Baptist is portrayed as an ascetic living in the wilds around the Jordan. Passages in various Christian sources indicate that celibacy was considered a good option for living, especially as the world came to an end. In most Syrian churches, Christians were required to be celibate before baptism. There is evidence that their pre-baptismal celibacy was performed as proof that after baptism they would be able to remain celibate and not fall into sexual sin. Marcion too asked his followers to practice a form of Christian discipline that included celibacy and vegetarianism. So there was precedent for Tatian's emphasis on the sinfulness of eroticism and sexual activities, even within marriage, which he considered fornication (Iren., *Haer.* 1.28).

Tatian, even during his lifetime, became labeled as a deviant by some in the west. We first hear about this from Irenaeus of Lyons (180 CE) who says that Tatian left the Roman church after Justin died to start his own church in Syria. We do not know what exactly caused him to secede. Irenaeus thinks his secession indicates that Tatian became a heretic, pointing to Tatian's views that Adam could not be redeemed, his belief that marriage was sinful, and his cosmogenic (origin of world) system. This identification of Tatian's secession with heresy is problematic because there is little scholars can find about Tatian's teachings that is not aligned with accepted Christian discourse at the time. Tatian's teachings about creation are very much in line with Justin's, developing the Logos mythology and advancing the-fall-of-the-angels scenario. His advocacy of celibacy is not out of place either, especially in Syria where celibacy was the Christian ideal well into the third century. While Irenaeus may not have agreed with Tatian's views on Adam, this seems minor when it comes to the types of descriptions of heresy found throughout the rest of Irenaeus' work.

So what do we make of the fact that Irenaeus thought that Tatian was a heretic, a position maintained in the west (because of Irenaeus' influence) but is not common in the east until the tenth century (Agapius of Hierapolis, *Kitab al-'Unvan*)? Irenaeus also mentions that Tatian was an arrogant teacher who went his own way when he left the Roman church and set up shop in Syria under his own name. This suggests that the real issue was not theological but sociological. Rather than continuing within the ecclesiastical network that had begun linking emergent Apostolic Catholic churches together under the care of duly elected bishops, Tatian decided to open his own church and run his own show as an independent operator and teacher beyond the reach of the bishops. This seems to have led to his condemnation and ruined his reputation in Rome. His reputation in Syria, however, remained strong as the skilled philosopher who created a wonderful Gospel harmony in which he preserved the real order of the things said and done by Jesus (cf. 'Abd Iso' bar Berika, *Nomokanon*).

Timeline

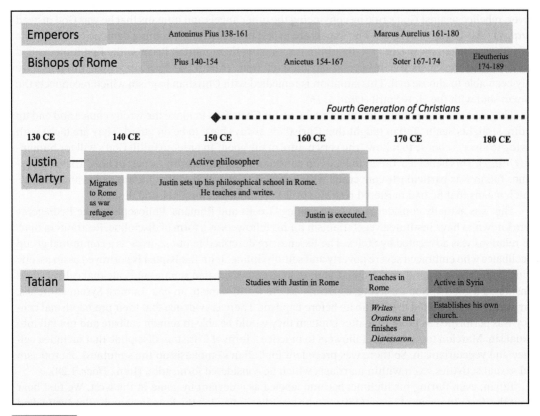

Emperors	Antoninus Pius 138-161			Marcus Aurelius 161-180	
Bishops of Rome	Pius 140-154	Anicetus 154-167	Soter 167-174	Eleutherius 174-189

Fourth Generation of Christians

130 CE	140 CE	150 CE	160 CE	170 CE	180 CE

Justin Martyr — Active philosopher

Migrates to Rome as war refugee

Justin sets up his philosophical school in Rome. He teaches and writes.

Justin is executed.

Tatian — Studies with Justin in Rome | Teaches in Rome | Active in Syria

Writes Orations and finishes *Diatessaron.*

Establishes his own church.

FIGURE 6.4   Timeline for Justin Martyr and Tatian.

Pattern Summary

In this chapter, we encountered a number of Yahwist Christians who held differing opinions on the value of the Law (see Figure 6.5). Justin and Tatian were Moderates who distinguished the ceremonial Jewish Laws from God's moral commandments. They made this distinction in order to create a Christian identity that separated Christians from Jews, arguing that Jews observed the ceremonial Laws while Christians did not. Of course, Justin knows that this was not true; he is aware of Christians who faithfully keep the ceremonial Laws including circumcision. These groups – the Ebionites, Nazoreans, and Elchasaites – were Maximalists who worshiped YHWH as they believed Jesus taught them to do. Justin debates with himself about whether they are Christians or Jews since his definition excludes them. In the end, he compromises with himself, that as long as they do not impose these unnecessary rules on the rest of the Gentile Christian population, they are saved as Christians.

Aside from their differing positions on the Law, this lot of Christians deploy the same cluster of patterns. They all worship YHWH and believe him to be the CREATOR of the world and their special PATRON and CARETAKER. They fault humans for suffering and evil, and teach that righteous living in accordance with God's commandments is necessary to achieve salvation. They are all DUALISTS who believe that there will be a BODILY RESURRECTION at the end of time when they will be judged by God, with the exception of Tatian who argued for the ascent and immortalization of the souls of the saved (who avoid reincarnation). Christology remains dynamic, with the old ADULT POSSESSION PATTERN being favored by the Ebionites and the Elchasaites, while Justin and Tatian play with the notion that the Logos functioned as Jesus' soul (ENSOULMENT PATTERN).

Family Pattern Chart
Justin, Tatian, and Jewish Christians

X=Definitely > L=Likely

THEODICY	Faulty-God	Faulty-Human	Other
Justin		X	
Ebionites		L	
Echasaites		L	
Nazoreans		L	
Tatian		X	

SOTERIOLOGY	Gift from God	Human achievement	Minimalist	Moderate	Maximalist
Justin		X		X	
Ebionites		X			X
Echasaites		X			X
Nazoreans		X		X	X
Tatian		X		X	

CHRISTOLOGY	Adult possession	Fetal possession	Hybrid	Ensoulment	Visitation	Human who received revelation
Justin				X		
Ebionites	X					
Echasaites	X					
Nazoreans			L			
Tatian				X		

ANTHROPOLOGY	Mono	Dual	Triad	Quad
Justin		X		
Ebionites		X		
Echasaites		X		
Nazoreans		X		
Tatian		X		

COSMIC DEMIURGY	Autocrat	Administrator	Caretaker	Patron	Justice	Villain	Rebel	Ignorant	Impaired
Justin	X	X	X	X	X				
Ebionites	L	L	L	L	L				
Echasaites	L	L	L	L	L				
Nazoreans	L	L	L	L	L				
Tatian	X	L	X	X	L				

RESURRECTION	Body reunites with soul	Body discarded and soul immortalized	Body and soul discarded and spirit rises	God-element separates from body soul, and spirit and rises
Justin	X			
Ebionites	L			
Echasaites	L			
Nazoreans	L			
Tatian	X			

FIGURE 6.5 Summary of patterns of Justin Martyr, Tatian, and Jewish Christians.

SCRIPTURES									
	Jewish	Gospel	Pauline letters (10)	Pauline letters (13)	Hebrews	Acts	Catholic letters	Revelation	Other
Justin	X	Mt/Mk/Lk/Jn/Harmony		X				X	
Ebionites	X-partial	version Mt (Gos. Ebion.)							
Elchasaites	X-partial	version Mt							ApocElch
Nazoreans	X	version Mt (Gos. Naz.)							
Tatian	X	Diatessaron/Mt/Mk/Lk/Jn/L-GosThom		L					

ECCLESIOLOGY							
	Consolidation movement	Reform movement	Secessionist movement	Counter movement	Innovative movement	Trans-regional	Regional
Justin	X					X	
Ebionites					X		X
Echasaites					X		X
Nazoreans					X		X
Tatian			X				X

All these Christians formed their own social groups. Justin, while part of the CONSOLIDATING Apostolic Catholic network, operates out of a Christian philosophical school in his apartment in Rome. Tatian left the Apostolic Catholic network of bishops and opens his own independent SECESSIONIST church in Syria, a move which led Irenaeus to brand him a heretic. The Ebionites, Elchasaites, and Nazoreans each have their own INDEPENDENT CHURCHES and social communities with particular rules and leaders in place that are not part of the Apostolic Catholic ecclesiology. Baptism and eucharist ceremonies are performed by all, but under different conditions and according to different liturgical calendars. Lifestyles among most of these Christians tend toward asceticism, with Tatian the most extreme, considering even marriage a state of sin. Justin is more moderate, emphasizing the need to follow God's commandments and stay away from heresy.

Takeaways

1. Justin Martyr was not the first Christian philosopher but was one among several Christian teachers who presented themselves as philosophers and Christianity as a philosophy. Justin thought that his scholarship recovered a universal and perennial philosophy about the origin of the world in a transcendent God whose Logos created the world, souls, and human beings. Christianity, Justin argued, is older than Judaism.

2. Justin was a refugee from Samaria fleeing the aftermath of the Bar Kochba Revolt. Justin converted from Platonism to Christianity after becoming convinced that the Jewish scriptures contained universal truth older than the Greek philosophers.

3. Justin argued that the pre-existent Logos incarnated in Jesus' flesh. The Logos also appeared on earth before Jesus' advent, as evidenced in the scriptural stories about the Angel of the Lord.

4. Because all humans (including those before Jesus' advent) contain the soul (*logos spermatikos*), they had the capacity to partially recognize the existence of the true God who created the world with is Logos.

5. The origin of suffering is traced to fallen angels who raped women and fathered demons. The demons convinced humans that they were Gods (i.e. Greek Gods) and ought to be worshipped through sacrifices and the creation of idols.

6. In Justin's era, some Christians began framing Christianity as a new or third race that was perceived to be universal (geographical) and traditional (appropriating Jewish God and scriptures).

7. Justin knew of law-observant Christians and characterizes their practices as unnecessary.

8. Justin disparages the Jews as people who God punished for their idolatry and insolence by giving them the Law.

9. Historical records indicate that various law-observant Christians (Maximalists) lived in the Transjordan and Mesopotamian regions in the second century. They were known by different names, including Nazoreans, Ebionites, and Elchasaites.

10. Justin traces heresy to the activity of the demons who are trying to hide the Christian God from everyone so that they themselves will continue to be worshipped (as the Greek Gods, etc.).

11. Justin was using and likely editing a Gospel harmony that included the Gospels of Matthew and Luke. His student Tatian finished the book after Justin's death. This book is known as the *Diatessaron* and was the Bible of Syrian Christianity for centuries.

12. Tatian further developed Justin's Logos Christology and seceded from the Apostolic Catholic ecclesiological network of bishops to start his own Christian church when he returned to Syria.

Questions

1. How does Justin argue that Christianity is older than Judaism? Why was this argument important for Justin?

2. When Justin turns Christianity into a universal philosophy, he degrades Judaism. How and why does he do this?

3. How does Justin's view of Judaism compare with the author of the *Epistle of Barnabas*? Melito's sermon?

4. How did Justin remap the binary Jew–Gentile to advantage Christians?

5. How and why did Christians like Justin or Diognetus begin framing Christianity as a new race?

6. How did Roman stereotypes and slander of Christians play into the formation of Christian identity in Justin's writings?

7. Compare the different law-observant Christian groups that populated the Transjordan and Mesopotamian regions in the second century.

8. How does Justin explain the origins of heresy within early Christianity? What makes Simon, Marcion, Valentinus, and Basilides heretics in his opinion?

9. How does Justin explain Christian pluralism? How does he see his own Christian identity within this plurality?

10. Why was Tatian identified as a heretic in Rome (while he was alive), but not in Syria (until the tenth century)?

Resources

Denise Kimber Buell. 2005. *Why This New Race: Ethnic Reasoning in Early Christianity.* New York: Columbia University Press.

M. David Litwa. 2022. Chapters 2, 3, 5, 6, and 19. *Found Christianities: Remaking the World of the Second Century CE.* London: T&T Clark.

Terence L. Donaldson. 2020. *Gentile Christian Identity from Cornelius to Constantine: The Nations, the Parting of* the Ways and Roman Imperial Ideology. Grand Rapids: Eerdmans Publishing Company.

René Falkenberg. 2014. "Tatian". Pages 67–80 in In Defense of Christianity: Early Christian Apologists. Early Christianity in the Context of Antiquity 15. Edited by Jakob Engberg, Anders-Christian Jacobsen, Jörg Ulrich. Translated by Gavin Weakley. Frankfurt am Main: Peter Lang.

Jarl Fossum. 1987. "The Simonian Sophia Myth." SMSR 53: 185–197.

Jarl Fossum. 1989 "Sects and Movements." Pages 293–389 in The Samaritans. Edited by Alan D. Crown. Tübingen: Mohr Siebeck.

Paul Foster. 2007. "The Epistle of Diognetus." Pages 147–156 in The Writings of the Apostolic Fathers. Edited by Paul Foster. London: T&T Clark.

Justo L. González. 1970. (revised ed.). Pages 101–112. A History of Christian Thought from the Beginnings to the Council of Chalcedon. Volumes 1. Ashville: Abingdon Press.

Stephen Haar. 2003. Simon Magus. The First Gnostic? Berlin: Walter de Gruyter.

Andrew Hayes. 2017. Justin against Marcion: Defining the Christian Philosophy. Minneapolis: Fortress Press.

Emily J. Hunt. 2003. Christianity in the Second Century: The Case of Tatian. London: Routledge.

Daniélou Jean. 1964. The Theology of Jewish Christianity. Translated and edited by John A. Baker. Chicago: The Henry Regnery Company.

A.F.J. Klijn. 1992. Jewish-Christian Gospel Tradition. Leiden: Brill.

Peter Lampe. 2003. Chapters 25 and 26 in From Paul to Valentinus: Christians at Rome in the First Two Centuries. Translated by Michael Steinhauser and Marshall D. Johnson. Minneapolis: Fortress Press.

Petri Luomanen. 2008. "Nazarenes". Pages 279–314 in A Companion to Second-Century Christian 'Heretics'. Edited by Antti Marjanen and Petri Luomanen. Leiden: Brill.

Petri Luomanen. 2012. Recovering Jewish-Christian Sects and Gospels. Supplements to Vigiliae Christianae Vol. 110. Leiden: Brill.

Gerard P. Luttikhuizen. 1985. The Revelation of Elchasai. Texte und Studien zum Antiken Judentum Volume 8. Tübingen: Mohr Siebeck.

Gerard P. Luttikhuizen. 2008. "Elchasaites and Their Book." Pages 335–364 in A Companion to Second-Century Christian 'Heretics'. Edited by Antti Marjanen and Petri Luomanen. Leiden: Brill.

Claudio Moreschini and Enrico Norelli. 2005. Chapters 2.8, 10.3–4. Early Christian Greek and Latin Literature: A Literary History. Volume 1: From Paul to the Age of Constantine. Translated by Matthew J. O'Connell. Peabody: Hendrickson Publishers.

James Carleton Paget. 2007. "The Epistle of Barnabas." Pages 72–80 in The Writings of the Apostolic Fathers. Edited by Paul Foster. London: T&T Clark.

Sara Parvis and Paul Foster (eds.). 2007. Justin Martyr and His Worlds. Minneapolis: Fortress Press.

Anders Klostergaard Petersen. 2014. "Heaven-borne in the World: A Study of the Letter of Diognetus." Pages 125–138 in In Defense of Christianity: Early Christian Apologists. Early Christianity in the Context of Antiquity 15. Edited by Jakob Engberg, Anders-Christian Jacobsen, Jörg Ulrich. Translated by Gavin Weakley. Frankfurt am Main: Peter Lang.

William L. Petersen. 2008. "Tatian the Assyrian." Pages 125–158 in A Companion to Second-Century Christian 'Heretics'. Edited by Antti Marjanen and Petri Luomanen. Leiden: Brill.

Häkkinen Sakari. 2008. "Ebionites." Pages 247–278 in A Companion to Second-Century Christian 'Heretics'. Edited by Antti Marjanen and Petri Luomanen. Leiden: Brill.

Jörg Ulrich. 2014. "Justin Martyr." Pages 51–66 in In Defense of Christianity: Early Christian Apologists. Early Christianity in the Context of Antiquity 15. Edited by Jakob Engberg, Anders-Christian Jacobsen, Jörg Ulrich. Translated by Gavin Weakley. Frankfurt am Main: Peter Lang.

Stephen G. Wilson. 1995. Related Strangers: Jews and Christians 70–170 CE. Minneapolis: Fortress Press.

Oliver Larry Yarbrough. 2012. "The Shadow of an Ass: On Reading the Alexamenos Graffito." Pages 239–252 in Text, Image, and Christians in the Graeco-Roman World: A Festschrift in Honor of David Lee Balch. Edited by Aliou Cissé Niang and Carolyn Osiek. Eugene: Pickwick Publications.

CHAPTER 7

Holiness Movements in Asia and Syria

Left: Marble statue of Cybele. Roman (first or second century CE). She is holding a tympanum used in ecstatic dances. Her eyes would have been inlaid with glass or colored stone. San Antonio Museum of Art, Texas. Photo courtesy of April D. DeConick. Right: Marble relief of Dionysus. Roman (second century CE). San Antonio Museum of Art, Texas. **Source:** Courtesy of April D. DeConick

"I am pursued like a wolf from the sheep. I am not a wolf. I am word and spirit and power."

This is one of the only sayings that has survived from Maximilla

KEY PLAYERS
Montanus – Maximilla
Priscilla – Themiso
Thomas the Apostle

KEY TEXTS
Montanist Oracles
1 Corinthians
Revelation – Didache
Gospel of Thomas
Thomas the Contender
Acts of Thomas

In this textbook, we have met Christians like Valentinus who were convinced that the pinnacle of faith is not belief. The pinnacle of faith is Gnosis. So they established Gnostic rituals to guide Christians through ecstatic soul journeys to meet the transcendent God face-to-face. These types of out-of-body transcendent experiences were not the only types of ecstasy that the early Christians fostered. Some Christians were keen to

Comparing Christianities: An Introduction to Early Christianity, First Edition. April D. DeConick.
© 2024 John Wiley & Sons Ltd. Published 2024 by John Wiley & Sons Ltd.

cultivate the "gifts of the spirit" that Paul discusses in his letter to the Corinthians, especially the gifts of prophecy and visions. In this chapter, we will travel to two areas of the ancient world – Asia Minor and eastern Syria – where Christian churches developed that were devoted to fostering these gifts and promoting the lifestyle of holiness as the antidote for sin.

7.1 A Failed Exorcism

COMPANION READINGS
Eusebius, *Ecclesiastical History* 5.16–19
Epiphanius, *Refutation of All Heresies* 48.11–12

Themiso did not know when they were coming, but he had heard rumors that Zotikos and Julian, the bishops from the neighboring cities Cumane (modern Gönen) and Apamea (modern Dinar), were planning to come all the way out to the villages of Pepuza and Tymion to exorcise Maximilla (cf. Eus., *Eccl. Hist.* 5.16, 18) (Figure 7.1). Themiso was aware that this was not the first attempt to exorcise his church's prophets. A few years earlier, Bishop Aelius Publius Julius from Debeltum had tried to exorcise Priscilla, but the congregation refused to give Julius the opportunity he needed to get the job done (Eus. *Eccl. Hist.* 5.19).

Since Themiso had taken over the Church of New Prophecy after the deaths of Montanus and Priscilla, two of its founding prophets, he was tasked with protecting its remaining prophet, Maximilla. So he was ready for the bishops when they arrived at his home during the Sunday service. In fact, Maximilla had already fallen into a frenzied trance and was babbling in a language only she knew, when the bishops showed up at the door. Even though the bishops tried to push in, the congregation pushed them back. But still, they managed to muscle their way into the room. As the bishops opened

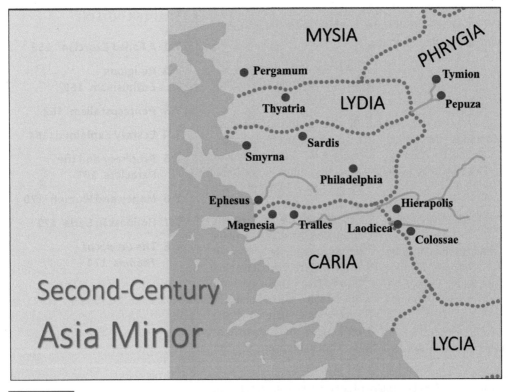

FIGURE 7.1   Map showing the locations of the Montanus camps in Tymion and Pepuza.

their mouths to address the demon that the bishops were certain possessed her, no words came out. They were speechless as Maximilla fell to the floor, shouting out, "I am pursued like a wolf from the sheep. I am not a wolf. I am word and spirit and power" (Eus., *Eccl. Hist.* 5.16).

The Church of New Prophecy did not begin as a church separate from the regional Apostolic Catholic church congregations in Phrygia, a province in Asia Minor. In fact, 10 years earlier, the congregation in Pepuza had just baptized its most recent convert, a man named Montanus. The members of the church must have rejoiced that they had saved a man who was known to have been a priest of Apollo (*Debate* 4.5). Some had heard that he had been initiated into Cybele's mysteries as well (Jer., *Ep.* 41.4). Yet they had triumphed over paganism. They had convinced him of the Christian truth, training him from the Gospel of John about the Lord and from the Book of Revelation about the future.

But then, during the Sunday service, something extraordinary happened. Montanus suddenly began trembling, falling into a frenzied trance before their eyes. His body contorted this way and that, and he babbled nonsense. No one could understand a thing he said. Some among them tried to intervene, worried that a demon might be responsible for his frenzied state of madness. But the demon would not respond, and Montanus continued rolling around and crying out. The frenzy and babbling intensified to the point that some in the congregation wondered if, in fact, an angelic spirit had possessed him. So they encouraged him, calling out to him and asking the angel to identify itself (Eus., *Eccl. Hist.* 5.16). In a climactic moment, Montanus shouted back, (his words reminiscent of Isaiah 63:9), "I am neither angel nor messenger, but I the Lord God the Father have come" (Epiph., *Pan.* 48.11). The congregation was stunned.

But that was not half of it. The religious enthusiasm in the room was contagious. Two women in the congregation also began thrashing around, babbling in nonsensical language. As their frenzy intensified and the congregation began asking the spirits in them to identify themselves, Maximilla responded in a fevered pitch, "Hear not me, but hear Christ" (Epiph., *Pan.* 48.12). Likewise, Priscilla's spirit identified itself with the Paraclete, the name given the Holy Spirit in the Gospel of John (cf. Tert., *Exh.* 10.5; John 14:16–17; 15:26; 16:13).

The congregation could hardly believe it. God had chosen three from among them to be his next prophets. They were convinced that the Trio was like Quadratus and Ammia, the famous Christian prophet and prophetess who lived in the neighboring environs around Philadelphia (Eus., *Eccl. Hist.* 5.16–17). They began broadcasting that the latter-day prophets God promised in Joel 2:28–32 were among them, successors of Agabus (Acts 11:27–28), Judas Barsabbas, Silas (Acts 15:22, 27, 31), and the daughters of Philip (Acts 21:9).

Their latter-day prophets were extra special in their eyes because they had received the fullness of the Paraclete, not just the pledge of the Spirit that the apostles had received at Pentecost (Acts 2; cf. Orig., *Princ.* 2.7.3; *Comm. Matt.* 15.30; *Debate*; Fil., *Haer.* 49). The Trio had been filled with the Paraclete, the spirit of Christ, which Jesus had promised to send after his death to forecast God's will and continue God's revelation of the truth (John 14:16–18). Jesus' prophecy had been fulfilled in their church.

Had their revelations been only about the end of the world or an intensification of morality, the Trio may have been received by the surrounding churches on better terms. But once they began building an egalitarian community dedicated to holiness at the foot of the mountain near Pepuza and started talking about themselves as "spiritual" people (pneumatics) who understood the truth and other Christians as "soul" people (psychics) who did not know how to live as God preferred, the pot was stirred and trouble began to brew.

7.2 Religious Enthusiasm

COMPANION READINGS
1 Corinthians 12–13
Acts 2
Didache 1–16

Trance states were not novel in antiquity. They are described in terms of ecstasy, as involuntary states that seize people and put them out of their "right" mind. Such states were associated with speaking in tongues, prophesying, clairvoyance, frenzied movements, shouting furiously, body tremors, out-of-body experiences, and other forms of "madness." The ancients had one explanation for these physical fits. They believed that spirits – either good or bad – possessed people. Ecstasy was the result of divine or demonic enthusiasm that took over the person. If divine, the person was a prophet or seer and was considered an authority who had access to divine knowledge. If demonic, the person was ill or insane and required treatment, usually exorcism.

For as long as anyone could remember, the God Apollo was known to possess his priestesses, who in frenzied states babbled his oracles in free vocalization that only Apollo's priests could interpret and then scribe in poetic verse for the petitioner. The rites of various religions devoted to the mysteries of different deities often included frenzied states. Consider the Bacchanalia, the fevered carnivals in the forests of groups of mostly women possessed by Dionysus, who danced to music and screamed throughout the night. The intensity of their madness was so great that, according to ancient reports, as they ran through the woods, they hunted, tore animals apart limb-by-limb, and devoured them. People who lived in Phrygia were particularly familiar with the mysteries of Cybele, the Great Mother Goddess native to Anatolia, whose rites rivaled Dionysus' in their revelry and ecstasy with frenzied dance circles fueled by loud percussive music.

Religious enthusiasm was not limited to pagan religions. It was foundational to the Christian story with Paul's report of his own revelation (Greek: *apocalypsis*) of Christ (Gal. 1:11–12) – "whether in the body or out of the body" (2 Cor. 12:1–4) – and his claim that Christ's mind and spirit was in him as well as in all who had been baptized (Gal. 2:20; 1 Cor. 2:6; Phil. 2:5). Paul is very clear that the spirit of Christ possesses converts at baptism (Rom. 8:9). Possessed with Christ, the converts experience Christ's death and resurrection (Rom. 6:1–11).

Paul's converts clearly understood the religious enthusiasm within their communities as exhibitions of their divine possession, what they called "gifts of the spirit" (1 Cor. 12:4–11). Paul reports that religious enthusiasm gripped his churches in the form of tongue-speaking, tongue-interpretation, prophecy, communication of divine knowledge, miracle-working, healing, and discernment (the ability to distinguish holy possession from demonic possession). His communities were so enthused to have access to divine knowledge and authority that Paul tried to get things under control by imposing a loose hierarchy of divine offices (apostles, prophets, teachers, miracle-workers, healers, tongue-interpreters, and tongue-speakers) and emphasizing the common good of the church over the diversity of its gifts (1 Cor. 12: 12–30). He also recognized charitable work and faithfulness as more significant than tongue-speaking, prophesizing, and the communication of divine knowledge, enthusiastic activities in his churches that, according to Paul, were accompanied by percussive music: banging on gongs and clanging cymbals together (1 Cor. 13:1–13).

Stories of the apostles and other first-generation Christians as powerful healers, miracle-workers, prophets, and seers were well-known to later Christians. The author of the book of Acts writes about the origins of his church in an ecstatic moment when the Holy Spirit, as fiery tongues, descended on the apostles while they were gathered in a house in Jerusalem. Possessed by the Spirit, the apostles were able to speak in non-native tongues so that everyone – no matter where they came from – could understand the apostles. Some scoffed at the enthusiasm that gripped the apostles, suggesting that they must be drunk (Acts 2:1–13). The author of Acts said otherwise. He told the story as the fulfillment of God's promise in Joel 2:28–32 to send his Spirit to Israel's daughters and sons so that they would prophesize, see visions, and have dreams that would help them discern what they needed to know about the advent of the last days (Acts 2:17–21).

Prophets and prophecy were a matter of fact among early Christians, many of whom had heard about Agabus, who had predicted a severe famine that took place during the reign of Claudius (Acts 11:27–28), Judas Barsabbas and Silas, who were itinerant prophets from Jerusalem (Acts 15:22, 27, 31), the four unmarried prophetesses who were daughters of Philip (Acts 21:9), and Anna, the daughter of Phanuel (Luke 2:36). An early church handbook (ca. 100 CE) called the *Didache* reports that itinerant prophets were the norm, wandering from church to church, prophesizing during church services as holy guests.

But prophecy was not something that occurred only in Christian memory. It was alive and well in the mid-second century when the Trio was around. Justin Martyr tells Trypho that "the prophetic gifts remain with us, even to the present time" (Just., *Dial.* 82). And Irenaeus, the Trio's contemporary, knows Christians in his church who possess the spiritual gifts of prophecy, miracle-working, healing, and discernment. He also shares a great deal of information about Marcus the Valentinian, whose church services featured frenzied prophetesses (Iren., *Haer.* 2.32.4; 5.6.1). So it would be wrong to see the Trio as a revival of prophecy that had died out in the churches, as scholars used to speculate. Prophecy was alive and well when Montanus, Maxmillia, and Pricilla came online.

Prophets and prophecies only became problematic for churches when what the prophets communicated was in conflict with the messages of the resident church presiders and council of presbyters or elders. Discerning the type of spirit – whether holy or demonic – that possessed the itinerant prophets became critical in these situations. The spirit would be judged "holy" if its message agreed with the teachings of the resident leaders. If the messages differed, the spirit would be exorcised as a demon.

The author of the *Didache* boiled discernment down to a few simple judgments. If the prophets teach something different from the teachings laid out in the *Didache* (*Did.* 1–4), they are false prophets. If the prophets overstay their visits – if they stay more than two days – the prophets are false prophets. If they ask for money for themselves, they are false prophets. If the activities of the prophets are unseemly or unethical, they are judged to be false prophets. Only true prophets should be heeded and fed (*Did.* 11, 13).

The escalating tension between the presiders and elders of the churches and the prophets is visceral in early Christian texts. For instance, in the *Ascension of Isaiah*, we hear from the prophets themselves about the tension between them and the resident church leaders. The prophets complain about resident leaders who love being in office so much that they "make ineffective the prophecy of the prophets" (cf. *Asc. Isa.* 3:13–4:22).

It is within this context of escalating tension between prophets, presbyteries, and presiders that the Trio emerges and must defend themselves as true prophets. They do so by turning to Jewish scriptures. They point to Abraham, Moses, Miriam, Deborah, Huldah, Isaiah, Ezekiel, Daniel, and others as their prophetic exemplars. They also reference Adam, whom, in the Greek translation of Genesis 2:21–24, God put into "ecstasy of sleep" before Adam prophesized about the future. They also point to their own Christian exemplars, especially John of Patmos, the author of the book of Revelation (Figure 7.2). But it is the authority of the Gospel of John that they wield most powerfully, claiming

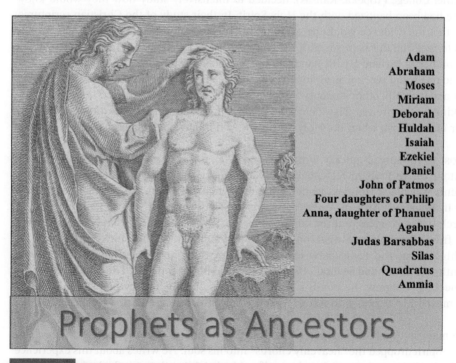

FIGURE 7.2 Montanists understood Genesis 2:21–24 to say that God put Adam in an "ecstasy of sleep." Etching of God putting Adam to sleep before operating on him. G. B. Leonetti, C. Cencioni, and Nicola Pisano (ca. 1250). **Source:** Wellcome Collection / Public Domain.

that their prophets are not just filled with a holy spirit, but the Paraclete that Jesus had promised to send to his followers in order to inspire and lead people to God after Jesus' death (John 14:16–17; 15:26; 16:13).

7.3 Pentecostalism

Christian religious enthusiasm is not confined to early Christianity and the Montanists. Their ecstatic performances during worship combined with their emphasis on a holiness lifestyle have comparatives in modernity, especially within the Pentecostal tradition. The type of frenzied trance and tongue-speaking exhibited by the Trio is the type of behavior reported to have occurred, for instance, at the Methodist Holiness camp meetings and revivals in the late 1800s, which laid the groundwork for the emergence of modern Pentecostalism. The nineteenth-century Holiness Movement, like the ancient Church of New Prophecy, recognized that it was not enough to be baptized and saved. While it was true that original sin had been forgiven in the washing, how was the Christian supposed to stay clean? Something had to happen after baptism to prevent backsliding.

Holiness preachers began to teach new converts that what was really important was what happened to them after baptism. How did they plan to live their lives in Jerusalem, the holy city? What did a holy life look like? To prepare them to live in the heavenly Jerusalem to come, Holiness preachers held camp meetings, which they set up to prefigure heavenly Jerusalem and the tabernacle (tent temple). Holiness preachers taught that Christian holiness is a voluntary practice of the human will supported by the constant revelation of Christ to the soul by the Holy Spirit. At their revivals, the religious enthusiasm was such that those baptized by the Spirit would shout, scream, speak in tongues, fall into trances, and "even get the jerks."

In 1900, over Christmas break, a group of Bible school students and their holiness teacher, Charles F. Parham at Bethel College (Topeka, Kansas), decided to intensively study how they would know whether someone had been baptized with the Holy Spirit. In their study of the Christian scriptures, they determined that the evidence would be speaking in tongues of foreign languages (Acts 2). The students wanted to replicate this baptism with the Holy Spirit. On 1 January 1901, Agnes Ozman felt the power come on her as Parham lay his hands on her and prayed. Suddenly she began to babble in a language that no one could recognize, although some thought perhaps it was Chinese. After weeks of fervent prayer and worship, other students along with Parham himself fell into ecstasy, experiencing tongue-speaking for themselves. They determined that tongue-speaking was the proof of the Holy Spirit, the power of Pentecost, when the Holy Spirit was said to have descended upon the Apostles (Acts 2:1–31).

The Pentecost fervor spread quickly. From 1901 to 1906, the Pentecostal experience occurred mainly in Houston, where Parham relocated (1905) and opened the Houston Bible College. One of his first students was black Holiness leader William Seymour. Parham and Seymour started to preach together in Houston's African-American churches. Then Seymour was invited to preach in a Holiness Church in Los Angeles, but the congregants there were convinced that he was teaching heresy. He was fired after only one week on the job. A sympathetic family took him in, and he continued teaching about the Pentecostal experience from their home on Bonnie Brae Street. Within two months, Seymour and several others began speaking in tongues. The popularity of his house-church meetings outgrew the family's home almost as quickly as they had started. That is when Seymour moved his meetings to Azusa Street, where his message started a three-year-long revival meeting.

Frank Bartleman, an eyewitness to the events, describes what took place in those early days. He says it felt like the Spirit dropped the "heavenly chorus" into his soul. He writes about this experience in his ever-popular book *Azusa Street*, "I found myself suddenly joining the rest who had received this supernatural gift [tongue-speaking]. It was a spontaneous manifestation and rapture no earthly tongue can describe." The power was contagious, Barlteman explains, "A dozen might be on their feet at one time, trembling under the mighty power of God." Then, he says, "Suddenly the Spirit would fall upon the congregation. God Himself would give the altar call. Men would fall all over the house, like the slain in battle, or rush for the altar en masse, to seek God." Bartleman reports, "The presence of the Lord was so real."

Parham and Seymour began conducting revivals across the country, which caught media attention. The press began to refer to the Pentecostals in these revivals as "holy rollers," while their Methodist ancestors were "holy jumpers." By September 1906, the movement had grown to 13,000 converts in the United States, and within the year, Pentecostalism had crossed the oceans into Asia and Europe. Today, over 200 million people across the globe identify as Pentecostal Christians.

What are Pentecostal experiences like? The testimony of William H. Durham, who was a Holiness preacher from Chicago in the formative years of Pentecostalism, provides a glimpse. When he visited Azusa Street Mission, he was overcome with the Spirit, his body jerking and quaking for three hours. The power worked its way through his whole body, he relates, one section at a time. It started in his limbs, worked inward to his torso, head, face, chin, and finally hit his vocal cords when it spoke through Durham in unknown tongues. All the while, Durham says, he was aware that a "living person" had come into him, that he literally was possessed with the Spirit, which took hold of his vocal cords and spoke any language it chose through him (*The Apostolic Faith*, Los Angeles, 1 no. 6 [Feb.–Mar. 1907] 4).

Phenomenologically, what Durham describes is quite similar to Montanus' description of his own ecstatic state. Montanus likened himself to a lyre, a stringed instrument that is plucked by the Spirit's hand to speak what the Spirit wills. As this happens, Montanus says that he is asleep, involuntarily acted upon by the Spirit, who stirs up his deepest feelings and emotions (Epiph., *Pan.* 48).

> "Behold, the human is like a lyre, and I flit about like a pick.
> The human sleeps, and I awaken him.
> Behold, it is like the Lord who changes humans
> and gives humans a heart."
>
> *A saying of Montanus recorded by Epiphanius, Panarion 48.4 (trans. DeConick)*

The phenomenon both men describe is known as glossolalia (Greek: *glossai lalein*, to speak in tongues), the ability to involuntarily speak unlearned languages. The early Christian texts differentiate the phenomenon, sometimes describing it as the ability to speak unknown angelic languages (angelolalia), or to speak unlearned foreign languages (xenolalia), or to speak a language that everyone hears in their own native tongues (heteroglossolalia). Inarticulate speech that needed to be interpreted in order to be understood was considered angelolalia by the Christians. Of course, if the prophet was believed to be demon-possessed, the prophet's babble would amount to nothing more than demonic communication or quackery.

While the first Pentecostals believed that they were speaking in unlearned foreign languages, they have come to understand their glossolalia in terms of speaking the language of God. In fact, investigation into the modern phenomenon agrees that there is no evidence that any form of human language is being spoken. Rather tongue-speech consists of familiar phonetic sounds strung together and repeated again and again. The first-known recording of a tongue-speech is demonstrative. It was made by the ethnomusicologist Jeff Titon in 1977 at a Pentecostal revival meeting (Titon 1978). The phonetic symbol "?" indicates a guttural sound emitted in the back of the esophagus (Figure 7.3).

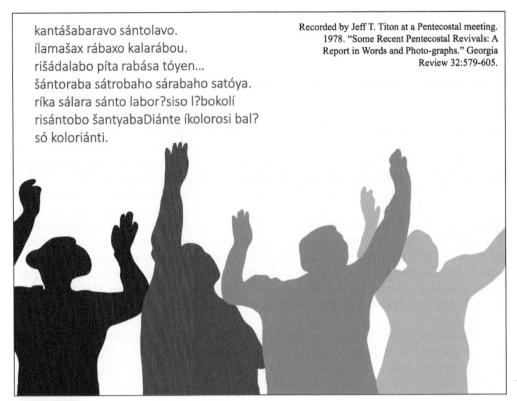

kantášabaravo sántolavo.
ílamašax rábaxo kalarábou.
rišádalabo píta rabása tóyen...
šántoraba sátrobaho sárabaho satóya.
ríka sálara sánto labor?siso l?bokolí
risántobo šantyabaDiánte íkolorosi bal?
só koloriánti.

Recorded by Jeff T. Titon at a Pentecostal meeting. 1978. "Some Recent Pentecostal Revivals: A Report in Words and Photo-graphs." Georgia Review 32:579-605.

FIGURE 7.3 Illustration of Pentecostal meeting 1941, Chicago Illinois.

7.4 Ecstasy Explained

Most scholars have tried to use epilepsy (damaged neurology) and schizophrenia (mental illness) as explanations for these ecstatic states of mind. In other words, the Trio were either having seizures or hallucinations. But this explanation breaks down when we study modern subjects (like the Pentecostals) and are not dealing with epilepsy or schizophrenia. In fact, ecstatic states of mind are phenomena that are universally and historically attested in physically and mentally healthy people.

According to cultural anthropologists, all societies acknowledge and distinguish special "spiritual" experiences from ordinary experiences, and, in every society, some people are known as religious specialists who induce and enter ecstasy for the purpose of communicating with a spirit entity to acquire information to help their group. Anthropologists study these altered states of consciousness under the rubric of shamanism, the practice of trance by specialists in hunter-gatherer societies to communicate with spirits and interact with the spirit world for the benefit of their communities: to heal the sick, foretell the future, and generally improve the lot of the living. Glossolalia is associated with some shamanic rituals. As societies become more complex and sedentary, the shaman is replaced by mediums, priests, prophets, healers, and sorcerers, and glossolalia turns up in new contexts.

Anthropologists who study shamans have known for a long time that entheogens, psychoactive substances like psilocybin (a substance derived from mushrooms and used in certain religious ceremonies) stimulate ecstasy. But studying the biology of this has been difficult since, in 1968, psychoactive drugs became illegal and research funding dried up. However, in 2000, Roland Griffiths at John Hopkin's Center for Psychedelic and Consciousness Research, received a grant to study the clinical effects of psilocybin on alcoholism, anorexia, depression, and Alzheimer's disease. Publications of this research have been showing that controlled use within clinical settings decreases anxiety and depression, even people's fear of death, and vastly improves their ability to control their addictions.

While these therapeutic benefits are significant findings in-and-of themselves, it is not all. The Pahnke-Richards Mystical Experience Questionnaire revealed that 85% of clinical participants rated their psilocybin trip as one of their most meaningful and spiritually significant experiences, with many rating it as a "complete mystical experience." Karin Sokel, one of the clinical subjects, related to Michael Pollen (2018, 71) that her trip climaxed with an encounter with the God "I Am," who merged with her in an "explosion of energy." The power penetrated her body so that her fingers went "electric." She understood, not intellectually, but in the deepest sense possible, that "we are divine" and that love is "the core of our being." When asked if this were some dream or drug-induced fantasy, Sokel replied, "This was as real as you and I having this conversation. I wouldn't have understood it either if I hadn't had the direct experience. Now it is hardwired in my brain so I can connect with it and do it often." Although the researchers have not yet been able to determine the exact brain mechanism involved in altering consciousness via psilocybin, their research continues and very likely will impact how we come to understand the induction of states of ecstasy in the future.

Entheogens, however, are not the lone stimulants of ecstasy. Ecstasy is more complicated than that. There are other correlates. For instance, numerous studies have shown that rhythmic stimuli. as we find in religious rituals, often induce altered states of consciousness. This includes low-key repetitive behaviors like chanting or drumming and rapid, repeated behaviors like all-night dancing. Prolonged fasting, meditation, and prayer can also stimulate them, resulting in an altered sense of the self and its boundaries, disembodiment, and feelings of transcendence, ineffability, and timelessness.

Ecstatic states also have been linked with what is known in the psychological sciences as dissociative or fugue mental states. These states are characterized by feelings of depersonalization or detachment from the immediate surroundings, even separation from one's own body and memories. As such, they are often triggered by traumatic events that people have experienced. People with dissociative disorders like Post-Traumatic Syndrome Disorder (PTSD) often report feelings of derealization, when they feel like they are slipping away from normal reality. Feelings of possession are also quite common, as are sensations of self-fragmentation and the emergence of an "other" self. In these cases, the alteration of consciousness is negative and maladaptive (which is why psychologists and psychiatrists call it a dissociative disorder), rather than positive and adaptive (which is why in other contexts the dissociation is called a religious experience).

Prevailing research has begun to map the biological basis of altered states of consciousness. Much of this research was pioneered by Andrew Newberg (and the late Eugene D'Aquili) who ran controlled experiments on Buddhist practitioners, and then later on Franciscan nuns. In order to investigate the biological basis of ecstasy, Newberg used SPECT brain scan imaging on the subjects while they were engaged in meditative and prayer activities that the practitioners felt achieved transcendent "mystical" or peak experiences. Newberg discovered that the altered states of consciousness described by religious adepts are not necessarily hallucinations, delusions, or the misfiring of a neurologically damaged brain, as so many people over the years have assumed. Rather ecstatic experiences rely on our normal biological hardware.

The brain structures that Newberg identified involve a circuit of the limbic system (Figure 7.4). The circuit starts in the prefrontal cortex when attention is directed away from the external senses. This triggers a decrease in the activity of the parietal lobe and the right orientation association area. The right hippocampus is stimulated, leading to the activation of the quiescent centers of the right amygdala and hypothalamus. This arouses the autonomic nervous system, leading to changes in the midbrain and feelings of peacefulness. The continual stimulation of this circuit results in the deafferentation of the orientation association area and feelings of transcending space, time, and self. This brain circuit is regulated mainly by dopamine and serotonin neurotransmitter systems. During ecstatic states, serotonin levels fall and dopamine levels rise.

The basic biology supporting ecstatic states relies on overstimulation of the autonomic nervous system. The autonomic nervous system has two main modes of operation–the sympathetic and parasympathetic modes. The sympathetic mode is responsible for our body's ability to become instantly alert. It produces our body's fight-or-flight reaction and the corresponding emotions of anxiety, fear,

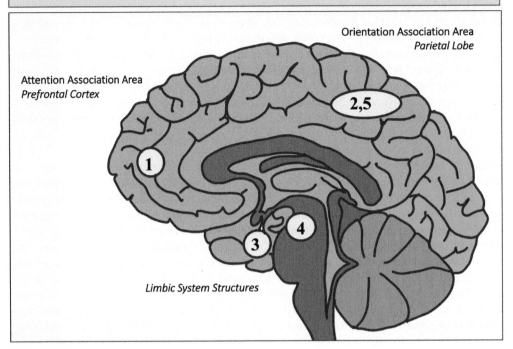

FIGURE 7.4   Illustration of the brain and the cycle of activity when meditating.

and panic. When this mode is triggered, it immediately increases heart rate and breathing, pumps adrenaline into the bloodstream, and dilates our pupils, as it gets the body ready for instant action. The parasympathetic mode is our body's natural response to relax by decreasing heart rate and breathing, lulling us into rest and sleep, and quieting us so that we can digest food and mate. When this system is operationally dominant, we tend to be emotionally peaceful.

Scientific research is demonstrating that the induction of ecstatic states of mind correlates with hyperstimulation of either the sympathetic or parasympathetic modes. The parasympathetic mode can be overstimulated, even to the point of producing a total loss of bodily sensations, through intentional stillness and silence or low-key repetitive behaviors like chanting or drumming. This effects a hyper-quiescent state and an extraordinary state of relaxation, bliss, and oceanic tranquility.

The sympathetic mode can be intentionally overstimulated by engaging in deliberate trauma, excessive behaviors, and extreme activities. While this hyperstimulation has its own correlation to ecstatic states of boundless energy and flow, when pushed to the extreme, the sympathetic mode can run on high until the body becomes exhausted and collapses. At this point, the parasympathetic system kicks in, and we are back to oceanic tranquility, but now with an orgasmic, rapturous rush. It appears that the type of ecstasy reported to have taken over the Trio as well as the modern Pentecostals (frenzied body movements, dashing to the ground, shouting, and inarticulate tongue-speaking) is related to the hyperstimulation of the sympathetic mode of the autonomic nervous system.

Which brings us back to glossolalia. How is it explained by scientists? Again, Newberg pioneered this area of research, conducting for the first time ever brain scans on Pentecostal tongue-speakers. Newberg describes the experience of watching his first subject, "Sharon," start to sing one of her favorite gospel songs, dancing and shouting, "Hallelujah! Thank you, Jesus!" She continued singing for an hour while Newberg ran a series of scans to record her brain activity as she sang. Then Sharon began swinging her arms and rocking from side to side. Within minutes, Sharon started babbling. Newberg reports that, to him, it sounded like a foreign language.

When Newberg analyzed the brain scans of his five subjects taken while they were tongue-speaking and compared them with the scans taken while they were singing, he discovered a decrease in the activity in the frontal lobes and increased activity in the thalamus. The scans of praying Franciscan nuns showed an increase in the activity of the frontal lobes, which makes sense since this is the language area of the brain. So a decrease in the activity of this area of the brain during tongue-speaking is an unusual finding, according to Newberg. It suggests to him that the language is being generated in a way that differs from the ways we normally process speech. He hypothesizes that there may be another circuit, possibly associated with the thalamus, responsible for the production of glossolalic speech. Another possibility is that glossolalia is a kind of vocalization that is not actually speech. Because it does not involve linguistic accuracy, it may not be indicated by activity in the frontal lobes.

Newberg also speculates that, for the tongue-speaker, this may be why the experience feels like proof that another entity had actually spoken through them involuntarily. Decreased activity in the frontal lobes produces the conscious experience that someone else is in charge. Newberg observed that Sharon interrupted her normal consciousness by losing herself in the strong rhythmic patterns of gospel music. As her frontal lobe activities decreased, her memory functions were suspended. In this cognitive state, Newberg says, the internal rules that govern the construction of language begin to disengage. What begins as random babbling moves into a series of repetitive sounds that mimic the structure of ordinary speech but is not language.

The babbling is interpreted by people according to the established religious beliefs that they or their religious community already believe to be true. The community judges the soundness of the practitioner's ecstasy, whether holy or diabolical, prophetic or mad. Ultimately, the explanations of ecstatic states are dependent on their cultural location. What is called God possession in one location may be demon possession in another. While the Trio and the Pentecostals understood their ecstasy to be genuine manifestations of the Holy Spirit, others around them were not so sure. Demons might be on the loose.

[7.5] **Prophecy and the Paraclete**

COMPANION READINGS
Revelation 21
Debate of a Montanist and an Orthodox

Little is left of the published versions of the Trio's prophetic sayings. These oracular collections were considered authoritative new revelation by members of the Church of New Prophecy. In fact, Tertullian of Carthage (ca. 200–220 CE), who affiliated with the Church of New Prophecy later in life, referred from time to time to these collections as authorities of Christian truth. Themiso, the prophet who replaced Montanus after his death (ca. 175 CE), was known for writing an epistle, styled after Paul's letters, that he distributed to the regional churches to instruct them about the true Christian faith. The leaders of those churches were not impressed and accused him of blasphemy (Eus., *Eccl. Hist.* 18.5).

For centuries, the Montanists read these sacred revelations alongside other Christian scriptures until John of Ephesus (on orders of Emperor Justinian and accompanied by a band of soldiers) went to Pepuza to put an end to the Church of New Prophecy (550 CE). He went to their basilica, dug up the sacred relics of the church – the bones of the Trio – and retrieved their holy books. Then he set fire to it all, burning the church to the ground amidst the weeping and wailing of the Montanists who were there (Michael the Syrian, *Chron.* 9.33).

All that remains of the Trio's teachings are a dozen quotations of their sayings found smattered in the writings of other authors who opposed them. Only Tertullian, as a Montanist himself, quotes the prophets as authorities on Christian living. This dearth of information is not much to go on, but combined with the arguments that their opponents made against them and the praise that Tertullian heaped upon them, we can make out the broad strictures of their message.

We have already seen that the Trio's activities were believed to be manifestations of the Paraclete, the Holy Spirit, which Jesus promised to send to believers after his death to guide them as he had guided them during his life. There are two oracles that confirm that when Montanus spoke in ecstasy, he was speaking as the Lord God the Father (Epiph., *Pan.* 48.11). His ecstasy, Montanus reported, was an involuntary process when the Spirit possessed him and spoke through him. As we already learned, he likened the experience to the way a stringed instrument sings when it is plucked (Epiph., *Pan.* 48.4).

> "I am the Lord God, the Almighty dwelling in man."
>
> "Neither angel nor envoy, but I the Lord God the Father has come."
>
> *Sayings of Montanus recorded by Epiphanius, Panarion 48.11*

Likewise, Maximilla claimed to speak as the "word, spirit, and power" (Eus., *Eccl. Hist.* 5.16). Maximilla claims to be a true prophet pursued like a wolf, a false prophet (Matt. 7:15). Her oracular words, she said, were not her own but the words of Christ himself (Epiph., *Pan.* 48.12). She talks about having the knowledge of God forced upon her. She had no choice in the matter but to prophesize (Epiph., *Pan.* 48.13). She understands her compulsory role as an enthusiast, revelator, and interpreter, to alleviate suffering and teach people about God's covenant so that they can be heirs to his promises (Epiph., *Pan.* 48.13).

> "Hear not me, but hear Christ."
>
> "The Lord has sent me as partisan, revealer, and interpreter of this suffering, covenant, and promise. I am compelled to come to understand the knowledge of God whether I want to or not."
>
> "After me there will no longer be a prophet, but the end."
>
> *Sayings of Maximilla recorded by Epiphanius, Panarion 48.2, 12–13*

A couple of the known oracles are prophetic predictions about the end of the world. In one of these oracles, Maximilla predicts that she will be the last prophet because, after her death, the end will occur (Epiph., *Pan.* 48.2). In another, Priscilla (or Quintilla, a later prophetess; Epiphanius is unclear) says that Christ came to her in a dream as a woman, dressed in a bright robe. Christ gave her wisdom, revealing to her that Pepuza is a holy place. It is the very place that the new Jerusalem will descend from heaven (Epiph., *Pan.* 49.1). These sorts of predictions reflect knowledge of the book of Revelation.

> "They are flesh, and they hate the flesh."
>
> "Having assumed the form of a woman, Christ came to me in a bright robe and put wisdom in me, and revealed to me that this place is holy, and that it is here that Jerusalem will descend from heaven."
>
> *Sayings of Priscilla recorded by Tertullian, Resurrection 11.2 and Epiphanius, Panarion 49.1*

Whether the Trio picked up Chiliasm from Revelation as Justin did is debated. Tertullian certainly did. He mentions a New Prophecy oracle that identified the Church of Prophecy as the prefiguration of the heavenly Jerusalem, which would descend to earth in the future. Tertullian said that the new Jerusalem would be a sub-celestial kingdom for a thousand years (Tert., *Marc.* 3.24). It is likely that the Trio taught something similar.

Montanus did in fact call Pepuza Jerusalem. He summoned people from everywhere to come to Phrygia and gather in Jerusalem (Pepuza) to receive the Paraclete and God's "spiritual gifts" (Eus., *Eccl. Hist.* 5.18; Epiph., *Pan.* 48.1; *Debate*). In a secluded location, the Montanists baptized pagan converts and the dead, ritually consecrated the camp, and hoped to have a vision of Christ (Epiph., *Pan.* 48.14; 49.1; Fil., *Haer.* 49). There are reports that they tattooed baptized children with God's name (Eus., *Pan.* 48.14–15; Aug., *Haer.* 26). This ritual, which is mentioned in Revelation (3:12; 14:1; 22:4), marks God's name on the foreheads or hands of the baptized in order to identify them as God's Elect in contrast to the damned (Rev. 13:1, 6, 16–17; 14:9–11; 16:2; 19:20; 20:4).

Women whom they called Virgins took center stage in their meetings, carrying torches as they joined the assemblies. The women came to prophesy to the people. They would fall into frenzied trances. Soon the crowd would be caught up in the "enthusiastic inspiration" and "Bacchic frenzy," weeping and wailing violently for repentance (Epiph., *Pan.* 49.2–3). Charged, the crowd was compelled to take on the disciplined Christian life that the Trio demanded (Epiph., *Pan.* 48.13).

How did the holy lifestyle work? Wasn't baptism enough to sanctify a Christian? According to the Trio, baptism should not be the end goal for the convert. While baptism granted absolution for sins committed before baptism, it did nothing for post-baptismal sins. Everyone knew this. The Trio, however, insisted that the forgiveness of post-baptismal sins was not as easy as Christians in other churches believed, who relied on a one-time penance that the other churches offered to forgive sins that were committed after baptism. The Trio was reluctant to grant post-baptismal absolution because, they said, people would only sin again (Tert., *Mod.* 21.7). Jerome relates that they supported their opposition to post-baptismal pardon with reference to the book of Hebrews 6:4–6 (Jer., *Ep.* 41 *ad Marc.* 3).

Among Christians more broadly, Christians facing martyrdom were also believed to have the power to forgive sins, even forgiving those who had denied Christ when they were arrested and tried (Tert., *Mart.* 1.3. 6; Eus., *Eccl. Hist..* 5.2.5). This privilege to forgive sins was extended to "confessors" as well, Christians who were arrested and tortured but not executed (Eus., *Eccl. Hist..* 5.2.2–4). Yet, in his Montanist writings, Tertullian says that even the martyrs did not exercise the power to forgive sins. While the Church of New Prophecy encouraged Christians to be prepared to embrace martyrdom (Tert., *Flight* 9.4), Tertullian had been convinced that their martyrdoms only absolved the martyrs of their personal sins, not the sins of others (Tert., *Mart.* 1). In the Church of New Prophecy, it is clear that absolution was not freely handed out.

If forgiveness of post-baptismal sins was withheld, then what was the solution for sin? The Trio's solution was to make Christians commit to a disciplined lifestyle that would be free of sin. The Christian, filled with the Holy Spirit, was obligated to live a disciplined life of holiness in accordance with the new revelation provided by the Trio. Their holiness lifestyle centered on disciplining their bodies when it came to diet and sex.

In terms of diet, they reformed the fasting practices of Christians by increasing the number and length of fasts, as well as imposing "dry" fasting or xerophagy. The reasoning behind xerophagy had to do with their understanding of ancient physiology and controlling the excesses of the body's humors. The ancients believed that excess fluid in the body would be turned into semen, and with this, the need for sexual release. So prescribing a dry diet (eating uncooked, soaked legumes; raw radishes; avoiding meat, succulent fruit, and wine) would purge the body of excess fluid, reducing the production of semen. Dry diets were adopted by the ancient Christians to curb sexual excesses. Since the Trio led a charismatic group seeking the continual revelation of the Spirit, they also imposed fasting on the Lord's Day (Sunday) as well as the Sabbath (Saturday) whenever visions were being sought (Tert., *Jej.* 1; 13; *Comm. Dan.* 4.20).

To curb sexual sins, the Trio limited sexual activities by codifying (as the Paraclete's revelation) Paul's personal opinion on marriage, that to remain celibate is preferred to marriage since the end of the world is near (1 Cor. 7:7–8, 26, 29, 40). So exalted was singlehood, that the Trio went so far as to permit divorce for devotional reasons (1 Cor. 7:32–35). Apollonius reports that Priscilla and Maximilla immediately divorced their husbands once they became filled with the Spirit, setting a precedent for others to follow suit (Eus., *Eccl. Hist.* 5.18). After her divorce, Priscilla took on the title Virgin (Eus., *Eccl. Hist.* 5.18). She was the first to hold this office in the Church of New Prophecy. Digamy or remarriage after a spouse had died was outlawed altogether. Anyone who was in a second marriage was not allowed in their church (Epiph., *Pan.* 48.9).

This discipline was supposed to be exemplified in the lifestyle of the clergy. Priscilla preached that the clergy needs to know how to cultivate the holiness lifestyle because holiness produces harmony and facilitates visions and verbal revelations of secrets that will be beneficial to the church (Tert., *Chastity* 10.5). Montanus encouraged Christians to maintain a disciplined lifestyle because the righteous "will shine a hundred times brighter than the sun," and the children who are saved "will shine a hundred times brighter than the moon" (Epiph., *Pan.* 48.10). The disciplined Christians of the Montanist camp meetings identified themselves as "spiritual Christians" or pneumatics over and against the average Christians, whom they recognized as "soulish Christians" or psychics (Clem. Alex., *Strom.* 4.13.93.1; Tert., *Fasting* 1; *Marc.* 4.22; *Haer.* 1.86).

> "Why do you call the more excellent person saved?
> For the just will shine a hundred times brighter than the sun,
> and the children among you who are saved
> will shine brighter than the moon."
>
> *Saying of Montanus recorded by Epiphanius*, Panarion 48.10

When all the evidence is amassed, we can see that the Trio started the first Christian charismatic revival movement, complete with camp meetings fueled by religious enthusiasm. The comparison with nineteenth-century Methodist and Holiness revival camps is instructive. Like those enthusiastic meetings of the Holiness preachers, the Trio's camp was designated as Jerusalem, and the pursuit of holiness was their dominant message. The Trio called Christians to pursue sanctification, the outpouring of the Spirit, which, they believed, would empower Christians to resist the temptation to sin and all but guarantee their salvation. Their meetings included preaching, prayer, prophecy, and baptism, all bolstered by a religious enthusiasm that gripped all who attended. Campers left, going home to nearby Cumane, Otrous, and Hieropolis, committed to a disciplined life of holiness that would cleanse them from sin, and committed to follow the new revelations given by the Trio about fasting, marriage, and absolution.

7.6 Money and Women

COMPANION READINGS
Eusebuis., *Ecclesiastical History* 5.18.2–11
Epiphanius., *Panarion* 49.2–3
Didymus of Alexandria, *Trinity* 3.41

When the movement first started, Christians around Phrygia flocked to the camp to see what all the fuss was about. Local bishops and presbyters from neighboring cities were particularly interested in observing the Trio and figuring out what was going on. Everyone knew that their claim to prophecy had to be tested.

Up until then, false prophets had been determined when their messages deviated from the teachings of the established regional churches, when they prophesied about a God other than YHWH or taught that Jesus was not a human being. But everyone agreed that this was not the case with the Trio's message. They did not "preach another God" or "dismiss Jesus Christ" or "overturn some Canon of Truth" simply because they taught that fasting ought to be more frequent and marriages ought to be more limited (Tert., *Fasting* 1; Epiph., *Pan.* 48.1). The regional churches also glorified virginity and celibacy, praised chastity and widowhood, and honored marriage while forbidding prostitution, adultery, and unrestrained sex (Epiph., *Pan.* 48.9). In agreement with the other churches in the area, the Trio taught about the same Father, Son, and Holy Spirit, used the same Jewish and Christian texts as their scriptures, and instructed that there will be a resurrection from the dead (Epiph., *Pan*. 48.3–4). Even the Trio's claim that the church is the recipient of the spiritual gifts of prophecy – both their daughters and sons – was aligned with the other churches (Epiph., *Pan*. 48.5). The other church leaders did not know how to respond at first, except to observe how things developed and hold meetings to discuss the camp revivals among themselves.

The leaders of the regional churches noticed a few things that raised their eyebrows. First, the revivals were becoming so popular that the Trio decided that they needed help running them. They began hiring (yes, hiring!) preachers and paying them salaries out of the donations they collected from the congregants (Eus., *Eccl. Hist*. 5:18.2). As far as they could tell, the collections were pouring into the Trio's coffers. They were receiving gold and silver from wealthy patrons, and luxurious gifts. The Trio began wearing expensive clothing and jewelry when they preached. They started using cosmetics and had their hair fashionably coiffed. They had collected so much money that they had begun giving out loans (Eus., *Eccl. Hist*. 5:18.4, 11) and appointed a financial officer, Theodotus – an ecstatic who claimed to have been taken up to heaven – to take care of it all (Eus., *Eccl. Hist*. 5.16.14).

While the regional leaders agreed that it was acceptable for resident prophets and teachers to be supported by the congregation through "first-fruit" gift-offerings of bread, wine, meat, oil, money, clothes, and other possessions (cf. *Did*. 13), the gifts going into the Trio's coffers seemed excessive to them. And of course, the Trio's tithing success could impact their own coffers in the not-so-distant future. If Christians went to their revivals and tithed excessively there, how would the regional leaders be able to fund their own churches?

Second, the regional leaders noticed the prominence of the prophetesses, who were treated as equals to Montanus. The women were justifying their prominence by referring to Paul's statement that "in Christ Jesus there is neither male nor female" (Gal. 3:28) (Epiph., *Pan*. 49.2), as if Paul was referring to social equality rather than spiritual equality. If this were not enough, now the regional leaders had heard that the Trio was organizing a whole crew of lay presbyters to assist them, women among them. And all the while, the enthusiasm spread, leading the Trio to appoint more and more women to assist in the camp meetings, giving them more opportunities to prophesy and preach.

Wasn't this overstepping things, the regional leaders asked? To allow them to speak so publicly? What about the fact that Paul had forbidden women to teach (1 Tim. 2:12)? Or the fact that he told women to be silent and to defer to their husbands (1 Cor. 14:33–36). Everyone knew that Eve had been the one to deceive Adam and therefore was subordinated by God to her husband (1 Tim. 2:14) (Did. Alex., *Trin*. 3.41). This reminded them of the fact that the prophetesses had divorced their husbands in order to serve the Lord. They wondered about the women in their own congregations. What if they started going to the revival meetings only to return home and make similar demands?

And then there was the *way* the Trio prophesied and the kind of religious enthusiasm that spread among the congregants during the revival meetings. They were acting like Bacchants possessed by Dionysus and celebrants enthused by Cybele, not Christians gifted with the Spirit. Christian prophets didn't jump and flit around; they didn't fall down and thrash around for hours. They didn't lose consciousness. They didn't act like crazed people (Epiph., *Ref*. 48. 3–8).

The more the regional leaders talked about the Trio and their revival meetings, the more they speculated that they were facing demonic possession and false prophets. Finally, when Apollonarius became bishop of Hierapolis in 171 CE, he took charge of the situation. He convened a meeting of twenty-six sympathetic local church leaders to make a judgment about the whole affair (*Syn. Vet*. 5). The regional leaders determined that the Trio was demon-possessed and that anyone who attended their revivals was no longer welcome in their churches (Eus., *Eccl. Hist*. 5.16). The judgment was written up, signed by everyone present, and sent around to all the regional churches (*Syn. Vet*. 5). Then Apollonarius went to work composing the first of many books that would be written against the Church of New Prophecy (Eus., *Eccl. Hist.*. 4.27).

The response of the Trio is not surprising, especially given the fact that they had access to significant financial resources. They established the Church of New Prophecy as a separate Christian institution. They opened up regional house churches and put in place a hierarchy of officers to manage them. They appointed bishops, bodies of presbyters, and financial officers. They honored prophets and virgins in their assemblies. They held in high regard confessors and martyrs. The confessors were known as Companions (from Greek: *koinonos*) to the martyrs, who were Pillars (from Greek: *stylos*) – those who were so filled with the Spirit that they endured torture and death, their example providing support for others. All of these offices were open to women, and the liturgical duties of the offices (baptism, eucharist, preaching, prophecy) were discharged by women because of the Trio's belief in the Spirit's capacity to empower women and men equally. This point they took from their reading of Galatians 3:28.

Over time, the Church of New Prophecy developed a rich biblical platform that supported women clergy and women authors of new scriptures (Orig., *Comm. Matt.* 28; Eus., *Eccl. Hist.* 3.21.2–4; 27.1; Epiph., *Pan.* 49.2–3; Did., *Trin.* 3.41). As precedents, the New Prophets referenced Deborah (Judg. 4–5), Huldah (2 Kg. 22:14–20; 2 Chron. 34:22–28), Miriam (Exod. 15:20–21), Philip's daughters (Acts 21:9), Mary the mother of Jesus (Luke 1:48), and Anna (Luke 2:36–38). Women prophesied in Paul's churches, they pointed out (1 Cor. 11:5). Because Eve was the first to eat from the tree of knowledge, they regarded her highly (cf. Gen. 3:6). They granted her grace, considering her the foremother of the knowledge-filled and prophetic women in their churches. Despite the criticism heaped upon them by their Apostolic Catholic opponents, the Church of New Prophecy continued until its destruction by the Catholics to be a church devoted to women leaders with no distinctions between what they could or could not do within the churches because of their gender (Tert., *Soul* 9.4; Orig., *Cat. Cor.* 14.36; Pass. Perp.; Cyprian, *Ep.* 75.7–10; Epiph., *Pan.* 49.1; Amb., *Comm. Tim.* 3.8–11; Aug., *Haer.* 27; 86; John Dam., *Haer.* 87).

They continued with their message that the Spirit had been poured out onto the Church and that Christians had to receive the gifts of the Spirit in order to live consecrated lives. They continued to honor new prophecies, recognize new visions, value the many ways that the Holy Spirit assisted the Church, and, most of all, honor the Spirit whom Jesus sent to administer its gifts to the baptized (*Pass. Perp.* 35.4).

⌗7.7⌗ Holiness in Syria

COMPANION READINGS
Thomas the Contender
Acts of Thomas 1–16

The Church of New Prophecy was not alone in its concentration on sanctity and the promotion of a holiness lifestyle among believers. In eastern Syria, sanctity was front and center in the Christian churches at large. We saw in Chapter 6, Tatian the Syrian insisted on sexual continence, even when it came to marriage. In fact at this time in eastern Syria, the churches-at-large demanded celibacy and asceticism before converts could be baptized. The literary evidence from Syrian sources (i.e. *Gospel of Thomas, Acts of Thomas, Book of Thomas the Contender, Odes of Solomon*) all point to an indigenous form of Christianity in Syria which was encratic, a lifestyle that celebrated the solitary life over the marital. Celibacy was the benchmark of sanctity and the precondition of God's gift of ecstatic visions.

This position on the solitary life shifted with the monastic Aphraates, who is the earliest known author of the Syriac Orthodox Church in Persia (ca. 350). His writings show us that these demands of celibacy were eventually relaxed, perhaps under the pressure of western Catholic bishops who taught the sanctity of the marriage bed. By the time that Aphraates was writing in Persia, the average Syrian Christian could marry. The celibacy requirements now were reserved for a privileged class of the Syrian Church, a community of monastics that Aphraates calls the Sons and Daughters of the Covenant.

Yet for centuries prior to Aphraates, the encratic form of Christianity was the norm. For these Christians, baptism, followed by daily washings and renunciatory sexual practices that extinguished desire, sanctified their bodies as non-binary or androgynous beings. They believed that remaking the body a non-binary or androgynous body made it possible for them to restore their souls to the glorious Image of God that they read about in Genesis 1. They would live as Adam before sin even existed, when God made the original human being as male–female.

Their belief that the human being was not sexually differentiated before Adam sinned – an idyllic state of human purity before the Fall – was shaped by the features of the creation of the first human narrated in the opening chapters of Genesis. The narrative is fractured at Gen. 2:4 where the author of the book of Genesis stitched together two separate accounts of creation (Gen. 1–2:4a and Gen. 2:4b-3) to appear as a sequence of events rather than two different accounts. This made it possible for readers to understand the creation of the human being in Genesis 1 as referring to the creation of an ideal human prototype, a glorious being who was God's Image. The second account was read as the creation of the human Adam, who became the locus of sin once Eve was taken out of him and they became sexual. In this reading of the narrative, the forbidden fruit was the sexual awakening of the first couple, when they experienced shame and covered their bodies (Gen. 2:25; 3:7).

> "These are the generations of the heavens and the earth when they were created **[[the end of a creation story]]**
>
> **[[The beginning of a second creation story]]** In the day that the Lord God made the earth and the heavens,..."
>
> *Genesis 2:4*

The second odd feature of the narrative is Genesis 1:27 which reads literally, "So God created **man** in his image, in the image of God he created **him**; male and female he created **them**." Readers noticed that God produced the singular human being **man** and **him** as the plural **them**, which was both male and female (and thus neither male nor female). They also noticed that God, as the creator, spoke in verse 26 as a plural: "Let **us** make man in **our** image, according to **our** likeness." This led to the belief that the ideal human being was male–female (i.e. androgynous, hermaphrodite, non-binary, asexual; these were equivalents in the ancient mind) and so was God, in whose image the ideal human was created. In addition, the ideal hermaphrodite human being was a male androgyne: a male externally but female internally, a "man" from whom God extracted the female Eve.

This reading of the creation story in Genesis led some early Christians to believe that it was possible to regain Paradise lost by living as sanctified non-binary or androgynous creatures. They mimicked the ideal human – male–female – by curbing the sexual body and refusing to wed. In renunciation, they believed that they eliminated the gender binary, that "in Christ" they experienced "neither male nor female" as Paul taught (Gal. 3:28). They were glorious hermaphrodites recreated in God's Image. Their true spouse was no human, but their divine double, Jesus, as the story of the ideal bride underscores in the popular *Acts of Thomas*. In this narrative, the apostle Judas Thomas has a spiritual or angelic twin who looks just like him – Jesus.

This idea ultimately was derived from the fact that the name Thomas is not so much a name in Aramaic as it is a title, the Twin. Among the Christians, the apostle Judas (not Iscariot) was known as Judas the Twin, just as Peter was known as the Rock and James and John, the Sons of Thunder. Scholars have speculated that Judas may have been Jesus' look-alike little brother. Jesus did have a brother named Judas, as well as James, Joseph, and Simon (Matt. 13:55; he has sisters too, but their names are not remembered: Matt. 13:56). So this is possible.

Whatever the historical derivation, the Syrian stories have the heroic apostle Judas Thomas as the spitting image of Jesus, so much so that, when Jesus appears in the stories, he is mistaken for Judas. Judas Thomas – Judas the Twin – becomes the metaphor in Syrian literature for all believers whose divine double is Jesus. Judas' hallmarks are chastity and celibacy, which the believers are called to imitate (*Thom. Cont.* 139.31–141.2).

This reading of the Genesis story by many Syrian Christians is not confined to antiquity. Christians even in modernity have read these verses and found in their interpretations support for a male–female God and a celibate lifestyle. Consider the eighteenth-century Shakers, so-called because of their ecstatic behavior during worship services when they sang, danced, twitched, shouted, and jerked in the Spirit. They followed the lead of Mother Ann Lee, a charismatic preacher who had visions about Adam and Eve and their sex life. Basing herself on Genesis 1:27, she preached that God had no gender but was both "male and female." Jesus represented the first coming of Christ to earth as the "male" aspect of God, while Mother Ann was the second coming of Christ to earth as the "female" aspect of God. Adam's sin was interpreted to be "sex" with Eve.

Mother Ann constructed a celibate egalitarian community that valued the contributions and leadership of women and men equally since, she said, both men and women are equal in the eyes of God. Because the community outlawed sex and procreation, the men and women were segregated in their housing and work areas. She considered the Shaker community to be God's utopia, Paradise realized on earth. The Shakers ran successful farms and became known for their exquisite yet simple craftsmanship of furniture, like Shaker chairs. They composed thousands of songs, many of which have become part of standard Christian hymnals (i.e. "Simple Gifts"), American folk music, and other popular compositions. The last active Shaker community was the Sabbathday Lake Shaker Village in Maine.

7.8 The *Gospel of Thomas*

COMPANION READINGS
Gospel of Thomas

The asceticism of Judas Thomas, valorized in the *Acts of Thomas* and the *Book of Thomas the Contender*, has a long history within Syrian Christianity. The *Gospel of Thomas* – a gospel of Jesus' sayings finalized in the mid-second century but based on earlier sources – is presented as the secret sayings that the living Jesus told Judas Thomas. As we will see, many of the sayings in this gospel idealize celibacy.

The *Gospel of Thomas* was found in 1945 in Nag Hammadi, Egypt. Early scholarship on this gospel revealed that it was related to another find from Oxyrhynchus, Egypt. In the late 1800s, Bernard Grenfell and Arthur Hunt from Oxford University had excavated one of the chief centers of early Christianity in Egypt, the city of Oxyrhynchus. It is located about 120 miles south of Cairo, on the edge of the desert. Professors Grenfell and Hunt unearthed the old town dump, where they found scores of papyri (ancient paper made from reeds), mainly in Greek, which had been discarded with the rubbish.

There was quite an enthusiastic reaction to the original publication by Grenfell and Hunt of the "lost sayings" of Jesus (cataloged today as P. Oxy. 1, 654, and 655). It was not until 1952, however, that the French scholar Henri-Charles Puech made the connection between these fragments and the Coptic *Gospel of Thomas* found at Nag Hammadi. While in the Coptic Museum in Cairo examining the *Gospel of Thomas* with the Dutch scholar Gilles Quispel, Puech realized that the Oxyrhnychus fragments were pieces of the *Gospel of Thomas*. This is quite significant because it meant that the Coptic was a translation from an earlier Greek version of the Gospel. Since one of the Greek papyri from Oxyrhynchus has been dated to 200 CE, this means that there is manuscript evidence for the *Gospel of Thomas* that is 150 years older than the fourth-century Coptic version from Nag Hammadi. Since Grenfell and Hunt had argued from internal evidence that the original composition of this Greek fragment could be dated to the late first or early second century – no later than 140 CE – suddenly the *Gospel of Thomas* became very interesting to scholars of early Christianity.

Professors Quispel and Puech published some of the earliest opinions on the *Gospel of Thomas*. Quispel was convinced that the *Gospel of Thomas* was based on an old, lost gospel, either the *Gospel of the Hebrews* or the *Gospel of the Nazoreans* (which we learned about in Chapter 6). He argued that the sayings in the *Gospel of Thomas* have no literary connection with our Greek New Testament Gospels, but represent an independent early tradition of sayings associated with James the leader of the

Jerusalem Church and probably known in Aramaic. He and Puech wrote extensively about the encratic flavor of the sayings of Jesus in this gospel, and Quispel argued that Tatian may have used this gospel when he created the *Diatessaron*.

By the early 1960s, however, scholars were not convinced by Quispel's theory, mainly because his arguments relied on fragmentary evidence of the *Gospel of the Hebrews* (which was composed in Greek, not Aramaic) and the *Gospel of the Nazoreans* (which was an Aramaic translation of a Greek original). The versions of the sayings and the thematic parallels, he identified in these sources, varied enough from their parallels in the *Gospel of Thomas* to raise doubts. This led scholars to turn to a more colorful, even exotic explanation, developing the opinion that the *Gospel of Thomas* was a Gnostic Gospel that drew its sayings from the New Testament Gospels.

Scholars who first thought that the *Gospel of Thomas* was a Gnostic Gospel set out to prove that it belonged to a specific Gnostic group, like the Valentinians. But it was soon recognized that the concepts in the *Gospel of Thomas* do not cohere to the teachings of any known Gnostic group. This led scholars to try another angle. Could the *Gospel of Thomas* represent a generic form of Gnostic religion? If so, perhaps the Gospel was an exemplar of an ancient religion, which scholars coined "Gnosticism." In a circular fashion, some scholars went so far as to suggest that the very existence of Gnosticism was proven by the existence of the *Gospel of Thomas*. This interpretation of the *Gospel of Thomas* became standard even though no scholar could account for the fact that the text does not have terminology characteristic of Gnostic mythology.

To account for this terminological silence, some scholars started to think of the *Gospel of Thomas* as a precursor to what they began to call "full-blown" Gnosticism. It was a text in transition, on its way to becoming a Gnostic gospel, but not-quite-there-yet. According to this hypothesis, the *Gospel of Thomas* was a Gnostic gospel, not in the sense of a fully mature Gnostic system, but in a proto-Gnostic sense. Helmut Koester championed this position. He argued that in this gospel Jesus is not portrayed as a prophet, but as a sage who speaks with the authority of heavenly Sophia (or Wisdom). Through his words, Jesus grants salvation to those who hear his words and understand them. He admonishes people to recognize themselves, particularly their inner divinity and destiny, in order to overcome death. The Kingdom, far from being a future end-of-the-world or eschatological experience, is present in the person of Jesus and the believer. Renunciation of the world is preached, along with liberation of the soul from the body.

In Koester's opinion, Jesus does not simply teach everyday wisdom to the common folk. He is characterized as a "living" mystagogue, a hierophant, teaching "hidden sayings" and "mysteries" to a chosen few. Koester considered this a "spiritualization" of proverbial wisdom. In other words, the author of this gospel turns everyday proverbs into Gnostic-like koans. Koester characterized this spiritualization as a "natural progression" of sapiential or wisdom teachings into Gnostic instructions.

Yet, Koester also noticed that when he compared the versions of *Thomas*' sayings with their New Testament parallels, the sayings in *Thomas* often lacked secondary interpretations and developments. This led him to conclude that the author of the *Gospel of Thomas* probably had access to a very old collection of Jesus' sayings that predated the New Testament gospels. It is this unresolved tension between a very old collection of sayings and Gnosticism that complicates Koester's hypothesis. He seems to be aware of this, admitting that the "natural" progression makes it difficult to sort out which sayings belong to the original composition and which are later proto-Gnostic expansions.

As scholars continued to study the *Gospel of Thomas*, it became increasingly clear that there was nothing "natural" about Koester's progression from proverbial wisdom to Gnosticism. This was his own construction of ideas placed into a linear trajectory in order to explain the origins of a generic form of Gnosticism that earlier scholars had constructed. Although it is certainly possible that Jesus' proverbial sayings were reused by specific Gnostic authors, like we find in the Valentinian *Gospel of Philip*, they can also be reused by authors who have other goals. For instance, in the case of the *Book of Thomas the Contender* (another Nag Hammadi book), Jesus' proverbs are reused in an encratic context to promote the celibate lifestyle at the expense of the married. The *Teachings of Silvanus* (another Nag Hammadi book) shows a continued interest in the proverbial sayings of Jesus among the Catholic Christians in Alexandria, who recycle the sayings for their own theological purposes.

This led scholars to begin to analyze and describe the contents of the *Gospel of Thomas* as an oracular text with its own agenda. What does the gospel have to say for itself? The most obvious fact is that many of the sayings in the *Gospel of Thomas* honor the life of solitary or single people above marriage. In fact, the noun *monachos* (unmarried celibate person) is used for the first time in Christian literature in the *Gospel of Thomas*. It is a word that, in the fourth century, will come to identify the monk. In the *Gospel of Thomas*, the *monachos* is blessed with finding the Kingdom, the place from where the *monachos* originated (*Gos. Thom.* 49). Similarly, the *monachos* will be admitted to the bridal chamber, a metaphor identifying the anticipated Kingdom of Heaven (*Gos. Thom.* 75; see Matt. 15:1–13).

The Christians who authored this gospel took seriously the call to celibacy, believing that sexual renunciation aided them in the recreation of their bodies in God's Image. This state is described as androgynous (*Gos. Thom.* 22, 114), infantile or youthful (Adam was believed by some Christians to have been a child before his sexual awakening and sin; *Gos. Thom.* 4, 21, 22, 37), non-binary (*Gos. Thom.* 11, 22, 106), non-familial (*Gos. Thom.* 16, 101, 105), shameless (cf. Gen. 2:25; *Gos. Thom.* 37), and better-than-the-sinful-Adam (*Gos. Thom.* 85). These Christians advocated a holy life as God's Elect (*Gos. Thom.* 23, 49). They encouraged each other to imitate Jesus whom they believed had conquered his passions at his crucifixion (*Gos. Thom.* 55, 56, 58, 80, 87, 112). They believed that it was necessary to renounce the world, to fast from the world, and to guard against temptations and worldliness (*Gos. Thom.* 21, 27, 110). They taught that the eucharist helped make the holy life possible since they were convinced that the power of the divine food and drink rendered the person "equal" to Jesus (*Gos. Thom.* 13, 61, 108).

As they transformed their sexual bodies into celibate non-binary or androgynous bodies, the believers were encouraged to study the words of Jesus contemplatively (*Gos. Thom.* 1). Through this lifestyle of extreme body renunciation and contemplation, they sought revelation and mystical vision, including ecstatic journeys into heaven to see Jesus and the Father (*Gos. Thom.* 15, 27, 37, 59). Renunciates memorized the information that they would need to know in order to make safe passage through the divine realms (*Gos. Thom.* 50). They hoped to be able to enter heaven safely and gaze upon God before death in order not to die (*Gos. Thom.* 59).

The collection of sayings in the *Gospel of Thomas* tells the story of Christians in Syria whose members were not waiting for death or the end of the world in order to enter the Kingdom or achieve immortality. Instead of waiting for heaven to come to them, they were invading Eden as consecrated bodies, as holy hermaphrodites, hoping to gaze upon God as the first human had in Paradise before everything went awry. They were living what came to be known in Christian literature as the "angelic life."

While many scholars have classified the *Gospel of Thomas* as a Gnostic or proto-Gnostic gospel, this is incorrect. The *Gospel of Thomas* is theologically the predecessor of eastern Syrian Christianity. It is one of our earliest, if not our earliest ancestor to Orthodox thought. The Orthodox Church emerged out of the Great Schism of 1054 CE, when the Catholic Church split into Roman Catholicism and Eastern Orthodoxy. The Orthodox Church teaches about a mysticism of the heart and the progressive transformation of the soul into the glorious Image of God. In the West, the Augustinian position on original sin reigns. Original sin severed humans from the Image of God, leaving them lost, helpless, and damned. The lost are saved through grace and atonement, which is completed in the eucharist, a sacrificial meal. In Eastern Orthodoxy, however, the glorious Image is not lost, but only diminished or stunted by Adam's decision. The Image can be recovered in part through human actions by living virtuously and ingesting the divine body of Christ during the Eucharist. This works like divine medicine, helping transform the soul into the Image of God. The believer is called to self-knowledge, renunciation of the body through temperance in marriage or the eremitic (hermit) life, purification of the passions, the path of virtue, imitation of Jesus, and contemplation. This leads to a gradual glorification of the believer, and ultimately to Gnosis and *theoria*, the vision of God as uncreated light. The *Gospel of Thomas* is consistent with early Syrian Christianity as described in the oldest literature from the area.

The mystical tradition in the *Gospel of Thomas* is very old, and emerges out of Christian apocalypticism. Once the end of the world did not manifest as most of the first Christians expected, the Syrian Christians remodeled the familiar sayings of Jesus by shifting their focus from eschatology to the mystical or ecstatic dimension of apocalypticism, fostering visions and revelations of divine secrets. Central to the *Gospel of Thomas* is the cultivation of a holy life in imitation of what Adam was imagined to have been like before he was split into two genders and experienced sexual awakening with Eve. Living as the non-binary celibate, Adam had its perks. Not only would they be gifted with visions of God in this life, but they were also guaranteed entry into the Kingdom where they would live with God in the afterlife. It also meant that women could choose not to wed, avoiding the likelihood of serial pregnancies, the traumatic loss of their babies to disease, and their own deaths in childbirth.

Timeline

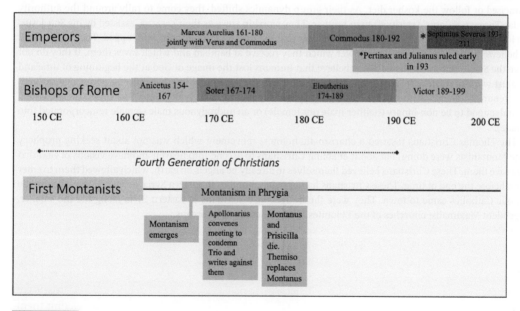

FIGURE 7.5   Timeline for the first Montanists.

Pattern Summary

While the Montanists eventually are forced to establish their own Church of New Prophecy, they begin their holiness charismatic revivalist movement within the Apostolic Catholic network and ecclesiology. Even after they secede, they pronounce the Apostolic Catholic Rule of Truth in their church and consider the (other) Apostolic Catholics lazy and lax. All the sources agree that, dogmatically, they were identical to the Apostolic Catholics (see Figure 7.6). They worship YHWH as their CREATOR, PATRON, and JUDGE. They believe that humans are responsible for the evil and suffering in our world, and that to be saved, humans have to follow God's commandments. They are DUALISTS who hope for the RESURRECTION OF THEIR BODIES in the afterlife at the end of time. Given their belief that the Holy Spirit possessed their prophets, it is likely that they promoted the ADULT POSSESSION PATTERN when it came to trying to sort out the Binitarian Problem. They reference the Jewish scriptures, at least the ten letters of Paul, Acts, the Gospel of John, and the book of Revelation.

Eventually they develop their own egalitarian ecclesiology, camp meetings, and charismatic churches which compete with the Apostolic Catholic network. They promote the idea that, once baptized, there can be no lapsing. Holiness must be lived everyday, guided by the Holy Spirit. The Montanus leaders refused to give absolution after baptism for fear that their congregations would become lax in the knowledge that they could receive a second baptism or make confession and receive forgiveness. They upped the commitment of their congregants by extending fasts beyond the regular hours observed by the Apostolic Catholics and adding a two-week dry fast to their liturgical calendar. Because they believed that they were living in the end times, they lived urgently as Paul recommended, unmarried and celibate. On occasion, women divorced their husbands and became Virgins in the church. Their church was the first known Christian group to salary its leaders. It was able to do so because the Trio drew in substantial donations and surplus money.

The *Gospel of Thomas* represents the views of Christians in eastern Syria who were originally Maximalist and followers of James, Jesus' brother. By the third generation, however, when this gospel took its final form, these Christians had moderated their position on the Law due to an influx of Gentile converts who did not want to be circumcised or follow the kosher diet. As their group dynamics shifted, they come to rally around the authority of Judas Thomas as Jesus' (spiritual) twin brother. They worship YHWH as their CREATOR, assisted by his Son Jesus. YHWH is the "living God" in contrast to the dead idols that the pagans around them worshipped. They are DUALISTS who believe that the Spirit is an extra power which they receive at baptism and which saves them. If they do not receive the Spirit, they are doomed. They believe that humans lost the image of God at the beginning of time and now must work to retrieve it. This is not just an idea for them, but something that must be performed through bodily renunciation, singlehood, and celibacy. They were remaking their bodies into God's holy Image, which they understood to be non-binary (neither male nor female) or an androgynous male (female reincorporated into the male).

The Thomas Christians fostered a charismatic holiness movement which was not about seeking prophecy (as the Montanists were doing) but about enabling Christians to ascend into heaven and have visions of God that would save them. These Christians believed themselves to already be angels on earth, which allowed them to enter heaven before the end of time. These Christians had popular churches in eastern Syria, around Edessa, before the Apostolic Catholics came to town. They were the indigenous Christians of eastern Syria alongside the smaller, independent Maximalist churches of the Ebionites, Elchasaites, and Nazoreans.

Family Pattern Chart
Montanist Trio

X=Definitely > L=Likely

THEODICY

	Faulty-God	Faulty-Human	Other
Montanists		L	

SOTERIOLOGY

	Gift from God	Human achievement	Minimalist	Moderate	Maximalist
Montanists		X		X	

CHRISTOLOGY

	Adult possession	Fetal possession	Hybrid	Ensoulment	Visitation	Human who received revelation
Montanists	L					

ANTHROPOLOGY

	Mono	Dual	Triad	Quad
Montanists		X		

COSMIC DEMIURGY

	Autocrat	Administrator	Caretaker	Patron	Justice	Villain	Rebel	Ignorant	Impaired
Montanists	L	L	L	L	L				

RESURRECTION

	Body reunites with soul	Body discarded and soul immortalized	Body and soul discarded and spirit rises	God-element separates from body soul, and spirit and rises
Montanists	X			

SCRIPTURES

	Jewish	Gospel	Pauline letters (10)	Pauline letters (13)	Hebrews	Acts	Catholic letters	Revelation	Other
Montanists	X	John	X			X		X	

ECCLESIOLOGY

	Consolidation movement	Reform movement	Secessionist movement	Counter movement	Innovative movement	Trans-regional	Regional
Montanists		X	X			X	

FIGURE 7.6 Summary of the Trio's patterns.

Takeaways

1. Across Asia Minor and Syria, Christian churches emerged that were devoted to fostering charismatic gifts and promoting the lifestyle of holiness as the antidote for sin.

2. The Church of New Prophecy did not begin as a church separate from the regional Apostolic Catholic church congregations in Phrygia, a province in Asia Minor.

3. The Church of New Prophecy traced its prophetic activities through a line of ancestors that started with Adam and included a number of women.

4. The Montanists understood themselves to be pneumatic Christians, while other Christians were psychics.

5. Religious enthusiasm, trance states, and glossolalia are cross-cultural and transhistorical phenomena which can be explained as altered states of consciousness involving derealization and dissociation.

6. The Trio claimed to be vessels or instruments through which God, Christ, and the Paraclete spoke to the community.

7. The Trio demanded that Christians take up the holiness lifestyle which they said included regular dry fasts (xerophagy), celibacy, and no remarriage (digamy). The Trio refused to bind and loose absolution after baptism, so the only remedy for post-baptismal sin was the adoption of the holiness lifestyle.

8. The regional Apostolic Catholic churches determined that the Trio was demon-possessed, which resulted in the Trio establishing their own independent church. This determination was not influenced by the Trio's beliefs (which the bishops admitted were in line with their own). What influenced this decision was the equal status of women leaders in the Church of New Prophecy and the immense popularity of the holiness camps, which drew financial resources away from neighboring churches.

9. Until the fourth century, the Syrian churches valued the holy lifestyle, demanding celibacy of its converts before and after baptism.

10. The apostle Thomas served as the hero of the holiness lifestyle in Syria, especially around Edessa.

11. The holiness lifestyle was largely based on reading Genesis 1:26–27 and 2:4 in ways that imagined God and the primal human (Adam with Eve inside of him) as non-binary (what ancients called male–female, androgynous, hermaphrodite, or asexual). This imaginary provided Syrian Christians with an ideal to imitate.

12. The *Gospel of Thomas* is not a Gnostic text, but a holiness text promoting a renunciatory and contemplative lifestyle for the purposes of attaining visions and revelations. It represents an early form of Syrian Orthodoxy.

13. Living as the non-binary celibate Adam had its perks, especially for women who could choose not to wed, avoiding the likelihood of serial pregnancies, the traumatic loss of their babies to disease, and their own deaths in childbirth. It also put them on the same hierarchal level as men, providing them opportunities to be leaders in their churches.

Questions

1. How did the Montanists argue for the value of prophetic leaders and authorize them as holy men and women?

2. What was the position of women within the Church of New Prophecy? How did the Church of New Prophecy argue for the legitimacy of women leaders?

3. Why did the other Apostolic Christians decide that the Montanist prophets were demon-possessed? How did they go about making this decision and applying social pressure?

4. How does the holiness lifestyle of the Asian Montanists compare to the Syrian Christians? What reasons did these two groups give for demanding this lifestyle?

5. How might we explain the strong similarities between the holiness camps of the Montanists and the Methodists? How might we explain the strong similarities between the "spiritual" activities of the Montanists and the Pentecostals?

6. Do you think the *Gospel of Thomas* is Gnostic? Why or why not? Why does it matter that the *Gospel of Thomas* is Gnostic or not?

7. What kind of social movement was the Church of New Prophecy? How was it the same and how was it different from other Apostolic Catholic churches in Asia?

8. What kind of social movement might be reflected in the Thomas literature? How do you think Syrian Christians actually lived the "angelic life" in the everyday?

Resources

Sebastian P. Brock. 1973. "Early Syrian Asceticism." *Numen* 20: 1–19.

April D. DeConick. 2005. *Recovering the Original Gospel of Thomas: A History of the Gospel and Its Growth.* LNTS 286. London: T & T Clark.

April D. DeConick. 2008. "The Gospel of Thomas." Pages 13–29 in *The Non-Canonical Gospels.* Edited by P. Foster. London: T&T Clark. Reprint from *Expository Times* 2007.

April D. DeConick. 2018. "Naturally Supernatural." *Religion, Brain and Behavior* 8: 1–36.

Dell'Isola, Maria. 2020. "'*They are not the words of a rational man': Ecstatic Prophecy in Montanism." Pages 71-86 in Lived Religion in the Ancient Mediterranean World: Approaching Religious Transformations from Archaeology, History and Classics.* Edited by Valentino Gasparini et.al. Berlin: De Gruyter.

Jonathan A. Draper. 2007. "The Didache." Pages 12–20 in *The Writings of the Apostolic Fathers.* Edited by Paul Foster. London: T&T Clark.

B.P. Grenfell and A.S. Hunt. 1897. *Sayings of Our Lord from an Early Greek Papyrus.* London: The Egypt Exploration Fund.

B.P. Grenfell and A.S. Hunt. 1904. *New Sayings of Jesus and Fragment of a Lost Gospel from Oxyrhynchus.* London: The Egypt Exploration Fund.

Ronald E. Heine. 1989. *The Montanist Oracles and Testimonia.* North American Patristic Society Patristic Monograph Series 14. Macon: Mercer University Press.

Antti Marjanen. 2008. "Montanism: Egalitarian Ecstatic 'New Prophecy." Pages 185–212 in *A Companion to Second-Century Christian 'Heretics'.* Edited by Antti Marjanen and Petri Luomanen. Leiden: Brill.

Claudio Moreschini and Enrico Norelli. 2005. "Chapter 9.7." in *Early Christian Greek and Latin Literature: A Literary History.* Volume 1. *From Paul to the Age of Constantine.* Translated by Matthew J. O'Connell. Peabody: Hendrickson Publishers.

Robert Murray. 1975. *Symbols of Church and Kingdom: A Study in Early Syriac Tradition.* Cambridge: Cambridge University Press.

Andrew Newberg and Mark Robert Waldman. 2007. *Born to Believe: God, Science, and the Origin of Ordinary and Extraordinary Beliefs.* New York: Free Press.

McNamara Patrick. 2009. *The Neuroscience of Religious Experience.* Cambridge: Cambridge University Press.

JamesRobinson and Helmut Koester (eds.). 1971. *Trajectories through Early Christianity.* Philadelphia: Fortress Press.

W. Stewart Mccullough. 1982. *A Short History of Syriac Christianity to the Rise of Islam.* Chico: Scholars Press.

William Tabbernee. 2007. *Fake Prophecy and Polluted Sacraments: Ecclesiastical and Imperial Reactions to Montanism.* Supplements to Vigiliae Christianae 84. Leiden: Brill.

J.T. Titon. 1978. "Some Recent Pentecostal Revivals: A Report in Words and Photographs." *Georgia Review* 32: 579–605.

Christine Trevett. 1996. *Montanism: Gender, Authority and the New Prophecy.* Cambridge: Cambridge University Press.

Michael Winkelman. 2016. "Shamanism and the Brain." Pages 355–372 in *Religion: Mental Religion. Macmillan Interdisciplinary Handbooks.* Edited by Niki Kasumi Clements. New York: Gale, Cengage Learning.

CHAPTER 8

The Expansion of Gnostic Churches

The Samaritan woman at the well, detail from the Stories of the New Testament, 1072–1078, Byzantine-Campanian school frescoes, right side of the nave of Basilica of Sant'Angelo in Formis, Sant'Angelo in Formis, Campania. Italy, 11th century. **Source:** DEA / A. DAGLI ORTI / Getty Images.

"That the Law was ordained through Moses, my dear sister Flora, has not been understood by many people. They do not have accurate knowledge of the one who ordained it nor of its commandments...If the Perfect God is good by nature (in fact he is, since our Savior declared that there is only a single good God, his Father whom he manifested) and if the (Devil) with the opposite nature is evil, wicked, and unjust, then the (Creator and Lawgiver) who is situated between these two is neither good nor evil nor unjust, it is proper to call him Just, since he is the arbitrator of his justice...In making these brief statements to you, my sister Flora, I have not grown weary...These points will be of great benefit to you in the future, if like fair and good soil you have received fertile seeds and go on to show forth their fruit."

Ptolemy wrote this in a letter composed to Flora who was being instructed before her initiation into the Valentinian mysteries.
Selections from Epiphanius, Pan. 33.3–7 (trans. DeConick)

Comparing Christianities: An Introduction to Early Christianity, First Edition. April D. DeConick.
© 2024 John Wiley & Sons Ltd. Published 2024 by John Wiley & Sons Ltd.

In Chapter 3, we were introduced to Valentinus and other third-generation (110–150 CE) Ophian and Sethian Christians who worshipped a transcendent God separate from the Biblical Creator God and who favored the flipped reading of the Genesis story. In Chapter 5, we met Basilides and Carpocrates, Christians who also started movements that targeted the worship of the transcendent Source of Life. Their Transtheistic mythologies were not dependent on the Barbeloite, Ophian, or Sethian Combo Myth, but instead reflected their cultural embeddedness in Egyptian lore, Stoicism, Cynicism, and Platonic thought.

During the watch of the fourth-generation of Christians (150–190 CE), these movements did not die out. They attracted new members by expanding their geographical reach and developing their religious thought in ways that reflected the genius of their founders' students. The Christian Sethian assemblies flourished, migrating from Alexandria to Rome, and into Syria and Mesopotamia too. At the same time, new innovative Gnostic teachers emerged in a variety of urban areas and launched their own distinctive Christian Gnostic movements. To say the least, the desire for esoteric knowledge was attractive for many Christians. Especially appealing was the promise to be initiated into advanced Christian mysteries, which peaked in a Gnostic experience of the True God.

Initiatory religions were popular in the Roman world, so it is not surprising that the Gnostic Christian groups modeled their assemblies along these lines. In antiquity, initiatory religions were called mystery religions, which advertised the revelation of secret knowledge during a protracted course of induction. Demeter's mysteries were known for their spectacles when the initiates carried torches and wandered around in the dark, crying like Demeter as they sought her kidnapped daughter Persephone in Hades. The Roman Plutarch says that the initiates were dragged around in the dark and deep mud, hiking in circles along frightening paths, shivering, trembling, sweating, and terrified, until they were shown a holy vision of light (Plut., *Frag.* 178). Each mystery religion included the initiates in dramatic performances of the particular mythology associated with the mystery God, whether Demeter and Persephone, Dionysus and Orpheus, Isis and Osiris, or Cybele and Attis. The closest example of this audience-involved religious theater today may be passion plays that not only include actors from the congregation, but also the congregation itself, which stands in for the crowds who wept and scoffed at Jesus' suffering.

By participating in this dramatic theater, the initiates put themselves under the authority of the God, whom they met face-to-face during the performances. Their theatrical participation was not nightly entertainment. The dramas were simulations, virtual realities that fully immersed the initiates bodily and emotionally. They were reenacting the God's mythology which counted the initiates among the original participants in the myth. They trusted that their submission to the God in this context would guarantee them a better fate in this life and the afterlife.

Gnostic Christian groups offered similar dramatic initiations to guide the human spirit back to its transcendent home. Their highly structured ceremonies took place within private meetings, not in spaces open to the public. Many of these events may have taken place in private homes like the Christian house unearthed in Dura-Europos (an excavated ancient city in Syria) with its specially built baptistery, or in villas like the one in Pompeii whose dining room sported life-size murals depicting the mysteries of Dionysus, or in theaters rented for the private event. There are references to some Gnostic Christian groups using special costumes and headgear in their mysteries, possibly even animal masks (lions, bulls, serpents, eagles, bears, and dogs), as well as torches to light their way. Some Valentinian Gnostics put on the helmet of Hades, which they believed made them invisible to the judges of the dead in the underworld. The Gnostic Christian texts are filled with examples of recitations, lyrics, dialogues, and visions, suggesting that these virtual dramas were regularly performed in their churches and involved ecstatic experiences.

Their virtual dramas psychologically reinforced what the initiates already had learned about reality from their catechism, which they studied before taking part in the ceremonies. Each Gnostic Christian group prided itself on owning the "real" map that would guide the spirit back to its transcendent home. Each group advertised its own variation on this mystery journey to a hidden place beyond the underworld purgatories and stars in the skies. The leaders of these churches staged otherworldly journeys along secret routes through the underworld, the skies, and the transcendent realms. During the ceremonies, the initiates confronted and overcame the Archons, while they embraced the transcendent beings. Their initiations were curated to be virtual realities created so that the initiates experienced complete transformation of their humanity into full-fledged divine beings.

Because of their focus on the myth of the fallen suffering soul, Gnostic initiations were innovative in antiquity, offering a form of psychological therapy that was unheard of in other mystery religions. Gnostic Christian initiations were meant to be therapeutic. They were meant to awaken, purge, mature, and integrate the alienated human spirit, the real self, with its transcendent Source. The goal was to heal the separation anxiety that had started it all when the spirit was severed from God, its primal root. These groups claimed that Jesus had been sent down from the transcendent world in order to teach them the necessary ceremonies to guide their spirits home.

Each Gnostic Christian group had its own specific rituals, including ceremonies performed as virtual underworld journeys that were effective to awaken or quicken the unconscious or sleeping spirit. Other ceremonies were cathartic, used to separate the soul from the body so that it could ascend through the celestial realms and gradually expel its demons. Once purified, the spirit could separate from the soul and enter the transcendent realms, where it had to mature into a full-fledged divinity. Rituals were also involved to separate and mature the spirit. Ultimately, the spirit had to be integrated into God, so additional rituals were curated for this purpose, offering the initiate direct contact with God, what they called Gnosis. All these rituals were performed to bring the initiates into ecstasy, to alter their normal state of consciousness, to bring them into feelings of disembodiment, the loss of their souls or egos, and (re-)unification with the transcendent God.

In this chapter, we follow Valentinus' students as they developed the Valentinian metaphysical system and practices. We also meet other Gnostic Christians including Justin the Gnostic, the Ophians, the Naassenes, and the Peratics, who established independent Christian movements with complex cosmologies, mythologies, and rituals to guide the spirit on an astrological journey into the transcendent realm.

8.1 My Dear Flora

COMPANION READINGS
John 1:1–18
Epiphanius, *Refutation of All Heresies* 33.3,1–7,10
Irenaeus, *Against Heresies* 1.8
Justin, *2 Apology* 2

Before his death, Valentinus trained several students who were Einsteins like himself. For a teacher to inspire so many prominent intellectual powerhouses is mostly unheard of. If a teacher promotes one such thinker, it is a feat. But to promote several (that we know of!) is beyond the pale. It says something about the charisma of Valentinus and just how much the system he developed made sense to Christian intellectuals in antiquity who were obviously attracted to it. Among Valentinus' students were Agathopous (an Alexandrian [likely]), Heracleon (a Sicilian who taught in Rome), Marcus (an Alexandrian who organized a church in Lyons), Ptolemy (a prominent Valentinian scholar in Rome), Secundus (a Latin name, a Roman [likely] scholar, whom Irenaeus mentions), and Theodotus (an early Valentinian teacher associated with Asia Minor and Alexandria).

We know by name several other Christians who joined the Valentinians during the fourth-generation, including Axionicus (an Antiochean who may have authored the *Gospel of Philip*), Flora (a Roman woman who was considering Valentinian initiation), Prodicus (an Alexandrian), Rheginus (an Alexandrian [likely]), Theotimus (a Roman [likely] who authored the lost *On the Images of the Law*), and Flavia Sophe (a Valentinian Roman woman whose tombstone survives).

Another name associated with Valentinianism pops up in the writings of Irenaeus: Florinus. Florinus was a Christian stationed within Polycarp's household in Smyrna (Asia Minor) when Irenaeus studied with Polycarp. Florinus immigrates to Rome, where he eventually becomes a presbyter in a Roman Apostolic Catholic congregation. During Bishop Victor's tenure (189–199 CE), Florinus authors a book on theology that unsettles Irenaeus. Irenaeus responds by writing a letter to Florinus and a book called *On the Ogdoad* (this is lost but likely is a refutation of Valentinus' Ogdoadic Godhead). Eusebius, preserves a fragment from Irenaeus' personal correspondence with Florinus about the sole sovereignty of God and why God did not author evil, in which Irenaeus chides Florinus for spouting unsound doctrine that is "inconsistent with the Church," and tells him that their teacher Polycarp would not have approved (Eus., *Eccl. Hist.* 5.20). There is a fragment of a second letter of Irenaeus about Florinus (*Frag.* L1). This letter is addressed to Bishop Victor of Rome informing him that Florinus is a retrobate presbyter, a closet-Valentinian, who is teaching "false doctrines about God." Irenaeus works to have Florinus removed from office.

All this is to say that Valentinianism was popular among esoterically-minded urban Christians. Many of these named individuals were teachers in their own right who used Valentinian doctrines to think about primal existence, creation, and the human condition. Tertullian claims that there were as many constructions of the Valentinian myth as there were Valentinian teachers, which amounted to a confusing array of materials and no one in charge of it all. Most of the Valentinian teachers were independent operators who ran churches that mirrored the Apostolic Catholic congregations in terms of their Sunday worship services. In addition to these worship services, they offered advanced training and initiations for more spiritually-minded Christians. With the exception of Marcus who pioneered a pneumatics-only church, most teachers governed split-level groups (the group included both pneumatics and psychics). On the one hand, this split-level organization allowed Valentinian teachers to organize and govern their own groups outside the emerging ecclesiology of the Apostolic Catholics while poaching them. On the other hand, it also allowed Christians like Florinus to maintain their Apostolic Catholic identity and affiliations, while considering their forays into Valentinianism as some kind of religious supplement or advanced esoteric endeavor which gave them access to God's full mysteries.

We gain more insight into this split-level organization in a letter that the popular Valentinian teacher in Rome, Ptolemy (ca. 160 CE) wrote to a woman named Flora. While we do not know much about Ptolemy as a person, we do know that he led a Valentinian Christian congregation that sought to initiate Apostolic Catholic Christians (psychics) into the spiritual or pneumatic mysteries of God. We know this because Epiphanius, the fourth-century bishop of Salamis, chronicles a letter that Ptolemy wrote to a wealthy Christian woman, Flora. In it, he addresses questions that she had asked him about God. In his response, he encourages her to be initiated into the pneumatic ranks, when, Ptolemy says, her spiritual seed will be planted in fertile soil (Epiph., *Pan.* 33.3,1–7,10).

From Ptolemy's remarks, we can tell that Flora was worried about what Ptolemy has already told her about God. Perhaps she was even having second thoughts about going through with the second baptism (chrism). She did not know what to think about the fact that Ptolemy had just explained to her that what she thought she knew about God was all wrong. Flora had been taught, like other Apostolic Catholics, that the supreme God of worship is the Biblical God YHWH, the Creator and Ruler of the universe. She believed like her Apostolic Catholic brothers and sisters that this supreme God had given certain commandments to humans for the purpose of ensuring righteousness, and he expected humans to observe them. These laws were written in the five books of Moses, the Torah. As we saw with Justin Martyr, this connection to the Jewish scriptures was fundamental to their faith. Not only had Christians been arguing for decades that the Jewish scriptures had prophesied Jesus' advent, but also the connection with Jewish scripture gave their religion at least the façade of a natural history and, with it, a tradition that could boast some authority.

But Valentinian Christians like Ptolemy found the issue much more complex than the Apostolic Catholics. As we saw in Chapter 3, Valentinus questioned whether the Father Jesus revealed in the Christian scriptures, the God of grace and goodness, could really be the cruel and arrogant God they saw when they read the Jewish scripture. Valentinus and his students came to distinguish the Creator God YHWH from Jesus' transcendent Father. They saw this as a spiritual truth that outplays all others.

Christians like Flora, who were trying to decide whether or not to be initiated into the spiritual mysteries and become pneumatic Christians, had to be told the truth, that the Supreme God of worship, the true Father, transcends the Creator God YHWH. Ptolemy tells her that this Supreme God is the one and only good God whom Jesus called his Father, and he is not the Biblical Creator God (Epiph., *Pan.* 33.7,5, quoting Matt. 19:17). Ptolemy likely told her that the Supreme God is the Unbegotten Father, whose existence and form are impossible to conceive. Speech cannot convey him, the eye cannot see him, and bodies cannot grasp him because of his inscrutable greatness, incomprehensible depth, immeasurable height, and illimitable will. He transcends all wisdom, intellect, glory, beauty, sweetness, and greatness. He is simply unknowable by anything except himself (cf. *Tri. Tract.* 54.13–26). While male pronouns are used to identify him, Ptolemy may have explained to Flora, that God transcends the gender binary. God is really a hermaphrodite He–She, a Father–Mother paired (a syzygy), and capable of conceiving and producing all the Aeons. The original Ogdoad of Aeons, as Ptolemy taught, is referred to in the Gospel of John as Father, Grace, Only-Begotten, Truth, Word, Life, Man, and Church (John 1:1–18; Iren., *Haer.* 1.8).

For Flora, the news that there was another God more transcendent than the Biblical Creator God came as a shock since it contradicted everything she had known to be true up to that point. Ptolemy's handling of Flora's questions reveals her conflict about this teaching. She is unsettled about this new view of reality that Ptolemy shares with her. If true, she wondered, what would it mean for the Bible and the commandments she had been taught to follow as a Christian? She feels that the Scripture has added value to her life, particularly the Ten Commandments, which Christians like herself thought were the moral core of the Torah. If Ptolemy were right, then where did the Torah really come from and what was its purpose?

Ptolemy is nuanced in his response to Flora's questions. He is careful. He does not want to frighten Flora away from initiation, so he does not want to make the Biblical Creator God out to be evil, as he knows other Gnostic teachers were doing. So rather than emphasizing YHWH's arrogance and cruelty, his irrationality and capriciousness, Ptolemy instead focuses on YHWH's justice. He softens YHWH's rough edges by telling Flora that the Biblical Creator is a God who operates by enforcing laws that he established to govern his creation. While he is a lesser God, he is fair, ruling by enforcing laws. He is the God of Justice, whose nature falls between the good nature of the transcendent Father and the evil nature of the Devil (Epiph., *Pan.* 33.7,2–5).

From this position, Ptolemy reasons through Flora's concerns about the Law, knowing that the Ten Commandments in the Jewish scriptures have been important to Flora's faith. He wants her to weigh the options for authorship of the scriptures given the fact that some laws have more moral value than others. While Ptolemy acknowledges that the Ten Commandments are good laws, he reminds Flora that other laws are not so good. How do we explain the tension between Exodus 20:15, which commands us not to kill, and Leviticus 24:17, which allows us to execute murderers, particularly when they require retribution that contradicts the Ten Commandments? This inconsistency in the Mosaic laws, Ptolemy says, is proof that all of the rules were not put on the books by the same lawmaker. Since YHWH is a just God, he is responsible for some of the better content of the Law. But everything else, which is most of the Law, was authored by men. Here he points his finger at Moses and the Jewish elders, whose legislation, in Ptolemy's eyes, often contradicted YHWH's better intentions. To make his point, he refers to the famous story about Jesus' discussion of divorce, that it was Moses who had made the law allowing for divorce, while YHWH had never intended this (Epiph., *Pan.* 33.4,1–10, quoting Matt. 19:6–8).

All of this Ptolemy knows is disturbing news for Flora, whose entire metaphysical orientation has just been flipped. It is not what Flora, the psychic Christian, expected when she decided to pursue God's spiritual mysteries with Ptolemy. Ptolemy asks Flora to stay calm and try to take it in. Once she can accept that YHWH is a lesser God than Jesus' Father, he promises to reveal the next teaching in the catechism: the unfolding of the Father into the spiritual, psychic, and material dimensions of existence. But Ptolemy reassures her that this revelation can wait until she is ready.

We do not know whether Flora went through with the initiation unless we take a curious story reported by Justin Martyr as a reference to Flora (Just., 2 *Apol*. 2). He speaks about a hedonistic woman who converted to Christianity and became a student of a teacher named Ptolemy. When she did so, she no longer wanted to engage in hedonistic parties with her husband and filed for a divorce. In retaliation, her husband denounced her as a Christian to the Roman authorities. She filed a petition asking the Emperor to allow her some time to sort through her affairs before her case went forward, a petition which the Emperor granted. What Justin refers to as her "affairs" likely included a sizable dowry that had to be returned to her once the divorce was final. When the Emperor grants her petition, her husband is forced to return her dowry. Unable to get his revenge on his wife, he decided to denounce Ptolemy instead. Ptolemy was arrested, brought before Quintus Lollius Urbicus, and sentenced to death.

Are the people in this story Flora and the Valentinian Ptolemy? It is not clear. Ptolemy was a common enough name in antiquity that this identification is not necessary. Additionally, Justin characterizes the martyred Ptolemy as a "lover of truth," neither deceitful nor false. Since Justin considers Valentinians to be heretics (Just., *Dial*. 35), it is more likely that the martyred Ptolemy was an Apostolic Catholic teacher aligned with Justin than Flora's Valentinian instructor. If he was the Valentinian Ptolemy, then Justin could not have known the details about Ptolemy's Valentinian teachings. This might suggest that Ptolemy did not broadcast the fact that he had been baptized a second time as a Valentinian initiate himself.

[8.2] Three Classes of People

COMPANION READINGS

John 4:5–42; 4:46–54; 8:44

Fragments of Heracleon

Tripartite Tractate (NHC I,5)

118.29–35

We learned in Chapter 3 about the way in which the Valentinians classified humans into the pneumatics (themselves), the psychics (Apostolic Catholics), and the hylics (everyone else). Irenaeus, Clement, and Origen present the Valentinians as resolute determinists, while the Apostolic Catholics as believers in free choice. Were they right about this? This becomes the question of the hour among fourth-generation Valentinians, who work hard to try to explain and defend themselves against this charge.

The Valentinian who discusses this the most is the Sicilian Heracleon (ca. 170 CE), another pupil of Valentinus. History has left us with a handful of extracts from his famous *Commentary on the Gospel of John* (the first ever written), quoted at length by the third-century theologian, Origen of Alexandria. There is also a long untitled writing discovered in the Nag Hammadi Collection that we call the *Tripartite Tractate* because it is divided into three main parts. Some scholars have attributed this work to Heracleon because some of the ideas correspond with Heracleon's *Commentary on John*. But this correspondence is better explained as the dependence of a third-century author on Heracleon's commentary since the issues taken up in the *Tripartite Tractate* interface with Origen's theology and his theory about the eternal generation of the Son (which we will learn about in Chapter 11). This interface points to the possible authorship of the *Tripartite Tractate* by the fifth-generation Valentinian Candidus who debated Origen in Athens about these issues in 228 CE (and won!) (Jer., *Apol. adv. Ruf.* Ii.512).

In his *Commentary on the Gospel of John*, Heracleon finds three stories about Jesus interacting with people that Heracleon believes reflect the three different classifications of people as either pneumatics, psychics, or hylics. The first is the story about the Samaritan woman at the well from John 4:5–42. As they talk, Jesus tells her about God's gift of living water that will quench her thirst immediately. Without hesitation, she accepts his offer of water. They go on to discuss her serial marriages, her improper understanding of God, and her faulty manner of worship. When she accepts Jesus' gift of grace, the waters of eternal life, all of this changes for her. She instantly comes to know that the real Father is a God of the Spirit who is not worshiped as a stone or wooden idol, nor identified with the God of the Jews and his temple. The true God of worship is pure and invisible. This God should be worshiped by the human spirit, rather than through material objects and in specific physical locations (John 4:21–24; Orig., *Comm. John* 13.97, 102, 104, 117–118, 147–148).

Heracleon keys into the Samaritan woman's immediate response to Jesus and her acceptance of Jesus' teachings about the true God in contrast with YHWH, the God worshiped in the Jewish and Samaritan temples. According to Heracleon, the Samaritan woman exemplifies the pneumatic. She is someone who directly converts to the Valentinian faith. She did not convert to Apostolic Catholicism first.

In both Heracleon's *Commentary on John* and the later *Tripartite Tractate*, the pneumatic is defined as a social category that identifies people who immediately, without hesitation, become advanced Gnostic Christians when they hear the voice of Jesus (Orig., *Comm. John* 13.57–66; *Tri. Tract.* 118.29–35). This is why Heracleon identifies the Samaritan woman as a pneumatic. She leaves behind her old life of decadence and passion as she accepts the water of life, the gift of grace, measured out into her vessel by Jesus the Savior (Orig., *Comm. John* 13.57–60, 149, 187–191). Jesus tells her to go and call her husband, which Heracleon explains does not refer to her human husband (which she did not have) but refers to her angel bridegroom who lives in the transcendent world. With this, Jesus leads her into union with her angel twin, and she is redeemed (Orig., *Comm. John* 13.67–72). She becomes a spokeswoman for the pneumatics, converting many people to the faith.

The psychics are Apostolic Catholics. Their conversion is exemplified for Heracleon by the story of the royal official whose dying son is healed from a distance by Jesus (John 4:46–54; Orig., *Comm. John* 13.416–426). Heracleon explains that the royal official (the *basilikos* or *petty king*) refers to YHWH the Creator and King of the world and human souls. YHWH's *diseased son* is the soul of an unconverted person. The soul is gravely ill because it has been trapped in *Capernaum* (matter, ignorance, and sin). Jesus came into the world to heal the soul and give it life. This happens when people convert to Apostolic Catholicism.

Heracleon, however, thinks that Christian conversion heals the convert's soul from its sins and forgives it. The soul, at the end of time, will abide in the darkness outside the divine Pleroma. This means, when people choose to become Apostolic Catholics, water baptism cleanses their souls. In this cleansed state, the souls have the chance of awakening their immortal spirits, so that one day, the converts might be baptized a second time in the Valentinian ceremony of redemption (chrism) and be fully redeemed. Heracleon explains that the conversion process involving first Apostolic Catholic conversion, and then pneumatic conversion, is slow, requiring signs, wonders, and a lot of persuasion.

The third type of response is refusal to convert to Christianity. Heracleon calls these people hylics (earthy or material). He thinks that John 8:44 points to pagans and Jews who chose not to convert and lapsed Christian apostates who have fallen away from Christianity or denied Christ (Orig., *Comm. John* 20.168–170, 211–219). Those hylics who further aligned themselves with the Devil by intentionally engaging in debauchery and wantonness were unlikely to ever convert, according to Heracleon.

The Valentinians have been misunderstood as determinists. In fact, their writings never indicate that only some humans are redeemable because they are born with spiritual seeds. Rather, they argue that everyone has the potential to be converted into a pneumatic, but not everyone would choose to do so. Not only was it possible for everyone to be converted, but, as Heracleon explains, there is more than one path to enlightenment. God gave humans two routes. The fastest and most direct route is for the pagan or Jew to be converted immediately into a pneumatic (a Valentinian). The slower route is for the pagan or Jew first to convert to Apostolic Christianity as a psychic, then later to be baptized a second time with oil (chrism) and enter the pneumatic ranks. The potential problem with the slower route is that converts might get stuck in the psychic rank, making their redemption second-rate. They would end up outside the Pleroma at the end of time instead of inside it with the pneumatics. But at least they would not be destroyed with the hylics and the physical cosmos.

8.3 Sacred Marriage

COMPANION READINGS
Gospel of Philip (NHC II,3)
Clement of Alexandria, *Excerpts from Theodotus* 63–65
Clement of Alexandria, *Miscellanies* 2.8

The Valentinians were lovers, which made them unique among third- and fourth-generation Christians, who for the most part lived in temperate marriages or as single celibates. As we have seen, the early Christians generally were suspicious of eroticism and sex because of its powerful lure toward sin. Like the Stoics, they worried that desire and lust could pull them into adulterous relationships and other sexual catastrophes. This was aggravated by their belief that the world would be ending any day. Many Christians wondered what the point of having children was if the world was soon to pass away. So they refused to marry and have sex as they hunkered down and waited for the skies to light up and Jesus to come out of the clouds and rescue them.

The Valentinians, however, believed that marriage is what grounds humans and makes them whole. It is primordial and it is eternal because marriage is not just a human institution, but a sacred mystery. It is an existential relationship in which God exists along with the married couple. As we learned in Chapter 3, the Valentinian hermaphrodite God is a syzygy, a pairing or fusion of the male–female into a whole. This fusion is imagined in terms of their erotic and procreative relationship which is necessary for the creation and maintenance of the transcendent and cosmic realms.

While the mating of the divine couples in their sacred marriages is the source of all existence and the greatest of all mysteries, it is also the fault line. When Sophia is unable to maintain her own spousal relationship with her husband Will because of her obsession to know the Father, her sacred marriage ruptures and all hell breaks loose. The traumatized Sophia is cast out of paradise, her raw emotions (desire, anxiety, fear, ignorance, repentance) are separated from the transcendent world. As we have seen, they become the substances from which the physical world, including the human psyche or soul, are constructed. In other words, God is fractured with divorce and God's severe emotional response is inscribed in human hearts.

When the Jesus Aeon leaves the Pleroma to rescue Sophia, as she delights in his beauty, Sophia births human spirits that are twins to a host of guardian angels who attend Jesus. The human spirits exist separately from the guardian angels, who are imagined as their divine male fiancés. The spirits become imprisoned in human souls and suffer embodiment apart from their twin fiancés. The *Gospel of Philip* uses the story of Adam and Eve to illustrate this condition. According to this Valentinian Gospel, humans feel naked and afraid because they have been separated from their angelic twins, their male counterparts. Like Eve, they have been cut out of Adam's side. They are two longing to be one.

How is this terrible situation of separation and suffering rectified? The Valentinian teacher Theodotus (ca. 160–180 CE) envisioned the end of the world as an exquisite mass wedding and banquet celebrated on the outskirts of the Pleroma. The mass wedding is kicked off with the marriage of Sophia and the Jesus Aeon. Then all the human spirits who have been redeemed marry their fiancés, their guardian angels, who have been waiting for them since the beginning of time. After the wedding banquet, the brides and grooms undress (leave their souls behind), enter the Pleroma, and join each other naked in their bridal beds. The couples become syzygies, the newlyweds embracing each other in an eternal moment of love-making and consummation (Clem. Alex., *Exc. Theo.* 63–65).

While there is much to look forward to in the erotic afterlife, the Valentinians believed that their human marriages should mirror or prefigure this ideal by engaging in a type of marriage that they called "sacred" and "pure." The Valentinians were tasked with managing their marriages as a holy sacrament. The purpose of the marriage was not the sex act itself, but procreation in imitation of the profundity of the Aeons. Because of this, the Valentinans defined "pure" marriage as heterosexual and monogamous. The sex act was performed intentionally between spouses as an act of love. At the moment of conception, the couple were supposed to raise their spirits in prayer to the transcendent God. The lovers believed that their angelic twins would be drawn down from the transcendent realm and join them in their erotic embrace. They were convinced that babies conceived within this holy embrace of spirits and angels would be born with spirits ready to immediately receive the Gnostic message (*Gos. Phil.* 78.12–79.14).

Because psychic Christians had not been initiated into this truth about marriage, the Valentinians believed that it was better for Apostolic Catholics to abstain from sex altogether, live in completely celibate marriages, or as single people. Irenaeus of Lyons considered this a double standard, one that he did not like. The Valentinians, however, insisted that the consequences of sex are too vast to loosen these standards. Sex is existential; its creative power is foundational to all of existence. When sex goes out of bounds, when intentions are misdirected or desire is misplaced, the creative act goes awry, as it did with Sophia.

While it is true that their marriages sacralized sex and eroticism (which the Valentinians distinguished from lust), it is also true that they taught that hermaphrodism was the sacred state of God, which they conceived as a procreative heterosexual syzygy. This meant that the mythology and practices of the Valentinians only served to reinforce and justify heterosexual marriage as the dominant institution of patriarchy because it gave marriage holy credentials and meaning as the replication of Aeonic syzygies. The holy state was marriage, and women had to have sex the right way in order to birth spiritual offspring. This reduced women to incubators of God's children. The pressure to conceive "perfect" children must have been enormous for women converts. The salvation of her children depended on her ability to perform sex properly. Should her children fall away from the faith, she would be the one to blame. Infertility, likewise, would have been her fault.

These ideas impacted the lives and deaths of the Valentinians. A group of Valentinians who congregated in the southeast quarter of the suburbs of Rome have left behind physical evidence of these ideas in the form of two tombstones. These stones (from the late second century) are our earliest archeological evidence of Christians. Stones like these tell uncensored stories. These stones tell us about the death and redemption of two Valentinians and how central sacred marriage was to them.

One of the tombstones is so fragmented that the name of the deceased is missing. The tombstone reads, "For my baths, the brothers of the bridal chamber bear the torches. In our chambers, they hunger for banquets. They praise Father and glorify the Son. There is a flow of solitary Silence and Truth in that place" (NCE 156, Capitoline Museum, Rome; trans. DeConick). The epigraph reveals that the deceased had already been redeemed through baptism. The ceremony is depicted as a wedding banquet attended by brothers, the groomsmen of the bridal chamber. The baptismal ceremony had been a preview of the deceased's final ascent to the bridal chamber, to the place where the Father and Son are praised, where Silence and Truth flow.

The second tombstone reveals the name of the deceased to have been Flavia Sophe. Her husband, also a Valentinian, wrote about her faith on her tombstone. The front of her tombstone says in verse, "Sophe, my dear sister and bride, you yearn for the light of the Father. You have been anointed with immortal holy oil in the baths of Christ. You have sought eagerly to gaze upon the divine faces of the Aeons, upon the great angel of the great counsel, the true Son. You have gone to the bridal chamber and ascended to the house of the Father" (CIG 4:9595a; Museo Nationale, Rome; trans. DeConick). From this inscription, it is clear that Sophe's husband considers her his sister and bride in Christ. They are companions in faith and sacred marriage. Her Valentinian initiation, when she sought out the Aeons, prepared her for the final ascent at death. Because she has received the second baptism of redemption when holy oil was spread on her body, her spirit now is able to make the journey into the house of the Father and enter God's Pleroma, which is described as a bridal chamber.

A second inscription is etched onto the backside of Sophe's tombstone. It reads, "This deceased woman did not have a typical end to her life. She died, yet she lives, and sees a truly immortal light.

She really is living among the living, and is dead to the dead. Earth, why are you astonished by this dead body? Are you terrified?" (CIG 4:9595a; Museo Nationale, Rome). It is shocking how atypical the description of Sophe's death is when compared to other Roman tombstones, which usually announce the ending of a life well-lived ("Remember me as you pass by" or "I was not; I was; I am not; I do not care"). Sophe is not described as a mortal dying, turning to dust in the earth, but as an immortal rising to the light of a transcendent world. She is an immortal living among the Gods, not a corpse interned among the dead. Her husband notes in the epigraph how terrifying her death must be to the cosmic powers, who do not have the authority to detain her in the shadow world or force her into another body.

Why did Sophe's husband think that the cosmic powers were afraid of Sophe? One of Valentinus' letters (which we referred to in Chapter 3) provides a possible answer (Clem. Alex., *Strom.* 2.8). As we noted earlier in this textbook, Valentinus describes the moment when Adam is first created and the Archons stand around him in awe of his beauty. The Archons had created Adam in the likeness of a transcendent Man they saw in the skies. Adam turned out to be so much more lovely than they themselves were. The Archons noticed another difference too. Adam seemed to know things that they did not. They were ignorant of the fact that Adam had been endowed with a seed of the divine spirit. Because the spirit is literally truth, this means that Adam had the ability to speak the truth, which the ancient Greeks called *parrhesia* or bold speech. And his truth-telling struck terror in his creators, who realized that Adam knew more than they did.

Parrhesia was considered a basic duty of Greek citizens in the Athenian democracy. The Greeks understood that freedom of speech and frank criticism are necessary for democracy to be successful. Citizens were obligated to maintain the welfare of the city-state by speaking the truth, even when the majority of the population may not agree. In the later Hellenistic period (when kings ruled instead of citizens), the king's advisors were supposed to speak the truth in order to help the king make sound decisions and prevent him from abusing his power. For those in power, such truth-telling can be terrifying because they may threaten the king's positions and plans. Socrates discovered how real the risk was when he was executed for his bold vision. John the Baptist faced the same risk when he criticized Herod and lost his head.

Sophe's tombstone exemplifies the terror that Gnostic truth incites. Sophe is among the saved because she stopped believing the lies of the Archons. She came to know that she was more than her material body and mortal soul. The real Sophe – her spirit – transcends this cosmos and its Gods. She ascends to the transcendent world as a glorified immortal. There, she embraces her lover, the angel who has been waiting for her since the beginning of time.

8.4 The Pneumatic Church

COMPANION READINGS
Irenaeus, *Against Heresies* 1.13–21
Hippolytus, *Refutation* 6.39–41

Marcus the Valentinian (ca. 170 CE) is one of the most flamboyant characters among the early Christians (Iren., *Haer.* 1.13–20). During his lifetime, Christianity was spreading north of Italy into Gaul, where a new flourishing center of Christian conversion had emerged. When Marcus was called to be a Christian missionary, he made it his mission to proclaim Jesus' true spiritual message to the Gauls. This is why Marcus settled near Irenaeus in the Rhone Valley and opened a Valentinian church that competed with Irenaeus' church.

Marcus built his church on a psychological principle that contemporary mega-church leaders have only rediscovered lately. When it comes to church, forget the creeds. People want to feel God. They want to be emotionally moved. They want their brokenness to be acknowledged and healed. They want to be swept up in the promise of something bigger and better.

Like Valentinus, Marcus' mission started with his own vision when, he said, Silence (the primal Mother-God) descended to Marcus. Since her male form could not be endured, the Mother-God stood before Marcus as a beautiful female angel. Her transgender reflects the fact that Marcus perceives the primal deity in terms of the unfolding of a series of divine hermaphrodites, who are gender fluid.

Marcus listens to her story, how she came into being when the primal God first uttered thirty separate letters. These thirty separate letters became the thirty divinities, she explained, that populate the transcendent world of the Pleroma. These divinities only knew the sound of their own letters and could only utter their own sound. They were incapable of vocalizing the entire string of letters, which means that they were not able to comprehend the primal God who is the sound of the whole string.

The Mother-God then revealed to Marcus the truth about the transcendent God. The truth turns out to be Truth, a second angel, also a beautiful female. Rather than representing an individual aspect of the primal God as the thirty divinities did, Truth embodies the whole primal God in one human-shaped divinity called Anthropos or Man. Truth was produced when God's name, I-Ê-S-O-U-S (Greek spelling for Jesus) was verbalized. The angel of Truth explains that the name IESOUS is shorthand for God's longer secret name, the twenty-four-letter Greek alphabet.

Marcus believed that the powerful secret sounds of creation were revealed to him by these angels. Before the Jewish Kabbalists in the Middle Ages taught that creation occurred when God pronounced his ineffable name YHWH, Marcus was already teaching that creation occurred when the primal God spoke the name IESOUS. Marcus went on to develop a complex system of esoteric practices based on the numerology of the divine thirty and the pronunciation of the twenty-four letters of the alphabet. He believed that these practices harnessed the power of the thirty transcendent divinities.

For example, the pronunciation of the eight semi-vowels L-M-N-R-S-DZ-KS-PS channeled the powers of Word and Life, while the intonation of the nine mute letters P-K-T-B-G-D-PH-CH-TH harnessed the powers of the Father and Truth. The seven vowels A-E-Ê-I-O-U-Ô drew on the powers of Man and Church (Iren., *Haer.* 1.14.5). To bring into harmony the chaotic seven heavens ruled by YHWH and his Archons, the Marcosian congregation intoned the seven vowels consecutively AAA-EEE-ÊÊÊ-III-OOO-UUU-ÔÔÔ. Because Marcus taught that the original utterance of each vowel had generated the seven heavens in primordial time, their ritual intonation was able to control the spheres now. They believed that the ritual intonation of the seven vowels floated up to the transcendent world, praising the divinities Anthropos and Church.

Marcus did not conjure up these vowel vocalizations himself. For centuries, Egyptian priests had been intoning the vowels in ceremonies in order to ensure heaven's harmony (Ps.-Dem., *Style* 71). This practice shows up in many ancient contexts. We find it in many magical spells from Egyptian and Greek sources, as well as in the liturgies of the Hermetics and other groups in antiquity. The evidence suggests that ancient people used vowel chanting to maintain order in the universe, heal their bodies, and force powerful divinities to do their biddings. Marcus simply shifted the practice to control also the transcendent world known to the Gnostics. Marcus' congregants, by imitating the sounds of creation, were convinced that they were tapping into the primal power of the divine world and harnessing it to heal their world and themselves.

Marcus was known for his therapeutic services. In order to relieve his congregants' personal difficulties and stresses, the members of his congregation ritually intoned the long vowel ôôô. They believed ô is a universal letter of healing because whenever infants are suffering or in need, they make this sound. According to Marcus, when the distressed soul cries out this vowel, the soul's angelic twin hears it and sends relief down from the transcendent world. Marcus also guided his congregation in the unison pronunciation of the prayer AMEN. He said that its intonation has restorative properties, harnessing the mighty powers of the thirty separate divinities as if they were one (Iren., *Haer.* 1.14.7–8).

Marcus gained the reputation of a magician among his detractors. While this label was meant to be a slight, it reflected the fact that Marcus led his congregation in the invocation of words of power for healing and created theatrical rituals for his church. Marcus wanted his congregation to experience an emotional enthusiasm that the standard Apostolic Catholic service did not deliver. Marcus wanted his congregation to experience the presence of God. So he hyped up the standard eucharist so that the ceremony was more like the drinking ceremonies used to induce ecstasy among initiates inducted into the Greek mysteries.

Marcus' ecstatic eucharist started with Marcus as the presider filling a number of cups with a light-colored wine beverage. He kicked off the ceremony with a prayer meant to draw God's grace into their midst, petitioning Grace, "May the Unknowable and Ineffable Grace that is prior to all things fill your inner self. May she multiple her knowledge in you, sowing the grain of mustard seed in good soil" (Iren., *Haer.* 1.13.2; trans. DeConick). Next, he invited the congregants to come forward to each take a cup. As they did so, the wine in one of the cups turned blood red, as if the blood of Grace had flowed into it, raining down from the transcendent world above. The lucky person who held the cup of red wine was blessed. Marcus said that this person had been especially elected by the Aeon Grace that day to lead the congregation. This election could happen to either a woman or a man, so women often were congregational leaders in Marcus' church. The elected leader consecrated the blood red wine in the cup and then shared it with everyone present, so that God's grace would flow among them all.

After all the congregants had drunk from the cup, Marcus held up a large empty chalice. He asked the leader-of-the-day to pour the remainder of the blood red wine into the chalice. As this was done, Marcus prayed for Grace to fill the elected person so that the person might prophesy for the congregation. Marcus said, "My wish is for you to share in the grace that I have. The Father of all is constantly looking upon your angel who is in his presence. But the place of the mighty (angel) is in us. We must be restored to one. First, from me and through me, receive grace. Prepare yourself as a bride awaiting her bridegroom, so that you may be what I am and I may be what you are. Consecrate the seed of light in your bridal chamber. From me, receive (your) bridegroom. Hold him and be held by him. Behold grace has descended upon you. Open your mouth and prophesy" (Iren., *Haer.* 1.13.3; trans. DeConick).

At this moment, the liquid in the chalice bubbled and overflowed the rim. Marcus gave the chalice to the elected person who drank the divine liquid and became the community's prophet-of-the-day too. Instantly, the person's heart rate increased and body perspired. The person became visibly enthused and prophesied before the congregation (Hipp., *Ref.* 6.39–41).

Given the testimony of the physical alteration of the color of the wine, the effervescence of the wine in the chalice, and the physiological and mental changes of the elected leader, Marcus must have put something in the wine. Hippolytus, in fact, reports that drugs were involved. Likely Marcus smeared a special plant compound in one of the initial cups. When the compound mixed with the wine, the chemical reaction altered its color, so that it became the color of blood when the cup was held. We can imagine how thrilling it must have been for the person when the wine changed color right before her eyes, believing herself to have been selected by Grace to be the congregational leader and prophet for the day.

The bubbling of the wine in the large chalice must have been produced likewise. A chemical compound must have been smeared on the inside of the chalice, so that a bubbling reaction resulted as the red wine was poured in and mixed with it. Whatever the nature of the drug, when it was ingested, it stimulated the person's body almost instantly. While the carnivals of Dionysus relied on wine for their religious enthusiasm, and the mysteries of Demeter used a special barley brew called *kykeon*, Marcus mixed a drug in a wine beverage. With this hyped up eucharist, Marcus made sure that all of his congregants experienced on an emotional, if not a psychedelic high.

Marcus gave the average Apostolic Catholic service a shot of adrenalin. While his eucharist was still about communing with God, the communion was on a level of enthusiasm unprecedented in Apostolic Catholic and other Valentinian churches. While Marcus' congregation still prayed to God the Father, Marcus included therapeutic chanting to the Mother. While his church still ended their prayers with the traditional AMEN, they did so as a long chant to harness the entire power of the divine world. His prayers and liturgies differed enough from those of the Apostolic Catholic churches that Marcus' church was not the split-level church of the other Valentinians who catered to the Apostolic Catholics. There was no second-level baptism. Marcus was the first to build a *spiritual* or *pneumatic* Christian Gnostic church. The people who attended his church came to join the pneumatics. From the start, they were seeking Gnostic redemption, an ecstatic ceremony when the initiates ascended to the transcendent world and united with their twin angels.

Because his random selection of service leaders made it just as likely for women as for men to be leaders and prophets in his church, Marcus was extremely successful recruiting women. It is not surprising that Irenaeus, bishop of Lyons, complains that a number of leading women withdrew their membership from the Apostolic Catholic church and joined Marcus' congregation, perhaps protesting the more restrictive gender policies of the Apostolic Catholics when it came to church leadership.

One particular event seems to have been the tipping point for Irenaeus. One of Irenaeus' deacons had Marcus over for dinner. Not long after, the deacon's wife dropped out of the Apostolic Catholic church and joined Marcus'. She became so involved in the ministry of Marcus' church that she traveled on missions with him. This situation became so tense that the presbyters from Irenaeus' church pursued her, persuading her "with no small difficulty" to return to Irenaeus' church. They forced her to publicly confess that she had been sexually seduced and then abused by Marcus (Iren., *Haer.* 1.13.4–5). It was obvious to the presbyters that Marcus had seduced her since, in their eyes, there was no other reason why a faithful married Catholic woman would have joined Marcus' church and traveled around with him. We will return to Marcus in Chapter 9 when we study how Irenaeus used his knowledge of Marcus' activities to construct Catholic orthodoxy.

8.5 The Travelers

COMPANION READINGS

Hippolytus, *Refutation* 5.12.1–17.13 As we have seen, a number of regional Valentinian churches were established and operated by Valentinus' students after his death. These churches had their differences, but they all depended on the general terminology and broad strokes of the Valentinian myth and used liturgies that were closely related to their Apostolic Catholic counterparts. They all offered full redemption to initiates, an oil ceremony that functioned as a second baptism for pneumatics.

Other Gnostic Christian groups also were around in the mid-second century. These groups had their own histories, unrelated to the Valentinians. What they had in common with the Valentinians was the worship of the supreme Source of Life, a God beyond the Biblical Creator, and their tenacity to read the Jewish scriptures in a way that flipped the traditional Jewish and Christian readings, so that the Creator God is not the hero, but the villain of the story. Their mythologies and liturgies were innovative and distinctive, reflecting regional differences and cultural variety. All of these groups were ecstatic groups whose leaders took initiates on soul journeys to meet the supreme God. The personal experience of God – Gnosis – was their goal.

To achieve Gnosis, these groups had a heightened interest in mapping the soul journey astrologically along paths that wound through the Zodiac constellations. The constellations were conceived as gates guarded by the Gods who ruled the constellations. In the ancient mind, the planets and constellations are the traditional gods and heroes. Zeus, for instance, is the planet Jupiter, and Kronos is Saturn. The constellations are legendary heroes like Hercules and Perseus. The realms of the underworld are the territories of Hades and Persephone. Each of these groups marketed their innovative paths through the constellations as their own exclusive trademark mysteries.

One of these groups was the Peratics (Hipp., *Ref.* 5.12.1–17.13). Their Greek name means Travelers. They tell us that they are called Travelers because they alone know the road the soul travels to get into the world and the path the soul journeys to get out of it. They also claim to know an exclusive route through the underworld. Alone, as Travelers, they claim to know how to pass by mortality (Hipp., *Ref.* 5.16.1). In their view, traversing mortality requires that the human spirit – what they call "the seed of divine potential" – be awakened from its sleep and grown into a divinity that is able to journey back to its transcendent home.

We learn about these second-century Gnostics from Hippolytus who is writing in Rome at the beginning of the third century. According to his description, the Peratics envisioned Ultimate Reality as a fountain spewing forth or emanating three streams of existence. One stream is Transcendent Being, which they call the Perfect Good, the Great Father, and the Unbegotten. The second generates itself and manifests itself as Divinities or Gods. The third stream of existence is everything that is created.

Each of these streams represents superjacent levels of reality. The Peratics believed that the first level of reality, the Unbegotten Good, flows into the second level of reality, the Self-Generating Good. The flow continues into the third level of reality, the material cosmos and humanity, leaving humans filled with spirits, the seeds of divine potential.

The Peratics believed that there was a primordial insurrection when some of the good Divinities who controlled the created universe revolted and became evil. The Peratics identified these treasonous Divinities with the traditional Greek Gods. Their mythology is a complicated religious blend of popular astrological lore, legends about the monstrous Titans, and myths of fallen angels like Lucifer and Samael. The result is a unique Gnostic story about the apostasy of the traditional Greek Gods who turned to the dark side and took control of the universe.

The consequence of this primordial insurrection is that as Archons, they incarcerate human spirits in the bodies they create. The Archon reigning over all creation is Kronos, the violent Titan who quakes the earth and spews the waters of Tartarus upward into the ocean. Kronos is identified as the creator God who brings forth human life only to destroy it. He is the father God who murders his children by eating them, trapping their spirits in the cosmos.

This wretched situation requires drastic intervention from the two other levels of reality. The transcendent Good and the upright Divinities must do something to alter this horrible predicament and liberate the spirit. Here the Peratic story takes on a decisively Christian turn. Following the narrative arc of the Gospel of John, the Peratics teach that Christ is sent down from the Good to save creation. Christ, they said, is a powerful Deity who embodied all three levels of reality, the transcendent, the divine, and the human. He is the Son of Man who, when crucified, was lifted up like the serpent that Moses lifted up. The Peratics said that this means that Christ joined the other celestial Rulers as a God, taking control of the highest and brightest constellation, the serpentine Draco. In this way, Christ became the good guardian of the Draco stargate which, they believe, controls the flow of existence from the transcendent sphere into the cosmos and back up again. Christ opened the Draco portal, they say, establishing a flow of divinity into and out of the cosmos every time the celestial sphere rotates. This is how the Peratics understood the Christian aphorism attributed to Jesus in the Gospel of John, "I am the door" (John 10:7).

The Peratics claimed to know the secrets about how the human spirits could make their way back to the transcendent realm through Draco's stargate. The secrets were gradually revealed during initiations that began with a journey through hell, and then, a dangerous and terrifying skywalk through the heavens. The final ceremony, they called the Mystery of Eden, when the initiates were drawn into the transcendent Father's world along a star river that flowed through the mouth of Draco.

8.6 The Wise Serpent

COMPANION READINGS
Origen, *Against Celsus* 6.24–38

The pagan philosopher Celsus decribes a Christian rite called The Seal, which he witnessed being performed (Orig., *Cels.* 6.24–38). He says that he saw a person lying on the ground. The priest or "Father" anointed the person with oil. The person said in response, "I have been anointed with white oil from the tree of life." Celsus reports that this ritual caused the person's soul to separate from the body, allowing it to fly up through the celestial spheres. This is the resurrection.

This might sound like the Catholic ritual known as the Last Rites, when a person on their deathbed is anointed with oil. This is done to prepare the soul for death by providing the dying person with absolution for sins. But Celsus was not witnessing a Catholic ritual. What is being described is an initiation ceremony performed by a specific group of Gnostics. According to Celsus' description of these people, they are Christian "fools" who believe that the soul, when it separates from the body, has to journey home along a specific secret route (that they alone know) through the planets.

Celsus is writing his critique of Christianity in the year 178 CE. He describes this particular group of Gnostic Christians in his book. He says that they believe in Jesus, the crucified son of a carpenter, who established laws that contradict the laws of the Jewish God. He says these Christians call the Jewish God "Cursed" because this is the God who cursed the serpent in Paradise for giving the first humans knowledge of good and evil. Instead of worshiping the Creator God of Jewish scripture, these Christians, Celsus says, worship another God whom they have been taught by Jesus is the authentic Father God.

Celsus reports that he was familiar enough with the group's presbyters that they showed him some of their books in which foreign names of demons and prophecies were written. He witnessed their purification rites. He heard their hymns of redemption. He listened to the sounds they made when they healed their sick. He learned how they used particular costumes, numbers, stones, plants, and roots as therapeutic remedies (Orig., *Cels.* 6.40). Celsus considers all of this dangerous rather than beneficial, and thinks of it as magic meant to deceive gullible and uneducated people.

Celsus says that their presbyters talk repeatedly about "the tree of life" and believe that resurrection "from" the flesh, rather than resurrection "of" the flesh, is made possible by applying oil from this tree on the initiates' bodies. The application of the oil causes the initiates' souls to separate from their bodies. Once separated, the soul is free to journey through the planetary spheres to the transcendent world. To assist their journey, the initiates use a diagram that is a map of the celestial realms complete with the names, shapes, and locations of all the Archons who guard each sphere.

We know even more about these Gnostics and their celestial initiation rite because Origen, the early third-century theologian from Alexandria, writes about them. He identifies them, not as Christians, but as Ophians. They appear to be users of the Ophite Myth that we learned about in Chapter 3. This name stems from the Greek word for snake, *ophis*, which refers to their belief that the serpent in Eden was wise and that he spoke the truth to Eve in the garden. Origen tells us that he was able to find a copy of the map that Celsus had seen, although it does not appear to be an exact replica of the one Celsus saw. Origen's map was inscribed with the names of the Archons plus the actual prayers that the initiates memorized and recited along the way. Origen gives us enough information that we can reconstruct the secret path that the Ophian Christians believed the soul took to ascend through the cosmic spheres (Figures 8.1 and 8.2).

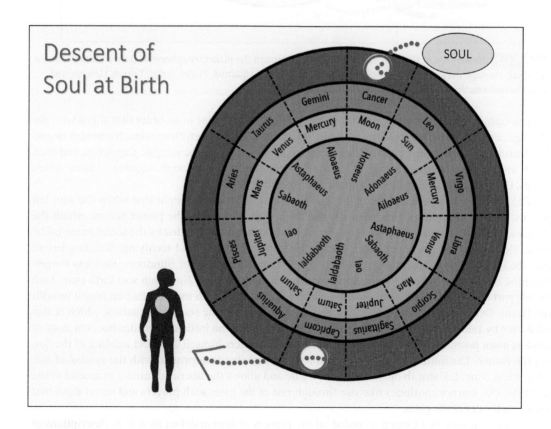

FIGURE 8.1 Illustration of the path that the soul takes through the planetary spheres as it descends through the stargate in Cancer, then flies through Leo, Virgo, Libra, Scorpio, Sagittarius, and leaves the heavens through the stargate in Capricorn where it falls into a body.

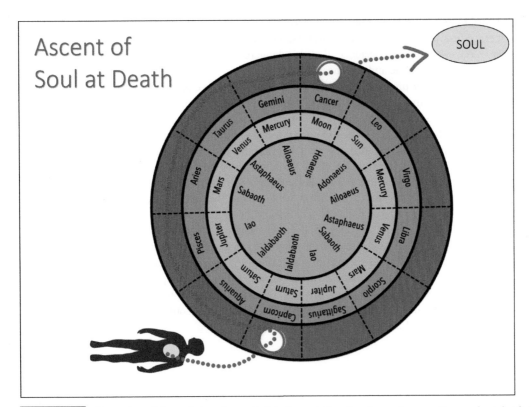

FIGURE 8.2 Illustration of the path that the soul takes through the planetary spheres as it ascends at death out of the body through the stargate in Capricorn, then flies through Aquarius, Pisces, Aries, Taurus, Gemini, and enters the heavens through the stargate in Cancer.

The Ophian path was a sky trek through the houses of the Zodiac in an order that aligns with the astrological teaching of a second-century Neo-Pythagorean philosopher, Numenius. Numenius taught that the soul, when journeying out of the body, ascends first through the stargate Capricorn, and then travels around the nocturnal houses of the Zodiac from Capricorn through Aquarius, Pisces, Aries, Taurus, Gemini, and exiting into the upper realm via Cancer.

The Ophian Christians, following this same astrological pattern, taught that when the soul left its body, it flew through the Capricorn stargate. Capricorn is ruled by the planet Saturn, which the Ophians identified with the chief Archon, the Jewish God whom they called by the secret name Ialdabaoth. He also carried the angel name Michael, who is lion-shaped and terrifying. Standing before him, the initiate is supposed to pray, "Greetings! Solitary King, Bond of Blindness, Reckless Forgetting, First Power. I am guarded by the Spirit of Pronoia and by Sophia. Now I am sent forth pure. I am already part of the light of the Son and the Father. May Grace be with me. Yes, Father, may it be with me" (trans. DeConick). The initiate is released and continues to the stargate Aquarius, which is also ruled over by Ialdabaoth. A second prayer is recited in which the initiate identifies his own *nous* or mind as more powerful than Ialdabaoth. The initiate considers himself a perfect product of the Son and the Father. The initiate shows Ialdabaoth a secret seal that is imprinted with the symbol of life. Once this is done, Ialdabaoth opens the cosmic gate and allows the liberated initiate to ascend to the next gate. The journey continues likewise through rest of the gates with prayers and secret signs that thwart each ruler of the gates.

We are fortunate that Origen recorded all the prayers of demon defeat as well as descriptions of the various objects or signs that were used along the Zodiac route. We are also lucky that one of the Ophian's ritual objects has survived the centuries. In 1949, Professor Bonner published an article in which he identified a green jasper gem as an Ophian amulet. A lion-headed god is carved on the front of the gem. The inscription reads: Ialdabaoth and Ariel (the Lion of God) (see Figure 3.7). This carving reveals how the Ophians imagined Ialdabaoth's appearance. He is a humanlike God with the ferocious head of a lion. He is dressed as a Roman solider, holding a staff. Listed on the gem's reverse side are the seven Ophian planetary Rulers Ia(ldabaoth), Iao, Sabaoth, Adonai, Eloaeus, Horaeus, and Astaphaeus. This remarkable gem was once worn by an Ophian initiate, either as a pendant or ring of power.

8.7 Justin the Gnostic

COMPANION READINGS
Hippolytus, *Refutation* 5.26.1–27.5 Justin the Gnostic swore to anyone who would join his movement that he would give them "what no eye has seen and no ear has heard and what has not been conceived by the heart" (Hipp., *Ref.* 5.26.1–27.5). As their guru, he promised to conduct them directly to the Good Father. Justin claimed for himself and his followers the name Gnostics because, he said, they had exclusive knowledge about the whereabouts of the Father whom they had met during their ecstatic flights.

Justin wrote a book about the truth as it was revealed to him. Justin operated by blending what he knew about Greek literature with Christian piety and a flipped reading of the Genesis story. According to Justin's book *Baruch*, from eternity three unbegotten primordial Gods exist. The first is the Father, the Good. Since the Good Father ultimately is responsible for the design of everything that exists, he is known and worshiped throughout the Mediterranean world as the Greek fertility god, Priapus. The second is Elohim, the Father of everything that is begotten. He is the Creator God from the Jewish scriptures, the Lord of the skies. The third is Eden, the female earth Goddess, whom Justin treats as the personification of the garden of paradise.

In Justin's mythology, Elohim and Eden are attracted to each other and marry. They are happy newlyweds in the honeymoon phase. Their erotic lovemaking births all the Divinities that populate the skies and the underworld. Their lovemaking also creates the human being, as males and females. Eden gives them their souls, while Elohim their spirits. The first human couple follow the example of Eden and Elohim. They marry, become lovers and populate the earth with their children.

Problems arise in Paradise when it dawns on Elohim that he is the sky God. It is his nature to rise up. Eden, however, cannot follow him since she is the earth below the sky. Elohim ascends. Reaching the summit of the heavens, he comes to a stargate whose light is brighter than anything he himself had created. He calls out, "Open the gates!" (Ps. 118:19). From the other side of the gate, a voice calls back, "This is the gate of the Lord. Through this gate the righteous enter" (Ps. 118:19). The stargate opens and Elohim ascends through it. On the other side of the gate, Elohim sees the Good Father. The Good Father enthrones Elohim on his right hand and does not allow him to ever leave again.

When Eden realizes that Elohim has abandoned her, she tries to lure him back with her beauty and erotic gestures. But Elohim does not return to her. Abandoned, she falls into despair, grief, and anger. To punish Elohim, the resentful Eden declares war on the human spirit, which Elohim had given human beings. She finds all ways possible to make it suffer. Because of this, the soul and spirit are locked in a perpetual battle with each other.

Elohim tries to liberate the spirit from its suffering by sending his angel Baruch as a divine envoy to humans. The most important visit was when Baruch appeared in Nazareth to the twelve-year-old boy Jesus. Baruch reveals the existential damage to Jesus. He tasks Jesus the mission to show people how to ascend to the Good Father and take their place next to Elohim. Jesus takes on the task. When he is crucified by Eden's angels, he leaves his natural body behind in Eden's hands. His spirit ascends to the Good Father, revealing the path for other human spirits to follow.

Justin claimed to know this path because it had been revealed to him in the *Book of Baruch*. Justin guided his initiates to the stargate that Elohim and Jesus had used. At the stargate, they chanted the same line from the Psalms, "Open the gates!" (Ps. 118:19). Once the portal opened, Justin's initiates entered the realm of the Good Father and gazed upon him. As living spirits like Elohim, they were offered drink from a fountain of life-giving bubbling water, and then they were told to bathe in it. The bath was therapeutic, ending the suffering of their spirits.

8.8 Adamas the Man

COMPANION READINGS
Hippolytus, *Refutation* 5.6.3–11.1

One of the most complex descriptions of a Gnostic group is the report about the Naassenes (Hipp., *Ref.* 5.6.3–11.1). This name is inspired by the Hebrew word for snake, *nachash*, and was likely given to them by their opponents. The group did not call themselves Naassenes. They called themselves Gnostics because, they said that they alone had experienced the depths of knowledge (Hipp., *Ref.* 5.6.3–4).

In line with the Egyptian primordial myths about Atum and Amun, the Naassene Gnostics believed that the God from which everything originates is serpentine. He lives in the moist essence of the primordial universe. This God is a hermaphrodite, a primal Man, whom the Naassene Gnostics call Adamas (derived from Gen. 1:26-27). Adamas is the source of all life, which flows from him like a river with three currents: the noetic, psychic, and earthy. This river and its currents flow from Adamas' transcendent realm down into the realm of chaos.

The Naassene Gnostics were ancient perennialists. They promoted the idea that the same universal God Adamas was behind all the different religions of the world. They preached that this serpentine God-Before-Gods is the reality beneath the worship of every one of the Gods at the world's shrines and temples, and in every religious ceremony and mystery initiation, although the glory of Adamas had been tarnished by trying to capture Adamas in statues, temples, and myths.

According to the Naassene Gnostics, Adamas has a son, who is known as the Perfect Man and the Son of Man. He is a microcosmic version of Adamas, containing within himself the noetic, psychic, and earthy currents. The Son serves as the template for the first human being, Adam, who is molded out of clay from the earth (Gen. 2:7) by the Archons of Chaos and Esaldaeus, the fiery solar God whose name most scholars think is a garbled form of one of the names for YHWH in the Bible, El-Shaddai (Exod 6:3). Playing on the story of Narcissus, the Son is so enamoured with his beautiful look-alike that he orgasms and his semen falls into Adam (Hipp., *Ref.* 5.6.35–36). This seed is the vivifying human spirit, which now must suffer because it dwells in an environment unnatural for it.

Because the Perfect Man strayed sexually, the Naassene Gnostics understand the Greek god Attis to be his reflection. Attis is a famous God because he was the husband of the Great Mother Goddess Cybele. Although there are many versions of his story, they all point to Attis, a God handsome to a fault, who has an affair that breaks Cybele's heart. Her wrath brings down Attis' lover, and Attis goes mad. He is driven to castrate himself out of his grief and guilt (Ovid, *Fasti*. 4.222FF). Hippolytus tells us that the Naassene Gnostics, like the priests of Cybele, value castration, although they do not remove their scrota. Rather, he says that the Naassene Gnostics refuse to procreate by abstaining from heterosexual intercourse and engaging in same-sex relationships instead. In this way, they make up for the mistake of the Son, making sure that his spirit will not continue to be passed on in the semen that seeds new children (Hipp., *Ref.* 5.7,38–41).

As for spirits already entrapped, they have to be rescued through a process of initiation. In order to reveal these mysteries of ascent, the Son incarnates as Jesus, born of Mary, bringing with him secret knowledge of the holy way back to the realm of Primal Man (Hipp., *Ref.* 5.10,1). Prior to the initiation, the initiates had to take vows of abstinence from heterosexual relations. The Naassene Gnostics thought that abstinence from heterosexual relations was a practice that made them hermaphrodites, new creatures that no longer played binary male and female roles. By refusing to participate in heterosexual sex, they had become male–female creatures like the Primal Man (Hipp., *Ref.* 5.7,14–15).

Initiation into their "Angelic Church" occurred in three stages: defeating mortality, ascension through the spheres, and rejoining Adamas in the House of God (Hipp., *Ref.* 5.8,4). The initiates first embarked on a journey to defeat death, being reborn as a Paidos or Child. During this ceremony, the initiates were awakened in the realm of the dead and journeyed out of it following Christ as Hermes. Chanting a secret password, the initiates were resurrected from the grave, their souls leaving their bodies behind.

During the second ceremony, their souls ascend through the heavenly spheres and advance to the level of Ephêbos or Youth. This level was kicked off with a drinking ritual followed by an ecstatic flight along the Milky Way, the river that they believed streamed downward from Adamas. By following the river upward they believed that they were reversing the Fall. They were headed to the Gate of Heaven, which they had identified as Venus, the third gate. At this gate, the initiates chant a prayer they lifted from Psalm 24:7–9, "Your leaders, lift up the gates! Ancient doors be lifted up! That the King of Glory may come in!" The initiate was identified as the King of Glory who has been mighty in battle because he had repudiated his heterosexual body and morphed into a hermaphrodite. The initiate shouts a secret password and the stargate opens to them. As a communal display of their new status as an Ephêbos, the initiates' bodies are anointed with oil from the horn of David (Hipp., *Ref.* 5.9.21–22).

The mysteries of the Angelic Church are completed at the third level where the Youth becomes an Anêr or Adult Man (Hipp., *Ref.* 5.8,19). In the previous stages of initiation, the soul had left behind the body. Now the spirit leaves behind the soul as it calls out another secret password, passing through Venus' stargate and entering the transcendent realm, the House of God (Hipp., *Ref.* 5.8.44–45). When the Son of Man who guards the House of God hears this, he greets them as his bridegrooms. As a communal display of their new status, they are fed milk and honey. Its taste is said to have been transformative (Hipp., *Ref.* 5.8.30). The initiates unite with the hermaphrodite God himself.

8.9 Revelation of Secrets

Each of these Gnostic groups prided itself on owning the real map to eternity, the map that would guide the lost spirit safely through the underworld purgatories and the stars in the skies to the transcendent world from which it had fallen. Each of these Gnostic groups charted very particular and distinctive initiatory paths through these realms. The distinctive catechisms and mythologies feature flipped readings of the Genesis story. The Peratics, Justinians, and Naassenes appear to have developed their readings independently of the Ophite, Barbeloite, or Simonian Myths. All are Christian thinkers whose indigenous knowledge about Greco-Roman and Egyptian religion is blended with their flipped interpretations of the Genesis story. While their mythologies and regional programs of initiation are diverse, they all promoted a series of ritual activities that served to awaken or quicken the spirit, purge it, mature it, and integrate it into the divine Source of Life.

The expansion of the Gnostic churches among fourth-generation Christians demonstrates that Christians capitalized on the claim to know and be able to reveal God's mysteries and Jesus' secrets. This claim to secret knowledge attracted converts who yearned to participate in ecstatic practices that disclosed to them the afterlife journey before they died and promised them the vision of the Highest God. They found homes in these churches because they were attracted to their therapeutics, especially the promise that their suffering would be alleviated through the grace of God.

While the ecstatic and therapeutic messages of these churches were attractive, there is no evidence to suggest that any of these churches sought to consolidate into a network such as the Apostolic Catholics were creating. The Valentinians developed their own ecclesiology which included bishops, but their church remained decentralized and their urban congregations were led by scholars who expressed competing opinions on many issues. The Peratic church, the Ophian church, the Justinian church, and the Angelic Church of the Naassene Gnostics remained independent ecstatic churches that were regional. Over time, their independence and regionality resulted in their isolation. Since most of these churches did not thrive beyond the third century, they likely had difficulty managing the transfer of leadership and knowledge to the next generation of church-goers or were unable to maintain rates of conversion necessary for their churches to survive. The rate of conversion likely was curtailed once the Apostolic Catholics in the early third century realized that they could outdo the Gnostic churches at their own game by promising to reveal to potential converts a Catholic secret tradition. But this story must wait until Chapter 11.

Timeline

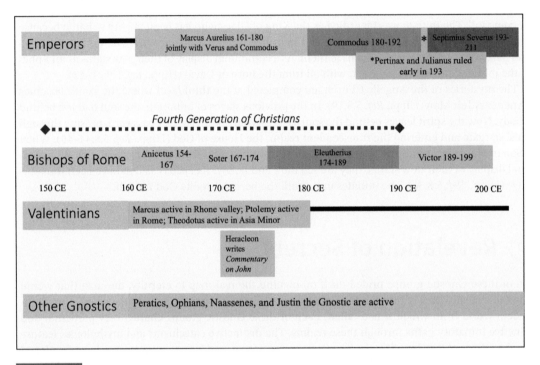

FIGURE 8.3 Timeline for the expansion of Gnostic groups.

Pattern Summary

While these Gnostic groups have divergent opinions about the details of their Christian mythologies and practices, their patterns are remarkably similar (see Figure 8.4). All these groups are TRANSTHEISTIC, agreeing that the Biblical God is the CREATOR who fashions the human being and the world with the assistance of his Archons. All groups consider the Biblical God to be a bad guy, a VILLAIN, or a lesser deity who creates a problematic universe in which suffering pervades. The human is conceived to be TRIADIC, and redemption focuses on the spirit, which is released from the soul after the death journey through the cosmic spheres. These groups all appear to use the ADULT POSSESSION PATTERN, or the ENSOULMENT PATTERN, or some combination of these when sorting out the Binitarian Problem.

These patterns are blended with indigenous religious knowledge of the Greco-Roman Gods (Peratics; Justinians), Egyptian Gods (Valentinians; Naassenes), and Neo-Pythagorean astrology (Ophians). The result of these blends are divergent and distinctive mythologies, rituals, and lifestyles that were advertised and marketed as God's mysteries.

Family Pattern Chart
Fourth-Generation Gnostics

X=Definitely > L=Likely

THEODICY	Faulty-God	Faulty-Human	Other
Ptolemy	X		
Heracleon	X		
Theodotus	X		
Marcus	X		
Peratics	X		
Ophians	X		
Justin the Gnostic	X		
Naassenes	X		

SOTERIOLOGY	Gift from God	Human achievement	Minimalist	Moderate	Maximalist
Ptolemy	X		X		
Heracleon	X		X		
Theodotus	X		X		
Marcus	X		X		
Peratics	X		X		
Ophians	X		X		
Justin the Gnostic	X		X		
Naassenes	X		X		

CHRISTOLOGY	Adult possession	Fetal possession	Hybrid	Ensoulment	Visitation	Human who received revelation
Ptolemy	L			L		
Heracleon	L			L		
Theodotus		L				
Marcus	L			L		
Peratics	L			L		
Ophians	L					
Justin the Gnostic						X
Naassenes		L		L		

ANTHROPOLOGY	Mono	Dual	Triad	Quad
Ptolemy			X	
Heracleon			X	
Theodotus			X	
Marcus			X	
Peratics			X	
Ophians			X	
Justin the Gnostic			X	
Naassenes			X	

COSMIC DEMIURGY

	Autocrat	Administrator	Caretaker	Patron	Justice	Villain	Rebel	Ignorant	Impaired
Ptolemy	X	X	X	X	X	X	X	X	X
Heracleon	X	X	X	X	X	X	X	X	X
Theodotus	X	X	X	X	X	X	X	X	X
Marcus	X	X	L	L	L	L		X	X
Peratics	X	X					X		
Ophians	X	X				X			
Justin the Gnostic	L	X				X			
Naassenes	X	X				X	X		

RESURRECTION

	Body reunites with soul	Body discarded and soul immortalized	Body and soul discarded and spirit rises	God-element separates from body soul, and spirit and rises
Ptolemy, Heracleon, Theodotus			X	
Heracleon		X		
Theodotus		X		
Marcus		X		
Peratics		X		
Ophians		X		
Justin the Gnostic		X		
Naassenes		X		

SCRIPTURES

	Jewish	Gospel	Pauline letters (10)	Pauline letters (13)	Hebrews	Acts	Catholic letters	Revelation	Other
Ptolemy, Heracleon, Theodotus	X-partial	X-Mt/Mk/Jn	X						X-1Jn PrPet GosTr
Marcus	X-partial	X-Mt/Mk/Lk	X					L	
Peratics	X-partial	X-Jn							
Ophians	X-partial								
Justin the Gnostic	X-partial	X-Lk							X-Gnostic Baruch
Naassenes	X-partial	X-Mt/Mk/Lk Jn/GosThom/ GosEgyp							

ECCLESIOLOGY

	Consolidation movement	Reform movement	Secessionist movement	Counter movement	Innovative movement	Transregional	Regional
Ptolemy			X			X	
Heracleon			X			X	
Theodotus			X			X	
Marcus			X				X
Peratics					X		X
Ophians					X		X
Justin the Gnostic					X		X
Naassenes					X		X

FIGURE 8.4 Summary of the patterns of the different Gnostic movements.

Takeaways

1. Gnostic movements expanded in fourth-generation Christianity. This expansion built on the desire among Christians for esoteric knowledge and initiatory experiences. Initiatory religions were popular in antiquity. They were known as mystery religions and they involved participation in virtual realities that reenacted the group's myth and took initiates on journeys to the underworld and celestial realms.

2. The fourth-generation Valentinian leaders were teachers who independently operated churches and schools that reflected their own take on Valentinian mythology. No single Valentinian was in charge.

3. While most Valentinian churches ran services that mirrored Apostolic Catholic services, they operated outside the ecclesiastical reach of the Apostolic Catholics. Their services contained both psychic (Apostolic Catholic) and pneumatic (initiated Valentinians) Christians.

4. Ptolemy's *Letter to Flora* reveals the types of concerns facing Apostolic Catholics who were receiving instruction to prepare them for Valentinian initiation. The first part of the catechism was the revelation that the Biblical Creator was not the ultimate God, but that a transcendent God exists beyond him. This raised concerns among the proselytes about the character of the Biblical Creator (was he good or evil?) and the status of the Law (which they had been taught previously to follow).

5. Heracleon was the first Christian to write a commentary on a Christian text, in this case the Gospel of John. Heracleon was reading the Gospel of John to uncover spiritual truths rather than reading it to establish its literal meaning. He read several passages allegorically in order to argue for exemplars of the Valentinian tri-division of humanity into pneumatics, psychics, and hylics.

6. The Valentinians understood their marriages to be sacramental because they mirrored Aeonic syzygies. They limited procreation to pneumatic (initiated) heterosexual monogamous couples for the purpose of conceiving pneumatic children. While these marriages sacralized sex, they also reduced women to incubators of God's children. This not only reinforced the dominant institution of patriarchy, but also gave it holy credentials.

7. Marcus opened a church for the pneumatics and revved up the Eucharist ceremony with a spiked drink. The ceremony brought Grace upon the assembly and selected one congregrant to be the prophet-of-the-day. Women were reputed to have been attracted to Marcus' church and involved in his missionary work. They were known to have opportunities to lead his congregation as prophetesses.

8. Marcus used chanting and silent meditation as cosmic and personal therapy.

9. A number of independent Christian Gnostic churches emerged in the mid-second century. Their mythologies and liturgies were innovative and distinctive, reflecting regional differences and cultural variety.

10. The independent Christian Gnostic churches had in common with the Valentinians the worship of the transcendent God and their reading of the Jewish scriptures in a way that the Biblical Creator is not the hero, but the villain.

11. The independent Christian Gnostic churches were ecstatic groups whose leaders took initiates on astrological soul and spirit journeys through stargates to meet the supreme God in the world beyond ours and achieve Gnosis.

Questions

1. What role did women play in these various Christian groups? Describe the roles. Why did the groups create these roles for women?

2. All these groups had to recruit new members. How did each group go about recruiting? What was different about Valentinian recruitment? Which group do you think would have been most successful with recruitment? Why?

3. How did these groups interpret Jewish and Christian scriptures? Give specific examples. How were they similar interpretations? Where did they differ? What do these similarities and differences suggest to you about the Genesis story, the process of reading, a reader's prior knowledge, a reader's social situation?

4. Did these groups produce scriptures themselves? If so, what types of writings did they produce? What was the content and purpose of the writings? How did they make their writings convincing to others?

5. Was there any advantage for the groups to operate as independent private churches? If so, what was the advantage? Were there any downsides? If so, what were they?

6. For all of these groups sex (the sex act) is about producing children. Explain each group's position on this and how their view impacted the social lives of their members.

Resources

Campbell Bonner. 1949. "An Amulet of the Ophite Gnostics." *Hesperia Supplements* 8: 43–48.

M. David Litwa. 2022. Chapters 8, 15, 16, 17, 22, 25 in *Found Christianities: Remaking the World of the Second Century CE*. London: T&T Clark.

April D. DeConick. 2012. "From the Bowels of Hell to Draco: The Mysteries of the Peratics." Pages 3–38 in *Mystery and Secrecy in the Nag Hammadi Collection and Other Ancient Literature: Ideas and Practices. Studies for Einar Thomassen at Sixty*. Edited by Christian H. Bull, Liv Ingeborg Lied, and John D. Turner. Nag Hammadi and Manichaean Studies Volume 76. Leiden: Brill.

April D. DeConick. 2013. "The Road for the Souls Is through the Planets: The Mysteries of the Ophians Mapped." Pages 37–74 in *Practicing Gnosis: Ritual, Magic, Theurgy and Liturgy in Nag Hammadi, Manichaean and Other Ancient Literature. Essays in Honor of Birger A. Pearson*. Edited by April D. DeConick, Gregory Shaw, and John D. Turner. Nag Hammadi and Manichaean Studies Volume 85. Leiden: Brill.

April D. DeConick. 2016. Chapters 6, 7, and 8 in *The Gnostic New Age: How a Countercultural Spirituality Revolutionized Religion from Antiquity to Today*. New York: Columbia University Press.

Ismo Dunderberg. 2008. "The School of Valentinus." Pages 64–99 in *A Companion to Second-Century Christian 'Heretics'*. Edited by Antti Marjanen and Petri Luomanen. Leiden: Brill.

Peter Lampe. 2003. Chapter 23 and 27 in *From Paul to Valentinus: Christians at Rome in the First Two Centuries*. Translated by Michael Steinhauser and edited by Marshall D. Johnson. Minneapolis: Fortress Press.

Maria Grazia Lancellotti. 2000. *The Naassenes: A Gnostic Identity among Judaism, Christianity, Classical and Ancient near Eastern Traditions*. Forschungen zur Anthropologie und Religionsgeschichte Volume 35. Münster: Ugarit-Verlag.

Tuomas Rasimus. 2009. *Paradise Reconsidered Gnostic Mythmaking: Rethinking Sethianism in Light of the Ophite Evidence*. Nag Hammadi and Manichaean Studies Volume 68. Leiden: Brill.

van den Broek Roelof. 1973. "The Shape of Edem according to Justin the Gnostic." *Vigiliae Christianae* 27: 35–45.

Einar Thomassen. 2010. "Heracleon." Pages 173–210 in *The Legacy of John: Second-Century Reception of the Fourth Gospel*. Edited by Tuomas Rasimus. Supplements to Novum Testamentum Volume 132. Leiden: Brill.

Roelof van den Broek. 2003. "Gospel Tradition and Salvation in Justin the Gnostic." *Vigiliae Christianae* 57: 363–388.

CHAPTER 9

The Construction of Orthodoxy

Fresco depiciting "The Resurrection of the Dead" from the Gospel of Vysehrad. Dated 11th century. Source: Photo 12 / Universal Images Group / Getty Images.

"It is said that God came down from heaven, and from a Hebrew virgin assumed and clothed himself with flesh, and the Son of God lived in a human daughter. This is taught in the gospel, as it is called, which for a short time was preached among them...This Jesus, then, was born of the race of the Hebrews. And he had twelve disciples in order that the purpose of his incarnation might in time be accomplished. But he himself was pierced by the Jews, and he died and was buried. And they say that after three days he rose and ascended to heaven. Thereupon these twelve disciples went forth throughout the known parts of the world, and kept showing his greatness with all modesty and uprightness" (Aris., *Apol.* 2).

Aristides wrote this to Emperor Antoninus Pius in order to explain to him how Christianity originated (Apology 2).

Comparing Christianities: An Introduction to Early Christianity, First Edition. April D. DeConick.
© 2024 John Wiley & Sons Ltd. Published 2024 by John Wiley & Sons Ltd.

KEY PLAYERS

Irenaeus – Hegesippus – Marcus
Aristides – Athenagoras – Theophilius

KEY TEXTS

Gospels of Matthew, Mark, Luke, and
John – Book of Acts
Irenaeus, *Against Heresies*;
Demonstration
1 Clement – Aristides, *Apology*
Theophilus, *To Autolycus*
Tripartite Tractate (NHC I,5)
Athenagoras, *Treatise on*
the Resurrection – Treatise on the
Resurrection (NHC I,4)

As the Gnostic churches expanded, the Marcionite churches multiplied, and the Church of New Prophecy spread, the Apostolic Catholic Christians found themselves in a conundrum. Roman outsiders had a difficult time distinguishing the different movements, thinking that all of them were crazy Christians. How could this confusion be cleared up? How could the Romans be made to understand that the real Christians had a long traditional history, reasonable beliefs, and ethical practices that could be traced back to the apostles? The Apostolic Catholics needed to explain that if there were crazy Christians, it was not them, but those other "so-called" Christians. As writers like Hegesippus and Irenaeus wrote to distinguish genuine Christians from heretics, they not only helped construct Christian heresy (what Christianity is not) but also Christian orthodoxy (what Christianity is).

9.1 Martyrs in Lyons

COMPANION READINGS

Eusebius, *Ecclesiastical History* 5.1–4

In 177 CE, Irenaeus traveled southeast over 600 miles from Lyons, Gaul (modern France) to Rome (Figure 9.1). He carried with him a letter from the newly established churches in Lyons and Vienne, along with letters written and signed by several imprisoned confessors awaiting their executions (Eus., *Eccl. Hist.* 5.3.4). Bishop Pothinus had sent Irenaeus with the letters, commissioning him to be their ambassador. He was sent to communicate to Eleutherus, Bishop of

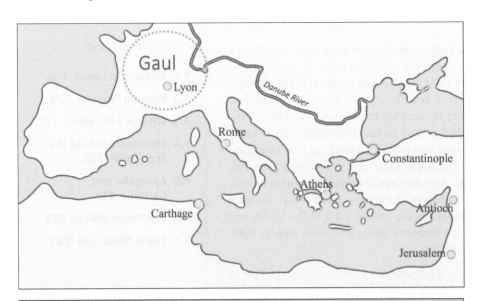

FIGURE 9.1   Map situating Gallic Christianity in relationship to Rome and Asia Minor.

Rome, the Gallic churches' decision about the Church of New Prophecy, hoping to foster peace in the churches. Pothinus also sent copies of these documents to the churches in Asia Minor and Phrygia.

Several prominent Christians in Lyons and Vienne were immigrants from Asia Minor and Phrygia, so there were strong connections between the new Gallic churches and those in Asia Minor (*Mart. Lyon.* 1.3). The new Gallic churches were under Roman jurisdiction, so they may have been started by Asian immigrant churches already established in Rome. Irenaeus himself was from Smyrna, having been a student of Polycarp (Eus., *Eccl. Hist.* 5.20.5–6). He was serving as Pothinus' presbyter, helping organize and run the church in Lyons.

The regional churches in Gaul had just held a meeting to decide what to do about churches which professed that the Trio were real prophets. They had heard that in Phrygia the Trio had been disaffiliated from the the Apostolic Catholic church network after Bishop Apollinarius had called a meeting of the regional bishops and they ruled to kick them out. Should they do the same in Gaul? Eusebius reports that the decision of the Gallic churches aligned with the decision that came out of Apollinarius' meeting since he calls it a "most orthodox judgment." Yet he also reports that the decision reflected their "own prudent" judgment too. While they agreed that the Trio were decidedly false prophets, they also may have felt that this did not mean that prophecy as a whole or the Gospel of John were invalidated as some were arguing (Iren., *Haer.* 3.11.9). Eleutherus and his successor Victor (189–198 CE) agreed and excommunicated the Church of New Prophecy (Tert., *Prax.* 1.5). Bishop Zephyrinus briefly overturned this ruling as we see in Chapter 10.

Once Irenaeus returns to Lyons, he finds the Gallic churches devastated by a pogrom of arrests and executions. Forty-eight Christians were martyred in Lyons while he was gone, Pothinus among them (Eus., *Eccl. Hist.* 5.1–4). He was told how Christians had been beaten and dragged before the city authorities by an enraged mob. The mob, concerned about the rising numbers of Christians in their city, feared the anger of their own Gods as they prepared for the Festival of the Three Gauls which celebrated the Imperial cult. They believed that the executions of the treasonous Christians who refused to participate in the civic religion that upheld the Empire was called for. In the wake of these executions, Irenaeus finds himself elected and installed as the next Bishop of Lyons.

9.2 Wanton Women

COMPANION READINGS
Irenaeus, *Against Heresies* 1.13.3, 5, 7

Apostolic Catholic churches like Irenaeus' were not the only churches in the area. Gaul was a new center for the Christian mission, and the Valentinians were active in the area too. In Chapter 8, we met Marcus, the Valentinian. He and his followers founded and ran several churches for the Pneumatics (Spirituals) in the Rhone Valley (Iren., *Haer.* 1.13.7). They seem to have come onto Irenaeus' radar because he started to notice that several women from his church had been persuaded to attend Marcus' Spiritual Church. Some decidedly stayed in the Spiritual Church and resigned from Irenaeus'. Others returned to Irenaeus' church and gave public confession of their sins in order to be readmitted. These women confessed to being overwhelmed by passion, making it easy for Marcus to seduce them and take them as his lovers. Irenaeus says that Marcus gave the women love potions which made them mad for him. Still other reprobate women wanted nothing to do with public confession. They returned to Irenaeus' church as fence sitters, attending but refusing to confess anything. In Irenaeus' opinion, their refusal meant that they had committed sins so shameful that they were not able to admit them in public. Did it ever cross his mind that these women probably did not feel that they had any sins to confess?

This situation called for an intervention (Iren., *Haer.* 1.13.5). One of Irenaeus' deacons, an immigrant from Asia Minor like Irenaeus, invited Marcus to his house presumably to find out who Marcus was and what he was all about and report back to Irenaeus. But the unexpected happened. The deacon's wife was persuaded by Marcus. She not only abandoned her husband's church, but became so committed to the Spiritual Church that she traveled around with Marcus for an extended period of time most likely on official church business. The men in Irenaeus' church, her husband surely among them, kept arguing with her and cajoling her to leave Marcus' church and return to their own. After a great deal of difficulty, she relented and, like the other women, had to make public confession in order to be fully readmitted. Like the others, Irenaeus says, she admitted to being Marcus' lover.

While it is certainly possible that Marcus had affairs with some women in his church – this type of abusive relationship is a stereotype of new religious movements, where charismatic gurus have been known to become sacred sex partners with the devoted – this may also have been the only way that the men in Irenaeus' church could have imagined why their once-faithful wives had chosen to join another church. In their minds, their women must have become wanton. Their imagination reflected the fact that in the ancient mind, there were only two types of women: the chaste virgin or wife and the wanton woman or prostitute. The domain of the virgin and wife was the domicile. When she went out in public, she was escorted by a member of the household or in the company of her husband. The wanton woman was a public woman who went about unescorted. She was believed to be sexually available. This categorization of women made it easy for Irenaeus to think that the reason for the defection of their good wives must mean that the women were morally weak and had been overpowered by sex-magic.

Yet from Irenaeus' reports it is glaringly apparent that the gender equity and prophetic experience in Marcus' church was attractive to Christian women whose leadership roles in the Apostolic Catholic churches were being severely restricted. If Irenaeus' report is accurate, the women were quite literally flocking to the new Pneumatic churches that were popping up in the valley. This meant that the wives of men who attended the Apostolic Catholic churches began claiming to be pneumatics – spiritually awakened and resurrected – while their husbands remained psychics. This distinction had repercussions in the conjugal bed. Since, according to the Valentinians, pneumatics should only be having "pure" sex with their pneumatic spouses, and psychics were supposed to be chaste, this meant that the husbands would have been abandoned in bed. To make matters worse, the women were wealthy and aristocratic wives who had large dowries that would have been on the line should divorce proceedings be filed, which was starting to happen (Iren., *Haer.* 1.6.2–4; 1.13.3). It is no wonder that the men in the Apostolic Catholic congregations were forceful in their attempts to get their wives back to their own churches, making them publicly confess how sinful they had been and lucky to be forgiven for their sexual trysts.

[9.3] What Is a Heretic?

COMPANION READINGS
Justin, *First Apol.* 26 and 56
Justin, *Dialogue with Trypho* 35
Eusebius, *Ecclesiastical History* 4.22
Irenaeus, *Against Heresies* Pref.; 1.22, 29–31
1 Timothy 6:15–21

The defection to Marcus' Spiritual churches was so bad that Irenaeus decides to get educated in order to deal with Marcus. He needed to learn as much as he could about Marcus in order to take him down. He begins by collecting written materials that Marcus had published. He turns to his Roman contacts and begins to collect materials written by Ptolemy and others who, as we learned in Chapter 8, were Valentinians active in Rome at this time. Among other things, he also finds copies of the *Gospel of Truth*, the *Gospel of Judas*, the Ophite Myth, the Barbeloite Myth, and Justin's *Syntagma against Heresies* (which he calls *Against Marcion*; Iren. *Haer.* 4.6.2). He also has Papias' *Interpretation of the Lord's Sayings* (Iren. *Haer.* 5.33.4), a text he may have brought with him from Asia Minor.

Relying on these sources, Irenaeus tries to sort out the diversity of the Christian movements he knows. He observes that the diversity is so great that the movements are like mushrooms popping up here and there and everywhere. He is not certain where they each came from nor how they might relate to each other, although he has read Justin's *Syntagma*, which suggests that Simon Magus and his movement was the first post-Christian heresy to arise, followed by the Marcionites, Valentinians, Basilidians, Saturnilians, and others (cf. Justin, *1 Apol.* 26, 56; *Dial.* 35). As we learned when we discussed Justin, because these movements all centered on the worship of a supreme deity who is not identified with the God of Abraham, Isaac, and Jacob, Justin said that the demons put these movements in place. The demons did this to divert attention away from the worship of the true God, the Biblical Creator. This trick meant that people would worship the demons instead of the Creator, whom Jesus proclaimed.

Justin clearly plays on the ancient concept of heresy, which meant at the time "school of choice." In other words, heresies were groups or sects that people chose to join. So, for example, while people might be born as Jews and attend their local synagogues, they also might choose to join any number of sectarian Jewish movements like the Essenes, the Pharisees, the Zealots, or the Christians.

This understanding of heresies is evident in *The Memoirs* (Greek: *Hypomnemata*), a five-volume work of early Christian records put together by Hegesippus. This work survives mainly in fragments quoted by the fourth-century Christian, Eusebius. Hegesippus was Irenaeus' contemporary. He traveled around the Mediterranean, collecting information from the regional churches he visited in order to create records for the Roman church of its affiliate churches. He did this by first compiling a list of the succession of Apostolic Catholic bishops in Rome and outlining their teachings about the Law, the Prophets, and the Lord. He considered this to be orthodoxy. He then used this orthodoxy as a measuring stick or canon to judge the orthodoxy of the regional churches he visited. If the regional church's teaching was aligned with Rome's teaching about "the Law, the Prophets, and the Lord," Hegesippus determined that the particular church was orthodox, a determination he made for a congregation at Corinth that he had visited. Then he registered the regional church's succession of their own bishops as part of the Apostolic Catholic network (Eus., *Eccl. Hist.* 4.22.2–3).

"And the church of the Corinthians continued in the orthodox faith up to the time when Primus was bishop in Corinth. I had some dealings with them on my voyage to Rome, when I spent several days with the Corinthians. During my stay, we were mutually refreshed by the orthodox faith. On my arrival at Rome, I drew up a list of the succession of bishops down to Anicetus, whose deacon was Eleutherus. To Anicetus succeeded Soter, and after him came Eleutherus. But in the case of every succession, and in every city, the state of affairs is in accordance with the teaching of the Law and of the Prophets and of the Lord."

Eusebius says that Hegesippus wrote this
in his Commentaries on the Acts of the Church *(trans. DeConick)*

In his travels, Hegesippus ran across many congregations of Christians that did not measure up to this Roman standard. What was he to think about them? Where did they come from? Because their diversity was so great, he reasoned that their origins must be very early within the timetable of the Christian movement. But since he also believed that Roman orthodoxy could be traced back to the apostles, the origin of heresy had to have happened in Jerusalem after James had been martyred and his (and Jesus') cousin Simon (not Peter) had become the second bishop of the Jerusalem church (Eus., *Eccl. Hist.* 4.22.4–7). Hegesippus said that Thebuthis (likely Theudas from Acts 5:36-37) had lost the bishopric to Simon, and thwarted, began teaching ideas he was familiar with from his contact with seven Jewish heresies (Essenes, Galileans, Hemerobaptists, Masbothei, Samaritans, Saducess, and Pharisees).

Here Hegesippus is feeding on the idea that had gained real traction among Gentile Christians by the mid-second century as we saw when we studied Marcion and Ignatius: that Christians should not "Judaize." This idea that Christians should not "Judaize" made it easy for Hegesippus to suggest that multiple heresies were developed by people who listened to Thebuthis' Judaized teachings, including the Simonians (founder: Simon), Cleobians, Dosithians, Goratheni, Masbothei, Menandrians, Marcionists, Carpocratians, Valentinians, Basilidians, and Saturnilians. Hegesippus characterizes these movements as promoting false doctrine "against God and against his Christ," false prophets, false messiahs, and false apostles which were meant to destroy the unity of the church. In other words, the origin of Christian heresy came out of Christian groups that "Judaized."

We are familiar with the association of "Judaizing" with "bad" Christians from previous chapters, including when we learned that this very idea was used by Marcion to suggest that the apostles had "Judaized" the Gospel or by Ignatius, who decided that law-observant Christians in the Asia Minor churches were "Judaizing" heretics. This prevailing idea ultimately derived from Gentiles reading Paul's letters and focusing attention on Paul's criticism of the Law. In Paul's letters, we read that the Gentiles should not be forced to be circumcised, or eat kosher, or observe other regulations of the Jewish Law. Paul argued that the Jewish Law had come to an end with Christ who showed people that the heart of the Law is love and mercy, which take precedence over the rest of the Law. Hegesippus understood Paul to mean that Christians must not allow themselves to be regulated by the Jewish Law, and if they do, they are doing so in error. Ignatius had a similar understanding, as we have already seen in Chapter 4, presenting Judaism as "old sour leaven" and Christians who "Judaize" as heretics. Irenaeus too knows this argument, and, for this reason catalogues the Ebionites (Law-abiding second-century Christians) as heretics (Iren., *Haer.* 1.1.26.2).

Yet Irenaeus does not write about heresy with Hegesippus' agenda. Irenaeus wants to take down Marcus more than anything else and "Judaizing" will not fit the bill. As he settles into his work, he sorts through the texts he has in hand and, in a very academic fashion, compares the mythologies he reads about in these texts against what he can determine about Marcus' mythology. He contextualizes Marcus' mythology as a variation of Valentinian mythology. He identifies the premier exemplar of Valentinian mythology with Ptolemy, and suggests deviations in Ptolemy's mythology come from Marcus' personal revelations.

But where did the Valentinians come from? Irenaeus tries to map out what Valentinus himself taught based on the changes Ptolemy's students said they made to his system. He notices structural similarities when he compares the Valentinian mythology to what he reads in the Barbeloite Myth and the Ophite Myth which features Seth and Ialdabaoth. Based on this analysis, Irenaeus concludes that Valentinus must have based his mythology on the Ophite Myth broadcast by the Gnostics (*Gnostikoi*), and from there a many-headed hydra of Valentinian sects emerged (Iren., *Haer.* 1.11, 30–31).

Irenaeus acknowledges that Valentinian churches are often mistaken for Apostolic Catholic churches because their liturgies and scriptures match what the Apostolic Catholics use. What makes them distinct – and false Christians in Irenaeus' opinion – is the fact that they interpret these liturgies and scriptures in ways that the Biblical Creator God is no longer understood to be the supreme God (Iren., *Haer.* Pref.; 1. 22). It is this difference that Irenaeus uses to contextualize the Valentinians – and specifically Marcus – within the totality of other heresies. On this point, he follows Justin, who had made the argument that heresy arose during the apostolic period beginning with Simon Magus. The demons had used Simon to draw attention away from the apostolic mission and its preaching about the true Creator God. Like Justin, Irenaeus catalogues these Other-God heresies as introduced and spread by Simon, Menander, Saturnilus, Basilides, Carpocrates, Cerinthus, Cerdo, and Marcion (Iren., *Haer.* 1.23–27).

Irenaeus categorizes these groups using theology as the distinguishing criterion, that these groups do not worship the Biblical Creator as God, but another deity. We should keep in mind, however, that there was not a single theology that actually linked these groups. Marcionites worshiped a God from another universe, while Saturnilus, Basilides, Carpocrates, and the Valentinians worshiped a transcendent God who is the source of life for our universe. Simon's God was far-removed from our world and had hermaphrodite traits (which he probably derived from reading Genesis 1:26–27), generating the mother God as his first thought and sending his son as his manifestation to earth to save humankind. Justin, and likely Irenaeus in his wake, believed that the Simonians worshiped Simon and his wife Helen as Father and Mother Gods.

Even though these groups do not share a common theology, they all promoted the worship of a God other than the Biblical Creator. And based on this alone, Irenaeus identifies the groups as inauthentic Christians and assigns them the name "Gnostic," punning on 1 Timothy 6:15–21. Irenaeus does this because he is aware that the Gnostic category was already being used to identify people who claimed to know a transcendent God who was not the Biblical Creator. This is how very different and unrelated systems got lumped together in his catalogue and got mixed up with the Judaizing heresies (i.e. Ebionites) and the extreme lifestyle groups (i.e. Nicolas, Tatian) that Irenaeus also disapproves of.

In Irenaeus' study, it becomes apparent to him that the Other-God theology of the heretics has considerable consequences. It means that the God whom Irenaeus worships is a demon or some subordinate God. This inflames Irenaeus, so he concentrates his energies on assailing it. In his assault, Irenaeus' criteria for the categorization of heretics shifts so that the Other-God theology takes a back seat to his assault on their belief in a separate Creator or Demiurge. In this way, Irenaeus binds the concept of heresy with demiurgy, the idea that a subordinate or lesser being created the universe. With demiurgy came the crime of polytheism, since in the systems studied, the creator Gods were rebellious or ignorant subordinates of a supreme God. When Irenaeus is done, heresy is a category defined by errant demiurgic beliefs and polytheism. And Gnostics – the Valentinians among them – are unmasked as nothing other than pagan polytheists.

Irenaeus' crafting shifts attention away from the fact that the groups he identifies as heretics were actually monotheistic groups who worshipped the transcendent God. While their systems included angels and demons (yhwh was usually envisioned as a fallen or malformed angel), they were not worshipping these as divinities. They would not have considered themselves polytheists, nor would they have defined themselves as polytheists based on the fact that a subordinate demiurge turned up in their mythologies. They defined themselves as transcendentalists who claimed direct experience of the one and only real God, who was the object of their worship.

9.4 Measurements of the True Faith

COMPANION READINGS

Aristides of Athens, *Apology* 2

Irenaeus, *Against Heresies* 1.10, 30.13; 3.4.2; 3.16.6; 3.18.1; 4.38.3; 5.2–3

Irenaeus, *Demonstration of the Apostolic Preaching* 3–7

Athenagoras, *Treatise on the Resurrection* 1–16

Treatise on the Resurrection (NHC I,4) 43.-50.18

Romans 5:12–21

1 Corinthians 15: 20–23, 45–49

Irenaeus' construction of heresy provides him with a backdrop to continue to develop the parameters and define the boundaries of Apostolic Catholicism around a statement of faith called the Canon of Truth (a.k.a. Rule of Faith). Aristides of Athens, who likely wrote to try to convert Emperor Antoninus Pius (138–161 CE), may be the earliest author to encapsulate the Canon of Truth in full. Aristides defines Christians as a new race that differs from the three other races (the Barbarians, the Greeks, and the Jews). This is based on Aristides' understanding that Christians trace "the beginning of their religion from Jesus the Messiah, and he is named the Son of God Most High. And it is said that God came down from heaven, and from a Hebrew virgin assumed and clothed himself with flesh, and the Son of God lived in a daughter of man. This is taught in the gospel, as it is called, which a short time was preached among them... This Jesus, then, was born of the race of the Hebrews. And he had twelve disciples in order that the purpose of his incarnation might in time be accomplished. But he himself was pierced by the Jews, and he died and was buried. And they say that after three days he rose and ascended to heaven. Thereupon these twelve disciples went forth throughout the known parts of the world, and kept showing his greatness with all modesty and uprightness" (Aris., *Apol.* 2).

In this early canon, Aristides emphasizes that Jesus and his disciples were Hebrews. Aristides goes on to establish that the Christian race is connected to the Jews because both races worship the same God. Compared with the Barbarian race and the Greek race, Aristides says that the Jews had come close to finding real knowledge because they exclusively worship the Creator God and received his commandments. However, he says, they actually do not worship God correctly when they celebrate the sabbaths and festivals, fast, circumcise, and eat kosher meat. It is not God they actually serve with these behaviors, but the angels. In contrast, he says, the Christians are known by their morality, based on the fact that they actually follow the Ten Commandments (i.e. abstain from idolatry; do not commit adultery; do not bear false witness; do not covet; etc.) and direct their worship exclusively toward the Creator in a manner that does not involve the Jewish ceremonial laws.

With Ignatius and Polycarp, we saw how the Apostolic Catholic network of churches promoted the Canon of Truth to standardize Christian identity and mark Marcionites as deviants. Verbatim wording was not yet institutionalized, although stock phrases were common in their statements, phrases that could be fine-tuned to deal with the continuing rise of competing Christian teachers and leaders. Verbatim wording did not matter as much as a set of essential ideas set forth in the statement. The statement came to be used by the Apostolic Catholics as a canon or ruler to measure the authenticity of different Christ movements. It was used as an Apostolic Catholic litmus test, taught to converts, and probably recited at baptism.

As we learned in Chapter 4, the Canon of Truth published by Ignatius and Polycarp (cf. Ign., *Trall.* 9; *Eph.* 18; 20; *Smy.* 1–3; Poly., *Phil.* 2) referenced the belief in Jesus Christ as David's descendent, born of Mary. Jesus had been persecuted, suffered, and crucified under Pontius Pilate. Jesus had been resurrected from the dead. In the same way, the faithful will also be raised. This statement was created out of Romans 1:1–6, which mentioned that Jesus was born "according to the flesh." This phrase was interpolated by Ignatius in order to combat Marcion's angelic Jesus.

Justin refers to the same Canon of Truth several times in his writing (Justin, *1 Apol.* 13; 21.1; 31.7; 42.4; 46.5; 61.3; *Dial.* 63.1, 85.2, 126.1, 132.1). In his version, Jesus Christ was the descendent of Jacob and Judah, conceived virginally and born a human being. He was crucified, died, and resurrected. He ascended into heaven. Justin expands these statements to include also the teaching that is most near-and-dear to him – that Jesus Christ as the Logos is the first born of God – an expansion dependent upon John 1:1–2. He also acknowledges God as the Father and Lord of the universe, a reference to 1 Corinthians 8:6 (Just., *1 Apol.* 61.3).

Irenaeus' version emphasizes this core (Iren., *Haer.* 1.10; 3.4.2; 3.16.6; *Demo.* 3–7). His version is the first time we see the Canon of Truth presented in a full creedal format as a complete statement of the "true" faith. Irenaeus' version begins with the acknowledgment, lifted from 1 Corinthians 8:6, that there is only one supreme God and he is the creator of the heaven and the earth and all its creatures, including humans. His language is quite different from Justin's. The reason for this is obvious. Since Irenaeus used demiurgy and polytheism as a way to define heresy, Irenaeus expands the creedal tradition of his church network to distinguish it from the Valentinian network and any other Christian movement that Irenaeus defines as heretical. He makes it clear that the true Christian worships the Biblical Creator as the one-and-only God.

Irenaeus' version also makes it clear that Jesus was resurrected and ascended into heaven, not as a spirit, but in the flesh. The future resurrection of human beings will be the same: their fleshly bodies will be raised up. Again, the reason for this emphasis is obvious since it works to distinguish Irenaeus' church network from the Valentinian network, which was all about saving the pneumatic or spiritual people using rituals that prefigured the after-death ascension of the soul into the heavens when it left the flesh behind. According to the Valentinian faith, at the end of time, the immortal spirit would strip off even the mortal trappings of the soul and ascend into the Pleroma.

The belief in the resurrection of the dead was an idea that Christians had in common with most Jews, although there was no established teaching about what this would look like. The idea originated during the Maccabean Revolt when Jews were being tortured to death by the Greek colonizers for circumcising their children and observing the rules of Torah. The belief arose that, at the end of time, God would raise up the righteous people – those who had suffered and died for the faith – in order to reward them for their faithfulness (i.e. Dan. 12:1–3).

Beyond this core belief, among the Christians there were many questions about how this would all work out. Would the physical bodies of the faithful come up out of the graves and walk around

(Matt. 27:52–53)? Or would the faithful be given some kind of angelic heavenly bodies (1 Cor. 15:42–54)? Would their resurrected bodies be tangible (Luke 24:36–39; John 20:27)? Would they be able to walk through closed doors (John 20:26)? Would they be able to eat (Luke 24:41–52)? Or should the phrase be read resurrection *from* the body instead of resurrection *of* the body (as an ablative instead of a genitive)? In this case, would the soul leave the body and be immortalized on its ascent to heaven (Iren., *Haer.* 1.30.13)?

Irenaeus was a big believer in the resurrection *of* the flesh. But not everyone was, as Athenagoras of Athens makes abundantly clear in his treatise on the subject (ca. 177 CE). Many Christians objected to the idea that bodies that had decomposed completely in the grave would be brought out of the grave as persons (Athen., *Res.* 2). They seem to have envisioned it as some kind of zombie apocalypse, considering it gross and absurd. They thought it unreasonable that the dead person would remain in the grave until the end of time and the final judgment, when they would be raised to immortality. "What happened in the meantime?" they asked. In their minds, the body decayed and the soul went on into the heavens and was immortalized. A doctrine that kept them in their graves until the end of the world was untenable in their opinion and went against everything they knew about the soul from popular Platonic philosophy (Athen., *Res.* 16).

Athenagoras argues that what God created once, he can and will create again (Athen., *Res.* 3). Even for those deprived of proper burial – when animals or fish had eaten them and digested their bodies – it is possible for God the Creator to restore them particle by particle (Athen., *Res.* 4). Athenagoras claims that resurrection is a proven fact because it fulfils God's original purpose to create the human being to be immortal, a composite of soul and body (Athen., *Res.* 13–15). As for the soul of the deceased, Athenagoras claims that it will exist in a sleep state until the day the graves are opened and everyone is resurrected (Athen., *Res.* 16).

The Valentinian *Letter to Rheginos* (a.k.a. *Treatise on the Resurrection*) about the resurrection also mentions that not all Christians agreed when it came to the topic of resurrection (*Treat. Res.* 43.9–10). In this letter, we see the opinion expressed that so angered Athenagoras and Irenaeus. The author confirms with Rheginos that Jesus was both divine and flesh, but that his death conquered the perishable world and transformed him into an immortal being. Jesus' death provided humans with the way to their own immortality as Paul said, "We suffered with him, and we arose with him, and we went to heaven with him." This means, according to the author, that the spirits of the deceased are drawn up to heaven like the beams of the sun, when both mortal flesh and soul are discarded (*Treat. Res.* 45.15–46.2). This is how the dead are raised (*Treat. Res.* 46.8–9). The transformed bodies that rise from the grave resemble the luminous bodies of Elijah and Moses who appeared to Jesus in the Gospel (*Treat. Res.* 48.4–20; Mark 9:2–8). The fleshy body stays in the grave, while the living members of the body rise like sun rays immediately upon death. There is no delay (*Treat. Res.* 47.31–48.3). Rheginos is told the good news that if he lives so that he does not conform to the flesh, he has already experienced the resurrection (*Treat. Res.* 49.10–16).

For Irenaeus, this type of thinking is nonsense. The resurrection of the body meant the resurrection of the flesh. It was nothing less than the restoration of the human body to its primal condition. This primal body was Adam's mortal body, which, Irenaeus pointed out, had been created in God's glorious image and likeness from the dust of the earth, animated by the psyche or soul, and given life by the breath of God's Spirit. God created Adam as a child who would look and act like his father. Adam was supposed to grow up under the guidance of God so that as an adult he would resemble the Creator as closely as a mortal creature could and eventually be gifted immortality (Iren., *Haer.* 4.38.3). This growth was interrupted, however, when Adam wielded his free will as a disobedient child. Once Adam became tainted with sin, the glory of the primal body of flesh and blood lost its shine. This loss was universal.

The incarnation of Jesus Christ was the remedy to this situation. Just as Adam had universally lost the glory of the primal body, Jesus Christ's incarnation universally restored the body's original state. Irenaeus believed that the whole of human reality was contained in Christ, so when Christ incarnated, humanity got a new start. His incarnation literally jumpstarted humanity's growth. The image and likeness that was lost with Adam now could be recovered in Jesus Christ (Iren., *Haer.* 3.18.1, 7). Irenaeus famously quips, "He became what we are in order to enable us to become what he is" (Iren., *Haer.*, 5.pref.). He calls this idea recapitulation, a term he picks up from Ephesians 1:10, which says that God's plan for redemption includes the "gathering in" of all things in Christ.

How exactly did this work? Building on Paul's comments in Romans (5:12–21) and 1 Corinthians (15: 20–23, 45–49), Irenaeus presents Jesus as a second Adam who had to fix what Adam had screwed up, by being obedient to God even unto death. Just as Adam's action affected all his descendants, so Christ's actions affected the whole human race going all the way back to Adam (Iren., *Haer.* 3.22.3; cf. Luke 3:23–38). Like Adam was generated from the virgin earth, so Jesus Christ was born of the Virgin (Iren., *Haer.* 3.21.10). Christ resisted the temptations of the Devil so that Adam's original temptation could be redone (Iren., *Haer.* 5.21.2–3). Jesus obediently went through all the stages of life, even death on the tree (Iren., *Haer.* 3.18.1; 2.22.4). Irenaeus sees a parallel between the disobedience of Adam at the tree in the garden which brought death and Jesus' obedience to be crucified on the tree of the cross which brought life. Through Jesus' obedience, the fall is reversed and humanity is restored to its original state. This means that humans can once again grow into the beautiful creatures that God had originally intended, that they would be like Gods.

While this is all well and good, it was obvious that humans were still mortal and that sins were still being committed. To remedy sin, Irenaeus emphasizes that Jesus' death – specifically his blood – served as a sacrificial appeasement to God for the sins of humankind initiated by Adam (*Haer.* 3.16.9; 4.5.4; 5.17.1). People benefit when they join the body of Christ and are gifted with his immortal Spirit in baptism. Their sins are forgiven and their resurrection as immortals is guaranteed. This transformation is aided by the Eucharist. The argument here is that we are what we eat. By ingesting the body and blood of the immortal Christ in the Eucharist meal, the body of the converts are being gradually immortalized according to Irenaeus (Iren., *Haer.* 5.2.3).

Irenaeus uses his version of the Canon of Truth to distinguish the Apostolic Catholic church's teachings from the Valentinians, but also from the Marcionites and other Christian movements he considers deviant because they either degrade the Biblical Creator or "Judaize." He appends to the core canon the consequences of failing to heed the Canon of Truth. The heretics will be prosecuted at the last judgment as ungodly, unrighteous, wicked, and secular. Their fate is to be tortured in everlasting fire, while those faithful to the canon will be conferred immortality and bask in everlasting glory (Iren., *Haer.* 1.10.1).

[9.5] Apostolic and Catholic

COMPANION READINGS
Justin, *1 Apology* 49–50
Irenaeus, *Against Heresies* 3.1–5, 11; 4.26.2–5
1 Clement

Irenaeus promotes this Canon of Truth as traditional, as a set of teachings and practices that faithfully represents the teachings of Jesus and the teachings about him. In fact, the network of churches in which Irenaeus participates taught that they preserved the authentic Christian tradition which was based on what the prophets had foretold about Jesus' mission and what the apostles had learned from Jesus. This two-fold appeal to the prophets (Jewish scriptures) and the apostles (gospels or memoirs) was standard fare in the literature of the Apostolic Catholics. Polycarp's directive to the Philippians to accept as standard the teaching of "the apostles who preached the gospel to us and the prophets who announced out Lord's coming in advance" is illustrative (Poly., *Phil.* 6.3). It was common among these Christians to claim that their interpretation of the prophets and the gospels was actually the faithful transmission of the truth from the apostles to their churches (cf. Clem. 42; Just., *1 Apol.* 49–50).

As we saw in Chapter 4, Hermas considered the apostles to be the superstars of his church. He claims that the bishops, presbyters, and deacons of his church have always been in agreement with each other and have always taught what the apostles had taught (Herm., *Sim.* 8.18, 25). As we learned in the same chapter, Ignatius considered the teachings of the bishops in his Asian and west Syrian church networks to be apostolic. He claimed that the teachings of the bishops came from the apostles through an established chain of transmission (Ign., *Trall.* Intro.; Poly., *Phil.* 6). He used this idea to authorize the teachings within the Asian network by arguing that the transmission of teachings from apostle to bishop had resulted in consistent teachings that reflected faithfully the golden age of Jesus' teaching to his appointees. Ignatius leveraged this idea to the advantage of the local bishops because Ignatius thought that the bishops rather than the presbyters should be the sole authorities in their congregations (Ign., *Smy.* 8). These apostolic teachings were not only about the doctrinal elements expressed in the Canon of Truth. Justin traces the practice and explanation for baptism and the Eucharist to the apostles too (Just., *1 Apol.* 61.9; 66.1–3).

When Irenaeus wrote, he elevates the apostolic tradition above the prophetic as the supreme authority (Iren., *Haer.* 3.2.1–2). He does this to combat the Valentinians and others he believed to be heretics because these groups, he says, appeal to a secret tradition as their authority, rather than the Jewish scriptures or the apostles' writings. They do this because they think that the Jewish scriptures contain a mixture of messages that has to be sorted. What came from the Demiurge? What from the true God? What from human hands? As for the apostles, when writing, they added erroneous materials about the Law that sullied Jesus' teachings. For these reasons, these groups do not rely on scriptures to authorize their teachings, but a tradition of hidden wisdom that they claim has been transmitted to them via revelation. They believe that this secret tradition reveals to them the unadulterated truth which the presbyters and the apostles had adulterated.

To counter this, Irenaeus doubles down on the idea that his church's tradition originates with the apostles and that its authenticity and truthfulness has been safeguarded and preserved by an orderly succession of presbyters in his church network (Iren., *Haer.* 3.2.1–2). The authenticity of the apostles' teaching is credited to the Pentecost experience (rather than Jesus' public ministry or his post-resurrection teaching), when the apostles were filled with the Holy Spirit. Irenaeus says that in this moment they received all of the Spirit's gifts, including perfect knowledge.

After receiving perfect knowledge, the apostles went out and preached the universal gospel of God, which they also recorded in written documents, specifically, the Gospels of Matthew, Mark, Luke, and John. For the first time in Christian history, we learn the names of the four gospels that will later become canonized in the Catholic New Testament. The idea that there are four authentic Gospels (rather than one) is an idea that Irenaeus formulates. Prior to this, Marcion talked about one gospel, the *Evangelion*, which was supposed to represent the gospel that Jesus revealed to Paul. Justin and Tatian knew about multiple written gospels which they understood to be memoirs of the apostles. To compete with Marcion, they worked on crafting a gospel harmony, that is one complete gospel created from multiple written gospels. This could be viewed as more authentic because it contained all the information that was known about Jesus in one story. Irenaeus takes another approach, disliking Tatian's *Diatessaron* project enough to include him in his heresiological catalog. Irenaeus wants to market Apostolic Catholicism as old and traditional, so he does not want to rely on a newly composed gospel harmony. To combat Marcion, he decides to take the four gospels he knows and argue that they are older than Marcion's *Evangelion* or Tatian's *Diatessaron* because they are written by the apostles themselves. He does not edit them, but allows them to stand with their differences as old testimonies, believing that four testimonies are better than one.

Irenaeus authorizes these four gospels as legitimate repositories of the perfect apostolic knowledge by giving them apostolic lineages and arguing that four gospels are necessary to be able to preach to the whole world, which has four zones and four winds (Iren., *Haer.* 3.1.1; 3.11.8). For Matthew and Mark, he relies on Papias' testimony, although Irenaeus specifically calls the texts gospels, while Papias does not. Irenaeus says that while Peter and Paul preached in Rome, Matthew wrote a Gospel in Aramaic for

Jewish converts. Irenaeus understands this to be the writing we know today as the (Greek!) Gospel of Matthew probably because this text reads as a Maximalist text supporting the Jewish Law as taught by Jesus and aligning prophetic passages with events in Jesus' life. Mark, Irenaeus says, was a student of Peter. He wrote down what Peter preached. Irenaeus identifies this with the gospel we call today the Gospel of Mark (even though this text does not contain any preaching of Peter). According to Irenaeus, Luke was Paul's companion and his gospel represents Paul's preaching. He links Luke's authorship to the text we call the Gospel of Luke. About the text we know as the Gospel of John, Irenaeus associates it with John the son of Zebedee. According to Irenaeus, John lived in Ephesus and it was there that he published his gospel. The apostles are presented as disciples of truth, incapable of teaching falsehoods or even adapting the truth to different audiences (Iren., *Haer.* 3.5.1).

While this apostolic knowledge was embedded in the gospels, it could be (and was) communicated independently from written documents (Iren., *Haer.* 3.4.1–2). The apostolic tradition Irenaeus has in mind is the Canon of Truth, the belief in one God who created heaven and earth and everything in them, Jesus Christ born a virgin, suffered under Pilate, was resurrected, and will judge the saved and damned (Iren., *Haer.* 3.4.2). This ought to be used as the benchmark for any interpretation made of the Jewish scriptures or the Christian writings. At the same time, the Canon of Truth revealed how "off" the scriptural interpretations of other Christian movements were (Iren., *Haer.* 2.27.2).

According to Irenaeus, this apostolic tradition remains constant across the individual churches in his network, no matter the differences between them in language or culture (Iren., *Haer.* 1.10.2). The churches in his network (he cites churches in Germany, Spain, Gaul, East, Egypt, Libya, and around the Mediterranean) possess the same tradition, he says. He compares this to the sun shining on everyone in the world in the same manner. This continuity is guaranteed, he says, through a strict line of succession from one bishop to the next in the Roman see (Iren., *Haer.* 3.3.3). In Irenaeus' record (which was based on Hegesippus' list), the lineage starts with the apostles who make Linus (1 Timothy 4:21) the first bishop of Rome. Following him is Anacletus, then Clement, who Irenaeus thinks also authored a letter to the Corinthians. Irenaeus references Clement's letter as the earliest exemplar of the apostolic tradition.

Irenaeus and Hegesippus are the first to mention a letter of Clement to the Corinthians. Hegesippus thought it was written during the reign of Domitian (81–96 CE; Eus., *Eccl. Hist..* 3.16; 4.22.1). Irenaeus says that Clement was the first to write about the tenets of the apostolic tradition, proclaiming the one God, omnipotent, Creator of heaven and earth and humans. He is the God who brought the flood, called Abraham, led the people out of Egypt, spoke to Moses, gave the Law, sent the prophets, prepares the punishments for the Devil and his ministers. According to Irenaeus, Clement's letter shows how Jesus' Father was preached by the churches at an early time.

The letter that both men refer to is known today as *1 Clement*. The body of the letter itself does not mention Clement as the author. The linkage of the letter with Clement of Rome only comes with Hegesippus and Irenaeus, so it is not clear when the letter was actually written or who actually wrote it. Likely, it was authored by someone among the third-generation Christians when they were developing ecclesiastical structures and procedures for installing bishops.

The Christians who carried the letter from Rome to Corinth are mentioned in the letter: Claudis Ephebus, Valerius Bito, and Fortunatus. The concrete circumstances of the letter center around a hostile takeover of the Corinthian leadership by the youth who replaced the established bishop and the church elders (presbyters). While the precise reasons for the takeover are not explicitly discussed, the dynamics of the issues can be pieced together from the advice the letter gives to squash the takeover.

We learn from the letter that women and their children were involved. The women and youth of the congregation were in disagreement with the male elders, which meant that not only was the congregation disrupted but also their families and the running of their households. Some women were starting to ask for divorce (*1 Clem.* 1; 6; 11–12; 21; 55).

What had led to this discontent? The women and youth were challenging the interpretation of Jewish scriptures that their elders had established and the lifestyle rules that they were imposing based on their reading of the Jewish law. The women and youth were pointing out passages where God acted unjustly, when, for instance, faithful people were put into terrible situations by God. They drew attention to Daniel who was cast into the lions' den; Ananais, Azarias, and Misheal, who were thrown into a fiery furnace; and Job, who had to endure horrible things that God let happen (*1 Clem.* 17; 45). They pointed out that the God of Abraham demanded circumcision, that God wanted Isaac to sacrifice his own son to him, and that Jacob tricked his father Isaac, his brother Esau, and his uncle Laban in order to receive an inheritance that was not rightfully his (*1 Clem.* 31). They worried for all the Egyptians whom God had killed with plagues (*1 Clem.* 17). What kind of God would do that, they asked? The Creator God had some flaws. Perhaps he was not the supreme omnipotent God after all. Might there be another God that deserved their worship (*1 Clem.* 33; 35; 46)?

The discontents, however, had not given up on the Jewish scriptures completely like Marcion did. Instead, like the Valentinians, they surmised that the scriptures contained fake or forged passages that needed to be distinguished from the true ones (*1 Clem.* 45). As Minimalists, they were highly critical of the Jewish Law, believing that they were not bound to heed its ordinances (*1 Clem.* 3; 20; 37; 40; 43; 49–50). They questioned Moses' authority and the prophets, whom they said were mere goatherders (*1 Clem.* 17; 43). They were not so sure about the doctrine of the resurrection of the dead, whether a future resurrection of the body from the grave really made sense (*1 Clem.* 24).

These disagreements led the women and youth to believe that the bishop and the elders were not good stewards of the truth. In their opinion, the elders were promoting false teachings. They demanded a congregational election, which went in their favor. By doing this, they challenged the legitimacy of the previous appointment of the bishop and presbyters. In their congregation, the previous appointment did not involve an election by the congregation. Instead, when a bishop or presbyter died, the elders – the preeminent men – appointed the next in line. The elders claimed that this process was legitimate because it allowed for a succession of leaders that could be traced back to the apostles. This, they said, meant that Jesus Christ endorsed them (*1 Clem.* 49).

The ousted leaders of this particular congregation considered themselves part of the emergent Apostolic Catholic network because they appealed to the Roman bishop for help. When news of the removal of the bishop and the board of elders reached Rome, the Roman church responded with a strong letter to persuade the church to rejoin the network. The advice provides us with insight into the beginnings of the Apostolic Catholic tradition. The author of the letter argues that the Biblical Creator God is the authentic God of worship (*1 Clem.* 14; 19–20; 33; 35; 38). The author justifies the genuineness of the prophets based on the fact that they foretold the advent of Christ (*1 Clem.* 32). Abraham is presented as an honorable "friend of God," while Job as "God-fearing," and Moses as "faithful in all God's house" (*1 Clem.* 32). The commandments are upheld as "holy" and presented as a sacred moral code that Christians are required to observe. The author links Peter and Paul, considering both to be apostolic authorities. He references 1 Corinthians and Romans, using Paul's admonitions against the Corinthian factionalism to chide them to return to the body of Christ (*1 Clem.* 47; 32; 35). With reference to the book of Hebrews, Jesus is portrayed as a High Priest who intervenes on our behalf (*1 Clem.* 36). The author preserves fragments of Roman liturgies that include references to Jesus Christ, his incarnation in flesh, and his sacrificial death (*1 Clem.* 7; 21; 49; 58). The author admonishes them to confess as the church did in Rome, "Jesus Christ our Lord gave his blood for us by the will of God. His flesh for our flesh. His soul for our souls" (*1 Clem.* 49).

The author assures the congregation that the previous bishop and elders had been appointed properly using a method that he traces back to Jesus. Jesus, he says, appointed the apostles and then the Holy Spirit who filled the apostles before they went out and preached. These spirit-filled apostles appointed the first bishops and deacons after testing that the Spirit had also filled them. The author claims that this way of appointment is approved by God and has been established since antiquity (*1 Clem.* 42, with reference to Isa. 60:17 LXX). He says that the apostles gave instructions to their appointees, that when the appointees should die, other men would need to be "approved" by those appointees still alive. These approved men would be installed as their successors. This is the same process that Ignatius refers to in his letter to Polycarp (Ign., *Poly.* 7).

In the end, the Roman congregation chides the Corinthian congregation to void the improper election, reinstall the old bishop and presbyters, and obey their appointed leaders from this point out. We do not know if the Corinthian church did so, or if this church in Corinth split so that the original elders met with those Christians who were persuaded by the Roman congregation while the challengers met with those who sided with their perspective. Given the fact that the challengers had already installed themselves and had the majority of the congregation on their side, it is likely that the church splintered in Corinth. Decades later when Hegesippus visited Corinth, he claims to have found a church there that was aligned with Rome's teaching about the Law and the Prophets. So at least that faction survived as a church in Corinth. That said, this does not mean that the other faction did not make it in Corinth too.

The letter's contents reflect the consolidation of Apostolic Catholicism and the respect for the opinion of the Roman bishop that we see occurring in Anicetus' reign (154–167 CE) when Polycarp traveled to Rome to sort out with Anicetus the date of Easter. So, it is possible that the letter was penned by Anicetus. Pius (140–154 CE) is another possibility since he was actively consolidating the Roman see by kicking out Marcion. Did he also assert his authority over other churches in the Catholic network by cracking down on dissonant Christians abroad? In any case, *1 Clement* was written by a Roman bishop who was attempting to intervene in the Corinthian Christians' affairs on behalf of Claudis Ephebus, Valerius Bito, and Fortunatus who traveled to Rome requesting the Bishop's help.

Irenaeus, however, follows Hegesippus' lead. Irenaeus is satisfied that the author of this letter was Clement, the Bishop of Rome, because it supports his argument that the apostolic tradition was earlier than the Valentinian tradition (i.e. Clement was bishop of Rome before Valentinus arose to eminence). Irenaeus says that Clement is succeeded in office by Evaristus, Alexander, Sixtus, Telephorus, Hygius, Pius, Anicetus, Soter, and finally Eleutherius. While the bishops in Rome have safeguarded the tradition, Irenaeus claims, bishops in other locations were also beacons of the tradition, transmitting the same teachings that Rome had preserved. Irenaeus mentions specifically Polycarp who, according to Irenaeus, had a connection to the apostles through his many conversations with those who had seen Christ. He had been appointed Bishop of Smyrna by these very same apostolic people. Polycarp always taught faithfully the same apostolic tradition as Rome, as did many of the Asiatic churches. Like Hegesippus, Irenaeus is using the teachings of the Roman bishops as the standard to measure the orthodoxy of other churches. There appear to have been a number of churches in Asia that met this standard and were included in this Roman network.

Against competing Christian movements, Irenaeus weaponizes the idea that this network of bishops possesses the truth from the apostles. He argues that any Christian who does not obey the bishops or who affiliates with a group outside the Roman succession of bishops is a heretic who has fallen away from the truth. The disobedient heretics will all end up in hell (Iren., *Haer.* 4.26.2–5). In this, Irenaeus is not all that far removed from Ignatius, who, we learned in Chapter 5, taught similarly about the authority of the bishops and fate of the heretics, although how much power Ignatius thought that the Roman church exercised is debatable (cf. Ign., *Rom.* Inscr.).

Irenaeus is authorizing the teachings and practices of his church network with reference to the apostolic tradition. For him, this not only refers to the teachings of the twelve apostles, but also the transmission of their teachings through a line of bishops recognized by some Roman churches. This teaching is encapsulated in the Canon of Truth as presented by Irenaeus and others before him. This canon was linked to the baptismal and eucharist liturgies (Iren., *Haer.* 4.18.4–5; 4.32.1). Like Ignatius, Irenaeus understands this Canon of Truth to be catholic or universal (Iren., *Haer.* 1.10.3), that is one-and-the-same in all the churches in the network from Germany to Egypt, from Rome to Syria (Iren., *Haer.* 1.9.4; 1.10.1–2; 1.22.1).

9.6 The Proof of Acts

COMPANION READINGS
Irenaeus, *Against Heresies* 3.12–14
Acts 1–4, 7–8
Luke 1:1–4

While the Montanists certainly referenced the book of Acts to link their prophets into the lineage of the prophets mentioned in Acts, Irenaeus is the first author to make extensive use of the written book of Acts. This is all the more interesting because he uses its stories and speeches to bolster the apostolic tradition and the Canon of Truth against belief in a supreme God beyond the Biblical Creator. He singles out Marcion and Valentinus as promoters of this belief. He also promises to take on Marcion more fully in a future volume, but that work never made it off his desk (Iren., *Haer.* 3.12.12). Even so, we can make out the broad outline of the arguments he planned to direct against Marcion. The book of Acts played prominently in this plan.

Irenaeus launches his argument by insisting that the Holy Spirit had descended on the apostles and made them God's prophets and spokesmen of the truth. This God is the same God as the Biblical God who promised to send his Spirit on the whole human race in the last days (Iren., *Haer.* 3.12.1; Acts 2:22–27). The speeches of Peter, Philip, and Stephen in Acts, he says, reference the God of Abraham, Isaac, and Jacob as Jesus' Father, that the God they preach is the Lawgiver and inspired the Prophets to foretell Jesus' advent (Iren., *Haer.* 3.12.2–8, 10; Acts 2, 7, 8:26–40).

Irenaeus thinks that there was an original church of the apostles, an idea evident in Acts. He sees Marcion and Valentinus as latecomers who subverted the apostolic truth (Iren., *Haer.* 3.12.5). He insists that every church across the world, which the apostles established, must reflect the teachings of the original church, that the Jewish God is one-and-the-same as the Christian God. Irenaeus authorizes this apostolic message as "truly perfect" because the apostles had been "perfected by the Spirit" at Pentecost (Iren., *Haer.* 3.12.5).

What is interesting here is the fact that Irenaeus has to make this argument. The "perfection" of the apostles was not universally attested among early Christians, as even the Gospel of Mark suggests with its digs about the ignorance and faithlessness of the disciples. Various groups, including the Marcionites, promoted the idea that the disciples misunderstood Jesus and preached the Jewish God erroneously after Jesus' death (Iren., *Haer.* 3.12.6, 12). Instead, Marcionites said that Paul was the only authentic apostle, chosen to receive the gospel directly from Jesus via revelation. And this gospel disclosed that Jesus' Father was not the Jewish God, but an unknown God who was not responsible for the creation of our universe. They thought that Paul's letter to the Galatians, in particular, showed how Paul was in dispute with the apostles over their insistence to "Judaize" the non-Jewish converts.

It was difficult to argue against this read of Galatians without the account in the book of Acts, where Paul and Peter are in agreement throughout, teaching a unified message to both Jews and Gentiles. The presentation of Paul in Acts is domesticated, so that Paul and Peter preach the same message to the same groups of people, a picture that reflects the sentiment expressed in *1 Clement*, that Peter and Paul were illustrious pillars of the church who preached the same faith to the whole world (*1 Clem.* 5). To this end, Irenaeus quotes at length the famous speech in Acts where Paul proclaims that God is the Creator and Lord of the heavens and the earth and everything in it (Acts 17:22–32).

Irenaeus loves this and sees it as absolute confirmation of his position. He believes that Acts is a very old book. Yet he never stops to wonder why Marcion (or any other Christian before Irenaeus and the Montanists) does not mention Acts, either to draw support from it or to disagree with it. What Christians prior to fourth-generation Christians knew about Paul came only from his letters, first the ten letters and later the thirteen letters with the composition of 1 and 2 Timothy and Titus (ca. 135–140).

The Paul of Acts does not come into the debate until he pops up in Irenaeus' writing (ca. 182 CE). The Paul of Acts, in fact, looks different from the Paul that Christians knew from his letters. Paul's message that Gentiles are justified by their faith is absent. Instead, his message is aligned with Peter's mission to the Jews and reflects the basic outline used by Apostolic Christians that the scriptures were proof-texts for their Canon of Truth, that Jesus was crucified and resurrected from the dead as foretold by the prophets (cp. Acts 2 and Acts 13). The details about the Jerusalem Council appear very differently (cp. Acts 15:1–35 and Gal. 2:1–10). If nothing else, it is clear that whoever authored Acts felt compelled to erase the conflict and differences between Paul and Peter so that Paul and Peter were on the same page.

Even though Irenaeus is aware of the discrepancies between Paul's letters and Acts, he promotes the idea that Paul's letters are identical with the story of Paul presented in Acts (Iren., *Haer.* 3.13.3). To give this suggestion authority, Irenaeus tells us that Acts was written by the author of the same Gospel that Marcion had shortened (Iren., *Haer.* 3.12.12; 3.14.1–3). The author was none other than Luke, a physician and Paul's companion (Iren., *Haer.* 3.14.1). This is the first time we hear this story. No one prior to Irenaeus mentions a gospel written by Luke, nor that the author of this gospel was Paul's companion.

It is quite likely that Irenaeus puzzled out this authorship himself (Iren., *Haer.* 3.14.1) by comparing the sections in Acts where the first-person "we" occurs, so that it seems that the author of Acts journeyed with Paul from Troas to Philippi (Acts 16:10–17), from Philippi to Troas (Acts 20:5–15), from Miletus to Jersualem (Acts 21:1.18), and from Caesarea to Rome (Acts 27:1–28:16). Who could this have been? Irenaeus wondered. Looking back at Paul's letters, Irenaeus found his answer. There he read how Paul complimented Luke as the only companion who remained always with him, while Demas, Crescens, and Titus had taken their leave to journey elsewhere (1 Tim. 10–11). This association was cinched when Irenaeus noted that Paul also called Luke his "beloved" physician (Col. 4:14). Irenaeus must have been so delighted to have thought that he cracked the code and discovered the author of Acts and its companion book, the third Gospel. For him, this was a double whammy to Marcion, that the Gospel Marcion used (Irenaeus thought this was a shortened version of the Gospel of Luke) was actually written by the same person who wrote the Acts of the Apostles. In Acts, Luke knew that Paul had preached about the Lord and Creator of the world and all that is in it, not an alien God. If Marcion were to listen to Luke's full account in Acts, he would be convicted (Iren., *Haer.* 3.14.4).

This raises the question about when Acts was written, who wrote it, and why. Traditionally, scholars have placed it around 110 CE and understood the author to be the same person who wrote the third Gospel in 85 CE. The reason that scholars have thought that these two books were written by the same person is the fact that Acts opens with a reference to Theophilus, the same person that the third Gospel mentions in its introduction, and claims to be the second book in the series (Acts 1:1; Luke 1:1–4). If the third Gospel were written in 85 CE, then Acts must have been written soon after that. Very little attention has been given by scholars to the fact that this continuity could be part of an author's conscious efforts to link his new composition – Acts – to the authority of an earlier gospel which may not have been authored by him.

The 110 CE date has always been suspect, however, because notable references to the written book of Acts first appear among fourth-generation Christians, with the exception of a possible allusion to Acts 20:53 in *1 Clement*. These types of queries have led scholars today to challenge the traditional dating of Acts. If not 110 CE, then when? Acts is clearly a rewriting of Christian social memory that works to align Paul's letters with an emerging Apostolic Catholic tradition in much the same way that the Pastorals epistles strive to do. If 1 Clement alludes to Acts 20:53, could this mean that the same author wrote both texts? Could Acts have been written by someone who wanted to bring Marcion down? Was this purpose realized by Irenaeus who uses it as an anti-Marcionite text that supports the apostolic tradition? If so, that would place its composition later, likely between 135–145 CE, when Marcion was in conflict with the Roman church and forced out.

Such a re-dating has repercussions for our understanding of the third Gospel. It suggests that an Apostolic Christian around the time of Polycarp revised a version of the third Gospel (which had affinities with Marcion's *Evangelion*) to serve as the prelude to Acts, as the first volume of a two-volume series about the history of the church. One of the hopes was that these books would definitively put Marcion to rest. Irenaeus realizes this purpose and more. He uses the books to combat Marcion along with any other Christian who posited a God other than the Biblical Creator.

The years around 140 CE appear to be a turning point for the Moderate Christians. It was "the" moment when they began to define themselves as a church network separate from others, constructing for themselves a long history which they anchored in apostolic memory and teaching. As we learned in earlier chapters, between 138–140 CE, Marcion and Cerdo were the first Christians to officially be removed from the Moderate church in Rome, an excommunication that other Moderate churches in Asia Minor and Syria supported (as the writings of Ignatius and Polycarp demonstrate). Marcion reorganized as a separate church with a New Testament scripture which he had edited. At the same time that this was going on in Rome, Valentinus was trying to get elected as Bishop of Rome in order to reform the church into a grace-based Minimalist church. But that did not happen either. Instead, Pius was installed and Valentinus split, developing his own ecclesiology with a split-level model of pneumatic (Gnostics) and psychic Christians (Ignorant; Apostolic Catholics). With these events (and likely under the direction of Pius), the construction of Apostolic Catholicism was set in motion. A writing campaign was undertaken to integrate Paul into the historical memory as a Moderate (Pastorals; Luke-Acts) and emphasize the church's continued connection to Judaism (1 Peter; Hebrews; Ep. *Barn.*). This writing campaign extended into the Asian and Hellenic network of churches (as the salutations of their pseudonymous letters indicate), where the Apostolic Catholics found themselves competing with Marcion and other Minimalist Christians who were questioning the morality and authenticity of the Biblical God (*1 Clement*; Ignatius; Polycarp).

9.7 The Infinite God

COMPANION READINGS

Aristides of Athens, *Apology* 1 and 15
Theophilus of Antioch, *To Autolycus* 1.1–5, 2.2–8, 22, 26
Irenaeus, *Against Heresies* 2.30.9
Tripartite Tractate (NHC I,5) 51.6–57.8
Apocryphon of John (NHC II,1) 2.34–4.26

In Jewish scriptures, God is described in mythical terms as a being who strolls in the garden (Gen. 3:8) and talks to a serpent (Gen. 3:14–19) and Adam and Eve (Gen. 2:16–18; 3:1, 3). He seems ignorant of the whereabouts of Adam and Eve (Gen. 3:9) and claims to be jealous of other Gods (Exod. 20:4–6). He has a face (Exod. 33:20), mouth (Gen. 2:7), voice (1 Kgs. 19:12), hands (Isa. 66:2), and buttocks (Exod. 33:24). He stands on walls (Amos 7:7) and sits on a throne (Isa. 6:1). These anthropomorphic descriptions (and others!) of the Biblical Creator God were problematic for Christians, since they had earned the God of the Jews a reputation for being a jealous, ignorant, and vengeful God. In the minds of many ancient people, this made him no different from the pagan Gods.

In fact, Jews had been questioned about this long before Christianity emerged. The response of Jewish intellectuals like Aristobulus of Alexandria (181–124 BCE) and Philo of Alexandria (ca. 20 BCE–50 CE) was that Moses (whom they believed authored the Jewish scriptures) used these images as metaphors, since they believed that it was not fitting to talk about God in this manner. To do so would be a monstrosity. The anthropomorphic descriptions should not be taken literally, but allegorically, so that, for instance, the hand of God means God's reason or power.

In this, they were aligned with the arguments of Greek intellectuals like Xenophanes (ca. 570–479 BCE) and Chrysippus (ca. 281–208 BCE) who faced the same problem with descriptions of the Greek Gods in their myths. Among the philosophers, anthropomorphic descriptions of the Gods were viewed as naïve and absurd, written to placate the uneducated folk. Intellectuals had been theorizing about the primal cause of the universe for centuries and they knew it to be noetic (reason or wisdom) or an ethereal or fiery substance that was either incorporeal or spherical. This was the first God.

But all of this philosophizing did not make the Biblical Creator God with all his ignorance, jealousy, and vengeance go away. He kept appearing every time the Biblical texts were read or consulted. The beauty and simplicity of the theologies of Marcion and Valentinus was the way in which they detached God from human characteristics and emotions by distinguishing the true God from the Creator God of the Jewish scriptures. Marcion's God was the God of Love and Mercy that Marcion deduced from Paul's letters and the *Evangelion*. He was the Father of Jesus, who existed in another universe outside or beyond our own, and intervened to save us from the suffering we endured under the rule of the Creator God of Jewish scriptures.

Valentinus' God was the first God of the philosophers and the Egyptians, the transcendent primal source of our universe, whose offspring were responsible for creation. In the Valentinian literature, like in the writings of Middle Platonists such as Albinus (ca. 149–157), the true God is described in negative theological or apophatic terms – what he is not – because his nature is beyond human speech and description. God is inimitable, immutable, unbegotten, immortal, unchangeable, irreducible, unattainable, inscrutable, incomprehensible, unfathomable, immeasurable, unknowable, and ineffable (*Tri. Trac.* 51.6–57.8). Such language is very similar to what Sethian Gnostics used to describe their transcendent God (*Apoc. John* 2.34–4.26). These apophatic theologies made good sense to ancient people who were familiar with the idea that a primal source of life existed before the other secondary Gods.

So if the Creator God of the Jewish scriptures – who showed signs of ignorance, anger, and capriciousness – was to be promoted also as the primal source of life, a case had to be made. How could the awkward Creator God in the scriptures also be the ineffable source of life imagined by the philosophers? As we saw in *1 Clement*, third-generation Christians were starting to ask questions about the unjust actions of the Biblical God who allowed horrible things to happen to righteous people. The Apostolic Christians responded by referencing the scriptures, seemingly trying to reinforce as authoritative the declaration that God is "the Father and Creator of the entire cosmos" (*1 Clem.* 8.2; 19.2; cf. Herm., *Mand.* 1; *Vis.* 1.3.4), and the "Lord Almighty" who governs the universe (*Barn.* 21.5).

But the questions continued and the Valentinian and Marcionite solutions made sense to enough Christians that by the middle of the second century, the Apostolic Christians realized that the Biblical theology on its own was not sufficient to meet the challenge. Christians began to comb philosophical resources in order to integrate the Biblical Creator God with philosophical speculations about the origins of the universe. The earliest example from the Apostolic Christians comes from Aristides (ca. 140 CE) who argues that the Biblical Creator God is none other than Aristotle's Prime Mover. He is uncreated, incorruptible, unchanging, invisible, without beginning or end. He has no form, no limits, and no gender. He cannot be contained by the heavens, but, instead contains them. This is why, Aristides says, Christians acknowledge him as "creator and demiurge of all things...and apart from him worship no other God" (Aris., *Apol.* 1; 15). As we saw in Chapter 6, Justin applies Platonic descriptors, considering the Creator God to be everlasting, ineffable, unnameable, changeless, impassible, and ungenerated, who created all things out of formless matter (Just., *1 Apol.* 9.3; 10:2; 13.4; 14.1; 25.2; 58.1; 61.11; 63.1). Athenagoras (ca. 175–180 CE) similarly says that "[God is] one, unbegotten and eternal and invisible and impassible and incomprehensible and infinite, apprehended by the mind and reason alone, surrounded by light and beauty and spirit and inexpressible power." This is the same God who ordered and holds together everything that exists through his Word (Athen., *Leg.* 10.5; 13.2).

Theophilus of Antioch (169–182 CE) likewise insisted that the Biblical Creator God was uncreated, without beginning, immutable, immortal. He is the supreme God who is above all things and holds all things – heavens, abysses, and the world – in his hands (Theoph., *Autol.*, 1.5). Theophilus' description is particularly insightful since he frames his work as responses to questions that people are asking him about the Christian God. "What does God look like?" he is asked. Theophilus reacts by describing God as ineffable, indescribable, invisible, incomprehensible, unfathomable, inconceivable, incomparable, unrivaled, inimitable, unutterable. While Theophilus uses philosophical language to describe the Christian God, he does not want to leave the impression that the Christian God is exactly what the philosophers theorize. He goes to some length to distinguish the Christian God from the Greek Gods and the opinions of the philosophers concerning the first God, particularly the Platonic idea that matter is uncreated. Theophilus says that God created from nothing, an idea that may have originated with Basilides (Theoph., *Autol.*, 2.2–8).

Yet there is still the problem of the Biblical story about the Creator God in the garden. His congregants are asking him about it, and he responds with a point-by-point rendering of the meaning of the entire creation account in Genesis. They ask him, "Since you said that God is uncontainable, how is it that he walked in Paradise?" Theophilus explains that it was not God who walked there, but his Son the Logos or Word who stepped into his Father's shoes and walked around the garden (Theoph., *Autol.*, 2.22). What about the fact that God had to ask "Where are you Adam?" Theophilus replies that this does not show that God was ignorant but that God gave Adam a chance to repent and confess (Theoph., *Autol.*, 2.26). When asked, "Is God angry?", Theophilus does not deny this, but, instead, agrees with the qualification, "God is angry *with sinners*" (Theoph., *Autol.*, 1.3).

Irenaeus continues to address these same issues as he presses back against groups that read the Genesis story in such a way that the Lord God is the antagonist and rival of another supreme God. Their readings focus on a limited number of passages. Genesis 1:26 (God said, "Let us make humankind in our image, according to our likeness") signaled that God was not a lone creator, but others were involved in creation, either Aeons or lesser angels. Sometimes, this passage was read in conjunction with Genesis 1:28 ("So God created man in his image, in the image of God he created them; male and female he created them") to reveal that God himself was male–female, some kind of primal hermaphrodite (Iren., *Haer.* 1.5.1–2; 1.18.2). Some Christians objected to the morality of a Creator who would be so envious of Adam and Eve that he drove them out of the garden once he realized that they had become powerful Gods in their knowledge (Gen. 3:22–3; Iren., *Haer.* 3.23.6). The wise serpent had told the truth and freed Adam and Eve from their ignorance of the trickery and treachery of the Creator (Gen. 3.1–7; Iren., *Haer.* 1.3–7; 1.5.3; 2–3.23.3). Adam was right, some thought, to hide from his enemy God, to try to escape him (Gen. 3:8–10; Iren., *Haer.* 3.23.5). They were confident that the Creator God admits his ignorance when he has to ask Adam where he is (Gen. 3:9) and when he proclaims himself the only God who exists (Isa. 45:5–6; 46:9; Iren., *Haer.* 1.5.3–4). He was proud of his jealousy (Exod. 20:5; Iren., *Haer.* 1.29.4). What a cruel God to allow poor Jonah to be eaten by a whale (Jonah 3:8–9; Iren., *Haer.* 3.20.1).

To disabuse these opinions, Irenaeus sets forth two major arguments. First, the plurality of creators in Genesis 1:26 has nothing to do with Aeons, or angels, or lesser Gods. Irenaeus says that the Lord is the Creator, but that he created by using his Son or Logos and his Wisdom or Spirit, as his hands (Iren., *Haer.* 2.30.9; 3.18.1; 3.24.2; 4.20.1–4). The Logos here is not the second God who partners with God in creation as was the case according to Justin. Yet, like Justin, Irenaeus says that the Son – who is comprehensible and visible – brought forth the Incomprehensible and Invisible. The Son reveals the Father (Iren., *Haer.*, 3.11.5–6). He is the Logos from Gospel of John that incarnates in the flesh as Jesus Christ (Iren., *Haer.* 3.11.8).

Second, to deal with all the times that God is said to have interacted with humans – when he spoke to Adam, Abraham, Noah, and Moses – when he brought judgment upon the Sodomites – when he wrestled with Jacob – these interactions were not God, according to Irenaeus, but Christ as God's manifestation (Iren., *Haer.* 4.5.2; 4.10.1; 4.36.4). Irenaeus emphasizes how the actions of God and Christ are just and good, even using Plato's writings as support for this view (Iren., *Haer.* 2.30.9; 3.25.2–5).

Once Irenaeus establishes this, he is able to read the Genesis story as the miserable downfall of the first humans. It was obvious to him that God cast Adam out of the garden because he pitied Adam. He did not want Adam to be a sinner throughout eternity should he next eat from the tree of life before he repented. So he caused man to die to his sin, so that he could begin to live with God (Iren., *Haer.* 3.23.6). Adam recognized his error and hid from God because he was confused. Knowing that he transgressed God's command, he did not feel worthy to talk to God. Adam showed that he was repentant by wearing irritating fig leaves that gave him an uncomfortable rash on his lustful genitalia. It was the merciful God who removed the leaves and clothed him in a skin tunic instead (Iren., *Haer.* 3.23.5). It was the serpent who tricked Adam and Eve, not the other way around (Iren., *Haer.* 4.pref.4).

As for Jonah, God was not cruel, but long-suffering and patient. He had foreknowledge that Jonah would be saved and a purpose that dwarfed Jonah's personal suffering. He wanted the Ninevites to repent and convert through this awesome miracle. And even more, Irenaeus said, Jonah's story foreshadows the Lord's death and resurrection (Iren., *Haer.* 3.20.1).

By arguing that the Logos and Wisdom were the two hands that God used to create (Iren., *Haer.* 4.19.2; 4.20.1) and that the Son interacted with humans rather than the Father, Irenaeus was able to distance God the Creator from the garden and from emotions like anger and envy (Iren., *Haer.* 2.13.3). This allowed him to link God the Creator with the transcendent primal source of life that the philosophers described. He devotes Book 2 to the project of explaining and defending God's transcendence, that he is truly perfect, all light, all mind, all substance, and the font of all good (Iren., *Haer.* 2.28.4–5; 4.11.2). He is the one God who established everything and contains all things, but is not himself contained (Iren. *Haer.* 2.1.1; 4.20.2). He is the Creator, Framer, Builder, Founder with his hands, Logos and Wisdom. He is one and the same God as the God of Abraham, Isaac, and Jacob (Iren. *Haer.* 2.30.9). He is the supreme God and there is no other above him (Iren. *Haer.* 2.1.2; 2.2.1; 2.30.9). He is indescribable and unspeakable who created everything from nothing (Iren. *Haer.* 2.13.4; 2.28.6; 4.38.3). This, according to Irenaeus, is the apostolic tradition received and transmitted faithfully by the Catholic church. Anything else is wrong (Iren. *Haer.* 2.9.1; 2.30.9).

Timeline

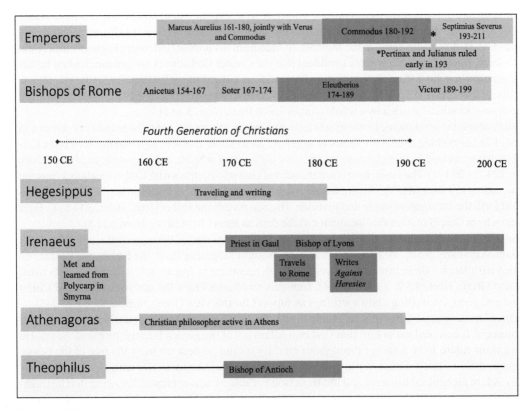

FIGURE 9.2   Timeline for early Apostolic Catholics.

Pattern Summary

The Christians we learned about in this chapter – Aristides, Hegesippus, Irenaeus, Athenagoras, and Theophilus – were all Moderate Yahwist Christians. Although we do not have much evidence of Aristides' or Hegesippus' patterns, we can determine the others, which cluster in ways that are comparable to Hermas, Ignatius, Polycarp, Justin Martyr, and Tatian.

Family Pattern Chart
Irenaeus, Athenagoras, and Theophilus

X=Definitely > L=Likely

THEODICY

	Faulty-God	Faulty-Human	Other
Irenaeus		X	
Athenagoras		X	
Theophilus		X	

SOTERIOLOGY

	Gift from God	Human achievement	Minimalist	Moderate	Maximalist
Irenaeus		X		X	
Athenagoras		X		X	
Theophilus		X		X	

CHRISTOLOGY

	Adult possession	Fetal possession	Hybrid	Ensoulment	Visitation	Human who received revelation
Irenaeus		X				
Athenagoras						
Theophilus						

ANTHROPOLOGY

	Mono	Dual	Triad	Quad
Irenaeus		X		
Athenagoras		X		
Theophilus		X		

COSMIC DEMIURGY

	Autocrat	Administrator	Caretaker	Patron	Justice	Villain	Rebel	Ignorant	Impaired
Irenaeus	X	X	X	X	X				
Athenagoras	X	L	X	X	X				
Theophilus	X	L	X	X	L				

RESURRECTION

	Body reunites with soul	Body discarded and soul immortalized	Body and soul discarded and spirit rises	God-element separates from body soul, and spirit rises
Irenaeus	X			
Athenagoras	X			
Theophilus	L			

SCRIPTURES

	Jewish	Gospel	Pauline letters (10)	Pauline letters (13)	Hebrews	Acts	Catholic letters	Revelation	Other
Aristides	L	John	1 Cor						
Irenaeus	X	Mt/Mk/Lk/Jn		X	X	X	1 Pet	X	1 Jn/2 Jn/?-Jms
Athenagoras	L	Mt	1 Cor						
Theophilus	X								

ECCLESIOLOGY

	Consolidation movement	Reform movement	Secessionist movement	Counter movement	Innovative movement	Trans-regional	Regional
Irenaeus	X					X	
Athenagoras	X					X	
Theophilus	X					X	

FIGURE 9.3 Summary of the Moderate Yahwists' patterns of beliefs and practices.

These Christians worship the Biblical God and link him to the transcendent God, whom they understand to be all-Good. They had to defend this position against Christians who were convinced that the Biblical God was immoral and not transcendent. As Yahwists, they blamed humans for suffering (theodicy) and held the opinion that humans had to follow God's commandments in order to achieve salvation and avoid heresy. While God was gracious, God also had rules that humans had to obey in order to grow into the God-like creatures humans were originally intended to be.

Resurrection of the body continued to be a hard sell for fear of a zombie apocalypse, but sell it they did. Both body and soul were understood by these Christians to be mortal and left in the grave until the end of the world. At that time, the whole person – body and soul – would come out of its grave as a creature fit to live in God's Kingdom (even if God had to recreate it cell-by-cell). Their writings are evidence of an expanding network of Apostolic Catholic churches who were constructing an apostolic tradition, a Canon of Truth, and a Roman ecclesiology (Figure 9.3).

Takeaways

1. Marcus' Spiritual church was attractive to women because they offered more opportunities for women's leadership and social mobility.

2. Irenaeus responds to Marcus by educating himself about the Valentinians and clumps together a number of distinct groups under the rubrics "heretics" and "so-called" Gnostics.

3. Hegesippus was a Roman Christian who traveled to other churches around the Mediterranean to create a record of the churches that agreed with Rome's teaching about the Law, Prophets, and the Lord.

4. Hegesippus developed his idea of Christian heresy by reading Paul and identifying Thebuthis as a Judaizer.

5. Irenaeus creates a lineage for the Valentinians in which Valentinus was influenced by the Gnostics who developed the Ophite interpretation of the Genesis story. He categorizes the "so-called" Gnostics as people who do not worship the Biblical Creator God. In so doing, he makes demiurgy and polytheism the calling cards of the Gnostics.

6. Irenaeus presents us with a complete Canon of Truth/Canon of Truth for the first time. Other authors including Aristides, Ignatius, Polycarp, and Justin refer to earlier renditions of this Canon.

7. The doctrine of the resurrection of the dead was hotly contested among the Christians. The Apostolic Catholics develop the idea that the resurrection is a fleshly one and will occur at the end of time. The Valentinians believed that the flesh would stay in the grave and the spirit would ascend as a luminous body into the Pleroma.

8. Irenaeus is the first to name the four Gospels as authored by Matthew, Mark, Luke, and John. He likely picked up these names from Papias (who was not referring to same writings as Irenaeus) and his own reading of Acts.

9. Irenaeus developed the concept of the apostolic tradition in order to counter the claims of other groups to secret post-resurrection teaching and to bolster the troubled reputation of the apostles as ignorant. He uses the Pentecost story from Acts to argue that the apostles had complete knowledge before they went out to preach.

10. *1 Clement* was likely written by a third-generation Christian from Rome (Pius or Anicetus) to bring the Corinthian church back into the emerging Apostolic Catholic network.

11. The book of Acts is first discussed by Irenaeus, although his contemporaries, the Montanists relied on it to authorize their activities. The author of *1 Clement* mentions the Pentecost experience.

12. The book of Acts was composed by a third-generation Christian to align Paul's letters with an emerging Apostolic Catholic tradition in much the same way that the Pastoral letters strive to do. This book was written at the same time by the same author who revised the third Gospel (which had affinities with Marcion's *Evangelion*).

13. Irenaeus uses Acts as an anti-Marcionite text.

14. Theology (who is God?) was also hotly contested among fourth-generation Christians. Irenaeus and Theophilus of Antioch provide point-by-point refutations of readings of the Jewish scriptures that suggest that God has a body, emotions, and is often capricious. Their solution is that the transcendent God is the Biblical God, but that all references to his body and interactions with humans refer to the Logos. They also say that God and everything he does is for our own good.

Questions

1. Explain the debate around the doctrine of the resurrection of the dead among third- and fourth- generation Christians. What are the issues that the debate raised about the way that ancient people imagined the afterlife?

2. If you were a woman in antiquity, why might Marcus' church have been attractive? Why might you have gone back to Irenaeus' church? Why would you have publicly confessed to having been Marcus' lover, if you weren't?

3. What are the main points that Christians argued about when they were discussing the Biblical God? What troubled them specifically? Were they biblical literalists? Why or why not?

4. How did Theophilus and Irenaeus respond to Christians who proved from the scriptures that the Biblical God was not the transcendent God? Why was it important to Theophilus and Irenaeus that the Biblical God is the transcendent God too?

5. In what directions did Irenaeus develop the Canon of Truth? Why did he develop the Canon of Truth in these directions? What made his arguments compelling?

6. Explain what Hegesippus was doing. Who do you think authorized him to do these activities? Why would this have been an important strategy for the emerging Apostolic Catholics? How does it relate to the sociological idea of consolidation?

7. You learned several possibilities for possible dates and authors of *1 Clement*. How do you sort this out for yourself?

Resources

John Behr. 2013. *Irenaeus of Lyons: Identifying Christianity.* Oxford: Oxford University Press.
M. David Litwa. 2022. Chapter 13. *Found Christianities: Remaking the World of the Second Century CE.* London: T&T Clark.
April D. DeConick. 2013. "Gnostic Spirituality at the Crossroads of Christianity: Transgressing Boundaries and Creating Orthodoxy." Pages 148–184 in *Beyond the Gnostic Gospels: Studies Building on the Work of Elaine Pages.* Edited by Eduard Iricinschi, Lance Jenott, Nicola Denzey Lewis, and Philippa Townsend. Tübingen: Mohr Siebeck.
Jakob Engberg. 2014. "Theophilus." Pages 101–124 in *In Defense of Christianity: Early Christian Apologists* Early Christianity in the Context of Antiquity 15. Edited by Jakob Engberg, Anders-Christian Jacobsen, and Jörg Ulrich. Translated by Gavin Weakley. Frankfurt am Main: Peter Lang.
Justo L. González. 1970. (revised ed). Chapter 6. *A History of Christian Thought from the Beginnings to the Council of Chalcedon.* Volume 1. Ashville: Abingdon Press.
Andrew Gregory. 2007. "*1 Clement*: An Introduction." Pages 21–31 in *The Writings of the Apostolic Fathers.* Edited by Paul Foster. London: T&T Clark.
Anders-Christian Jacobsen. 2014. "Athenagoras." Pages 81–100 in *In Defense of Christianity: Early Christian Apologists* Early Christianity in the Context of Antiquity 15. Edited by Jakob Engberg, Anders-Christian Jacobsen, and Jörg Ulrich. Translated by Gavin Weakley. Frankfurt am Main: Peter Lang.
Peter Lampe. 2003. Chapter 21 in *From Paul to Valentinus: Christians at Rome in the First Two Centuries.* Edited by Michael Steinhauser and edited by Marshall D. Johnson. Minneapolis: Fortress Press.

Denis Minns. 2010. *Irenaeus: An Introduction*. London: T&T Clark.

Claudio Moreschini and Enrico Norelli. 2005. Chapters 9.8, 10. 2, 5–6 and 13.1. *Early Christian Greek and Latin Literature: A Literary History. Volume 1: From Paul to the Age of Constantine*. Translated by Matthew J. O'Connell Peabody: Hendrickson Publishers.

Odd Magne Bakke. 2001. *"Concord and Peace: A Rhetorical Analysis of the First Letter of Clement with an Emphasis on the Language of Unity and Sedition."* Wissenschaftliche Untersuchungen zum Neuen Testament 2. Reihe 143. Tübingen: Mohr Siebeck.

Richard I. Pervo. 2006. *Dating Acts: Between the Evangelists and the Apologists*. Santa Rosa: Polebridge Press.

Rick Rogers. 2000. *Theophilus of Antioch: The Life and Thought of a Second-Century Bishop*. Lanham: Lexington Books.

Geoffrey S. Smith. 2015. *Guilt by Association. Heresy Catalogues in Early Christianity*. Oxford: Oxford University Press.

Jörg Ulrich. 2014. "Aristides." Pages 35–50 in *In Defense of Christianity: Early Christian Apologists* Early Christianity in the Context of Antiquity 15. Edited by Jakob Engberg, Anders-Christian Jacobsen, and Jörg Ulrich. Translated by Gavin Weakley. Frankfurt am Main: Peter Lang.

Gérard Vallée. 1993. *A Study in Anti-Gnostic Polemics: Irenaeus, Hippolytus, and Epiphanius* Studies in Christianity and Judaism 1. Waterloo: Wilfrid Laurier University Press.

CHAPTER 10

Church Reform

Statue representing Hippolytus of Rome. Third-century statue heavily restored in sixteenth century. Discovered with no head in a Roman cemetery (1515 CE). The chair is inscribed with a handful of Hippolytus' works as well as information about the Paschal and Easter calendars. Apostolic Library, Vatican. **Source:** Everett Ferguson.

> "We are priests of the one God."
>
> *Tertulllian's motto*

KEY PLAYERS
Tertullian
Theodotus the Cobbler
Praxeaus – Noetus – Sabellius
Hippolytus – Hippolytus of Asia

KEY TEXTS
Gospel of Luke
Tertullian, *Apology, On Chastity, On Modesty, On Veiling of Virgins, On Repentance, Against Hermogenes, Against the Valentinians, Against Marcion*
Martyrdom of Perpetua and Felicity
Hippolytus of Asia, *Against Noetus*
Hippolytus, *Refutation*

We have seen in the last few chapters that in the fourth-generation (150–190 CE), Christians were busy expanding and defining their movements, building ecclesiastical structures and networks, and constructing memories and traditions to affirm their beliefs. The Apostolic Catholics were creating a consolidated movement. They were occupied with the construction of the apostolic tradition and ecclesiology, placing more authority in the hands of their

Comparing Christianities: An Introduction to Early Christianity, First Edition. April D. DeConick.
© 2024 John Wiley & Sons Ltd. Published 2024 by John Wiley & Sons Ltd.

bishops with the expectation that the bishop of Rome would rule on the major disputes (i.e. Easter calendar; Montanism).

In eastern Syria, Christian churches had a different regional shape, especially when it came to lifestyle which was much more demanding and ascetic than in the west. They appear to have operated as regional churches independent of the ecclesiastical network developing among Apostolic Catholics in the west. The introduction and consolidation of Apostolic Catholic churches in eastern Syria and Mesopotamia does not appear to have taken place until the late second century when Bishop Serapion of Antioch (191–211 CE) installed Palut as Bishop of Edessa. Palut is said to have brought a revised edition of the Jewish scriptures combined with the four Gospels, Acts, and fourteen letters of Paul with him to combat the *Diatessaron*. His scriptures became known as the Gospel of the Separatists and his collection was resisted by the majority of Christians in Syria at this time.

The Marcionite churches continued to flourish across the Mediterranean as a COUNTER MOVEMENT, a parallel Christian church, even in the way its ecclesiastical structures were built (presbyters, deacons, and bishops). Marcionite churches continued to demand a rigorous ethical lifestyle and condemn the Apostolic Catholics for their conspiracy to falsify the Gospel with a Jewish façade. Marcionites identified the Apostolic Catholics as Judaizers, and likely saw them as Christian heretics. The Marcionites relied on conversion for membership since procreation was prohibited. This meant that poaching members from Apostolic Christian congregations was becoming a problem that Apostolic Catholics took very seriously.

Montanism began within Apostolic Catholicism as a holiness REFORM MOVEMENT, but struggled to convince the majority of other Apostolic Catholics that their prophecies were not demonic. Even though they affirmed the Catholic Canon of Truth, they were forced to organize into a SECESSIONIST CHURCH known as the Church of New Prophecy replete with its own ecclesiology, which allowed for women leaders in all positions. They valued the Trio's prophecies, practiced prophecy themselves, and lived more rigorously than their Apostolic Catholic counterparts. They worked hard to persuade the Apostolic Catholics that they had become too lax and the Paraclete demanded that they change their ways before it was too late.

We also learned that independent Valentinian leaders emerged after Valentinus' death. They were busy establishing independent Valentinian churches to try to absorb the psychic (soulish) Apostolic Catholic congregations into their initiatory groups. They poached Apostolic Catholics like Flora by setting up parallel churches that were practically indistinguishable from Apostolic Catholic churches. They advertised their congregations as spiritual churches that offered advanced knowledge (gnosis) and an additional ecstatic initiation into God's Kingdom (the realm of the Transcendent God). In this period, the Valentinians do not seem to have an overseer or a way for differences to be arbitrated among themselves. They are not linked into the ecclesiastical network of the Apostolic Catholics but appear to be a SECESSIONIST MOVEMENT made up of independent congregations with famed teachers like Ptolemy or Marcus as their leaders. This gives the Valentinian movement the character of a school with opinionated and innovative teachers running independent congregations.

Other independent Gnostic churches like the Basilidians formed in the fourth generation (e.g. Justinians, Ophians, Naassenes) although these churches were not Apostolic Catholic reform or secessionist movements. Rather, they emerge regionally as INNOVATIVE MOVEMENTS with their own distinct Christian histories.

As we approach the fifth generation of Christianity (190–230 CE) in the next chapters, the tensions between all these Christianities escalate. This forces the movements to figure out what is important to defend, what needs clarification, and what should be appropriated or mirrored from other movements. As Christian literature continues to be written, edited, revised, and published, Christian scholasticism intensifies with serious attention given to what Christian knowledge has to do with Athens (Greek philosophy) or not.

10.1 Out of Africa

COMPANION READINGS
Tert., *Apology* 24, 50
Martyrdom of Perpetua and Felicity

While early Christianity spread to Alexandria by the beginning of the second century, the first we hear about Christianity in western Africa is at the beginning of the third century with the Latin publications of Quintus Septimus Florens Tertullianus (ca. 160–240 CE) from Carthage. Details about Tertullian's life are scant and unreliable. What we can know about him with certainty, we derive from his own writings.

He relates that he was a born and raised pagan (Tert., *Repent.* 1.1). He was married but also admitted that he had an affair with another woman (Tert., *Wife*; Tert., *Res.* 59.3). His marriage and adulterous liaison resulted in an existential crisis, which he appears to have written about in a now-lost book called *To a Philosopher Friend*. The topic? How difficult it is to be a philosopher while also being married. Tertullian's concerns likely focused on themes that would become accentuated in his later Christian writings, such as the trouble with passions and divided attentions. Not surprisingly, Tertullian's philosophical leanings were in the direction of Stoicism as articulated by Seneca (4 BCE–65 CE) whose ethic was all about harnessing the passions through self-control. Ethical rigor was always on Tertullian's mind.

In 197 CE, Tertullian converted to Christianity. He appears to have done so after observing Christians on trial before their execution (*Apol.* 50.15). He was curious about their obstinacy while being examined by the jurists. So he started asking the condemned, "Why?" He wanted to know what was at the bottom of their stubborn determination to refuse to participate in the civic cult. Whatever they told him persuaded him to look deeper into their teachings. When he did so, he not only became convinced of their truth, but jumped in whole hog, willing to defend Christians against what he perceived to be Roman legal injustice.

Tertullian may have known the young Roman mother, Perpetua, who in 203 CE was arrested in Carthage with four other Christians and condemned when they refused to sacrifice to the emperor. We have a record of her imprisonment, nightmares, and visions mainly because we have her diary embedded in the *Martyrdom of Perpetua and Felicity*. She describes her feelings as a nursing mother on death row and her hopes for forgiveness and salvation through martyrdom. She considered herself privileged, asking God for a vision of her future, and receiving four dreams that she believed forecast her exaltation to heaven as a martyr. Her dreams involved visits with her dead brother who was suffering in the afterlife, with Christ in the heavenly garden at the top of a ladder of torture, and with an Egyptian gladiator with whom she sparred and conquered (having become a man of mighty power herself). Perpetua's diary was edited by a later hand. Some scholars have suggested that Tertullian may have been the editor.

While we will never know if Tertullian had a hand in editing Perpetua's diary, it is evident from writings like his letter *To the Martyrs* that Tertullian was impressed with their faith and considered them heroes. His first post-conversion writing is the *Apology*, which challenges the legality of the charges against Christians and the executions carried out following their convictions. The writing demonstrates that he had extensive knowledge of the Roman law and the juridical status of Christians. It is not implausible that he had legal training as a young man and was involved enough in the judicial system before his conversion that he was present when Christians were on trial and had the opportunity to question them.

The *Apology* reads like a law brief arguing to the Roman court why Christians are being wrongly convicted. Tertullian highlights that the Romans allow freedom of religion among all the conquered people, and yet "by taking away religious liberty and forbidding theological free choice so that I may no longer worship according to my inclination," the Romans act irreligiously and capriciously toward Christians (Tert., *Apol.* 24). He goes on to argue that Rome did not become an empire because of its fealty to the Gods, when, in fact, this ought to be attributed to wars and the victories of superior armies (Tert., *Apol.* 25). While Christians do not offer sacrifices to the emperor, they do pray for his safety, a practice which demonstrates that Christians are not traitors to the state (Tert., *Apol.* 27–34). Christians do not threaten the public since their behaviors and ethics are impeccable (Tert., *Apol.* 35–45). He concludes his exhibits by upending the wrongful conviction, stating that execution is not a deterrent but instead, "the blood of Christians is seed." The more Christians are "mown down," the "more in number" they grow. Their outrageous deaths expose the injustice, savagery, and cruelty of the Empire rather than demonstrating that the Roman law is a civilized system of government (Tert., *Apol.* 50). It may be that the Tertullian understood their actions to be something akin to what we have theorized as civil disobedience in modernity, although it is questionable whether he (or any other Christian) believed that their actions would have any effect on Roman imperialism.

Tertullian went on to write and publish over 30 influential books as a Christian, yet nowhere does he suggest that he became a bishop. Instead, he seems to include himself in the laity, although this may be a rhetorical gesture to make the point that all Christians (himself included) should live like priests even though they are not formally ordained (Tert., *Chast.* 7.3; *Monog.* 12.3). Tertullian, however, mentions preaching about the soul one Sunday while a sister became enraptured with the Spirit (Tert., *Soul* 9.4). This suggests that at some point in his career he became a presbyter or elder in a church in Carthage. He not only assumed responsibility for presiding or leading services but also tested at least one prophetess and discussed her visions with her after the services concluded.

His mention of this prophetess suggests that Tertullian considered women legitimate prophets. And yet he followed a conservative decorum that relegated the reports of their revelations to after church, to coffee hour (Tert., *Soul* 9). As far as we know, Tertullian never supported women as liturgical leaders. In agreement with Apostolic Catholics, he opposed women's ordination (which was a regular occurrence among other Christian groups he labels "heretics"). In his estimation, women should not be allowed to speak in church during the services, teach, debate, preside over the eucharist, baptize, heal, or exorcize demons (Tert., *Veiling* 9; *Prescr.*41).

Regardless of the status of his ordination, Tertullian was an avid reader of Irenaeus and became an influential scholar among the Latin-speaking Christians. The scholarship he generated about Christianity is not only enormous but also erudite. Later Christian writers in the west relied heavily on his works, considering them classics. Cyprian the bishop of Carthage in the middle of the third century is rumored to have asked his secretary every day, "Hand me the teacher," by which he meant one of Tertullian's writings (Jerome, *Epist.* 22.22; *Jov.* 1.13).

Tertullian is a complicated figure in the history of early Christianity. While he converted to an African form of Apostolic Catholicism, around 207 CE, he began to identify with the Church of New Prophecy (Montanism) and became their staunch defender, even criticizing Eleutherius, the bishop of Rome (alternatively dated to 171–177/185–193 CE), for a ruling Eleutherius had made against them (Tert., *Prax.* 1). Late in life, however, even Montanist rigor was not sufficient for him. Wishing for more ethical rigor than was customary for either the Apostolic Catholics or the Montanists, Tertullian formed an ultra-rigorous group of Christians in Carthage which Augustine later knew as the Tertullianists. Augustine says that he successfully reintegrated this Carthaginian group into the Catholic fold (Aug., *Her.* 86).

10.2 We are Priests of the One God

COMPANION READINGS
Tertullian, *On Repentance* 9–12
Tertullian, *On Chastity* 1–2, 5
Tertullian, *On Modesty* 1–2
Tertullian, *On Veiling Virgins* 1

If Tertullian had a motto, it would have been "We are priests of the one God" (cf. Rev. 1:6; Tert., *Chast.* 7.3; *Fast.* 11). This image reflects the type of ethical rigor and moral discipline that Tertullian believed was essential for Christian life. Tertullian believed that God created humans to reflect his Image and to become his Likeness. For Tertullian, this meant that it is necessary for Christians to make themselves holy just as God himself is holy (Tert., *Chast.* 1). While it is true that the rigor Tertullian imagined as ideal increased after he aligned himself with the Church of New Prophecy, he was never not rigorous in his expectations for a holy life. For instance, prior to his affiliation with New Prophecy, he preferred that widows and widowers remain unmarried (Tert., *Wife* 1.1). After affiliating with New Prophecy, he compared marriage to monotheism, insisting that widow and widowers never take a new spouse (Tert., *Monog.* 1). It was his love of rigor that drew him to the obstinate displays of the Christian martyrs in the first place, and then to the disciplined principles that New Prophecy adopted in regard to remarriage, post-baptismal sin, fasting, and chastity.

Tertullian always identified the erotic with trouble, before and after his conversion to Christianity, as well as before and after his introduction to New Prophecy. For Tertullian, the erotic should be kept under lock and key at all times because of its potential to compel us to sin. Tertullian mapped chastity onto all stages of life from childhood to widowhood (Tert., *Chast.* 1). Childhood was a virgin state of happiness before sexual awareness. After baptism, adult Christians were expected to continue their virtuous practices of chastity, limiting sex to times when the spouses consented, and leaving behind sex when the spouses were widowed. Those who were most glorious in their virtue took chastity even more seriously. According to Tertullian, these were spouses who suspended sex with each other completely and lived in chaste marriages.

Not far-removed from his position on chastity was his position on post-baptismal sin. Even before affiliating with New Prophecy, he took a harsh stance with those who sinned after baptism. Although he permits exomologesis or confession one time after baptism, he characterizes it as a protracted and humiliating discipline (Tert., *Repent.* 9–12). He writes, "While it abases people, it raises them; while it covers them in squalor, it renders them clean; while it accuses, it excuses; while it condemns, it absolves." He shames sinners who ask for merciful treatment, who dread wearing sackcloth, covering themselves with ashes, mourning their sins publicly, and fasting until their faces are sunken in hunger and sorrow. What else should they expect when expunging eternal punishments for idolatry, murder, and adultery?

Once Tertullian became associated with the New Prophecy, he complained about sinners who tried to flatter God with their confessions, and he openly criticized the Bishop of Rome for pandering to them (Tert., *Mod.* 1–2). He thinks it dangerous to count on God's mercy, and instead says that Christians need to worry about God's justice. He argues that the severity of God's judgment ought to cause their constancy and invigorate their discipline. Exomologesis should not provide sinners with a loophole that encourages lax behavior. New Prophecy and the teachings of the Paraclete had convinced him that there is no exomologesis that should alleviate God's punishment for post-baptismal sin (Tert., *Mod.* 5).

The disciplined life that Tertullian promotes, focused on controlling the appetites of the body at the ground level so that sin would not be able take root in the first place (Tert., *Fast.* 17). For Tertullian, this discipline starts with curbing the fork, a practice which he thinks served as a type of perpetual exomologesis (Tert., *Fast.* 9). He advocates following the more regimented fast protocol put into place by Montanus, Maximilla, and Priscilla, rather than the more lenient fasting schedule established by the Apostolic Catholics, who placed their faith in their love for God and neighbor and not in "the emptiness of their lungs and intestines" (Tert., *Fast.* 3). For Tertullian, this laxity is a slippery slope that make Christians vulnerable to gluttony, lust, and adultery (Tert., *Fast.* 1).

Normally, Christians fasted on Wednesdays and Fridays until 3 p.m., but Tertullian, like other Montanists, extended these fasts to 9 p.m. During the weekdays for two weeks out of every year, Tertullian, along with other Montanists, observed xerophagy, when they ate only "dry" foods, following a diet similar to a vegetarian diet without fruit or wine. They mainly ate cooked vegetables and bread without moistening them with juices or oil. They also abstained from bathing (Tert., *Fast.* 1, 15). Tertullian feels that this austere diet prepares the Christian for the prison food that martyrs were forced to eat. He likens the diet to what Daniel ate in captivity when he grew stronger by refusing to eat the gourmet foods cooked for the king's court. The association of Adam's sin with eating the forbidden fruit was not lost on Tertullian either, who recognizes that death is the product of "tasting." Tertullian quips, "Adam yielded more readily to his belly than to God, heeded the meat rather than the mandate, and sold salvation for his gullet!" (Tert., *Fast.* 3).

Like the Montanists, Tertullian distinguishes those Christians who prescribe to this austerity as pneumatics or spiritual Christians, while the lax Christians are psychics or soulish Christians who will run into real trouble at God's judgment for their negligence and permissiveness. Considering John 16:12–13, Tertullian was convinced that following Jesus' death, Jesus had sent the Paraclete as the Vicar of discipline: to guide his followers and inaugurate a period of increasingly rigorous rules for a new holy people (Tert., *Prescr.* 28; *Veil.* 1). These rules were delivered by the Montanist prophets, who were mouthpieces of the Holy Spirit (Tert., *Soul* 9).

Tertullian periodizes rigor and righteousness as "stages of growth." Tertullian associates the time of the Law and the Prophets with infancy, when God bestowed rudimentary righteousness on his people. God's next set of demands for righteousness – the Youth stage – was shared when the Gospel was proclaimed. Tertullian argues for a third period of adulthood when the Paraclete guides Christians into even more rigorous discipline proclaimed by the Church of New Prophecy (Tert., *Veil.* 1). Tertullian was frustrated by the majority of Christians, including the Roman bishops, whom he criticizes for being content to never grow up and take on the rigors of adulthood.

What was Tertullian's relationship to Apostolic Catholicism and the bishopric in Rome? He shares the Montanist point of view that the Apostolic Catholics had become lazy and overconfident in their faith. He believes that Christians are being called by the Spirit to shape up and get ready for God's imminent judgment when the heavenly Jerusalem will descend to earth (Tert., *Marc.* 2.24.4). Confident that the final years of the world were at hand, Tertullian aligns himself with the Montanist prophets who demanded that Christians reform the church so that they could live a more disciplined daily life as they waited for the End.

In seven books on ecstasy that are now lost, Tertullian defends the legitimacy of the Montanist prophets, glossolalia, and individual inspiration. The church in Carthage which Tertullian attended featured a woman prophetess who, Tertullian reports, enjoyed many gifts of the Spirit (Tert., *Soul* 9). After the services, she shared stories about her ecstatic experiences and the revelations she had when she was "in the Spirit," when she talked to angels and the Lord. She was known to have these experiences at various points in the service: during scripture reading, when chanting hymns, while the sermon was being preached, as prayers were being offered.

As mentioned earlier, one time while Tertullian preached about the soul, the prophetess went into a trance. After the service, she told them that a soul appeared to her as a transparent ethereal body that she could touch (it was soft), see in color (the color was delicate), and observe in form (it was humanlike). She likened it to the appearance of the Spirit which regularly came to her and lifted her into ecstasy. Tertullian admits to testing her "with the most scrupulous care" and being convinced of the authenticity of her communication. It likely helped that her vision coincided with Tertullian's Stoic position that souls had actual bodies. In Tertullian's judgment, soul bodies were a kind of ethereal substance, a condensation of the breath that God breathed into Adam's nostrils. Adam's body served as a kind of mold for the congealment of the "living soul" as it impressed and condensed inside of Adam's physical body.

Tertullian understood the Church of New Prophecy as an Apostolic Catholic reform movement that was supposed to correct the laxity of other Apostolic Catholics. He is quite clear that apostolic teaching and the Apostolic Catholic Canon of Truth are the backbone of his faith. He repeats on occasion that it is "immoveable and irreformable" that there is "one only God omnipotent, the Creator of the universe, and his Son Jesus Christ, born of the Virgin Mary, crucified under Pontius Pilate, raised again on the third day from the dead, received in the heavens, sitting now at the right hand of the Father, destined to come to judge the quick and dead through the resurrection of the flesh."

Tertullian understands that this Canon of Truth is part of a broad *traditio* or tradition of truth that has been passed on from generation to generation, from the mother church founded by the apostles down to the Apostolic Catholic churches in Tertullian's time. This tradition included the Apostolic Catholic catechism taught to proselytes preparing for baptism, and the exclusive right to interpret the scriptures.

While Tertullian insists that the Apostolic Catholic Canon of Truth and the *traditio* from the apostles is a constant truth, he also argues that when God saw how mediocre Christians were becoming, he sent the Paraclete to correct them and, little by little, bring lax Christians to perfection through the teachings of the Montanists (Tert., *Veil.* 1). Since the Montanists in Pepuza were invalidated by the agreement of local bishops around 170 CE and Eleutherius, the Bishop of Rome, ruled against the Montanists shortly thereafter (Tert., *Prax.* 1), it is safe to conclude that reformers like Tertullian likely worshipped in separatist assemblies that stuck to the Apostolic Catholic Canon of Truth while, at the same time, encouraging prophecy in their services and rigorous discipline in their daily practices. They considered themselves advanced spiritual Catholics and held out an olive branch to their psychic Catholic brothers and sisters, hoping to convince them to reform before it was too late.

10.3 Dressing the Part

COMPANION READINGS
Tertullian, *On Apparel of Women* 1.1–4 and 2.9

The austere daily practices of holiness espoused by Tertullian included a dress code which he thought was necessary to make Christians distinct from other Romans who used fixed dress codes to signal peoples' class, gender, ethnicity, and even vocation. In Rome, social status was immediately evident in a person's attire. A wrapped blanket or short handspun toga was used by peasants as a practical work garment. For the wealthy males, beautifully appointed long togas were worn over white tunics. Married women were expected to wear a stola, a long woolen outer garment which draped over their tunics and disguised their bodies in folds. They also wore a facial veil and a palla, a shawl-like scarf that served as a hood. This attire was meant to signal their modesty and marital status. When in mourning, dark wool togas and stolas were donned instead of colorfully dyed and embroidered ones. Purple edging on garments signaled a magistrate, priest, or aristocrat. Freedmen and slaves wore clothing appropriate to their jobs, and any proposal that they all ought to wear similar costumes was abandoned out of fear that once the slaves saw their tremendous numbers, they would realize how vulnerable their masters actually were to revolt.

Tertullian wrote treatises on Christian grooming and attire, toilette and dress, and veiling practices, harnessing the power of fashion for his social and religious agendas. In doing so, he thought deeply about what type of dress would best signal the truth about the character and virtues of Christians (Tert., *Apparel* 2.9). In his opinion, what a Christian wore ought to demonstrate what a Christian is. In so doing, Tertullian does not abandon Roman garb, but repurposes traditional attire by linking Christian values to existing dress codes, to mark the emergence of a new holy people.

It is telling that at the end of his career, Tertullian wrote an entire track on the pallium, the short cloak that Greek philosophers wore. Tertullian tells us that he set aside his toga for the pallium, a change of attire that he hoped would signal his identity as a man who had adopted a strict code of Christian ethics, stricter than any ethics prescribed by "other" philosophers. While Tertullian did not think that Greek intellectualism could contribute substantially to the Christian faith – he famously asked, "What does Athens have to do with Jerusalem?" – he certainly positioned Christianity as a "way of life" alternative to the "way of life" characteristic of the Greek philosophies. His selection of attire for himself signaled these new values.

What are these values and how did Tertullian want them to be staged in everyday grooming and clothing? Unlike other Romans who used dress codes to signal their wealth, status, and ambition, Christians ought to use dress codes to signal opposing values. The most important value to display, according to Tertullian, is the shame and humility of the repentant sinner. This is particularly true of women who, Tertullian says, "are each an Eve" (Tert., *Apparel* 1.1).

Tertullian reads the Genesis story as a righteous justification for misogyny. He designates Eve as the absolute cause of sin and the horrors of the entire human predicament. According to Tertullian, she is responsible for destroying God's Image, man, so that all men everywhere are subject to death because of her. Man originally had been created in the Image of God, not in his fleshly makeup, but in the fact that he had the power to act freely like a God. God charged man to live virtuously, to choose obedience or resistance (Tert., *Marc.* 2.5–9). But through woman, the world has been cursed and men have been corrupted. This corruption is passed on to the souls of their children because Tertullian, like Stoics, thought that souls were corporeal. Just as their bodies come from their parents' bodies when babies are conceived, Tertullian said that their souls also are derived from the corrupted souls of the parents. This doctrine is called Traducianism. This means that Eve is blamed for the original sin that children, in turn, inherit from their parents in a perpetual cycle. This doctrine becomes the basis for Augustine's (354–430 CE) own doctrine on original sin. While Augustine abandons the belief in the corporeality of souls, he retains Tertullian's notion of the hereditary nature of sin.

Because of Eve's original sin, Tertullian notes with indignance, it became necessary for the Son of God to die. Eve has only herself to blame for her own suffering, for the pain she suffers in childbirth, for her erotic desire for her husband, and for her utter subjugation to him as a slave to a master (Tert., *Apparel* 1.1; *Marc.* 2.11). Tertullian calls woman "the Devil's Gateway," blaming her for eating the forbidden fruit, deserting the divine law, and persuading man to sin too. If they do not already, Tertullian says, women should feel such guilt and shame that they cover their bodies with the humble garb of a repentant sinner. They should present themselves as perpetual mourners.

The second value that Tertullian wanted performed by Christians was chastity. He traces the problem of sexual temptation and promiscuity to women who wear cosmetics, dye their hair, and adorn themselves with jewelry in order to catch the eye of men and seduce them (Tert., *Apparel* 1.2–4). Referencing The Book of Enoch, Tertullian argues that women were first taught these practices by fallen angels who wanted to have sex with them. To enhance their lustful trysts with the women, the angels gifted women with beautification techniques. They taught them how to make and wear jewelry, how to dye wool scarlet and purple, and how to manufacture black powder to make their eyes more prominent. According to Tertullian, such habits reflect the prostitute, not "handmaidens of God," who are valued for their humility and chastity, not their voluptuousness and beauty.

Modesty is the third value that Tertullian invokes. Here he addresses the dress of both men and women. Modesty is necessary, he thinks, because the Christian body is possessed by the Holy Spirit. The body ought to be treated like priests who care for temples, keeping out everything that is impure. On this front, Tertullian argues that men and women ought to groom and dress to reflect nature, which he considered the primary and pure state, and not custom, which he identified as secondary and impure. For Tertullian *au naturel* meant that men ought not to cut their beards short, pluck their facial hair, shave around the mouth, style or dye their hair, depilate their body hair, use women's hair gel, exfoliate their skin, or check their looks in mirrors (Tert., *Apparel* 2.8). Likewise, women ought not to dye their hair blond or try to cover their gray with black. The use of cosmetics, elaborate hairstyles, wigs, and braids are forbidden. Dyed fabrics, pierced ears, and jewelry are prohibited. All these practices are chalked up to customs that disfigure God's natural design for men and women (and sheep who are not born purple or scarlet!).

Tertullian was particularly concerned about how adult virgin women ought to dress. This was a hot debate among Christians in Carthage. Since married women were veiled in Roman society, some adult virgins in the Carthaginian churches never bothered to take on the veiled dress of a matron. Tertullian expresses alarm, worried that the church's adult virgins will be viewed as prostitutes for hire, since adult women who were prostitutes did not wear the attire of the modest matron either. Tertullian is very clear that adult virgins should take on the veil. Although they did not have human husbands, they were married to Christ, he says.

10.4 When A Human Becomes God

COMPANION READINGS
Eusebius, *Ecclesiastical History*. 5.28
Tertullian, *Against Praxeas* 1

Fifth-generation Christians (c. 190–230 CE) like Tertullian were not only distant from the historical time of Jesus, the apostles, and Paul, but they also had accumulated a pastiche of Christian traditions and practices that were often dissonant and incompatible. For over a century and a half, Christians had understood stories in the Jewish scripture to indicate that the Jewish God (YHWH) himself as the great angel of the Lord, the angel who bore God's Name (YHWH). In other words, God and his angelic manifestation were equivocal. Some

Christians believed this divine angelic manifestation to have been Christ the Son. Because the Son bore God's Name, he exercised God's power. In this way, the Son was the Father, and monotheism was safeguarded. As long as the Christians thought in these biblical categories, there was little controversy.

But once a philosopher like Justin came along and began to blend the biblical categories with the philosophical, problems surfaced. While Justin agreed that the Son was the Angel of the Lord (and thus the manifestation of the Father), he also argued that the Son issued from the Father as God's Logos. This, Justin admitted, meant that the Son clearly was the Father's subordinate. Those reading Justin wondered whether Jesus was God or some second deity worshiped alongside the Father.

The subordination of the Son became exacerbated when Justin fully assimilated the Jewish creator God with the universal transcendent God whom philosophers had posited as the origin of life and Gnostic groups were worshiping as the supreme deity (in contrast to the Jewish God). If the Christian God was *also* the universal transcendent God, how could his Son ever be equivocal to him? Since the Son came to earth, was born and died, he clearly was not a transcendent deity. This put the Christians' claim to be monotheists on even shakier ground.

Between 180–190 CE, Theodotus, a cobbler and Christian philosopher from Byzantium (a.k.a. Constantinople; modern Istanbul) worked out the problem in a way that he believed honored scriptures while preserving God's monarchy, his sovereignty as the *sole* source and ruler of universe, what today we call monotheism (Eus., *Eccl. Hist.* 5.28; Epiph., *Pan.* 54.1). Theodotus was an ancient monotheist in a unitarian sense. He believed in the absolute Oneness of God. Since Theodotus believed that God-Is-One, he taught that the man Jesus was not an incarnate God, but had instead *acquired* the Christ as a divine power or *dynamis*. This type of Christology has come to be called Dynamic Monarchianism and while it was originally formulated in antiquity, it was reinvented in Transylvania by two European Unitarians, Lelio Sozzini (1525–1562 CE) and his nephew Faustus Socinus (1539–1604 CE) under the name Socinianism. The Socinians denied the pre-existence of Christ. They believed that the Son did not exist until he was conceived, that he was born merely a human being. This idea is referred to as psilantropism from the Greek *psilo* meaning "merely or only" and *anthropos* meaning "human."

Theodotus was convinced that the Apostolic Christian teaching was wrong that Jesus was a heavenly entity who came down into the Virgin's womb and assumed flesh (Figure 10.1). Instead, he promotes a version of the ADULT POSSESSION PATTERN, explaining that Jesus Christ was born a natural human being (though the Holy Spirit assisted with his conception in the Virgin's womb). The young Jesus lived so piously that when he was baptized, the Holy Spirit as the Christ came down upon him. When he received the Christ, he received the power or *dynamis* that he needed to perform miracles and fulfill his special mission. It was at this moment that he also became God's Son, although not as a divine being. Instead, there was a power or force working through the man Jesus, but no substantive divine presence in him.

To preserve the Christian conviction about God's oneness, Theodotus sacrificed the idea that Christ was a full deity. Because Theodotus teaches that Jesus is not God but a human being through whom God worked, Theodotus preserves God's monarchy, and monotheism is saved. Some of Theodotus' disciples argue that Jesus was elevated to a divine status at his resurrection, but Theodotus does not appear to have taught this himself (Hipp., *Ref.* 7.35). Even those followers of Theodotus who argued for Jesus' glorification at his resurrection believed that Jesus was a human who only *became* God after his death. Either way, Jesus was viewed as someone who was made God and was clearly subordinate to the Father, who was God from eternity.

In 190 CE, Theodotus traveled to Rome and had an audience with Bishop Victor (189–199 CE). He set before Victor his neat solution, arguing that he had recovered the earliest understanding of Jesus, a Christology that dated back to the apostles. Artemon, a later proponent of Theodotus' solution (ca. 230 CE), divulges the type of reasoning Theodotus must have used (Eus., *Hist.* 5.28). Acts 2:22 was leveraged, where the apostles identify Jesus as "a *man* attested to you by God by means of powerful deeds." It was pointed out that the apostle Paul too understood "the man Jesus Christ" to be the mediator between God and men (1 Tim 2:5). Passages in the Gospels were referenced where Jesus is identified as

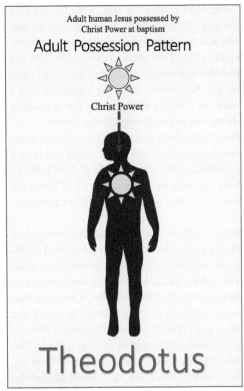
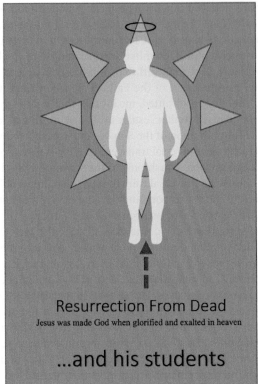

FIGURE 10.1 Left: Theodotus' Christological solution. Right: Teaching about Jesus' resurrection by Theodotus' students.

a "man" (i.e. John 8:40). The Mosaic prophecy long attached to Jesus by the Christians, that the Lord would raise up a prophet like Moses from their brothers (Deut. 18:15), was used as evidence that Jesus was a human being chosen by God, like Moses. Another prophetic passage that Apostolic Catholics identified with Jesus, Isaiah 53:3–4, was shown to speak about the suffering of a "man" not a God.

Victor was not convinced. He excommunicated Theodotus from the Roman church. This is why, under his successor Bishop Zephyrinus (199–218 CE), Theodotus' student, also named Theodotus (a banker by trade instead of a cobbler), founded an independent church. He installed Natalius, a native of Rome, as the salaried bishop of his church. There is a story that Natalius eventually returned to the Apostolic Catholic church after he was afflicted with nightmares of angels flogging him because of his heresy.

The ideas that Theodotus assembled were hardly new. As we saw in Chapter 6, other Christians like the law-observant Ebionites held similar views of Jesus. Likewise, Cerinthus (who was an early transtheist Christian from Asia Minor) taught that Jesus was born a natural child of Mary and Joseph, but that he grew to be more righteous than other men (Figure 10.2). At his baptism, Christ descended upon him in the form of a dove. From then on Jesus proclaimed the Father and performed miracles. At the crucifixion, Christ departed from Jesus, so that Jesus the man suffered and rose again, while Christ the Spirit remained impassible (Iren., *Haer.* 1.26.1; 3.3.4). Cerinthus is remembered by Irenaeus as a contemporary to the apostle John.

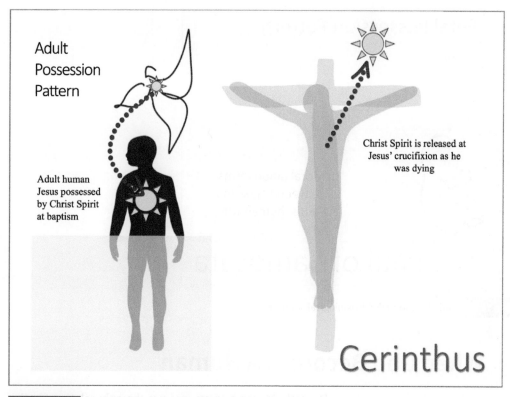

FIGURE 10.2 Cerinthus' Christological solution.

Theodotus' Christology then was not novel, but a product of early Christian speculation about Jesus that was ongoing especially in Asia Minor and Mesopotamia even after Theodotus' excommunication. The most well-known proponent of Dynamic Monarchianism came half a century after Theodotus in the teachings of the sixth-generation Christian (ca. 230–270 CE), Paul of Samosata, Bishop of Antioch (260–268 CE) who was jested to be a follower of Artemon. Paul's Christology follows the FETAL POSSESSION PATTERN (Figure 10.3). For Paul, God's monarchy was more important than the distinctions between the Father and the Son. He argued that only the Father is God. The Son only comes to be after he is conceived in the Virgin's womb with the assistance of the Holy Spirit. This is when the Logos, as an impersonal Power, indwelt the man Jesus. The indwelling Logos was no more than God's wisdom which had similarly possessed other prophetic men, but to a greater degree in Jesus. The union between the man Jesus and the Logos was not an ontological union but rather a moral one. That is, their union became stronger as Jesus aligned himself morally with God until his human will was inseparable from God's, and Jesus was perfected. In other words, Jesus practiced goodness in order to progressively become Good. This means that Jesus was not God-become-man but man-become-God. He was able to work miracles because of the indwelling Power, but also suffered because he was a man. Paul's ideas were heavily debated at three separate councils before his Christology was condemned and he was deposed in 269 CE.

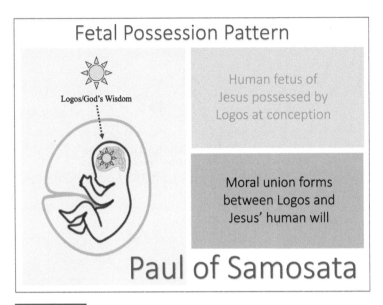

FIGURE 10.3 Paul of Samosata's Christological solution.

10.5 When God Becomes A Human

COMPANION READINGS

Hippolytus of Asia, *Against Noetus*
1–2, 6–7, 16

Tertullian, *Against Praxeas* 1–2, 9,
23, 26–27, 29

Dynamic Monarchianism was not the only solution fourth-generation Christians invented to preserve the monarchy of God and the unitarian Godhead. The other more popular solution – since it preserved *both* the monarchy of God *and* the full deity of Christ – was Modalist Monarchianism. This is the teaching that there is only one God who manifests himself in different modalities: as Creator and Lawgiver, he is called the Father; as the incarnate Savior, he is called the Son. These different modalities were not separate entities but masks that God wore (Figure 10.4).

Already in Justin's time, there were some Christians who objected to Justin's insistence that the Son is a Power begotten by the Father in a manner that made him numerically distinct from the Father, like fires lit from a fire. His detractors disagreed, arguing that the Power issuing from God is actually a projection of God, indivisible and inseparable from him, distinct only in name, whether Angel or Logos, so that the Father appeared in whatever forms pleased him (Jus., *Dial.* 128.3).

This teaching gained traction with Noetus, a presbyter who was active in Smyrna at the end of the second century. Noetus believes that the Logos in prologue to the Gospel of John is a figure of speech. Noetus rejects the position that the Logos incarnated as an entity separate from God (Hipp. Asia, *Noet.* 16). If this were the case, how could the Gospel of John go on to identify Jesus with the Father, Noetus asks (John 1:18; 10: 30; 14:8–10; Hipp. Asia, *Noet.* 2, 6–7)? Noetus took as his starting point what Christians took for granted, that Christ was God. In this case, Noetus reasons, Christ must be identical with the Father who, by definition, is God. This means that when Christ suffered, so did the Father. Noetus says that there is nothing wrong with glorifying the one and only God, Christ, who was born, suffered, and died (Hipp. Asia, *Noet.* 1). For this, Noetus was examined twice by the presbyters of his local church. The second examination ended in his expulsion.

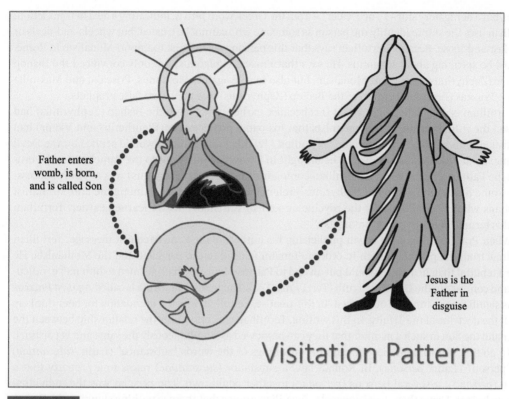

Father enters womb, is born, and is called Son

Jesus is the Father in disguise

Visitation Pattern

FIGURE 10.4 Modalist Christological solution.

Noetus continued to teach anyway, considering his unitarian position proper. He cultivated an influential school. His disciple Epigonus carried Noetus' teachings to Rome and persuaded Cleomenes to help publicize them and convince the Christian leaders in Rome to stop worshiping two Gods (the Father and the Son) (Hipp., *Ref.* 9.2, 5–6). Epigonus and Cleomenes convinced Bishop Zephyrinus (199–217 CE) and his righthand advisor Callistus (and next Bishop of Rome; 218–222 CE) that the Father and the Son are one and the same person (Latin: *persona*; Greek: *prosopon*) appearing with different names. They compared God to the universal monad that the philosopher Heracleitus (ca. 502 BCE) had speculated about, a being comprised of different qualities that were at once divisible and indivisible, created and uncreated, mortal and immortal. God is himself from himself, they explain, called by the names Father or Son depending on the situation. The Father appeared to us as the Son, was birthed, suffered, and died.

According to Tertullian, the Modalists claimed, that the Father himself "made himself a Son to himself" so that the Son is "a Father to himself" (Tert., *Prax.* 9). The Father proceeded from himself as the Son and returned to himself after the crucifixion (Tert., *Prax.* 23). Relying on Luke 1:35 ("The Spirit of God will come upon you and the power of the Highest will overshadow you; therefore the Holy Thing that will be born of you *will be called the Son of God*"), the Modalists argue that the Father is the High Power who entered the Virgin's womb and after his birth was called the Son (Tert., *Prax.* 26). Because the Son was the Father with a different name, the Father suffered as the Son suffered (Tert., *Prax.* 29). Not surprisingly, the Modalists became known as the Patripassian party (literally: The-Suffering-Father party). Modalist Christology is a variation of the VISITATION PATTERN Christology where the Father descends, enters the womb, is born, and walks around as the Son. Or to put it differently, Jesus is the Father in disguise.

Tertullian comes into this debate because of his personal interactions with an anti-Montanist and Modalist from Asia Minor whom Tertullian identifies as Praxeas. This name is not the name of an actual person, but a derogatory slur – "The Dealer" – from the Greek word *praxis*, indicating a deal or transaction. Tertullian uses the slur to identify the person as someone who cannot be trusted, but wheels-and-deals or plays-fast-and-loose. Because Tertullian says that this person was the first to import Modalism to Rome, he must be speaking about Epigonus. He says that Praxeas (Epigonus) not only convinced the Bishop of Rome (Zephyrinus) to support Modalism, but also to rule against Montanus, Priscilla, and Maxmilla because Praxeas (Epigonus) proved to the Bishop (Zephyrinus) that they were false prophets.

Tertullian is especially angry about this because earlier in his reign the Bishop (Zephyrinus) had reversed the rulings against the Montanists that his papal predecessors (Eleutherius and Victor) had established. This is why Tertullian famously quips, "By this Praxeas did a twofold service for the Devil at Rome: he drove away prophecy and he brought in heresy; he put flight to the Paraclete and he crucified the Father" (Tert., *Prax.* 1). Tertullian complains that Praxeas (Epigonus) was not only successful in Rome during the Bishop's (Zephyrinus') reign, but also in Carthage among the anti-Montanist Christians whom Tertullian calls the psychic or soulish Christians (as we learned earlier, Tertullian uses this term to identify non-Montanists).

When Praxeas (Epigonus) began publicizing his anti-Montanist and Modalist message, Tertullian withdrew from the psychic church in order to remain faithful to the Paraclete and the Montanists. He wrote a rebuttal that, he hoped, would put an end to Patripassianism which seemed to him naïve, ridiculous, and contrary to the Canon of Truth (Tert., *Prax.* 1–2). The treatise he wrote is called *Against Praxeas* and its significance cannot be overstated. In this treatise, Tertullian lays the foundation for later thinkers to craft the doctrine of the Trinity. In this writing, Tertullian conceptualizes the relationship between the Father and the Son in such a manner that they can be viewed as simultaneously the same and yet distinct.

To do this, Tertullian relies on statutory meanings of the words "substance" (Latin: *substantiae*) and "person" (Latin: *persona*). In Roman law, a substance (*substantiae*) refers to a property that a person (*persona*) or several persons (*personae*) together could own. The *persona* was the individual property holder. Using these legal concepts, Tertullian argues that there is nothing stopping the Father from sharing his divine monarchy with his Son. This does not split the monarchy into two properties. Instead, the single monarchy is administered or managed (Latin: *dispensation*; Greek: *oikonomia*) by the Son (Tert., *Prax.* 2). This would have made sense to Romans who were used to Emperors sharing their reigns with their sons. Such situations did not end up with two separate reigns, but one managed by different people. When this idea is applied to God, Tertullian concludes that the Father and Son share the same property or substance (they are consubstantial) in their monarchy while being distinct persons in its administration.

What is most fascinating is that Tertullian does not stop here, but brings the Paraclete into the equation. Not only does Tertullian create a rebuttal to Noetus' teaching about relationship of the Father and the Son, but he also goes after Epigonus' anti-Montanist bravado by incorporating the Paraclete into the divine monarchy and its administration. By establishing equal footing for the Father, Son, *and* the Paraclete, the discussion is no longer limited to the relationship of the Father and Son, but now also includes the Holy Spirit's relationship to them. This is a bold move on Tertullian's part that shapes what had been a binitarian (two-in-one) controversy into a trinitarian (three-in-one) controversy.

Tertullian does this in order to legitimize the Montanist understanding of the Paraclete as the Vicar of holiness and perpetual revelator and regulator of church discipline. Tertullian fashions the doctrine of the Three-In-One God (Figure 10.5), that the Father, Son, *and* Holy Spirit share in one single undivided substance as three different persons, "not in condition, but in degree; not in substance, but in form; not in power, but in aspect" (Tert., *Prax.* 2). He uses natural images to exemplify the relationship: like beams from the sun; like fruit and plants from the root; like rivers from the spring. That said, Tertullian goes on to play up the distinctions between the persons in the Trinity in ways that led other Christians to label him a subordinationist (the Son is subordinate to the Father) because he also said that the Father is the "entire substance" while the Son is a "derivation and portion of the whole" (Tert., *Prax.* 9).

How could it be that the Son is consubstantial with the Father but also be a human being? Tertullian sorts this dilemma out by using the same Roman property law which, in addition to stating that

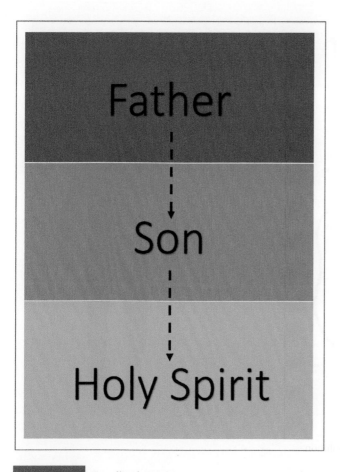

FIGURE 10.5 Tertullian's Trinity.

more than one person (*persona*) could own a single property (*substantia*) also stated that a single person (*persona*) could own more than one property (*substantia*). In Jesus' situation, the Son could own the God-substance while also owning the human substance. In other words, the Son shared two properties: the divine nature (spirit) and human nature (flesh and soul).

It was obvious to Tertullian that the Son was the Logos in flesh. What was not obvious was how the Logos became flesh. Tertullian asks, "Was he metamorphosed into flesh, or did he clothe himself in it?" (Tert., *Prax.* 27). A transfiguration of God into flesh was unthinkable to Tertullian who imagines it as a monstrous mixture or amalgam that was the result of changing God and the human being into something else entirely. This means that the HYBRID and the ENSOULMENT PATTERNS were out. The only real solution in Tertullian's mind was to build on the FETAL POSSESSION PATTERN (Figure 10.6) because this was the only way to safeguard both Jesus' humanity (he had his own body and soul) and his full divinity (the Logos dwelled in him). But the possession was not ordinary. It was extraordinary because both substances were conjoined unaltered and unimpaired in Jesus, so that each one preserved its own qualities and activities: the spirit performed miracles and the humanity (flesh and soul) endured sufferings and death. "We observe a twofold condition, not confused but conjoined, Jesus, in one Person at once God and human" (Tert., *Prax.* 27). The conjoined but separate natures of Jesus allowed Tertullian to argue against Patripassianism, ruling that the human substance of Jesus suffered and died, while the divine substance did not.

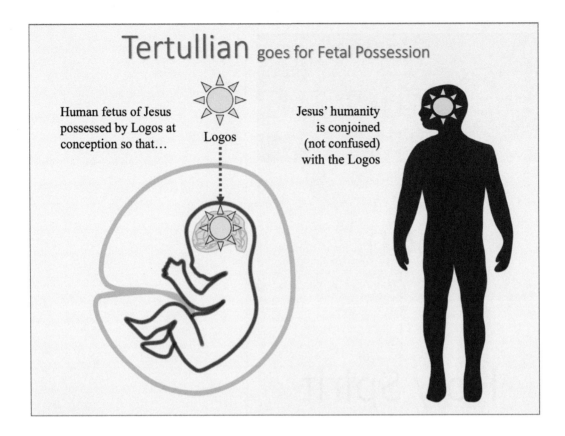

FIGURE 10.6 Tertullian's Christological solution.

[10.6] The God Crisis

COMPANION READINGS
Hippolytus, *Refutation* 9–10 Soon after Tertullian published *Against Praxeas* (ca. 213 CE) at the end of Bishop Zephyrinus' tenure (199–217 CE), Sabellius, a Christian theologian from Libya (North Africa), arrived in Rome and took over where Cleomenes left off. He appears to have responded to the criticism waged by Tertullian against Noetus' naïve formulation of Modalism, giving it a more sophisticated philosophical shape that also included the Holy Spirit in the equation (Hipp., *Ref.* 9.11). Sabellius said that *God* is a Son–Father (Greek: *huiopator*) monad that expressed itself through a process of dilation (Figure 10.7). He taught that the Father and the Son are the *same God* (Greek: *homoousios*; Basil, *Ep.* 9.2), a monad that reveals itself in three ways when creating, redeeming, and sanctifying. This expansion took place so that when the monad acted to create and give the Law we call God the Father, to redeem we call God the Son, and to sanctify and inspire we call God the Holy Spirit. For Sabellius, there only is a Trinity of names, not a Trinity of persons. He envisions the dilation of the monad to be like the sun projecting a ray, withdrawing it, and then projecting it again in consecutive order. This is how Sabellius maintained monotheism while at the same time tried to distance himself from Patripassianism: the Son suffers as *God*, but not as the *Father*.

While in Rome, Sabellius had the support of Bishop Zephyrinus and his successor Callistus (218–222 CE) until another Roman theologian, Hippolytus became relentless in his campaign against

God dilates as Father
to create and give Law

God dilates as Son
to redeem

God dilates Holy Spirit
to sanctify

Sabellius

FIGURE 10.7 Sabellius' solution to the Trinity.

the two bishops and Sabellius. Hippolytus of Rome wrote the *Refutation Against All Heresies* after Callistus' death in order to bring down Modalism and other movements he considered heretical (Hipp., *Ref.* 9.12). Hippolytus of Rome is not the same author as the Hippolytus of Asia who wrote *Against Noetus*. Both authors, however, positioned themselves as Tertullian did: as critics of Modalism. Hippolytus of Asia took on Noetus, while Hippolytus of Rome took on Sabellius and the two bishops of Rome.

In the case of Hippolytus of Asia who wrote *Against Noetus*, he thinks that God is one with many powers inside himself that issue forth like light from light, water from a spring, a sunbeam from the sun. When the Logos becomes visible as the Son, he does so by incarnating as Jesus Christ. When the Logos fashions the universe, it is God's Wisdom or Spirit that adorns it. He views these as a triad of persons: Father, Son, and Spirit (Hipp. Asia, *Noet.* 10–11). As for Hippolytus of Rome who wrote the *Refutation*, he believed in one God whose inner thought was the Logos and mediator of creation. In his incarnation, he recapitulated the stages of human life from infancy to death, redeeming all through his resurrection (Hipp., *Ref.* 10.32–34).

Bishop Zephyrinus and Bishop Callistus found themselves in a bind. On the one hand, Modalism was popular in Rome during their tenures. Tertullian, Hippolytus of Rome, and Hippolytus of Asia were considered Ditheists (believers in two Gods) by many Christians. Their new talk of "persons" of the Godhead was viewed with suspicion. On the other hand, the less popular idea that the Father suffered continued to be linked with Modalism even as it was reformulated by Sabellius.

By 220 CE, Callistus could avoid a ruling no longer. Even though he sympathized with Modalism, he decided to excommunicate Sabellius for making no real distinction between the Father, Son, and Spirit. At the same time, he excommunicated Hippolytus of Rome for ditheism. To avoid the danger he had identified in both these positions, Callistus tried to work out a compromise that accounted for the real distinctions between the Father and the Logos while insisting that they were manifestations of one divine Spirit.

Callistus, wanting to put an end to ditheism, continues to emphasize God's unity, that the Father, Son, and Spirit are one and the same reality, being, or person (Greek: *prosopon*). God is the Spirit which pervades the universe as a single being or person, he says. He believes that this Spirit as the

Logos, which really incarnated in Jesus, is the Father while the visible flesh is the Son. Callistus states, "I will not profess belief in two Gods, Father and Son, but in one. For the Father, who subsisted in the Son himself, after he had taken on our flesh, raised it to the nature of God, by bringing it into union with himself, and made it one. Thus Father and Son must be styled one God, and that this Person being one, cannot be two" (Hipp., *Ref.* 9.12.18). This means that the Father did not suffer, but the Father only suffered in union with the Son. Although his was not the final formulation of the Trinity or the problem of the two natures of the Son, Callistus served as a bridge between both forms of Dynamic and Modalist Monarchism while holding ditheism at bay.

Modalism, however, has never been put to rest partly because the scriptures used to formulate Modalism are part of the Christian canon. For instance, in modernity, Modalism re-emerges through the Pentecostal "revelations" of R.E. McAlister and John G. Schaepoe who taught that baptisms ought to be performed only in the name of Jesus (as the scripture says: Acts 2:38; 8:16; 10:48; 19:3–5; 22:16; 1 Cor. 1:13) rather than the Trinitarian formula. By 1916, a schism formed over this teaching and Oneness Pentecostalism was born. Oneness Pentecostals, like ancient Modalists, believe that there is one indivisible God with no personal distinctions in God's essence. The Father, Son, and Holy Spirit are merely titles reflecting the different ways that the One God reveals himself to us. Many of the scriptures the Oneness Pentecostals point to are the same passages used by Modalist theologians in antiquity. As long as these scriptures exist, Modalism will re-emerge as a Biblical explanation for the nature of the God and his relationship to the Son.

10.7 Counterfeit Christians

COMPANION READINGS
Tertullian, *Against Hermogenes* 2–3, 11, 18, 20, 33–34, 40
Tertullian, *Against the Valentinians* 1–2, 4–5, 39

Tertullian attempted to bar particular Christians from being able to use the scriptures on the grounds that the Apostolic Catholics were their only legitimate owners (Tert., *Prescr.* 15). He bases this argument on a legal argument called the *longi temporis praescriptio*, the defense in Roman law that someone who possessed land for a long period of time was considered its legitimate owner. Tertullian argues that the Apostolic Catholic church is the long-time heir of Christ's teaching, which had been entrusted to the apostles as the Canon of Truth and then transmitted to the churches they founded. Given this history, he declares that the scriptures are the rightful possession of the Apostolic Catholics and that its Canon of Truth is true.

The Christians who had no right to the scriptures and perverted or rejected the Canon of Truth are characterized by Tertullian as heretics. In Tertullian's mind, heretics are newcomers who distorted the Catholic tradition when they forged their own tradition from a supposed "secret tradition" they traced back to Jesus. Tertullian thinks that this secret tradition is something they fabricated to make their movements appear to be old when, in fact, they were new and their faith counterfeit. Tertullian never considers the creation of his own apostolic tradition in similar terms: as the fabrication of an old apostolic lineage to authorize the Canon of Truth.

Tertullian considers his Christian Carthaginian contemporary, the artist and painter Hermogenes of Antioch, a heretic. He writes an entire work against Hermogenes, although Tertullian's exposition (ca. 204–207 CE) may rely on the earlier lost work of Theophilus of Antioch who also wrote against Hermogenes (170–180 CE). Hermogenes disagreed with the teaching that God created from nothing (*creatio ex nihilo*). *Creatio ex nihilo* was something that the Christians had been discussing since at least the time of Basilides.

According to Hermogenes, there are three possibilities when it came to how demiurgy worked. Either God had made all things out of himself, or out of nothing, or out of something that pre-existed (Tert., *Herm.* 2). Hermogenes ditches the first possibility because this would mean that God sliced and diced himself or dissolved himself into parts. The second possibility is equally problematic because if

God is all good, it is impossible for him to will or make anything evil. But experience tells us, Hermogenes says, that evil exists and its existence is best explained as a fault of something. This is what led him to stand by the long-established Platonic model that the world of matter had always existed and that it was acted upon by God when the world was created.

In Hermogenes' opinion, God and matter are co-eternals. He accepts the Aristotelian argument that since God is Lord, this implies that he has to be the Lord of something and that this something has to also exist eternally (Tert., *Herm.* 40). Through this schematic, Hermogenes is able to deal with the problem of evil, positing evil as the result of the chaotic motion of matter rather than God (Tert., *Herm.* 11). Hermogenes finds support for his position in the account of creation according to Genesis which states that in the beginning "the earth was without form, and void." Hermogenes understands this to mean that matter ("matter") pre-existed ("was") in a state of chaos ("formless and void") (Tert., *Herm.* 23).

His reading aligns with the way creation is described in other ancient stories of creation written by people who lived around the Mediterranean basin. His reading would have been perceived to be the normative reading of the Genesis account, with the exception of some Christians like Tertullian who started from the position that God is omnipotent and matter is perishable and inferior to God (Tert., *Herm.* 34). Tertullian develops the position that, as the Canon of Truth states, only God is uncreated and undivided. God's Thought, Wisdom, or Logos, he argues, is what God used to create from nothing (Tert., *Herm.* 18, 20, 33). Here Tertullian proposes for the first time that the Logos is coeternal with God. Even so, he wants to make clear that God exclusively is eternal. To make this argument, Tertullian insists that "God" refers to the eternal divine substance, while the designations "Lord" and "Father" refer to God's power. Lord and Father are names that are accrued once the Son was begotten (Tert., *Herm.* 3).

A more disturbing heresy, according to Tertullian, started with the teachings of Valentinus. Tertullian identifies the Valentinians as a group who, because they have so many differing opinions and versions of their doctrines, are comparable to a courtesan who changes her dresses everyday (Tert., *Val.* 4). Tertullian understands their diversity to be a disadvantage because it leaves the Valentinians divided into separate social groups each following a different leader whose opinions and revelations do not necessarily agree with other leaders. In his mind, this diversity showcases how far they have strayed from the Canon of Truth into the territory of heresy. He sees their aberrant doctrinal growth as spreading into a Gnostic forest (Tert., *Val.* 39).

Tertullian's knowledge of Valentinian doctrines mainly is dependent upon Irenaeus although he mentions relying also on Justin Marytr, Miltiades, and Proculus (Tert., *Val.* 5). He knows about Valentinians in the past (Ptolemy, Heracleon, Secundus, and Marcus) who have all developed Valentinus' teachings in their own unique and sometimes contradictory directions. Uniquely, Tertullian tells us about his own contemporary, the Valentinian Axionicus of Antioch. Axionicus appears to have understood how confusing the Valentinian systems had become with all the variations that had emerged since Valentinus' death. So Axionicus jumps in, conducting historical research to recover Valentinus' original teachings so that they can be reinstated as authoritative church doctrine (Tert., *Val.* 4). Because Axionicus' reform movement was ongoing while Tertullian was writing, we do not know if he was successful. But given the fractured nature of Valentinian systems and their belief in continued revelation, it is unlikely that he had long-term success reforming Valentinian diversity.

While Tertullian finds their diversity annoying, what he really vexes over is how much Valentinian church services mirror Catholic services, a point that Irenaeus also makes. But Tertullian reports to know why this is the case. Tertullian perceives the Valentinian movement to be a SECESSIONIST MOVEMENT that was started by Valentinus after he lost the election to Pius who assumed the bishopric of Rome instead (ca. 140 CE). Tertullian concedes that Valentinus was a brilliant theologian and teacher (he calls him a genius) who was considered part of the Apostolic Catholic church until after his campaign for election failed. Tertullian does not even entertain the possibility that Valentinus was excommunicated – Valentinus clearly was not – but rather, he says that Valentinus seceded from the Roman church and founded a parallel church for spiritual seekers (Tert., *Val.* 4).

The Valentinians whom Tertullian knows, however, do not consider themselves anything but Christian. They reject the name Valentinian that other Christians have assigned them (Tert., *Val.* 4). Tertullian says that they affirm to be part of the same community of faith as the Apostolic Catholics (Tert., *Val.* 1). How can this be? Tertullian explains that they think that the community of faith consists of an advanced group of wise spiritual people (the serpents) and a beginner group for simple souls (the doves) (cf. Matt. 10:16; Tert., *Val.* 2). The advanced group undergoes a catechism based on the revelation of secret esoteric mysteries over a long time period (Tertullian says five years) until the full divinity is revealed at the climax of the initiation (Tert., *Val.* 1). They view themselves as the advanced initiated Christians while the non-Valentinians are the simpletons.

While they claim to be part of the Christian community of faith and may organize their Sunday worship services to mirror Apostolic Catholic churches, they should not be confused with the Apostolic Christians for whom the Roman Bishop was becoming the principal leader. Tertullian remarks about the Valentinians' loose independent ecclesiastical structure, that "today one person is a bishop and tomorrow another; the person who is a deacon today, tomorrow is a reader; the one who is a priest is a layman tomorrow; for they even impose on laymen the functions of priesthood" (Tert., *Presc.* 41). Ordination includes women who "are bold enough to teach, to dispute, to exorcise, to heal – it may be even to baptize" (Tert., *Presc.* 41). During Tertullian's time, the Valentinians were a parallel Gnostic Christian church that billed themselves as the Spiritual Apostolic Catholic church, offering special knowledge (gnosis) and advanced initiations (second baptism; ecstatic journeys). They relied on the continual revelations of their leaders to sustain their identity, authority, and doctrines.

⟦10.8⟧ The Two Testaments

COMPANION READINGS
Hebrews
Tertullian, *Against Marcion* 1.19;
3.14; 3.22; 4.1; 5.2

As we learned in Chapter 2, Marcion founded a Christian church that worshipped an Alien God of Goodness (XENOTHEISM). Marcion saw the Jewish scriptures as the possession of Jews, not Christians, being a record of the Jew's history and relationship with YHWH the Creator of this universe and their patron God. Marcion saw the need for a unique set of scriptures for Christians. He created a set of Christian scriptures – The New Testament – that consisted of an edited version of the *Evangelion* and ten letters of Paul. He organized his counter movement to parallel the Apostolic Catholic churches and had immense success, especially in Asia Minor, Syria, and Africa.

Marcion's success had to be confronted by the other Christians who continued to worship YHWH and use the Jewish scriptures as authoritative sacred writings. To top Marcion, Justin and Tatian worked to create a better Gospel that harmonized several Gospels into one story, *The Apostles' Memoirs*. Tatian's ultimate harmony publication, the *Diatessaron*, became the Bible for early Syrian Christians. Both authors avoid Marcion's language: they do not use the name Gospel (*Evangelion*) and New Testament for their own publications, although the concept of the gospel as the good news of Jesus Christ and the establishment of the new covenant (Greek: *diathêkê*; Latin: *testamentum*) as prophesied by Jeremiah 31:31–34 were assumed. The "newness" of Christianity was reframed in supersessionist language by them. Christianity was not a new separate religion from Judaism as Marcion taught, but a religion that surpassed Judaism, both succeeding it and preceding it in its universal philosophical scope.

Another third-generation strategy undertaken by an opponent of Marcion involved rewriting a version of the *Evangelion*, to showcase the connection that Jesus' life had with Judaism. This became known as the Gospel of Luke. The same scholar likely wrote the book of Acts as a sequel. It is the first church history written to relocate Paul as a friend of the apostles and co-worker within the synagogues. Paul's message about God is clarified, so that Marcion's God is put to rest. In a famous speech set in Athens, Paul proclaims that the God of worship is not the Unknown and Foreign God (of Marcion), but the Creator of the world who will judge the world through Jesus and resurrect the faithful from the dead just as he did Jesus (Acts 17:16–32). Similarly-minded Christian scholars were responsible for writing *1 Clement* and/or the Pastoral Epistles (1 and 2 Timothy and Titus), which legitimatize the ecclesiastical offices that were emerging in the Apostolic Catholic network and clarify the God of worship as the Creator and sole Sovereign over the universe. In the Pastoral letters, Paul presents himself as a heresy-hunter and considers the Law to be good when it is used legitimately. These three pseudepigraphic letters were appended to Marcion's collection of ten letters, so that it appears that Paul banned Marcionism before it was even conceived.

A generation later, Irenaeus took another approach. He collected four Gospels together, arguing that four is better than (Marcion's) one. He provides names for the Gospels (Matthew, Mark, Luke, and John) and backstories about the authors in order to give the four Gospels direct links to apostolic tradition. He is the first Christian to extensively use the book of Acts and he uses it to make out Marcion to be a fool. We get a sense from Irenaeus that, to displace Marcion's canon, the Apostolic Christians have been in the process of constructing a set of scriptures that include, as their core, the four Gospels, Acts, and thirteen letters of Paul. That said, Irenaeus never calls this set of scriptures The New Testament.

By the fifth-generation when Tertullian takes up the cause against Marcion, the Apostolic Catholics have established the parameters of their Christian scripture so that Tertullian makes use of the books that are in the modern Christian New Testament (with the exception of 2 and 3 John, James, and 2 Peter). He considers the scripture to include the Law and the Prophets and the writings of the evangelists and apostles (Tert., *Presc.* 36.5). In his works, Tertullian is the first Apostolic Catholic to distinguish The Old Testament and The New Testament as two sets of scriptures. By his time, these appear to be popular designations for the Jewish scripture (The Old Testament) and the Christian scripture (The New Testament) probably due to the fact that the Marcionite church had broadcast this distinction for decades (Tert., *Marc.* 4.1). While Marcion was long dead, his impact continued to be felt among the fifth-generation Christians whose conceptualization of their scriptures bore Marcion's imprint.

Because of the popularizing of the terms Old and New Testaments, Tertullian chooses to appropriate the designations in order to co-opt them from the Marcionites. To do so, he finds it necessary to clarify exactly what the terms mean. He is not completely comfortable with these designations because Marcion made the distinction to highlight the difference between the Alien God and the Biblical God, assigning the New to the Alien God and the Old to the Biblical God (Tert., *Marc.* 1.19). Tertullian reframes the separation of the Old from the New not as a difference in deities, but a difference in how and why the same God disciplines differently as needed (Tert., *Marc.* 5.2). Tertullian understands the difference in terms of progressive justice: what is demanded of infants (Law and Prophets) is different from what is demanded of young people (Gospel) and adults (Montanist revelations) (Tert., *Veil.* 1.10).

Tertullian agrees with Marcion, that there is a difference between the Law and the Gospel and that they can be understood as two separate testaments (Tert., *Marc.* 3.14; 4.1; 5.2). But Tertullian doubts that the Law of the Creator should be excluded from the Gospel of Christ as Marcion had done (Tert., Marc. 3.22; 5.2). For Tertullian, the Law is part of the discipline. Prophecy has been fulfilled. In Tertullian's reframing, the Old Testament is supplemented by the New as God's discipline unfolds (Tert., *Marc.* 4.1). It is in this context that Tertullian describes Gentile converts as those who are "turning aside from Judaism" and exchanging "the obligations and burdens of the Law for the freedom of the Gospel" (Tert., *Marc.* 3.22). Clearly, Tertullian did not wish to preserve the relevance of Judaism, but only anchor the identity of the Christian God as the same God who gave the Law to the Jews. The language of newness was not about discontinuity as Marcion taught, but superiority, supplementation, renewal, and extension. The Old Testament is not to be abandoned as irrelevant, but retained as a separate and still-relevant set of scriptures as Apostolic Catholic Christians understand them.

Tertullian makes these arguments within a five-volume critique of Marcion called *Against Marcion*. This is the most comprehensive and extensive treatment of Marcion to survive from antiquity. Book 1 handles Marcion's Alien God, while Book 2 Marcion's Creator God (the Biblical God).

Book 3 rebuts Marcion's VISITATION CHRISTOLOGY. Book 4 provides a verse-by-verse textual analysis of the *Evangelion* compared to the canonical Gospel of Luke. Book 5 presents a similar textual analysis of the *Apostolicon* compared to the Apostolic Catholic version of the letters of Paul. In both cases, Tertullian determines that the *Evangelion* and the *Apostolicon* are abridged versions of the Apostolic Catholic texts created by Marcion through a process of editing ("mutilating") the Apostolic Catholic texts to make them conform to Marcion's theology and Christology.

Tertullian's conclusion (that Marcion "mutilated" Luke and Paul by cutting out what did not conform to his teachings) has come under intense scrutiny recently by scholars who have been working on this issue. Scholars working on this problem have been coming to the conclusion that canonical Luke is actually an expansion of a version of the *Evangelion* largely because Marcion's edition of the *Evangelion* contains materials that do not conform to Marcion's teachings. It is most likely that the creation of the Gospel of Luke was done in reaction to Marcion, who had published his New Testament, a Christian scripture that included his own distinctive editions of the *Evangelion* and the *Apostolicon*. To compete, an Apostolic Catholic author took an edition of the *Evangelion* and expanded it into the Gospel of Luke. He wrote Acts as a sequel to reconfigure Marcion's Paul. As we have seen previously, the author of Acts did this by aligning Peter and Paul, so that both men are in agreement on issues of Judaism and the Law.

As for Paul's letters, Marcion's ten-letter collection was first expanded by the Apostolic Catholics into a thirteen-letter edition, with the addition of the anti-Marcionite Pastoral epistles. This thirteen-letter edition was expanded again to include the Epistle to the Hebrews, which appears to be another anti-Marcionite text written by a third-generation Christian. But this second addition to Paul's letters was not universal. Hebrews is known as a letter of Paul by some fifth-generation Christians and survives in our oldest manuscript of Paul's letters, P^{46} (ca. 200 CE), although it is noteworthy that Irenaeus, Tertullian, and Hippolytus do not recognize it as a letter of Paul and its authenticity as Paul's letter was disputed until the fourth century.

In the collection of Paul's letters that contained it, however, Hebrews worked in an anti-Marcionite fashion: to certify how Paul's theology ought to be understood properly, explaining in great detail Jesus' relationship to the old covenant (or testament), the Jewish cult, and Jewish scripture. The importance of the prophets as they relate to Jesus are mentioned in the opening of the letter. Immediately God is identified with the Biblical Creator, and what he creates is said to reflect his glory and imprint (Heb. 1:1–3). Jesus is presented as the super-angel who is God's High Priest in the order of Melchizedek. He both conducts the divine rites (sacrifice for atonement) and serves as the offering (his own blood) in the heavenly temple. The worship and sanctuary of the Jews (as it is related in the Jewish scripture) is linked to the first covenant. This is presented as a mere imitation of the heavenly cult and a foreshadowing of the new covenant, when Jesus interceded as the final sacrifice. Jesus, as the High Priest, mediates eternal life when he enters the heavenly temple and appears in God's presence on our behalf and sacrifices himself. In this way, the author of Hebrews, like Ignatius, Polycarp, Justin, and other third-generation authors, appropriates Jewish scripture and the Jewish cult, while arguing for the supersession of Christian theology and eucharistic practices.

By the time of Tertullian, the Apostolic Catholics in the west had determined the basic parameters of their New Testament in direct competition with Marcion and other Christian groups. The earliest list of their books is located in the Muratorian Canon, which purports to be from Rome (ca. 200 CE). The beginning of the list is missing so it starts with Luke (which it also calls the third Gospel) and John (the fourth of the Gospels). So Matthew and Mark were likely included in the missing fragment as the first and second Gospels. After John came Acts, the thirteen letters of Paul, Jude, two letters of John, the Wisdom of Solomon, the Apocalypse of John, and the Apocalypse of Peter. About the Apocalypse of Peter, the text says that some people do not allow it to be read in church. Also, it says that the *Shepherd of Hermas* should be read but does not have the authority of scripture. Not surprisingly, the list mentions Marcion, explaining that two letters of Paul ought to be avoided (To the Laodiceans and To the Alexandrians) because they were "forged in Paul's name to further the heresy of Marcion." Outed also is a Marcionite psalm book composed by Miltiades. Also unacceptable is anything written by Valentinus, Basilides, and Arsinous (we are unsure who Arsinous was, but a heroic woman Arsinoe is mentioned in the *1 Apocalypse of James* from the Nag Hammadi Collection).

While the New Testament canon of the Apostolic Catholics is not yet completely determined (the exact list comes in 367 CE in a letter written by Athanasius to the churches in his bishopric), the foundational material is set. Largely to combat the success of Marcionite Christianity and the genius of Marcion's New Testament canon, Apostolic Catholics carefully curated their own New Testament by selecting, editing, and even authoring new Christian scriptures as part of their *traditio*.

Timeline

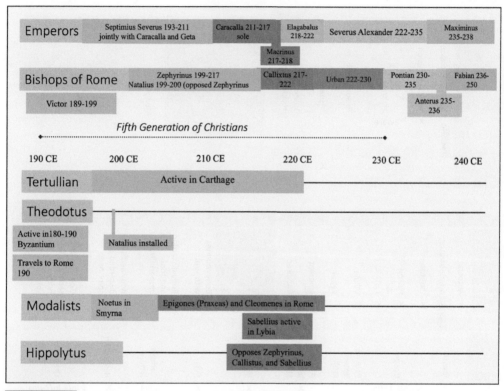

FIGURE 10.8   Timeline for fifth-generation Christians in Rome and Carthage.

Pattern Summary

Tertullian, the Dynamic Monarchians, and the Modalists were representatives of the YAHWIST FAMILY and considered themselves to be Apostolic Catholics (see Figure 10.9). This identity is interesting since Tertullian identified as a Montanist (Pneumatic) at a time when the Montanists were once-and-for-all expelled by Pope Zephyrinus, and both the Dynamists and the Modalists were expelled at various synods. Tertullian's writings are evidence of an increase of infighting among the Apostolic Catholics, who continue to consolidate through exclusion. Since the Transtheists and Marcionites had been excluded in previous generations, now the fight turned on issues of Maximalism (excessive holiness and rules) and the Binitarian Problem, which had been created once the Apostolic Catholics merged the Biblical God with the Transcendent God of the philosophers. What Tertullian, the Dynamists, and the Modalists agreed upon was that YHWH is the Creator and God of worship. God was considered a fair JUSTICE

Family Pattern Chart
# Tertullian
X=Definitely > L=Likely

THEODICY			
	Faulty-God	Faulty-Human	Other
Tertullian		X	Traducianism

CHRISTOLOGY						
	Adult possession	Fetal possession	Hybrid	Ensoulment	Visitation	Human who received revelation
Tertullian		X	aware			
Theodotus	X					
Noetus					X	
Paul of Samosata	X					

SOTERIOLOGY					
	Gift from God	Human achievement	Minimalist	Moderate	Maximalist
Tertullian		X		X	

ANTHROPOLOGY				
		Mono	Dual	Triad	Quad
Tertullian			X		

COSMIC DEMIURGY									
	Autocrat	Administrator	Caretaker	Patron	Justice	Villain	Rebel	Ignorant	Impaired
Tertullian	X	X	X	X	X				

RESURRECTION				
	Body reunites with soul	Body discarded and soul immortalized	Body and soul discarded and spirit rises	God-element separates from body soul, and spirit and rises
Tertullian	X			

SCRIPTURES									
	Jewish	Gospel	Pauline letters (10)	Pauline letters (13)	Hebrews	Acts	Catholic letters	Revelation	Other
Tertullian	X	Mt/Mk/Lk/Jn		X	X	X	1 Pet	X	1 Jn/2 Jn/?-Jms

ECCLESIOLOGY							
	Consolidation movement	Reform movement	Secessionist movement	Counter movement	Innovative movement	Trans-regional	Regional
Tertullian	X	X	X			X	X

FIGURE 10.9 Summary of the western Apostolic Catholic patterns of beliefs and practices among fifth-generation Christians.

and a PATRON to the Apostolic Catholics. Human beings were RESPONSIBLE FOR SIN and had to work for their purity and salvation. The FLESH WOULD BE RESURRECTED in some form at Judgment. They disagreed on how to sort out the Binitarian Problem, which directly impacted their Christological Patterns.

Takeaways

1. The first known Christian author from North Africa is Tertullian of Carthage. Tertullian converted to Christianity because he was impressed with the culture of martyrdom and ethics of the Christians.

2. Tertullian aligned himself with the Montanists because he favored their holiness lifestyle. He believed that the Apostolic Catholics had become too lax in their behaviors and were not following the teachings of the Holy Spirit.

3. While Tertullian honored women prophets he could test, he did not support women's leadership in the church.

4. Tertullian fashioned a dress code for Christians that signaled their chastity, modesty, and everyday holiness.

5. Theodotus the Cobbler was instrumental in the promotion of Dynamic Monarchianism, which declared that an impersonal Power possessed the morally upright Jesus. This teaching safeguarded monotheism because Jesus was not God, but a man possessed by a divine Power.

6. The unitarian Godhead was also safeguarded by the Modalist Monarchians who taught that there is only one God who manifests himself in different modalities as the Father, Son, and Spirit. Noetus and Sabellius were Modalist Monarchians.

7. Tertullian wrote *Against Praxeas* to argue against Epigonus, a Modalist. He accused the Modalists of teaching that the Father suffered. Because of this, he called them Patripassians.

8. Tertullian developed his Trinitarianism in response to the Modalists, arguing that the three persons of the Trinity shared the administration of the single monarchy.

9. Tertullian argued for the FETAL POSSESSION PATTERN, stating that the Son shared both human and divine properties that were conjoined but not mixed or confused.

10. Sabellius attempted to resolve the Modalist problem by arguing that God dilated himself as Father, Son, and Holy Spirit.

11. Tertullian believed that only the Apostolic Catholics had the right to use the scripture because they had "owned" it longer than heretics like Hermogenes, Valentinus, and Marcion.

12. Tertullian appropriated the Marcionite division of the Old Testament and the New Testament. He reframes the division to refer to how God disciplines differently as needed rather than signaling two different Gods as Marcion had it.

13. Tertullian critique against Marcion is the most comprehensive and extensive treatment of Marcion to survive from antiquity. Tertullian determines that the *Evangelion* and the *Apostolicon* are abridged editions of the canonical texts created by Marcion through a process of "mutilation."

14. The Epistle to the Hebrews was added to some collections of the thirteen letters of Paul in order to combat Marcionism.

Questions

1. How did Marcion's canon affect the development of the Apostolic Catholic New Testament? How were Paul's letters a factor in this development? What was the importance of Jewish scripture in this development?

2. Compare and contrast Dynamic Monarchianism and Modalist Monarchianism? What is the same about these two positions? What is different? What were these positions trying to safeguard?

3. Explain Tertullian's position on the Trinity. How does his position take on Modalism? How does it interface with Montanism?

4. How and why did Tertullian begin to call the Catholic Christian scriptures The New Testament? How did he distinguish this from Marcion's New Testament? How did the terminology of the old covenant or old testament come into play?

5. What do we learn about Marcion from Tertullian's critique? How does Tertullian explain the *Evangelion* and the *Apostolicon* in comparison with the Catholic letters of Paul and their versions of the written Gospels?

6. What do we learn about Montanism from studying Tertullian? Why was he attracted to it? What did he believe about prophecy and the Holy Spirit?

7. How and why did Tertullian think the Apostolic Catholic church should reform?

8. What did Tertullian think about martyrdom? What actions did he personally take to clear the Christian name?

Resources

M. David Litwa. 2022. Chapters 18 and 21 in *Found Christianities: Remaking the World of the Second Century CE*. London: T&T Clark.

Geoffrey D. Dunn. 2004. *Tertullian*. London: Routledge.

Everett Ferguson. 1993. "Early Christian Martyrdom and Civil Disobedience." *Journal of Early Christian Studies* 1: 73-83.

Justo L. González. 1970 (revised edition). Chapter 7 in *A History of Christian Thought from the Beginnings to the Council of Chalcedon*. Volume 1. Ashville: Abingdon Press.

Wolfram Kinzig. 1994. "Kainê Diathênê. The Title of the New Testament in the Second and Third Centuries." *Journal of Theological Studies* 45: 519–544.

Peter Lampe. 2003. Chapter 33 and 34 in *From Paul to Valentinus: Christians at Rome in the First Two Centuries*. Translated by Michael Steinhauser and edited by Marshall D. Johnson. Minneapolis: Fortress Press.

Lee Martin McDonald. 2007. *The Biblical Canon. Its Origin, Transmission, and Authority*. Peabody: Hendrickson Publishers.

Claudio Moreschini and Enrico Norelli. 2005. Chapter 18.2. *Early Christian Greek and Latin Literature: A Literary History*. Volume 1: *From Paul to the Age of Constantine*. Translated by Matthew J. O'Connell. Peabody: Hendrickson Publishers.

Laura Nasrallah. 2003. *An Ecstasy of Folly: Prophecy and Authority in Early Christianity*. Cambridge: Harvard University Press.

Eric Osborn. 1997. *Tertullian, First Theologian of the West*. Cambridge: Cambridge University Press.

Joyce E. Salisbury. 1997. *Perpetua's Passion. The Death and Memory of a Young Roman Woman*. New York: Routledge.

Vinzent, Markus. 2019. "Hippolytus of Rome: A Manifold Enigma." Pages 162-195 in *Writing the History of Early Chrisitanity: From Reception to Retrospection*. Cambridge: Cambridge University Press.

Niels Willert. 2014. "Tertullian." Pages 159–184 in *In Defense of Christianity: Early Christian Apologists* Early Christianity in the Context of Antiquity 15. Edited by Jakob Engberg, Anders-Christian Jacobsen, and Jörg Ulrich. Translated by Gavin Weakley. Frankfurt am Main: Peter Lang.

CHAPTER 11

The Mystical Church

Roman death masks. **Source:** Hisham Ibrahim / Getty Images.

"The maxim, 'know yourself' shows many things. That you are mortal, and that you were born a human being...And it means, 'Know for what you were born, and whose Image you are. And what is your essence and what your creation, and what your relation to God, and the like.'"

Clement's summary of his beliefs about Gnosis and the true Gnostic Christian

KEY PLAYERS
Clement of Alexandria
Origen – Plotinus

KEY TEXTS
Clem. Alex., *Christ the Instructor; Exhortation to the Greeks; Miscellanies*
Origen, *On First Principles; Dialogue with Heraclides; Commentary on the Song of Songs*
Allogenes – Zostrianos

In Chapter 10, we saw how the Christians in the fifth generation (190–230 CE) continued to argue over God. They had many opinions on which God to worship and how Jesus relates to him. Christians in all the various groups were trying to justify their worship of Jesus while explaining that they were not polytheists (like the pagans) but proper monotheists devoted to The One God (which the Jews and the philosophers knew about but did not worship correctly). Tertullian and Hippolytus of Rome continued to publish catalogs describing and labeling certain groups as heretics while insisting that their church and interpretations of scriptures were natural and normative. Their hermeneutics (interpretations) were presented as the intended meaning of the original authors, which had been passed down through the lineage of the twelve apostles and bishops. They presented these "plain" or "literal" interpretations over and against other groups that claimed to have learned God's mysteries by uncovering them through their own (often allegorical and inspired) interpretations of the scriptures.

Those Christians whom Tertullian and Hippolytus of Rome hereticized in their catalogs, however, were not easily undermined because these groups, by the third century, had constructed a different and powerful lineage for themselves based on an idea that turns up in Acts 1:1–3, that Jesus taught his disciples for 40 days after his resurrection about the Kingdom of God. Christians wanted to know about the mysteries of God mentioned by Paul in his letters and the secrets that Jesus alludes to in the Gospel (Mark 4:10–12; 1 Cor 4:1; 13:2; 14:2: Rom. 16:25; Eph. 3:3–4, 9; 6:19; Col. 1:26–27; 2:2; 4:3; 2 Thess. 2:7). Christian Gnostic groups claimed that they were heirs of this esoteric or secret teaching, which amounted to their own doctrine directly taught by Jesus to his inner disciples after his resurrection. These Christians understood that Jesus had a public or exoteric mission as recorded in the Gospels. They believed that the mysteries of God, however, were communicated by Jesus privately after his resurrection to his inner circle (mysteries which they equated with their own doctrines). This mention of post-resurrection teaching in Acts continues to prick the imagination of contemporary Christians, conveniently providing a way to authorize new revelation. For instance, in the modern world, it serves to authenticate Joseph Smith's story in the Book of Mormon about how Jesus after his resurrection appeared to the Nephites (North American Indigenous People) and revealed Mormonism to them.

In Alexandria, the Valentinians, Christian Sethians, Basilidians, and Carpocratians persuaded converts to join their churches because their claims to esoteric knowledge were convincing to the proselytes. They had no problem assuring potential converts that Jesus had not taught the mysteries of God in his public ministry, but did so after he was resurrected, especially since the esoteric scripture that they produced presents itself as authentic revelation received from Jesus by his inner circle. Their esoteric scripture presents the insights of this inner circle, which included people who were not necessarily among the twelve but beloved by Jesus, such as Paul, Jesus' brother James (not the son of Zebedee), and women like Mary Magdalene and Salome. These groups authored texts like the *Gospel of Philip* and the *Gospel of Mary*, the *Apocalypse of Paul* and the *Apocalypes of James*, and the *Secret Book (Apocryphon) of John* and the *Secret Book (Apocryphon) of James* as records of Jesus' esoteric teachings. These groups also relied on esoteric hermeneutics, believing that the Jewish and Christian scriptures contained hidden truth. These groups advertised their readiness to disclose God's mysteries to converts via initiations that resembled initiations into the Greek mysteries proper. This resemblance with the Greek mysteries made their Christian movements both familiar to pagan converts and popular with them.

The Apostolic Catholics found themselves in something of a bind when it came to the claim to esoteric tradition and scriptural knowledge. While it is clear that the authors of the Gospel of Mark and Acts used the esoteric claim to authorize their own writings, the Apostolic Catholics in the fourth generation had worked hard to construct their religious tradition as public-facing rather than private (Iren., *Haer.* 3.2–4). They did this to avoid Roman sanctions on private meetings and allay suspicions that they were an underground revolutionary group. Writers like Irenaeus pinned the esoteric label on the Christians they identified with heresy in order to point the finger and Roman attention at Christians other than themselves. They hoped that by doing so, they would be able to further distance the Apostolic Catholic churches from Roman skepticism about private Christian assemblies and their political motives.

This move to construct a public message and religion made it difficult for the Apostolic Catholics to compete with Christian groups who were organized around the attractive claim to reveal esoteric knowledge, especially when this revelation included a Gnostic event, an ecstatic visitation with the true God in his transcendent home. All the heresiologists complain about the popularity and attractiveness of the Christian Gnostic initiations and provide various reasons for why people were so excited to join in. This is all to say, the advertisement of secrets by these groups had wild appeal. The fifth-generation Christians had to come to terms with the fact that Jesus esoterica was not going away.

11.1 Leveling Up

COMPANION TEXTS
Clem. Alex., *Miscellanies*
5.6; 7.2; 7.16–17;
Christ the Instructor 1.1–3.3

Clement of Alexandria is uniquely situated in the Christian conversation about Jesus esoterica because he was a famed Christian philosophical teacher who had first-hand knowledge of the Valentinians, Basilidians, and Carpocratians in Alexandria. He was born around 150 CE, probably in Athens (Epiph., *Ref.* 32.6) and trained as a philosopher, learning from several teachers hailing from Greece, Syria, Mesopotamia, Palestine, and Egypt. Clement settles in Alexandria and becomes a pupil of the Christian teacher Pantaenus, a fourth-generation Christian.

Pantaenus operated an independent Christian philosophical school in Alexandria such as Justin had done in Rome. He was aligned with the Apostolic Catholic network (also like Justin). His student Clement (and later Clement's student Origen) were similarly aligned. Clement, in fact, views the Apostolic Catholic church as the Christians' Mother just as God is their Father. He admonishes believers to be faithful to her. He legitimizes the Catholic Church by arguing that she is older than the churches of other Christians who, he claims, deviated from her (Clem. Alex., *Misc.* 7.17).

Pantaenus had been a Stoic philosopher prior to his religious conversion and Clement appears to have received a form of Christian Stoicism from him. Legends built up around Pantaenus that he evangelized India in the wake of the apostle Bartholomew who had left the Gospel of Matthew with the Indian converts before Pantaenus arrived (Eus., *Eccl. Hist.* 5.10). Pantaneus left behind no writings. Yet Clement lauds Pantaenus as a charismatic teacher. It appears that Pantaenus preferred to pass on his knowledge orally to those he hand-selected to be his pupils. Clement speaks to how much he benefited from Pantaenus' wealth of utterances and mentions his own reluctance to write down Pantaenus' teachings because he considered much of it to be special secret teaching for advanced Christians that should only be communicated orally.

This explanation is important because it suggests that the Apostolic Catholic esoteric tradition was so new that Clement did not have esoteric Catholic texts at his disposal. To argue for the antiquity of this new esoteric tradition, Clement promoted the claim that the materials were so secret that they had to be safeguarded by being transmitted only by word-of-mouth. Clement's argument is that the Jesus esoterica were not mentioned by other Apostolic Catholic authors, not because they had yet to be invented, but because they were so dangerous and holy that authors prior to him refused to write them down.

Upon Pantaenus' death, Clement takes over Pantaenus' school. He immediately decides that if he is to be successful he must wrestle the esoteric tradition away from his Valentinian and other Christian Gnostic competitors. So it is with Clement that we see the first robust effort within the Apostolic Catholic network to construct an esoteric tradition for itself. To do so, Clement reforms the school, establishing a three-tiered curriculum which he outlines in his book *Christ the Instructor* (ca. 180–190 CE). He creates the tiers so that they function as an initiation that advances the proselytes gradually from conversion to the faith to their perfection in Christ.

Clement's first level of Christian education is about conversion. It covers how the Logos exhorts humans to leave behind paganism and follow Christ. Clement's textbook for this level is his book, *The Exhortation to the Greeks* (ca. 195–197 CE). This textbook falls into the ancient category of protreptic books, that is, books meant to persuade readers to join a philosophical school. In the book, Clement critiques Greek religion, mystery cults, astrology, sacrifice, fatalism, and polytheism which, like Justin, he characterizes as the worship of demons. As for Greek philosophy, like Justin, Clement thinks that sages like Plato were inspired by reason (the Logos) to say something about the Truth and God. Even more so, the prophets were inspired by reason (the Logos) to convey knowledge of the true God. With the advent of the Logos as Jesus Christ, the true God can now be revealed to everyone who harkens to the Christian call. In this way, Clement suggests that Greek culture is a natural segue into Christianity, which asks all to align themselves with the Logos, universal reason. Clement's arch is similar to Justin's in that he presents Christianity as the system of true philosophy that has been percolating throughout history with partial revelations of the Logos. This revelation was fully disclosed with the incarnation of the Logos in Jesus Christ.

Was the incarnation of the Logos conceived by Clement as a POSSESSION or ENSOULMENT of the Logos? In other words, was the Logos a divinity who possessed a fully human Jesus who had his own body and soul? Or was the Logos Jesus' soul? Clement's language is varied enough that scholars debate this point. Clement speaks about Jesus being "God in human form." The Logos came down and "clothed himself with man" in order to voluntarily subject himself to human experiences and passions (Clem. Alex., *Instr.* 1.2; *Rich* 37). The mystery of the incarnation is "God in man, and man in God" (*Instr.* 3.1). In these instances, is Clement using the concept of "human form" or "man" to refer to the complete human being with body and soul? If this is the case, then he is pedaling a POSSESSION CHRISTOLOGY.

But Clement also says that the Lord took on flesh, carried around flesh like a garment, entered the flesh, or attached himself to it. He understands the flesh to be the "outward man." In this same passage, the "inner man" or reasoning faculty appears to be the Logos which assumed Jesus' flesh, making his flesh passionless (*Misc.* 5.6; 7.2; *Instr.* 3.1). In other words, Jesus' flesh was divinized because of the incarnation, so that Jesus did not really need to sleep or eat or drink, although Jesus does it for show. This left Clement open to the accusation that he was a Docetist, although clearly he was not. Did Clement consider Jesus' flesh to be a container for the Logos which functioned as Jesus' psyche? If so, he would be conveying an ENSOULMENT PATTERN. Whichever Christological pattern he intended to convey (or perhaps he was not clear on this himself), Clement understood Jesus' soul to be the perfect Image of God which serves as a model for our own moral formation.

The second level of Christian education is about the moral formation of the Christian, which Clement writes about in his book, *Christ the Educator*. This level comprises how the Logos helps Christians control their passions and align their actions with the Logos' moral expectations. The readers are addressed as baptized Christians – "children" – who need to align their lives with their Christian faith as they move forward toward gaining perfect knowledge or Gnosis. They are told that, because it is impossible for humans not to sin, the Logos must become the guide of both Christian men and women, healing their passions and educating them properly.

In this education, the Logos leads us by using both the Law (which he gave to Moses) and the grace that comes through Jesus. He led Jews by the Law to fear God, and now he leads Christians by grace to love God. He leads by providing an ideal to model, but also through chastisement and punishment. Clement thinks that divine goodness and retributive justice are not incompatible as the Marcionites and Gnostic groups assumed. Taking up the Stoic argument, Clement says that because God is good, retributive justice is good for us (Clem. Alex., *Instr.* 1.63.1–1.64.2). Like a good parent, God threatens chastisement before carrying out the punishment in order to stir up fear in his children, warning them what will happen if they continue misbehaving. Clement emphasizes that God is retributive, not out of hatred or revenge, but because he must correct the sinner he loves.

Throughout this textbook, Clement sets down a catechism of practical moral rules, discussing everything from eating, drinking, and sleeping to home furnishings, banquet etiquette, and how to laugh. His rules are related in minute detail. In these details, we discover that Clement is something of a moderate when it came to everyday affairs. He does not completely reject pagan banquets, spectacles, hair and clothing styles, and adornments. He considers his rules to represent a reasonable kind of morality. The rules are meant to help Christians know how to maintain moderation in all situations, even when invited to attend a pagan meal with non-believing friends. Christian women ought to choose perfumes that do not make men swoon. Men should avoid perfumes altogether because they might cause them to lose their virility. Drinking wine should not lead to drunkenness. Possessions should not be disposed of. Rather the desire for wealth should be rooted out. Marriage ought not to be avoided. Marriage, in fact, is the remedy for out-of-control passions.

The third level of Christian education is the Gnostic-level, when Christians learn "the mysteries of ecclesiastical Gnosis" (Clem. Alex., *Misc.* 7.16). This consists of the Logos' instructions about how to attain *gnosis* or perfect knowledge, a knowledge which Clement insists is in line with the Church's Canon of Truth (Clem. Alex., *Instr.* 1.1–3.3). By constructing the Gnostic-level, Clement appropriates and reframes the claim of Christians like the Valentinians and the Basilidians to have Gnosis of the transcendent God *beyond* the Biblical Creator God. Clement reframes this claim by making perfectly clear that the Gnosis he is talking about is Gnosis of the transcendent God who *is* the Biblical Creator God. Clement is the master of the game; if-you-can't-beat-'em-join-'em.

11.2 The Authentic Gnostics

COMPANION TEXTS
Clem. Alex., *Miscellanies.*
1.1; 2.1–5; 4.3.1–2; 4.22–23;
5.4; 6.14; 7.1

Clement never wrote the third textbook about the Gnostic-level. Rather, he left us with his research notebooks about subjects he planned to include in the third-level Gnostic textbook once he got around to writing it. The notebooks are called the *Miscellanies of Gnostic Notes According to the True Philosophy* (ca. 198–203 CE). In the chapters, Clement reflects on subjects that he feels are necessary to prepare the Gnostic-level student to ascend and receive the grand vision of the Creator God (Clem. Alex., *Misc.* 4.3.1–2). These subjects include discussions about the true origin of the world, the compatibility of faith (pistis) and knowledge (gnosis), proper marriage, martyrdom, the Logos as the source of knowledge, the spiritual interpretation of scriptures, and why other Christians are not real Gnostics. In these notes, Clement is laying out how Christians can be real Gnostics (in contrast to inauthentic Gnostics like the Valentinians, Basilidians, and Carpocratians) and worship the right God (the Biblical Creator God) as the supreme transcendent God. Clement includes the martyrs in the rank of Gnostics, arguing against Basilides that martyrdom is a punishment for sins committed in a previous lifetime.

Also, in contrast to Basilides, Clement writes that faith is not an intuition devoid of proof. Nor is it the mark of simpleton Christians as the Valentinians teach. For Clement, faith (pistis) is the believer's voluntary allegiance to the Logos. As such it is the foundation and prerequisite for acquiring knowledge (gnosis). Pisits is the first step in the progression toward Gnosis. Out of faith comes virtue. Virtue leads believers to love God. Those who are lovers of God contemplate God and receive knowledge of God (gnosis), which Clement defines in Platonic fashion as a beatific vision of God (Clem. Alex., *Misc.* 2.1–55). As a first step, faith inspires believers to search for divine truth through an analytical process of scripture-reading and study of the good qualities of the world (Clem. Alex., *Misc.* 5.1–18; 5.65–88).

Clement defines the Gnostic-level Christian as a believer who has conformed to the Image of God, which is the Logos (Clem. Alex., *Misc.* 2.56–102). This Image is primal. It had been stamped on Adam's soul. In other words, Adam's psyche was molded to reflect God's mind. But when Adam gave in to pleasure and was seduced by lusts, his mind degraded, warping the mold. Adam's soul no longer reflected God's glorious Image, but was deformed. Adam's story, according to Clement, is about the fall of the soul when the soul descends into the body, is engendered, and weighed down with the appetites, left unconscious and weakened (*Misc.* 4.22–23; 6.14; *Instr.* 1.2–3; 1.12; 3.1; *Exh.* 11).

Only the call of the Logos can awaken the soul and instruct the soul about its situation and how to get out of this mess. The call of the Logos is a call to self-knowledge, to know your true divine Self, the image that was lost with Adam's sin. This divine self is not a piece of God as Christian Gnostic groups taught. Clement never says that the human soul is consubstantial with God. Rather, for Clement, the soul is the Image of the Logos who is the Image of God, but in a deformed state. Its original condition as the Image of the Logos has to be restored. Clement says that if we know ourselves, we will know God, and knowing God, our psyches will be remade or transformed into their original form, reflecting God's glorious Image once again (Clem. Alex., *Instr.* 3.1). He writes, "The maxim, 'know yourself' shows many things. That you are mortal, and that you were born a human being...And it means, 'Know for what you were born, and whose Image you are. And what is your essence and what your creation, and what your relation to God, and the like'" (Clem. Alex., *Misc.* 5.4).

The knowledge of the true form of the psyche comes when people put themselves under the tutelage of the Logos. As a teacher, he is the exemplar to model. Clement compares this educational process to the softening of wax to receive Jesus' stamp (Clem. Alex., *Misc.* 7.12). What does this process entail? The Logos expects his pupils to cure the passions that haunt their souls. They must become impassible so that the original mold of their psyches can be restored to reflect the shape of the Logos. In other words, they must make their souls like Jesus' whose incarnation and life enacted the whole drama of human salvation (Clem. Alex., *Instr.* 1.2–3; 1.12; 3.1; *Misc.* 1.1; 4.22; 7.2; *Exh.* 10; 12).

Clement fills an entire notebook with his feelings about passion and marriage (Clem. Alex., *Misc.* 2.137–47; 3). He makes it clear that controlling the passions does not mean giving up marriage or refusing to wed in order to live as celibates. While celibacy remains a viable option, Clement thinks that marriage is a good institution because, when properly conducted, the passions should stay in check (as Paul suggests in 1 Cor. 7). Clement thinks about marriage in the same terms as Stoic teachers, that it ought to be conducted chastely. In other words, desire (*eros*) should not inflame the partners to have sex. Sex ought to be about procreation between married partners, not hedonistic orgies.

Clement considers the Gnostic-level Christian to be someone who has achieved perfection and is now privy to mystical teachings and true philosophy that have been hidden from the unholy (Clem. Alex., *Misc.* 7.106–108). Perfect Christians are Gnostics who no longer fear God but love him (Clem. Alex., *Misc.* 4.89–172). Real Gnostics are so entirely liberated from their passions that they no longer need the virtues to help them resist the passions.

Real Gnostics also are the only people who are able to understand the spiritual meaning of the scriptures, a meaning that is more advanced than readings based on simple faith. Clement calls the faith reading "letter-by-letter" because it works to clarify the plain meaning of the text. The spiritual meaning, he calls "according to the syllables" because it represents the esoteric meaning of the text (Clem. Alex., *Misc.* 6.131.2–3). Clement claims that this dual-hermeneutics (simple and advanced levels of interpretation) is distinctive and authentic in ways that undermine the hermeneutics of heretics, which he thinks are one-sided and do not represent what the Lord originally intended (Clem. Alex., *Misc.* 2.54.1; 4.134.3–135.1; 7.89–111). The Lord's original intention, which the Catholic Gnostic understands, is a meaning that reflects the norms of the Apostolic Catholic church (Clem. Alex., *Misc.* 6.125.2–3; 7.1). These norms mean that the Law, the Prophets, and the Gospel revelation are in harmony, not opposed to each other, and that the interpretation should avoid personal biases or idiosyncratic agendas. These norms must be assumed by the hermeneut (interpreter) as scripture is read and studied. Notably, Clement changes up the opinion broadcast by earlier Apostolic Catholics like Irenaeus that the "plain" or "literal" reading of the scripture reflects the author's original intent and the Lord's actual teachings.

The real Gnostic life is a mystical life, according to Clement. By this, he means that Gnostics are able to ascend into heaven, see God, join the ranks of the angels as they worship God, and partake of other heavenly delights because they have become like the Logos and can enter and exit divine realms (Clem. Alex., *Misc.* 6 and 7). They do this by intensely training in contemplative exercises. The climax of their practices is the moment when the Gnostic-level Christians ascend to God and receive visions of the Creator's glorious light (Clem. Alex., *Misc.* 4.116–117). Mystically, they partake of the intelligible world (Clem. Alex., *Misc.* 5.40.1; 7.13.1–2) and get a taste of what their future lives will be like in heaven (Clem. Alex., *Misc.* 7.56.3–57.1).

While we have access to Clement's notes about the Gnostic-level, we do not have his intended textbook. Clement, however, did compose another esoteric work meant to be read by students who made it to the third level. This composition is called *Extracts from the Prophets*. In this text, he teaches his Gnostic-level students about baptism and its connection to the waters of creation in the Genesis story. He writes about how the faith of the baptized has to be completed by fidelity to the Gnostic life. He concludes with a description of the geography of the heavens, the location of the angels, and the ascent of the Gnostic's soul to its Creator (the Biblical God).

Clement also appears to have taught a seminar meant to critique the teachings of the Valentinian Theodotus and friends. Clement left us with an anthology containing Theodotus' teachings interspersed with Clement's own personal notes and comparable teachings from other Valentinians. We might imagine that this was the notebook Clement used to teach his seminar on this subject. It is called *The Excerpts from Theodotus.*

Clearly Clement approached the problem of the popularity of Christian Gnostic movements differently from Irenaeus who worked to distance Apostolic Catholicism from charges of privatization, secret meetings, and hidden agendas. Irenaeus did this by pointing the finger at Christian Gnostic groups, which authenticated themselves by claiming to be privy to private post-resurrection teachings of Jesus or to have the hermeneutical keys to unlock the secrets hidden in the scriptures. Irenaeus exposed these teachings as obvious quackery and secured the plain or literal reading of the text as its authentic meaning. Clement realized that the fascination with Jesus esoterica and mystical experiences was not going away. If Apostolic Catholicism was going to undermine the authority of Christian Gnostic groups, it was not enough to expose their esoteric traditions as foolish and unnecessary in light of the public traditions that the Apostolic Catholics touted as Truth. Clement recognizes that the claim of Christian Gnostic groups to esoteric tradition and Gnosis had to be co-opted. He does so by appropriating from these groups the Jesus esoterica and reframing them to fit within the Apostolic Catholic Canon of Truth.

This is why Clement emphasizes that God can be good, but also a God who metes out divine retribution. Also, this is why Clement teaches that knowledge of God (Gnosis) and the revelation of esoteric teachings is not achievable because (certain) humans possess a divine nature capable of intuiting God and his mysteries. Gnosis and esoteric teachings, Clement says, are only available to humans because the Logos incarnated and after his resurrection entrusted his mysteries to James, John, and Peter who, in turn, taught the other disciples about them. The disciples taught the mysteries to the seventy apostles (mentioned in Acts), including Barnabas. Paul also received this same revelation (Clem. Alex., *Misc.* 1.11.3; 1.13.2; 6.61.3; 6.68.2). Clement believed that Paul taught about how "Gnosis, which is the perfection of faith, advances beyond religious instruction *(catechesis)*, in accordance with the magnitude of the Lord's teaching the Canon (i.e. the Canon of Truth) of the church" (Clem. Alex., *Misc.* 6.18.165.1).

Significantly, Clement does not trace the esoteric teachings through the bishops, but rather he traces them through Christian teachers like Pantaenus who, he says, received them from their teachers, who received them from the apostles, who received them from the resurrected Christ (Clem. Alex., *Misc.* 1.1.11–13). These esoteric teachings of Jesus were never written down, but, according to Clement, were delivered orally from teacher to student, beginning with the resurrected Jesus who declared in the Gospels that he had secret teachings which were meant for the ears of a few, not the many (Clem. Alex., *Misc.* 1.1).

Clement talks about his reluctance to write down the orally transmitted mysteries he claims to have learned from Pantaenus. He reflects on how "the writing of these memos of mine is weak when compared with that spirit, full of grace, which I was privileged to hear" (Clem. Alex., *Misc.* 1.1). He says that he is concerned that the esoterica may fall into the wrong hands or be wrongly interpreted once they are written down. Yet he contends that already he has forgotten so much of what Pantaenus taught him that if he does not get the esoterica written down soon, all will be lost. In the end, he decides to write most of the esoterica down, omitting only the esoterica that, he says, require the oral instructions of a teacher who has walked the walk.

This is how Clement cunningly constructs an independent lineage for his church's esoteric teachings that countered point-by-point the claims that Christian Gnostic groups made to possess the esoteric post-resurrection teachings of Christ. This meant that the Jesus esoterica (of the Apostolic Catholics) were transmitted in a manner that differed from but ran alongside the exoteric or public teachings that Jesus transmitted to the apostles and then to the bishops (Figure 11.1). Clement constructed an esoteric

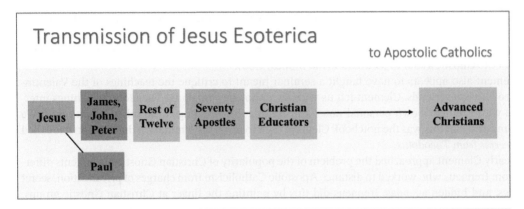

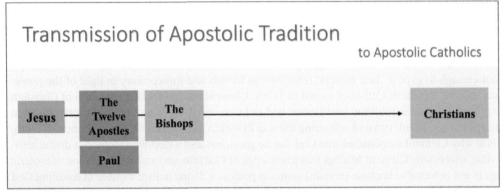

FIGURE 11.1 Illustration of how Clement envisioned the difference between the transmission of esoteric traditions and the exoteric teachings of the Apostolic Catholic church.

tradition for the Apostolic Christians that was meant to do more than mirror similar claims by Christian Gnostic groups. His construction was meant to beat them at their own game. According to Clement, the esoteric tradition is not located in the private teaching of Jesus to a few, but in the distribution of that teaching to the approved heroes of the Apostolic Catholic church, from Peter to Paul, and then to the Christian scholars and educators. Nor is this esoteric teaching reserved for a predetermined Elect. Rather, it can be learned by any Christian who has faith and is devoted to virtuous living and the contemplation of God (Clem. Alex., *Misc.* 2.31.1–2). The divine mysteries are discovered, Clement concludes, by reading the scriptures on the spiritual level ("according-to-the-syllable"), conforming to the teachings and demands of the Logos, and contemplating the Creator.

11.3 | Textual Erotics

COMPANION TEXTS
Origen,
On First Principles 1–4

Origen was born into a Christian family in Alexandria (185–254 CE). He was highly educated, both in the Greek literature and the Bible as disciplines. His father had him memorize scriptures on a daily basis. Origen was fully exposed to the Jewish scriptures (in Greek) and the Apostolic Catholic New Testament, which included at the very least the four Gospels, the thirteen letters of Paul, Acts, 1 John, 1 Peter, Jude, Hebrews, and Revelation. He seems to have suspicions about the authenticity of James and never mentions 2 Peter, or 2 and 3 John. Origen loved the Epistle to the Hebrews (he references it over 200 times), but he is reluctant to acknowledge Paul as its author, stating that the style and composition belong to another author, perhaps a follower of Paul who had reflected on Paul's teaching. He says that some in the Church had assigned the authorship of Hebrews to Clement of Rome, others to

Luke who authored the Gospel and Acts. After debating the point, Origen concludes, "Honestly, who wrote the letter, only God knows" (Eus., *Eccl. Hist.* 6.25.11–14). Origen had elevated opinions of other texts, including *1 Clement*, *Epistle of Barnabas*, and the *Shepherd of Hermas*.

The pinnacle of Origen's Greek education (we may think of it as his graduate studies) was his training in philosophy. It is contested in scholarship whether this training happened under the famous Ammonius Saccas (175–242 CE) in the same classroom with the equally famous Plotinus (204–270 CE), the father of Neo-Platonism (Eus., *Eccl. Hist.* 6.19.7). As a young man, Origen's parents enrolled him in his church's program for catechumens who were receiving instructions as they prepared to be baptized. Given Origen's continuity with Clement's teachings and the fact that both men affiliated with the Canon of Truth endorsed by the Apostolic Catholics and overlapped in their time in Alexandria, Origen likely received his catechism from Clement. In 202 CE, when Origen was 17, his father Leonides died as a martyr in the persecution of the Roman Emperor Septimius Severus (193–211 CE) and the family's possessions were confiscated by the state.

After his father's death, a wealthy Christian Gnostic woman financially supported Origen so that he could pursue his dream to establish himself as a Biblical scholar. This woman was also the patron of a scholar from Antioch who was a Gnostic as well. We only know that the man's name was Paul and that he had come to stay with the woman and Origen in Alexandria. Eusebius, who tells us about this biographical detail, makes sure to distance Origen from their Gnostic influence by claiming that Origen never prayed with them (Eus., *Eccl. Hist.* 6.2.13).

Because Origen was the eldest of the children in his family, he was still responsible for the care of his mother and siblings. To support his family, he began to teach Greek literature. He also began to teach the Christian catechism on the side to potential converts who asked him for instruction. Origen stepped in because there was a dearth of catechists in Alexandria in the wake of Severus' persecution of the Christians. They had either been martyred or gone into hiding. This included Clement who left the city in 202 CE. A letter written by Bishop Alexander of Caesarea in Cappadocia to Origen in 215 CE assumes that Clement is dead, but we do not know what exactly happened to him.

Between 206–210 CE, a second wave of persecution hit Alexandria. Several of Origen's students were martyred. But Origen survived. When the persecution subsided and it was safe, Bishop Demetrius returned to Alexandria and officially put Origen in charge of the catechetical instruction for the Apostolic Catholic church in Alexandria. This allowed Origen the luxury to give up teaching Greek literature. He sold his library of the classics and devoted himself to asceticism. Rumors had it that he was so serious about this new ascetic life that he took Matthew 19:12 literally and castrated himself, fully devoting himself to the Lord. He would later argue against the literal interpretation of this passage, so perhaps he learned from his own experience that not everything in scripture ought to be taken literally.

In fact, Origen became known for his nuanced approach to hermeneutics or scriptural interpretation. Like Clement, Origen comes to understand that the hermeneutical process ought to be conducted on different levels. Origen is convinced that every word, even every letter of scripture, is pregnant with secret knowledge, ripe with mysteries to be revealed to the advanced hermeneut.

This idea is not particularly distinctive since Christians, with the exception of the Marcionites, had been interpreting the Jewish scriptures in ways that they claimed signaled Christ. Since the beginning of the movement, Christians had been reading the Jewish scriptures to forecast or prefigure Christ's advent as well as to signal some higher reality beyond the literal text. This perspective led them to accuse the Jews of obstinacy and ignorance regarding God's (Christian) plan because, they said, the Jews took the Bible too literally. As we have seen repeatedly in this textbook, the Jews were accused of being incapable of discerning Christ in the prophecies or the true moral interpretation of the Jewish ceremonial and cultic laws. Similar arguments were leveled against Marcion, who also was accused of reading the Jewish scriptures too literally.

What Origen does is systematize this approach (Figure 11.2) and use it to legitimize the construction of the Apostolic Catholic esoteric tradition that Clement had advanced. Origen believed that the apostles deliberately left some teachings vague so that philosophers like himself would have material to speculate about to "display the fruit of their ability" (Orig., *Princ.*, preface. 2–3). He thinks God's mysteries

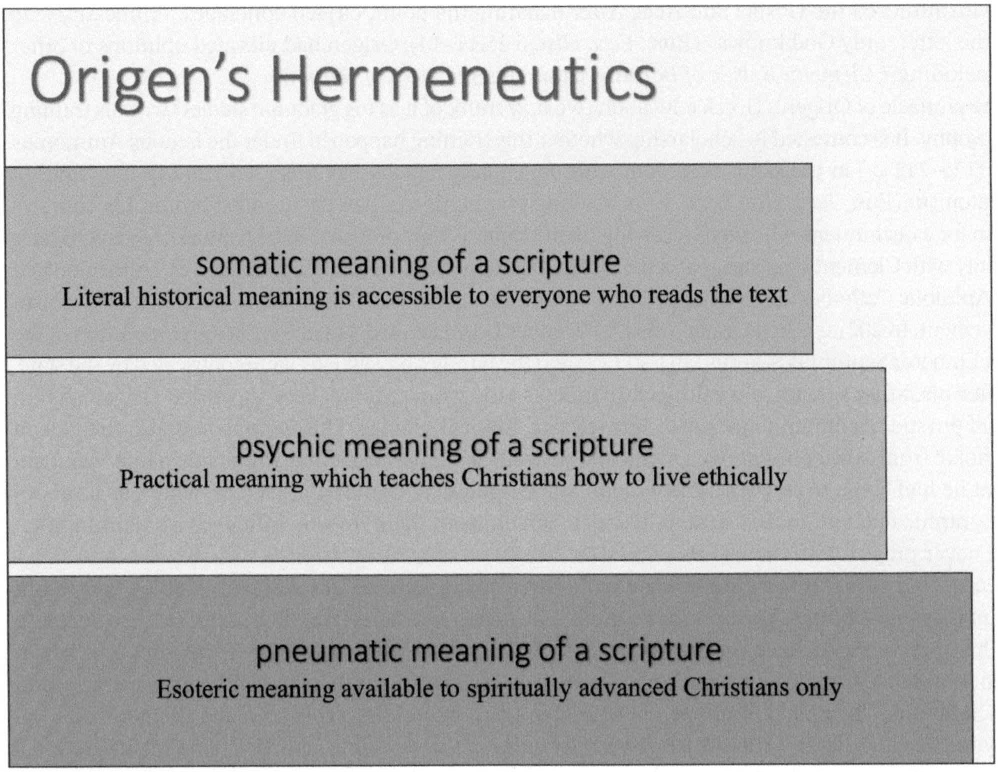

Origen's Hermeneutics

somatic meaning of a scripture
Literal historical meaning is accessible to everyone who reads the text

psychic meaning of a scripture
Practical meaning which teaches Christians how to live ethically

pneumatic meaning of a scripture
Esoteric meaning available to spiritually advanced Christians only

FIGURE 11.2 Illustration of how Origen explained the scriptural interpretative process.

are hidden beneath the literal meaning of the scriptures, what he calls the bodily (*somatic*) meaning of the text. Armed with historical and philological knowledge, the literal meaning of a text, is accessible to all reasonable people, he says. This type of interpretation is comparable to the way that students are trained to read Biblical texts in modern secular universities.

Origen felt that the literal meaning is a veil that hides the truer and deeper moral (psychic) and spiritual (pneumatic) meanings, safeguarding this divine knowledge from people who are not yet worthy to know them. He thought that the moral meaning of the text (the soul of the text) is discovered when we ask how the text can be applied to our personal spiritual development and inform us practically, so that we use the text as a guide for our ethical formation. This type of reading resembles the hermeneutics taught in seminaries today that work to prepare clerics to preach from the pulpit or assist with religious education.

As for the pneumatic readings, these are the most advanced readings and are taught to advanced Christians whom Origen calls the "perfect," a word that is commonly used to identify people in the ancient Roman world who have gone through initiation successfully (in either a mystery religion or Gnostic movement). Like Clement, these advanced Christians are the ones who possess Gnosis. They are seeking to understand the "spirit" of the text, which may contradict the "letter" of the text.

Origen establishes criteria for determining when the hermeneut ought to seek the deeper level of meaning hidden in the literal. He considers the text to be a conduit for God's "unspeakable mysteries" which are revealed to us in counsel with the Holy Spirit. First, he points us to examine texts that appear on the surface to be unedifying or even immoral and determine how they are really edifying or moral, such as may be the case with many of the ceremonial and cultic laws in Leviticus. Second, the hermeneut ought to determine if the text, taken literally, would be absurd. He creates a list of texts that are absurd if they are taken in their most obvious sense, such as Matthew 5:29. Origen wonders why we would pluck out our right eye because it made us sin. Is the right eye more guilty of sin than the left? He concludes that these passages require deeper allegorical reflection to uncover their true spiritual meaning. Origen also watches for any discrepancies in the texts, especially between the different Gospel narrations of Jesus' life. He views any discrepancies or contradictions as red lights, indicating that a deeper spiritual meaning lies in wait for discovery.

What are the spiritual mysteries that are learned when the scriptures are studied in this way? Origen explains in his theological treatise, *On First Principles*, that the mysteries he has come to know from his own personal study of the scriptures are about the care of the soul, that is, what souls have to do to achieve perfection. Theology – who the real God is – is the foremost mystery that souls need to know. Alongside this is Christology, specifically what the Son's nature is and how he is the Son. The next mystery is accurate knowledge of the Son's incarnation, what caused him to descend and become human, and why he did it. Additional mysteries include knowledge of the whereabouts of other beings (angels and demons), the reasons for the existence of different kinds of souls, the creation of the universe, and the spread of evil on earth (Orig., *Princ.* 4.2.7).

Origen reveals these mysteries largely in his book *On First Principles*, although this knowledge informs his other writings. Origen argued that creation itself is eternal, not in its physical reality, but as an intellectual world that Origen considered superior to Plato's doctrine of the World of Forms. This world consisted of *logikoi* (rational or intellectual beings) whose only purpose was to contemplate God via his Logos or Mind. Origen understood the logikoi to be non-binary beings created as "male and female;" they had no sexual distinctions (Gen 1:27–28). This concept of the initial Godhead is not so far removed from Valentinus' Pleroma of syzygitic Aeons, who were emanated to contemplate the Father through his Son (Figure 11.3). Origen went on to explain that everything that will come to be already

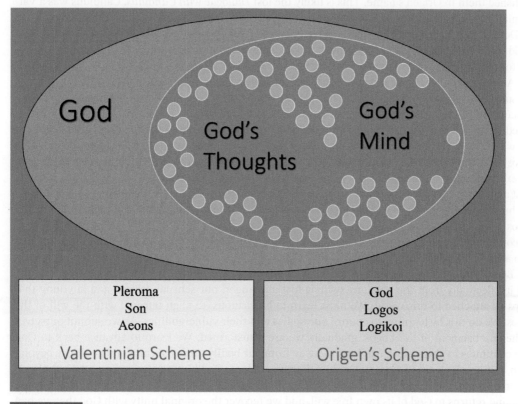

FIGURE 11.3   Comparison of Valentinian and Origen's protogony.

existed in God's Mind, a concept that Plotinus played around with as well, but can also be traced to Basilides as we learned in Chapter 5.

Origen explains the origin of the world and evil as the consequence of the fall of the logikoi who had free will. This is slightly different from the Valentinian explanation that Wisdom took things into her own hands with disastrous results because, in the Valentinian systems, her fall is inevitable. Because she is God's Wisdom, she has to try to know the unknowable Father, which turns out to be impossible to do on her own. In Origen's schematic, the logikoi had free will and could potentially stop contemplating God. Indeed, that is exactly what happened. They turned their intellect away from God and when they did so, they became souls. Relying on a word play in Greek, Origen understands this to mean that they became souls or psyches when their love for God cooled off (Greek: *psychesthai*).

According to Origen, not all logikoi cooled off similarly. Souls that did not cool off as much as others, became a higher order of beings: angels whose bodies are ethereal. Souls who cooled off the most became demons, who have extremely coarse bodies. In the middle of the hierarchy of souls are humans. Our souls moderately cooled off and fell into this world, taking on the flesh and sexual distinctions per Genesis 2–3.

The world was created by God through his Son (who is also Wisdom) for the purpose of providing an arena for souls to make better use of their freedom to regain the unity with God that they had lost. It is possible (although by no means certain) that Origen thought that this may take souls several lifetimes to achieve (Orig., *Princ.* 1.6.3; 2.11.6). Origen also seems to have speculated that it was possible for any rational creatures, including the demons, to regain what they had lost. Whether Origen actually taught that the Devil would or could be saved is debated, but it is a position his detractors identified him with and carried on about. Origen denies the accusations, saying that his teachings had been distorted. This is quite possible because we know of two occasions when fake news went out about Origen. In one case, a Christian whom he debated in public altered the minutes of the debate and then published them in Origen's name. This is likely the lost *Dialogue with Candidus*. Candidus was a Valentinian who debated Origen on the subjects of the eternal generation of the Son and the salvation of the Devil. Candidus actually won that debate, much to Origen's chagrin. Another Christian, who was afraid to debate Origen in public at Ephesus, forged and distributed a fake debate with Origen. Origen had to travel to Antioch to debunk the author.

According to Origen, we all face the fact that we have been handicapped in the fall. Sin has marred our souls (our psyches) so that we are incapable of using our free will to liberate ourselves from the human condition. Christ incarnated to jumpstart us. He destroyed the power of the Devil over us, liberated us from death and the underworld, and he enlightened us about the road home. The Son did this when the Logos united with the one logikos that had not fallen but had remained with God. This Logos-logikos incarnated in a human body in a birth process that matched all other human births with the exception that the baby had the Logos-logikos as his soul. It seems that Origen's Christology is most akin to the ENSOULMENT PATTERN, since the Logos is not a separate entity possessing a human body and human soul (Figure 11.4). The logikos is supposed to be functioning as Jesus' human soul with the Logos as an addition. But, by definition, the logikos is not a soul because it did not cool off, which is the condition Origen says creates the soul. In the end, Jesus' "soul" is actually the divine Logos melded with a logikos. Both descend united into flesh.

Because Jesus is God in flesh, when we see him, we learn how we can separate ourselves morally and intellectually from the passions such as lust and anger, our sensual desires, and anything that keeps us attached to this world. We must learn to be virtuous, to align our will with the will of the Logos. We do this by learning to control our bodies and their vulnerabilities. As we submit ourselves to the chastisement of the Logos, gradually we are transformed. We learn to advance back to God who continues to always love us. We turn away from our bodily senses to contemplate things beyond them, things which are incorporeal and intellectual, indeed, God himself (Orig., *Princ.* 4.4.10). When the time comes, the resurrection of our bodies will mirror our moral and intellectual progress, when our mind returns to God of its own free will, and we recover the original unity with God that we had originally lost.

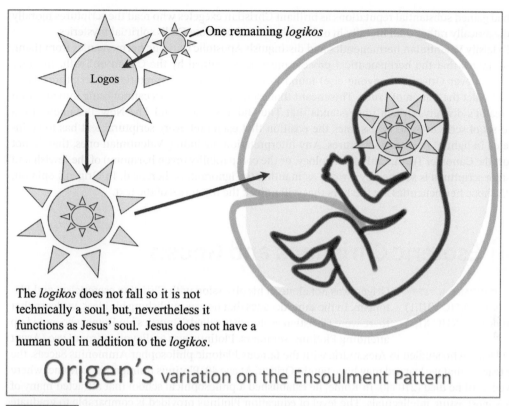

The *logikos* does not fall so it is not
technically a soul, but, nevertheless it
functions as Jesus' soul. Jesus does not have a
human soul in addition to the *logikos*.

Origen's variation on the Ensoulment Pattern

FIGURE 11.4 Illustration of the union of the Logos and logikos and their descent into the womb.

These are the mysteries that Jesus taught according to Origen, mysteries which he claims to have recovered through his devoted study of the scriptures. He is convinced that the erotics of intellectual activity provides the Christian the means of initiation into the mysteries of existence. Indeed, Origen believes that such intellectual activity is the only way that we can come to know God (Gnosis), which Origen imagines as our falling into love with God again. It is with Origen that the study of scripture and philosophical reasoning become the means to achieve Gnosis, which is for him an erotic reunion with God.

By way of example, we might consider Origen's *Commentary on the Song of Songs*. Origen understands the pneumatic soul to be like a bride who prepares herself to receive the Logos as her groom. She does this by studying the Bible. Like the second verse in the Song of Songs, the soul cries out to God, "O that you would kiss me with the kisses of your mouth!" urging God to help her understand the obscure passages of the Bible. She longs for the kisses of the Logos which are insights into the meaning of the text. The Logos, as the bridegroom, praises the soul for having the "eyes of a dove," which indicates that the soul is spiritually advanced (the Spirit descended onto Jesus at his baptism in the form of a dove, Origen reminds us). With the eyes of a dove (the Spirit's inner eye), the soul will be able to see the true meaning of the Bible. The beauty of the bridegroom's chest is identified with the hidden meaning of the Bible, which John learned when he leaned against Jesus' chest at the Last Supper. Origen identifies the bridal chamber in the Song of Songs with a private room reserved for the revelation of secrets between the bride and groom. It is reserved for those souls that are advanced in their practice of holiness and their depth of knowledge.

Ultimately, Origen's hermeneutical practice was aimed at shaping an esoteric tradition for the Apostolic Catholic church. Like Clement, the popularity of Valentinian esotericism seems to have been the driving force behind Origen's push to shape the Catholic esoteric tradition by systematizing a Catholic hermeneutical process to rival the Valentinian. He wished to outperform the Valentinians, who had gained substantial reputations as brilliant Christian exegetes who read the scriptures morally and allegorically rather than literally in order to learn and promote God's spiritual mysteries.

To falsify Valentinian hermeneutics and distinguish Apostolic Catholic hermeneutics from them, Origen argues that the hermeneutical process must be restrained by the Canon of Truth. In other words, whatever Origen (or anyone else) found in their exegesis (interpretation of scripture) could not contradict the Canon of Truth. This meant that esoteric hermeneutics cannot bring into question the Creator's divinity. Origen understands that The Old Testament and The New Testament are a united set of scriptures, so he assumes the position that each and every scriptural text has to be interpreted in light of the other scriptures. Any interpretation, including Valentinian ones, that do not support the Canon of Truth, Catholic theology, or the compatibility (even harmony) of the Jewish and Christian scriptures is scorned by Origen as inauthentic, ignorant, or heretical. In Origen's opinion, only Catholic hermeneutics are the keys that will unlock the mysteries of the text.

11.4 Esoteric Christians and Gnosis

COMPANION TEXTS
Zostrianos (NHC VIII,1)
Allogenes (NHC XI,3)

Origen was not alone in his obsession with Christian esotericism and Platonism. In the same decades that he was publishing his ideas, we learn that there were Christian esotericists called "Gnostics" in Rome who ended up attending Plotinus' seminars. Plotinus was an Egyptian from Lyco (Asyut or the Delta) who studied in Alexandria with the famous Platonic philosopher Ammonius Saccas, the same teacher that we learned may have taught Origen. At age 40, Plotinus immigrated to Rome, where he lived until he died (270 CE). In Rome, he established a philosophical school that attracted many of Rome's most astute intellectuals. The level of education Plotinus provided is comparable to graduate education in universities today.

Plotinus taught about the existence of the transcendent God as the Undivided One, the Good, and the Beautiful. This God exists beyond all categories of being and non-being. The One is the Potentiality or Power (*Dynamis*) of all life that will come to be. From the One emanates multiplicity in levels that become less and less perfect, although the process of emanation does not dilute the One or change the One in any way.

Plotinus' concept of the primal God and his emanation sounds very much like the doctrines of the Valentinians and the Sethian Christians. In fact, scholars are now considering the possibility that Plotinus was exposed to Valentinianism and Sethianism while in Alexandria, and went to Rome to distinguish his philosophy from the aspects of Gnostic thinking he grew to dislike. It is not surprising that Plotinus would end up in a debate with Christian Gnostics who enrolled in his lectures in Rome. They were interested in interacting with Plotinus and debating with him about the identity and accessibility of the transcendent God, believing that Plato had not actually reached the depths of the primal Intellect, nor had he understood the fallen nature of the natural world. While we often refer to these Christian Gnostics as Platonists, they were actually highly critical of Plato and saw their own philosophical work as correcting or superseding Plato.

Plotinus' disagreements with them were organized by Porphyry (Plotinus' student and biographer) in a book called *Against the Gnostics* (*Enn.* 2.9). Plotinus considered the Gnostics arrogant to believe that they were able to ascend into the realms of the transcendent God because they believed themselves to be consubstantial with God. Plotinus also did not think that the world was as fallen a place as they did, nor that it was crafted by a Demiurge who was equally fallen. For Plotinus, the world had been created as optimally as it could be. He felt that the Christian Gnostics had introduced novelties into Plato's teachings by suggesting that the emanation of divinities resulted in a damaged Creator and universe and that the soul should be blamed for its incarceration in the body. So arrogant were they, Plotinus remarks, that they believed their own intellects surpassed famous philosophers including Plato.

What is even more fascinating is the description of the Christians that Porphyry presents in the *Life of Plotinus* 16. Porphyry calls these particular Christians "heretics" because they attended the philosophical schools of Adelphius and Aculinus and had learned their bad Platonism there. In other words, he describes them as heretical or sectarian Platonists. While we do not know anything about Adelphius, we do know that Aculinus was a Platonist and competitor of Plotinus. Porphyry says that these Christian philosophers brought with them to Plotinus' seminars many texts authored by Alexander the Libyan, Philocomus, and Demonstratus of Lydia. We know from Tertullian that Alexander the Libyan was a Valentinian, but the others remain mysteries since all their texts are lost.

But these Christians did not just possess texts authored by others. Porphyry says that they also brought with them texts that they themselves had produced, texts that they marketed as the ancient revelations of Zoroaster, Zostrianos, Nicotheus, Allogenes, Messos, and others. Porphyry considers that these Christians had been deceived in the past by other philosophers, and now were deceiving people by publishing these revelations. The titles of two of these revelations – *Zostrianos* and *Allogenes* – are books that have been recovered in the Nag Hammadi Collection. We have a very good idea about the content of the books that these Christians were said to have composed and passed off as ancient revelation.

The content of these books takes Sethian wisdom and modifies it, so that the emanations in the primal Godhead are presented as three Platonic ontological metaphysical levels: The One, The Intellect, and The Soul. Similar ontology is found in two other Nag Hammadi texts: the *Three Steles of Seth* and *Marsanes*. Together these texts are known as the Platonizing Sethian treatises. These Roman Christian Gnostics were busy authors, turning Sethian mythology into revelations containing technical Platonic terminology.

What modifications did they make to the Sethian mythology they likely knew about from earlier Sethian Christian texts like the *Apocryphon of John*? They abandon the Father (Spirit)–Mother (Barbelo)–Son (Autogenes) triad in favor of an absolute unitarianism they pick up from Plato's writing *Parmenides*. While there are some differences across the Platonized Sethian treatises, generally the primal Unknown God is presented as an absolute monad, The One existing in the highest realm *beyond* or *before* Being itself (Figure 11.5). In these treatises, the Beyond-Being God comes into being as Existence, Vitality, and Mentality in one Aeon called The Triple-Powered One. This Aeon generates an intelligible realm of pure incorporeal being called Barbelo. Barbelo is no longer the female Mother, but the Triple-Male-Child, The Intellect which consists of the realm of Platonic contemplated Ideas (presided over by the Aeon Kalyptos), the contemplating Mind (presided over by the Aeon Protophanes), and the demiurgic Mind (presided over by the Aeon Autogenes). Autogenes generates an incorporeal realm of The Soul, which includes residences for purified disembodied souls, repentant souls, and souls who are not self-motivated. Below these realms are the atmosphere where disembodied souls roam who have yet to be purified (ghosts?) and earth where souls are embodied.

The Platonizing Sethian treatises are very fragmentary. The surviving bits do not address in detail how the physical material realm came into existence, except that Sophia's descent and generation of the Demiurge are implicated (e.g. *Zostr.* 8.9.2–10.20). Plotinus, however, summarizes the views of the Christian Gnostic authors (*Enn.* 2.9). According to him, these Christian Gnostics wrote wrongly that the physical material realm is deficient and in need of rectification. The universe resulted from the willful action of the Aeon Sophia who did not contemplate the Aeons above her, but instead looked down into the darkness below her, illuminating it. When she did this, she generated a son, the Demiurge, who gazed even deeper into the depths. Seeing matter, he revolted against Sophia, took hold of matter and created the physical universe out of this nasty substance. Like Sophia, the souls looked down instead of up, so they ended up falling into physical bodies.

Why was this remapping of the universe so important to these Christian Gnostics? Philosophers like them were actually interested in determining what we have to do to get back to the Source of Life. If they could map how we came to be on earth, they could map how to get out of here. These Christians envisioned their souls as resident aliens, as foreigners trying to get home. So the Nag Hammadi books of *Zostrianos* and *Allogenes* are actually initiatory texts, providing how-to instructions for the person's ascent back to The One, an initiation that prefigured and enacted the death journey. Along this journey,

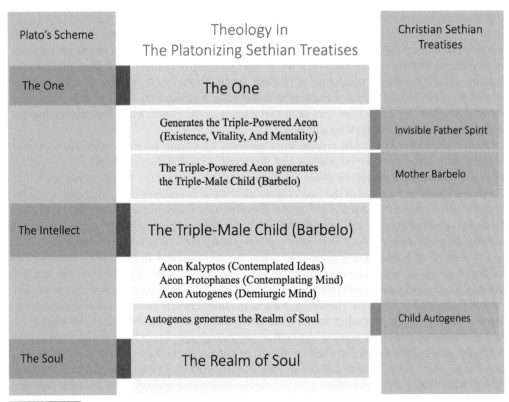

FIGURE 11.5 Comparison of theology in Plato, Platonized Sethian treatises, and the earlier Christian Sethian treatises.

souls pass through the celestial realms of the Moon and the Milky Way, and the Soul realms of Autogenes. Beyond this, the soul is shed and the spirit ascends into the Intellectual realms of Barbelo, all the way back to the Invisible Father. Notably, the "ascent" in these texts appears to have been less about an astral journey through the realms of existence, and more about internal acts of contemplation and visualization that the initiate used to experience the various ontological levels of cognition, angelification, and deification.

Even though the ascent was conducted through contemplative activities, this interior journey was made possible through a ritual they called "The Five Seals," which was a baptismal ritual that they repeated at each successive realm in their ascent. They used "living water" which they identified with the "light" of the celestial realms, oil, and invocations or prayers. They were probably performing this ritual in rivers since baptism in "living water" turns up in many Christian texts that refer to river immersions. Because of the reflective nature of water, water is equivalent with light even in the highest realms. This is why, when the transcendent God is described, we find stories about God peering into a pool of light and seeing its own reflection in these waters.

It was their initiations that gave these Christian Gnostics the edge on Plotinus, or so they said. They believed that they alone were the true philosophers because they alone had observed the Intellect firsthand and united with it mystically, something that Plato had not done. Their initiations were marketed by them as the exclusive way to apprehend the primal Source of Life and achieve enlightenment or Gnosis. I wonder if their claim to exclusivism is what ultimately got to Plotinus who himself claimed to have ascended and united with the One through intense contemplation (although his writings have left us with little evidence of practical instructions to achieve this unification).

Who were these Gnostic Christians? Most scholars refer to them as third-century Sethians because the texts they wrote reflect knowledge of Sethian mythology. But I question whether this is the most accurate description of them. They certainly were philosophers who studied Plato and believed that they had come to know more than Plato based on their initiatory experiences. This means that they were involved in an esoteric group that performed initiations. Their literacy is remarkable, so much so that they are probably best described as scholastics and theologians interested in metaphysics. In this capacity, they authored the revelations of *Zostrianos*, *Allogenes*, and others. Their texts work to authenticate a new unitarian theology that fuses Platonic metaphysics with the Barbeloite Myth which they likely read about in Sethian sources. They completely reimagined the Sethian Godhead and installed above the old Sethian God an Unknown God of Non-Being who proceeds the existence of the Invisible Father.

Does this make them Christian Sethians, part of an intergenerational church movement of the Seed of Seth? Or were they philosophers who appropriated older Christian Sethian and Valentinian texts (i.e. Alexander the Libyan)? Did they reengineer the mythology to authorize new esoteric knowledge? Did they choreograph similar rituals to promote their own private Christian initiatory club in Rome, where they taught the path to the primal God beyond all religions and philosophies, including Sethian Christianity and Valentinianism? Whatever we might conclude, the evidence is clear that the interaction between all of these people and texts in both Alexandria and Rome reflected a network of distributed and entangled knowledge and identities that blurred the boundaries between philosophy, Christianity, Gnostic movements and the texts they produced, with a fecund fascination with ancient esotericism and metaphysics.

11.5 God Thoughts

COMPANION TEXTS
Origen, *Dialogue with Heraclides*

In 212 CE, the Alexandrian Ambrose, a wealthy educated Valentinian, decided to pay Origen a visit at the catechetical school. He had heard about Origen's growing reputation as a Biblical scholar and likely hoped to have an audience with Origen about matters of the interpretation of scripture. They hit it off. Eventually, Origen was able to convince Ambrose that Valentinus (and Marcion) had it wrong, that the Apostolic Catholics possessed the true faith and the key to interpret the scriptures as they were meant to be understood.

Ambrose became Origen's constant companion and a deacon in the Alexandrian Church. Even more importantly, Ambrose became Origen's patron, supplying Origen with all the books he needed for his studies as well as stenographers (so that he could easily dictate his compositions) and the resources to publish and circulate his books. This financial support meant that Origen was prolific and his work widely distributed even in his own lifetime. The more he wrote and published, the more his reputation and fame as a top theologian burgeoned. Ambrose particularly encouraged Origen to write commentaries on scriptural texts and take on other commentators like the Valentinian Heracleon (who, we learned in Chapter 8, wrote a commentary on the Gospel of John) and the pagan philosopher Celsus (who wrote a treatise attacking Christians as fools). Everything that Origen wrote after 218 CE is dedicated to Ambrose, including his *Commentary on John* and *Against Celsus*.

Origen traveled extensively, visiting Rome, Antioch, Athens, Nicomedia, and Caesarea where he offered wealthy Christians instructions, like Julia Mammaea, the mother of Emperor Alexander Severus who was interested in Christianity. She had heard about Origen and asked him to come to her in Antioch to teach her. He also traveled on invitation to preach in different churches (279 of his homilies have survived). He was particularly well-liked by Bishops Alexander of Jersualem and Theoctistus of

Caesarea. Theoctistus, in fact, ordained him as a priest. Origen's growing fame and ordination (which was not done in Alexandria by Bishop Demetrius of Alexandria nor with his permission), raised the ire of Demetrius who wrote to the Bishop of Rome, accusing Origen of believing that the Devil will be saved. In 230 CE, Demetrius managed to have Origen barred from the Alexandrian church.

Because of this, Origen never returned to Alexandria, but settled in Caesarea. There he continued to flourish, writing his scriptural commentaries, theological treaties, and a reference book he called *The Hexapla*. This was Origen's critical edition of the Jewish scriptures. *The Hexapla* consisted of four Greek editions of the Jewish scriptures (the Septuagint and three other Greek translations made by Aquila of Sinope, Symmachus the Ebionite, and Theodotion in the second century). These were laid out in columns next to one column of the text in Hebrew (consonants only) and another column of the Hebrew text in Greek characters (including vowels). Origen recognized that the texts of the Hebrew manuscripts varied as much as the Greek translations. His goal was the creation of a synopticon to aid him in correcting the errors in the popular Septuagint text so that his new Greek translation would reflect as closely as possible what he determined to be the original text of the Jewish scriptures.

Origen died either in Caesarea or Tyre in 254 CE following a brutal persecution of the Christians in 250 CE by Emperor Decius. Origen was arrested and tortured, but did not succumb immediately to the violence done to him. He was still alive when Decius died in 251 CE. Origen's own death likely was the result of the injuries he sustained from his interrogation and imprisonment.

The proliferation and distribution of Origen's writings demonstrate how learned Origen was. He is perhaps the most learned of all Christian theologians in antiquity. He knew the Jewish and Christian scriptures backward and forward (by heart we would say). He knew how the Valentinians and other Christians interpreted the scriptures and was able to debate them point-by-point. This is why Bishops Alexander and Theoctistus took Origen with them when they were called to conferences in order to judge the orthodoxy of bishops and clerics who were accused of heresy. We know a great deal about the case of Bishops Beryllus of Bostra and Bishop Heraclides (who led another church in Arabia) because we possess the minutes of Heraclides' interrogation (244–249 CE). Heraclides faced the accusation that he was a Modalist Monarchian who downplays the divinity of the Son in order to emphasize monotheism. Recall that the Modalists argued that the Son is only the name the Father uses when he comes to earth to redeem humanity.

In these minutes, we get a picture of Origen's conceptualization of God and the relationship of the Father to the Son. Foremost, he rejects the Modalist position. He reasons that, if the ontological reality of the Son is removed (if the Son is only a name and not an actual divine being), then the ontological reality of the Father is also removed because a father cannot be a father without a son. Origen insists on the reality of both the Father and the Son as individual divinities. They are not simply names or modes of expression. Here he pushes Heraclides to accept the position that the Father and Son are "two Gods" whose divine "power (*dynamis*)" is one."

What does Origen mean here? Is he a polytheist? While he certainly was accused of polytheism by his detractors (as were Tertullian and Hippolytus), Origen's other writings make his position clearer. We find that Origen was devoted to the Apostolic Catholic Canon of Truth whose first article refers to the belief in one God. Origen understood this one God to be the transcendent God who was also the Biblical Creator of the world. Origen is adamant that God is One and that this One is invisible and incomprehensible. Any anthropomorphic language about God in the Biblical texts either refers to the Logos or otherwise must be allegorically interpreted.

This One God, however, is a trinity, which Origen understands to be a triad of beings not a triune being. He is a Father, a Son, *and* a Holy Spirit. Origen, like Tertullian, takes on the task of explaining how exactly this triadic relationship works. As we will see shortly, after his death, Origen's opinion on these matters is disputed among Catholics who either identified as right-wing Origenists or left-wing Origenists. So much did this debate consume the Apostolic Catholics that the landscape of Christian thought changed markedly around 250 CE. Disputes over Origen's doctrines paved the road to Nicaea (325 CE).

Origen said:	Since once an inquiry has begun it is proper to say something upon the subject of the inquiry, I will speak. The whole church is present and listening. It is not right that there should be any difference in knowledge between one church and another, for you are not the false church. I charge you, father Heraclides: God is the Almighty, the Uncreated, the supreme God who made all things. Do you hold this doctrine?
Heraclides:	I do. That is what I also believe...
Origen:	Is the Son distinct from the Father?
Heraclides:	Of course. How can he be Son if he is also Father?
Origen:	While being distinct from the Father is the Son himself also God?
Heraclides:	He himself is also God.
Origen:	And do two Gods become a unity?
Heraclides:	Yes.
Origen:	Do we confess two Gods?
Heraclides:	Yes. The power is one.
Origen:	But as our brethren take offence at the statement that there are two Gods, we must formulate the doctrine carefully, and show in what sense they are two and in what sense the two are one God. Also the holy Scriptures have taught that several things which are two are one. And not only things which are two, for they have also taught that in some instances more than two, or even a very much larger number of things, are one... In this way we avoid falling into the opinion of those who have been separated from the Church and turned to the illusory notion of monarchy, who abolish the Son as distinct from the Father and virtually abolish the Father also. Nor do we fall into the other blasphemous doctrine which denies the deity of Christ.

Transcript of Origen's interrogation of Bishop Heraclides who was accused of Modalism

The reason for the Origenist debate centered around two opposing tendencies in Origen's opinions about the divinity of the Son, which we see emerge in the way Origen interrogated Heraclides. On the one hand, Origen affirms the divinity and eternity of the Son, making him equal to the Father. There can be no Father without the Son existing. If there was such a time (which there was not), this would result in the conclusion that there was a time when the Father did not exist. Origen called this mystery the Eternal Generation of the Son. The Son's generation is not an emanation, but resembles the way that thoughts proceed from the will or brightness from light. This generation is eternal, by which Origen means, there was no time that the Son did not exist. There was no time that the Father lacked the Son.

To explain their relationship further, Origen uses two Greek words that more or less meant the same thing: *ousia* and *hypostasis*. Both words mean "being" or "existence" and were used to translate the Latin *substantia* or substance. Origen says that the Son is "from the hypostasis of the Father." Here he is referring to Hebrews 1:3 which describes the Son as an impression of the Father's hypostasis ("God's very being"). Based on this passage, Origen uses the word hypostasis not to mean the generic idea of "being" or "what exists," but to indicate a being that exists with its own personal identity. Origen restricted the word to mean a personal or individual being, which enables him to read Hebrews to mean that the Son is a separate hypostasis from the Father. Origen uses this concept of personal identity to argue against Modalists who did not credit the Son with a hypostasis of his own. Origen applies the same term to the Holy Spirit, so that he argues that the Father, Son and Holy Spirit are three hypostases (persons). While he understands the three to be distinct personal beings (hypostases), he also perceives them to be eternally generated and united by the harmony of their will, love, and action. They all possess a distinctive ousia, a generic essence of divinity. In other words, the hypostases are distinct from all other beings because only they participate in the divine ousia which Origen defines as goodness, truth, life, and power. Origen used the generation of steam from water as an analogy.

While Origen insisted that the Son was utterly different from all other beings because he shared the Father's ousia, he also presented the Son as a mediator (the Logos) between the Father and the world. This led Origen to say that only the Father is truly God, while the Son is God by his participation in the Father. This he affirmed from his reading of John 1:1, "In the beginning was the Logos, and the Logos was with **the** God, and the Logos was God." Origen noted that the article **the** was present when referring to God, but was not present when referring to the Logos, which confirmed the Son's lesser divinity. Origen saw the Son not as God but as God's Image. He argued that it is appropriate to pray to the Father through the Son, but prayers ought not to be offered to the Son by himself.

These two tendencies led Catholics after Origen to divide into two camps, those who emphasized Origen's teachings about the divinity and Eternal Generation of the Son because they were scandalized by Paul of Samasota's Dynamist teachings (right-wing Origenists) and those who emphasized Origen's teachings about the subordination of the Son because they feared Sabellius' Modalist teachings (left-wing Origenists). Their debate ultimately led to the Arian crisis which precipitated the Nicene Council in 325 CE.

Arius was an Alexandrian left-wing Origenist and presbyter in the Alexandrian church which was run by a right-wing Origenist, Bishop Alexander (313–328 CE). Arius was a populist preacher who taught that the Son must be subordinate to the Father and that there must have been a time when the Son was not, otherwise he would be the Brother of the Father, not the Son. God is not eternally Father, but in fact, God *created* the Son from nothing. While the Logos (God's thought) always existed, he did not exist as the first-born of all creation until he was created. This meant that the Son was not divine in his ousia, but became like God when God adopted him prior to the creation of the world. The Son is not equal to God, nor is he one in essence with God.

Arius' opinion was like a spark hitting cinder. Christians took to the streets of Alexandria proclaiming, "There was when he was not! There was when he was not! There was when he was not!" Bishop Alexander responded by deposing Arius in a synod packed with Egyptian bishops he had called for this purpose. Rioting broke out. As the violence in the streets continued, Emperor Constantine got wind and intervened, calling the Council of Nicaea and forcing the Apostolic Catholic bishops who traveled there to make a decision about Arius. Arius was deposed and the Nicene Creed established as the official expression of their faith, specifically declaring that the Son is "from the ousia of the Father" and "homoousios" (the same substance or essence) with the Father while maintaining the distinctions between the Father, Son, and Holy Spirit. The creed from that first council reads:

"We believe in one God, the Father Almighty, Creator of all things visible and invisible. And in one Lord Jesus Christ, the Son of God, begotten of the Father, the only-begotten; that is, of the essence (*ousia*) of the Father, God of God, Light of Light, very God of very God, begotten, not made, consubstantial (*homoousia*) with the Father; by whom all things were made both in heaven and on earth; Who for us men, and for our salvation, came down and was incarnate and was made man; He suffered, and the third day he rose again, ascended into heaven; From thence he shall come to judge the quick and the dead. And in the Holy Spirit. But those who say, 'There was a time when he was not;' and 'He was not before he was made,' and 'He was made out of nothing,' or 'He is of another substance' or 'essence' (*ousia*), or 'The Son of God is create,' or 'changeable,' or 'alterable' – they are condemned by the holy Catholic and Apostolic Church."

Form of the Nicene Creed agreed upon in 325 CE

Notice that nothing is explained about these declarations. This left the creed open to interpretation. The Catholics continued to debate the legitimate interpretation of the creed. There was fierce fighting over what homoousios meant and whether it was a Modalist term. Many bishops wondered if perhaps hom**oi**ousios was better, acknowledging that the Son was *like* (-**oi**-) the Father's ousia.

Eventually, they become convinced by Bishop Athanasius of Alexandria that homoousios should be retained as long as it is understood that they did not mean it in the same sense as the Modalists (that the Father and the Son are the same entity with different names). They decided it was a necessary term which establishes that Jesus is not a semi-divine power or inferior to the Father, but a divinity equal to the Father and able to mediate salvation. This was settled in the Council of Constantinople in 381 CE and the creed rewritten to calm the controversy. This rewritten version is considered the Catholic Church's official declaration of the Nicene Creed.

> "We believe in one God, the Father, the Almighty, maker of heaven and earth, of all that is, seen and unseen. And in one Lord, Jesus Christ, the only-begotten Son of God, eternally begotten of the Father, Light from Light, true God from true God, begotten, not made, of one being with the Father. Through him all things were made. For us, humans, and for our salvation, he came down from heaven, was incarnate of the Holy Spirit and the virgin Mary, and became fully human. For our sake he was crucified under Pontius Pilate. He suffered death and was buried. He rose again on the third day in accordance with the Scriptures. He ascended into heaven and is seated at the right hand of the Father. He will come again in glory to judge the living and the dead, and his kingdom will have no end. And in the Holy Spirit, the Lord, the giver of life, who proceeds from the Father, who in unity with the Father and the Son is worshiped and glorified, who has spoken through the prophets. In one holy universal and apostolic Church. We acknowledge one baptism for the forgiveness of sins. We look for the resurrection of the dead and the life of the world to come. Amen."
>
> *Form of the Nicene Creed agreed upon* in 381 CE

The official Nicene Creed, however, left the two-natures of Jesus in limbo. While the creed declares that Jesus was "very God" and "was made man" the details were not worked out. This debate went on for several decades before the details were agreed upon in the Council of Chalcedon (451 CE). At this council, Jesus Christ is declared to be "truly God and truly man." He is the Son, only-begotten of the Father. But he also had his own human body and soul, born like us from a human mother. In him existed two natures "unconfusedly, unchangeably, indivisibly, inseparably." The properties of both natures were not altered by the incarnation. The incarnation, however, meant that the two natures "concurred" in "one person" and "one hypostasis."

The official Nicene Creed also provided more details about the Holy Spirit which proved most problematic later. The Spirit is declared to have been involved in Jesus' conception in the virgin Mary. The Spirit is the Lord and Giver of Life, who proceeds from the Father, who is worshiped in conjunction with the Father and the Son, and who inspired the prophets. This version of the Creed establishes the Godhead as three persons in one substance. It does not explain how their relationships ought to be understood. This explanation came in the fourth-century writings of three Catholics known as the Cappadocian Fathers (Basil of Caesarea, Gregory of Nyssa, and Gregory of Nazianzus). Using Stoic and Aristotelian logic, they argue that God's ousia is a universal and undifferentiated substrate (a general property) that is the basis for individual existence expressed in individual qualities (particular concrete examples). We might think of three different horses who share the property of horsiness, which makes them horses. They applied this logic to the problem of God.

Beyond this, we are in the dark. They argued that we cannot know *what* God is (the ousia remains a mystery) but only *how* it is expressed as the Father, Son, and Holy Spirit. No amount of debate or reasoning is going to reveal what our minds cannot conceive, they said. Gregory of Nyssa writes about this in the *Life of Moses*, "This is the true knowledge of what is sought; this is the seeing that consists in not seeing, because that which is sought transcends all knowledge, being separated on all sides by incomprehensibility as by a kind of darkness." According to the Cappadocians, the most we can say about the ousia is what it is not, not what it is. This is called apophatic theology. They conclude, like

Job, that God's ways are greater than ours, and that we have to find a way to live in the face of an apophatic mystery. They recommend participating in the Eucharist when the mystery is laid on the altar and we experience God in this communion.

Timeline

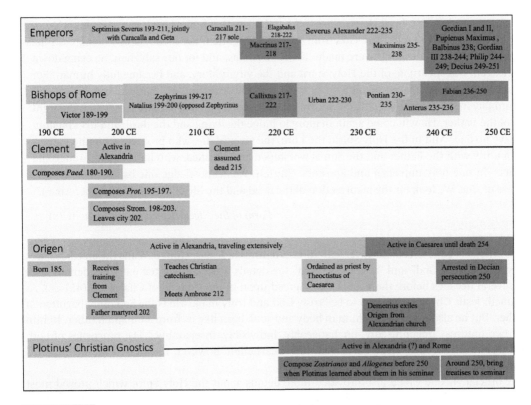

FIGURE 11.6 Timeline for Clement, Origen, and Plotinus' Christian Gnostics.

Pattern Summary

All of the figures we engaged in this chapter are concerned with developing esoteric wisdom for their churches or philosophical clubs. Theology is still being debated across Christian Families. While Clement and Origen agree with other Apostolic Catholics that the God of worship is the Biblical Creator, who is their PATRON (they are resolute YAHWISTS), they are still having to promote this theology because they are in intense competition with the Valentinians, who are well-known and respected TRANSTHEISTS in Alexandria and abroad. In Rome, the Christian Gnostics known to Plotinus have rekeyed Sethian mythology so that Plato's concept of The One precedes and supersedes the Sethian Father God. They have written new apocalypses to distribute their theology. Like other YAHWISTS, Clement and Origen FAULT HUMANS (primordially in Origen's scheme) for the fall into sin and corruption. Humans must work toward their salvation and BODILY RESURRECTION.

Family Pattern Chart
Clement and Origen

X=Definitely > L=Likely

THEODICY

	Faulty-God	Faulty-Human	Other
Clement of Alexandria		X	
Origen		X	Fall of *logikoi*

SOTERIOLOGY

	Gift from God	Human achievement	Minimalist	Moderate	Maximalist
Clement of Alexandria		X		X	
Origen		X		X	

CHRISTOLOGY

	Adult possession	Fetal possession	Hybrid	Ensoulment	Visitation	Human who received revelation
Clement of Alexandria		X		X		
Origen			aware	X		

ANTHROPOLOGY

	Mono	Dual	Triad	Quad
Clement of Alexandria		X		
Origen		X		

COSMIC DEMIURGY

	Autocrat	Administrator	Caretaker	Patron	Justice	Villain	Rebel	Ignorant	Impaired
Clement of Alexandria	X	X	X	X	X				
Origen	X	X	X	X	X				

RESURRECTION

	Body reunites with soul	Body discarded and soul immortalized	Body and soul discarded and spirit rises	God-element separates from body soul, and spirit rises
Clement of Alexandria	X			
Origen	X			

SCRIPTURES

	Jewish	Gospel	Pauline letters (10)	Pauline letters (13)	Hebrews	Acts	Catholic letters	Revelation	Other
Clement of Alexandria	X	Mt/Mk/Lk/Jn		X	X	X	1 Pet	X	1 Jn/2 Jn extensive apoc
Origen	X	Mt/Mk/Lk/Jn		X	X	X	1 Pet	X	1 Jn/2 Jn Some apoc

ECCLESIOLOGY

	Consolidation movement	Reform movement	Secessionist movement	Counter movement	Innovative movement	Trans-regional	Regional
Clement of Alexandria	X					X	
Origen	X					X	

FIGURE 11.7 Summary of Clement and Origen's patterns of beliefs and practices.

The fight over the Gnostic tag is in high gear. Clement and Origen work to take the label away from the Valentinians, and Plotinus knows that the Christian philosophers in his seminars are using it to identify themselves as knowers of the God-of-Non-Being-Before-Being (likely against Christians such as Clement and Origen who are using it to promote the Biblical God). It appears that in the third century, the word Gnostic takes on a more generic meaning, used by Christians who were metaphysicians searching for the universal and perennial truth about human existence (Figure 11.7).

Takeaways

1. Clement of Alexandria constructed an esoteric tradition for the Apostolic Catholics to rival Valentinian esotericism. Clement taught that the esoteric tradition was revealed by Jesus to a select number of disciples, who went on to reveal it to the twelve and then the seventy apostles. In turn, the apostles revealed it to Christian educators, who passed on the tradition orally.

2. Clement of Alexandria created a school curriculum to educate Christians on three levels, the most advanced being the Gnostic level when the Christian was taught to contemplate the Creator and achieve Gnosis of him. Clement of Alexandria wrote two of the three textbooks he had planned for each level in his school.

3. According to Clement of Alexandria, the Gnostic life is a mystical life when the advanced Christians ascend to heaven, see God, and join the angelic ranks.

4. Origen most fully develops the concept that the esoteric tradition is hidden in the scripture, which must be read at an advanced level (pneumatic level) in order to recover it. Origen believed that scripture had three meanings: somatic, psychic, and pneumatic.

5. Origen had a complicated origin story for the human soul which began as logikoi that fell into bodies as their love for God cooled off.

6. Origen developed the ENSOULMENT PATTERN, teaching that the Logos combined with the one remaining logikos. This entity served as Jesus' soul.

7. Plotinus personally knew and interacted with esoteric Christian philosophers he called Gnostics. He said that they authored books including *Zostrianos* and *Allogenes*. These books reimagine Sethian cosmogony and cosmology by aligning mythological language with technical Platonic language about the first principles.

8. Origen persuaded Ambrose to give up Valentinianism. Ambrose became Origen's patron and most ardent supporter.

9. Origen taught that the Son is eternally generated, but also that the Son is a distinct hypostasis from the Father who shares the Father's ousia.

10. Origen's massive corpus and reputation helped to shift Christian discourse and paved the way for the Arian controversy and the Council of Nicaea.

Questions

1. How and why did the Apostolic Catholics create an esoteric tradition in the fifth generation (and not before)? How did this relate to other Christians who had already created an esoteric tradition? How and why did they create their esoteric traditions?

2. How did the authors of *Zostrianos* and *Allogenes* realign Sethian mythology with technical Platonic terminology about the first principles? What does this tell us about who the authors might have been and what they were up to?

3. What is the difference between somatic, psychic, and pneumatic readings of scripture? Select three passages from the Bible that Origen might have identified as in need of a spiritual interpretation. How did he identify these kinds of passages? Provide different levels of interpretation for the three passages you chose.

4. Did Clement teach an ENSOULMENT PATTERN? Why or why not? How does Clement's Christology compare with Origen's. What was it about the ENSOULMENT PATTERN that they may have found beneficial? How did they nuance or adjust the pattern?

5. Compare Origen's Christology with the Valentinian pattern of the first principles. How close or far apart do you judge Origen to be from the Valentinian pattern?

6. Compare Origen's Christology with Valentinian Christology. How does Origen's understanding of Christology relate to Origen's understanding of the first principles? Consider also how Valentinian Christology is related to their understanding of the first principles. What are the points of similarity and difference between Origen and the Valentinians on this subject?

7. Were the Christians who attended Plotinus' seminar in Rome Sethian Gnostics? Why or why not?

8. Throughout this textbook, the subject of the relationship between the Father and the Son has been a constant refrain. Summarize the main positions from Justin to Arius. Include the Holy Spirit as a third element once Tertullian turns the Binitarian Problem into a Trinitarian one. What do you make of this controversy and the solutions various thinkers provided?

Resources

Denise Kimber Buell. 1999. *Making Christians: Clement of Alexandria and the Rhetoric of Legitimacy*. Princeton: Princeton University Press.

Dylan M. Burns. 2014. *Apocalypse of the Alien God: Platonism and the Exile of Sethian Gnosticism*. Philadelphia: University of Pennsylvania Press.

Paul B. Decock. 2011. "Origen: On Making Sense of the Resurrection as a Third Century Christian." *Neotestamentica* 45: 76–91.

April D. DeConick. 2018. "Deviant Christians: Romanization and Esoterization as Social Strategies for Survival among Early Christians." *Gnosis: Journal of Gnostic Studies* 3.2: 135–176.

Justo L. González. 1970. (revised ed.). Chapter 8 in *A History of Christian Thought from the Beginnings to the Council of Chalcedon*. Volume 1. Ashville: Abingdon Press.

Jesper Hyldahl. 2014. "Clement of Alexandria: Paganism and Its Positive Significance for Christianity." Pages 139–158 in *In Defense of Christianity: Early Christian Apologists* Early Christianity in the Context of Antiquity 15. Edited by Jakob Engberg, Anders-Christian Jacobsen, and Jörg Ulrich. Translated by Gavin Weakley. Frankfurt am Main: Peter Lang.

Salvatore R. C. Lilla. 1971. *Clement of Alexandria: A Study in Christian Platonism and Gnosticism*. Oxford: Oxford University Press.

Alexander J. Mazur. 2021. *The Platonizing Sethian Background of Plotinus's Mysticism*. Nag Hammadi and Manichaean Studies 98. Leiden: Brill.

Claudio Moreschini and Enrico Norelli. 2005. Chapters 14 and 15. *Early Christian Greek and Latin Literature: A Literary History*. Volume 1: *From Paul to the Age of Constantine*. Translated by Matthew J. O'Connell. Peabody: Hendrickson Publishers.

Joseph Wilson Trigg. 1973. *Origen: The Bible and Philosophy in the Third-Century Church*. Atlanta: John Knox Press.

John D. Turner. 2001. *Sethian Gnosticism and the Platonic Tradition* Bibliothèque Copte de Nag Hammadi 6. Québec: Les Presses de L'Université Laval.

CHAPTER 12

A Family History

Remains of the earliest known house church. Baptistery wall painting: Procession of women, ca. 240–245 CE, Paint on plaster, 95 × 140 cm (37-3/8 × 55-1/8 in). Syria, Dura-Europos, Roman. **Source:** Sepia Times / Getty Images.

In this textbook, we have approached the history of early Christianity by decentering the standard linear stories of Christian origins by starting in the middle with Christian literature that we can reliably date and position geographically (ca. 120–220 CE). This retrospective approach means that the end has not determined the beginning of the story nor has the beginning of the story determined the end. Rather we are firmly located in the middle, which has given us a clear picture of the plurality of third-, fourth-, and fifth-generation Christians. The picture that has emerged is a web of interactions between Christians, Jews, and pagans in a variety of regional settings, rather than a linear positioning of Christians that tells the story from the perspective of the Catholics and their memories.

So you might wonder, "What now?" What more can this web of interactions tell us about the early Christians? From this stage, we are reasonably positioned to construct "biographies" of the earlier generations. There are three provisos, however, that we ought to keep in mind as we construct these biographies in this chapter. First, the biographies must account for the emergence of the different Christian movements and their intergenerational struggles for survival while also staying tuned into the shape of the Christian family network. Second, these biographies must explain the origins of Christian pluralism and offer reasons for their differing memories of Jesus and

Comparing Christianities: An Introduction to Early Christianity, First Edition. April D. DeConick.
© 2024 John Wiley & Sons Ltd. Published 2024 by John Wiley & Sons Ltd.

the Christian past. How is it that each of them was able to authenticate themselves as true Christians? Third, these biographies must present reasonable accounts of the composition of early Christian literature *independent* of the conceptualization of the Apostolic Christian New Testament canon, which is a late anti-Marcionite development.

12.1 Who Is Christian?

In this textbook, we have met dozens of people who started or joined Christian movements that were popular in antiquity. The movements were highly pluralistic and varied, so much so that it begs the question: how do we define Christianity? There are different possibilities for approaching this question. A SUBSTANTIVE DEFINITION lays out crucial characteristics that define what Christianity is and what it is not. This type of definition is prescriptive and exclusive. In other words, if a group does not have all the characteristics, it is excluded. This is the type of definition that the Apostolic Catholics put into play. They developed a cluster of beliefs and practices that defined the true Christian. This began as a pronouncement they called the Canon of Truth, which became the basis for the Nicene Creed (325 CE). They organized their memories to trace their beliefs back to apostolic times and give them apostolic credibility. They wrote and rewrote scriptures and developed hermeneutics to reflect their memories and support their beliefs and practices. They used the Canon of Truth, the Apostolic tradition, and their versions of scriptures and interpretations to define Christianity and exclude other movements that had differing beliefs, historical memories, interpretations, and credentialing stories. SUBSTANTIVE DEFINITIONS are incredibly persuasive because they are narrow and easy to measure. But because they are so narrow, they are also the most restrictive. They are unable to capture religious diversity so that groups like the Valentinians or the Marcionites or the Ebionites cannot be understood as anything other than heresies.

A second approach to defining Christianity is to create a FUNCTIONAL DEFINITION, to state what Christianity did for its converts. In this case, we could define Christianity as a movement that provided people in the Roman world with the means to struggle with their ultimate concerns. Their churches provided them with a common myth and rituals to feel, think, and act in ways that gave their lives purpose and meaning. Their churches were particularly attractive to colonialized and oppressed populations, including slaves and women. In this sense, Christianity functioned to destabilize, disrupt, and dislocate society's norms and hierarchies, providing a new social order and power to people who had little social mobility or resources. Their communities were charitable, providing food, clothing, and medical care to those in need, and burial and the promise of a good afterlife when they died. Functional definitions like this are useful because they are able to transcend differences in beliefs and practices. But they tend to be so inclusive that it becomes difficult to distinguish Christianity from other movements in antiquity. Other religions (i.e. Judaism; mystery religions) and non-religious groups (i.e. philosophical schools, burial clubs) in antiquity functioned similarly.

A third approach, which we take up in this textbook, is to create a FAMILY RESEMBLANCE DEFINITION. The idea is that families share some physiological traits, which distinguishes them from other families even though each family member is unique and every family member will not share all the same traits. Using this type of definition, Christianity is defined as a family network of religious movements that shares clusters of related attributes when it comes to beliefs, rituals, religious experience, and social form. On the one hand, these common attributes make Christianity a distinct religion. On the other hand, these common attributes are arranged in different clusters or patterns across the varied Christian movements. That said, the patterns are not prescriptive. There may be arrangements that do not share all the same patterns, but are still Christian, just as games do not all share dice, footballs, or video screens.

The strength of the FAMILY RESEMBLANCE DEFINITION is that it has the power to define what Christianity is and what it is not without being overly exclusive. Christians do not have to fall into the categories of orthodox and heretic. The definition also allows for us to compare the different Christian movements with each other by looking at how the common patterns are arranged. This has the potential of helping us understand the history of the movements and their relationships with each other.

What does the Christian Network of Families look like in antiquity? We have charted at the end of each chapter the PATTERNS used by the individual Christians we have studied. Now we are ready to do comparative work with reference to a chart that aggregates this information. This chart is located at the end of this chapter (Figure 12.8). This chart is meant to facilitate the organization and comparison of the family patterns. It is not meant to be exhaustive or prescriptive, but representative of the Christians covered in this textbook. When we study the PATTERNS, it is clear that three distinctive families of Christian movements can be delineated based on their patterns of THEOLOGY. Their THEOLOGY, in turn, impacted their patterns of DEMIURGY, which, in turn, largely determined the rest of patterns in the family grouping.

TABLE 12.1 Christian Families Organized by Theology

Yahwist Family	Transtheist Family	Xenotheist Family
Papias (Hierapolis)	Cerinthus (Asia Minor)	Marcion (Sinope, Rome)
Hermas (Rome)	Cerdo (Syria, Rome)	Miltiades
Ignatius (Antioch)	Valentinus (Alexandria, Rome)	Apelles (devalued YHWH to angel)
Polycarp (Smyrna)	Agathopous (Alexandria?)	?-Philumene
Author of Canonical Luke-Acts	Christian Sethians (Alexandria)	Potitus
Author(s) of Pastoral Epistles	Basilides and Isidore (Alexandria)	Basilicus
Author of Hebrews	Carpocrates and Epiphanes (Alexandria)	Syneros
Author of 1 Clement	Marcellina (Rome)	
Justin Martyr (Rome)	Ptolemy (Rome)	
Ebionites (Syria, Mesopotamia)	Flora (Rome)	
Nazoreans (Syria)	Theodotus the Valentinian (Asia Minor, Alexandria)	
Elchasaites (Syria,Mesopotamia)	Heracleon (Italy)	
Tatian (Syria)	Marcus (Gaul)	
The Trio: Montanus, Maximilla, Priscilla (Pepuza; Asia Minor)	Flavia Sophe (Rome)	
Encratic Syrian Christians	Secundus (Rome)	
Hegesippus	Axionicus (Antioch)	
Irenaeus (Antioch, Lyons)	Prodicus (Alexandria)	
Aristides (Athens)	Rheginus (Alexandria ?)	
Athenagoras (Athens)	Theotimus (Rome)	
Author of Letter of Diognetus	Florinus (Smyrna, Rome)	
Author of Letter of Barnabas	Peratics	
Author(s) of Catholic Letters	Ophians	
Tertullian (Carthage)	Justin the Gnostic	
Theodotus the Cobbler (Constantiople)	Naassenes	

(continued)

TABLE 12.1   **Christian Families Organized by Theology** *(continued)*

Yahwist Family	Transtheist Family	Xenotheist Family
Artemon (Modalist) (Rome)	Platonizing Sethian Christians	
Theodotus the Banker (Rome)		
Natalius (Rome)		
Paul of Samosata (Antioch)		
Noetus (Smyrna)		
Epigonus (Rome)		
Sabellius (Libya)		
Hippolytus of Rome		
Hippolytus of Asia		
Hermogenes (Antioch, Carthage)		
Clement of Alexandria		
Origen (Alexandria, Caesarea)		

The YAHWISTS are Christians who worship the Biblical Creator God. By 150 CE, this God comes to be identified with the universal transcendent God of the Greek philosophers. The TRANSTHEISTS are Christians who worship the transcendent primal Source of Life, but not the actual Creator of the universe. This God beyond the created universe has characteristics of the Egyptian primal God (i.e. Atum, Aten, Amun) and the Greek philosophical God. The XENOTHEISTS are Christians who worship an alien transcendent God who is an intruder in our universe. He does not have any connection to the creation of the human being or the world. This God is truly Unknown from a distant place. He is a religious innovation in antiquity.

It is important to recognize that all Christians across the three Families believe that the Biblical God created the cosmos as an AUTOCRAT who had an ASSISTANT or ASSISTANTS. All the Christians think that YHWH had help from certain Powers (Wisdom, Logos, Angels, Archons, etc.) when creating the world. This is probably a result of the plural references (us, our) in Genesis 1:26–27. All Christians also believe that YHWH's justice and punishment is based on his Law, which he, his angels, or his Archons gave to Moses. The difference between the Families' opinions on DEMIURGY are qualitative: whether YHWH and his helpers were good, bad, or ugly. Once the groups determined their opinion about YHWH, the rest of their patterns of belief rationally follow suit.

Equally important is the observation that all Christians across the three Families believe that God intervened to save humanity and that Jesus' death is instrumental in this act. All groups believed themselves to be exclusive (i.e. the Elect), that, in order to be redeemed, the person had to join their group, participate in their rituals, and live a life that reflected their redeemed status. The question they debated was whether humans had to achieve their salvation through human actions too. In other words, was their salvation also dependent on whether they observed certain laws that God required them to follow? Again we find ourselves faced with the initial divide between those first Christians who were Jewish sectarian Maximalists, Moderates, and Minimalists. This divide continued to determine the formation and maintenance of Christian differences generations later.

12.2 Xenotheist Family

We begin our summaries of the individual Families with the Xenotheist family because Christians in this family were the first to establish their movement as a distinct Christian religion separate from Judaism (Figure 12.8). In addition, the Apostolic Catholic network constructs their own Christian identity largely in response to them so it makes sense to start with their overview.

We observe that the Xenotheists are the least diverse family, consisting only of Cerdo, Marcion and his followers. Since Cerdo operated an esoteric school that did not survive intergenerationally, the only church movement in this family is the Marcionite Church and Marcionite factions. There simply are no other Christian churches that worship a God who was completely alien and unattached to our world. While the Transtheists worship a superior God who lives in a transcendent realm, this God is always the primordial initiator of life in the universe. In Transtheist systems, God's coming-into-being consequently results in the creation of the cosmos by a lesser divinity. This is a different theology from that held by the Marcionites who believed in an utterly Good alien God living in an unknown world of his own, very distant from our universe. The Marcionite God is in no way the cause of life in our universe. Perhaps this innovative theology proved to be too much for some like the Marcionite Apelles who modified Marcion's theology by suggesting a connection between the Supreme transcendent God and a subordinate fiery angel who created this world. It seems that Apelles may have been trying to modify Marcionism so that it was closer to the theology taught by the Transtheists.

From careful study of the Jewish scriptures and Paul's letters, the Marcionites configured their DEMIURGY PATTERN, determining that YHWH is a capricious God who created our universe and patronized the Jews, leaving Gentiles suffering without recourse. Not surprisingly, when it comes to their THEODICY PATTERN, the Marcionites ascribed all suffering to the Biblical Creator. In his capriciousness, he elected to help the Jews while forsaking everyone else to a miserable existence with no hope of afterlife liberation. YHWH has a Law which he uses to reward and punish the Jews. He promises to send the Jews a Messiah to save them at the end of time. Gentiles, however, suffer in a system that the Creator God has rigged against them. They had no hope until the Alien God, out of his goodness and grace, intervened in the affairs of another God's world. Since salvation is entirely an act of grace, the Marcionites were Minimalists.

To save humanity, the alien God sent his own Son, Jesus, as an ambassador to earth. His Son took the form of an angel. He was like the Angel of the Lord who, in the Jewish scriptures, appeared on earth as a human being and interacted with the Jewish Patriarchs. The Marcionites are very clear that Jesus did not have a real human body but appeared as an angel. Because they deployed this VISITATION PATTERN to present their Christology, the Marcionites are characterized by their detractors as Docetists.

Marcionite use of the VISITATION PATTERN, however, makes sense with the rest of their beliefs. They did not feel that it was necessary for Jesus to have a physical body because Jesus was here only to retrieve souls and transfigure them into spiritual entities that would be able to live in the alien God's spiritual world. Their physical bodies were not going to be saved, but would be left behind in the grave. Clearly, the Marcionites were DUALISTS when it came to anthropology. But because the goal was to leave behind YHWH's world for an afterlife in the Alien God's spiritual world, they believed that the resurrection of the dead referred to the ascension of the mortal soul to the alien God's world where it would be transfigured into an IMMORTAL SPIRITUAL ENTITY. In other words, the mortal soul was changed into the alien God's substance – spirit – so that it could live happily ever after in the alien God's spiritual world.

12.3 Transtheist Family

The Transtheists posit that their native land is a realm beyond the cosmos, the home of a superior primal God who initiated life (Figure 12.8). They worship this superior Deity as the primordial God. In terms of DEMIURGY, all the Christian movements in the Transtheist family assume that YHWH is an AUTOCRAT WITH ASSISTANTS who create the cosmos and the human being. Some Transtheists ratchet the identities of the Biblical Creator and his archons by associating them with Greek and Egyptian Gods. In the case of Justin the Gnostic, he sees two Biblical Creator Gods in Genesis: Elohim and Eden. He uses these names to create a very idiosyncratic mythology.

The Transtheists characterize the Creator God in relationship to the superior God as a VILLAIN. He is a rebellious, arrogant, lustful, ignorant, or deformed angel. As proof of his angelic status, they referred to Biblical stories about YHWH's appearance on earth as the Angel of the Lord (Angel of YHWH). Because the Biblical God proclaims in the Jewish Scripture that he is jealous and creates woe, the Transtheists understand this angel to have fallen or been demoted like Lucifer. That said, Satan or the Devil is usually discussed as a separate figure (probably because he is distinct from the Biblical God in scriptures like Job).

The rebellious Creator fashions an imperfect world and binds humans into his system in order to keep the divine power that was either stolen from the superior God, ignorantly blown into Adam's nostrils, or is somehow locked into Adam's body. This incarceration of the spirit exacerbates human suffering and ignorance. THEODICY falls to the Gods. Transtheist writings trace human suffering to the primordial God, when God's generation of life inevitably caused a rupture of divinity and/or its mixture in the material realm. This suffering is exacerbated by the Creator God who fashions an imperfect world that locks the divinity within this condition with laws that make it impossible for the soul and spirit to be freed without help from the primordial God.

Most Transtheists emphasize that SALVATION IS A GIFT of the primordial God's grace. Because the Law is the instrument of the Creator, obedience to its rules will not save humans. That said, this did not mean that Transtheists believed that it was acceptable for humans to sin. Isidore, for instance, said that the human compulsion to sin must be resisted for human suffering to be alleviated. Carpocrates thought that it was necessary for humans to resist the passions and despise or reject the Law in order to be released from the cycle of reincarnation. Yet Carpocrates did not think that this was possible without the Power that the transcendent God sends at baptism. This is what made him different from other Platonists who saw their release from reincarnation accomplished by their human efforts, not God's intervention.

Since the Transtheists posited a native spiritual land beyond the cosmos, they also tended to split the human into THREE ASPECTS: the physical body, soul/psyche, and spirit. The body was made from the earth, the soul from ethereal substance of the celestial sphere, and the spirit from divine substance that makes up the transcendent world. Only Basilides and Carpocrates appear to be outliers. Basilides claimed there was a realm higher than the spirit realm, likely to distinguish his system from Stoic philosophy and the Valentinian system. Basilides is the only QUADRATIC Christian in antiquity. Carpocrates identified himself as a trained Platonist, so his system included only the body and the immortal soul, which traveled through many lifetimes trying to conquer the passions. The goal of his system was perfection and the liberation of the soul from imprisonment within the Creator's order. If Carpocrates believed in a spirit in addition to the soul, the sources are such that we will never know.

The Transtheists offered a variety of CHRISTOLOGICAL solutions, but most agreed that Jesus was possessed by a divine Power at his baptism and that it departed at his death. This pattern was probably the oldest Christological solution. Because they posited a transcendent realm in addition to the cosmic, the Valentinians complicated the ADULT POSSESSION PATTERN by splitting Christ into two figures, so that the psychic Christ (formed by the demiurge) enters Jesus at his birth as his soul (ENSOULMENT POSSESSION PATTERN). The pneumatic Christ (produced by Sophia) generates the Aeon Jesus as his mobile representative, who leaves the Pleroma, descends at the baptism, and possesses Jesus (ADULT POSSESSION PATTERN). When Transtheists discuss the Logos in the prologue of the Gospel of John, he is an emanation associated with the transcendent God and the coming-into-being of the Pleroma. For instance, Heracleon believed that the Logos was an Aeonic emanation who, in turn, caused the Demiurge to create the world. Origen contests this interpretation, saying that the Demiurge (YHWH) worked through the Logos to create the world, not the other way around.

Importantly, the literature produced by Transtheists indicates that these groups believed Jesus to be a complete real human being. This includes Justin the Gnostic who said that Jesus was a human boy who was visited by an angel and received a revelation. The Transtheists have been mistakenly characterized as Docetists because of their insistence that Christ did not suffer or die. But this is an unfair depiction, because when these groups refer to "Christ" they are not usually referring to the physical man Jesus but the spiritual entity that possessed the human Jesus at his baptism and departed at his death as the Gospel narratives indicate.

12.4 Yahwist Family

Because the Yahwists worshipped the Biblical God and came to identify him with the philosophical transcendent God of the Greeks who was all-Good (Figure 12.8), the Yahwists characterized the Biblical God as a good, caring, and just God who was their PATRON (after giving up on the Jews). He created using his Wisdom, Powers, or Logos. All Biblical passages that describe God in anthropological and emotional terms are explained as condescending stories or allegories, or they are attributed to the Logos. Once the Gospel of John came into play, some Apostolic Catholics like Justin promoted the idea that Jesus is God's pre-existent Logos who visits with Adam and the Jewish patriarchs as the Angel of the Lord. Eventually, they argued, the Logos possesses Jesus either at his baptism (ADULT POSSESSION PATTERN) or his conception (FETAL POSSESSION PATTERN).

Theodotus the Dynamist is likely correct that the earliest understanding of Jesus among Christians followed the ADULT POSSESSION PATTERN; the FETAL POSSESSION PATTERN is an idea that develops later. When the virgin birth stories were composed by second- or third-generation Christians, they suggest a HYBRID CHRISTOLOGY, that Jesus is a demi-God, a fusion of his human and divine parentage comparable to the birth stories of heroes in Greek myths. Origen is aware of this and considers them condescending tall-tales for simple-minded Christians who need stories like the Greek myths to assist their faith. But no Apostolic Catholic scholar seems to have taken seriously hybridity as an option because such a model suggests that Jesus was not really human or God, but, as Tertullian argued, a monstrosity in-between the two. Apostolic Catholic scholars read the virgin birth stories to mean that the fetus is possessed by the divine element, although Justin and Tatian surmise that the Logos stands in for Jesus' soul (ENSOULMENT PATTERN) rather than functioning as a divine element in addition to Jesus' human soul (POSSESSION PATTERN).

The Modalists are the only Apostolic Catholics who believe that Jesus is the Father visiting earth, where he is called the Son. They made this Christological decision because they were ancient unitarians, believing that God is One and Only One. Their VISITATION PATTERN, however, was very different from the Marcionite Visitation pattern. According to the Modalists, the Father was born, suffered, and died as Christ. Because they believe that Christ is born of Mary, it is debatable whether the Modalists were Docetists, although they were accused of this because they said that the Father appeared as the Son. They resisted the belief that Jesus was the descendent Logos, so they said that the prologue of John must be read allegorically.

The other ancient unitarians were the Dynamists who held onto the early belief that Jesus was a righteous human possessed by the Holy Spirit at his baptism. This made Jesus little more than a special prophet (who may have been transformed into a divine being when he was resurrected). At least some of the Dynamists seceded from the Apostolic Catholic network, given that they established a separate ecclesiology and appointed Natalius as their first Bishop, a position that he eventually abandons after being plagued with nightmares.

The THEODICY and SOTERIOLOGY charts (Figure 12.8) reveal that the Yahwist family faulted humans for suffering, rather than God. The Yahwists all believed that humans had to be obedient to the Biblical God's laws to achieve salvation, although there was debate about exactly what these laws included, whether sins committed after baptism could be resolved, and what sins were unforgivable.

This debate over the exact nature of the laws and forgiveness separated the Yahwists into two main sub-families: Apostolic Catholics (who created a network by mainly consolidating the Moderates) and Maximalist groups like the Ebionites, Elchasaites, and Nazoreans (who operated as independent groups). It is curious that these same issues fueled reformers within the Apostolic Catholic network, such as Hermas, the Trio, and Tertullian, who pushed for more lax (i.e. Hermas) or more demanding laws (i.e. the Trio, Tertullian).

Examining the ANTHROPOLOGY and RESURRECTION charts (Figure 12.8) shows that the Yahwists were all DUALISTS, believing that the human being consisted of a physical body and a mortal psyche in need of immortalization. They all affirmed that THE RESURRECTION OF THE DEAD would occur at the Eschaton when the physical body (the flesh) was raised from the grave and reunited with the soul so that the whole person would survive in the afterlife.

Their insistence on the raising of the flesh is residue from their Jewish monist legacy. Resurrection of the body was a concept that developed among Jews who were monists, believing that the body–mind were a single unit. When a person died, the body–mind died. All that was left was a shadow of the person, a ghost that flitted around Sheol, the dark abode of the dead. In the Maccabean period, when Jews were tortured and executed by the colonial Greek king and his administration, the idea of the resurrection developed so that God could reward the martyred Jews for their faithfulness and punish the Greeks for their torments. The resurrection of the dead meant just that, the resurrection of the person (the body–mind unit) from the grave.

Resurrection made sense within the Jewish monist anthropological system. The deceased existed as a ghost in an underworld and the person would be raised from the dead at final judgment. But once people started to think along dualistic lines as Plato taught, that the person is an immortal soul fallen into a physical body, the resurrection of the dead became difficult to understand. Gentiles were not familiar with the monist pattern, so we see all the Yahwist Christians working to understand the doctrine of the resurrection of the dead from a dualist perspective. This is why there were so many questions raised in their literature about what happened to the soul while the body was in the grave and whether the resurrection would be like a zombie apocalypse. In the end, the Yahwists came to think that the flesh will be raised from the grave and the mortal soul will be reunited with it and then immortalized at the eschaton.

12.5 Surveying What We Know

While three distinct Christian Families are evident from the third generation onward, we have yet to determine how different Christian movements within the Families emerged as competing churches. As we learned in Chapter 1, scholars since the Enlightenment have provided a variety of descriptions of the origins of the first Christians. They have mainly done so by relying on the New Testament literature which they have posited as our earliest reliable historical record of the Christians.

In this textbook, our retrospective approach has revealed that a fair amount of the New Testament literature was composed by third-generation Apostolic Catholics to combat Marcion (at the very least, Luke-Acts; the Pastoral Letters; Hebrews; and likely, the Catholic Letters too). We have also learned that the first and oldest New Testament was Marcion's canon of the *Evangelion* and ten letters of Paul. The New Testament scriptural canon that the Apostolic Catholics eventually constructed is responsive to Marcion. Not only is the canonical collection anachronistic to the first four generations of Christians, it contains a significant number of books that were composed to authorize the social and historical memories of the third-generation Apostolic Catholics (see Table 12.2). What scholars generally have reconstructed as the history of the first Christians from the New Testament texts is more accurately a reflection of the memories of the third-generation Apostolic Catholics and their construction of their own past.

What does Christian history look like if we build it based on what we can know about Christianity from sources we can confidently date and locate geographically? What is immediately evident from the following map (Figure 12.1), which locates the location of third-generation Christians, is that Yahwists populate eastern Syria and Mesopotamia. Interestingly, these Yahwist groups are all Maximalist (with the exception of the Thomas Christians which had become more moderate as their social constituency came to depend on Gentile conversion). Looking to the west, we see that Antioch, Asia Minor, and Greece are populated by both Moderate Yahwists, Minimalist Transtheists, and Marcionites. Alexandria is a stronghold for Minimalist Transtheist groups. Rome is a mixture of all Families. Marcion and

TABLE 12.2 First-Known Locations of Major Christian Writings

Location	First Generation 30–70 CE	Second Generation 70–110 CE	Third Generation 110–150 CE	Fourth Generation 150–190 CE	Fifth Generation 190–230 CE
Palestine					
Eastern Syria/ Mesopotamia			L-*Gospel of Thomas*	*Gospel of Ebionites* *Gospel of Nazoreans* Tatian, *Oration* Tatian, *Diatessaron*	L-*Acts of Thomas* L-*Odes of Solomon* L-*Thomas the Contender*
Western Syria/ Antioch			Ignatius' letters Gospel of Matthew (Ignatius)	?-*Gospel of Philip* ?-Justin, *Baruch* Theophilus, *To Autolycus* *Gospel of Peter* Hermogenes' writings	
Asia Minor/Greece	Paul's Letters		*Evangelion* Gospel of John Pastoral Letters Papias' fragments Book of Matthew (sayings of Jesus in Aramaic) Book of Mark (=Preachings of Peter?) Polycarp to *Philippians* Matthew (Polycarp) 1 Peter (Polycarp)	Montanist Oracles L-Acts (Montanists) Revelation Aristides, *Apology* Athenagoras, *Treatise on the Resurrection*	*Tripartite Tractate* (L-Candidus)

(continued)

TABLE 12.2 First-Known Locations of Major Christian Writings *(Continued)*

Location	First Generation 30–70 CE	Second Generation 70–110 CE	Third Generation 110–150 CE	Fourth Generation 150–190 CE	Fifth Generation 190–230 CE
Egypt/Alexandria			?-*Valentinus*' letters and writings Gospel of John ?-*Gospel of Truth* (Valentinus) L-*Trimorphic Protennoia* Basilides' *Exegetica, Odes,* and early version of *Secret Doctrine* Isidore, *On the Inseparable Soul* and *Exposition of the Prophet Parchor* Epiphanes, *On Righteousness*	?-*Valentinian Exposition* ?-*Apocalypse of Adam* ?-*Coptic Gospel of Egyptians* ?-*Letter of Barnabas* ?-*Letter of Diognetus* ?-*Letter to Rheginos* Teachings of Theodotus (Valentinian) L-*Apocryphon of John*	Clement of Alexandria's writings *Gospel of the Hebrews* *Greek Gospel of the Egyptians* Origen (early writings)
North Africa/Carthage					Tertullian's writings

Rome	?-Valentinus' letters and writings Marcion's *Evangelion* *Apostolicon* *Antitheses* Gospel of Matthew Gospel of John *1 Clement* Hermas' writings ?-*Gospel of Truth* (Valentinus) Justin Martyr's writings *Memoirs of the Apostles* Gospel of Mark (Justin) Revelation (Justin)	Hegesippus Tatian's *Diatessaron* Ptolemy, *Letter to Flora* Heracleon, *Commentary on John* ?-*Valentinian Exposition* ?-*Letter to Rheginos*	*L-Allogenes* *L-Zostrianos* Hippolytus of Rome's writings
Gaul		Irenaeus' writings Marcus' writings Canonical Luke-Acts	

TABLE 12.3   Regional Locations of First Christians

Location	First Generation 30–70 CE	Second Generation 70–110 CE	Third Generation 110–150 CE	Fourth Generation 150–190 CE	Fifth Generation 190–230 CE
Palestine	Paul Peter James John	Menander			Alexander of Jerusalem Theoctistus of Caesarea Origen
Eastern Syria/ Mesopotamia			Elchasaites Ebionites Nazoreans Thomas Christians	Tatian Thomas Christians Elchasaites Ebionites Nazoreans L-Peratics	Palut
Western Syria/ Antioch	Paul Peter Barnabas Men from James		?-Evodius Cerdo Satornil Ignatius	Irenaeus Hermogenes Theophilus	Serapion Paul of Samosata Axionicus
Asia Minor/Greece	Paul Apollos Timothy Silvanus Paul's named co-workers	Cernithus	Marcion Papias Polycarp	Hippolytus of Asia Theodotus (Valentinian) Florinus Montanus Trio Aristides Athenagoras L-Naassenes	Theodotus (Cobbler) Noetus Candidus (Valentinian)

Egypt/Alexandria	Valentinus	Pantaneus	Clement of Alexander
	L-Agathopous	Theodotus (Valentinian)	Leonides
	L-Christian Sethians	Marcus	Valentinian woman (Origen's first patron)
	Basilides and Isidore	?-Rheginus (Valentinian)	Origen
	Carpocrates and Epiphanes	Ophians	Heraclas
		Apelles	Demetrius
			Ambrose (former Valentinian)
			Prodicus
			Ophians
North Africa/Carthage		Hermogenes	Tertullian
			Sabellius
			Montanists
			Marcionites

(continued)

TABLE 12.3 Regional Locations of First Christians *(Continued)*

Location	First Generation 30–70 CE	Second Generation 70–110 CE	Third Generation 110–150 CE	Fourth Generation 150–190 CE	Fifth Generation 190–230 CE
Rome	Prisca and Aquila	?-Linuis	Marcion	Tatian	?-Naassenes
		?-Anacletus	Valentinus	Hegesippus	?-Peratics
		?-Clement	Cerdo	Anicetus	Theodotus (Cobbler)
		?-Evaristus	Hermas	Soter	Theodotus (Banker)
		?-Alexander	L-Author of Luke-Acts	Eleuterius	Natalius
			L-Author of Pastoral Epistles	Marcellina	Hippolytus of Rome
			L-Author of Hebrews	Florinus	Epignonus
			L-Author of Catholic Epistles	Ptolemy	Cleomenes
			Author of 1 Clement	Flora	Zephyrinus
			Justin Martyr	Heracleon	Callistus
			Telesforus	Flavia Sophe	Artemon
			Hyginus	?-Rheginus	Theotimus
			Pius	Secundus	Platonizing Sethian Christians
				L-Justin the Gnostic	
				?-Apelles	
				?-Miltiades	
				?-Philumene	
				?-Potitus	
				?-Basilicus	
				?-Syneros	
Gaul				Pothinus	
				Irenaeus	
				Marcus	

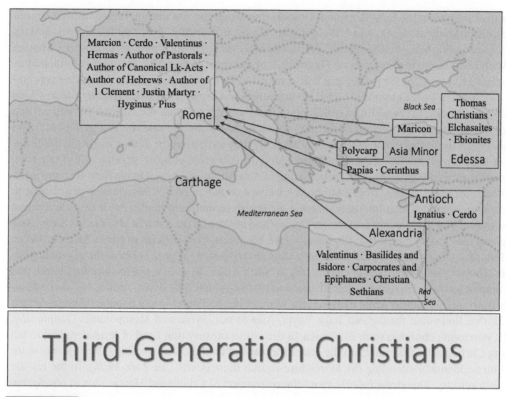

FIGURE 12.1   Map showing the location of the known third-generation Christians.

the Transtheists in Rome, however, have migrated there from Asia Minor, Antioch, and Alexandria. Notice that the Minimalist Christians largely established themselves in the areas of Paul's missions, overlapping and competing with the Moderates in western Syria, Asia Minor, and Greece. A group of Minimalists also appears to have gone south establishing a church or churches in Alexandria, but it is unclear if this mission occurred in the first or second generation. By the third generation, however, Minimalist Transtheist forms of Christianity are firmly established in Alexandria.

12.6 | A Biography of the Marcionite Church

How does this geographical spread of Christian Families help us explain the emergence of the different Christian churches? Again we start with Marcion's Church which was established by Marcion, a Minimalist Christian who catered to Minimalists. What do we make of the observation that, in the third generation, all the Minimalists were either Marcionite or Transtheist? Where are the Minimalist Christians who were worshiping YHWH? While their footprints seem to be almost invisible by the third generation, we know that they were around earlier. For instance, the Gospel of Mark presents as a Yahwist text with an understanding of the Law cogent with a Minimalist interpretation of Paul's letters. The Gospel of Mark's original title was the "Evangelion of Jesus Christ" (Mark 1:1), a phrase which harkens back to Paul's insistence that he had received the authentic gospel of Christ through revelation (i.e. Gal. 1:6–12). The author of the *Evangelion of Jesus Christ* understood his composition to represent the gospel that Paul received, spelling out in narrative format the salvific function of Jesus' death that Paul wrote about in his letters (i.e. 1 Cor. 15: 3). The apostles are characterized as ignorant and faithless, and Peter is actually identified with Satan himself (cp. Mark 8:33 and 2 Cor. 11:14). The laws are presented as unnecessary Jewish traditions that fail to recognize that what God really wants from his people is the cultivation of a natural inner morality (i.e. Mark 7:1–23; cf. Rom. 13:8–10).

Critical analysis of the New Testament Gospels shows that there is a literary relationship between the Gospels of Matthew, Mark, and Luke. Scholars almost universally agree that the Gospel of Mark (what we are calling here the *Evangelion of Jesus Christ*) comes to be incorporated into other Christian texts. With reference to the numbers on Figure 12.2, my analysis of Marcion's *Evangelion* (which Marcion believed to represent the gospel as it was revealed to Paul) suggests that the *Evangelion* was created by a Christian in Asia Minor [2]. This person edited and expanded the *Evangelion of Jesus Christ* (the Gospel of Mark) [1a] by adding a collection of Jesus' sayings to it that the Maximalists had written earlier [1b]. Marcion has a version of this text which he knows by the title the *Evangelion*. Marcion may have been the author of the *Evangelion*, that is, he may have been the author who took the *Evangelion of Jesus Christ* (the Gospel of Mark) and added the collection of Jesus' sayings to it. If not, then Marcion revises the *Evangelion* already circulating in Asia Minor and puts it in his New Testament [3].

Either way, Marcion came from a Minimalist Yahwist church in Pontus. Marcion, however, came to question YHWH's morality after intensely studying the Jewish scriptures in tandem with Paul's letters and the *Evangelion*. This led Marcion to create XENOTHEISM and missionize the Yahwist Minimalists across Asia [4]. He may also have been the first Christian to take his message to Carthage in North Africa in 144 CE since Tertullian tells us that the local Marcionite Church recognized the year 144 CE as the advent of Marcionism. This is the earliest report of Christianity in North Africa. By 200 CE, the Marcionite Church was firmly entrenched in North Africa as Tertullian's massive five-volume take-down, *Against Marcion*, attests.

By the time Epiphanius wrote in 375 CE, the Marcionites had developed a popular COUNTER-CHURCH network that flourished throughout Italy, Egypt, Asia Minor, Syria, and Mesopotamia (Epiph., *Ref.* 42.1.2). Marcionite churches were so popular in the fourth century that Cyril of Jerusalem had to tell traveling Christians to find the Catholic church in the towns they were visiting. They did not want to end up accidentally attending the Marcionite church there (Cyril, *Cat. Lect.* 18.26). In the middle of the fifth century, Theodoret reports about the conversion of a thousand Marcionites in one Syrian

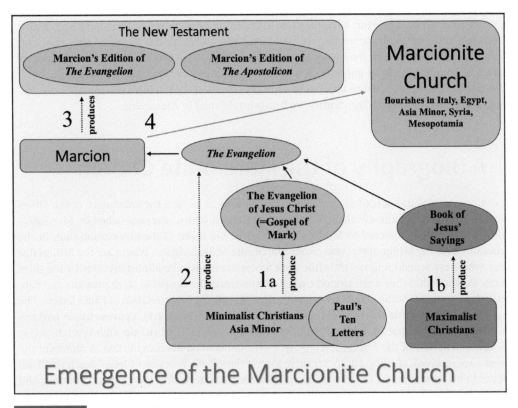

FIGURE 12.2   Illustration of how the Marcionite Church formed.

village alone. He says that there were eight Marcionite villages in his region (Theod., *Letter* 113). When exactly the Marcionite Church failed to continue as an intergenerational movement is unknown, but Muslim sources still reference them in the tenth century.

12.7 Biographies of the Transtheist Churches

The Transtheist family is the most diverse of the Christian Families, so mapping the history of each of the movements within the family is a very complex task. First, we observe that Transtheist movements were started by Christian Minimalists. Second, we note that all the movements in this family represent different systematizations of Gnostic Spirituality, so it is important for us to determine how these movements interfaced with Gnostic Spirituality. Third, we know that each Transtheist leader formed an independent movement with independent ecclesiastical structures and historical memories. Given this complexity, we can only provide a provisional map that takes into account and explains the evidence based on the logic set forth in this textbook.

With reference to the numbered avenues on Figure 12.3, we identify how Gnostic Spirituality interfaced with Christianity via three main avenues. We note that one channel [Avenue 1] is the adaption of the Ophite Myth which was created by sectarian Jews in Alexandria during Philo's lifetime. Jesus Christ was grafted into the Ophite mythology later by Christians whom Origen called Ophians. A Christianized version of the Ophite Myth also was combined with the Barbeloite Myth by another group, and out of this combination Sethian Christianity emerged. The Sethians formed initiatory churches with multiple baptisms and anointing ceremonies called the Five Seals. In the early third

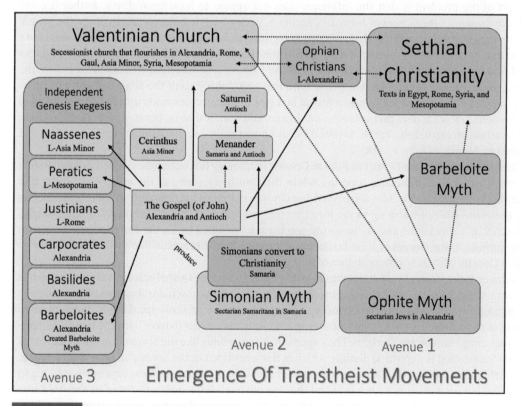

FIGURE 12.3 Illustration of the relationship of the Transtheist Movements to each other, the Gospel (of John), and the Ophian Myth.

century, the Sethian mythology becomes highly Platonized by esoteric Christians who were metaphysicists interested in correcting Plato. The Valentinians also used the Ophite Myth.

Given this situation, how do we map the relationship between the Ophian Christians, Sethian Christians, and Valentinians? Which movements drew upon the Ophite Myth directly from their interactions with Jewish scholars in Alexandria? Did any of the movements draw the Ophite Myth from each other? If so, how so? Because we have not yet been able to make these determinations confidently, I have used dotted lines to denote these possible relationships in Figure 12.3.

We observe that the second channel of Gnostic Spirituality [Avenue 2] is a Christianized version of the Simonian Myth that substituted Jesus for Simon. In this textbook, we have called this movement Ex-Simonian Christianity and have seen that Menander was an early exemplar. But we have not yet explained where Ex-Simonian Christianity came from. As we have seen in this textbook, the Simonians who believed Simon to be the Great Power and Son of God were robust religious competitors during the expansion of Christians in the first generation of Christianity, so it is almost certain that the Christians would have tried converting the Simonians and vice versa (a detail that actually turns up in the Book of Acts: 8:4–25). As the Simonian converts switched allegiances from Simon to Christ, they replaced Simon in their mythology with Jesus.

The heresiologists were not completely wrong when they proposed that Simon was the ancestor of the Christian Gnostics. Of course, their insistence that Simon was their only ancestor and direct ancestor does not make any sense because Simon was not Christian, but Simonian. He and Helen operated a distinct religion that was the main competitor to the first-, second-, and third-generation Christians. The author of Acts tries to manage this important detail by composing a story that takes Simon down by having Simon convert to Christianity (Acts 8:4–25). But the fact remains that in the heresiological sources, Simon is not a Christian. Menander, Simon's disciple, is. This suggests to me that the heresiologists did not know how the Christians came to be influenced by the Simonian Myth.

Part of the problem is that the influence does not appear to have been direct. Rather it came indirectly by way of the Gospel of John. In Chapter 5, we learned that Simon taught about the primal Father's Image and a great Power that contains everything that will come-to-be. He said this was God's Logos. Simon taught that he himself descended from the Father, as this Great Power. His believers called him the Son of God and believed him to be the Father's manifestation who was sent to save the world. This is the storyline of the Gospel of John and only John, except the Gospel of John presents Jesus (instead of Simon) as the Logos, a divine being of Light, who descends into the dark cosmos to save humankind. Jesus does this as God's Son, Image, and manifestation. Because he is the true God's manifestation on earth, Jesus is able to reveal the unknown Father so that humans may know him and be saved by his grace (John 1:1–18).

The relationship of the Gospel of John to Gnostic mythology has never been settled in scholarship. A century ago, Rudolf Bultmann tried to explain the Gnostic elements of the text by proposing that the authors of the Gospel of John were rewriting Gnostic materials to combat them. But most scholars after Bultmann did not warm up to the idea that the Gospel could actually contain Gnostic thought. Most scholars today land somewhere on the spectrum established by Elaine Pagels, that Gnosticism is not intrinsic to the Gospel of John but imposed on it by later Christians like the Valentinians who made it Gnostic with their interpretation of it.

Whatever else we might say about the Gospel, whoever wrote the Gospel of John was very concerned to legitimize the conversion of some group of Samaritans, as Biblical scholar Raymond Brown argues. The Johannine author did this by including an expansive story of Jesus speaking to the Samaritan woman at the well (John 4:4–42). But these Samaritans do not appear to have been the typical Samaritan worshiping YHWH on Mt. Gerizim. They appear to be sectarians like the Simonians who believe that the true Father God is a spiritual divinity which is not worshiped in the Jewish or Samaritan temples. In the Johannine story of the Samaritan woman at the well, the theology Jesus lays out is striking in its contrast between the true Father God and the God of Israel. Jesus makes it clear that there is a true God who is Spirit and that there are true believers who worship this true Father. Those who think that they are worshiping the Father in the Jewish temple in Jerusalem or in the Samaritan temple on

Mt. Gerizim are ignorant. They think they are worshiping the Father, when in fact, they are not. Only the true believer knows the Father and worships him. This is the Father who sent Jesus as the universal Savior of the world.

In other Johannine passages, this contrast of Gods bears out. Jesus makes it clear that the Jews do not know Jesus' Father even though they think they do (i.e. John 8:19, 55). They are blind, he says (John 9:41; 12:39–40). Jesus differentiates between his Father and the God of the Jews (8:42, 47) whom he identifies with the Devil's Father (8:44). Since the Jews carry out the desires of their Father (8:44), the implication of the rest of Jesus' story in this Gospel is that YHWH works through the Jews to murder Jesus (cf. John 14:30). Jesus calls YHWH a liar and a murderer because YHWH duped the Jews into believing that he is the real God and because he is responsible for crucifying Jesus (John 8:44).

While we can build different scenarios to explain this evidence, the most plausible solution begins with a group of Minimalist Christians who headed to Samaria where they encountered and converted a group of Simonians. The new converts switched allegiances from Simon to Jesus, writing Jesus into Simon's Myth. They developed their own regional movement, identifying themselves as the Children of Light believing themselves to be followers of Jesus, a Being of Light who came down into the world from another realm (John 1:4–9; etc.). They believed that Jesus had enlightened them, that they were privy to special knowledge of the true God. Menander likely was part of this regional Ex-Simonian Christian movement before he moved from Samaria to Antioch where he organized and led an Ex-Simonian Christian congregation.

This would mean that the Gospel of John does not just contain the social memories of Samaritan converts, as Brown proposed, but the social memories of sectarian Samaritans who had converted to Christianity from Simonianism. It was composed to legitimize their unique Christian Gnostic identity and their understanding that the Biblical God was the Father of the Jews. He was distinct from their own God, Jesus' Father (i.e. John 8:19, 42, 44). It also authorized their position that the Jews had their own Law given by Moses which contrasted with the grace and truth that Jesus gave (i.e. John 1:17; 8:17). It was probably originally published as *The Gospel* (such as was the case with the other second-generation Gospel compositions), the attribution to John of Zebedee being late.

The Children of Light, as they called themselves, missionized along the Jordan Valley, traveling as far south as Alexandria. They had some success converting followers of John the Baptist along the way. From Figure 12.3, we observe that the Gospel of John was used by most Transtheist groups in Alexandria, and it was fully integrated into Valentinian theology. The Children of Light also carried the Gospel of John to Antioch and then along the coast of Asia Minor where Moderate Yahwist Christians became so interested in it that they revised *The Gospel*, developed a Yahwist interpretation of it (as evident in 1 John), and by Polycarp's time, had given it Johannine credentials. This is how it came to be the property of both the Valentinians (in Alexandria) and the Apostolic Catholics (in Antioch, and then Asia Minor).

The third channel of Gnostic Spirituality (Avenue 3) was the Genesis story itself. In other words, independent interpreters of the Genesis story like Justin the Gnostic, Carpocrates, Basilides, the Peratics, the Naassenes, and the Barbeloites developed convergent idiosyncratic readings of the Genesis story. Justin, Carpocrates, Basilides, the Peratics, Barbeloites, and Naassenes all concluded that the Biblical God is bad or ugly, and that life started with a primal God who was not him. They formulated their unique Transtheist systems from that position.

How did each of these Transtheist movements get started? In Alexandria, around 120 CE, Valentinus is taught about Christianity mainly from the letters of Paul and *The Gospel* (of John). He likely learns how to interpret the letters and *The Gospel* (of John) from the Ex-Simonian Christians. He probably also was in conversation with a group of Christians using the Ophite Myth. Valentinus develops his own Egyptianized version of Christian Gnosticism from there. It may be that Valentinus carried *The Gospel* (of John) to Rome and was the one to introduce it to the Christians in Rome. Or perhaps someone (Ignatius or Polycarp?) brought the Catholic version from Antioch or Asia Minor to Rome. Whatever the case, *The Gospel* (of John) does not appear to have made it to Rome earlier than 140 CE because the first non-Valentinian Christian in Rome to make use of it is Justin Martyr.

Valentinus moved from Alexandria to Rome as an influencer, trying to reform Apostolic Catholicism into a grace-based religion (Minimalist) rather than works-based (Moderate). He failed to be elected bishop of Rome, and we have argued in this textbook that, as Tertullian testifies, Valentinus seceded. He established a split-level church that poached Apostolic Catholics in order to coax them into a second baptism (chrism) and, with it, Gnosis and the revelation of God's mysteries. His church was not tied to the ecclesiology of the Apostolic Catholics, but authorized itself with reference to the ongoing revelation of its scholastic leaders and the secret teaching Jesus delivered to certain apostles, Mary, and Paul.

Valentinus' disciples continued with this type of split-level organization. Marcus was the exception. In Gaul, he innovated and established the first Spiritual Church for pneumatics only. The Valentinians do not ever seem to have established a powerful central organization. Various leaders continually debated and innovated Valentinian mythology, hermeneutics, and practices. They also actively debated Apostolic Catholics, such as the Valentinian Candidus who debated Origen in Athens (230 CE). They established churches across the Mediterranean (Rome, Gaul, Alexandria, Athens, Cyprus, Asia Minor, Antioch, Carthage, eastern Syria, and Mesopotamia).

Their movement survived intergenerationally. Ambrose tells us that the Catholics burnt down a Valentinian church near the Euphrates River in 388 CE (*Letter* 40.16). The Valentinians are anathematized as late as the seventh and eighth centuries, but whether this is rhetorical or a reference to existing Valentinians is debatable. Valentinus is remembered as the one who first framed the concept of the Trinity. He is also an early framer of the idea that salvation is entirely a gift of grace from God, an idea that later Protestants developed on their own by reading Paul in a way that paralleled Valentinus' Minimalist reading of Paul's letters. Valentinian hermeneutics and esoteric traditions were co-opted by the Apostolic Catholics in the fifth generation by Clement and Origen and ultimately bloomed into the apophatic Platonic-inspired mysticism of Ps.-Dionysus.

The Transtheist family consists of a number of other groups which formed churches with their own ecclesiologies and memberships. They had in common a claim to secret teachings and initiatory rites to reveal the mysteries of God gradually to their members. They privatized the revelation of their special knowledge by organizing socially in ways that reserved their secrets for their members only. Some of these groups survived intergenerationally, others did not.

Basilides originated the idea that God created from nothing and that divine Providence is good, that suffering has educational value. Both of these ideas, for better or worse, still survive in Christian thought today. The Basilidean church, however, never grew beyond Egypt. It remained a small collection of regional churches in Alexandria and in the western reach of the Nile Delta, between the Mediterranean Sea and Memphis. Our last reference to them is in the fourth century when Eusebius records that they were still viable as a regional church (Eus., *Pan.* 68). Some later writers connect the origins of the Priscillians of Spain (a fourth-century Gnostic group) with a Basilidian man from Memphis named Marcus (e.g. Jerome, *On Illustrious Men* 121; Ep. 75.3; Severus, *Chron.* 2.46). It may be that the Basilidians made a concerted effort in the fourth century to expand their regional church beyond Egypt and sent Marcus as a missionary to Spain. Since we do not hear of Basilidian missionary activity anywhere else in the Mediterranean, it is more likely that the Basilidian Marcus immigrated to Spain on his own and spread his Gnostic faith in his new homeland.

The Christian Ophians were known to Celsus, Origen, Epiphanius, and Theodoret. Their groups were run by presbyters who cared for their sacred secret books, some of which contained therapeutic magic spells and ascent liturgies. They also had priests they called "Father." They used baptism and anointing as initiatory rituals, believing that the oil from the Tree of Life assisted in the separation of the soul from the body and its ascent into the spheres. They appear to have been located mainly in Alexandria where Celsus (170 CE) and Origen (240 CE) were able to obtain copies of their map for soul ascent through the celestial realms of the Archons. The existence of the Bonner Ialdabaoth Gem (Figure 3.7), which was carved in the third or fourth centuries, confirms their extended survival, although there is no evidence that their movement ever made it out of Alexandria.

By the late fourth century, the Sethian Christians had proliferated across Egypt to Rome, eastern Syria, and Mesopotamia. Plotinus may have entertained some of them in his seminars in

Rome. At least he entertained Christians he called Gnostics who showed him the books of *Allogenes* and *Zostrianos*, both Platonizing Sethian texts in the Nag Hammadi Collection. By the late fourth century, Epiphanius' testimony suggests that a number of distinct sects (Archontics, Phibionites, and Stratiotics) had broken away from the Sethians. Their ideas appear to have continued influence among Christian esotericists in late antiquity and the early Middle Ages, given the mixture of Sethian theology with Catholicism in the seventh- or eighth-century Coptic grimoire known as the *Macquarie Papyri*.

The other Transtheist movements do not appear to have survived beyond the third century. The Carpocratians remained a small regional church-commune in Alexandria until the beginning of the third century when Clement of Alexandria takes them on for what he believed was promiscuity. He says that he knows about an isolated group of fifth-generation Christians who venerated Epiphanes in Cephalonia, but this testimony from Clement of Alexandria likely has mixed up Carpocrates' son with the festival of the Epiphany (a sun–moon festival) celebrated at the Samê Temple (Clem. Alex., *Strom.* 3.2.5). We know that Marcellina immigrated to Rome around 150 CE where she established a Carpocratian church-commune in the empire's capital. In the beginning of the third century, Hippolytus, in Rome, writes his refutation of the heresies, never mentioning Marcellina or the Carpocratians. Marcellina's Roman church must not have survived beyond her death. While she was alive, they organized as a private commune and hosted Eucharists as part of their charity meal program (Agape meals).

Justin the Gnostic was located in Rome too at the end of the second century. He was a mystagogue who privately initiated his followers into the mysteries using two water baptisms. No other leaders rose to take over his movement once Justin died. The Naassenes, most likely located in Asia Minor, had preachers and priests who led their regional Angelic Church. They privately initiated members using water and oil rituals, and served the eucharist as a heavenly banquet of milk and honey. They do not appear to have lasted beyond the third century, perhaps because they valorized castration as a measure of holiness. Likewise, the Peratics were a regional initiatory church in Greece or Mesopotamia that did not survive beyond the third century.

12.8 A Biography of the Yahwist Churches

The Yahwist family also has a complex history in terms of how the Yahwist movements formed. We observe that the Christians who migrated north and east out of Judea were mainly Maximalist and Yahwist (Figure 12.1). The Ebionites, Elchasaites, and Nazoreans formed isolated congregations, each with their own ecclesiology, hierarchies, beliefs, and practices (Figure 12.4). They all were baptizing groups, living along the Euphrates, Tigris, and neighboring rivers. Because these groups believed that Jesus did not approve of the Jewish sacrificial system, their eucharist meals look like vegan Passover meals, with unleavened bread and water distributed to the church's members. They likely performed them to offer thanks to God for their redemption. Their baptisms were daily and served a variety of purification and therapeutic purposes. Their ideal lifestyle emphasized bodily holiness framed by strict fasting, vegetarianism, and sexual regulations (either celibacy or controlled marriage). They rejected Paul as an authority, although, according to the heresiological record, the later Nazoreans were not as harsh in their views about Paul as the other groups. Initially, these Maximalist groups heavily recruited Jews and Gentile proselytes (God-Fearers) from synagogues, but by the second generation, their literature suggests that they also were recruiting Gentiles from public spaces.

These third-generation groups all had unique versions of the Gospel of Matthew which they read alongside Jewish scripture [4a]. We can infer from the Gospel of Matthew itself that it was composed in the Transjordan region [1a, 4a] because the author credentials the Transjordan Christian community as directly established by Jesus, who crosses the Jordan from Galilee, followed by a large group of people (Matt. 19:1). This migration of Christians into the Transjordan is also mentioned in Matthew 4:15, where it is further legitimized by the author as the fulfillment of prophecy (Isa. 9:1–2).

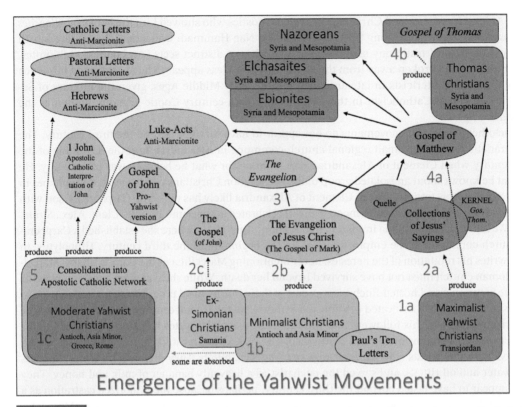

FIGURE 12.4 Illustration of the network of Christians and literature that developed as the Apostolic Catholic network consolidated.

While the Gospel of Matthew was composed in the Transjordan region, it did not stay put. By the third generation, the Gospel of Matthew had migrated west through Antioch (Ignatius may have used it) to Rome where Marcion comes across it. Marcion quotes from it in his *Antitheses* and complains that Paul's gospel has been Judaized by the apostles. Marcion is probably correct: the author of the Gospel of Matthew probably had a copy of the *Evangelion of Jesus Christ* (=Gospel of Mark) which he completely rewrites to correct it and align with it a Maximalist position [4a]. The author of Matthew also had access to a collection of Jesus' sayings similar to the collection that the author of the *Evangelion* used [2a, 4a]. The Matthean author distributes these sayings differently in his composition.

The Thomas Christians started as a Maximalist Christian group, but they were much more successful converting non-observant Gentiles than the other Maximalist groups. This changed the makeup of the group and its orientation to the Law. As more and more non-observant Gentiles converted, the Maximalist view on the Law was called into question and their original Gospel (Kernel Thomas) was rewritten to minimalize the Law (i.e. *Gos. Thom.* 6, 14, 53) [4b]. But their holiness lifestyle remained in place to the extent that marriage became recognized as a state of sin.

As they repositioned themselves, they justified their holiness lifestyle with reference to the non-binary Adam in the Genesis story who only became a sexual being after the Fall. Before the Fall, they thought, he reflected God's Image. He was a male–female who was neither male nor female. To imitate the non-binary Adam, they demanded celibacy (no sex) and singlehood (no marriage) from their converts. Fasting was expanded to include the practice of voluntary abstinence from the world and its pleasures. As the *Acts of Thomas* and the *Odes of Solomon* demonstrate, conversion involved a one-time baptism, full-body anointing, and the eucharist meal. Their churches developed their own ecclesiological structures, prayers, and hymns that included references to the Spirit as the Mother.

At the beginning of the fifth-generation, Palut is appointed the Apostolic Catholic bishop in Edessa. With this, Apostolic Catholicism is established as a competitor to the indigenous Maximalist and Thomas movements. Even then, Palut and his canon were resisted by the Syrian Christians who preferred Tatian's *Diatessaron* and lifestyle that emphasized extreme holiness and the forsaking of marriage. The Apostolic Catholics take a century to establish their ecclesiology, scripture, and marital lifestyle in eastern Syria and Mesopotamia. Syrian Orthodoxy, which emerges in the fourth century (i.e. Aphrahat; Ephrem) appears to be a merger of Apostolic Catholicism with these maximalist indigenous Christian traditions.

We also observe (Figure 12.1) that Moderate first-generation Christians headed north and west out of Judea, concentrating their mission on western Syria, Asia Minor, Greece, and Rome. The churches that grew out of their mission were mainly Moderate and Yahwist [Figure 12.5: 1c]. They established individual congregations in territories across Asia Minor and Greece, where Minimalist Christians had also established a presence. They primarily recruited Jews and Gentile proselytes (God-Fearers) from the synagogues, but once they were no longer welcome in the synagogues, they turned to recruit Gentiles from public places where they competed with the Minimalists for converts. Their early mission to Rome established their brand of Christianity as the oldest in that city.

The main impetus for the emergence of the Apostolic Catholic network was the desire to defend Yahwism against Marcionism around the year 140 CE [5]. Consider the fact that, in the fourth- and fifth-generation, Apostolic Catholics wrote at least 15 treatises against Marcion. The Apostolic Catholics appear to have realized how vulnerable the Yahwist Minimalist congregations were to Marcion's popular message that established a Gentile Christian identity separate from Judaism. The Apostolic Catholics like Ignatius, Polycarp, and the authors of *1 Clement*, Luke-Acts, Hebrews, and the Pastoral Epistles must have targeted Yahwist Minimalist churches themselves, persuading and absorbing into

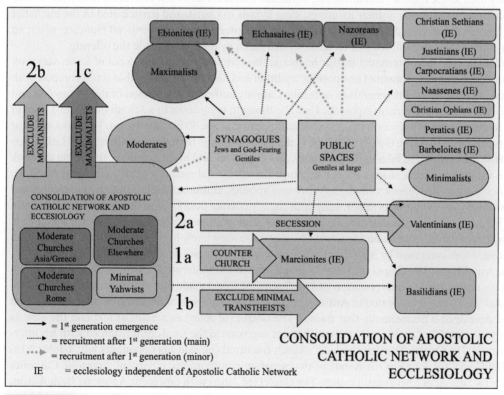

FIGURE 12.5 Illustration of the consolidation of the Apostolic Catholic network and ecclesiology.

their Moderate network any Yahwist churches that had not turned Marcionite and converting any ones that had. That is to say, the Apostolic Catholic network and ecclesiology begins to emerge as some of the third-generation Moderate churches around 140 CE decide that it is in their best interest to consolidate and band together against Marcion (Figure 12.5). In so doing, they not only exclude Marcionites as Docetists [1a], but also Minimalist Trantheists as Polytheists [1b]. Further, they exclude the Maximalists as Judaizers [1c]. As time goes on, they resist any group in their network like the Church of New Prophecy that tries to form a holiness reform movement [2b], viewing them as Maximalists (even though they were not) because their practices were considered excessive and their additional rules unnecessary.

To compete with the Transtheists (especially the Valentinians) [2a], the consolidating Apostolic Catholic churches updated their Yahwist theology, as we see in Justin Martyr's works. By framing the Biblical Creator as the transcendent God, they co-opted the transcendent God whom the Transtheist Christians worshiped separately and the Greek philosophers discussed. They developed explanations for the Biblical God's anthropomorphic characteristics (i.e. condescending stories and/or descriptions of the Christ as the Angel of YHWH) and bad behavior (i.e. he rightly punishes sinners).

To make their traditions legitimate, they connected and authorized their beliefs, practices, and ecclesiology to the twelve apostles (Apostolic) and claimed that their tradition had universal reach (Catholic). By the beginning of the fifth generation (ca. 190 CE), the Roman bishop had gained a significant amount of power within the Apostolic Catholic network, acting as an arbitrator who was consulted about a variety of disagreements and whose judgment affected churches in the network beyond the local Roman see.

This process of inclusion and exclusion resulted in the development of the Canon of Truth, the Apostolic tradition, and the exploitation of the concept of heresy to disadvantage and marginalize Maximalist Yahwist and Minimalist Transtheist Christian movements. The Moderates in this network came to define themselves as worshipers of the Biblical Creator God, upholders of the Jewish scriptures, and believers in his Son who was born, suffered, and was crucified for the salvation of humanity. They used single baptism and anointing to initiate members into their churches, read from Jewish scriptures and the Gospels at their meetings, sang hymns to Christ, and participated in the eucharist meal. The meal was considered atoning or redemptive, interpreted as a sacrificial banquet, when an animal was ritually slaughtered and its cooked flesh eaten by those who made the offering.

Following the logic presented in this textbook, the composition of the Gospel of Luke-Acts took place in Rome mainly to construct an apostolic tradition and historical memory that could compete with Marcion. To do this, a third-generation Apostolic Catholic author took a version of the *Evangelion* and revised it to represent emergent Apostolic Catholic thought, tying Jesus to a Jewish birth and a human youth in order to rebut Marcion's belief that Jesus appeared at age 30 in Capernaum. The Lukan author appears to have in hand the Gospel of Matthew, details of which he harmonizes with his new Lukan version of the *Evangelion* (i.e. John the Baptist story, Jesus' baptism, and his temptation). In writing the book of Acts, the author selects, shapes, creates, and organizes the social memories of the emergent Apostolic Catholics in a way that gives credibility to the twelve apostles, authorizes their tradition as apostolic, and domesticates Paul so that he is in harmony with their Moderate position and firmly connected to Judaism. This makes the composition of Luke-Acts anti-Marcionite, as were the Pastoral Epistles which were also written by a third-generation Moderate Christian who most likely lived in Asia Minor. Hebrews and 1 Peter were also composed by Apostolic Catholics as anti-Marcionite documents, likely in Rome.

In Asia Minor, *The Gospel* (of John) is first disputed by Moderate Christians. The letter known as 1 John represents the interpretation of *The Gospel* (of John) made by a third-generation Moderate presbyter who likely was located in Antioch or Asia Minor. Analysis of his interpretation reveals that he had developed a hermeneutic that framed *The Gospel* (of John) as a Yahwist text and the Law as not only necessary but positive. He tells us that not everyone in the local church agreed with his interpretation of *The Gospel*. This left the local church fractured (he said his opponents left: 1 John 2:19) and *The Gospel* (of John) in the hands of two separate communities: emergent Apostolic Catholics and the Ex-Simonian Christians. To align *The Gospel* (of John) with emergent Apostolic Catholicism, a third-generation Moderate author revises John along lines that Ignatius and Polycarp would have approved: to emphasize the reality of the flesh of Jesus' body, which was ritually shared in the Eucharist (i.e. John 6:51b-59 which contradicts 6:62–63). We do not know the extent of the revisions that *The*

Gospel (of John) underwent once it fell into the hands of the emergent Apostolic Catholics in Antioch or Asia Minor, but scholars have pointed to several passages like John 6:51b-59 and John 21 that show that *The Gospel* (of John) was revised heavily.

By the time of Tertullian, the Apostolic Catholics had composed and distributed new anti-Marcionite scriptures (Luke-Acts; Pastoral Letters; Hebrews; 1 Peter), revised and domesticated the interpretation of *The Gospel* (of John) via the publication of 1 John, and agreed upon a basic form of their own New Testament canon (four Gospels, Acts, thirteen letters of Paul, 1 John, 1 Peter, Hebrews, and Revelation). They promoted a public image that their meetings were not clandestine and that they kept no secrets, that is, until the fifth-generation in Alexandria when Clement and Origen constructed an esoteric tradition that they claimed was orally transmitted from Jesus to a select few of his disciples to later Christian educators including themselves.

12.9 Judaism and the Christian Race

The Family Network Model makes Christianity's relationship with Judaism clearer (Figure 12.6). While Christianity in the first generation was a Jewish sectarian movement with a Gentile mission that brought converted Gentiles into the People of Israel, the members of the movement were divided on how to apply the Law to the converted Gentiles. This division into Maximalist, Moderate, and Minimalist parties was inherent to Christianity. In other words, there was never a time when the early movement was not divided by these three opinions. The first Christians were Jews who, previous to joining the Christian movement, already held a range of opinions about the Law and its applicability to non-Jews who wanted to convert to Judaism.

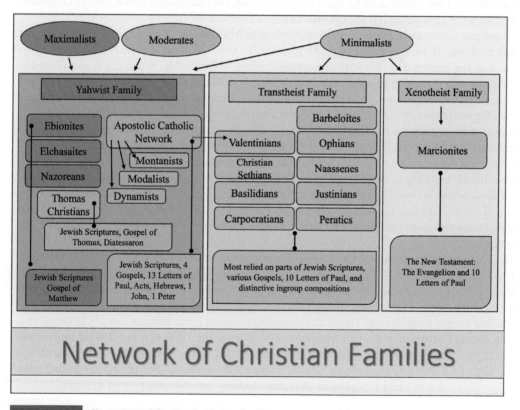

FIGURE 12.6 Illustration of the Family Network of Christian movements.

This intrinsic pluralism means that the first Christians developed concurrent competing models for the incorporation of Gentiles into the movement. The Maximalists believed that the Law was traditional and necessary so that Gentile converts had to be circumcised, follow the dietary code, observe Sabbath, and other prescriptions they believed that Jesus had given them. They thought the Law was good and that Jesus had come to teach them how to observe the Law according to God's original intent. They promoted James as their founder and hero. They followed a KINSHIP MODEL of leadership, considering James to be the logical "heir" to Jesus' movement because he was Jesus' brother. James was not one of Jesus' disciples, but his closest relative. This is the same kind of leadership model that resulted in the Shi'a movement after Muhammad's death, when a Muslim group formed around the leadership of Muhammad's cousin and son-in-law Shi'atu Ali.

The Christian Maximalists were centralized in Judea and mainly missionized Jews and Gentile God-Fearers in synagogues. Their home-base was a church they established in Jerusalem. After the Roman–Jewish War (66–74 CE), most of the Maximalists became refugees in the Transjordan area. They established independent baptizing movements along the rivers up into Edessa. One of these groups began to further authorize themselves as recipients of Judas Thomas' wisdom, a disciple they identified as Jesus' twin brother (also the KINSHIP MODEL).

All of these groups held on to their Jewish identity and practices for a longer time than other Christians. The late second-generation Thomas Christians are the first of the Maximalist groups to question the continued validity of the Law for incoming Gentiles and moderate their position. To secure their new moderated position on the Law, they elevated the brother relationship between Judas Thomas and Jesus, identifying Jesus as Thomas' *divine* twin or doppelganger rather than biological brother.

Christians like Paul fell on the opposite end of the spectrum from the Maximalists. They believed that the Law was unnecessary for Gentile converts and anyone who said otherwise was a "Judaizer." They argued that God did not require circumcision to make Gentile converts righteous because Abraham was considered a righteous man; he was chosen by God not because he was circumcised or followed the Mosaic Law, but because he was a believer. In fact, the Minimalists noted, both circumcision and the Law were added after Abraham's election.

Minimalist Christians first established themselves in Antioch, Asia Minor, and Greece, the areas of Paul's missions. In fact, Paul was *the* (only) Apostle in their traditions, commissioned directly by Jesus to lead the movement. This is the CHARISMATIC MODEL of leadership, when the leader claims to receive credentials through revelation or some other kind of divine calling.

Minimalist Christians tended to missionize Gentiles at large rather than working the synagogues. As time progressed and their local communities consisted (almost) entirely of Gentile converts, they began to perceive the Law as not only unnecessary but negative. Many of them either distanced YHWH from the Law, saying that the Law was inferior because it was given by angels, or they distanced the real God from YHWH the Lawgiver, who they began to suspect was a fallen archangel or vainglorious God.

This line of reasoning resulted in a reexamination of key Jewish scriptures including the Genesis story. This is where Marcion came in. His reexamination led him to innovate theology and develop XENOTHEISM. He was the first Christian to completely distinguish Christianity from Judaism. It appears that the Marcionites were the first to embrace the name Christian because they wanted to make this distinction clear.

The name first came into use, however, in the context of Roman denouncements – to mark the group as illegal deviants – as Pliny's *Letter to Trajan* suggests (Letters 10.96–97; ca. 111–113 CE). The use of the name by Marcionites to voluntarily identify themselves must have caused consternation among those like Ignatius who were facing martyrdom as "Christians." Ignatius did not want others to think that he was a Marcionite. This is an interesting proposal given that the word "Christian" first crops up among Christians in the anti-Marcionite literature written between 140–150 CE: in Acts and Ignatius (Eph. 9; 11; 14–15; Magn. 4; 10; Trall. 6; Rom. 3; Philad. 6; Smy. 2; Poly. 1; 7). The book of Acts says the name Christian was first used in Antioch, although the author of Acts predates this attribution to the first-generation in order to legitimize the name. Notably Ignatius also is from Antioch.

It is reasonable to think that Ignatius of Antioch was the first Apostolic Catholic to try to take the name away from the Marcionites, who, he says, are really unbelievers because they do not use the Jewish scriptures or believe that Jesus was a real man. Ignatius says that these unbelievers falsely call themselves Christians. He goes on to argue that the name Christian ought to be embraced by the Apostolic Catholics because the Marcionites are not really Christians, we are! Ignatius argues that the name is valuable because it allows him to distinguish the movement itself from Judaism and his network of churches from Christian Maximalists, he calls "Judaizers." This is not so different from Marcion's use of the name Christian, although Marcion accused the Moderates of being "Judaizers" because they continued to use the Jewish scriptures, worship the Jewish God, and require converts to follow some of the commandments.

Marcion is the framer of Christianity as a distinct new religion with its own set of scriptures, the New Testament. He does not necessarily reject the Jewish scriptures and the Jewish God because he is anti-Semitic. Marcion recognizes the Jewish scriptures as the property of the Jews and the Jewish God as an ethnic God who patronizes a particular nation. His position on Judaism is very much in line with what most Jews at the time claimed, that they worshiped a national God who elected them, had unique scriptures, and awaited the coming of a Messiah who was not Jesus. Marcion agreed with the majority of the Jews who said that the prophecies in their scriptures had nothing to do with Jesus, a crucified Messiah, but someone yet-to-come.

In Marcion's opinion, Christians were not Jews and Jews were not Christians. Christianity was a Gentile religion with universal scope. He believed that the Christian God, because he was all-Good and all-Merciful, was better than and superior to the Jewish God who was jealous, arrogant, and angry. Marcion hoped that the unresponsiveness of the Jews to Jesus would not always be the case. He considered their conversion still possible, but it came with a heavy price: the abandonment of their national faith and traditions. Otherwise they would have to rely on YHWH to save them according to his own plan.

Marcion's innovative theology was not the only response among Minimalist Christians. Others developed TRANSTHEIST systems that recognized that the capriciousness of the Biblical God could not be synchronized with the Source of Life that philosophers imagined. These Christians believed that the Jewish scripture and Law may contain some truths, but these are hidden gems buried in stories, sentences, phrases, and words that require reinterpretation informed by revelation. In other words, the traditional ways that both Jews and Yahwist Christians read and understood scripture left Jews and the Yahwist Christians blind and duped into worshiping a jealous arrogant God who was either a rebellious archangel (an Archon) or Titan (a Greek God) or demon.

Because the Trantheists villainize the Jewish God, they have been characterized by scholars as thoroughly anti-Semitic. But this needs to be reassessed. First, the villainization of YHWH largely came about through reading Jewish scriptures literally: YHWH calls himself a jealous God who makes weal and woe; he mistakenly and arrogantly claims that he is the only God and there is no other God but him. Because the Transtheists believe that this self-professed ignorant God cannot be the primal Source of Life, they disparage his worship and those who worship him.

Second, Transtheists considered *everyone* who worshiped YHWH to have been blinded or tricked into worshiping a fallen angel or demon. In other words, their configuration of the ethno-racial categories meant that the Jewish category included everyone, even Christians, who worshiped the Biblical God YHWH. We ought to recognize that this ethno-racial configuration reflects how most pagans viewed the Christians, as a sectarian group of Jews who all worshiped the God of Israel. In establishing themselves as separate from those who worship YHWH, Trantheist thinkers deploy this ethno-racial configuration to elevate their status above YHWH-worshipers. All the Transtheist groups believed their group to be a superior "race" (*genos*) or people (*laos*) that originated from a divine realm. Because of this origin, the members of their group share a divine nature (i.e. seed, spark, light) that outsiders do not share or do not access.

The Valentinian author of the *Gospel of Philip* calls Yahwist Christians "Hebrews" because they worship YHWH, while he calls the Valentinians "Christians" because they know and worship the true

God. The Sethian Christians also saw themselves as superior to the Jews and Christians (the thirteen tribes or kingdoms who inadequately understand Christ's advent in the *Apocalypse of Adam*). The Sethian Christians do not make much of a distinction between Jews and Christians because all of them worship the Biblical God whom the Sethian Christians call The Fool (Aramaic: Saklas). The Sethian Christians do not appear to have called themselves either "Jews" or "Christians," but instead call themselves the Elect, Seth's Children, and the Immovable Race. Basilides thinks similarly. He says that he and his followers are no longer Jews but not Christians either, because he believes that he and his group transcend all YHWH-worshipers (Jews *and* Christians), including the Valentinian Pneumatics. Better than everyone else, the Basilidians claim to be the Elect, the true God's Kin.

While these groups all marketed themselves as the sole possessors of this divine nature, it is more complicated how they got this nature to begin with, whether their divine nature was pre-determined or not. For instance, most Valentinians appear to have thought that everyone is born with a spiritual seed, but the seed has to be grown in the right soil to mature enough to recognize the truth and be saved (as a Valentinian). Yet they also believed that, from the beginning, God already had identified the Called by writing their names in the Book of the Living. The Sethian Christians trace themselves back to Seth, an ancestor who is distinct from Cain and Abel. Cain is the ancestor of the Hylic (non-Christians) race, while Abel of the Psychic (Christians) race. The Sethian race differs from the other two races because its members are born with Sophia's *pneuma*. The other two races get a fake-*pneuma* manufactured by Ialdabaoth. Basilides is clear on this as well. There is only so much Filial substance mixed in with the other substances, and Basilidians are the only ones born with it.

So were these groups pre-deterministic like later Calvinists? Or did they recognize an individual's freewill? Was salvation a choice? This is complicated because, in all these Transtheist cases, the claims to be the possessors of the divine nature from birth do not depend on some birth characteristic that can be observed. They depend solely on whether people join the Elect group, which sociologically happened through peoples' own choices. The choice to join the group is interpreted by the group as evidence of the convert's innate divinity. And vice versa. The choice not to join or to leave the group is interpreted as evidence that the person does not or never did possess the spark. The Valentinians at least appear to have believed that many names are written in the Book of the Living and are called, but not everyone chooses to respond in a way that would guarantee their full redemption.

The Moderates had difficulty differentiating themselves from Jews because they worshiped the Jewish God and they straddled the fence when it came to the Law. They believed that converted Gentiles should not be forced to be circumcised, but other commandments did apply, whether they were the Noahide Laws (rules God imposed on Noah) or the Decalogue (Ten Commandments) or more extensive behavioral laws such as Hermas or the Montanists recognized. Under pressure to compete with Marcion's separation from Judaism and the Law, the Moderates rallied to consolidate into a network of like-minded churches in Asia Minor, western Syria, and Rome. In this process, they found it necessary to distinguish their movement from Judaism, even while maintaining their connection to Judaism.

They did this by first defining Jews as people who observe all the Mosaic Laws. This allowed Moderate Christians like Ignatius and Hegesippus to point their finger at the Maximalist Christians, identifying them as the real "Judaizers" and Christianity's first heretics, even though they knew the Maximalist groups were Christian, as Justin Martyr testifies.

Second, the Moderate Christians defined how their observation of the Law differed from the practices of the Jews. They stressed that they followed the original intent of the Torah, which was the Torah's moral core: the exclusive worship of the Jewish God, discontinuance of idolatry, and the practice of charity, chastity, and faithfulness. They distanced themselves from the rites of circumcision and the ceremonial laws (i.e. Sabbath observation; Jewish calendar and festivals). When it came to these laws, the Moderate Christians interpreted them metaphorically. For example, they argued that God did not want the foreskin to be circumcised, but converts' hearts. God did not want bloody sacrifices but devotion.

But even this type of spiritual interpretation was not enough to distinguish the Moderate Christians from Jews (many of whom were moderately minded themselves and read certain laws metaphorically).

As the pressure grew to define Christianity as Marcion did – as completely distinct from Judaism – the Moderates had to do more to prove that they were not Jews or Judaizers as Marcion alleged. This is when the Moderate Christians realized that they had to make everyone understand that they were Christians who had ancestors older than Marcion. They identified these ancestors as the twelve apostles.

This meant that the Apostolic credentialing of their movement developed along the ASSOCIATE MODEL of leadership, when leadership is linked to the closest associate(s) of a movement's founder. This is comparable to the Sunni Muslims who define themselves as followers of Muhammad's devoted companion Abu Bakr who, they think, most closely modeled Muhammad's example. In the case of the Moderate Christians, they linked their consolidating church network to the authority of Jesus' twelve disciples. This gave their church network the façade of antiquity – that the apostles had founded them – making them older and more authentic than Marcionism which was "new."

This link to the apostles, however, did not alleviate the accusation lodged by Marcion, that they were Judaizers. It only served to reinforce the impression because it was known that the apostles were Jews. It did not help that the Moderates had appropriated the Jewish scriptures, which they believed predicted Jesus' advent and Messiahship.

To prove that they were not Judaizers, some Moderate Christians begin making anti-Semitic remarks in their writings: that the Jewish nation had failed God; circumcision had been forced on the Jews to mark them as sinners; the Law was given to discipline and punish them; they remain an insolent people; they killed God's Son. We saw how this anti-Jewish sentiment was summarized in Melito's sermon.

By disparaging the Jews in this manner, the Moderates reconfigured the ethno-racial boundaries, arguing that God established a new universal (*catholic*) race (*genos*), nation (*ethne*), and people (*laos*) of Gentiles that succeeded, superseded, or replaced the Jewish nation. In other words, even though their apostolic ancestors were Jewish, the apostles had started a movement that surpassed Judaism, because the Jews not only failed to recognize Jesus as their Messiah, but murdered him too.

Were the Moderates the only Christians to characterize Jews and Judaism this way? This is a difficult question to answer because of the lack of sources from the Marcionites and Transtheist groups. The negative portrayal of the Jews in *The Gospel* (of John) may suggest that the Ex-Simonian Christians had developed anti-Semitic views, but this may also reflect the historical animosity between the Samaritans and the Jews rather than a Christian construction of anti-Semitism. What we do know is that this characterization of Jews and Judaism is found consistently in the literature written by the Apostolic Catholics. This characterization of Jews and Judaism has had a long, ugly, and horrific afterlife. It has been used to justify violence against the Jews (including expulsions and massacres) and their forced conversion by Catholics. Jews were continually segregated into ghettos in Catholic countries, made to wear distinctive clothing, and targeted with anti-Jewish legislation.

Jews fared no better with Protestants. In fact, Martin Luther's anger against the Jews because of their rejection of Jesus led him to write, "We are at fault for not slaying them. Rather we allow them to lie freely in our midst despite their murder, cursing, blaspheming, lying and defaming" (Luther, *On the Jews and Their Lies*; 1543 CE). While the Holocaust had many causes, we cannot minimize the fact that Luther's opinion was emphasized by the Nazis. It was not until 1983, that the Missouri Synod Lutheran Church renounced Luther's opinion. It took until 1994 for the Evangelical Lutheran Church in America to do the same.

Horrendous stereotypes of Jews that developed in the Middle Ages (e.g. blood libel, alleged greed, conspiracy against humanity) continue to persist today, leaving Jewish communities vulnerable to continued violence such as we witnessed with the mass shootings at the Pittsburg Tree of Life Synagogue in 2018 and the San Diego Chabad of Poway Synagogue in 2019. In 2021, anti-Semitic incidents reached an all-time high. According to the Anti-Defamation League's audit, 2717 assaults, harrassments, and vandalisms targeted Jews in 2021 alone (seven incidents a day), a 34% increase from 2020. It remains to be seen what the anti-Semitic abusive language of social influencers like Nick Fuentes and music icons like Kanye (Ye) West will do to these numbers in years to come.

12.10 Sex and Survival

It has been a long-standing problem in scholarship to figure out how Christianity not only survived but flourished in late antiquity. A.D. Nock proposed that Christians were able to convert large numbers of pagans because they structured their religion to incorporate the most appealing features of Greco-Roman philosophy and mystery religions. This appeal led to successful conversions and the rapid growth of Christianity (1933). Ramsay MacMullen said that it happened through mass conversions of pagans who were impressed with Christian displays of miracles (1984). The sociologist Rodney Stark, who studies how new religious movements emerge and why they are successful, argued that mass conversions were not necessary and did not happen. Rather Christianity was able to rapidly expand because conversion involved entire households and grew through kinship networks that targeted child-bearing women and intellectuals who helped create a movement that was intellectually appealing to Romans (1996).

While it is true that missionary activities, attractive features, conversion, and child-bearing all played a role in Christianity's survival and growth, these studies all assume Christianity to be a monolithic movement and Catholicism to be the heir apparent. Given what we have learned in this textbook, we ought to be asking first why Christianity ultimately survived in the shape that the Apostolic Catholics gave it, and not the shape that the Valentinians, the Marcionites, or the Ebionites gave it.

Consider, for instance, the fact that all these Christian groups had active and successful missions that included outreach to Gentiles. Gentiles were attracted enough to their various messages that most Christian movements survived intergenerationally for at least a hundred years, if not centuries. As for the conversion of intellectuals, it appears that all forms of Christianity had its scholars who shaped the individual movements in ways that accommodated Greek philosophy and Greco-Roman religious practices, including mystery religions.

While on the surface it seems a no-brainer that, if a movement targets women for their child-bearing capacity, the movement should survive intergenerationally. More children equals better survival. The problem with this folk wisdom is that it does not necessarily bear out historically. The Marcionites discouraged marriage and procreation, and yet their movement lasted in eastern regions of Mesopotamia into the tenth century. The Syrian Christians considered marriage a sinful state and targeted women who wanted to become virgins. They were successful and did not adjust their position on marriage until a century after Palut arrived in Edessa. The Montanists gave women the opportunity to divorce their husbands and become virgins and prophets. This seemed to be very attractive and their movement survived for centuries. On the other hand, the Valentinians elevated marriage and procreation to sacred levels, and yet their movement did not have the survival rate that the Apostolic Catholics had, who did not elevate marriage and procreation to the same divine status. The Carpocratians, who dissolved individual marriage because they did not believe in owning individual property (i.e. wives) and wished to imitate the natural order in the world's first free-love movement, did not survive past the third century.

Something else is at play in the survival of Christianity in the shape that the Apostolic Catholics gave it. What was so effective about the emergence of this particular shape of Christianity? Apostolic Catholicism, unlike all the other Christian movements, emerged through the consolidation of churches with a moderate standardized message and a public profile that reflected Roman values. All of these characteristics worked in tandem to give the Apostolic Catholics an advantage.

Consider how socially powerful it can be to take a number of already-existing like-minded churches and bring them together into a network, standardize their beliefs and practices, and then centralize leadership. Compare this to Marcion who establishes his own church with a theology that is innovative. He is at an immediate disadvantage. He is only as successful as the number of churches he can establish. Marcion knew this, so rather than trying to start new churches, he went around and poached the Minimalist-leaning churches to join his movement. But even then, he had to compete with the Apostolic Catholics who went after the Minimalist churches too in order to incorporate them into their moderate network. Marcion was successful and built a counter-church with a standardized New Testament and centralized leadership, but he was always embattled with the Apostolic Catholics. This embattlement with the Apostolic Catholics stalled his movement more in the west than in the east where the competition was not so fierce because the Catholics took longer to establish themselves there.

We can also compare this consolidation model to Valentinus' church. Valentinus seceded from the Apostolic Catholic network to do his own thing. For whatever reason, he did not centralize leadership, so even two generations after his death, the Valentinian churches were being led by independent scholastic leaders who were unable to standardize their mythology or practices. The Valentinians set up their churches in a split-level model to poach Apostolic Catholics into the ranks of the initiated. They had the appeal of esoteric secrets and so, for a time, were successful poaching the Catholics. But once Catholics like Clement of Alexandria and Origen constructed an equally attractive esoteric tradition for themselves, the Valentinians lost this advantage.

The standardization of a moderate message also is powerful socially. Moderate messages appeal to the largest number of people, while messages that are innovative or countercultural have smaller audiences. They might initially "grab" converts who are dissatisfied with the status quo and are looking for something new or revolutionary, but this appeal does not have longevity. Messages with the best survival rate need to have a distinctive edge (this is what gives the group its identity) while also reflecting and improving upon some of the important values of the rest of society (this is what makes the message marketable).

The Moderate Christians had this advantage from the get-go because they were flexible when it came to the conversion of Gentiles and the Law. They were in the middle when it came to the Law. They did not make Gentiles undergo circumcision or be kosher, so they could still go to the gymnasiums and work out in the nude without being identified as a Jew and they could hold dinner parties with their pagan kin and friends. But they had distinctive rules around chastity, charity, and exclusivity of worship that they had to follow as well. This Moderate message meant that the early missions had high success rates among God-Fearers and pagan Gentiles. Their only real competitors were the Minimalists, whose no Law message was also appealing to Gentile converts.

What made the difference then between the survival of the messages of the Moderates and the Minimalists since both were attractive to Gentiles? The Moderates edged out Minimalists when they standardized the Moderate message in the form of the Canon of Truth and composed and publicly distributed anti-Marcionite literature. As Hegesippus' mission to identify like-minded moderate churches relates, this standardization and public distribution of literature made it possible for the Apostolic Catholics to construct a network of churches that included those who agreed with their message and excluded (and perhaps stranded) those churches that disagreed. It gave the Apostolic Catholics the platform to weaponize Christian difference into Judaizing (Maximalist) and Polytheistic (Minimalist) heresies and position themselves in the golden middle as we saw the heresiologists do. This weaponizing of difference continued to define the Apostolic Catholics in the fourth and fifth centuries, serving to exclude (and strand) dissident Catholics and their positions until they were able to come to a consensus (the middle again) and normalize their opinions in official creeds.

I am reminded of the social power of consolidation whenever I hear people question where all the women country musicians have gone today. It is an understatement to say that country music has become principally a male format in less than 20 years. According to *Rolling Stone*, in 2019 for every one female artist played on the radio, 9.7 men were played. Since 2000, there has been a 66% decline in the number of songs held by women on the year-end country airplay reports, a descent from 33.3% to 11.3%. The financial disparity between male and female artists is so great that *Rolling Stone* says that women artists are no longer financially viable, including top performers. And now we have a whole generation of young girls that has grown up hardly hearing women on the radio, believing that country music is defined by male voices and brash patriotism.

What happened? The decline of female artists is largely the result of the Telecommunications Act of 1996, which allowed single companies to purchase multiple stations in a single market. This resulted in the consolidation of independently owned and operated stations within one mega-company like Clear Channel (now iHeartMedia), which grew from 40 stations in 1996 to 1,240 stations in 2002. Artists like Billy Bragg complained in his Tell Us the Truth Tour (2003) that Clear Channel was "a great hulking Frankenstein monster gobbling things up."

This consolidation allowed the owner of Clear Channel to redefine country music. Following 9–11, when patriotism began to rise, the decision was made to lay-off the country love ballads and social action songs that women artists had made famous and, instead, have the stations almost exclusively play the patriotic songs that some of the men had started to compose and sing. It became an increasingly threatening and intimidating environment for women artists who were critical of the political scene and who questioned the radio's shift toward patriotic songs like "Courtesy of the Red, White and Blue" by Toby Keith. So, in 2003, when Natalie Maines of the Dixie Chicks told an audience in London that they were "ashamed the President of the United States is from Texas" because they did not support his invasion of Iraq, Clear Channel told its stations to pull the Dixie Chicks. Future artists became so fearful of being branded a heretic and canceled by the industry that the slang "don't be dixie chicked" came into vogue. Clear Channel went on to force their radio stations to use exclusive monetized playlists that determined not only which artists would be played, but also the frequency that men and women artists could be played. They ruled that women artists could not be played back-to-back, while men could. Further, the lists functioned to authenticate certain artists while excluding others. This ended up standardizing and normalizing country music around these lists.

Consolidation around a standard list (or creed in the case of the Apostolic Catholics) is a powerful social process that uses inclusion and exclusion to construct and market movements, whether we are talking about the redefinition of country music or the emergence of Apostolic Catholicism. While the consolidation and standardization of a public message may explain why Apostolic Catholicism emerged to dominate Christian discourse and become the "natural" form of Christianity, it does not explain why pagans chose to join a Christian movement in the first place. Here again, the issue is complex and has more moving parts than we are able to identify here. So the following should not be taken as an exhaustive list, but as indicators of strong social factors in the growth of Christian movements more broadly.

First, many pagans were drawn to Christianity because they were attracted to religious enthusiasm like prophecy and the types of religious experiences and esoteric lore that some of the groups marketed as the best mystery religion in town. They were familiar with oracle Gods like Apollo and mystery initiations as a mode to experience the (under)world of the Gods. Some may have thought that Christianity trumped all the other mystery inductions because its rites would take them into a transcendent world where they would meet the Source of Life.

Second, some marketed Christianity as a philosophy, as a way of life that was more authentic or universal than other philosophies. This was very attractive to intellectuals who were looking for the perennial philosophy, the truth behind all philosophies and religions.

Third, some were (morbidly) fascinated at the faith of people who would rather suffer and die than deny Christ. Wondering what was going on with this culture of martyrdom, they set out to investigate only to find themselves converted by the enthusiasm and devotion of the Christians they interviewed.

Fourth, by the late second century, the message of Christianity had been fine-tuned to draw attention to Roman values like charity and chastity. Charity was especially important to pagans struggling to make ends meet or those unable to cover funeral expenses. Christians took care of each other and provided for their own. Chastity was also a long-standing Roman value, especially as it applied to Roman married women who dressed and lived so that their bodies remained the property of their husbands. Once Christians began equating chastity with virginity and virginity with adult (divorced) women, a whole new possibility for women opened up that allowed them to be freed from the terrors of childbirth and forced marital (heterosexual) sex. It also opened up the possibility for divorced women to regain their substantial dowries from ex-husbands.

Fifth, fealty to the Gods, another Roman value, was remodeled into devotion to a single God. Pagans valued the worship of their Gods and connected this to their prosperity and the health of their cities. Pagans respected the fact that Jews worshiped their national ancestral God. As long as Christians were considered a Jewish sect, the worship of a single God was not problematic. Gentiles who converted understood that they were converting to Judaism and they respected the fact that they were giving fealty to the Jewish national God. But when Christians began distinguishing themselves from Jews, the Jewish national God became problematic for Gentiles. Why were they worshiping the Jewish national God when they were not Jews?

This question caused the Christians to turn to the transcendent God of the philosophers and argue that this transcendent God was the real object of their worship, although they disagreed among themselves if this transcendent God was YHWH. Long before Christianity emerged, Greeks and Romans had already conceptualized a transcendent universal God, the Source of Life. Many pagans had been worshiping this One God under the name of Zeus or Apollo at temples devoted to the One Highest God. It was not difficult to convince pagan converts that this One God was not Zeus or Apollo, but the Jewish Creator God or Jesus' Father. If Christians had not made the argument that the Christian God was the same God that the philosophers had proposed as the Source of Life, their movements may not have lasted, because the capricious national God of the Jews was a hard sell to Gentiles who understood that they were joining a new race (*genos*) or made up a new nation (*ethnos*) that was not (or no longer) Jewish.

Sixth, all Christian movements marketed themselves as revealing the "true" worldview. While the patterns of beliefs differed across movements, they share a stable core. All Christians worshiped an exclusive transcendent One God who, they believed, sent his Son as an ambassador to earth. His Son walked around as Jesus of Nazareth, taught humans what God wants from them, and was executed by the Romans. His crucifixion was connected to the liberation of humanity from the dark powers that rule the world. Believers understood themselves to belong to an Elect group that had been freed from these dark powers who had controlled their fate. As the Elect, they were part of a new race that was promised resurrection and immortalization.

Why was this belief-system so attractive to people in the Roman world? We can imagine that this message was particularly attractive to colonized and enslaved populations who experienced trauma in their daily lives, as well as sporadic revolts, wars, and massacres. We can imagine why colonized people idealized scenarios that separated everyone into their "original" (pre-colonial) states and elevated their Christian race in a hierarchy that gave them the best real estate in heaven while everyone else (unconverted Romans) destruction. This is not to say that socially mobile and powerful Romans did not convert. Certainly, they did. Emperor Constantine, perhaps, is the primary exemplar of a colonizer appropriating the imagery (and magic) of the cross to secure military victory for himself at the Battle of Milvian Bridge (313 CE).

But the Christian message was particularly well-suited to provide oppressed people with a sense of autonomy and personal control. While their lived reality as colonized and enslaved people was out-of-their-control, the monstrous cosmic Powers at the root of the chaos might be controlled through ritual interventions. While bloody revolutions had been unsuccessful in overthrowing Rome, they could protest the supernatural Powers that rule the world and their Roman accomplices without starting another war by using their bodies as sites of social protest and disruption (i.e. by refusing to marry or have children) and therapy (i.e. healing practices). This protest was peculiarly gendered. It gave women opportunities to be more than or other than a wife, without being labeled a whore. Christian women had more agency over their bodies which is why there was so much noise around women and female bodies in early Christian literature. True, some Christian movements afforded women more agency than others. Yet, depending on the movement, women could choose to be martyrs, patrons, prophetesses, apostles, teachers, presiders, baptizers, healers, virgins, hermits, or part of a divine conjugal syzygy. While this is a far cry from what we might think is equality today, it represented a shift in how ancient people thought about the agency of women's bodies. And this shift had much to do with the way in which Christians read and interpreted the Genesis story.

12.11 Where to End the Story

To end a textbook like this is difficult because we did not set out to end at a teleologically satisfying historical moment like the Nicene Council. We end with fifth-generation Christians embattled over the ownership of Jesus' esoterica. We observe, however, that with Clement and Origen's recalibration of esoteric lore, the type of Christian pluralism that had bloomed in the second century, had reached its peak. The fifth-generation Apostolic Catholics appropriated the claim to esoterica and the mystical path to achieve Gnosis, breaking the monopoly on esoteric tradition that had attracted converts and distinguished the Valentinian, Sethian, and other groups in the Transtheist family.

To make their esoteric tradition more esoteric and attractive than the Catholic, Gnostic groups were forced in future generations to esoterize even more. As they increased their privatization, they isolated themselves further, making proselytizing more and more difficult. This social dynamic stranded the independent Gnostic churches which already had been unable to centralize their leadership and churches earlier. While their churches shrunk and began to fail, their literature lived on in environments outside the churches that had produced and maintained them earlier. Their gospels, treatises, letters, and revelations were read and translated and copied by Christians who were interested in Jesus esoterica. New esoteric literature based on the second-century literature begins to be written by fifth- and sixth-generation Christians in eastern Syria and Mesopotamia where Apostolic Catholicism struggled to get a foothold in the third century.

This is where we end the story, in the middle of the next story which largely features Apostolic Catholics consolidating among themselves in the west and using "official" councils to do the work of exclusion of dissident Catholics. While in the eastern reaches of the Empire, the Christian scene remains competitive with Thomasine Christians, Marcionites, Valentinians, Elchasaites, Manichaeans, Sethian Christians, and independent esoteric teachers contesting with Palut and his Apostolic Catholic predecessors in something like the "wild west" (or better: "wild east") of late antique Christianity.

Timeline

Aggregated Timeline by Generation

Minimalists   Moderates   Maximalists

The arrangement of the layers of people and texts has no intended meaning. My goal was to arrange every generation in a condensed manner for layout purposes. Whenever possible, I grouped the Minimalists, Moderates, and Maximalists together. The Catholic traditional bishops are arranged in the first line as they were on the Timelines in the individual chapters.

First Generation

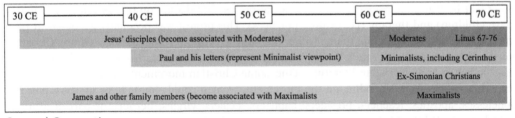

Second Generation

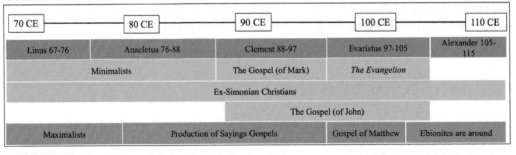

FIGURE 12.7 Composite timeline of the major thinkers in the first five generations of Christianity and the relative dates of their compositions.

Third Generation

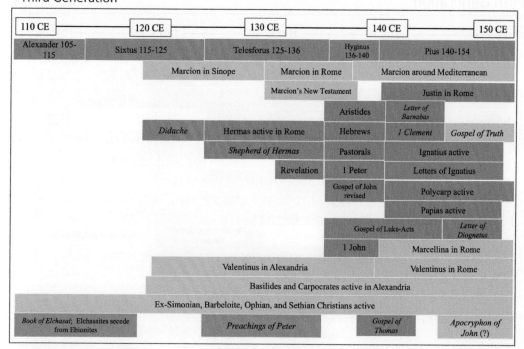

Fourth Generation

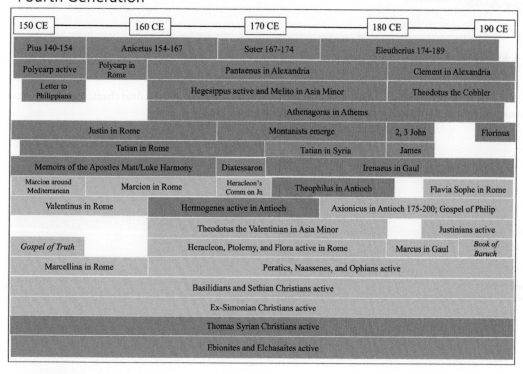

FIGURE 12.7 (Continued)

Fifth Generation

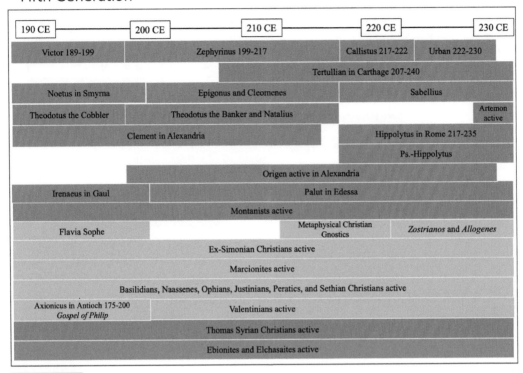

FIGURE 12.7   (Continued)

Pattern Summary

In every chapter, we have been charting the patterns of individual Christians. In this final chapter, we are able to assemble all of the individuals into one chart for comparative purposes.

Aggregated Family Patterns

■ Xenotheists   ■ Transtheists   ■ Yahwists

THEODICY

	Faulty-God	Faulty-Human	Other
Marcion	X		
Cerdo	X		
Valentinus	X		
Sethians	X		
Ptolemy	X		
Heracleon	X		
Theodotus	X		
Marcus	X		
Peratics	X		
Ophians	X		
Justin the Gnostic	X		
Naassenes	X		

SOTERIOLOGY

	Gift from God	Human achievement	Minimalist	Moderate	Maximalist
Marcion	X		X		
Valentinus	X		X		
Sethians	X		X		
Ptolemy	X		X		
Heracleon	X		X		
Theodotus	X		X		
Marcus	X		X		
Peratics	X		X		
Ophians	X		X		
Justin the Gnostic	X		X		
Naassenes	X		X		

THEODICY

	Faulty-God	Faulty-Human	Other
Basilides	X	X	
Carpocrates	X	X	
Hermas		X	
Ignatius		X	
Polycarp		X	
Justin		X	
Ebionites		L	
Echasaites		L	
Nazoreans		L	
Tatian		X	
Montanists		L	
Irenaeus		X	
Athenagoras		X	
Theophilus		X	
Tertullian		X	Traducianism
Clement of Alexandria		X	
Origen		X	Fall of logikoi

SOTERIOLOGY

	Gift from God	Human achievement	Minimalist	Moderate	Maximalist
Basilides	X		X		
Carpocrates		X	X		
Hermas		X		X	
Ignatius		X		X	
Polycarp		X		X	
Justin		X		X	
Ebionites		X			X
Echasaites		X			X
Nazoreans		X		X	X
Tatian		X		X	
Montanists		X		X	
Irenaeus		X		X	
Athenagoras		X		X	
Theophilus		X		X	
Tertullian		X		X	
Clement of Alexandria		X		X	
Origen		X		X	

FIGURE 12.8 Composite chart illustrating the relationships of the Family Patterns tracked throughout this textbook.

CHRISTOLOGY	Adult possession	Fetal possession	Hybrid	Ensoulment	Visitation	Human who received revelation
Marcion					X	
Valentinus	X			X		
Sethians	L				L	
Ptolemy	L			L		
Heracleon	L			L		
Theodotus	L			L		
Marcus	L			L		
Peratics	L			L		
Ophians	L					
Justin the Gnostic						X
Naassenes		L		L		
Basilides	X	Later				
Carpocrates	X					

ANTHROPOLOGY	Mono	Dual	Triad	Quad
Marcion		X		
Valentinus			X	
Sethians			X	
Ptolemy			X	
Heracleon			X	
Theodotus			X	
Marcus			X	
Peratics			X	
Ophians			X	
Justin the Gnostic			X	
Naassenes			X	
Basilides				X
Carpocrates		X		

	Adult possession	Fetal possession	Hybrid	Ensoulment	Visitation	Human who received revelation
Hermas	X					
Ignatius		X				
Polycarp		X				
Justin				X		
Ebionites	X					
Echasaites	X					
Nazoreans		L				
Tatian				X		
Montanists	L					
Irenaeus		X				
Athenagoras						
Theophilus						
Tertullian			X	aware		
Theodotus	X					
Noetus					X	
Paul Samo.		X				
Clement of Alexandria		X		X		
Origen				aware	X	

	Mono	Dual	Triad	Quad
Hermas		X		
Ignatius		X		
Polycarp		X		
Justin		X		
Ebionites		X		
Echasaites		X		
Nazoreans		X		
Tatian		X		
Montanists		X		
Irenaeus		X		
Athenagoras		X		
Theophilus		X		
Tertullian		X		
Clement of Alexandria		X		
Origen		X		

FIGURE 12.8 (Continued)

	COSMIC DEMIURGY										RESURRECTION			
	Autocrat	Administrator	Caretaker	Patron	Justice	Villain	Rebel	Ignorant	Impaired		Body reunites with soul	Body discarded and soul immortalized	Body and soul discarded and spirit rises	God-element separates from body soul, and spirit and rises
Marcion	X	L	X	X	X	X		X		Marcion		X		
Valentinus	X	X	X	X	X	X	X	X	X	Valentinus			X	
Sethians	X	X	X	X	L	X	X	X	X	Sethians			X	
Ptolemy	X	X	X	X	X	X	X	X	X	Ptolemy			X	
Heracleon	X	X	X	X	X	X	X	X	X	Heracleon			X	
Theodotus	X	X	X	X	X	X	X	X	X	Theodotus			X	
Marcus	X	X	L	L	L	L		X	X	Marcus			X	
Peratics	X	X				X				Peratics			X	
Ophians	X	X			X					Ophians			X	
Justin (Gn)	L	X			X					Justin (Gn)			X	
Naassenes	X	X			X		X			Naassenes			X	
Basilides	X	X	X	X		X		X	X	Basilides				X
Carpocrates	X	X	X	X		X		X	X	Carpocrates		X		
Hermas	X	X	X	X	X					Hermas	X			
Ignatius	X	L	X	X	X					Ignatius	X			
Polycarp	X	L	X	X	L					Polycarp	X			

	Autocrat	Administrator	Caretaker	Patron	Justice					Body reunites with soul			
Justin	X	X	X	X	X				Justin	X			
Ebionites	L	L	L	L	L				Ebionites	L			
Echasaites	L	L	L	L	L				Echasaites	L			
Nazoreans	L	L	L	L	L				Nazoreans	L			
Tatian	X	L	X	X	L				Tatian	X			
Montanists	L	L	L	L	L				Montanists	X			
Irenaeus	X	X	X	X	X				Irenaeus	X			
Athenagoras	X	L	X	X	X				Athenagoras	X			
Theophilus	X	L	X	X	L				Theophilus	L			
Tertullian	X	X	X	X	X				Tertullian	X			
Clement of Alexandria	X	X	X	X	X				Clement of Alexandria	X			
Origen	X	X	X	X	X				Origen	X			

FIGURE 12.8   (Continued)

	Jewish	Gospel	Pauline letters (10)	Pauline letters (13)	Hebrews	Acts	Catholic letters	Revelation	Other
SCRIPTURES									
Marcion		Ev/Mt	X						
Valentinus	partial	Jn Mt	X					L-GosTr	L-GosTr
Sethians	partial								
Ptolemy, Heracleon, Theodotus	partial	Mt Jn	X						1Jn PrPet GosTr
Marcus	partial	Mt/Mk/Lk	X					X	
Peratics	partial	Jn							
Ophians	partial								
Justin the Gnostic	partial	Lk							Gnostic Baruch
Naassenes	partial	Mt/Mk/Lk Jn/GosThom							GosEg
Basilides		Ev or Lk Mt/GosTh	X						
Carpocrates		Mt	X						
Hermas	X	Jn/Mt		L					
Ignatius	X	Mt/Lk/Jn		X					
Polycarp	X	Mt/Lk/Jn		X	X	?	1 Pet		1 Jn

	Jewish	Gospel	Pauline letters (10)	Pauline letters (13)	Hebrews	Acts	Catholic letters	Revelation	Other
Justin	X	Mt/Mk/Lk/ Jn/Harmony		X				X	
Ebionites	partial	version Mt (Gos. Ebion.)							
Elchasaites	partial	version Mt							ApocElch
Nazoreans	X	version Mt (Gos. Naz.)							
Tatian	X	Diatessaron Mt/Mk/Lk/Jn		L					L-GosTh
Montanists	X	Jn	X			X		X	
Aristides	L	Jn	1 Cor						
Irenaeus	X	Mt/Mk/Lk/Jn		X	X	X	1 Pet	X	1 Jn/2 Jn/?-Jms
Athenagoras	L	Mt	1 Cor						
Theophilus	X								
Tertullian	X	Mt/Mk/Lk/Jn		X	X	X	1 Pet	X	1 Jn/2 Jn/?-Jms
Clement of Alexandria	X	Mt/Mk/Lk Jn		X	X	X	1 Pet	X	1 Jn/2 Jn extensive apoc
Origen	X	Mt/Mk/Lk Jn		X	X	X	1 Pet	X	1 Jn/2 Jn Some apoc

**This scriptural chart reflects generally agreed upon academic assessments of the evidence of the people studied in this textbook; it does not reflect original research nor is it comprehensive of all early Christian literature.

FIGURE 12.8   (Continued)

ECCLESIOLOGY						
	Consolidation movement	Reform movement	Secessionist movement	Counter movement	Innovative movement	Transegional	Regional
Marcion				X		X	
Valentinus		X	X			X	
Sethians					X	X	
Ptolemy			X			X	
Heracleon			X			X	
Theodotus			X			X	
Marcus			X				X
Peratics					X		X
Ophians					X		X
Justin the Gnostic					X		X
Naassenes					X		X
Basilides					X		X
Carpocrates					X	Marcellina	

	Consolidation movement	Reform movement	Secessionist movement	Counter movement	Innovative movement	Transegional	Regional
Hermas	X					X	
Ignatius	X					X	
Polycarp	X					X	
Justin	X					X	
Ebionites					X		X
Echasaites					X		X
Nazoreans					X		X
Tatian			X				X
Montanists		X	X			X	
Irenaeus	X					X	
Athenagoras	X					X	
Theophilus	X					X	
Tertullian	X	X	X			X	X
Clement of Alexandria	X					X	
Origen	X					X	

FIGURE 12.8 (Continued)

Takeaways

1. Christian can be defined using a substantive definition, functional definition, or family resemblance definition.

2. The first Christians worshipped three different Gods. This difference in theology reveals how the Christians were divided into three Christian Families: Xenotheists, Transtheists, and Yahwists.

3. Biographies of each family can be constructed retrospectively although not conclusively.

4. The Marcionite church emerged from Minimalists who were using the *Evangelion* (which was an expanded version of the Gospel of Mark [=*Evangelion of Jesus Christ*]) and the ten letters of Paul. Marcion was a successful missionary convincing Minimalist Christians to join his counter church.

5. The Transtheist churches have varied origins, although they share a Minimalist perspective. Some of these churches developed their Gnostic mythology because they were exposed to the Ophite Myth or Barbeloite Myth. Others relied on the Gospel of John which applies the Simonian Myth to Jesus. Other churches developed their Gnostic mythology based on their own independent exegesis of the Genesis story. All these churches develop their own ecclesiologies and scriptures.

6. The Yahwists develop along Maximalist and Moderate lines. The Maximalist groups emerge in the Transjordan region. Moderate churches competed with Minimalist churches in Asia Minor and Western Syria. Eventually, the moderate churches consolidate into the Apostolic Catholic church.

7. While Christianity began as a Jewish sectarian movement, its relationship with Jews and Judaism becomes complicated as Gentiles flourished in the churches and Rome retaliated against the Jews for their political uprisings. Marcion pushed the Christians to make a decision about their religious identity. Because of Marcion, the Christians had to decide whether they were different from Jews and, if so, how so.

8. Apostolic Catholicism was the most successful Christian movement because of the social power generated via the consolidation of their church network and the public transparency of their activities. Christianity as a religious philosophy was attractive to pagans for a variety of reasons, including the draw of religious enthusiasm, the culture of martyrdom, extreme ethics, fealty to the One God (whom the philosophers had been discussing), and the attractiveness of a worldview that empowered the colonized.

Questions

1. How did different positions on the Law among the Christian Jewish sectarians result in three different Christian families?

2. How did three different theologies come to be?

3. How did different views on theodicy and soteriology emerge in connection with Christians' positions on the Law and God? How did this affect their lifestyle choices?

4. Consider how Christian identity was not necessarily about belief and practice, but ecclesiastical structures and leadership. Consider how and where different groups derived their authority and legitimated their group. How does this map onto the three different Christian families?

5. Compare and contrast Hermas', Valentinus', and Marcion's views on the nature of God. How does this view affect their positions on theodicy and resurrection?

6. Choose one Christian group and explain in detail how they legitimated themselves and defined themselves against one of the other groups.

7. Identify and discuss two or three early Christian debates that were also debated much later in history and even still go on today. What arguments do Christians use to support their positions on these issues? Why do these debates reoccur in history and appear to never be resolved across Christian groups?

8. How and why was the Canon of Truth created? Was it effective? How so?

9. How did different readings of Paul affect the formation of different Christian groups?

10. Compare people across generations: (a) Ignatius-Justin-Hegesippus-Tertullian; OR (b) Valentinus-Irenaeus-Clement-Origen; OR (c) Basilides-Carpocrates-Irenaeus-Origen.

11. How did the rise of early Christianity result in anti-Semitism? How does knowing this history help us confront anti-Semitism today and make positive changes? Write your response as a letter to the editor of your local newspaper.

12. We learned about six social reasons that helped Christianity survive intergenerationally and thrive in the Roman world. Brainstorm other reasons for its survival.

Resources

Daniel Boyarin. 1999. *Dying for God: Martyrdom and the Making of Christianity and Judaism*. Stanford: Stanford University Press.

Rudolf Bultmann. 1971. *The Gospel of John: A Commentary*. Translated by G.R. Beasley-Murray, R.W.N. Hoare, and J.K. Riches. Philadelphia: Westminster John Knox Press.

April D. DeConick. 2013. (revised ed.). *Holy Misogyny: Why the Sex and Gender Conflicts in the Early Church Still Matter*. New York: Continuum.

April D. DeConick. 2013. "Who is hiding in the Gospel of John? Reconceptualizing Johannine theology and the roots of Gnosticism." Pages 13-29 in *Histories of the Hidden God: Concealment and Revelation in Western Gnostic, Esoteric, and Mystical Traditions*. Edited by April DeConick and Grant Adamson. Gnostica Series. Durham: Acumen.

April D. DeConick. 2018. "Deviant Christians: Romanization and Esoterization as Social Strategies for Survival among Early Christians." *Gnosis: Journal of Gnostic Studies* 3.2: 135–176.

April D. DeConick. 2020. "The One God Is No Simple Matter." Pages 263–292 in *Monotheism and Christology in Greco-Roman Antiquity* Edited by Matthew Novenson. Supplements to Novum Testamentum 180. Leiden: Brill.

Bart D. Ehrman. 2018. *The Triumph of Christianity: How a Forbidden Religion Swept the World*. New York: Simon and Schuster.

John G. Gager. 1985. *The Origins of Anti-Semitism: Attitudes toward Judaism in Pagan and Christian Antiquity*. Oxford: Oxford University Press.

Keith Hopkins. 1999. *A World Full of Gods: The Strange Triumph of Christianity*. New York: The Free Press.

Larry Hurtado. 2016. *Destroyer of the Gods: Early Christian Distinctiveness in the Roman World*. Waco: Baylor University Press.

Judith M. Lieu. 2004. *Christian Identity in the Jewish and Graeco-Roman World*. Oxford: Oxford University Press.

Ramsay MacMullen. 1984. *Christianizing the Roman Empire*. New Haven: Yale University Press.

Elaine Pagels. 1972. *The Johannine Gospel in Gnostic Exegesis: Heracleon's Commentary on John*. Atlanta: Scholars Press.

Richard I. Pervo. 2010. *The Making of Paul: Construction of the Apostle in Early Christianity*. Minneapolis: Fortress Press.

Matt Recla. 2023. *Rethinking Christian Martyrdom: The Blood of the Seed?* Critiquing Religion: Discourse Culture Power. London: Bloomsbury Academic.

Rodney Stark. 1996. *The Rise of Christianity: How the Obscure, Marginal Jesus Movement Became the Dominant Religious Force in the Western World in a Few Centuries*. San Francisco: HarperCollins.

Benjamin L. White. 2014. *Remembering Paul: Ancient and Modern Contests over the Image of the Apostle*. Oxford: Oxford University Press.

A

abiogenesis   Origin of life

Abrasax   Well-known God who appears frequently on magical objects like charms and amulets and is referenced in esoteric literature and grimoires

achievement pattern   Soteriological scheme where salvation is something that humans have to do

active imagination   A Jungian meditative technique to stimulate a person's unconscious to release images that can be used therapeutically

Adamas   Primal Aeon who is source of all life in Naassene mythology

administrator pattern   Theological scheme that God creates the universe using an assistant or assistants like angels or attendant Gods

adult possession pattern   Christological scheme where the human Jesus is possessed by the Holy Spirit at his baptism; Jesus is viewed as a prophet

Aeons   Divinities or Eternities

agapê meal   Charity-meals

altered states   Qualitatively different from "ordinary" or "baseline" states of consciousness

angelolalia   The ability to speak unknown angelic languages

Anêr   Adult; highest level in the mysteries of the Naassenes

anthropology   Explanations of the human being

Anthropos   Greek, meaning man; Valentinian term for primal God in human shape

antinomian   Lawless; unregulated behavior; freedom from the laws and conventions

Antitheses   Marcion's book about the contradictions between the God in the Jewish scripture and Jesus' Father in the *Evangelion*

apocalypsis   Greek word meaning revelation; often associated with ecstasy

Apocrypha, Christian   Early Christian writings not collected in the New Testament canon

Apollo   Greek God associated with oracles

apophatic theology   Negative theology; explaining what God is by saying what he is not

apostates   Traitors; those who deny the Lord

apostle   Highest office of early Christian leaders who did missionary work, including Paul; retrospectively came to be associated with the twelve disciples of Jesus

apostolic   Tradition traced back to the twelve apostles

Apostolic Catholicism   Network of second-century churches that claimed their tradition came directly from the twelve apostles, their leaders were authorized via a direct succession from the apostles, and their church was universal (catholic) rather than an independent local variant; the bishop of Rome came to be the overseer or superintendent of the network; the traditions and practices this network develops in the second century are later claimed by Catholics, Orthodox, and Protestants as their official heritage

Apostolicon   Collection of ten letters of Paul that Marcion used, edited, and published

Apostolic Fathers   Considered the successors of the twelve apostles; collection of early Christian writings

archetype   Unconscious images with universal meanings (i.e. the Mother, the Maiden, the Crone, etc.); mental predispositions housed in the collective unconscious

Archon   Ruler of the world

ascetic   Renunciate

Associate Model   Leadership is transmitted and legitimized by linking it to the closest associate(s) of a movement's founder

Aten   Solar disk; considered the sole God of Egypt under Akhenaten

Attis   God who was the husband of the Great Mother Goddess Cybele

autocrat pattern   Theological scheme that the Creator God creates the universe by himself

autonomic nervous system   The part of the nervous system responsible for control of the bodily functions not consciously directed, such as breathing, the heartbeat, and digestive processes

B

Baal   Mesopotamian high God

Bacchanalia   Carnivals in the forests of groups of mostly women celebrating Dionysus

baptism   Water rite performed in Jesus' name; initiatory

Barbarians   The rest of the world's inhabitants from the viewpoint of the Greek and Romans

Barbelo   Name of the hermaphrodite Mother God in Sethian literature and Barbeloite Myth

basilica   Christian church building

Binitarian Problem   How the divine and human natures in Jesus Christ related to each other and worked together; see Two Natures of Jesus

bridal chamber   Valentinian ritual that signifies the culmination of one's journey entering into the house of the Father and God's Pleroma

Comparing Christianities: An Introduction to Early Christianity, First Edition. April D. DeConick.
© 2024 John Wiley & Sons Ltd. Published 2024 by John Wiley & Sons Ltd.

Bythus   Depth; Valentinian term for primal Father

C

canon   Authoritative documents or statement of faith; collection of texts considered authoritative

caretaker demiurge   Concept that the creator figure or figures are benevolent and conscientious

catechism   Christian instruction taught to proselytes preparing for baptism

catechumen   Converts preparing for baptism

Catholic   Christian Church which accepts the Roman Pope as its leader

catholic   Universal; transnational, widespread, and exclusive

Charismatic Model   Leadership is legitimized through revelation or divine calling

Christology   Explanations of Jesus' roles and nature (human/divine); theological view on the relation of Jesus to God, especially in his own nature and person

Chiliasm   Belief in the thousand-year reign of Christ at the end of time before the descent of Jerusalem; belief is dependent on the Book of Revelation

church   (1) Greek: *ecclesia*: body of assembled Christians in homes; (2) in sociological church-sect-cult typology: conventional religious organization

Church Fathers   Successors of the Apostolic Fathers; collection of early Christian writings

Church of New Prophecy   Movement founded by Montanus, Priscilla, and Maximilla; Phrygia, Asia Minor

circumcision   Ritual removal of foreskin from penis; affirmation of YHWH's covenant

Codex Sinaiticus   Earliest manuscript copy of the Christian Bible (ca. 350 CE)

collective unconscious   Shared archetypes that are part of the human mental hardware from birth; universal meanings

consolidated movement   Religious group created when two or more independent religious units form a network with common religious leadership

consubstantial   Share the same property or substance; in Gnostic systems, human beings share in God's nature; with reference to the persons in the Trinity sharing the same substance

Coptic   Ancient Egyptian language used by Egyptian Christians; latest stage in the Egyptian language

cosmogony   Explanations of how the universe was created or came into being

cosmology   Explanations of the structure of the universe

Council of Nicaea   First ecumenical council; Nicene Creed established as canon of faith; 325 CE

counter movement   Religious group formed in opposition to another religious group because it disagrees with the other group and attempts to compete with it for converts

covenant   Contract between YHWH and the people of Israel

Covenant Spirituality   God and his subjects are legally obligated to each other in a covenantal relationship; God established a set of laws or commandments that his subjects agreed to follow

creed   Common statement of faith to standardize Christian identity and mark anyone with differing beliefs as non-Christians

cult   Deviant religious organization with novel beliefs and practices in church-sect-cult typology

Cybele   Great Mother Goddess native to Anatolia

D

Demeter   Mother Goddess whose daughter Persephone was kidnapped by Hades at Eleusis; Greater and Lesser Mysteries associated with her worship

demiurge   From Greek: *demiurgos*, craftsman; God who creates the universe

demiurgy   Act of a God creating the universe

demon   Powerful evil supernatural being

derealization   Mental state when you feel detached from normal reality

determinism   A person's fate is determined before birth

diaspora   Jewish communities living outside Judea

Diatessaron   Syrian gospel harmony completed by Tatian (180 CE)

digamy   Remarriage

dilation   Modalist term that Sabellius used to describe how God is a Son–Father monad that expressed itself by dilating

Dionysus   God of wine and revelry; Mysteries of Dionysus are associated with his worship

discernment   Ability to distinguish holy possession from demonic possession

dispensation   Latin word meaning administration or management

dissociative disorders   Mental disorders that involve experiencing a disconnection and lack of continuity between thoughts, memories, surroundings, actions, and identity

ditheism   Belief in two Gods (Father and Son)

Docetism   Doctrine that Jesus did not have a fleshly body and, therefore, did not suffer in the flesh

dualistic pattern   Anthropological pattern where the soul is immortal; it enters a mortal body at birth and leaves it behind at death

Dynamic Monarchianism   Belief in the absolute Oneness of God; the man Jesus was not an incarnate God, but had instead acquired the Christ as a divine power

dynamis   Greek: divine power

E

ecclesiastic   Pertaining to the church; from Greek: *ecclesia*, church

ecstasy   Involuntary states that seize people and put them out of their "right" mind; out-of-body experiences

ego Center of the conscious mind; houses our accessible thoughts, memories, and emotions

encratism Greek: *encrateia*, self-controlled; lifestyle of extreme asceticism in which marriage is forbidden, often a sinful state; celebrated the solitary life over the marital

enculturation Adoption of the characteristics of the wider culture

entheogens Psychoactive substances like psilocybin that stimulate ecstasy

emanate Process of God coming into being by generating aspects of himself

ensoulment pattern Christological pattern where Jesus' soul is a special divinity

Ephêbos Youth; second level in mysteries of the Naassenes

episcopal Christians are subject to the authority of their local bishop (Greek: *episkopos*) as they are subject to Jesus Christ

Esaldaeus Sun God and Creator in Naassene system

eschatology End of the world

eschaton End of the world

esoteric Secret or hidden (teaching)

Essenes Jewish religious sect active in the early and mid-first century

ethnicity In antiquity, used synonymously with "race" to identify groups of people with shared territories, ancestry, language, religion, and physical traits

eucharist Thanksgiving meal where sacred bread and wine/water are eaten

Evangelion Early Christian gospel that Marcion used, edited, and published; similar to the Gospel of Luke

exegesis Explanation or interpretation of scripture

exegete As noun, Biblical interpreter; as verb, to interpret scripture

Exodus Story about the liberation of the Israelites from slavery in

Egypt which is narrated in Jewish scriptures

exomologesis Confession one time after baptism

exoteric Public (teaching)

F

family Group that shares overlapping similarities, not an essential feature common to all

family resemblances Variety of similarities that are shared by some but not all in a group

family resemblance definition Defines group identity as families that share some traits which distinguish them from other families, even though each family member is unique and every family member will not share all the same traits

faulty-God pattern Theodicy scheme where a God or Gods are responsible for suffering and death

faulty-human pattern Theodicy scheme where humans are responsible for suffering and death

fetal possession pattern Christological scheme where the human Jesus is possessed by an extraordinary Power while still in the womb

filial substance Literally: Sonship; sharing God's substance as his children

Five Seals Baptismal ritual common to Sethian texts

Forms Archetypal ideas in Platonic thought

functional definition Defines a group by what it does for its members

G

Gentile Non-Jew; pagan

gift pattern Soteriological scheme where salvation is something that God has to do

glossolalia Speaking in tongues (Greek: *glossai lalein*); speaking the language of God

Gnosis Knowledge of the supreme God via direct contact

Gnostic From the Greek word *gnosis* which means knowledge; used by early Christians to describe a countercultural spirituality dominated by the belief that it is necessary to directly experience or "know" the transcendent God via certain rituals and lifestyle practices; this God is the ultimate source of life (but not the world creator); the human spirit is consubstantial with the transcendent God

Gnostic Spirituality Metaphysical orientation that features a quest for reality that culminates in the direct knowledge of a supreme God who dwells beyond the cosmos

God-Fearer Jewish proselyte

gospel Greek: *evangelion*, good news

H

Hebdomad Realm of the Jewish God according to Basilides; the sublunar realm had been divided into seven areas: probably (1) the atmosphere between the moon and earth; (2) the earth; and (3) five underworld realms

Hellenization Adoption of Greek culture, religion, philosophy, language, and identity

Henotheism Worship of one God among many

heresy General meaning, "school of choice"; a sect people choose to join; Beliefs and/or practices that are labeled illegitimate by socially dominant Christians; label to mark opponents' teaching as deviating from the truth

hermeneut Interpreter

hermeneutics Interpretation, especially of the Bible and literary texts

Hermes Greek God; messenger and guide of the dead

heterodox Deviant from orthodox standards

heterogenous Multiform; mixed

heteroglossolalia The ability to speak a language that everyone hears in their own native tongues hierophant Teacher of "hidden sayings" and "mysteries" to a chosen few

Holiness Movement   Movement in nineteenth century Methodism that emphasized sanctification or perfection through disciplined behaviors; considered a second grace following baptism which had only cleansed convert from original sin

homoiousios   Greek: like substance; used by Apostolic Catholics who were afraid of Modalism to mean that the Son shares the similar substance with the Father

homoousios   Greek: same substance; used by Apostolic Catholics to mean that the Son shares the same substance with the Father

hubris   Godlike pride and vanity that is especially to be avoided because of the jealousy and wrath of the Gods

hybrid pattern   Christological pattern where Jesus is sired by God's Spirit in Mary's womb and is born a divine-human hybrid

Hypomnemata   Five-volume work of early Christian records put together by Hegesippus

hypostasis   Greek: being or existence; translates the Latin *substantia*; Origen uses it to indicate that the Son exists with its own personal identity

I

Ialdabaoth   Biblical Creator God in Sethian and Ophian Gnostic mythology; likely derived from phrase "Lord of Hosts" with reference to the warrior-like Jewish God who commands an army of angels

ignorant demiurge   Concept that the universe is created by a figure or figures who are fools or do not know any better

impaired demiurge   Concept that the creator figure or figures are diminished in their capacity, flawed, or deficient

Imperial cult   Civic religion of Roman Empire

indifferent   Greek: *adiaphora*; things are neither good or bad in and of themselves

individuation   Transformative journey to mental wholeness, when ego and the personal consciousness are reconnected

innovative movement   Religious group that emerges as a novel religious organization, generated as a product of innovation

Isis   Egyptian Goddess; wife of Osiris

J

Jesus Aeon   Aeon produced by the Pleroma; embodies all the qualities of each of the thirty Aeons; descends and enters the human Jesus at his baptism

Jew   People who worshipped YHWH, the God of the Judeans

justice demiurge   Concept that the creator figure rules his creation with a set of laws and judges human compliance

K

Kabbalah   Jewish mystical literature written during Middle Ages

kaulakau   Magical word derived from Isaiah 28:13; intonation of word opens door to the transcendent world

Kinship Model   Leadership is transmitted and legitimated along family lines

kosher   Food that is ritually fit for consumption in Jewish tradition

Kronos   Titan and Creator in Peratic system

kykeon   Barley brew used in the mysteries of Demeter

L

Law   *See* Torah

logikoi   Rational or intellectual beings whose sole purpose is to contemplate God via his Logos or Mind

Logos   Greek word meaning Reason; often translated Word

longi temporis praescriptio   Latin: defense in Roman law that someone who possessed land for a long period of time was considered its legitimate owner

Lucifer   Fallen angel

M

martyr   Christian who does not deny the Lord and endures torture and usually death

Maximalists   Jesus' followers who demanded circumcision and the full observation of the Law for all converts

Messiah   Anointed One; from Hebrew *mashiakh* and Greek *Christos*; Jewish end-time hero

Middle Platonism   Platonism as it was practiced from first century BCE - third century CE

mikveh, mikvot (pl.)   Special bathing pools with natural water sources often constructed next to synagogues

Minimalists   Jesus' followers who thought it was not necessary to burden the Gentiles with observing the Jewish Law; Paul likely is the originator of this opinion, arguing that Gentiles only had to devote themselves exclusively to the worship of the one God, love one another, and live temperately; some understood this to mean they should be antinomians

Mishnah   Codification of Oral Torah in second century

mitzvot   613 commandments and prohibitions found in the Torah or Law

Modalist Monarchianism   Belief that there is only one God who manifests himself in different modalities: as Creator and Lawgiver, he is called the Father; as the incarnate Savior, he is called the Son

Moderates   Jesus followers who thought that circumcision was not necessary for Gentile converts, but that other parts of the Law need to be intentionally observed like the Ten Commandments

monachos   Unmarried celibate person

monarchy   God's sovereignty as the sole source and ruler of universe; monotheism

monistic pattern   Anthropological scheme where the body and soul form a single indissoluble mortal unit

Monotheism   Belief that there is only one God

multivalency   Having many possible meanings

multivocality Containing voices of multiple authors or editors

Muratorian fragment First full list of Apostolic Catholic scriptures (ca. 200 CE)

mystagogue Leader who initiates a person into a mystery cult

mysteries of Cybele Great Mother Goddess native to Anatolia, whose rites rivaled Dionysus' in their revelry and ecstasy with frenzied dance circles fueled by loud percussive music

mystery religions Initiatory religions in the Greco-Roman-Egyptian world

myth Religious story

N

Nag Hammadi Collection Collection of thirteen books containing heterodox Christian writings; discovered in 1945, Nag Hammadi, Egypt

Neo-Pythagoreanism Revival of Pythagorean doctrines; originated in first century BCE and flourished during the first and second centuries CE

New Testament Closed canon of authoritative Christian documents; Marcion created the first New Testament

Noahide Laws Jewish laws for Gentiles which included prohibitions against idolatry, cursing God, murder, adultery, sexual immorality, theft, and eating flesh torn from a living animal, as well as the obligation to establish courts of justice

nous Greek word for the faculty of the human mind

O

Ogdoad Eight primal or original aspects of God; eight Gods of Hermopolis

oikonomia Greek: administration or management

Ophian Group name that stems from the Greek word for snake, *ophis*; name alludes to their belief that the serpent in Eden was wise and that he spoke the truth to Eve in the garden

Oral Torah A collection of authoritative oral rulings about the Law made by rabbis

original sin As defined by Basilides: Human inclination to sin; according to Augustine: children inherit sin from their parents in a perpetual cycle

Orpheus Legendary hero who learned music from Apollo and made a trip to the underworld

Orthodox Christian church in the east that recognizes the Patriarch of Constantinople as its leader; merged out of the Great Schism in 1054, when the Catholic Church split into the Roman Catholic and Orthodox Churches

orthodox Beliefs and/or practices that are labeled legitimate by socially dominant Christians

orthodoxy Teaching and practices judged "right" by Apostolic Catholics

Osiris Egyptian God of the dead

Oxyrhynchus City in Egypt where early Christian documents were excavated in late 19th century by Oxford University

P

Paidos Child; first initiatory level in mysteries of the Naassenes

palla Shawl-like scarf that served as a hood

pallium Short cloak that Greek philosophers wore

Pantheism All deities, forces of nature, etc. are aspects of God

Papacy Office and authority of the Pope

papyri Ancient paper made from reeds

Paraclete Spirit of Christ; Holy Spirit as named in the Gospel of John

parasympathetic mode Autonomic nervous system's response to relax by decreasing heart rate and breathing, lulling us into rest and sleep

parrhesia Greek, meaning bold speech

Pastoral Epistles 1 and 2 Timothy and Titus

Patripassianism The-Suffering-Father party; derogatory nickname for the Modalists

patron demiurge Concept that the Creator figure or figures are operating in discriminatory ways, showing favoritism or partiality to some of their creatures

penance Forgiveness of sin after baptism; which sins (if any) that could be forgiven was hotly contested among Christians

Pentateuch First five books of the Jewish bible; see Torah

Pentecost Celebration that commemorates the descent of the Holy Spirit upon the Apostles as described in Acts 2:1–31

Pentecostalism Protestant Christian movement that seeks a post-conversion religious experience, namely baptism with the Holy spirit

Pepuza Phrygian village where the Church of New Prophecy emerged (160–170 CE)

Persephone Demeter's daughter; kidnapped by Hades

Person Greek: *prosopon*; Latin: *persona*; in Roman law: the individual property-holder

Pharisee Separatist; Jewish sectarian group of laymen devoted to holiness

Pleroma Transcendent realm known as the Totality or Pleroma

pneuma Greek word for spirit; as defined by Stoics: the active principle that infuses and enlivens matter

pneumatic meaning "Spiritual" or esoteric meaning of the scripture; only accessible to advanced Christians

pneumatics According to Valentinians, they were advanced Christians who underwent chrism and achieved Gnosis; according to Montantists, they were spiritual people gifted with the Spirit and religious enthusiasm

polytheism Belief in and worship of more than one God

presbytery The committee of governing elders

Priapus Greek fertility god

proselyte   Person recruited and prepared for conversion

Protestantism   Christianity that separated from the Roman Catholic Church during the Reformation over disagreements regarding leadership, sacraments, and scripture (ca. 1517 CE)

Providence   The operation of divine reason in the world, determining all events

psilantropism   Belief that the Son did not exist until he was conceived, that he was born merely a human being

psyche   Greek word for soul, our rational and emotive self; what vitalizes the body; modern concept of our mental states

Psychic Christ   Son of the Demiurge; implanted as Jesus' soul at conception

psychic meaning   "Soulish" or moral meaning of the scripture; scripture as ethical guide

psychics   According to Valentinians, they were Apostolic Catholics who had been baptized and still worshipped the Biblical God; according to Montantists, Christians who had not received the fullness of the Spirit were merely "soul" people

R

rabbinic   Teachings and traditions of the rabbis

rebel demiurge   Concept that the universe is created by a rebellious figure or figures

recapitulation   God's plan for redemption when all things are gathered into Christ

Reformation   Protestant reformers separated from the Catholic Church and started churches under Protestant leaders such as Martin Luther and John Calvin (1517–1648 CE)

reformed movement   Religious group which has changed something about the religious group with which its members are already affiliated

reincarnation   Greek: *metempsychosis*; belief that the immortal soul goes through many life cycles to achieve perfection and liberation

restoration   Greek: *apokatastasis*; as defined in Basilides system: when the mixed natures are restored to their separate homelands

resurrection   Soteriological expectation that the deceased will be raised from the grave to live in a new utopian world

resurrection of the flesh/body   Physical body will be raised from grave at the end of time

S

Sabbath   Seventh day of the week; day of rest; from sundown Friday until sundown Saturday

sacrifice   Ritual slaughter (usually an animal) or tithing (agricultural product) to appease a God

Samael   Fallen angel; name for Demiurge according to some Christian Gnostics

Samaritans   Inhabitants of Samaria with historical ties to ancient Israel and the Torah; worship YHWH on Mt. Gerizim rather than at the temple in Jerusalem

schismatic movement   When a single religious movement splits into smaller segments

secessionist movement   Independent religious group formed when a segment splits off from a religious group and starts an alternative form of the parent group

sect   Deviant religious organization with traditional beliefs and practices in church-sect-cult typology

sectarian   Describes religious group or party with a distinct identity

sectarianism   Characterizes independently organized groups that claim to be the authentic representatives of the same religious tradition

Seth   Third son of Eve and Adam

Sethian   Gnostics who believed that Seth, the son of Adam, was their race's primogenitor

shadow   According to Jung, repressed memories and forgotten traumas, which were once conscious but are no longer accessible to the conscious mind

shamanism   Practice of trance by specialists in hunter-gatherer societies to communicate with spirits and interact with the spirit world for the benefit of their communities

Shema   Hebrew verb for "to hear"; denoting Jewish confession of faith

Sicarii   Group of Jewish nationalists known for assassinating Roman sympathizers with daggers

Sige   Silence; Valentinian term of primal Mother

Slave Spirituality   A worldview that deems humans slaves of the Gods in a way that God is a master who has the power to do anything he wants with his creatures

Socinianism   Dynamic Monarchianism as it was reinvented in Transylvania by two European Unitarians, Lelio Sozzini (1525–1562 CE) and hisnephew Faustus Socinus (1539–1604 CE)

sola scriptura   Protestant doctrine that the New Testament is the self-contained deposit of the revelation of Jesus

somatic meaning   "Bodily" or literal meaning of the scripture

soteriology   Explanations of salvation

Stoicism   Greek philosophical movement popular from the end of fourth century BCE to the end of second century CE

stola   Long woolen outer garment worn over tunics

subordinationist   Person who believes that the Son is subordinate to the Father

substance   From Latin *substantiae*; a property that a person (*persona*) or several persons (*personae*) together could own

substantive definition Defines group identity by specific characteristics; prescriptive and exclusive; if a group does not have all the characteristics, it is excluded from the identity

sympathetic mode Response of autonomic nervous system that is responsible for our body's ability to become instantly alert

synagogue House of prayer and worship for Jews

syzygy In Valentinianism, divine couple; divine male–female procreative pair joined together in such a way that they are one

T

tabernacle Before the Temple was built in Jerusalem, ancient Israelites who were nomadics worshipped in a mobile tent temple called the tabernacle

Talmud Codification of rabbinic opinions about the Mishnah in the fifth century CE

Tartarus Infernal regions in Greek mythology

theodicy Explanations for suffering and death, especially of righteous or good people; justification or defense of God in the face of suffering and evil

theology Explanations of God; reflection on the nature and being of God

theoria Vision of God as uncreated light; cultivated by Orthodox Christians

Titans Children of Gods Uranus (Heaven) and Gaea (Earth) and their descendants in Greek mythology

toga Practical work garment

Torah Jewish Law written in the first five books of the Jewish bible

traditio Tradition of truth that has been passed on from generation to generation, from the church founded by the apostles down to the Apostolic Catholic churches

traducianism Tertullian's doctrine that the souls of children are derived from the corrupted souls of the parents

transconfessional Not tied to a single religious group but crosses religious groups

Transtheism Belief that a transcendental primal God. who is the source of life but not the actual creator of the universe. is the God of worship

triadic pattern Anthropological pattern where the human being consists of body, soul, and Spirit; the Spirit is a divine aspect that gives the person the capacity to intuit truth

Trinity Fourth-century Christian doctrine developed to explain the triune Godhead (Father, Son, and Holy Spirit) as one God existing in three coequal, coeternal, and consubstantial persons

Two Natures of Jesus Fifth-century Christian doctrine developed to explain the hypostatic or real union between Jesus' divine and human natures

V

villain demiurge Concept that the Creator figure or figures are malicious

visitation pattern Christological scheme where Jesus is a descendent divine entity like an angel or a God that appears and performs in such a way that he is indistinguishable from humans

X

xenolalia The ability to speak unlearned foreign languages

Xenotheism Belief that a God who is a foreigner or alien intruder in our universe is the God of worship

xerophagy Dry fasting; eating only uncooked soaked legumes, raw radishes, avoiding meat, succulent fruit, and wine

Y

Yahwism Belief that YHWH, the Biblical Creator God is the God of worship

Yaldabaoth See Ialdabaoth

YHWH Name of Jewish national God; Creator of world; pronounced "Yah-weh"

Z

Zealots Group of Jewish nationalists at time of the First Roman–Jewish War

Zeus High God in the Greek pantheon

Glossary of People

A

Abraham Patriarch of the Israelites whose story is narrated in the book of Genesis

Adamantius Author of the dialogue *De recta in Deum fidei*, which disputes two disciples of Marcion and followers of Bardesanes and Valentinus (ca. 300 CE)

Agabus Early Christian prophet mentioned in Acts

Agathopous Valentinus' student; recipient of a letter from Valentinus

Agrippa Castor A third-generation Christian writer or apologist who refuted the heresy of Basilides

Albinus Middle Platonist (149–157 CE)

Alexander of Alexandria Bishop of Alexandria (313–328 CE); a right-wing Origenist and opponent of Arius

Alexander of Jerusalem Bishop of Jerusalem (d. 251 CE); supported Origen

Ambrose Alexandrian Valentinian who becomes Origen's patron

Ammia Christian prophetess who lived in Philadelphia at the time of Montanus or earlier

Ammonius Saccas Middle Platonist (175–242 CE); teacher of Plotinus and perhaps Origen

Andrew Disciple of Jesus and apostle

Anicetus Bishop of Rome (ca. 155–167 CE)

Anionicus Antiochean Valentinian who may have authored the Gospel of Philip

Antonius Pius Roman Emperor (138 to 161 CE)

Apelles Marcionite sectarian who modified Marcion's theology by suggesting a connection between the Supreme transcendent God and a subordinate fiery angel who created this world

Aphraates Earliest known author of the Syriac church in Persia (ca. 350)

Aphrahat Syrian Christian and author (270–345 CE)

Apollonarius Local Bishop in Asia Minor; opponent of early Montanists

Apollos A missionary Paul meets in Ephesus; visits Corinth

Apphia Woman leader of house church known to Paul

Aquila Jewish convert and apostle from Rome; Prisca's husband; known to Paul

Aristides of Athens Christian writer who likely wrote to try to convert Emperor Antoninus Pius (138–161 CE)

Aristion First-generation Christian teacher

Aristobulus of Alexandria Greek philosopher (181–124 BCE)

Arius An Alexandrian left-wing Origenist and presbyter in the Alexandrian church (256–336 CE) who taught that the Son must be subordinate to the Father and that there must have been a time when the Son was not; officially condemned at Nicea (325 CE)

Artemon Later proponent of Theodotus' Dynamic Monarchianism

Athanasius Bishop of Alexandria (296–373 CE); wrote Easter letter in 367 that listed the authoritative books in the Catholic New Testament

Athenagoras of Athens Early Christian apologist

Augustine Bishop of Hippo, one of the Latin Fathers of the Church and the most significant Christian thinker, who wrote *Confessions* and the *City of God*

B

Basilides Alexandrian Christian teacher and theologian in Alexandria during the time of Hadrian

C

Callistus Bishop of Rome (218–222 CE)

Calvin, John Christian reformer and theologian (1509–1564 CE)

Candidus Valentinian who debated Origen on the subjects of the eternal generation of the Son and the salvation of the Devil

Cappadocian Fathers Fourth-century theologians Basil of Caesarea, Gregory of Nyssa, and Gregory of Nazianzus; used Stoic and Aristotelian logic to explain the Trinity

Carpocrates Alexandrian Gnostic Christian

Celsus Roman philosopher who wrote *On the True Doctrine* critiquing Christians (170 CE)

Cerdo Christian philosopher and teacher in Rome; excommunicated from Roman church (ca. 138 CE); from Syria

Charito Woman who was Justin's student; arrested with Justin

Chariton Man who was Justin's student; arrested with Justin

Chloe Woman leader of a house church known to Paul

Chrysippus Greek philosopher (281–208 BCE)

Claudis Ephebus Christian who carried letter (*1 Clement*) to Corinth from Rome

Clemens Christian who helped Hermas publish his books

Clement of Alexandria Christian philosopher and teacher active in Alexandria (190–212 CE)

Clement of Rome Bishop of Rome who is mistakenly identified with the author of *1 Clement*

Comparing Christianities: An Introduction to Early Christianity, First Edition. April D. DeConick.
© 2024 John Wiley & Sons Ltd. Published 2024 by John Wiley & Sons Ltd.

Cleomenes   Persuaded by Epigonus to help publicize Noetus' teachings and convince the Christian leaders in Rome to stop worshiping two Gods (the Father and the Son)

Crescens   Philosopher was so embittered over Justin's teachings that he sought Justin's and Tatian's death

Cyprian   Christian theologian and bishop of Carthage (200–258 CE)

D

Damas   Bishop of Magnesia during the time of Ignatius

Darwin, Charles   English naturalist known for his major contributions to the science of evolution (1809–1882 CE)

Daughters of Philip   Early Christian prophetesses mentioned in Acts

Diogenes the Dog   Famous Cynic whose life showcases the philosophy's principles

Domitian   Roman emperor (81–96 CE)

Durham, William H.   Holiness preacher from Chicago in the formative years of Pentecostalism

E

Ebionites   Second-century law-observant Christian sect

Elchasaites   Second-century law-observant Christians whose beliefs were similar to the Ebionites

Eleutherius   Bishop of Rome (alternatively dated to171–177/185–193 CE)

Ephraem   Syrian Christian theologian and hymnographer (306–373 CE)

Epigonus   Carried Noetus' teachings to Rome

Epiphanes   Son of the Carpocrates who wrote a book entitled *On Righteousness*

Epiphanius   Bishop of Salamis in Cyprus who was a strong supporter of Nicaea and opponent of heresy (310–403 CE)

Esau   Son of Isaac in the Jewish scripture

Euelpistus   Imperial slave who was Justin's student; arrested with Justin

Euodia   Woman preacher with Paul

Euodius   First bishop of Antioch according to Catholic memory

Eusebius of Caesarea   Bishop of Caesarea in Palestine and church historian (ca. 260–340)

F

Flavia Sophe   Fourth-generation Christian; a Valentinian Roman woman whose tombstone survives

Flavius Josephus   Jewish historian and military leader in the First Roman–Jewish War; ca. 37–100 CE

Flora   Fourth-generation Christian; Roman woman who was considering Valentinian initiation; recipient of letter from Ptolemy

Florinus   Presbyter of the Roman Apostolic Catholic church who is accused by Irenaeus of being a Valentinian and writing a heretical book on theology

Fortunatus   Christian who carried letter (*1 Clement*) to Corinth from Rome

G

Glaucias   Basilides' teacher who was renowned for his interpretation of Peter's teachings

Grapte   Christian who helped Hermas publish his books

H

Hadrian   Roman Emperor (117–138 CE)

Hegemonius   Christian writer who wrote a book entitled *Acta Archelai*

Hegesippus   Contemporary with Irenaeus; constructed first records of the Apostolic Catholic network as aligned with Rome's teachings about the Law, Prophets, and the Lord

Helen   Co-founder (with Simon of Gitto) of Samaritan Gnostic sect called Simonianism (mid-first century)

Heracleitus   Greek philosopher (ca. 502 BCE)

Heracleon   Pupil of Valentinus from Sicily; wrote the commentary on the Gospel of John

Heraclides   Bishop of an Arabian church; interrogated by Origen for his Modalist beliefs (244–249 CE)

Hermas   Freedman convert in Rome; writes *Shepherd of Hermas* (ca. 125–135 CE)

Hierax   Slave from Phrygia who was Justin's student; arrested with Justin

Hippolytus of Asia   Late second-century or early third-century author whose principle work is *Against Noetus.*

Hippolytus of Rome   Early third-century author whose principal works are *Refutation of all Heresies* and the *Apostolic Tradition*

Hyginus   Bishop of Rome (ca. 136–140 CE)

I

Ignatius   Bishop of Antioch and martyr (ca. 130–150 CE); wrote a series of letters to various church communities in Asia Minor and Rome

Irenaeus   Bishop of Lyons (ca. 177–202 CE); wrote *Against Heresies* (ca. 180 CE); Christian theologian who described and refuted a number of gnostic groups and their theological ideas

Isaac   Son of Abraham in Jewish scripture

Isidore   Son of Basilides, who likewise dealt in Christian philosophy, writing several treatises that complemented his father's corpus

J

Jacob   Son of Isaac in Jewish scriptures

James   Brother of Jesus; leader of Jerusalem church after Jesus' death; a.k.a. The Just

James   Son of Zebedee; disciple of Jesus and apostle

Jerome   Church Father who translated most of the Bible into Latin and advocated the Church's acceptance of the canon of the Old Testament (ca. 342–420 CE)

Jesus of Nazareth   Jewish man born in Nazareth in 4 or 6 BCE; leader of Jewish messianic movement during the rule of Pontius Pilate

Johann A. Moehler   Catholic theologian and Church historian (1796–1838 CE)

John   One of the twelve disciples; son of Zebedee

John the Elder   First-generation Christian teacher and church leader

John of Ephesus   Destroyed the Church of New Prophecy (550 CE)

Judas Barsabbas   Early Christian prophet mentioned in Acts

Judas Thomas   Judas the Twin; apostolic hero in Syrian literature

Junia   Woman missionary and apostle known to Paul

Justinians   Followers of Justin the Gnostic who claimed themselves as the Gnostics because they had exclusive knowledge about the whereabouts of the Father whom they had met during their ecstatic flights

Justin Martyr   Christian who was a philosopher and teacher in Rome (ca. 100–165 CE); from Samaria

L

Lady   A female angel who represents the Church

Liberian   Man who was Justin's student; arrested with Justin

Linnaeus, Carl   Swedish botanist (1707–1778 CE); considered the father of modern taxonomy

M

Mani   Founder of Manichaeism; former Elchasaite (216–274/277 CE)

Marcellina   Famous woman leader of a Carpocratian group in Rome during the time of Bishop Anicetus (ca. 157–168)

Marcellus   Bishop of Ancryra (280–374 CE); attended Council of Nicaea

Marcus   Fourth-generation Christian; Valentinian who was living in the Rhone valley just north of Italy and gained the reputation of a magician among his detractor

Matthew   Disciple of Jesus and apostle

Matthias   Apostle who replaced Judas

Maximilla   Prophetess and co-founder of Montanism

Maximus   Christian who denied the Lord; Hermas knows him

Menander   Simon's disciple and next-generation leader of Simonianism (late first century)

Miltiades   Marcionite hymnographer

Montanus   Prophet and co-founder of Montanism

N

Naassenes   Fourth-Generation Christians; Group that called themselves Gnostics because they said that they alone had experienced the depths of knowledge

Natalius   Installed by Theodotus the Banker as the first (only?) salaried bishop of his church

Nazoreans   Aramaic-speaking Christians who lived in Syria and, by the end of the fourth century, were living in the northern city of Beorea (Aleppo, Syria)

Noetus   Presbyter who was active Smyrna at the end of second century

Numenius of Apamea   Middle Platonic and Neopythagorean philosopher (ca. 150–200 CE)

Nympha   Woman leader of house church known to Paul

O

Onesimus   Bishop of Ephesus during the time of Ignatius

Ophians   Fourth-generation Christians; Gnostic Christian group (etymologically stem from the Greek word for snake) who believe in Jesus and call the Jewish God "Cursed" because this is the God who cursed the serpent in the garden of Eden for giving the first humans knowledge of good and evil

Origen   Alexandrian theologian (185–253 CE)

ousia   Greek: being or existence; translates the Latin *substantia*; Origen uses it to indicate that there is a generic essence of divinity that the Father and the Son share

P

Paion   Man from Cappadocia who was Justin's student; arrested with Justin

Pantaenus   Fourth-generation Christian Stoic philosopher; Clement of Alexandria's teacher

Papias of Hierapolis   Bishop of Hierapolis in Asia Minor (died ca. 161 CE)

Parham, Charles F.   Holiness preacher, evangelist, and the director at Bethel Bible College

Paul the Martyr   Local martyr known to Polycarp

Paul of Samosata   Bishop of Antioch and Dynamic Monarchian (260–268 CE)

Paul of Tarsus   Jewish man born in Tarsus around the time of Jesus' birth; missionary and founder of Jewish sectarian churches that promoted Jesus as the Messiah.

Peratics   Group called "Peratics" or "Travelers" because they alone know the road the soul travels to get into the world and the path the soul journeys to get out of it

Persis   Christian woman co-worker of Paul

Peter   One of the twelve disciples of Jesus; apostle, missionary, and important leader of Jerusalem church

Philip   Disciple of Jesus and apostle

Phoebe   Woman leader and deacon of a house church; Christian co-worker known to Paul

Pius   Bishop of Rome (ca. 140–155 CE)

Plato   Greek philosopher (ca. 429–347 BCE); founder of the Platonic school

Pliny   Roman governor of Bithynia and Pontus (110–113 CE); author; a.k.a. Pliny the Younger

Plotinus   Father of Neo-Platonism (204–270 CE)

Polybius   Bishop of Tralles during the time of Ignatius

Polycarp   Bishop of Smyrna in Asia Minor and Christian martyr; died ca. 155 CE

Pontius Pilate Roman governor of Palestine who executed Jesus

Porphyry Plotinus' student and biographer (234–305 CE)

Pothinus Bishop of Lyons; Irenaeus succeeded him upon his martyrdom (ca. 177–178 CE)

Praxeas From the Greek word *praxis*, indicating a deal or transaction; a derogatory slur – "The Dealer" – meant to demean Tertullian's opponent, probably Epigonus

Prisca Jewish woman convert and apostle from Rome; Aquila's wife and leader of a house church in Rome

Priscilla Prophetess and co-founder of Montanism

Prodicus Alexandrian Valentinian known to Clement of Alexandria

Ps.-Tertullian Unknown author whose principal work, *Against All Heresies*, was ascribed spuriously to Tertullian of Carthage

Ptolemy Fourth-generation Roman Christian; Pupil of Valentinus; wrote *Letter to Flora*

Pythagoras Greek philosopher (ca. 570–495 BCE); founder of the Pythagorean school

Q

Quadratus Christian prophet who lived in Philadelphia at the time of Montanus or earlier

R

Reimarus, Hermann S. German Enlightenment philosopher

Rheginus Valentinian student; recipient of a theological letter (*The Treatise on the Resurrection*)

Rhodo Tatian's student in Rome (ca. 170 CE)

Rufus Local martyr known to Polycarp

Rusticus Roman prefect who judged and executed Justin

S

Sabellius Christian Modalist theologian from Libya (199–217 CE)

Secundus Roman Valentinian scholar known to Irenaeus

Seneca Stoic whose ethic was all about harnessing the passions through self-control (4 BCE-65 CE)

Septimius Severus Roman Emperor (193–211 CE)

William Seymour Black Holiness leader who traveled to Los Angeles, where he began to spread the message about the Pentecostal experience

Shepherd An angel (not Jesus) who is Hermas' guardian and disciplinarian

Silas Early Christian prophet mentioned in Acts

Simon of Cyrene Figure who compelled to carry Jesus' cross in the New Testament

Simon of Gitto Co-founder (with Helen) of Samaritan Gnostic sect called Simonianism (mid-first century)

Synthyche Woman preacher with Paul

T

Tatian Syrian Christian (ca. 120–180 CE); Justin Martyr's student and author of *The Diatessaron*

Telesforus Bishop of Rome (ca. 125–136 CE)

Tertullian Christian apologist, polemicist, and moralist from Carthage in the Roman province of Africa (ca. 155–220 CE)

Thales of Miletus Pre-Socratic philosopher, mathematician, and astronomer from the Greek city of Miletus in Ionia (624 BCE–546 BCE)

Thebuthis Originator of all the Judaizing heresies according to Hegesippus

Themiso Replaced Montanus after his death (ca. 175)

Theoctistus of Caesarea Bishop of Caesarea; ordained Origen as a priest

Theodotus Alexandrian Valentinian teacher whose quotations can be found in Clement's *Excerpts from Theodotus*

Theodotus the Banker Founded an independent Dynamic Monarchian church

Theodotus the Cobbler Christian philosopher from Byzantium who taught Dynamic Monarchianism

Theophilus of Antioch Bishop of Antioch (169–182 CE)

Theotimus A Roman Valentinian who authored the lost *On the Images of the Law*

Thomas Disciple of Jesus and apostle; a.k.a. Judas Thomas

Trajan Roman Emperor (98–117 CE)

Tryphosa Christian woman coworker known to Paul

Typhena Christian woman coworker known to Paul

V

Valerius Bito Christian who carried letter (1 Clement) to Corinth from Rome

Victor Bishop of Rome (189–199 CE)

W

Wittgenstein, Ludwig Austrian British philosopher who worked on logic, philosophy of mathematics, and philosophy of mind (1889–1951 CE)

X

Xenophanes Greek philosopher (570–479 BCE)

Z

Zephyrinus Bishop of Rome (199–218 CE)

NB *Italic* type refers to information contained in figures and tables.

Comparing Christianities: An Introduction to Early Christianity, First Edition. April D. DeConick.
© 2024 John Wiley & Sons Ltd. Published 2024 by John Wiley & Sons Ltd.